L WARNING

FINAL WARNING
A HISTORY OF THE NEW WORLD ORDER

David Allen Rivera

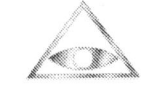

CONSPIRACY
An Imprint of InteliBooks *Publishers*
Oakland, California

All rights reserved.
Copyright © 1984, 1994, 1997, 2004 by David Allen Rivera.

This book may not be reproduced or utilized in whole, or in part, by any means or in any form, electronic, digital or mechanical, including mimeographing, photocopying, Xeroxing, recording, taping; or by any information storage and retrieval systems that would compress it for use in Word Processing software to be made available on a floppy disc or CD–ROM, or into files such as .html or .pdf formats that would enable the information to be accessed by others on an internet website, without the prior written consent of the author, except for brief quotes for use in reviews.

All Scripture quotations are taken from the Authorized
King James Version Text of the Holy Bible.

Cover design: Damion Gordon/BTP GRAPHX

ISBN: 0-9711391-9-9

This book was printed in the United States of America.
To order additional copies, contact:

InteliBooks, Oakland, California.
www.InteliBooks.com
orders@InteliBooks.com

Be sure to visit David Rivera's website at
www.viewfromthewall.com

DEDICATION

To my Mother and my Father,
who gave me the desire.

To my wife and my children,
who gave me the fire.

To my Lord and My God,
who lifted me higher.

CONTENTS

Preface / 11

Introduction / 14

Part One: The Physical Conspiracy

Chapter One: The Birth of Tyranny
The Illuminati / 27
The House of Rothschild / 33
Freemasonry / 37
The Illuminati Grows / 48
The German Union / 52
The French Revolution / 53
The Illuminati Spreads to America / 57
Phi Beta Kappa / 60
Skull and Bones / 61
Congress of Vienna / 62
The Masons Separate Themselves from the Illuminati / 64
The Illuminati in the United States / 66
The Illuminati Leadership Changes / 67

Chapter Two: Financial Background
The Beginning of Monetary Control / 71
The Federal Reserve Act / 79
The Federal Income Tax / 102
Foundations / 108
The Stock Market Crash and Depression / 124

Chapter Three: Bringing the World Together
World War I / 126
The League of Nations / 127
Symbol of the Illuminati / 128

Chapter Four: Domestic Tampering
The Illuminati Creates Racial Tension / 132
The Electoral College / 136

Chapter Five: The Council on Foreign Relations
British East India Company / 138
The Fabian Society / 139
The Round Table / 144
The Council on Foreign Relations / 147
The CFR Elects Nixon / 153
The CFR and Their Goals / 163
The Brookings Institution / 172
The Committee for Economic Development / 174

Chapter Six: Setting the Stage for World War II
The Protocols of the Learned Elders of Zion / 176
World War II and the Rise of Hitler / 185
The Deception of Pearl Harbor / 192

Chapter Seven: The Communist Agenda
The Origin of Communism / 201
The Rise of Karl Marx / 206
Lenin Takes Control / 209
The Russian Revolution / 211
China Goes Communist / 220
Korea Falls / 222
The Vietnam Conquest / 225
The Cuban Cover-Up / 227
Communists Fight Among Themselves / 231
The Spread of Communism / 231
Disarming America / 244
The End of Communism? / 250
The Ultimate Goal of Communism / 254

Chapter Eight: The Illuminati Influence on International Affairs
The United Nations / 256
The European Union / 269
The Bilderberger Group / 273
Atlas Shrugged / 278
The Seven Sisters / 281
The Club of Rome / 285
Independent Commission on International Development Issues / 292

Chapter Nine: Ready to Spring the Trap
The Trilateral Commission / 294
Regional Government / 308
Creating a Crisis / 315
Riot and Revolution / 317
Conclusion / 339

Part Two: The Spiritual Conspiracy

Chapter Ten: Setting the Stage for Destruction
When the Conspiracy Actually Began / 347
The Beginning of the End / 351
The Rapture / 356
The Dead Sea Scrolls / 363
Satanism / 374
The New Age Movement / 381
The World Church / 387

Chapter Eleven: The Shining Star
The War-Torn History of Israel / 422
The Ark of the Covenant / 431
Rebuilding the Jewish Temple / 437

Chapter Twelve: The Curtain Falls
Prieuré de Sion / 446
The Antichrist / 471
The Mark of the Beast / 477
The Invasion of Israel / 492

Afterword / 508

Appendix A / 511

Appendix B / 515

Sources Consulted / 517

About the Author / 535

PREFACE

As I sit here preparing my book for publication, I can't help but to think back to the time when this project was nothing more than a stirring of curiosity within me. What you are holding in your hands is the culmination of 25 years worth of reading, research, writing and effort to make people aware of the growing danger around them.

Back in 1978, I was given a cassette tape that had been recorded at the Open Door Church in Chambersburg, PA. The guest speaker was a gentleman by the name of John Todd. He identified himself as a former witch who was involved in a secret Order of the elite known as the Illuminati, who had been controlling world events for over 200 years, and whose ultimate goal was to establish a one-world government. I was quite shaken after listening to this tape, because in high school and college, I had begun to delve heavily into the facts and circumstances surrounding the assassination of President John F. Kennedy, and had come to the conclusion that there indeed was a conspiracy to kill him. I believed that this plot had been so pervasive and all-encompassing that it reached into the highest levels of government. Now, here was a man who was elaborating on the existence of a group who had the power, means, and motive to carry out such an act.

His tale was just so incredible, so unbelievable, that I couldn't get it out of my mind. So, I began to research the Illuminati, thinking I was going to easily disprove his wild claims. I also began to do some digging on Todd. It wasn't long before I began to realize that the history that is being taught in public school, and presented in the media, rarely reflects the accuracy of actual events. We are taught what they want us to know. Therefore we have grown up under the delusion of such misconception, that it has become inconceivable to believe anything other than what has been perceived as truth.

I was unable to prove or disprove that Todd was who he said he was. However, I was able to document about 90% of what he said about the Illuminati.

As I continued my research, the deeper I got, and the more disturbing it became. When I research something, I tend to have tunnel-vision so that my focus is so much on the subject, that I am totally immersed in it. This is very similar to what a Profiler does when they get into the mind of the criminal. So, when I discovered that this thing had been developing for so long, my initial reaction was to want to know why, and what the motive was. This would give me leads in any direction I needed to go to search for evidence.

When I sat in church as a child, and would hear what the Bible had to say about what was going to happen in the 'last days,' as outlined in Daniel, Ezekiel and Revelation, it was really hard to imagine how that all could be possible. But, I began to realize that prophecies made over 2,000 years ago were beginning to be fulfilled. I also realized that I could not approach this research from a physical standpoint, because it went far beyond a natural understanding. When you consider the spiritual foundation, then you can begin to comprehend what is now happening all around us.

For six years, I spent hundreds of hours into finding out all I could concerning the Illuminati. The result was a manuscript in 1984 titled *The Illuminati Conspiracy and the Coming One World Government*. A Christian bookstore in the area agreed to sell copies of it as I began to contact a few companies in the hopes of getting it published on a larger scale. There was nothing available at the time which pulled together all the different aspects into one reference source, so in that regard, it was a ground-breaking work. But alas, a first book, by a no-name writer, on a controversial subject, did not get any attention. The manuscript was filed away in a box.

Then, in 1990, during the Persian Gulf crisis, President George Bush began talking about a 'New World Order.' I immediately saw the connection to the Illuminati front organizations, and I began reworking the manuscript. I remember my wife standing in the doorway of my den saying: "You have been working on this book ever since I met you." It was self-published in 1994 as *Final Warning*, and sold in nearly all the Christian bookstores in eight central Pennsylvania counties, by mail order, and through four national distributors.

Again, I tried to get it published on a larger scale. I contacted over a hundred publishers, and even with proven sales in my target area, which projected into national sales of over 48,000, there was only one publisher, Huntington House, who seriously considered it.

After all the copies were sold, the manuscript was again filed away in a box.

Between 1996 and 1998, I received some very profound spiritual revelation in regard to my destiny, and my reason for being. I began to operate and function with a new degree of insight and purpose.

Early in 1998, I received a computer through Divine Providence, and on November 24, 1998 the book became available on my website, and since then has been copied onto other websites, linked to, downloaded, and printed by thousands of people. However, in mid-2003, many people began to request copies of the book.

It is now 20 years since the initial 'publication' of *Final Warning*, and many people have begun to see the many changes that have occurred in that time. The world is indeed a very dangerous place. But it is by design, and it is with purpose.

I have corrected some statistics, and added some new information in certain sections; but because of the space constraints, I decided not to completely update the book. Since much of the research was done between 1978 and 1984, the book may come across as being dated. However, I would like to remind the reader that this is a history book, and its focus is the origin and development of the movement toward one-world government.

In a sense, this book is a collection of files which provide a concise overview of the entire subject. Just as an attorney would do, I have taken it, pulled it apart, examined every piece, then put it all back together. The purpose for this is to systematically and methodically build my case, and produce the evidence that will prove my contention.

In addition, please understand that this is a reference work. One person, when he took it with him on vacation, expecting an easy read, likened it to a college textbook. Although, in reworking it, I have tried to change some of the dry language, rearrange, and edit some of the text, it is still a reference book. However, know that this incredible compilation of history and facts can not be found anywhere, in any one book. The story that will unfold before your eyes will grab a hold of you and never let go.

Come with me now on a trip to a not too distant past, and an uncertain future. It will be a journey of discovery and revelation.

David Allen Rivera
December, 2003

INTRODUCTION

Since the Persian Gulf War, the term 'New World Order' has become well known. However, there has never really been an explanation as to what the term actually meant, only that it represented a new spirit of cooperation among the nations of the world, in order to further the cause of peace. And peace is good, so therefore the New World Order is good and should be accepted. Not so fast. Like the old saying, you can't tell a book by its cover, there is more here than meets the eye.

In regard to the term, William Safire wrote in the *New York Times* in February, 1991: "…it's Bush's baby, even if he shares its popularization with Gorbachev. Forget the Hitler 'new order' root; F.D.R. used the phrase earlier."

The term 'New World Order' was actually first used many years ago.

In an address delivered to the Union League of Philadelphia on November 27, 1915, Nicholas Murray Butler said: "The old world order changed when this war-storm broke. The old international order passed away as suddenly, as unexpectedly, and as completely as if it had been wiped out by a gigantic flood, by a great tempest, or by a volcanic eruption. The old world order died with the setting of that day's sun and a new world order is being born while I speak, with birth pangs so terrible that it seems almost incredible that life could come out of such fearful suffering and such overwhelming sorrow."

In a 1919 subscription letter for the magazine *International Conciliation*, M. C. Alexander, the Executive Secretary of the American Association for International Conciliation wrote: "The peace conference has assembled. It will make the most momentous decisions in history, and upon these decisions will rest the stability of the new world order and the future peace of the world."

In August, 1927, Dr. Augustus O. Thomas, President of the World Federation of Education Associations said:

> "If there are those who think we are to jump immediately into a new world order, actuated by complete understanding and brotherly love, they are doomed to disappointment. If we are ever to approach that time, it will be after patient and persistent effort of long duration. The present international situation of mistrust and fear can only be corrected by a formula of equal status, continuously applied, to every phase of international contacts, until the cobwebs of the old order are brushed out of the minds of the people of all lands."

Adolf Hitler said: "National Socialism will use its own revolution for the establishing of a new world order."

In the 1932 book *The New World Order*, author F. S. Marvin said that the League of Nations was the first attempt at a New World Order, and said that "nationality must rank below the claims of mankind as a whole."

Edward VIII became King of England on January 20, 1936, but he was forced to abdicate the throne eleven months later, when he married a commoner. He became the Duke of Windsor, and in July, 1940, became the governor of the Bahamas. He is on record as saying: "Whatever happens, whatever the outcome, a new Order is going to come into the world ... It will be buttressed with police power ... When peace comes this time there is going to be a new Order of social justice. It cannot be another Versailles."

In a *New York Times* article in October, 1940, called "New World Order Pledged to Jews," comes the following excerpt: "In the first public declaration on the Jewish question since the outbreak of the war, Arthur Greenwood, member without portfolio in the British War Cabinet, assured the Jews of the United States that when victory was achieved an effort would be made to found a new world order based on the ideals of 'justice and peace'."

The "Declaration of the Federation of the World," written by the Congress on World Federation, which was adopted by the Legislatures of some states, including North Carolina (1941), New Jersey (1942), and Pennsylvania (1943), said: "If totalitarianism wins this conflict, the world will be ruled by tyrants, and individuals will be slaves. If democracy wins, the nations of the earth will be united in a commonwealth of free peoples; and individuals, wherever found, will be the sovereign units of the new world order."

From an article in a June, 1942 edition of the *Philadelphia Inquirer*: "Undersecretary of State Sumner Welles tonight called for the early creation of an international organization of anti-Axis nations to control the world during the period between the armistice at the end of the present war and the setting up of a new world order on a permanent basis."

According to a February, 1962 *New York Times* article called "Rockefeller Bids Free Lands Unite: Calls at Harvard for Drive to Build New World Order," New York Governor Nelson Rockefeller told an audience at Harvard University: "The United Nations has not been able— nor can it be able— to shape a new world order which events so compellingly demand ... (The new world order that will answer economic, military, and political problems) urgently requires, I believe, that the United States take the leadership among all the free peoples to make the underlying concepts and aspirations of national sovereignty truly meaningful through the federal approach." The Associated Press reported that on July 26, 1968, Governor Rockefeller said in a speech to the International Platform Association at the Sheraton Park Hotel in New York, that "as President, he would work toward international creation of a New World Order."

Richard Nixon wrote in the October, 1967 issue of the Council on Foreign Relation's (CFR) journal *Foreign Affairs*: "The developing coherence of Asian regional thinking is reflected in a disposition to consider problems and loyalties in regional terms, and to evolve regional approaches to development needs and to the evolution of a new world order." In 1972, while in China, in a toast to Chinese Premier Chou En-lai, Nixon expressed "the hope that each of us has to build a new world order."

Richard Gardner, former deputy assistant Secretary of State for International Organizations under Kennedy and Johnson, and a member of the Trilateral Commission, wrote in the April, 1974 issue of *Foreign Affairs* (pg. 558): "In short, the 'house of world order' will have to be built from the bottom up rather than from the top down. It will look like a great 'booming, buzzing confusion,' to use William James' famous description of reality, but an end run around national sovereignty, eroding it piece by piece, will accomplish much more than the old fashioned frontal assault."

Richard A. Falk, wrote in his article "Toward a New World Order: Modest Methods and Drastic Visions" (from the 1975 book *On the Creation of a Just World Order*): "The existing order is breaking down at a very rapid rate, and the main uncertainty is whether mankind can exert a positive role in shaping a new world order or is doomed to await collapse in a passive posture. We believe a new world order will be born no later than early in the next century and that the death throes of the old and the birth pangs of the new will be a testing time for the human species."

In 1975, 32 Senators and 92 Representatives in Congress signed "A Declaration of Interdependence" (written by the historian Henry Steele Commager) which said that "we must join with others to bring forth a new world order...Narrow notions of national sovereignty must not be permitted to curtail that obligation." Congresswoman Marjorie Holt, who refused to sign it, said: "It calls for the surrender of our national sovereignty to international organizations. It declares that our economy should be regulated by international authorities. It proposes that we enter a 'new world order' that would redistribute the wealth created by the American people."

In an October, 1975 speech to the General Assembly of the United Nations, Henry Kissinger said: "My country's history, Mr. President, tells us that it is possible to fashion unity while cherishing diversity, that common action is possible despite the variety of races, interests, and beliefs we see here in this chamber. Progress and peace and justice are attainable. So we say to all peoples and governments: Let us fashion together a new world order."

During the 1976 Presidential campaign, Jimmy Carter said: "We must replace balance of power politics with world order politics." In a February 14, 1977 speech, Carter said: "I want to assure you that the relations of the United States with the other countries and peoples of the world will be guided during my own Administration by our desire to shape a world order that is more responsive to human aspirations. The United States will meet its obligation to help create a stable, just, and peaceful world order."

Harvard professor Stanley Hoffman wrote in his book *Primacy or World Order*: "What will have to take place is a gradual adaptation of the social, economic and political system of the United States to the imperatives of world order."

Conservative author George Weigel, director of the Ethics and Public Policy Center in Washington, D.C. said: "If the United States does not unashamedly lay down the rules of world order and enforce them ... then there is little reason to think that peace, security, freedom or prosperity will be served."

In a December, 1988 speech, Mikhail Gorbachev told the United Nations: "Further global progress is now possible only through a quest for universal consensus in the movement towards a new world order."

The man who put the New World Order in the limelight, and did more than anyone to bring about its acceptance, was President George Bush. In a February, 1990 fundraiser in San Francisco, Bush said: "Time and again in this century, the political map of the world was transformed. And in each instance, a New World Order came about through the advent of a new tyrant or the outbreak of a bloody global war, or its end."

On Saturday, August 25, 1990, the United Nations Security Council voted unanimously to allow a joint military force to use whatever means necessary to enforce a UN blockade against the country of Iraq. That afternoon, Lt. Gen. Brent Scowcroft, a CFR member and former aide to Henry Kissinger, who was the National Security Advisor to Bush, was interviewed by Charles Bierbauer of the Cable News Network (CNN) and used the term "a New World Order." In August, 1990, (According to an article in the *Washington Post* in May, 1991) he said: "We believe we are creating the beginning of a New World Order coming out of the collapse of the U.S.-Soviet antagonisms." During a September, 1990 speech at the United Nations, he announced that "we are moving to a New World Order." Later, on the eve of the Gulf War, Scowcroft said: "A colossal event is upon us, the birth of a New World Order." In the fall of 1990, on the way to Brussels, Belgium, Secretary of State James Baker said: "If we really believe that there's an opportunity here for a New World Order, and many of us believe that, we can't start out by appeasing aggression."

In September, 1990, the *Wall Street Journal* quoted Rep. Richard Gephardt as saying: "We can see beyond the present shadows of war in the Middle East to a New World Order where the strong work together to deter and stop aggression. This was precisely Franklin Roosevelt's and Winston Churchill's vision for peace for the post-war period."

In a September 11, 1990 televised address to a joint session of Congress, Bush said:

> "A new partnership of nations has begun. We stand today at a unique and extraordinary moment. The crisis in the Persian Gulf, as grave as it is, offers a rare opportunity to move toward an historic period of cooperation. Out of these troubled times, our fifth objective— a New World Order— can emerge ... When we are successful, and we will be, we have a real chance at this New World Order, an order in which a credible United Nations can use its peacekeeping role to fulfill the promise and vision of the United Nations' founders."

The September 17, 1990 issue of *Time* magazine said that "the Bush administration would like to make the United Nations a cornerstone of its plans to construct a New World Order."

In a September 25, 1990 address to the UN, Soviet Foreign Minister Eduard Shevardnadze described Iraq's invasion of Kuwait as "an act of terrorism (that) has been perpetrated against the emerging New World Order."

In an October 1, 1990, UN address, President Bush talked about the "...collective strength of the world community expressed by the UN ... an historic movement towards a New World Order ... a new partnership of nations ... a time when humankind came into its own ... to bring about a revolution of the spirit and the mind and begin a journey into a ... new age." On October 30, 1990, Bush suggested that the UN could help create "a New World Order and a long era of peace."

Jeanne Kirkpatrick, former U.S. Ambassador to the UN, said that one of the purposes for the Desert Storm operation, was to show to the world how a "reinvigorated United Nations could serve as a global policeman in the New World Order."

On December 31, 1990, Gorbachev said that the New World Order would be ushered in by the Gulf War.

Prior to the Gulf War, on January 29, 1991, Bush told the nation in his State of the Union address:

> "What is at stake is more than one small country, it is a big idea— a New World Order, where diverse nations are drawn together in a common cause to achieve the universal aspirations of mankind; peace and security, freedom, and the rule of law. Such is a world worthy of our struggle, and worthy of our children's future." He also said: "If we do not follow the dictates of our inner moral compass and stand up for human life, then his lawlessness will threaten the peace and democracy of the emerging New World Order we now see, this long dreamed-of vision we've all worked toward for so long."

In a speech to the families of servicemen at Fort Gordon, Georgia on February 1, 1991, Bush said: "When we win, and we will, we will have taught a dangerous dictator, and any tyrant tempted to follow in his footsteps, that the United States has a new credibility and that what we say goes, and that there is no place for lawless aggression in the Persian Gulf and in this New World Order that we seek to create." Following a February 6, 1991 speech to the Economic Club of New York City, Bush answered a reporter's question about what the New World Order was, by saying: "Now, my vision of a New World Order foresees a United Nations with a revitalized peace-keeping function."

Bush said in a speech to the Congress on March 6, 1991: "Now, we can see a new world coming into view. A world in which there is a very real prospect of a New World Order. In the words of Winston Churchill, a 'world order' in which the 'principles of justice and fair play ... protect the weak against the strong.' A world where the United Nations, freed from cold war stalemate, is poised to fulfill the historic vision of its founders. A world in which freedom and respect for human rights find a home among all nations."

On August 21, 1991, after the failed coup in the Soviet Union, CNN reporter Mary Tillotson said that the President's "New World Order is back on track, now stronger than ever." In an interview with CNN at the height of the Gulf War, Scowcroft said that he had doubts about the significance of Mid-East objectives regarding global policy. When asked if that meant he didn't believe in the New World Order, he replied: "Oh, I believe in it. But our definition, not theirs." On January 25, 1993, Clinton's Secretary of State, Warren Christopher, said in a CNN interview: "We must get the New World Order on track and bring the UN into its correct role in regards to the United States."

In April, 1992, Sen. Joseph R. Biden Jr. wrote the article "How I Learned to Love the New World Order" for *The Wall Street Journal*.

While campaigning for the passage of NAFTA, Kissinger said: "NAFTA is a major stepping stone to the New World Order." In a July 18, 1993 *Los Angeles Times* article about NAFTA, Kissinger is quoted as saying: "What Congress will have before it is not a conventional trade agreement but the architecture of a new international system ... a first step toward a New World Order."

On May 4, 1994, Leslie Gelb, CFR President, said on "The Charlie Rose Show": "...you (Charlie Rose) had me on (before) to talk about the New World Order. I talk about it all the time. It's one world now. The Council (CFR) can find, nurture, and begin to put people in the kinds of jobs this country needs. And that's going to be one of the major enterprises of the Council under me."

On September 14, 1994, while speaking at the Business Council for the United Nations, David Rockefeller said: "But this present window of opportunity, during which a truly peaceful and interdependent world order might be built, will not be open for long. Already there are powerful forces at work that threaten to destroy all of our hopes and efforts to erect an enduring structure of global interdependence." He said at another time: "We are on the verge of a global transformation. All we need is the right major crisis and the nations will accept the New World Order."

In the July/August 1995 issue of *Foreign Affairs*, Arthur Schlesinger, Jr. wrote: "We are not going to achieve a New World Order without paying for it in blood as well as in words and money."

Former West German Chancellor Willy Brandt said: "The New World Order is a world that has supernational authority to regulate the world commerce and industry; an international organization that would control the production and consumption of oil; an international currency that would replace the dollar; a World Development Fund that would make funds available to free and Communist nations alike; and an international police force to enforce the edicts of the New World Order."

Somehow, the implications from these quotes, lends a sinister overtone to this New World Order. After 25 years of research, it is clear to me that this country has been infiltrated by conspirators, members of an organization who are dedicated to establishing a one-world socialist government— with them in control. It sounds unbelievable, like something out of a James Bond movie, yet, it is a fact. A fact that the media has refused to publicize, even attempting to cover it up, and deny its very existence.

In the 1844 political novel *Coningsby* by Benjamin Disraeli, the British Prime Minister, a character known as Sidonia (which was based on Lord Rothschild, whose family he had become close friends with in the early 1840's) says: "That mighty revolution which is at this moment preparing in Germany and which will be in fact a greater and a second Reformation, and of which so little is as yet known in England, is entirely developing under the auspices of the Jews, who almost monopolize the professorial chairs of Germany ... the world is governed by very different personages from what is imagined by those who are not behind the scenes." On September 10, 1876, in Aylesbury, Disraeli said: "The governments of the present day have to deal not merely with other governments, with emperors, kings and ministers, but also with secret societies which have everywhere their unscrupulous agents, and can at the last moment upset all the governments' plans."

On October 1, 1877, Henry Edward Manning, Cardinal Archbishop of Westminster, said of the trouble in the Balkan States: "It is not emperors or kings, nor princes, that direct the course of affairs in the East. There is something else over them and behind them; and that thing is more powerful than them."

In 1902, Pope Leo XIII wrote of this power: "It bends governments to its will sometimes by promises, sometimes by threats. It has found its way into every class of Society, and forms an invisible and irresponsible power, an independent government, as it were, within the body corporate of the lawful state." Walter Rathenau, head of German General Electric, said in 1909: "Three hundred men, all of whom know one another, direct the economic destiny of Europe and choose their successors from among themselves."

President Woodrow Wilson said in 1913: "Since I entered politics, I have chiefly had men's views confided to me privately. Some of the biggest men in the United States, in the field of commerce and manufacture, are afraid of something. They know that there is a power somewhere so organized, so subtle, so watchful, so interlocked, so complete, so pervasive that they better not speak above their breath when they speak in condemnation of it."

John F. Hylan, mayor of New York City (1918-25), said in a March 26, 1922 speech:

> "...the real menace of our Republic is this invisible government which like a giant octopus sprawls its slimy length over city, state and nation. Like the octopus of real life, it operates under cover of a self-created screen ... At the head of this octopus are the Rockefeller Standard Oil interests and a small group of powerful banking houses generally referred to as 'the international bankers.' The little coterie of powerful international bankers virtually run the United States Government for their own selfish purposes. They practically control both political parties."

In the December, 1922 edition of *Foreign Affairs*, Philip Kerr wrote: "Obviously there is going to be no peace or prosperity for mankind as long as (the earth) remains divided into 50 or 60 independent states until some kind of international system is created ... The real problem today is that of the world government."

In a letter dated November 21, 1933, Franklin D. Roosevelt wrote to confidant Colonel Edward House: "The real truth of the matter is, as you and I know, that a financial element in the large centers has owned the government ever since the days of Andrew Jackson."

In her novel, *Captains and the Kings*, Taylor Caldwell wrote of the "plot against the people," and says that it wasn't "until the era of the League of Just Men and Karl Marx that conspirators and conspiracies became one, with one aim, one objective, and one determination." Some heads of foreign governments refer to this group as "The Magicians," Stalin called them "The Dark Forces," and President Eisenhower described them as "the military-industrial complex." In the July 26, 1936 issue of the *New York Times*, Joseph Kennedy, patriarch of the Kennedy family, was quoted as saying: "Fifty men have run America and that's a high figure." In 1952, U.S. Supreme Court Justice Felix Frankfurter, said: "The real rulers in Washington are invisible, and exercise power from behind the scenes."

According to the California State Investigating Committee on Education (1953): "So-called modern Communism is apparently the same hypocritical and deadly world conspiracy to destroy civilization that was founded by the secret order of The Illuminati in Bavaria on May 1, 1776, and that raised its whorey head in our colonies here at the critical period before the adoption of our Federal Constitution."

This purpose of this book is to show the connection between the Illuminati, and what would become known as the New World Order. Through the years, the term 'Illuminati' has developed an anti-Semitic connotation, because some researchers have insisted that the move toward a one world government has been engineered as part of a Jewish conspiracy. This is not true. One of the documents that provided evidence concerning this has been proven to be a complete fabrication. Although some of the International Bankers which actually control this group are Jewish, there is no basis for indicting the entire Jewish race.

In 1966, Dr. Carroll Quigley, a professor of history at the Foreign Service School of Georgetown University, published a 1311-page book called *Tragedy and Hope: A History of the World in Our Time*. On page 950 he says:

> "There does exist, and has existed for a generation, an international Anglophile network which operates, to some extent, in the way the radical Right believes the Communists act. In fact, this network, which we may identify as the Round Table Groups, has no aversion to cooperating with the Communists, or any other groups, and frequently does so. I know of the operations of this network because I have studied it for twenty years and was permitted for two years, in the early 1960's, to examine its papers and secret records. I have no aversion to it or to most of its aims and have, for much of my life, been close to it and to many of its instruments ... my chief difference of opinion is that it wishes to remain unknown, and I believe its role in history is significant enough to be known ... because the American branch of this organization (sometimes called the 'Eastern Establishment') has played a very significant role in the history of the United States in the last generation."

On page 324, he elaborates even further by saying:

> "In addition to these pragmatic goals, the powers of financial capitalism had another far-reaching aim, nothing less than to create a world system of financial control in private hands able to dominate the political system of each country and the economy of the world as a whole. This system was to be controlled in a feudalist fashion by the central banks of the world acting in concert, by secret agreements, arrived at in frequent private meetings and conferences. The apex of the system was the Bank for International Settlements in Basle, Switzerland, a private bank owned and controlled by the worlds' central banks which were themselves pri-

vate corporations. The growth of financial capitalism made possible a centralization of world economic control and use of this power for the direct benefit of financiers and indirect injury of all other economic groups."

Bill Clinton, during his acceptance speech at the Democratic Convention, said: "As a teenager, I heard John Kennedy's summons to citizenship. And then, as a student at Georgetown (University where he attended 1964-68) I heard that call clarified by a professor I had named Carroll Quigley." This is where Clinton received his indoctrination as an internationalist favoring one-world government.

In the mid-1970's, Dr. Tom Berry, who was pastor of the Baptist Bible Church in Elkton, Maryland, said: "At most, there are only 5,000 people in the whole world who have a significant understanding of the plan."

Professor Arnold Toynbee (a founding member of the Round Table) said in a June, 1931 speech to the Institute of International Affairs in Copenhagen: "We are at present working discreetly with all our might to wrest this mysterious force called sovereignty out of the clutches of the local nation states of the world."

H. G. Wells, a member of the Fabian Society, wrote in his 1933 book *The Shape of Things To Come*: "Although world government has been plainly coming for some years, although it had been endlessly feared and murmured against, it found no opposition prepared anywhere."

Major General John Frederick Charles Fuller, a British military historian, said in 1941: "The government of the Western nations, whether monarchical or republican, had passed into the invisible hands of a plutocracy, international in power and grasp. It was, I venture to suggest, this semi-occult power which ... pushed the masses of the American people into the cauldron of World War I."

On June 28, 1945, President Harry Truman said in a speech: "It will be just as easy for nations to get along in a republic of the world as it is for us to get along in a republic of the United States." On October 24, 1945, Senator Glen Taylor (D-Idaho) introduced Senate Resolution No. 183, which called for the Senate to go on record as advocating the establishment of a world republic, including an international police force.

In 1947, the American Education Fellowship (formerly known as the Progressive Education Association) called for the "establishment of a genuine world order, an order in which national sovereignty is subordinate to world authority..."

Brock Chisholm, the first director of the UN World Health Organization said: "To achieve one world government it is necessary to remove from the minds of men their individualism, their loyalty to family traditions and national identification." On February 9, 1950, a Senate Foreign Relations subcommittee introduced Concurrent Resolution 66 which began: "Whereas, in order to achieve universal peace and justice, the present Charter of the United Nations should be changed to provide a true world government constitution."

James Warburg, a member of the Council on Foreign Relations, told the Senate Foreign Relations Committee on February 17, 1950: "We shall have world government whether or not you like it, by conquest or consent."

Sen. William Jenner said in a February 23, 1954 speech:

"Today the path to total dictatorship in the United States can be laid by strictly legal means, unseen and unheard by the Congress, the President, or the people ... Outwardly we have a constitutional government. We have operating within our government and political system, another body representing another form of government, a bureaucratic elite which believes our Constitution is outmoded and is sure that it is the winning side ... All the strange developments in foreign policy agreements may be traced to this group who are going to make us over to suit their pleasure ... This political action group has its own local political support organizations, its own pressure groups, its own vested interests, its foothold within our government."

In September, 1960, Elmo Roper, in an address called "The Goal is Government of All the World" said: "For it becomes clear that the first step toward world government cannot be completed until we have advanced on the four fronts: the economic, the military, the political and the social."

In a 1963 symposium (sponsored by the leftist Fund for the Republic, of the Ford Foundation) called "The Elite and the Electorate: Is Government by the People Possible?" Senator J. William Fulbright, the Chairman of the Senate Foreign Relations Committee said: "The case for government by elites is irrefutable ... government by the people is possible but highly improbable"

Sen. Russell Long of Louisiana, who for 18 years was the Chairman of the Senate Finance Committee, said that our "government is completely and totally out of control. We do not know how much long term debt we have put on the American people. We don't even know our financial condition from year to year..." He also said: "We have created a bureaucracy in Washington so gigantic that it is running this government for the bureaucracy, the way they want, and not for the people of the United States. We no longer have representative government in America."

Congressman Larry P. McDonald, who, in 1976 was killed in the Korean Airlines 747 that had been shot down by the Soviets said: "The drive of the Rockefellers and their allies is to create a one world government combining supercapitalism and Communism under the same tent, all under their control ... Do I mean conspiracy? Yes I do. I am convinced there is such a plot, international in scope, generations old in planning, and incredibly evil in intent."

Zbigniew Brzezinski, who was President Carter's National Security Advisor, said: "...this regionalization is in keeping with the tri-lateral plan which calls for a gradual convergence of East and West, ultimately leading toward the goal of 'one world government' ... National sovereignty is no longer a viable concept..."

Norman Cousins, the honorary Chairman of Planetary Citizens for the World We Chose (as well as the President of the World Federalist Association) is quoted in the magazine *Human Events* as saying: "World government is coming, in fact, it is inevitable. No arguments for or against it can change that fact."

During the 1991 Bilderberger Conference held in Evians, France, Dr. Henry Kissinger said:

"Today, America would be outraged if UN troops entered Los Angeles to restore order (referring to the riot caused by the Rodney King incident). Tomorrow they will be grateful! This is especially true if they were told that there were an outside threat from beyond, whether real or promulgated, that threatened our very existence. It is then that all peoples of the world will plead to deliver them from this evil. The one thing every man fears is the unknown. When presented with this scenario, individual rights will be willingly relinquished for the guarantee of their well-being granted to them by the World Government."

On October 29, 1991, David Funderburk, a former U.S. Ambassador to Romania (1981-85), told a group in North Carolina: "George Bush has been surrounding himself with people who believe in one-world government. They believe that the Soviet system and the American system are converging," and the manner in which they would accomplish that was through the United Nations, "the majority of whose 166 member states are socialist, atheist, and anti-American."

Time magazine on July 20, 1992, in an article called "The Birth of the Global Nation," Strobe Talbott, an Editor (later Clinton's Deputy Secretary of State) wrote: "In the next century, nations as we know it will be obsolete; all states will recognize a single, global authority. National sovereignty wasn't such a good idea after all ... But it has taken the events in our own wondrous and terrible century to clinch the case for world government." In 1993 he received the Norman Cousins Global Governance Award for the article and for what he has accomplished "for the cause of global governance."

Pope John Paul II said: "By the end of this decade (2000) we will live under the first one world government ... One world government is inevitable."

Haven't you wondered why things are the way they are. That even though a new President is elected and a new Administration takes over, executive policy does not change, nor does the State of the Nation— which continues to get worse. Is there some sort of group that has infiltrated both political parties, our government, and many other governments, which has for years been creating and controlling world events, and is only now being officially identified, because it is too late to stop this juggernaut? Yes, I believe there is. That is the purpose of this book, to trace the origin and growth of the group which has come to be known as the New World Order, and why there is such a massive campaign to accept it.

President Bill Clinton said in his first inaugural address: "Profound and powerful forces are shaking and remaking our world, and the urgent question of our time is whether we can make change our friend and not our enemy."

You need to know just exactly what these changes are, and how they will affect the lives and you and your family. Abraham Lincoln's pledge of "government of the people, by the people, for the people," has become a joke. After reading this book, you will know why things are the way they are; and when you hear that 'They' are responsible for something, you will know who 'They' are.

PART ONE

THE PHYSICAL CONSPIRACY

CHAPTER ONE

THE BIRTH OF TYRANNY

THE ILLUMINATI

When you talk about tracing the origin of an organization which is controlling the destiny of the world, it's obvious that you have to start at a period which would allow a movement of this magnitude, time to ferment. Changes like the ones which have, and are occurring do not take place overnight. We are dealing with a group which must have been growing for a long period of time, in order to obtain the power and influence necessary to achieve the global control now being exercised. When you think of it in that context, there is such a group. The Illuminati.

The leader of the Illuminati was a man named, Dr. Adam Weishaupt, who was born on February 6, 1748, the son of a Jewish rabbi. When his father died in 1753, he was converted to Catholicism by Baron Johann Adam Ickstatt, who turned the early training of the boy over to the Jesuits. Ickstatt, in 1742, had been appointed by the Jesuits to be the curator of the University in order to reorganize it. He had retired in 1765, but still controlled its policies.

Although Weishaupt later became a priest, he developed a distinct hatred for the Jesuits, and became an atheist. Given access to the private library of Ickstatt, his godfather, the young man became interested in the works of the French philosophers, and studied law, economics, politics, and history. One such philosopher, Voltaire (1694-1778), a revolutionary who held liberal religious views, had written in a letter to King Frederick II ('the Great', a Mason): "Lastly, when the whole body of the Church should be sufficiently weakened and infidelity strong enough, the final blow (is) to be dealt by the sword of open, relentless persecution. A reign of terror (is) to be spread over the whole earth, and ... continue while a Christian should be found obstinate enough to adhere to Christianity." It is believed that Weishaupt got his ideas concerning the destruction of the Church from Voltaire's writings. He studied in France, where he met Robespierre (who later led the French Revolution), and became friends with a few people in the French Royal Court. It is believed, that through these contacts, he was introduced to Satanism.

He graduated from the Bavarian University in Ingolstadt, Germany in 1768. He served four years as a tutor until he was promoted to Assistant Instructor. In 1770, he was chosen by Mayer Amschel Rothschild to develop an organization that he could use. In 1772, Weishaupt was made Professor of Civil Law. In 1773, he was made Professor of Canon Law, a post which had been held by the Jesuits for 90 years. They had founded most of the Universities, and kept strict control of them in order to eliminate Protestant influence.

In 1773, Weishaupt got married, against the wishes of Ickstatt, who denounced him. Two years later, at the age of 27, he was made Dean of the Faculty of Law. The Jesuits, worried about his quick progression, tried to thwart his influence by secretly plotting against him, and his liberal thinking. Not wanting to become a martyr for his free-thinking ideas, he began focusing on establishing his organization. To confuse his detractors, he based the organizational structure on the one used by the Jesuits, however, his intention was to have a secret coalition of liberalism.

He studied the anti-Christian doctrines of the Manicheans, whose teachings revolved around astrology, medicine, and magic. He had been indoctrinated into Egyptian occult practices by an unknown merchant named Kolmer, from Jutland (the area around the border of Denmark and West Germany), who had been traveling around Europe since 1771. He studied the power of the Eleusinian mysteries and the influence exerted by the secret cult of the Pythagoreans. Pythagoras was a 6th century B.C., philosopher who taught that men and women should combine their belongings— which became the basic philosophy behind Communism. Weishaupt also studied the teachings of the Essenes, and acquired copies of the 'Kabala,' 'The Major Key of Solomon,' and 'The Lesser Key of Solomon,' which revealed how to conjure up demons and perform occult rituals.

He studied the various Masonic writings after meeting a Protestant Freemason from Hanover. At first he thought about creating a superior Masonic-like organization that would be made up of men possessing superior abilities in all fields but concluded that Masonry was too open.

Weishaupt was instructed by the Rothschilds (who were also said to be Satanists), to leave the Catholic Church, and unite all the different occult groups. He created the coven known as the 'Golden Dawn' which, to this day, is alleged to be the Rothschilds' private coven.

Weishaupt spent five years working out a plan through which all of his ideas could be reduced to a single system which would be used to fight the oppression of religion, thereby loosening social ties. He wanted to replace Christianity with a religion of reason. An initial idea was to form an organization comprised of 'Schools of Wisdom,' whose goal was to "make of the human race, one good and happy family." They were to strive for the perfection of morals, so he thought about naming the group the 'Perfectibilists,' but it lacked the air of mystery and intrigue that he sought.

In 1774, he published a fictitious article called *Sidonii Apollinarus Fragment*, which he said, was to prepare the people for the doctrine of reason. Weishaupt wrote: "Princes and nations will disappear without violence from the earth. The human race will then become one family, and the world will be the dwelling of rational men." He wrote of their aims: "To make the perfecting of reasoning powers interesting to mankind, to spread the knowledge of sentiments, both humane and social, to check wicked inclinations, to stand up for suffering and oppressed virtue ... to facilitate the acquirement of knowledge and science."

On May 1, 1776, under the direction of the newly formed House of Rothschild (and Wessely, Moses, Mendelssohn; and the Bankers, Itzig, Friedlander, and Meyer), who instigated the American Revolution to weaken Great Britain, Weishaupt founded the Ancient Illuminated Seers of Bavaria, which became known as the Order of the Illuminati. Weishaupt said that the name was derived from Luciferian teachings, and means, 'Holders of the Light.' In Latin, it means, the 'enlightened ones.' In layman's terms, it means 'to illuminate,' or 'to give light.' It refers to someone who is enlightened, spiritually and intellectually. Satan, when he was an angel, was known as Lucifer, the 'Bearer of Light,' and being that the group's name evolved from this, we can see the underlying nature of its goals. In addition, May 1st was a great day for all communist nations, where it was known as May Day; and it is also known as a special day to witches.

There were some earlier groups, with similar names, such as a group known as the 'Illuminated Ones' which was founded by Joachim of Floris in the 11th century, who taught a primitive, supposedly Christian doctrine of "poverty and equality." The Rosheniah, or 'Illuminated Ones,' (which was influenced by an earlier group known as the Eastern Ismaelites, after Ismael, the son of Jaaffer; Batiniyeh, 'internal' or 'secret'; or just by their nickname, the 'Assassins.') was a group in Afghanistan during the 16th century, who sought the 'illumination' from the Supreme Being, who wanted a class of perfect men and women. After reaching the fourth degree, 'Enlightened One,' the initiate would receive mystical powers, and when the eighth and final degree was reached, they were told they had achieved perfection. An Afghan scholar said that their purpose was to influence people of importance to establish harmony in the world, and were devoted to fight the tyranny of the Moguls, who were the rulers of India. The group survived until the 1700's.

The Alumbrados ('enlightened' or 'illuminated') was a mysterious movement in Spain during the 16th and 17th centuries that believed that when a person achieved a certain degree of perfection, they experienced a vision of God, and then entered into direct communication with the Holy Spirit. At this point the soul would enter a state of limbo— not advancing or going back. Once this level was achieved, a person didn't have to perform any good works or get involved in any religious activity, because they had received the 'light.' Once they had received the 'light,' they would possess superior human intelligence.

Their members mainly came from reformed Franciscans, and the Jesuits. Their unusual claims caused them to be criticized and harassed, and the Inquisition issued Edicts against them in 1568, 1574, and 1623. Ignatius de Loyola, founder of the Jesuits, was put in jail for being a member. This condemnation forced the movement into France, where in 1654 they surfaced as the Illuminated Guerinets.

The 'Illuminati' was the name of an occultic German sect that existed in the 15th century that professed to possess the 'light' received from Satan. It was also the name of an organization that was influenced by the writings of Emanuel Swedenborg, which was established in 1760 at Avignon. This Swedenborgian philosophy also produced the Illuminated Theosophists in 1766 at Paris, then later in London, but was short lived.

Although it would certainly make for a more interesting story, there is no documentation to suggest that Weishaupt's Order of the Illuminati is a continuation of any of these groups. However, whether their teachings and philosophy had an influence on him is another question. Most assuredly, there is a spiritual lineage that ties them all together.

Starting with only five members (Weishaupt, and his inner circle— his friend Kollmer, Francis Dashwood of the Satanic Hellfire Club, Alphonse Donatien DeSade from whose name we get the word "sadism," and Meyer Amschel Rothschild), the Illuminati wasn't fully operational until 1778.

Weishaupt wrote: "The great strength of our Order lies in its concealment, let it never appear, in any place in its own name, but always covered by another name, and another occupation. None is fitter than the three lower degrees of Freemasonry; the public is accustomed to it, expects little from it, and therefore takes little notice of it." He also wrote: "For the Order wishes to be secret, and to work in silence, for thus it is better secured from the oppression of the ruling powers, and because this secrecy gives a greater zest to the whole."

The Order was made up of three degrees: Novice, Minerval, and Illuminated Minerval. It was organized in a manner similar to Freemasonry and the Jesuits. Even though he admired the structure of the Jesuit hierarchy, he wrote that no ex-Jesuits were to be admitted, except by special permission. He wrote that they "must be avoided as the plague." Their rites and ceremonies were similar to that of the Masons. Their aim, he said, was to have a one-world government, to allow the elite to govern the world, thus preventing future wars. One of their early programs was to distribute anti-religious material to criticize clerical leaders, who they saw as obstacles to social progress, and to oppose the "enemies of the human race and of society."

Weishaupt wrote: "How can the weak obtain protection? Only by union, but this is rare. Nothing can bring this about but hidden societies. Hidden schools of wisdom are the means which we will one day free men from their bonds..."

All members were required to adopt classical names. Weishaupt was called 'Spartacus' (who had been the leader of the slave insurrection in ancient Rome). His right-hand man, Xavier von Zwack, a lawyer to Prince von Salm, was known as 'Cato'; Nicolai, the bookseller, was 'Lucian'; Professor Westenreider was 'Pythagoras'; Canon Hertel was 'Marius'; Marquis di Constanza was 'Diomedes'; Massenhausen was 'Ajar' Baron von Schroeckenstein was 'Mohomed'; and Baron von Mengenhofen was 'Sylla.'

Their headquarters was in Munich, Germany, and known as the Grand Lodge of the Illuminati (or Lodge of the Grand Orient)— code-named 'Athens.' Among their other four lodges: Ingolstadt was known as 'Ephesus,' Heidelberg as 'Utica,' Bavaria as 'Achaia,' and Frankfurt was known as 'Thebes.'

The calendar was reconstructed, and the months known by names reminiscent of the Hebrew language: January was known as 'Dimeh,' and February as 'Benmeh,' etc. They dated their letters according to the Persian Era, named after the king who began to rule in Persia in 632 B.C., Jezdegerd. Their new year began on March 21st, which some sources say is New Years Day for witches.

In 1777, Weishaupt joined the Eclectic Masonic lodge 'Theodore of Good Counsel' in Munich, and towards the end of 1778, he came up with the idea of merging the Illuminati and the Masons. Zwack became a Mason on November 27, 1778, and working with a brother Mason, Abbé Marotti, he divulged the secret of the Order. By the middle of 1779, the Munich Masonic lodge was under the complete influence of the Illuminati.

During the first four years, about 60 active members had been recruited by a committee known as the 'Insinuators,' and close to 1,000 had become indirectly affiliated with the Order. Soon, three more lodges were established.

Few knew the supreme direction of the Order. Only those within the inner circle, known as the 'Areopagite' (meaning 'Tribunal'), were aware of their true purpose. To all others, Weishaupt said that he wanted a one-world government to prevent all future wars.

The book *World Revolution* (by Nesta Webster) stated: "The art of Illuminism lay in enlisting dupes as well as adepts, and by encouraging the dreams of honest visionaries or the schemes of fanatics, by flattering the vanity of ambitious egotists, by working on unbalanced brains, or by playing on such passions as greed and power, to make men of totally divergent aims serve the secret purpose of the sect."

Foolish, naive people, with money to burn, were especially welcomed. Weishaupt wrote: "These good people swell our numbers and fill our money box; set yourselves to work; these gentlemen must be made to nibble at the bait ... But let us beware of telling them our secrets, this sort of people must always be made to believe that the grade they have reached is the last." Weishaupt explained: "One must speak sometimes in one way, sometimes in another, so that our real purpose should remain impenetrable to our inferiors." And what was that purpose? It was "nothing less than to win power and riches, to undermine secular or religious government, and to obtain the mastery of the world."

Initiates were told that the Order represented the highest ideals of the Church, that Christ was the first advocator of Illuminism, and his secret mission was to restore to men the original liberty and equality they had lost in the Garden of Eden. Weishaupt said that Christ exhorted his disciples to despise riches in order to prepare the world for the community of goods that would do away with property ownership.

Weishaupt wrote to Zwack: "The most admirable thing of all is that great Protestant and reformed theologians (Lutherans and Calvinists) who belong to our Order really believe they see in it the true and genuine mind of the Christian religion." However, when one of Weishaupt's followers would reach the higher degrees, their secret was revealed: "Behold our secret ... in order to destroy all Christianity, all religion, we have pretended to have the sole true religion ... to deliver one day the human race from all religion."

Women were also enlisted. He wrote: "There is no way of influencing men so powerful, as by means of women. These should therefore be our chief study; we should insinuate ourselves into their good opinion, give them hints of emancipation from the tyranny of public opinion, and of standing up for themselves..." He also wrote: "This sex has a large part of the world in their hands." Female members were divided into two groups: one group of society women, to give the organization an air of respectability; and the other group "who would help to satisfy those brothers who have a penchant for pleasure." The Illuminati also used monetary and sex bribery to gain control of men in high places, then blackmailed them with the threat of financial ruin, public exposure, and fear of death.

Internal fighting soon developed because of Weishaupt's thirst for power.

Besides that, because only nominal dues were collected, the Order suffered financially.

In 1780, a new member, Baron Franz Friedrich Knigge (1752-1796), was recruited, and given the pseudonym of 'Philo.' Knigge was born on October 16, 1752. He studied law at Gottingen, served in the courts of Hesse-Cassel and Weimar, and was a well-known writer of romance, poetry and philosophy. He joined the Masonic lodge of Strict Observance, which was dedicated to the elimination of the occult sciences, which were widely practiced. Unable to do that, they were forced to accept it. Knigge achieved the rank of Brother Commander, and had the title of Knight of the Swan. He assisted in the establishment of a new Masonic lodge at Hanau. Because of his developing exposure and interest in the occult, magic and alchemy, he joined the Rosicrucians, a secret organization that dated back to the fourteenth century, and reportedly was an occult group who participated in human sacrifice rituals.

He later renounced alchemy, and devoted his studies to the development of a form of Masonry that would allow man to regain the perfection they once had before the fall of Adam and Eve. His idea was to reform Masonry, and he was going to make these proposals at the Congress of Wilhelmsbad. However, the Marquis of Constanza (known as "one of the most notorious of the Illuminati") informed him that the Illuminati had already done that. In order to lure him, Weishaupt portrayed the Order as representing the greatest advancement in science, and dedicated to philosophical advancement. Since this fell in line with Knigge's thinking, he was drawn into the Order.

Knigge was definitely a catch, because he had a talent for organization, and soon became the head of the Westphalia Circle. He was instrumental in pushing for a merger between the Masons and the Illuminati. Weishaupt wrote of him: "Philo is the master from whom to take lessons; give me six men of his stamp and with them I will change the face of the Universe ... Philo does more than we all expected, and he is the man who alone will carry it all through."

Knigge was firmly supported by members of the Areopagite, who felt that Weishaupt's supreme authority should be delegated to others, and they agreed with Knigge's proposed modifications for the organization. They were adopted on July 9, 1781. Knigge was able to recruit the most effective propagandists, and from 1780 on, the growth of the Order was very rapid because its expansion was facilitated through its affiliation with the Masonic lodges.

Their goal was now to achieve their aims by splitting mankind into opposing ideologies, and for them to fight among themselves, thus weakening national governments and organized religion.

An understanding was finally reached between the Masons and the Illuminati, and on December 20, 1781, a combined Order was proposed, which would add to the Illuminati organization, the first three degrees of Masonry. It wasn't until the Congress of Wilhelmsbad from July 16th to August 29th, 1781 (which was attended by Masons, Martinistes, and representatives from other secret organizations from Europe, America and Asia), that the alliance was official. Those at the meeting were put under oath not to reveal anything. Comte de Virieu, a Mason from the Martiniste lodge at Lyons, upon his return home, when questioned about the Congress, said: "I will not confide them to you. I can only tell you that all this is very much more serious than you think. The conspiracy which is being woven is so well thought out, that it will be, so to speak, impossible for the Monarchy and the Church to escape it." He later denounced the Illuminati, and became a devout Catholic.

Because of a movement begun by Dohm's book *Upon the Civil Amelioration of the Condition of the Jews* in 1781, and a book by Mirabeau in London, a resolution was passed at the Congress to allow Jews into the Lodges. It was obvious that it was done for financial reasons, because the Illuminati moved their headquarters to Frankfurt, Germany, a stronghold of Jewish finance. As the Order spread throughout Germany, money was contributed from such leading Jewish families as the Oppenheimers, Wertheimers, Schusters, Speyers, Sterns, and of course, the Rothschilds. Gerald B. Winrod wrote in his book *Adam Weishaupt: A Human Devil* that "of the thirty-nine chief sub-leaders of Weishaupt, seventeen were Jews." Arguments that the Illuminati was solely of Jewish origin, are completely unfounded.

After the Congress of Wilhelmsbad, the Illuminati functioned under the following organizational structure:

NURSERY
1) Preparation
2) Novice
3) Minerval
4) Illuminatus

SYMBOLIC (Masonry)
1) Apprentice
2) Fellow-Craft
3) Master

SCOTCH (Masonry)
4) Illuminatus Major (Scotch Novice)
5) Illuminatus Dirigens (Scotch Knight)

THE LESSER MYSTERIES
1) Presbyter (or Priest)
2) Prince (or Regent)

THE GREATER MYSTERIES
3) Magus
4) Rex

THE HOUSE OF ROTHSCHILD

No other name has become more synonymous with the Illuminati than the Rothschilds. It is believed that the Rothschild family used the Illuminati as a means to achieving their goal of world-wide financial dominance. Mayer Amschel Rothschild (1743-1812) was born in Frankfurt-on-the-Main in Germany, the son of Moses Amschel Bauer, a banker and goldsmith. Their name was derived from the 'red shield' ('rotschildt') that hung over the door of their shop, and had been the emblem of revolutionary Jews in Eastern Europe. A few years after his father's death, he worked as a clerk in a Hanover bank, which was owned by the Oppenheimers. He became a junior partner, and soon left to take over the business started by his father in 1750. He bought and sold rare coins, and later succeeded in buying out several other coin dealers.

In 1769, he became a court agent for Prince William IX of Hesse-Kassel, who was the grandson of George II of England, a cousin to George III, a nephew of the King of Denmark, and a brother-in-law to the King of Sweden. Soon Rothschild became the middleman for big Frankfurt bankers like the Bethmann Brothers, and Rueppell & Harnier. After expanding his business to antiques, wineries, and the importing of manufactured materials from England, the Rothschild family began to amass a sizable fortune.

Prince William inherited his father's fortune upon his death in 1785, which was the largest private fortune in Europe. Some of this money had come from Great Britain paying for the use of 16,800 Hessian soldiers to stop the revolution in America, because the money was never given to the troops. In 1804, the Rothschilds secretly made loans to the Denmark government, on behalf of Prince William.

In June, 1806, when Napoleon's troops pushed their way into Germany, Prince William fled to Denmark, leaving his money with Mayer Rothschild. History tells us that Rothschild secretly buried William's ledgers, which revealed the full extent of his wealth, a list of debtors and the interest required from them, and 600,000 pounds ($3,000,000), to keep Napoleon from confiscating it. Buderus von Carlhausen (Carl Buderus), the Treasury official who handled William's finances, was given 'power of attorney,' and he in turn made Rothschild his chief banker, responsible for collecting the interest on the royal loans. Napoleon announced that all debts being paid to Prince William, were to go to the French Treasury, and offered a 25% commission on any debts that he would collect. Rothschild refused.

Developing circumstances soon allowed the Rothschilds to formulate a plan which would guarantee them the financial control of Europe, and soon the world. It began with taking advantage of the outcome of the Battle of Waterloo, which was fought at La-Belle-Alliance, seven miles south of Waterloo, which is a suburb of Brussels, Belgium. Early in the battle, Napoleon appeared to be winning, and the first secret military report to London communicated that fact. However, upon reinforcements from the Prussians, under Gebhard Blucher, the tide turned in favor of Wellington. On Sunday, June 18, 1815, Rothworth, a courier of Nathan Rothschild, head of the London branch of the family, was on the battlefield, and upon seeing that Napoleon was being beaten, went by horse to Brussels, then to Ostende, and for 2,000 francs, got a sailor to get him to England across stormy seas. When Nathan Rothschild received the news on June 20th, he informed the government, who did not believe him. So, with everyone believing Wellington to be defeated, Rothschild immediately began to sell all of his stock on the English Stock Market. Everyone else followed his lead, and also began selling, causing stocks to plummet to practically nothing. At the last minute, his agents secretly began buying up the stocks at rock-bottom prices. On June 21, at 11 PM,

Wellington's envoy, Major Henry Percy showed up at the War Office with his report that Napoleon had been crushed in a bitter eight hour battle, losing a third of his men. This gave the Rothschild family complete control of the British economy, and forced England to set up a new Bank of England, which Nathan Rothschild controlled.

However, that wasn't the only angle he used to profit from the Battle of Waterloo. Mayer Amschel Rothschild sent some of William's money to his son Nathan in London, and according to the *Jewish Encyclopedia*: "Nathan invested it in 800,000 pounds of gold from the East India Company, knowing it would be needed for Wellington's peninsula campaign. He made no less than four profits: (1) on the sale of Wellington's paper (which he bought at 50¢ on the dollar); (2) on the sale of gold to Wellington; (3) on its repurchase; and (4) on forwarding it to Portugal. This was the beginning of the great fortune."

After Napoleon's defeat, Prince William returned to resume his rule. Buderus was made a Baron, and the Rothschilds were the richest bankers in Europe.

In 1817, France, in order to get back on their feet again, secured loans from a French banking house in Ouvrard, and from the Baring Brothers in London. The Rothschilds saw their chance to get a firm grip on the French economy, and on October, 1818, Rothschild agents began buying huge amounts of French government bonds, which caused their value to increase. On November 5th, they were dumped on the open market, creating a financial panic as their value declined. Thus, the Rothschilds gained control of France.

Mayer Rothschild had established banks in England, France, and Germany. His sons, who were made Barons of the Austrian Empire, were set up to continue and expand his banking empire. Amschel Mayer Rothschild (1773-1855, who in 1838 said: "Permit me to issue and control the money of a nation, and I care not who makes its laws.") was in charge of the bank in Frankfurt, Germany, which was known as M. A. Rothschild and Sons (which closed in 1901, after the deaths of Mayer Karl and his brother, Wilhelm Karl, the sons of Karl Mayer Rothschild). Salomon Mayer Rothschild (1774-1855) was the head of the bank in Vienna, Austria, known as S. M. Rothschild and Sons (which was closed during World War II after the Nazi occupation). Nathan Mayer Rothschild (1777-1836, who once said: "I care not what puppet is placed upon the throne of England to rule the Empire on which the sun never sets. The man who controls Britain's money supply controls the British Empire, and I control the British money supply.") was the head of the bank in London, England, which was known as N. M. Rothschild and Sons (and has occupied the same premises since 1809, at 2 New Court, St. Swithin's Lane in London, near the Bank of England and Stock Exchange). Karl Mayer Rothschild (1788-1868) was the head of the bank in Naples, Italy (closed in 1861). James Mayer Rothschild (1792-1868) was in charge of the bank in Paris, France, which was known as Messieurs de Rothschild Freres (whose name was changed to La Banque Rothschild in 1967).

This was the beginning of the House of Rothschild, which controlled a fortune estimated to be well over $300,000,000. Soon the Rothschilds spanned Europe with railroads, invested in coal and ironworks, financed England's purchase of the Suez Canal, paid for oil exploration in Russia and the Sahara Desert, financed the czars of Russia, supported Cecil Rhodes' diamond operations, aided

France in creating an empire in Africa, financed the Hapsburg monarchs, and saved the Vatican from bankruptcy. In this country, through their American and European agents, they helped finance Rockefeller's Standard Oil, Carnegie Steel, and Harriman's Railroad. Werner Sombart, in his book *The Jews and Modern Capitalism*, said that from 1820 on, it was the "age of the Rothschild" and concluded that there was "only one power in Europe, and that is Rothschild." In 1913, the family fortune was estimated to be over two billion dollars.

After Mayer Rothschild died on September 19, 1812, his will spelled out specific guidelines that were to be maintained by his descendants:

1) All important posts were to be held by only family members, and only male members were to be involved on the business end. The oldest son of the oldest son was to be the head of the family, unless otherwise agreed upon by the rest of the family, as was the case in 1812, when Nathan was appointed as the patriarch.

2) The family was to intermarry with their own first and second cousins, so their fortune could be kept in the family, and to maintain the appearance of a united financial empire. For example, his son James (Jacob) Mayer married the daughter of another son, Salomon Mayer. This rule became less important in later generations as they refocused family goals and married into other fortunes.

3) Rothschild ordered that there was never to be "any public inventory made by the courts, or otherwise, of my estate ... Also I forbid any legal action and any publication of the value of the inheritance."

American and British Intelligence have documented evidence that the House of Rothschild, and other International Bankers, have financed both sides of every war, since the American Revolution. Financier Haym Salomon, who supported the patriots during the American Revolution, then later made loans to James Madison, Thomas Jefferson, and James Monroe, was a Rothschild agent. As explained earlier, during the Napoleonic Wars, one branch of the family funded Napoleon, while another financed Great Britain, Germany, and other nations. Their boldest maneuver came prior to the Civil War.

The Rothschilds operate out of an area in the heart of London, England, the financial district, which is known as 'The City,' or the 'Square Mile.' All major British banks have their main offices here, along with branch offices for 385 foreign banks, including 70 from the United States. It is here that you will find the Bank of England, the Stock Exchange, Lloyd's of London, the Baltic Exchange (shipping contracts), Fleet Street (home of publishing and newspaper interests), the London Commodity Exchange (to trade coffee, rubber, sugar and wool), and the London Metal Exchange. It is virtually the financial hub of the world.

Positioned on the north bank of the Thames River, covering an area of 677 acres or one square mile (known as the "wealthiest square mile on earth"), it has enjoyed special rights and privileges that enabled them to achieve a certain level of independence since 1191. In 1215, its citizens received a Charter from King John, granting them the right to annually elect a mayor (known as the Lord Mayor), a tradition that continues today.

Both E. C. Knuth, in his book *Empire of the City*, and Des Griffin, in his book *Descent into Slavery*, stated their belief that 'The City' is actually a sovereign state (much like the Vatican), and that since the establishment of the privately owned Bank of England in 1694, 'The City' has actually become the last word in the country's national affairs, with Prime Minister, Cabinet, and Parliament becoming only a front for the real power. According to Knuth, when the queen enters 'The City,' she is subservient to the Lord Mayor (under him, is a committee of 12-14 men, known as 'The Crown'), because this privately-owned corporation is not subject to the Queen, or the Parliament.

There seems to be little doubt that the Rothschilds continue to influence the world economy, and it is known that they are squarely behind the movement to unite all the western European nations into a single political entity, which is just another step towards one-world government.

FREEMASONRY

Freemasons, or Masons, are members of a secret fraternal order known as the Ancient Free and Accepted Masons, whose goals are, supposedly, to promote brotherhood. One of the major sourcebooks of Masonic doctrine is *Morals and Dogma of the Ancient and Accepted Scottish Rite of Masonry*, written in 1871 by Albert Pike, and considered to be the "Masons guide for daily living." In it, he writes: "Masonry is a search after Light..."

According to early Masonic manuscripts, its origins can be traced back to Adam, who was said to be the first Mason. The apron of Masonry allegedly represents the fig leaves worn by Adam and Eve in the Garden of Eden. The knowledge received by Adam after eating from the forbidden tree, was carried on by his son Seth, and then Nimrod (who was responsible for the Tower of Babel), the great-grandson of Noah. Dr. Albert Mackey (33rd Degree), in writing his *Encyclopedia of Freemasonry*, referred to the 'York manuscript, No. 1' that contained information from a parchment dating back to the year 1560, which identified Babylon as the originator of Masonry. He also cited the Cooke Manuscript ("The Legend of the Craft," which was written in 1420, and is said to be the second oldest Masonic manuscript), which reveals that Nimrod taught the craft of Masonry to the workers at the Tower of Babel. When God confused their language, these secrets were said to be lost.

When King Solomon was building the Temple, it is taught that Freemasonry was revived. Mackey said that the "Masonic Lodges were initially dedicated to King Solomon, because he was our first Most Excellent Grand Master." However, Martin L. Wagner revealed in *An Interpretation of Freemasonry* that the "name Solomon is not the Israelitish king. It is the name in form, but different in its meaning. It is a substitute ... a composite, Sol-om-on, the names of the sun in Latin, Indian and Egyptian, and is designed to show the unity of several god-ideas in the ancient religions, as well as with those of Freemasonry."

A story recounted in Masonic tradition, has to do with Hiram Abiff, a Syrian Master Mason, known as the architect of Tyre, who was said to be hired by Solomon to build the Temple. He was killed by three Fellow-Crafts, when he would not reveal the secret Masonic word (so they could get Master's wages in foreign countries), which was engraved on a gold triangle he wore around his neck. Solomon found the triangle, and had it placed in a secret vault under the Temple. Abiff later became a Christ-like figure to the Masons. Mackey said that "Hiram represent(s) a popular Syrian god against whom the champions of Jehovah (the Jews) strove ceaselessly." Another Mason, Daniel Sickles, correlates him with an Egyptian god, and Pierson's *Traditions of Freemasonry* said that he actually represented all of the pagan sun gods, as does Mackey's *Lexicon of Freemasonry*. What this does, is to relate the message that it was the sun god who was the builder of the Temple, which makes this Temple symbolic, and not to be confused with the Jewish Temple. Pike said in his *Morals and Dogma*, that the "Temple of Solomon presented a symbolic image of the Universe; and resembled, in its arrangements and furniture, all the temples of the ancient nations that practiced the mysteries."

In ancient Greece, there were organized groups, or guilds (like our unions), such as the 'Dionysiacs,' and in Rome, the 'Collegium Muriorum,' who built the temples and stadiums. These groups, who were the forerunners of the Masons, were the draftsmen, builders, carpenters, and craftsmen who erected the huge cathedrals, castles, abbeys and churches during the Middle Ages. Because they 'lodged' or lived together during the construction, this is where the term 'masonic lodge' was originated.

The First Grand Lodge of England met at York in 926, where they adopted handsigns and passwords to identify themselves. Their workplace, or Lodges, was where their initiations, rites, rituals and ceremonies took place. Within their inner circles, witchcraft was practiced.

In the 13th century, they formed an association, headquartered at Cologne, with Lodges at Strasbourg, Vienna, and Zurich. They called themselves Free Masons, and had ceremonies for initiation. Near the end of the 16th century, people who weren't builders, were admitted into the fraternity, and were called 'Accepted' Masons. They were usually distinguished members of the community, or in short, a source of funding. Becoming more symbolic, the working masons and builders eventually quit, as did the Accepted Masons, who had become disappointed at what the organization really was.

The Bruton Vault

Sir Francis Bacon (1561-1626), an English Lord, the son of Elizabeth I, was recognized as the "founder of Free Masonry ... the guiding light of the Rosicrucian Order, the members of which kept the torch of the true universal knowledge, the Secret Doctrine of the Ages, alive during the dark night of the Middle Ages." Fluent in many languages, it has been believed by some that he was one of the editors of the King James Version of the Bible, as well as the true author of the plays attributed to William Shakespeare. He had been initiated by a secret society of intellectuals dedicated to civil and religious freedom. In his book *Instauratio Magna*, he wrote of a movement to "reorganize the sciences and restore man to the mastery over nature that he was conceived to have lost by the fall of Adam."

Bacon's novel, *New Atlantis*, published in 1627, a year after his death, by his secretary William Rawley, represented his vision for a new "Golden Age." It was about a crew of shipwrecked sailors who arrived on the shores a mysterious, unknown land, whose people had a much higher developed culture and possessed a technology unlike anything they had ever seen. He talked about buildings a half a mile high, flying machines, underwater vehicles, and a government of philosopher-scientists working in behalf of an enlightened group of people who were committed to learning, and a higher level of achievement.

Manly Palmer Hall (1901-1990), founder of the Philosophical Research Society in 1934, and one of the foremost experts in the realm of the metaphysical and the occult, authored over 200 books, and in six decades delivered more than 8,000 lectures. In his 1944 book *The Secret Destiny of America*, he revealed that even though the *New Atlantis* had been completed, the entire version was never published. He wrote: "The final (unpublished) chapters revealed the entire pattern secret societies had been working on for thousands of years to achieve the ideal commonwealth in the political world." It included details for nurturing the "New Order of the Ages," how this long range "Great Plan" would restore mankind to the original state that was intended to reflect the inner philosophical tradition of Freemasonry, and proposed timetables.

In *The Secret Destiny of America* Hall also wrote: "There exists in the world today, and has existed for thousands of years, a body of enlightened humans united in what might be termed, an Order of the Quest. It is composed of those whose intellectual and spiritual perceptions have revealed to them that civilization has a secret destiny ... The outcome of this 'secret destiny' is a World Order ruled by a King with supernatural powers. This King was descended of a divine race, that is, he belonged to the Order of the Illumined for those who come to a state of wisdom than belong to a family of heroes— perfected human beings."

The full-length version (which included the missing chapters) was taken to Jamestown in 1635 by his descendant Nathaniel Bacon, where it was buried under the altar of the old brick church. In 1676, it was moved to Williamsburg, Virginia, where it was buried "in a great vault beneath the tower center of the first brick church in Bruton Parish." The current church, known as the Bruton Parish Church (which was declared a National Historic Landmark), was built in 1715, and within the grounds of its graveyard (the site of the original church), and is where the Bruton Vault is located.

It is believed by many serious researchers that Sir Francis Bacon faked his death (actually dying in 1684), and constructed the vault with the help of his Wild Goose Club. It is a 10 ft. by 10 ft. brick vault, possibly part of an underground Freemasonry Lodge that is buried 20 ft. deep, and marked by certain strategically placed encoded memorials in the cemetery above.

The reason for the Rockefellers making such an investment to restore the town of Colonial Williamsburg, was the prospect of locating the fabled vault, which had three tunnels leading to it from homes in the area. Fortunately, ownership of the grounds remain in the hands of the Page and Bray families.

Deposited along with the unabridged copy of the *New Atlantis* were other secret documents, including ancient writings that had been in the possession of certain secret societies. One such artifact was the 'Book of Thoth,' which had been retrieved from a golden box out of an inner sanctuary in an ancient Egyptian temple. Known as the 'Sacred Torch,' the most important document ever given to Man, it is believed that anyone who is able to decipher it will have their consciousness enhanced to the point that they will be able to see the invisible Immortals and enter the presence of the Superior Gods. Manley Hall wrote in his book, *The Secret Teachings of All Ages* that the Book "was lost to the Ancient World with the decay of the Mysteries, but its faithful initiates carried it sealed to another land. The book is still in existence..."

The vault also contains instructions, maps, and documents that lead to 144 sacred burial sites of certain forefathers, patriots and early leaders in our country that in turn contain original writings, diaries and documentation that will prove how history has been rewritten today to reflect the biased political views of certain leaders in this country. Hall wrote in *The Secret Destiny of America*: "Not only were the founders of the United States Government Masons, but they received aid from a secret and august body existing in Europe, which helped them to establish this country for a peculiar and particular purpose known only to the initiated few."

Masonry was not always as it appears today. Many early Christian patriots during the foundational period of American history were part of the predominate York Rite, which promoted values, ethics, and brotherhood among its members. It has been reported that true Freemasonry Lodges were established in the cellars of Episcopalian and Presbyterian Churches. It was the Illuminati infiltration of the American Fraternal Lodges by the Jesuit-spawned Scottish Rite that moved through the ranks like a virus to take them over from within.

It is believed that the vault also contains a quantity of gold, an original edition of the supposed Bacon-edited King James Bible, inventions that were ahead of its time, and a device that will enable their codes to be deciphered.

There is some evidence to indicate that handwritten copies of certain documents were made during the administration of President Washington and hidden at a remote location in Virginia.

According to Colin Dyer in his book *Symbolism in Craft Masonry*, in 1804, Thomas Jefferson (3rd President) was the last person to examine the contents of this vault. It was believed that the contents were removed and placed in a secret location either at the University of Virginia (founded by Jefferson), or the capitol building in Washington, D.C. However, Manley Hall became a leading proponent for the Bruton Vault as being the location of this sacred repository. His quest to protect it from falling into the wrong hands cost him his life, because he was strangled to death by two members of the Skull and Bones Society— Morgan Brandt and Daniel Fritz. Luckily all of his research notes, documents, maps, books, photos, and artifacts relating to 50 years of work on the vault had already been sent to a secret location in Russia.

In *The Secret Destiny of America* Hall wrote: "America's true destiny will remain a secret as long as great masses of people have no knowledge whatsoever that enlightened humanitarians through thousands of years have in their own and succeeding generations remained united on the high purpose of eventually instituting democratic rule throughout the world. It is necessary to know, too, that it was anciently planned that leadership would fall to America— to a nation established on the Northern continent of the Western Hemisphere ... Long before Columbus, they were aware of the existence of the Western hemisphere, and selected it to be the site of the philosophic empire. The American continent was set apart for establishing here a great democratic nation, centuries before the founding fathers and colonists envisioned the Union..."

When President Theodore Roosevelt visited the site, and learned of its significance, he vowed to protect it, and out of appreciation, he was honored by having his image placed on Mount Rushmore. David Rockefeller and Queen Elizabeth have shown a particular interest in the vault's contents.

The contents of the Bruton Vault are priceless, and considered so important that it is referred to as the 'Seventh Seal.'

A group known as Sir Francis Bacon's Sages of the Seventh Seal have been the driving force behind the movement to uncover the vault. Though there were unsuccessful attempts in 1938 (which did discover the original church foundations) and 1992, they now believe that a spiral staircase exists beneath the pyramid-shaped monument that marks the centuries-old graves of David and Elizabeth Bray, and leads to the vault, which they refer to as a "Freemasonry library." Armed with new evidence from their continued research, the group has lobbied the Rev. Herman Hollerith IV, rector of the Episcopal Church, to authorize a new, controlled, archeological dig, to raise the vault, so that its contents can be studied, and protected from forces hostile to the information it contains.

The Growth of the Masonic Movement

Inigo Jones (1573-1652) reorganized the Lodges, introducing the Descartes rationalism, and they were now known as the Free and Accepted Masons. Elias Ashmole, a banker, Rosicrucian, and founder of the Oxford Museum, who became a Mason in 1648, established the three basic degrees:

1) Entered Apprentice
2) Fellow-Craft
3) Master Mason

On June 24, 1717, the four lodges in London were united into a Grand Lodge (sometimes called the Grand Mother Lodge) by three members who met at the Apple Tree Tavern, thus beginning the era of modern Freemasonry. Rather than being a guild of stone masons and builders, they altered their philosophy and became a pseudo-religion who "tried to cooperate with the Church so as to be able to work from the inside, rationalize the doctrine of Jesus and empty it gradually of its mystical content. Freemasonry hoped to become a friendly and legal heir to Christianity. They considered logic and the rules of scientific thinking as being the only absolute and permanent element of the human mind." By 1725, the movement had spread to France.

The members of the Grand Lodge of England brought their fraternity to America. In 1730, Daniel Core was appointed Provincial Grand Master of New York, New Jersey and Pennsylvania, after the first lodge was established in Philadelphia. A lodge was established in Boston in 1733. By the time of the American Revolution, there were 100 Masonic lodges. The Masons were firmly entrenched in the eastern colonies, but since 95% of the population identified themselves as Christians, they had to modify their philosophies to include Christian teachings. The Grand Lodge of the United States was established in 1777, which officially cut all ties to their British counterparts.

One writer summed up Masonry this way: "Freemasonry has incorporated bits of other systems in its initiations and higher degrees, such as mystery schools, Mithraism, the Egyptian priesthood, the system of the Pythagoreans, Essenes, Cabalists, Druids, the Orders of the Knighthood, Rosicrucians, Arabic secret societies, and the Knights Templar."

Masonry slowly spread throughout the world: France (1718-25), Ireland (1725-26), Spain (1726-27), Holland (1731), Germany (1730-33), Africa (1735), Scotland (1736), Portugal (1736), Switzerland (1737), Italy (1733-37), Russia (1731-40), Canada (1745), Sweden (1735-48), Prussia (1738-40), Austria (1742), Poland (1784), and Mexico (1825).

Originally against the Masonic Order, Benjamin Franklin became a Mason in 1731, at the age of 25. He became the Provincial Grand Master of Pennsylvania in 1734, and was the "appointed spokesman" of the secret societies. As ambassador to France, he was honored there at a major Masonic lodge. It is believed that while he was on a diplomatic trip to Paris to seek financing for the Revolution, he was initiated as a member of the Illuminati. George Washington joined the Fredericksburg Lodge #4 in Virginia, in 1752, and when he was elected President in 1789, he was the Grand Master of the Lodge (the highest official). He took his Oath of Office on a Masonic Bible, as did his Vice-President, John Adams, who was also a Mason. This Masonic Bible from the altar of St. Johns Lodge No. 1 in New York City, which was printed in London in 1767, was later used for other Oaths administered to Harding, Eisenhower, Carter, Reagan and Bush. This Masonic Bible has an introductory section that explains that Masonry is not a Christian fraternity, but in fact supports all religions. Eight of the signers of the Declaration of Independence were also members of the Fredericksburg Lodge. Actually, 51 of the 56 signers were believed to be Masons; however, only 8 were known to be members, while another 24 were suspected of being members.

It is also believed that 8 to 10 signers of the Articles of Confederation were Masons. There were 9 Masons that signed the Constitution, while 6 others later became members. Other sources have used the figure of 13, while some have said there were as many as 28 members who signed the Constitution.

Because of the disagreement between various books and on-line sources, representing Masonic and non-Masonic sources, it's easy to see how erroneous information becomes perpetuated as fact and truth. If the Masons can't even nail down the specifics of their own history, then the only thing we can hope to do, is to produce as accurate of a picture as possible, based on the facts.

Among the ranks of the Masons were: Patrick Henry (not all Masonic researchers agree on this), John Hancock, Paul Revere, John Paul Jones, Alexander

Hamilton, Benedict Arnold, John Marshall, Samuel Adams, Anthony Wayne, Francis Marion ('The Swamp Fox') and Ethan Allen. In the military, 24 of Washington's Major Generals, and 30 of his 33 Brigadier Generals were Masons (another fact that Masonic researchers do not agree on).

It was actually the Masons who instigated and carried out the American Revolution. The secrecy of the Masonic lodges allowed the Colonial patriots to meet and discuss strategy. It was commonly believed that the reason for the Revolution was "taxation without representation," when actually it was because the Parliament in the 1760's passed a law that no colony could issue its own money. The colonies had to issue bonds, and sell them to the Bank, who would then loan them money. This forced the colonies to pay interest on their money. The Revolution was ignited by the Boston Tea Party, which was planned during a dinner at the Bradlee home. The participants were from the St. Andrew Lodge in Boston, who dressed up as Mohawk Indians, and went aboard the Dartmouth, which was anchored in the harbor, and dumped its load of tea overboard. The British government responded by closing the port, and sending in British troops. Empress Catherine the Great of Russia, who wasn't controlled by the International Bankers, refused to send in 20,000 Russian troops against the colonists, when asked by King George III of England. The attack unified the colonies against England.

The Supreme Council of Scottish Rite Freemasonry was established in Charleston, South Carolina in 1801, because that area was geographically located on the 33rd parallel. They are an extension of French Freemasonry, and considered liberal. In 1755, the Ancient and Accepted Scottish Rite of Freemasonry had expanded to 32 degrees, and then they added a 33rd degree. In 1813, the Northern Supreme Council was established, consisting of 15 states, and was headquartered in Boston. They were an extension of English Freemasonry, and are considered conservative. The Supreme Council, which represented the Southern jurisdiction, relocated to Washington, D.C., and covers the remaining 35 states, the District of Columbia, and U.S. protectorates. It is considered the Mother Supreme Council of the World.

Among the Presidents who have been Masons: Washington, Jefferson (33rd Degree), Madison, Monroe, Jackson, Polk, Buchanan, Andrew Johnson (32nd Degree and Grand Master), Garfield, McKinley, Theodore Roosevelt, Taft, Harding (32nd Degree), Franklin Roosevelt (32nd Degree), Truman (33rd Degree and Grand Master), Eisenhower, Kennedy, Lyndon Johnson (1st Degree), Nixon, Ford (33rd Degree), Carter, Reagan (33rd Degree), and George H. W. Bush, Sr.

Many State Governors, U.S. Senators and Congressmen are Masons. The Masonic Bible says that "for well over 150 years, the destiny of this country has been determined largely by men who were members of the Masonic fraternity."

There is about 16,000 Blue or Symbolic Lodges, with a Grand Lodge in every state, which represent more than four million members. There are 150 Grand Lodges in the world, and a world-wide membership of over 6,000,000.

Members must be 21 years old; however, sons of members can be initiated at 18. Before consideration, an initiate must prove themselves to be "mentally and physically competent, of good moral character, and believe in the existence of a Supreme Being." Among their affiliated organizations: The Order of Demolay, The Order of Rainbow for Girls, and The Order of Job's Daughters, which allow children as young as 11 to become indoctrinated in Masonic teaching. The Order of the Eastern Star, Ancient Arabic Order of Nobles of the Mystic Shrine, and Daughters of the Nile are organizations closely aligned with the Masons.

Their literature claims that "Freemasonry is not a religion even though it is a religion in character ... does not pretend to take the place of religion nor serve as a substitute for the religious beliefs of its members ... (and) accepts men, found to be worthy, regardless of religious convictions." They claim that they exist "to make good men better through its firm belief in the Fatherhood of God, the Brotherhood of Man (and) consists of men bound together by bonds of Brotherly Love and Affection."

Examining Masonic Tradition

Any organization which strives to adhere to such a high moral standard certainly should deserve our admiration and respect. However, why have they elicited the criticism that they have? The Vatican has issued many Edicts condemning Masonry: Pope Clement XII in 1738, Pope Benedict XIV in 1751, Pope Plus VII in 1821, Pope Leo XII in 1825, Pope Plus VIII in 1829, Pope Gregory XVI in 1832, Pope Plus IX in 1846 and 1873, and Pope Leo XIII in 1884 and 1892. Pope Leo XXIII said that the goal of the Masons was the "overthrow of the whole religious, political and social order based on Christian institutions and the establishment of a state of things based on pure naturalism." Until 1974, the Roman Catholic Church had forbidden its members to be Masons, and on March 21, 1981, the Vatican warned that "all Roman Catholics who belong to Masonic lodges risk excommunication."

In 1784, and again in 1845, the Bavarian government considered Masonry a danger to the state. In 1814, The Regency of Milan and Governor of Venice echoed these same sentiments. King John VI of Portugal issued orders in 1816, and again in 1824, prohibiting the operation of the fraternity. In Russia, in 1820, Alexander I banished the Order.

Many writers in the late 1800's, such as Archbishop Meurin and Dr. Bataille, said that Masonry was just a cover organization for Satan worship, which occurred within its higher degrees, and was unknown to the ordinary member. In 1921, Dr. James Anderson wrote a booklet on Freemasonry called *The Anderson Constitution* in which he wrote: "Freemasonry rapidly expanded in Europe. In France, a number of the Masonic sects dabbled with magic and occultism. In Germany some were called Order of the Gold, and Rosy Cross (or Rosicrucians). In England, during the 1880's, the famous magical society, the Hermetic Order of the Golden Dawn adopted most of the Masonic grades." Many Druid ceremonies and witchcraft rites have been incorporated into Masonic rituals.

So, are the Masons a Christian organization? The answer is a resounding No! Their literature claims that Jesus was just a man, equal to Mohammed and Krishna, the Hindu God. He is called the "son of Joseph," not the Son of God. Initiates are told that Masonic rituals are "based on the Bible," however in Chase's *Digest of Masonic Law* it says that "Masonry has nothing whatever to do with the Bible ... it is not founded upon the Bible, for if it were it would not be Masonry, it would be something else." Chase said that the Bible is just one of the 'holy books' of man, equal to the Koran, Hindu Scriptures and others. Its literal meaning was meant only for the ignorant masses.

At the end of the initiation for the Royal Arch degree, the initiate has the lost name of 'God' whispered to him, which is 'Jebulon.' Mackey, in his *Encyclopedia of Freemasonry*, said that "Freemasonry is not Christianity," and indicates that this name actually represents a composite of the names of the sun god of three religions: 'Jah,' the Syrian form of Jehovah; 'Eel,' which is Baal; and 'On,' the Egyptian sun god. J. D. Buck (32nd degree) wrote in *Mystic Masonry* (1925): "The only personal God Freemasonry accepts is humanity in toto ... Humanity therefore is the only personal God that there is." Their Masonic philosophy is that God is whatever you want him to be and is referred to in general terms as the 'deity' and the 'Great Architect of the Universe,' but in higher degrees, he is identified as a force of nature, usually the sun.

Mackey, in his *Masonic Rituals* said that the elimination of the name of Jesus, and references to Him, in Bible verses used in rituals are "slight but necessary modifications." Mackey also wrote in his *Lexicon of Freemasonry*: "The religion then of Masonry is pure theism on which its different members engraft their particular opinions, but they are not permitted to introduce them into the lodge or to connect their truth or falsehood with the truth of Masonry ... A Christian Mason is not permitted to introduce his own peculiar opinions with regard to Christ's mediatorial office into the Lodge." No Masonic prayers in monitors, handbooks and guides, end in Jesus' name, and if it is discovered that they do, the Grand Lodge of that state will revoke their charter. Edmond Ronayne (a Master Mason), wrote on page 74 of the *Masonic Handbook* (later revised to eliminate the passage): "When a brother reveals any of our great secrets ... or whenever a minister prays in the name of Christ in any of our assemblies, you must always hold yourself in readiness, if called upon, to cut his throat from ear to ear, pull out his tongue by the roots, and bury his body at the bottom of some lake or pond." According to Morris in *The Freemason's Monitor* (or *Webb's Monitor*), which omits any reference to the name of Jesus: "Prayer ... should be of a general character, containing nothing offensive to any class of conscientious brethren."

Dr. Norman Vincent Peale (1898-1993), author of *The Power of Positive Thinking* was a 33rd degree Mason and his name appeared in many Masonic publications. In March, 1991, he was featured in the cover story of *The Scottish Rite Journal* (formerly known as the *New Age* magazine), and is quoted as saying that "Masonry became an early and essential part of my success." On Sunday, February 24, 1991, Peale had told the congregation of Robert Schuller's Crystal Cathedral in California: "Jesus Christ, Buddha and Krishna are examples of great philosophers who taught how to use mind power." In May, 1991, at a Dallas, Texas seminar for Christian writers, Dina Donahue, a contributing editor for *Guidepost* magazine (which Peale founded), said that any submission to the publication can never refer to the deity of Jesus, and claim that He is the only means by which salvation can be achieved. He can only be presented in a historical context as a prophet and philosopher. She said that the reason for this was that "*Guidepost* is an interfaith magazine, and Dr. Peale does not want to offend those who are not Christians."

In *Les Sectes et Societies Secretes* published in 1863, Le Couteulx de Canteleu wrote that the goal of the Masonic Order "was, is and will always be the struggle against the Church and the Christian religion..." Joseph Fort Newton wrote in *The Builders*: "Masonry ... is Religion, a worship in which all good men may unite, that each may share the faith of all ... Where else, except in a Masonic lodge, could men of many religions meet, each praying for all and all for one." Mackey wrote in his *Textbook of Masonic Jurisprudence*, that Masonry is "undoubtedly a religious institution"; and also in his *Manual of the Lodge*, he emphatically states that "Masonry is a religious institution." Buck wrote in *Mystic Masonry* that Masonry is "a world wide religion ... Masonry is the universal religion only because and so long as it embraces all religions."

High level Masons believe that Lucifer never fell to earth and that Lucifer is really God, and refer to Jehovah by the name of 'Adonay,' saying that he is the god of evil because he forces men to be subservient to his repressive dictates. Masonic books given to handpicked members of the 32nd and 33rd Degrees, say that Jesus was an impostor, and that Lucifer is the true God. The Masons have their own Luciferian based calendar. Where ours is based on the years before (B.C.) and after (A.D.) the birth of Christ, theirs counts its years with the suffix A.L. means Anno Lucis or 'Year of Light (Lucifer).'

In *Morals and Dogma*, Pike wrote: "Every Masonic lodge is a temple of religion; and its teachings are instruction in religion ... Masonry, like all religions, all the Mysteries, Hermeticism and Alchemy, conceals its secrets from all except the Adepts and Sages, or the Elect, and uses false explanations and misinterpretations of its symbols to mislead ... to conceal the Truth, which it calls Light, from them, and to draw them away from it ... The truth must be kept secret, and the masses need a teaching proportioned to their imperfect reason." He wrote that "every man's conception of God must be proportioned to his mental cultivation, and intellectual powers, and moral excellence. God is, as man conceives him, the reflected image of man himself." The next statement reduces the Masonic philosophy to a single premise. Pike writes: "The true name of Satan, the Kabalists say, is that of Yahweh reversed; for Satan is not a black god ... Lucifer, the Light Bearer! Strange and mysterious name to give to the Spirit of Darkness! Lucifer, the Son of the Morning! Is it he who bears the Light ... Doubt it not!"

These various passages should settle any arguments concerning the anti-Christian nature of the Masons. Their role in history seemed to be to act as a diluting factor, to lessen the impact of Christianity through tolerance, and to politically work towards the goals established by the Illuminati.

The Masonic Organizational Structure

The Blue Lodge (Symbolic Lodge of Masonry):
1) Entered Apprentice
2) Fellow-Craft
3) Master Mason

Albert Pike explained in *Morals & Dogma*: "The Blue Degrees are but the outer court or portico of the Temple. Part of the symbols are displayed there to the Initiate, but he is intentionally misled by false interpretations. It is not intended that he shall understand them; but it is intended that he shall imagine he understands them. Their true explication is reserved for the Adepts, the Princes of Masonry ... It is well enough for the mass of those called Masons, to imagine that all is contained in the Blue Degrees; and whoso attempts to undeceive them will labor in vain."

Lodge of Perfection (Scottish Rite or Ancient and Accepted Scotch Rite):
4) Secret Master
5) Perfect Master
6) Intimate Secretary
7) Provost and Judge
8) Intendant of the Building
9) Master Elect of Nine
10) Elect of Fifteen
11) Sublime Master Elected (Sublime Knights Elect of the Twelve)
12) Grand Master Architect
13) Master of the Ninth Arch (Knight of the Ninth Arch)
14) Grand Elect Mason

Council of Princes of Jerusalem:
15) Knight of the East (Knight of the Sword)
16) Prince of Jerusalem

Chapter of Rose-Croix
17) Knight of the East and West
18) Prince of Rose-Croix (Knight of the Eagle)

The Consistory (Council of Kadosh)
19) Grand Pontiff
20) Master Ad Vitam (Grand Master of all Symbolic Lodges)
21) Patriarch Noachite (Prussian Knight)
22) Prince of Libanus (Knight of the Royal Axe)
23) Chief of the Tabernacle
24) Prince of the Tabernacle
25) Knight of the Brazen Serpent
26) Prince of Mercy
27) Commander of the Temple
28) Knight of the Sun (Prince Adept)
29) Knight of St. Andrew
30) Grand Elect Knight of Kadosh

Consistory of Sublime Princes of the Royal Secret
31) Grand Inspector Inquisitor Commander
32) Sublime Prince of the Royal Secret

Supreme Council
33) Sovereign Grand Inspector General

The Mother Supreme Council of the World in Washington, D.C., awards all 33rd Degrees. It is the only degree that can't be earned— it is conferred "because of outstanding service to others which reflects credit upon the Order." All Illuminati members are 33rd Degree Masons.

Red Masonry or York Rite (or Craft Masonry):
All Masons go through the first 3 degrees of the Blue Lodge, and must then decide whether they want to enter either the Scottish or York Rites (Capitular Degrees).
Mark Master
Past Master
Most Excellent Master
Royal Arch Mason (Holy Royal Arch)
Royal Master
Select Master
Super Excellent Master
Order of the Red Cross
Order of the Knights of Malta
Order of Knights Templar

THE ILLUMINATI GROWS

From Bavaria, the Order of the Illuminati spread into the Upper and Lower Rhenish provinces, Suabia, Franconia, Westphalia, Upper and Lower Saxony; and outside Germany into Austria and Switzerland. Soon they had over 300 members from all walks of life, including students, merchants, doctors, lawyers, judges, professors, civil officers, bankers, and ministers. Some of their more notable members were: the Duke of Orleans, Duke Ernst Augustus of Saxe-Weimar-Coburg-Gotha, Prince Charles of Hesse-Cassel, Johann Gottfried von Herder (a philosopher), Count Klemens von Metternich, Catherine II of Russia, Count Gabriel de Mirabeau, Marquis of Constanza ('Diomedes'), Duke Ferdinand of Brunswick ('Aaron'), Duke Karl August of Saxe-Weimar, Johann Wolfgang von Goethe (a poet), Joseph II of Russia, Christian VII of Denmark, Gustave III of Sweden, and King Poniatowski of Poland.

By 1783, there were over 600 members; and by 1784, their membership reached nearly 3,000. By 1786 they had numerous lodges across the various German provinces, Austria, Hungary, England, Scotland, Poland, France, Belgium, Switzerland, Italy, Holland, Spain, Sweden, Russia, Ireland, Africa, and America.

By the time of the 3rd Masonic Congress in Frankfurt in 1786, the Illuminati virtually controlled all the Masonic lodges, and at this meeting their goals were stated as: "1) Pantheism for the higher degrees, atheism for the lower degrees and the populace; 2) Communism of goods, women, and general concerns; 3) The destruction of the Church, and all forms of Christianity, and the removal of all existing human governments to make way for a universal republic in which the utopian ideas of complete liberty from existing social, moral, and religious restraint, absolute equality, and social fraternity, should reign."

Students who were members of wealthy families, with international leanings, were recommended for special training in internationalism. Those selected by the Illuminati were given scholarships to attend special schools. Weishaupt wrote: "I propose academies under the direction of the Order. This will secure us the adherence of the Literati. Science shall here be the lure." He also wrote: "We must acquire the direction of education, of church, management of the professorial chair, and of the pulpit." Today, there are many such schools. Prince Philip, husband of Queen Elizabeth, was educated at an Illuminati school in Gordonstown, Scotland, at the insistence of Lord Louis Mountbattan (who became an admiral after the end of World War II, and had an uncle who was a Rothschild relative). Those trained at such schools were placed behind the scenes as experts and advisors to perpetuate Illuminati goals.

Weishaupt, worried that his control of the Order was diminishing, argued repeatedly with Knigge. While he preferred to work in secrecy, Knigge wanted to move on to more substantial things. In January, 1783, Knigge wrote in a letter to Zwack: "It is the Jesuitry of Weishaupt that causes all our divisions, it is the despotism that he exercises over men perhaps less rich than himself in imagination, in ruses, in cunning ... I declare that nothing can put me on the same footing with Spartacus as that on which I was a first." He also wrote: "I abhor treachery and profligacy, and I leave him to blow himself and his Order into the air." On April 20, 1784, Knigge quit, followed by Baron Bassus ('Hannibal'), Count Torring, Prince Kreitmaier, and others. In July, Knigge signed an agreement promising to return all documents in his possession, and to keep quiet on what he knew about their plans and activities. Some researchers believe that Knigge had also discovered that Weishaupt was a Satanist. He resumed his work as a writer, later becoming an inspector of schools at Bremen, where he died on May 6, 1796.

To insure that the activities of the Order would remain a secret, a warning as to the consequences of betraying the Order was including in the ceremony of initiation. They would point a sword at the initiate and say: "If you are a traitor and a perjurer, learn that all our Brothers are called upon to arm themselves against you. Do not hope to escape or find a place of safety. Wherever you are, shame, remorse, and the rage of our Brothers will pursue you, and torment you to the innermost recesses of your entrails."

In October, 1783, Joseph Utzschneider, a lawyer, who had dropped out of the Order in August, presented to the Duchess Maria Anna, a document which detailed the activities of the Illuminati. He was upset because he had been promoted too slow, and was constantly prodded to prove his loyalty. The Duchess gave the information to the Duke. On June 22, 1784, Duke Karl Theodore Dalberg, the

Elector Palatinate of Bavaria, after discovering from the information that the goals of the Illuminati were to "in time rule the world," by overthrowing all civil government, criticized all secret societies, and groups established without government sanction. On March 2, 1785, he issued a proclamation identifying the Illuminati as a branch of the Masons, and ordered that their Lodges be shut down. The government began a war against the Order by initiating judicial inquiries at Ingolstadt. In an attempt to preserve the secrecy of their motives, the Areopagite burned many of their documents, however, the government was able to seize many of their papers when they raided the Lodges.

After being replaced at the University in February, Weishaupt fled across the border into Regensburg, finally settling in Gotha, where he found refuge with another Illuminati member, the Duke of Saxe-Gotha.

In April, 1785, Utzschneider was able to convince three other members to come forward. They were fellow professors at the Marienburg (Marianen) Academy who had doubts about the validity of the organization's principles when they discovered that they would receive no mystical powers. They were also disgruntled over Weishaupt's tyranny. Cossandey, Grunberger, and Renner went before the Court of Inquiry on September 9, 1785, where they supplied valuable information, such as membership lists, and revealed their aims and goals, which they consolidated into the following six points:

1) Abolition of the Monarchy and all ordered government.
2) Abolition of private property.
3) Abolition of inheritance.
4) Abolition of patriotism.
5) Abolition of the family, through the abolition of marriage, all morality, and the institution of communal education for children.
6) Abolition of all religion.

The purposes of these six points were to divide the people politically, socially, and economically; to weaken countries and create a one-world government. They testified that "all religion, all love of country and loyalty to sovereigns, were to be annihilated..."

The government pardoned all public officials and military leaders who publicly admitted membership. Those who didn't, and were discovered to be members, lost their rank and standing, were removed from office, and openly disgraced and humiliated.

Weishaupt was preparing to set his plans into motion for the French Revolution, which was slated to begin in 1789. In July, 1785, he instructed Zwack to put their plans in book form. This book contained a history of the Illuminati, and many of their ideas for expansion and future endeavors. A copy was sent by courier (identified as Jacob Lanze) to Illuminati members in Paris and Silesia. However, after leaving Frankfurt, as the courier rode through Regensburg (another source says it was Ratisbon) on horseback, he was struck by lightning and killed. The authorities found the document and turned it over to the government. Another source indicates the possibility that he may have been murdered, and the documents planted on him.

FINAL WARNING

Xavier Zwack ('Cato'), a government lawyer, and one of the Order's most prominent leaders, whose name was on Renner's list, had his house in Landshut illegally searched by the police in October, 1785, and his papers seized. He was dismissed from his position. Many books, documents, papers and correspondence were discovered, including over 200 letters written between Weishaupt and the members of the Areopagite, which dealt with matters of the highest secrecy. The following year, more information was taken from the houses of Baron Bassus and Count Massenhausen ('Ajar'). Among the confiscated documents, were tables which contained their secret codes and symbols, secret calendar, geographical locations, insignias, ceremonies of initiation, recruiting instructions, statutes, a partial roster of members, and nearly 130 official seals from the government, which were used to counterfeit state documents.

Needless to say, all of this information shed more light on the Order, and the danger first realized by the government, had now become a national emergency. In 1786, the government gathered all of the confiscated documents, and published them in a book called *Original Writings of the Order and Sect of the Illuminati*, which was circulated to every government and crowned head in Europe, including France, to warn them of the impending danger.

The leaders of the Order who appeared before the government's Court of Inquiry, testified that the organization was dedicated to the overthrow of church and state. However, these revelations, and the publication of their documents, did little to alert the public, because of their unbelievable claims. New measures were taken by government officials. The leaders of the Order were arrested and formally interrogated, then forced to renounce the Illuminati. The final blow came on August 16, 1787, when Dalberg issued his final proclamation against the Illuminati. Anyone found guilty of recruiting members were to be executed, while those who were recruited, would have their property confiscated and then be deported.

Zwack, who was banished, sought sanctuary in the Court of Zweibrucken, where he was later appointed to an official position in the principality of Salm-Kyburg. He contributed to the Illuminati movement in Holland. He was later summoned by Dalberg, as the government tried to deal with the problem of fugitives who might attempt to reorganize the Order. Zwack fled to England.

On November 15, 1790, another Edict was announced against the members of the organization. Anyone found to be an active member, was to be put to death. The following year, a list of 91 names of alleged members was compiled. They were hunted down, and banished. This harassment didn't end until 1799, when Dalberg died.

The apparent demise of the Order was taken into stride by its highest members, who continued to operate underground. Weishaupt wrote: "The great care of the Illuminati after the publication of their secret writings was to persuade the whole of Germany that their Order no longer existed, that their adepts had all renounced, not only their mysteries, but as members of a secret society." Weishaupt had a contingency plan ready, and wrote: "By this plan we shall direct all mankind. In this manner, and by the simplest means, we shall set in motion and in flames. The occupations must be allotted and contrived, that we may in secret, influence all political transactions ... I have considered everything and so prepared it, that if the Order should this day go to ruin, I shall in a year re-establish it more brilliant than ever."

To hide their subversive activities, the highest members of the Order began to masquerade as humanitarians and philanthropists. Weishaupt fled to Switzerland, later returning to Germany, where the Duke of Saxe-Gotha gave him sanctuary. The Order moved their headquarters to London, where it began to grow again. Weishaupt told his followers to infiltrate the lodges of Blue Masonry, and to form secret circles within them. Only Masons who proved themselves as Internationalists, and were atheists, were initiated into the Illuminati.

THE GERMAN UNION

Dr. Charles Frederick Bahrdt (1741-1793), an Illuminati member, Mason, and German theologian, who was the professor of Sacred Philogy at the University of Leipzig, took advantage of the Illuminati's apparent demise by recruiting several of its members for his so-called 'German Union' in 1787. Bahrdt, the son of a minister, called his group the German Union for Rooting Out Superstition and Prejudices and Advancing True Christianity.

In 1785, Bahrdt had received an anonymous letter, containing the plans for the German Union, which was signed, "From some Masons, your great admirers." That same year, he was visited by an Englishman who urged him to establish the Union, promising to link it with the British Masonic structure. In 1787, he received another letter containing more details and organizational details.

Bahrdt had done some religious propaganda work for Weishaupt, "to destroy the authority of the Scriptures," and it was commonly believed that it was Weishaupt who was directing the activities of the organization behind the scenes in order to carry on the goals of the Illuminati.

The German Union appeared to be a Reading Society, and one was set up in Zwack's house in Landshut. Weishaupt wrote: "Next to this, the form of a learned of literary society is best suited to our purpose, and had Freemasonry not existed, this cover would have been employed; and it may be much more than a cover, it may be a power engine in our hands. By establishing reading societies, and subscription libraries, and taking these under our direction, and supplying them through our labors, we may turn the public mind which way we will ... A literary society is the most proper form for the introduction of our Order into any State where we are yet strangers." They planned about 800 such Reading Rooms.

The membership initially consisted of 17 young men, and about five of Bahrdt's friends. Knigge helped him to develop the organizational structure, which was divided into six grades:

1) Adolescent
2) Man
3) Elder
4) Mesopolite
5) Diocesan

6) Superior

The 'Society of the 22' or the 'Brotherhood' was its inner circle.

In a pamphlet entitled *To All Friends of Reason, Truth and Virtue*, Bahrdt wrote that the organization's purpose was to accomplish the enlightenment of people in order to disseminate religion, remove popular prejudices, root out superstition, and restore liberty to mankind. They planned to have magazines and pamphlets, but by 1788, Bahrdt had sunk over $1,000 into the group, and was spending all of his time working on it. Despite his efforts, they still only had 200 members.

Near the end of 1788, Frederick Wilhelm, the King of Prussia, worried about the growth of the organization, had Johann Christian von Wollner, one of his ministers, write an opposing view to Bahrdt's pamphlet, called the *Edict of Religion*. Bahrdt responded by anonymously writing another pamphlet of the same name to satirize it. In 1789, a bookseller by the name of Goschen, wrote a pamphlet called *More Notes Than Text, on the German Union of XXII, a New Secret Society for the Good of Mankind*, in which he revealed that the group was a continuation of the Illuminati.

The German Union, which represented Weishaupt's "corrected system of Illuminism," never really got off the ground because of its openness, which provoked hostile attacks from the government and members of the clergy. Bahrdt left the group and opened up a tavern known as 'Bahrdt's Repose.' The German Union ceased to exist after he died in 1793.

THE FRENCH REVOLUTION

The Illuminati had secretly spread to France by 1787 (five years after they had planned), through French orator and revolutionary leader Count Gabriel Victor Riqueti de Mirabeau (1749-1791, Order name 'Leonidas') who had been indoctrinated by Col. Jacob Mauvillon while he was in Berlin on a secret mission for King Louis XVI of France in 1786. Mirabeau introduced Illuminati principles at the Paris Masonic Lodge of the Amis Reunis (later renamed 'Philalethes'), and initiated Abbé Charles-Maurice de Talleyrand-Perigord (1754-1838, a court cleric in the House of Bourbon).

The most trusted members were brought into the 'Secret Committee of United Friends' (it is interesting to note that a group of the same name originated in 1771 as an occult group). The initiations took place at the Illuminati's Grand Lodge, about 30 miles from Paris, in the Ermenonville mansion owned by the Marquis de Gerardin. The famous impostor Saint Germain (1710-1780, or 1785) presided over the initiation ceremonies.

Germain was believed to be a Portuguese Jew, who was a member of the Philalethes Lodge. He was a Mason, a Rosicrucian, and belonged to several other occult brotherhoods. He spoke Italian, German, English, Spanish, French, Greek, Sanskrit, Arabic, and Chinese. He was said to be the son of Prince Rakoczy of Transylvania; raised by the last Medici, Gian Gastone; and was educated at the

University of Siena. He told people that he had lived for centuries, and knew King Solomon. He was arrested in London in 1743 for being a Jacobite spy, and he took credit for establishing Freemasonry in Germany. As an impostor, he posed as Comte Bellamarre, Marquis de Montferrat, and Chevalier Schoening.

During the initiation, new members were sworn to "reveal to thy new chief all thou shalt have heard, learned and discovered, and also to seek after and spy into things that might have otherwise escaped thy notice ... (and to) avoid all temptation to betray what thou has now heard. Lightning does not strike so quickly as the dagger which will reach thee wherever thou mayest be."

Count Alessandro de Cagliostro (also known as Giuseppe Balsamo), a Jew from Sicily, who was said to be one of the greatest occult practitioners of all time, was initiated into the Illuminati at Mitau (near Frankfurt) in 1780, in an underground room. He later said, that an iron box filled with papers was opened, and a book taken out. From it, a member read the oath of secrecy, which began: "We, Grand Masters of Templars..." It was written in blood. The book was an outline of their plans, which included an attack on Rome. He discovered that they had money at their disposal in banks at Amsterdam, Rotterdam, London, Genoa, and Venice. He found out that the Illuminati had 20,000 lodges throughout Europe and America, and that their members served in every European court. Cagliostro was instructed to go to Strasbourg, France, to make the initial contacts necessary for the instigation of the French Revolution. Identified as a Grand Master of the Prieuré de Sion, it is believed that he was the liaison between them and the Illuminati. He was arrested in 1790, in Rome, for revolutionary activities.

The French Masons had committed themselves to a plan for overthrowing the government, under the guise of liberty and equality; ending the autocratic regimes, in order to have government by and for the people. Jeremy Bentham and William Petty (Earl of Shelburne) planned and directed the French Revolution, then later directed the plot towards America.

In 1788, at the request of Mirabeau and Talleyrand, Johann Joachim Christoph Bode (1730-1793, 'Amelius'), a lawyer at Weimar, and a Mason, was summoned to France. He had been initiated into the Illuminati at the Congress of Wilhelmsbad, and later took over the Order in the absence of Weishaupt. Bode and Baron de Busche ('Bayard'), a Dutch military officer in the service of the Landgrave of Hesse-Darmstadt, in order to conceal the purpose of their presence in France, said they were there to investigate the influence of the Jesuits on the secret societies. However, the real reason for them being there, was to further the goals of the Illuminati in France. They operated out of the Lodge of the Amis Reunis, changing its name to 'Philalethes,' which means, 'searchers after the truth.'

The Marquis de Luchet, a friend of Mirabeau, wrote in his *Essay on the Sect of the Illuminati* in January, 1789: "Deluded people. You must understand that there exists a conspiracy in favor of despotism, and against liberty, of incapacity against talent, of vice against virtue, or ignorance against light! ... Every species of error which afflicts the earth, every half-baked idea, every invention serves to fit the doctrines of the Illuminati ... The aim is universal domination."

Intellectuals known as 'encyclopedists' were instrumental in spreading Illuminati doctrine. Soon other lodges become aligned with the Philalethes, such as the Nine Sisters; the Lodge of Candor, which included members like Laclos, Sillery,

D'Aiguillon; the Lameth Brothers, Dr. Guillotine, and Lafayette; and the Propaganda, which was established by Condorcet, Abbé Sieyes, and Rochenfoucault.

Revolutionary leaders in France, such as Maximilien Francois Marie Isidore de Robespierre (1758-1794), who was made head of the Revolution by Weishaupt; Marquis Antoine Nicholas Condorcet (1743-1794), philosopher and politician; Duke de la Rochenfoucault; George Jacques Danton (1759-1794); Marquis Marie Joseph de Lafayette (1757-1834), General and statesman; Jerome Petion de Villeneuve (1756-1794), politician; Philippe, Duke of Orleans, Grand Master of French Freemasonry; de Leutre; Fauchet; Cammille Benoit Desmoulins (1760-1794), D'Alembert; Denis Diderot (1713-1784), encyclopedist; and Jean-Francois de la Harpe (1739-1803), critic and playwright, all joined the Illuminati, who had eventually infiltrated all 266 Masonic lodges by 1789, even though the Masons weren't aware of it.

The Illuminati created situations in order to create dissention among the people. For instance, the Duke of Orleans instructed his agents to buy up as much grain as they could, then the people were led to believe that the King intentionally caused the shortage, and that the French people were starving. Fellow conspirators in the government helped create runaway inflation. Thus the people were manipulated into turning against a king whose reign had strengthened the middle class. The monarchy was to be destroyed, and the middle class oppressed. God was to be replaced by the Illuminati's religion of reason that "man's mind would solve man's problems."

During the first two years of the French Revolution, which started in April, 1789, the Illuminati had infiltrated the Masonic Lodges to such an extent, that they had ceased operation, and instead rallied under the name, "The French Revolutionary Club." When they needed a larger meeting place, they used the hall of the Jacobin's Convent. This revolutionary group of 1300 people emerged on July 14, 1789 as the Jacobin Club. The Illuminati controlled the Club, and were directly responsible for fermenting the activities which developed into the French Revolution. Lord Acton wrote: "The appalling thing in the French Revolution is not the tumult but the design. Through all the fire and smoke, we perceived the evidence of calculating organization. The managers remain studiously concealed and masked; but there is no doubt about their presence from the first."

In the playing out of a plan which called for the population to be cut down by one-third to one-half, over 300,000 people died, including the execution of King Louis and his family. This was done to insure the stability of the new French Republic. In August, 1792, after the overthrow of the government, the tri-colored banner was replaced by the red flag of social revolution, while the cry of "Vive notre roi d'Orleans" gave way to the Masonic watchword, "Liberty, Equality, Fraternity!" Those who responded with the proper Masonic handsigns, had their lives spared. By November, 1793, as the massacres had spread all over France, the churches had been reorganized along the lines of Weishaupt's contention that "reason should be the only code of man."

Talleyrand, who became the bishop of Autin in 1788, because of his radical reorganization of the Church, was excommunicated by the Pope. He became a deputy to the National Assembly. The Jacobins controlled the National Assembly, and for all intents and purposes, Mirabeau became France's leader. In true Democratic spirit, he said: "We must flatter the people by gratuitous justice, promise them a great diminution in taxes and a more equal division, more extension in fortunes, and less humiliation. These fantasies will fanaticize the people, who will flatten all resistance." The Revolution was considered at an end on July 28, 1794, when Robespierre was guillotined.

Thomas Jefferson, who served as minister to France for three years (1785-89), described the events as "so beautiful a revolution" and said that he hoped it would sweep the world. Treasury Secretary Alexander Hamilton said that Jefferson helped start the French Revolution, and wrote in a letter to a friend, dated May 26, 1792, that Jefferson "drank freely of the French philosophy, in religion, in science, in politics. He came from France in the moment of fermentation, which he had a share in inciting." Jefferson wrote to Brissot de Warville in Philadelphia, in a letter dated May 8, 1793, that he was "eternally attached to the principles of the French Revolution." In 1987, during a trip to the United States by Soviet leader Mikhail Gorbachev and his wife, where they visited the Jefferson Memorial, she referred to Jefferson as "one of the world's greatest thinkers."

It is interesting to note, that during the Communist revolution, Nikolai Lenin said: "We, the Bolsheviks, are the Jacobins of the Twentieth Century..."

An Illuminist, and member of the revolutionary French National Assembly, Vicomte de Barras, witnessed a 24 year old Napoleon repelling a siege at Toulon in 1793 by English and Spanish military forces. Barras, appointed by the Assembly as the Commander-in-Chief of the French military, in 1795 became a member of the five-man Directorate, which began to govern France, and soon became the most powerful political figure in the country. He chose Napoleon to lead the military forces. However, in 1799, Napoleon (a Knights Templar) broke his ties with Barras, because he feared Barras was attempting to restore the Monarchy. Napoleon eliminated the Directorate, and in 1804, with the support of Talleyrand (who served as his foreign minister), became Emperor. Unwittingly, as a puppet of the Illuminati, his reign brought about the total disruption of Europe, which was needed for the Illuminati to get control and unify it. He ended the Holy Roman Empire, and made his brother Joseph, the King of Naples in 1806. Joseph was replaced by Napoleon's brother-in-law Murat, when Joseph became the King of Spain in 1808. His brother Louis was made the King of Holland, and another brother Jerome, the King of Westphalia.

In 1810, Napoleon confiscated the contents of the Vatican archives, which amounted to 3,000 cases of documents, and took it to Paris. Although most were later returned to Rome, some were kept. By this time, Napoleon had changed the face of Europe, but, he settled his warring ways and ultimately the French Revolution had failed, because Europe had not been fully conquered. The Illuminati immediately took steps to dethrone him, which took five years. In order to get money to Wellington's English forces, Nathan Rothschild funneled money to his brother James (who handled financial transactions for the French government), in Paris, who got it to Wellington's troops in Spain. In addition, the Illuminati secretly worked to make agreements that shifted national alliances against France.

Upon his defeat at Waterloo, Napoleon was again exiled, this time, to the island of Saint Helena in the south Atlantic, which is where he died in 1821. He had written in his will: "I die before my time, killed by the English oligarchy and its hired assassins."

THE ILLUMINATI SPREADS TO AMERICA

In 1785, the Columbia Lodge of the Order of the Illuminati was established in New York City. Among its members were Governor DeWitt Clinton, Horace Greeley (politician and editor of the *New York Daily Tribune*), Charles Dana, and Clinton Roosevelt (the ancestor of Franklin D. Roosevelt). Roosevelt wrote a book called *Science of Government Founded on Natural Law*, in which he wrote: "There is no God of justice to order things aright on earth, if there be a God, he is a malicious and revengeful being, who created us for misery." He referred to himself and other members as the "enlightened ones," and said that the U.S. Constitution was a "leaky vessel" which was "hastily put together when we left the British flag," and therefore needed revision.

In 1786, a lodge was started in Portsmouth, Virginia, where allegedly, Thomas Jefferson was a member; followed by fourteen others in different cities of the thirteen colonies.

On July 19, 1789, David Pappin, President of Harvard University, issued a warning to the graduating class, concerning the Illuminati's influence on American politics and religion. In April, 1793, France sent new ambassador Edmond Genet to America, so he could collect payment for the American debt incurred during the American Revolution. The money was to be used to finance France's war with England. However, his real reason for being here, was to gain political favor for France, and spread Illuminism, which he did, through the establishment of 'Democratic Clubs.'

Washington said "they would shake the government to its foundations," while John Quincy Adams, oldest son of the 2nd President John Adams, who became our 6th President in 1825, said that these clubs were "so perfectly affiliated with the Parisian Jacobins that their origin from a common parent cannot possibly be mistaken." Because of the Illuminati threat, Washington and Adams lobbied Congress to pass the Alien and Sedition Act, which was "designed to protect the United States from the extensive French Jacobin conspiracy, paid agents of which were even in high places in the government."

In a letter from Adams to Jefferson, dated June 30, 1813, he wrote: "You certainly never felt the terrorism excited by Genet, in 1793 ... when ten thousand people in the streets of Philadelphia, day after day threatened to drag Washington out of his house, and effect a revolution ... nothing but (a miracle) ... could have saved the United States from a fatal revolution of government."

Thomas Paine, author and political theorist, helped the Illuminati infiltrate several Masonic lodges. He revealed his loyalty to them when his book *The Age of Reason* was published in 1794, which dealt with the role of religion in society. Although he believed in God, he could not accept the entire Bible as being fact.

A second volume was published in 1796. An unofficial third volume (subtitled: *Examination of the Prophecies*) also appeared, which seriously questioned the deity and existence of Jesus. In 1937, *The Times* of London referred to him as "the English Voltaire."

On May 9, 1798, Rev. Jedediah Morse, pastor of the Congregational Church in Charleston, South Carolina preached a sermon at the New North Church in Boston, about the Illuminati: "Practically all of the civil and ecclesiastical establishments of Europe have already been shaken to their foundations by this terrible organization; the French Revolution itself is doubtless to be traced to its machinations; the successes of the French armies are to be explained on the same ground. The Jacobins are nothing more nor less than the open manifestation of the hidden system of the Illuminati. The Order has its branches established and its emissaries at work in America. The affiliated Jacobin Societies in America have doubtless had as the object of their establishment the propagation of the principles of the illuminated mother club in France ... I hold it a duty, my brethren, which I owe to God, to the cause of religion, to my country and to you, at this time, to declare to you, thus honestly and faithfully, these truths. My only aim is to awaken you and myself a due attention, at this alarming period, to our dearest interests. As a faithful watchman I would give you warning of your present danger."

Later in July, Timothy Dwight, President of Yale University, told the people of New Haven: "Shall our sons become the disciples of Voltaire (a French writer) and the dragoons of Murat, or our daughters, the concubines of the Illuminati."

To infiltrate the Masonic lodges in Europe, Weishaupt had enlisted the aid of John Robison, who was a long time, high degree Mason in the Scottish Rite, a professor of Natural Philosophy at Edinburgh University in Scotland, a British historian, and Secretary-General to the Royal Society of Edinburgh. When he went to Germany, he was given Weishaupt's revised conspiracy plans to study, in order to expand the Illuminati's influence in the British Isles. However, Robison didn't agree with their principles, and after warning American Masons in 1789, published a book to expose the organization in 1798 called *Proofs of a Conspiracy Against All Religions and Governments of Europe, Carried On In the Secret Meetings of Freemasons, Illuminati, and Reading Societies* (which presented the Protestant view). He wrote: "I have observed these doctrines gradually diffusing and mixing with all the different systems of Freemasonry till, at last, an association has been formed for the express purpose of rooting out all the religious establishments, and overturning all the existing governments of Europe."

Also, that same year, Abbé Augustin Barruel (French patriot, Jesuit, and 3rd degree Mason) published his *Memoires pour servir a l'Histoire du Jacobinisme* or *Memoirs Illustrating the History of Jacobinism* (which presented the Roman Catholic view). Both books sought to warn America about the Illuminati conspiracy, but the warnings were not taken seriously. The January, 1798 edition of the *Monthly Magazine* contained a letter by Augustus Bottiger, Provost of the College of Weimar, who accused Robison of making inaccurate statements, and said that since 1790, "every concern of the Illuminati has ceased."

Thomas Jefferson, believed to be a member of the Virginia lodge of the Illuminati, and a Mason (who helped the Illuminati to infiltrate the New England Masonic lodges), denied all the allegations, and described Weishaupt as "an enthusiastic philanthropist" and called Barruel's revelations "the ravings of a Bedlamite (Bedlam was the name of a hospital in London for the mentally insane)."

During the summer of 1798, Rev. G. W. Snyder, a Lutheran minister, wrote a letter to President Washington and included a copy of Robison's book, expressing his concern about the Illuminati infiltrating the American Masonic lodges. In Washington's response, dated September 25, 1798, he wrote: "I have heard much about the nefarious and dangerous plan and doctrines of the Illuminati," but went on to say that he didn't believe that they had become involved in the lodges. A subsequent letter by Snyder, requesting a more reassuring answer, resulted in a letter from Washington, dated October 24, 1798, which can be found in *The Writings of George Washington* (volume 20, page 518, which was prepared under the direction of the U.S. George Washington Bicentennial Commission and published by the U.S. Government Printing Office in 1941). He wrote:

> "It was not my intention to doubt that the doctrines of the Illuminati and the principles of Jacobinism had not spread in the United States. On the contrary, no one is more satisfied of this fact than I am. The idea I meant to convey, was, that I did not believe that the lodges of Freemasons in this country had, as societies, endeavored to propagate the diabolical tenets of the first, or pernicious principles of the latter. That individuals of them may have done it, or that the founder or instruments employed to have found the democratic societies in the United States may have had this object, and actually had a separation of the people from their government in view, is too evident to be questioned."

Shortly before his death, Washington issued two more warnings about the Illuminati.

Around 1807, John Quincy Adams (said to have organized the New England Masonic lodges), who later became President in 1825, wrote three letters to Colonel William C. Stone, a top Mason, telling him that Thomas Jefferson, our 3rd President, and founder of the Democratic Party, was using the Masonic lodges for subversive Illuminati purposes. These letters were allegedly kept at the Rittenburg Square Library in Philadelphia, but have mysteriously vanished. Adams also wrote to Washington, saying that Jefferson and Alexander Hamilton were misusing Masonic lodges for Illuminati purposes and the worship of Lucifer (which is recorded in the *Adams Chronicles*).

Benjamin Franklin was also accused of being a member of the Illuminati, but there is no concrete proof of this. Jefferson seemed to be the main focus of everyone's ire. He was accused by the Federalists of being a Jacobin, and an atheist. There is some evidence to indicate that he did use the Democratic Societies and Jacobin Clubs in his 1796 battle with John Adams for the Presidency. The Rev. Jedediah Morse identified Jefferson as "an Illuminatus."

On July 4, 1812, Rev. Joseph Willard, the president of Harvard University, said in a speech in Lancaster, New Hampshire: "There is sufficient evidence that a number of societies, of the Illuminati, have been established in this land of Gospel light and civil liberty, which were first organized from the grand society, in France. They are doubtless secretly striving to undermine all our ancient institutions, civil and sacred. These societies are closely leagued with those of the same Order, in Europe; they have all the same object in view. The enemies of all order are seeking our ruin. Should infidelity generally prevail, our independence would fall of course. Our republican government would be annihilated..."

It has been suggested, that one of the reasons that the British looted and burned Washington in 1812, was to destroy secret documents that would have exposed the treason against the United States, by various people highly placed within the government.

When those advocating a strong central government organized the Federalist Party in 1791, the Anti-Federalists, who favored states' rights, and were against Alexander Hamilton's (Secretary of Treasury under Washington, 1789-1795) fiscal policies, which they felt benefited the wealthy, rallied under Thomas Jefferson, Washington's first Secretary of State (1789-93). They became an organized political party after the Constitutional Convention in 1787, led by New York Governor George Clinton (who was later Vice-President under Jefferson and Madison), Patrick Henry of Virginia, and Elbridge Gerry of Massachusetts (a signer of the Declaration of Independence). The Anti-Federalists were made up of the low class, farmers, and paper money advocates, who strongly opposed a strong central government as set forth in the U.S. Constitution of 1789, and succeeded in getting the Bill of Rights added. They were against a single, national government, upper class rule, and a weak program for the separation of powers.

The Jeffersonian Republicans, so named because of the anti-monarchy views of the Anti-Federalists, had power from 1801-1825. In 1796, the party split into the Democratic-Republicans, organized by New York State Senator Martin Van Buren (who became our 8th President, 1837-41), who concerned themselves with states' rights, farmers' interests and democratic procedures; and the National Republicans, led by John Quincy Adams, Henry Clay, and Daniel Webster, who merged with the Federalists in 1820. In 1826, the Democratic-Republicans became known as just plain Democrats, while the National Republicans became identified as only Republicans in 1854. That is how the two-party system was created in this country.

PHI BETA KAPPA

The fraternity known as Phi-Beta-Kappa was organized in 1776 by students at the College of William and Mary in Williamsburg, Virginia (the second oldest in the country, founded in 1694), as a secret debating club. It was later infiltrated, and used to introduce Illuminati principles to America.

Their name was derived from their Greek password and motto, 'Philosophia Biou Kuberuetes,' which means, 'Philosophy is the Guide of Life.' Open only to university students, their goal was to make philosophy, not religion, the guiding principle of man's actions. They had secret hand signals and handshakes up to 1831, when it was reorganized and changed from a social organization, to an honorary society for upper classmen with high scholastic standing.

During the 1700's, when it looked as through the fraternity would fold, one of its members, Elisha Parmele, received a grant to establish chapters at Yale in 1780 (Yale Professor of History, Gaddis Smith, said: "Yale has influenced the Central Intelligence Agency more than any other university, giving the CIA the atmosphere of a class reunion."), and at Harvard in 1781. They later grew to have chapters on 270 campuses, and with more than 500,000 members.

Among their member have been: Tom Brokaw (NBC commentator), Glenn

Close (actress), Francis Ford Coppola (noted film director), Henry Kissinger (U.S. Secretary of State, 1973 to 1977; Assistant to the President for National Security Affairs, 1969-75), Kris Kristofferson (singer/actor), Dean Rusk (Presidential advisor), Howard K. Smith (ABC commentator), Caspar Weinberger (U.S. Secretary of Defense, 1981-87), John D. Rockefeller, Jr., Nelson Rockefeller, President George H. W. Bush, President Jimmy Carter, President Bill Clinton, President Franklin Roosevelt, President Woodrow Wilson, Gov. Jeb Bush (from Florida), Sen. Joseph Lieberman (from Connecticut), Byron White (Supreme Court Justice), and Elihu Root (Secretary of State, 1905-1909; served in the U.S. Senate, 1909-1915; was president of the Carnegie Endowment for International Peace, 1910-1925).

To be fair here, I have to say that the inclusion of Phi Beta Kappa is by no means intended to downplay the academic achievements of its thousands of members, or to give it the connotation of it being an evil organization. However, its dubious beginnings, and the fact that many people in influential positions have come from their ranks, it certainly is reason enough to take note. But more than that, when you see their membership cross over into other organizations such as the Bilderbergers, Council on Foreign Relations, and Trilateral Commission; then you begin to see it as a possible breeding ground for people who are favorable to the international agenda that is leading to one-world government.

SKULL AND BONES

The Skull and Bones organization was founded at Yale University in 1832 by General William Huntington Russell (who later served in the Connecticut State legislature 1846-47) and Alphonso Taft (U.S. Secretary of War in 1876, Attorney General 1886-87, U.S. Minister to Austria 1882-84, U.S. Ambassador to Russia 1884-85, and the father of former president William Howard Taft); and incorporated in 1856 by Russell and Daniel Colt Gilman, under the name 'The Russell Trust Association.' Russell had visited Germany that year, where he was exposed to the Illuminati, and possibly initiated. He wanted to establish a similar group in America, where their sons could become members of a secret Order that would give them a favored status.

It became a black lodge of Freemasonry. In 1873, some Yale students broke into their headquarters, a windowless building called 'The Tomb' adjacent to the campus, where they discovered their insignia— the skull and bones, along with some real skulls and bones. They wrote in the Yale newspaper, the *Iconoclast*: "Year-by-year the deadly evil of the Skull and Bones is growing."

The Russell Trust is endowed by $54 million in alumni grants, and it is the alumni who control the group. Antony C. Sutton, a former Economics professor at Stanford University, wrote a four-volume series of books on the group, and revealed the names of 30 influential old-line American families who have contributed to its ranks (some of which can trace their lineage back to the 1600's, when they arrived from England), including Whitney, Lord, Phelps, Wadsworth, Allen,

Bundy, Adams, Harriman, Rockefeller, Payne, Davison, and Pratt. Every year, 15 juniors are chosen to be members, and are called 'Knights.' Upon graduation, they are called the 'Patriarchs of the Order.'

Since its inception, over 2500 Yale graduates have been initiated. Its members have assimilated themselves into every area of business and government. Members have included: W. Averell Harriman (governor of New York, and advisor to various Democratic presidents), William P. Bundy (editor of the CFR's journal *Foreign Affairs*), J. Hugh Liedtke (co-founder of Pennzoil Oil Corp.), John Kerry (U.S. Senator from Massachusetts), David Boren (U.S. Senator from Oklahoma), William Sloane Coffin (President of SANE/FREEZE, Phi Beta Kappa), William F. Buckley (conservative commentator, editor of the *National Review* magazine), Gifford Pinchot (father of the environmental movement), Potter Stewart (Supreme Court Justice), William H. Taft (27th President), Archibald MacLeish (founder of UNESCO), Harold Stanley (investment banker, founder of Morgan Stanley), Dean Witter, Jr. (investment banker), Henry Luce (head of *Time/Life* magazines), Henry P. Davison (senior partner of Morgan Guaranty Trust), Alfred Cowles (of Cowles Communications), Richard Ely Danielson (of the *Atlantic Monthly* magazine), Winston Lord (Chairman of the CFR, Ambassador to China and assistant Secretary of State in the Clinton administration), Russell Wheeler Davenport (of *Fortune* magazine), McGeorge Bundy (national security advisor for President John Kennedy), John Sherman Cooper (U.S. Senator from Kentucky), John H. Chafee (U.S. Senator from Rhode Island), Henry Stimson (Secretary of State for President Herbert Hoover), Robert A. Lovett (Secretary of Defense for President Harry Truman), George H. W. Bush. (41st President, Bilderberger, CFR and Trilateral Commission member until 1980), and George W. Bush (43rd President).

Nicknamed 'Bonesmen,' these establishment elites have become members of the Trilateral Commission and the Council on Foreign Relations, and have achieved high level positions in the Administrations of various Presidents, the Congress, and the government, in various capacities. From these positions, they can use their influence to work towards their common goal of one-world government.

Both the Skull and Bones, and Phi Beta Kappa, are indicative of the way the Illuminati functions. They know that if they can grab, control, and mold young minds, then they will have unwitting pawns to do their bidding, and could be called upon to contribute to their efforts. The early history of the Illuminati was nothing more than a seed that was planted. That is why there was a big emphasis on infiltrating educational institutions with their doctrine. As each class graduated through the educational systems of the world, the more people there were to perpetuate their plans. In time, the Illuminati knew they would have enough of the right people, in the right places, for them to secretly further their goals.

CONGRESS OF VIENNA

In 1802, Europe was made up of several hundred states, which were dominated by England, Austria, Russia, Prussia and France, which was the most powerful country. In 1804, when Napoleon Bonaparte took over France, his military exploits had led to the complete control of virtually all of Europe. Even today, France has more land than any other country in western Europe. In 1812, when Napoleon moved against Russia; England, Spain and Portugal were already at war with France. They were later joined by Sweden, Austria; and in 1813, Prussia joined the coalition to end the siege of Europe, and to "assure its future peace by the re-establishment of a just equilibrium of the powers." In 1814, the coalition defeated France, and in March of that year, marched into Paris. France's borders were returned to their original 1792 location, which had been established by the First Peace of Paris, and Napoleon was exiled to Elba, a small island off the Tucson coast of Italy.

After the Napoleonic Wars, the Illuminati thought the world would be tired of fighting, and would accept any solution to have peace. Through the Congress of Vienna (1814-15), the Rothschilds hoped to create a sort of League of Nations.

From September, 1814 to June, 1815, the four powers of the allied coalition, winners of the Napoleonic Wars, met at the Congress of Vienna, along with a large number of rulers and officials representing smaller states. It was the biggest political meeting in European history. Representing England, was Lord Robert Stewart, the 2nd Viscount Castlereagh; France, with Foreign Minister Charles-Maurice Talleyrand de Perigord; Prussia, with King Friedrich Wilhelm III; and Austria, with Emperor Franz II.

Other representatives were: Frederick VI, King of Denmark; Maximilian Joseph, King of Bavaria; Friedrich I, King of Wurttemburg; Napoleon II, King of Rome; Eugene de Beaurharnais, Viceroy of Italy; King Friedrich August I of Saxony; Count Leowenhielm of Sweden; Cardinal Consalvi of the Papal States; Grand Duke Charles of Baden; Elector William of Hesse; Grand Duke George of Hesse-Darmstadt; Karl August, Duke of Weimar; the King of Bohemia; the King of Hungary; and emissaries from Spain, Portugal, Denmark, Holland, and other European States.

The main concern of the Congress was to redistribute conquered territories, create a balance of power, restore the pre-Napoleonic order through King Louis XVIII, return the power to families who were ruling in 1789, and to return the Roman Catholic Church to its former power. Discussion revolved around the creation of a Federation of Europe that would establish a group of independent kingdoms which would be tied together through an administrative governing body that would, among other things, provide military defense. In their plan, Switzerland was made a neutral state that served as a repository for their finances.

In March, 1815, Napoleon left Elba, because the pension promised him by King Louis XVIII was discontinued, and he believed that Austria was preventing his companion, Marie Louise, and his son, the former King of Rome (who became the Duke of Reichstadt in Vienna) from being able to join him. Plus, he was made aware of the growing discontent with the King. Thus Napoleon returned, began the Hundred Days War, and was immediately labeled a "public enemy." The coalition at the Congress put aside their diplomatic business, and joined in the battle.

Shortly before Napoleon's defeat at Waterloo, negotiations at the Congress of Vienna were completed, and the treaty was signed on June 9, 1815. The Second Peace of Paris, in November, exiled Napoleon to St. Helena, an island 1,000 miles off the African coast, where he died in 1821. The Russian czar saw through the planned European Federation, recognizing it as an Illuminati ploy, and would not go along with it. On September 26, 1815, the Treaty of Holy Alliance was signed by Alexander I of Russia, Francis II of Austria, and Frederick William III of Prussia, while the allies were negotiating the Second Peace of Paris. The Treaty guaranteed the sovereignty of any monarch who would adhere to Christian principles in the affairs of State. The Treaty made them a "true and indissoluble brotherhood." Alexander claimed he got the idea from a conversation with Castlereagh. Castlereagh later said that the Alliance was a "piece of sublime mysticism and nonsense." Prussia and Austria claimed they went along with it, out of fear of Russian retaliation. Although the Alliance had no influence on matters, it did indicate to other countries that they had banded together against them, and it succeeded in temporarily crushing Europe's growing liberal movement.

Austrian Minister of Foreign Affairs, Prince Klemens Furst von Metternich, the most influential statesman in Europe, and a Rothschild agent, said that the purpose of his idea for a European Federation was only to preserve the social order, and he was convinced that Alexander was insane.

In actuality, the reason for the Congress of Vienna, was for the Illuminati to create a Federation, so they would have complete political control over most of the civilized world. Many of the European governments were in debt to the Rothschilds, so they figured they could use that as a bargaining tool. The Illuminati, in their first attempt, had come terrifyingly close to gaining control of the world. The head of the family, Nathan Rothschild, awaited the day that his family would get revenge by destroying the Czar and his family, which they did in 1917.

In 1916, the Senate *Congressional Record* (pg. 6781) reproduced a document known as the "Secret Treaty of Verona" which had been signed in November 22, 1822 by Austria (Metternich), France (Chateaubriand), Prussia (Bernstet), and Russia (Nesselrode); and was partially the reason for the establishment of the Monroe Doctrine. Its purpose was to make some changes to the treaty of the Holy Alliance, and Article One stated: "The high contracting powers, being convinced that the system of representative government is equally as incompatible with the monarchical principles as the maxim of the sovereignty of the people with the divine right, engage mutually, in the most solemn manner, to use all their efforts to put an end to the system of representative governments, in whatever country it may exist in Europe, and to prevent its being introduced where it is not yet known." Without a doubt, this document represented the intentions of the International bankers as they planned increasing domination over a growing world.

THE MASONS SEPARATE THEMSELVES FROM THE ILLUMINATI

In 1826, Captain William Morgan, a journalist and stonemason from Batavia, New York, who was a high degree mason in a local Masonic lodge, wrote an exposé of the Masonic Order in a book called *Illustrations of Masonry*, which revealed many of their secrets concerning the first three degrees. Shortly afterward, he was arrested and charged with stealing and indebtedness, and put in jail. The Illuminati tried him in absentia, convicted him of treason, and ordered five men, led by Richard Howard, an English Illuminist, to execute him. When he was released from jail, he was warned about the plot, and he attempted to flee to Canada. Howard caught him at the border, and took him to Fort Niagara, where he was held for a couple of days. The Freemasons that accompanied Howard, carried him off in a boat, and drowned him in the Niagara River.

This event was verified by the sworn statement of Avery Allen (said to be on file at the New York City Archives), who heard Howard give a report of the incident at a meeting of the Knights Templar at St. John's Hall in New York City. One of the three men who carried out the assassination, confessed on his deathbed in 1848.

Masonic leaders refused to cooperate with the lengthy investigation, which didn't get anywhere, since many of the police officers were Masons. The general consensus was that Morgan accidentally drowned himself in Lake Ontario. However, the press, religious leaders, temperance and anti-slavery groups, united to condemn the apparent murder. The murder caused over half of the Masons in the northeastern United States to break off their alignment with the Illuminati. The incident led to the creation of the country's first third party movement, the Anti-Masonic Party (1826-33) in New York. They wanted to stop the aristocratic conspiracy, and prevent all members of Masonic organizations from public service. Anti-Masonic candidates were elected to the New York Assembly in 1827.

A State Convention in Massachusetts in 1828 saw the establishment of a committee "to inquire how far Freemasonry and French Illuminism are connected." The Committee reported at a meeting at Faneuil Hall in Boston (December 30, 31, and January 1, 1829), and passed the following resolution: "Resolved, on the report of the Committee appointed to inquire how far Freemasonry and French Illuminism are connected, that there is evidence of an intimate connection between the high orders of Masonry and French Illuminism."

A National Convention was held in 1830 in Philadelphia, and another in Baltimore in 1831, where they nominated William Wirt, former U.S. Attorney General (under Monroe and John Quincy Adams, 1817-1829), as a Presidential candidate. They were represented by 116 Anti-Masonic delegates from 13 states. The movement caught on mainly in New England and the Mid-Atlantic states. Even though they won quite a few Congressional seats in 1832, Wirt only carried the State of Vermont, while Andrew Jackson, a Mason, won big.

The Party was phased out in 1836, because the anti-slavery movement began to overshadow their activities. They merged with the Whig Party (1834-60) in 1838. The Whig Party later assimilated themselves into the Democratic Party, the Liberty Party (1840-48), the Free Soil Party (1848-54), and the Republican Party.

Fifty years after Morgan's disappearance, Thurlow Weed (1797-1882), owner of the *Rochester Telegraph*, and Editor of the influential *Albany Evening Journal* (from 1830-1863), who helped found the Anti-Masonic Party, published information about Morgan's death. His grave was discovered in 1881 at Pembroke, in Batavia County, in New York. In the grave was a piece of paper that had the name John Brown written on it. Brown was said to be one of the people involved in the killing. A statue was erected in memory of Morgan in Batavia in 1882.

THE ILLUMINATI IN THE UNITED STATES

In 1829, the Illuminati held a secret meeting in New York, which was addressed by a British Illuminist named Frances 'Fanny' Wright, from Scotland, who was an associate of socialist Robert Dale Owen. She had come to America in 1818, then again in 1824. In 1828, she became the co-editor of the *New Harmony Gazette* with Owen. In 1829, they moved to New York, and called their publication the *Free Enquirer*. At the meeting, she spoke of equal rights, atheism, and free love, as she promoted a Women's Auxiliary of the Illuminati. Those present were told that an international movement of subversives was being developed along the lines of Illuminati principles, who would be used to ferment future wars. They were to be known as 'communists.' This movement was to be used to make the idea of a one-world government more appealing by bringing chaos to the world through war and revolution, so the Illuminati could step in to create order.

In 1843, poet Heinrich Heine, revealed what he knew about this new group, when he wrote a book called *Letece*, which was a compilation of articles he wrote for the *Augsburg Gazette* from 1840-1843. A passage from that book read: "Communism is the secret name of this tremendous adversary which the rule of the proletariat, with all that implies, opposes to the existing bourgeois regime ... Communism is nonetheless the dark hero, cast for an enormous if fleeting role in the modern tragedy, and awaiting its cue to enter the stage."

Clinton Roosevelt, Horace Greeley (1811-72, Editor of the *New York Tribune* which he founded in 1841), and Charles Dana (1819-97, City Editor on the *New York Tribune*, and later Editor of the *New York Sun*), prominent newspaper publishers at that time, were appointed to a committee to raise funds for the project, which was being financed by the Rothschilds. Incidentally, Greeley, because of his ambition for high public office, and his anti-slavery stand, helped organize the Republican Party in 1854. In 1872, he ran for the Presidency, against Ulysses S. Grant, on the Liberal Republican ticket. Grant defeated him 3,597,132 votes to 2,834,125.

In 1841, Clinton Roosevelt wrote a book called *The Science of Government Founded on Natural Law*, which was the blueprint of the conspiracy to eliminate the U.S. Constitution, and to communize the country, based on the principles of Weishaupt. It contained the detailed plan for the New Deal and the National Recovery Act that was implemented 92 years later by his direct descendant Franklin D. Roosevelt.

The Illuminati operated through a front organization known as the Locofoco Party (1835-45), which was organized by radical Jacksonian Democrats who were strongly influenced by the Working Man's Party (1828-30), and had labor support. The Working Man's Party merged into the Equal Rights Party in 1833, which later developed into the Socialist Party in 1901. The Locofocos got their name when they voted down the endorsed candidate for the Democratic Party Chairman, and the gas lights were turned off by Party regulars during the 1835 meeting in Tammany Hall. The matches they used to light candles, in order to continue the meeting, were called 'locofocos.'

With their political strength concentrated mainly in the Northeast, their goals were to establish an independent treasury and to enact anti-monopoly legislation.

They were absorbed into the States' rights movement of Sen. John C. Calhoun of South Carolina, Sen. Henry Clay of Kentucky, and Sen. Daniel Webster of Massachusetts, who joined with the Jeffersonian Republicans and the Anti-Masonic Party to form the Whig Party, which represented farmers, southern plantation owners, and northeastern business interests. Their main complaint was President Andrew Jackson's refusal to Charter the Second Bank of the United States. They succeeded in electing Gen. William Henry Harrison and Gen. Zachary Taylor to the Presidency, but were stymied by presidential vetoes when they tried to get their legislative projects passed, especially after the re-establishment of the National Bank. The Whigs later merged with the newly formed Republican Party.

THE ILLUMINATI LEADERSHIP CHANGES

After Weishaupt died on November 18, 1830, at the age of 82, Giuseppe Mazzini (1805-72), an Italian patriot, and revolutionary leader, was appointed head of the Illuminati in 1834. It was believed that Weishaupt rejoined the Catholic Church with a deathbed repentance.

While attending Genoa University, Mazzini became a 33rd degree Mason, and joined a secret organization known as the Carbonari (their stated goal in 1818: "Our final aim is that of Voltaire and of the French Revolution— the complete annihilation of Catholicism, and ultimately all Christianity."), where he became committed to the cause of Italian unity. In 1831, he was exiled to France, where he founded the 'Young Societies' movement, which included Giovane Italia (Young Italy), Young England, etc. This group united those who wanted to achieve unification through force. Mazzini moved to England in 1837, then returned to Italy in 1848 to lead the revolution against the Austrians. Again he was exiled. In the 1850's, he led more revolutionary activities, and through his actions, Italy became united in 1861, as a single kingdom, rather than the republic envisioned by Mazzini.

Mazzini, who became known as the 'Evil Genius of Italy,' tried to carry on the activities of the Illuminati through the Alta Vendita Lodge, the highest lodge of the Carbonari.

From 1814-48, the group known as the Haute Vente Romaine led the activities of most of Europe's secret societies. In April, 1836, the head of the Haute Vente, whose pseudonym was 'Nubius,' wrote to 'Beppo': "Mazzini behaves too much like a conspirator of melodrama to suit the obscure role we resign ourselves to play until our triumph. Mazzini likes to talk about a great many things, about himself above all. He never ceases writing that he is overthrowing thrones and altars, that he fertilizes the peoples, that he is the prophet of humanitarianism..."

In 1860, Mazzini had formed an organization called the 'Oblonica,' a name derived from the Latin 'obelus,' which means: "I beckon with a spit (dagger)." Within this group, he established an inner circle called the Mafia.

About 1,000 AD, after the Normans had driven the Arabs out of Sicily, they established a feudal system. Overseers to guard each feudi were chosen from known criminals. Skirmishes between the Barons were fought by these criminals. Although feudal privileges were abolished in 1812, these overseers retained control of the land through leasing arrangements. It was this band of criminals that Mazzini gave the name 'Mafia', which was an acronym for Mazzini, Autorizza, Furti, Incendi, and Avvelengmenti. Known as the Mafiosi, they were authorized by Mazzini to commit thefts, arson and murder. It was this organization that came to America during the 1890's with the beginning of Italian immigration.

In 1859, Albert Pike (1809-1891), a lawyer, and leader of the U.S. Scottish Rite Masonry (who was called the 'Sovereign Pontiff of Universal Freemasonry,' the 'Prophet of Freemasonry' and the 'greatest Freemason of the nineteenth century'), who was fascinated with the idea of a one-world government, was chosen to coordinate Illuminati activities in the United States. He said they needed to create a political party that would keep the world fighting, until they could bring peace. Pike said it would be done "with tongue and pen, with all our open and secret influences, with the purse, and if need be, with the sword..."

Pike was born on December 29, 1809, in Boston, went to Harvard, then later served as a Brigadier-General in the Confederate Army. He was appointed by the Confederacy to be the Indian Commissioner in order to create an army of Indian warriors. He became Governor of the Indian territory, and succeeded in creating an army consisting of Chickasaws, Comanches, Creeks, Cherokees, Miamis, Osages, Kansas, and Choctaws. He became known to them as the "faithful paleface friend and protector." The savagery of their attacks caused Jefferson Davis, the President of the Confederacy, to disband the Indian army. After the Civil War, Pike was found guilty of treason and jailed, only to be pardoned by President Andrew Johnson on April 22, 1866, who met with him the next day at the White House. On June 20, 1867, Scottish Rite officials conferred upon Johnson, the 4th-32nd degrees, and he later went to Boston to dedicate a Masonic Temple. The only monument to a Confederate general in Washington, D.C. was erected in Pike's honor, and can be found between the Department of Labor building and the Municipal Building, between 3rd and 4th Streets, on D Street, NW.

Pike was a genius, able to read and write in 16 different languages. A 33rd degree Mason, he was one of the founding fathers, and head of the Ancient Accepted Scottish Rite of Freemasonry. In 1869, he was a top leader in the Knights of the Ku Klux Klan. In 1871, he wrote the 861 page Masonic handbook known as the *Morals and Dogma of the Ancient and Accepted Rite of Freemasonry*.

Pike was said to be a Satanist, who indulged in the occult, and possessed a bracelet he used to summon Lucifer, with whom he had constant communication. He was the Grand Master of a Luciferian group known as the Order of the Palladium (or Sovereign Council of Wisdom), which had been founded in Paris in 1737. Palladism had been brought to Greece from Egypt by Pythagoras in the fifth century, and it was this cult of Satan that was introduced to the inner circle of the Masonic lodges. It was aligned with the Palladium of the Templars. In 1801, Issac Long, a Jew, brought a statue of Baphomet (Satan) to Charleston, South Carolina, where he helped established the Ancient and Accepted Scottish Rite. Pike, his successor, changed the name to the New and Reformed Palladian Rite (or Reformed Palladium). The Order contained two degrees: 1) Adelph (or Brother), and 2) Companion of Ulysses (or Companion of Penelope). Pike's right-hand man was Phileas Walder, from Switzerland, who was a former Lutheran minister, a Masonic leader, occultist, and spiritualist. His other closest aids were Gallatin Mackey (a Masonic leader), Longfellow, and Holbrook. Pike, along with Mazzini, Lord Henry Palmerston of England (1784-1865, 33rd degree Mason), and Otto von Bismarck from Germany (33rd Mason, 1815-1898), intended to use the Palladian Rite to create a Satanic umbrella group that would tie all Masonic groups together.

Because of Mazzini's revolutionary activities in Europe, the Illuminati had to again go underground. Pike established Supreme Councils in Charleston, South Carolina; Rome, Italy (led by Mazzini); London, England (led by Palmerston); and Berlin, Germany (led by Bismarck). He set up 23 subordinate councils in strategic places throughout the world, including five Grand Central Directories in Washington, DC (North America), Montevideo (South America), Naples (Europe), Calcutta (Asia), and Mauritius (Africa), which were used to gather information. All of these branches have been the secret headquarters for the Illuminati's activities ever since.

In a letter dated January 22, 1870, Mazzini wrote to Pike:

"We must allow all of the federations to continue just as they are, with their systems, their central authorities and diverse modes of correspondence between high grades of the same rite, organized as they are at present, but we must create a super rite, which will remain unknown, to which we will call those Masons of high degree whom we shall select (obviously referring to the New and Reformed Palladian Rite). With regard to our brothers in Masonry, these men must be pledged to the strictest secrecy. Through this supreme rite, we will govern all Freemasonry which will become the one International Center, the more powerful because its direction will be unknown."

In another letter, dated August 15, 1871, Pike wrote to Mazzini:

"We shall unleash the Nihilists and the atheists, and we shall provoke a formidable social cataclysm which in all its horror will show clearly to the nations the effect of absolute atheism, the origin of savagery, and of the most bloody turmoil. Then everywhere, the citizens, obliged to defend themselves against the world minority of revolutionaries, will exterminate those destroyers of civilization, and the multitude, disillusioned with Christianity, whose deistic spirits will from that moment be without compass, anxious for an ideal, but without knowing where to render its adoration, will receive the pure light through the universal manifestation which will result from the general reactionary movement which will follow the destruction of Christianity and atheism, both conquered and exterminated at the same time."

Another part of this letter was discovered in 1949, which graphically outlined plans for three world wars and at least two revolutions. The first world war was to enable communistic atheism to destroy the czarist government in Russia. This was accomplished. The second world war was to begin by pitting Great Britain against Germany, in order to destroy Naziism, and advance the cause of Zionism, so that

Israel could become a nation. This was accomplished. After this war, Communism was to be made strong enough to begin taking over weaker governments. In 1945, at the Potsdam Conference between Truman, Churchill, and Stalin, Russia was given a chunk of Europe, and that helped to sweep the tide of Communism into China. The plan also called for a third world war, which is to be ignited by firing up the aggression between the Zionists (Israel) and the Arab world, who will destroy each other, bringing the rest of the world into a final conflict. This conflict will be engineered to produce complete social, political, and economic chaos; out of which will emerge an Illuminati-controlled world government.

According to William Guy Carr, a retired Canadian Naval Commander, in his book *Pawns in the Game* (he also wrote *Red Fog Over America*), he said that for a short time this letter had been on display in the British Museum Library in London, where he wrote a copy of it. The British Museum has said that they never had such a letter in their collection. It was later discovered that Carr got the information from a book called *The Mystery of Freemasonry Unveiled* by Jose Maria Caro y Rodriguez, the Archbishop of Santiago, and the Cardinal of Chile. Some researchers believe the second letter to be fraudulent, and had been written much later than the first part, since the word 'Fascism' was not used until 1921, and the Arab/Jewish problem did not exist until after the 1917 Balfour Declaration. But then again, if they indeed planned and initiated these events, the document could very well be authentic.

After Mazzini's death on March 11, 1872, Pike appointed Adriano Lemmi (1822-1896, 33rd degree Mason), a banker from Florence, Italy, to run their subversive activities in Europe. Lemmi was a supporter of patriot and revolutionary Giuseppe Garibaldi, and may have been active in the Luciferian Society founded by Pike.

On July 14, 1889, Pike issued this statement to the 24 Supreme Councils of the world who were meeting in Paris:

"That which we must say to the crowd is: 'We worship a God, but it is the God one adores without superstition.'

To you, Sovereign Grand Inspectors General (33rd Degree Masons), we say this, that you may repeat it to the Brethren of the 32nd, 31st, and 30th degrees: 'The Masonic religion should be, by all of us initiates of the high degrees, maintained in the purity of the Luciferian doctrine.'

If Lucifer were not God, would Adonay (or 'Adonai,' Hebrew for the word 'Lord' which refers to Jehovah, the God of Israel, which they avoided using) whose deeds prove his cruelty, perfidy, and hatred of man, barbarism and repulsion for science, would Adonay and his priests calumniate him? Yes, Lucifer is God, and unfortunately Adonay is also God. For the eternal law is that there is no light without shade, no beauty without ugliness, no white without black, for the absolute can only exist as two Gods: darkness being necessary to light to serve as its foil as the pedestal is necessary to the statue, and the brake to the locomotive...

...Thus, the doctrine of Satanism is a heresy; and the true and pure philosophic religion is the belief in Lucifer, the equal of Adonay; but Lucifer, God of Light and God of Good, is struggling for humanity against Adonay, the God of darkness and evil."

CHAPTER TWO

FINANCIAL BACKGROUND

THE BEGINNING OF MONETARY CONTROL

Napoleon said: "When a government is dependent for money upon the bankers, they and not the leaders of the government control the situation, since the hand that gives is above the hand that takes ... financiers are without patriotism and without decency..." Karl Marx said in the *Communist Manifesto*: "Money plays the largest part in determining the course of history." The Rothschilds found out early, that when you control the money, you basically control everything else. So, while their political plans were being thwarted, they began to concentrate on tightening their grip on the financial structure of the world.

In the mid 1700's the Colonies were prospering because they were issuing their own money, called Colonial Scrip, which was strictly regulated, and didn't require the payment of any interest. When the bankers in Great Britain heard this, the British Parliament passed a law prohibiting the currency, forcing them to accept the debt money issued by them. Contrary to what history teaches, the American Revolution was not ignited by a tax on tea. According to Benjamin Franklin, it was because "the conditions were so reversed that the era of prosperity ended." He said: "The Colonies would gladly have borne the little tax on tea and other matters had it not been the poverty caused by the bad influence of the English bankers on the Parliament, which has caused in the Colonies hatred of England and the Revolutionary War."

In 1787, our new Constitution gave Congress the power to "coin money, (and) regulate the value thereof (Article 1, Section 8)." After Great Britain tried to destroy and control the currency of our new country, Congress realized the danger of fiat, or paper money created by law. In 1775, paper money had been issued to finance the war, and independent state legislatures passed laws requiring citizens to accept it as legal tender. Since it was created from nothing, and not backed by any precious metal, inflation developed. By the end of the war, it took 500 paper dollars to get one silver dollar. Our forefathers wrote in Article I, Section 10, of the U.S. Constitution: "No State shall enter into any treaty, alliance or confederation; grant letters of marque and reprisal; coin money; emit bills of credit; make any thing by gold and silver coin a tender in payment of debts; pass any bill of attainder, ex post facto law, or law impairing the obligation of contracts, or grant any title of nobility."

Alexander Hamilton, an Illuminist, and agent of European bankers, had immigrated to the colonies in 1772 from the British colony of Nevis, on the Leeward Islands in the British West Indies. He married the daughter of Gen. Philip Schuyler, one of the most influential families of New York. In 1789 he was appointed Secretary of the Treasury. Hamilton and Robert Morris successfully convinced the new Congress not to take this power literally, enabling the Bank of North America to be established in 1781, which was similar to the Bank of England. At the time, America had a foreign debt of $12,000 (in money borrowed from Spain, France, Holland, and private interests in Germany), and a domestic debt of $42,000.

In 1790, Hamilton, who favored Central Banking, urged the Congress to charter a privately owned company to have the sole responsibility of issuing currency, in order to handle the country's financial situation. His Plan called for Congress to create a Central Banking system, with a main office in Philadelphia, and smaller branches located in important cities throughout the country. It would be used to deposit government funds and tax collections, and to issue bank notes to increase the money supply needed to finance the country's growth. This Bank of the United States would have a capital stock plan of $10 million, with 4/5's to be owned by private investors, and 1/5 by the U.S. Government. It would be administered by a President, and 25 Board of Directors, with 20 to be elected by the stockholders, and 5 appointed by the government.

Central Banking was initiated by international banker William Paterson in 1691, when he obtained the Charter for the Bank of England, which put the control of England's money in a privately owned company which had the right to issue notes payable on demand against the security of bank loans to the crown. One of their first transactions was to loan 1.2 million pounds at 8% interest to William of Orange to help the king pay the cost of his war with Louis XIV of France. Paterson said: "The bank hath benefit of interest on all monies which it creates out of nothing." Reginald McKenna, British Chancellor of the Exchequer (or Treasury), said 230 years later: "The banks can and do create money ... And they who control the credit of the nation direct the policy of governments and hold in the hollow of their hands the destiny of the people."

Hamilton's elitist views and real purpose for wanting Central Banking came to light, when he wrote: "All communities divide themselves into the few and the many. The first are rich and well-born, the other the mass of the people. The people are turbulent and changing; they seldom judge or determine right."

In 1791, Jefferson said: "To preserve our independence, we must not let our rulers load us with perpetual debt. If we run into such debts, we (will then) be taxed in our meat and our drink, in our necessities and in our comforts, in our labor and in our amusements. If we can prevent the government from wasting the labor of the people under the pretense of caring for them, they (will) be happy." Even though Thomas Jefferson and James Madison (later to be our 4th President, 1809-17) opposed the Bill, Washington signed it into law on February 25, 1791. Alexander Hamilton became a very rich man. He and Aaron Burr helped establish the Manhattan Co. in New York City, which developed into a very prosperous banking institution. It would later be controlled by the Warburg-Kuhn-Loeb interests, and in 1955 it merged with Rockefeller's Chase Bank to create the Chase Manhattan Bank.

When Jefferson (1801-09) became President, he opposed the bank as being unconstitutional, and when the 20 year charter came up for renewal in 1811, it was denied. Nathan Rothschild, head of the family bank in England, had recognized America's potential, and made loans to a few states, and in fact became the official European banker for the U.S. Government. Because he supported the Bank of the United States, he threatened: "Either the application for renewal of the Charter is granted, or the United States will find itself in a most disastrous war." He then ordered British troops to "teach these impudent Americans a lesson. Bring them back to Colonial status." This brought on the War of 1812, our second war with England, which facilitated the rechartering of the Bank of the United States. The war raised our national debt from $45 million to $127 million.

Jefferson wrote to James Monroe (who later served as our 5th President, 1817-25) in January, 1815: "The dominion which the banking institutions have obtained over the minds of our citizens ... must be broken, or it will break us." In 1816, Jefferson wrote to John Tyler (who became our 10th President, 1841-45): "If the American people ever allow private banks to control the issuance of their currency, first by inflation, and then by deflation, the banks and the corporations that will grow up around them will deprive the people of all property until their children wake up homeless on the continent their father's conquered ... I believe that banking institutions are more dangerous to our liberties than standing armies ... The issuing power should be taken from the banks and restored to the Government, to whom it properly belongs."

On May 10, 1816, President James Madison signed the Bill, which created the second Bank of the United States. Inflation, heavy debt, and the unavailability of an entity to collect taxes, were some of the reasons given for its rechartering. The new charter allowed it to operate another 20 years, raised its capital stock to $35 million, authorized the creation of bank branches, and the issuing of notes with denominations no smaller than $5.00. The new bank now had the power "to control the entire fiscal structure of the country." The bank was run by the Illuminati, through such international banker 'front men' as John Jacob Astor, Stephen Girard, and David Parish (a Rothschild agent for the Vienna branch of the family).

In 1819, the Bank was declared constitutional by Supreme Court Justice John Marshall (a Mason), who said that Congress had the implied power to create the Bank.

People began to see how much power the Bank really had, and the voter backlash led to the election of Andrew Jackson as President in 1828. His slogan was: "Let the people rule." Jackson maintained: "If Congress has the right under the Constitution to issue paper money, it was given them to be used by themselves, not to be delegated to individuals or to corporations." Jackson said that the control of a central bank "would be exercised by a few over the political conduct of the many by first acquiring that control over the labor and earnings of the great body of people." During the 1828 presidential campaign, Jackson said in an address before a group of bankers: "You are a den of vipers. I intend to rout you out and by the Eternal God I will rout you out." He went on to say: "If the people only understood the rank injustice of our Money and Banking system, there would be a revolution before morning." Jackson said that if such a Bank would continue to control "our currency, receiving our public monies, and holding thousands of our citizens in dependence, it would be more formidable and dangerous than the naval and military power of the enemy..."

After fiscal mismanagement by its first President, former Secretary of the Navy, Captain William Jones, the Bank was forced to call in loans and foreclosed on mortgages, which caused bankruptcy, a price collapse, unemployment and a depression. However, the Bank began to flourish under its new President, financier Nicholas Biddle (1786-1844), who petitioned the Congress for a renewal of the Bank's Charter in 1832, four years before its current charter expired. The Bill for the new Charter passed the Senate, 28-20, and the House 107-85, and everyone knew how Jackson felt. Biddle threatened: "Should Jackson veto it, I shall veto him!" Jackson did veto the Charter, and abolished the Bank in 1832. He ordered the Secretary of the Treasury to remove all Government deposits from U.S. Banks and deposit them in state banks. On January 8, 1835, Jackson paid off the final installment on our national debt, and it was the only time in history that our national debt was reduced to zero, and we were able to accumulate a surplus, $35 million of which was distributed to the States. Nicholas P. Trist, the President's personal secretary, said: "This is the crowning glory of A.J.'s life and the most important service he has ever rendered his country." The *Boston Post* compared it to Christ throwing the money-changers out of the Temple.

James K. Polk, the Speaker of the House (who later became the 11th President in 1845) said: "The Bank of the United States has set itself up as a great irresponsible rival power of the government."

The Bank continued to operate until 1836, and it was used by Biddle to wreak havoc upon the economy by reducing loans and increasing the quantity of money. Jackson became the first President of the United States to be censured, which was done in March, 1834, "for removing the government's deposits from the Bank of the United States without the express authorization of the United States Congress." It is quite obvious that he did it because of the "abuses and corruptions" of the Bank, and the censure was later reversed by the Senate in 1837. The Bankers continued their attempts to revive the Bank. President John Tyler vetoed two bills in 1841 that would have rechartered the Bank of the United States.

In 1837, the Rothschilds sent another one of their agents to America. His name was August Belmont (real name, August Schonberg, a cousin of the Seligman family of Frankfurt, Germany). In 1829, as a 15 year-old, he started working for the bank in Frankfurt, and proved himself to be a financial genius. In 1832, he was promoted to the bank at Naples, so he could be fully integrated into international banking. He became fluent in English, French, and Italian. His mission was to stir up financial trouble within the southern banks. He ran a bank in New York City, and established himself as a leading figure in financial circles by buying government bonds, and later became a financial advisor to the President.

In 1857, the Illuminati met in London to decide America's fate. They had to create an incident which would allow the establishment of a Central Bank, and that had to be a war, since wars are expensive, and governments have to borrow to pay for them. Canada and Mexico weren't strong enough, as evidenced by Santa Anna's defeat in Texas the year before; England and France were too far away, and Russia wasn't under their control; so they decided to "divide and conquer," by fermenting a conflict between the North and the South. The North was to become a British

Colony, annexed to Canada, and controlled by Lionel Rothschild; while the South was to be given to Napoleon III of France, and controlled by James Rothschild.

In order to begin a movement that would lead to the secession of the South from the Union, the Illuminati used the Knights of the Golden Circle, which had been formed in 1854 by George W. L. Bickley, to spread racial tension from state to state, using slavery as an issue. War-time members included Jefferson Davis, John Wilkes Booth and Jesse James (1847-1882, a Mason, who after stealing gold from banks and mining companies, buried nearly $7 billion of it all over the western states in hopes of funding a second Civil War). The Ku Klux Klan, formed in 1867, were the military arm of the Knights. The states which seceded, united into the Confederate States of America, which meant they maintained their independence, and that if the South would win, each state would be like an independent country.

Abraham Lincoln informed the people that "combinations too powerful to be suppressed by the ordinary machinery of peacetime government had assumed control of various southern states." He had coastal ports blockaded to keep supplies from being shipped in from Europe.

The Rothschilds financed the North through emissaries August Belmont, Jay Cooke (who was commissioned to sell bond issues, arranging with Belmont to sell Union bonds in Europe), J. and W. Seligman and Company, and Speyer & Co.

Judah P. Benjamin (1811-84) of the law firm of Slidell, Benjamin and Conrad, in Louisiana, was a Rothschild agent, who became Secretary of State for the Confederacy in 1862. His law partner, John Slidell (August Belmont's wife's uncle) was the Confederate envoy to France. Slidell's daughter was married to Baron Frederick D'Erlanger, in Frankfurt, who were related to the Rothschilds, and acted on their behalf. Slidell was the representative of the South who borrowed money from the D'Erlangers to finance the Confederacy.

Towards the end of 1861, England sent 8,000 troops to Canada, and in 1862, English, French and Spanish troops landed at Vera Cruz, Mexico, supposedly to collect on debts owed them by Mexico. In April, 1861, the Russian Ambassador to America had advised his government: "England will take advantage of the first opportunity to recognize the seceded states and that France will follow her." On June 10, 1863, French General Elie-Frederic Forey, with the help of 30,000 additional French troops, took over Mexico City, and controlled most of the country. Through his representatives in Paris and London, Czar Alexander II in Russia discovered that the Confederates had offered the states of Louisiana and Texas to Napoleon III, if he would send his troops against the North. Russia had already indicated their support for Lincoln, but wanted something more to send their large navy to defend the country. On January 1, 1863, as a gesture of goodwill, Lincoln issued his Emancipation Proclamation to free the slaves, just as the Czar had done with the serfs in 1861. On September 8, 1863, at the request of President Lincoln and Secretary of State William H. Seward, Alexander sent the Russian fleet to San Francisco and New York, and ordered them "to be ready to fight any power and to take their orders only from Abraham Lincoln."

Lincoln said: "The privilege of creating and issuing money is not only the supreme prerogative of Government, but is the Government's greatest creative opportunity. By the adoption of these principles, the taxpayers will be saved immense sums of interest." On February and March, 1862, and March 1863, Lincoln received Congressional approval to borrow $450 million from the people by selling them bonds, or 'greenbacks,' to pay for the Civil War. They were not redeemable until 1865, when three could be exchanged for one in silver. They were made full legal tender in 1879.

Thus, Lincoln solved America's monetary crisis without the help of the International Bankers. The *London Times* later said of Lincoln's greenbacks:

> "If that mischievous financial policy which had its origin in the North America Republic during the late war in that country, should become indurated down to a fixture, then that Government will furnish its own money without cost. It will pay off its debts and be without debt. It will become prosperous beyond precedent in the history of the civilized governments of the world. The brains and wealth of all countries will go to North America. That government must be destroyed or it will destroy every monarchy on the globe."

Bismarck, the German Chancellor, said in 1876 about Lincoln: "He obtained from Congress the right to borrow from the people by selling to it the 'bonds' of States ... and the Government and the nation escaped the plots of the foreign financiers. They understood at once, that the United States would escape their grip. The death of Lincoln was resolved upon."

Before the Lincoln administration, private commercial banks were able to issue paper money called state bank notes, but that ended with the National Banking Act of 1863, which prohibited the states from creating money. A forerunner of the Federal Reserve Act, it began the movement to abolish redeemable currency. A system of private banks was to receive charters from the federal government which would give them the authorization to issue National Bank Notes. This gave banks the power to control the finances and credit of the country, and provided centralized banking, under Federal control, in times of war. The financial panic created by the International Bankers, destroyed 172 State Banks, 177 private banks, 47 savings institutions, 13 loan and trust companies, and 16 mortgage companies.

Salmon P. Chase, Secretary of the Treasury (1861-64) under Lincoln, publicly said that his role "in promoting the passage of the National Banking Act was the greatest financial mistake of my life. It has built up a monopoly which affects every interest in the country. It should be repealed, but before that can be accomplished, the people will be arrayed on one side and the bankers on the other, in a contest such as we have never seen before in this country."

Lincoln said: "The money power preys upon the nation in times of peace and conspires against it in times of adversity. It is more despotic than monarchy, more insolent than autocracy, more selfish than bureaucracy. I see in the near future a crisis approaching that unnerves me and causes me to tremble for the safety of my country. Corporations have been enthroned, an era of corruption in high places will follow, and the money power of the country will endeavor to prolong its reign by working upon the prejudices of the people until the wealth is aggregated in the hands of a few and the Republic is destroyed ... I feel at the moment more anxiety for the safety of my country than ever before, even in the midst of war."

FINAL WARNING

On April 14, 1865, Lincoln was shot by John Wilkes Booth, and that same evening, an unsuccessful attempt by his fellow conspirators was made on the life of Seward. In 1866, an attempt was made to assassinate Czar Alexander II, and in 1881, the Czar was killed by an exploding bomb.

In Booth's trunk, coded messages were found, and the key to that code was found among the possessions of Judah Benjamin. Benjamin had fled to England, where he died. It was always known that Lincoln's death was the result of a massive conspiracy. However, nobody realized how deep and far reaching it was. In 1974, researchers found among the papers of Edwin M. Stanton, Lincoln's Secretary of War, letters describing the conspiracy cover-up that were written to Stanton, or intercepted by him. They also found the 18 pages that were removed from Booth's diary, which revealed the names of 70 people (some in code) who were directly or indirectly involved in Booth's original plan to kidnap Lincoln. Besides Stanton's involvement in the conspiracy, Charles A. Dana, Assistant Secretary of War (and member of the Illuminati); and Major Thomas Eckert, Chief of the War Department's Telegraph Office, were also involved.

Journals and coded papers by Colonel Lafayette C. Baker, Chief of the National Detective Police, detailed Lincoln's kidnap and assassination conspiracy, and subsequent cover-up. The plot included a group of Maryland farmers; a group of Confederates including Jefferson Davis (President of the Confederacy) and Judah Benjamin (the Confederate Secretary of War and Secretary of State); a group of Northern Banking and Industrial interests, including Jay Cooke (Philadelphia financier), Henry Cooke (Washington, D.C. banker), Thurlow Weed (New York newspaper publisher); and a group of Radical Republicans who didn't want the south reunited with the North as states, but wanted to control them as military territories, and included Sen. Benjamin Wade of Ohio, Sen. Zechariah Chandler of Michigan, and Sen. John Conness of California. All of these groups pooled their efforts, and used actor John Wilkes Booth, a Confederate patriot. The original plan called for the kidnapping of Lincoln, Vice-President Andrew Johnson, and Secretary of State Seward. The National Detective Police discovered their plans, and informed Stanton. Planned for January 18, 1865, the kidnap attempt failed.

Captain James William Boyd, a secret agent for the Confederacy, and a prisoner of war in the Old Capitol Prison, was used by the National Detective Police to report on the activities of the prisoners, and to inform on crooked guards. He looked similar to Booth, and ironically, had the same initials. Stanton had him released, and Boyd took over the Northern end of the conspiracy, which had been joined by the Police and the War Department. The North wanted to kill Lincoln, while Booth wanted to kidnap him and use him as leverage to get Confederate prisoners of war released.

Booth failed twice in March, and then ended up shooting Lincoln at Ford's Theater. Boyd, warned that he could get implicated, planned to flee to Maryland. He was blamed for attacking Seward, which he didn't. Boyd was the one who was shot at Garrett's farm, and identified as Booth. The Police and Stanton discovered that it was really Boyd, after it was announced to the nation that it was Booth. The only picture taken of Boyd's dead body was found in Stanton's collection. The body was taken by Col. Lafayette Baker, to the old Arsenal Penitentiary, where it was buried in an unknown place, under the concrete floor.

Baker and Detectives Luther and Andrew Potter, knew the case wasn't closed, and had to find Booth to keep him from talking. They followed his trail to New York, and later to Canada, England and India. He allegedly faked his death and returned to the United States, where in Enid, Oklahoma, he revealed his true identity on his deathbed. The mortician, who was summoned, instead of burying the corpse, had it preserved, and it is still in existence today.

Baker broke off relations with Stanton, who was discharged from the Army and as head of the Secret Service in 1866. In 1867, in his book, *The History of the U.S. Secret Service*, he admitted delivering Booth's diary to Stanton, and on another occasion, testified that the diary was intact when it was in his possession. This means that Stanton did remove the pages to facilitate a cover-up, because the pages were found in his collection.

Andrew Johnson, who became President, issued the Amnesty Proclamation on May 29, 1865, to reunite the country. It stipulated that the South would not be responsible for the debt incurred, that all secession laws were to end, and that slavery was to be abolished. Needless to say, the Rothschilds, who heavily funded the south, lost a lot of money. In addition, the cost of the support of the Russian fleet cost the country about $7.2 million. Johnson didn't have the constitutional authority to give money to a foreign government, so arrangements were made to purchase Alaska from the Russians in April, 1867. It was labeled as 'Seward's Folly' because it appeared that Seward purchased what was then a worthless piece of land, when in fact it was compensation for the Russian Navy. In August, 1867, Johnson, failed in an attempt to remove Stanton from office, and impeachment proceedings were begun against him in February, 1868, by Stanton and the Radical Republicans. Johnson was charged with attempting to fire Stanton without Senate approval, for treason against Congress, and public language "indecent and unbecoming" as the nation's leader.

Sen. Benjamin F. Wade, President pro tempore of the Senate, next in the line of Presidential succession, was so sure that Johnson would be impeached, that he already had his Cabinet picked. Stanton was to be his Secretary of Treasury. The May 26th vote was 35-19, one short of the necessary two-thirds needed to impeach Johnson.

Col. Lafayette Baker, who threatened to reveal the conspiracy, was slowly poisoned till he died in 1868.

President James A. Garfield, our 20th President, also realized the danger posed by the bankers and said: "Whoever controls the money of a nation, controls that nation." He was assassinated in 1881, during the first year of his Presidency.

In 1877, in Lampasas County, Texas, a group of farmers formed a group called the Knights of Reliance, who were concerned about the financial power being "concentrated into the hands of a few." Later renamed the Farmers Alliance, it spread to 120 chapters throughout Texas, and by 1887, the movement stretched up to the Dakotas, and as far east as the Carolinas. By the time 1890 rolled around, this Populist philosophy had succeeded in establishing itself, and they had elected governors and congressmen.

They advocated a progressive income tax; for railroads, communications, and corporations to be regulated by the Federal government; the right to establish labor unions; and government mediation to stabilize falling commodity prices and the initiation of credit programs. They were against the gold standard, and the country's private banking system, which was centered at Wall Street. They were impressed with Lincoln's 'greenbacks,' because of its ability to adapt in order to meet the credit needs of the economy. They wanted the money supply to be controlled by their elected representatives, and not the money interests of Wall Street. They created the People's Party, and ran their own independent presidential candidate in 1892. And in 1896, they hitched their wagon to the campaign of Democrat William Jennings Bryan, who lost to McKinley, effectively ending the Populist movement.

This political movement created the initial stirrings for what eventually became the Federal Reserve Act.

THE FEDERAL RESERVE ACT

The end of the Civil War in 1865 ruined the Illuminati's chances to control our monetary system, as they did in most European countries. So, the Rothschilds modified their plan for financial takeover. Instead of tearing down from the top, they were going to start at the bottom to disrupt the foundation of our monetary system. The instrument of this destruction was a young immigrant by the name of Jacob Schiff.

The Schiff family traced their lineage back to the fourteenth century, and even claimed that King Solomon was an ancestor. Jacob Schiff was born in 1847, in Frankfurt, Germany. His father, Moses Schiff, a rabbi, was a successful stockbroker on the Frankfurt Stock Exchange. In 1865, he came to America, and in 1867, formed his own brokerage firm with Henry Budge and Leo Lehmann. After it failed, he went back to Germany, and became manager of the Deutsche Bank in Hamburg, where he met Moritz Warburg (1838-1910), and Abraham Kuhn, who had retired after helping to establish the firm of Kuhn & Loeb in New York.

Kuhn and Loeb were German Jews who had come to the United States in the late 1840's, and pooled their resources during the 1850's to start a store in Lafayette, Indiana, to serve settlers who were on their way to the West. They set up similar stores in Cincinnati and St. Louis. Later, they added pawnbroking and money lending to their business pursuits. In 1867, they established themselves as a well-known banking firm.

In 1873, at the age of 26, Jacob Schiff, with the financial backing of the Rothschilds, bought into the Kuhn and Loeb partnership in New York City. He became a full partner in 1875. He became a millionaire by financing railroads, developing a proficiency at railroad management that enabled him to enter into a partnership with Edward Henry Harriman to create the greatest single railroad fortune in the world. He married Solomon Loeb's oldest daughter, Theresa, and eventually bought out Kuhn's interest. For all intents and purposes, he was the sole owner of what was now known as Kuhn, Loeb and Company. Sen. Robert L. Owen of Oklahoma indicated that Kuhn, Loeb and Company was a representative of the Rothschilds in the United States.

Although John Pierpont Morgan (1837-1913), the top American Rothschild representative, was the head of the American financial world, Schiff was rapidly becoming a major influence by distributing desirable European stock and bond issues during the Industrial Revolution. Besides Edward H. Harriman's railroad empire, he financed Standard Oil for John D. Rockefeller (1839-1937), and Andrew Carnegie's (1835-1919) steel empire. By the turn of the century, Schiff was firmly entrenched in the banking community, and ready to fulfill his role as the point man in the Illuminati's plan to control our economic system, weaken Christianity, create racial tension, and to recruit members to get them elected to Congress and appointed to various government agencies.

In 1636, Miles, John, and James Morgan landed in Massachusetts, leaving their father, William, to carry on the family business of harness-making in England. Joseph Morgan (J. P. Morgan's grandfather), successful in real estate and business, supported the Bank of the United States. Junius Spencer Morgan (J. P. Morgan's father), was a partner in the Boston banking firm of J. M. Beebe, Morgan, and Co.; and became a partner in London's George Peabody and Co., taking it over when Peabody died, becoming J. S. Morgan and Co.

John Pierpont Morgan, or as he was better known, J. P. Morgan, was born on April 17, 1837. He became his father's representative in New York in 1860. In 1862, he had his own firm, known as J. Pierpont Morgan and Co. In 1863, he liquidated, and became a partner with Charles H. Dabney (who represented George Peabody and Co.), and established a firm known as Dabney, Morgan and Co. He later teamed up with Anthony J. Drexel (son of the founder of the most influential banking house in Philadelphia), in a firm known as Drexel, Morgan and Co. Morgan also became a partner in Drexel and Co. in Philadelphia. In 1869, Morgan and Drexel met with the Rothschilds in London, and through the Northern Securities Corporation, began consolidating the Rothschild's power and influence in the United States. Morgan continued the partnership that began when his father acted as a joint agent for the Rothschilds and the U.S. Government.

During the Civil War, J. P. Morgan had sold the Union Army defective carbine rifles, and it was this government money that helped build his Guaranty Trust Co. of New York. In 1880, he began financing and reorganizing the railroads. After his father died in 1890, and Drexel died in 1893, the Temporary National Economic Committee revealed that J. P. Morgan held only a 9.1% interest in his own firm. George Whitney owned 1.9%, and H. B. Davison held 1.2%, however, the Charles W. Steele Estate held 36.6%, and Thomas W. Lamont (whose son, Corliss, was an active communist) had 34.2%. Researchers believe that the Illuminati controlled the company through these shares.

In 1901, Morgan bought out Andrew Carnegie's vast steel operation for $500,000,000 to merge the largest steel companies into one big company known as the United States Steel Corporation (in which, for a time, the Rockefellers were major stockholders).

A speech by Senator Norris which was printed in the *Congressional Record* of November 30, 1941, said: "J. P. Morgan, with the assistance and cooperation of a few of the interlocking corporations which reach all over the United States in their influence, controls every railroad in the United States. They control practically every public utility, they control literally thousands of corporations, they control all of the large insurance companies. Mr. President, we are gradually reaching a time, if we have not already reached that point, when the business of the country is controlled by men who can be named on the fingers of one hand, because those men control the money of the Nation, and that control is growing at a rapid rate."

The House of Morgan grew larger in 1959, when the Guaranty Trust Co. of New York merged with the J. P. Morgan and Co., to form the Morgan Guaranty Trust Co. They had four branch offices, and foreign offices in London, Paris, Brussels, Frankfurt, Rome, and Tokyo. The firm of Morgan, Stanley, and Co. was also under their control.

Paul Moritz Warburg (1868-1932), and his brother Felix (1871-1937), came to the United States from Frankfurt in 1902, buying into the partnership of Kuhn, Loeb and Co. with the financial backing of the Rothschilds. They had been trained at the family banking house, M. M. Warburg and Co. (run by their father Moritz M. Warburg, 1838-1910), a Rothschild-allied bank in Frankfurt, Hamburg, and Amsterdam, which had been founded in 1798 by their great-grandfather. Paul (said to be worth over $2.5 million when he died), married Nina Loeb, the daughter of Solomon Loeb (the younger sister of Schiff's wife); while Felix, in March, 1895, married Frieda Schiff, the daughter of Jacob Schiff.

Their brother Max (1867-1946), a major financier of the Russian Revolution (who in his capacity as Chief of Intelligence in Germany's Secret Service, helped Lenin cross Germany into Russia in a sealed train) and later Hitler, ran the Hamburg bank until 1938, when the Nazis took over. The Nazis, who didn't want the Jews running the banks, changed its name to Brinckmann, Wirtz and Co. After World War II, a cousin, Eric Warburg, returned to head it, and in 1970, its name was changed to M. M. Warburg, Brinckmann, Wirtz and Co.

Siegmund Warburg, Eric's brother, established the banking firm of S. G. Warburg and Co. in London, and by 1956, had taken over the Seligman Brothers' Bank.

The Warburgs are another good example of how the Illuminati controls both sides of a war. While Paul Warburg's firm of Kuhn, Loeb and Co. (who had five representatives in the U.S. Treasury Department) was in charge of Liberty Loans, which helped finance World War I for the United States, his brother Max financed Germany, through M. M. Warburg and Co.

Paul and Felix Warburg were men with a mission, sent here by the Rothschilds to lobby for the passing of a central banking law in Congress. Colonel Ely Garrison (the financial advisor to Presidents Theodore Roosevelt and Woodrow Wilson) wrote in his book *Roosevelt, Wilson and the Federal Reserve Act*: "Mr. Paul Warburg is the man who got the Federal Reserve Act together after the Aldrich Plan aroused such nationwide resentment and opposition. The mastermind of both plans was Alfred Rothschild of London." Professor E. R. A. Seligman, head of the Economics Department of Columbia University, wrote in the preface of one of Warburg's essays on central banking: "The Federal Reserve Act is the work of Mr. (Paul) Warburg more than any other man in the country."

In 1903, Paul Warburg gave Schiff a memo describing the application of the European central banking system to America's monetary system. Schiff, in turn, gave it to James Stillman, President of the National City Bank in New York City. Warburg had graduated from the University of Hamburg in 1886, and studied English central banking methods, while working in a London brokerage house. In 1891, he studied French banking methods; and from 1892-93, traveled the world to study central banking applications. The bottom line, was that he was the foremost authority in the world on central banking. It is interesting to note, that the fifth plank in the 1848 Communist Manifesto had to do with central banking.

In 1906, Frank A. Vanderlip, of the National City Bank, convinced many of New York's banking establishment, that they needed a banker-controlled central bank, that could serve the nation's financial system. Up to that time, the House of Morgan had filled that role. Some of the people involved with Morgan were: Walter Burns, Clinton Dawkins, Edward Grenfell, Willard Straight, Thomas Lament, Dwight Morrow, Nelson Perkins, Russell Leffingwell, Elihu Root, John W. Davis, John Foster Dulles, S. Parker Gilbert, and Paul D. Cravath. The financial panics of 1873, 1884, 1893, 1907, and later 1920, were initiated by Morgan with the intent of pushing for a much stronger banking system.

On January 6, 1907, the *New York Times* published an article by Warburg, called "Defects and Needs of Our Banking System," after which he became the leading exponent of monetary reform. That same year, Jacob Schiff told the New York Chamber of Commerce, that "unless we have a Central Bank with adequate control of credit resources, this country is going to undergo the most severe and far reaching money panic in history." When Morgan initiated the economic panic in 1907, by circulating rumors that the Knickerbocker Bank and Trust Co. of America was going broke, there was a run on the banks, creating a financial crisis, which began to solidify support for a central banking system. During this panic, Warburg wrote an essay called "A Plan for a Modified Central Bank" which called for a Central Bank, in which 50% would be owned by the government, and 50% by the nation's banks. In a speech at Columbia University, he quoted Abraham Lincoln, who said in an 1860 Presidential campaign speech: "I believe in a United States Bank."

In 1908, Schiff laid out the final plans to seize the American monetary system. Colonel (an honorary title) Edward Mandell House (1858-1938), the son of British financier Thomas W. House, a Rothschild agent who made his fortune by supplying the south with supplies from France and England during the Civil War, was Schiff's chief representative and courier; and Bernard Baruch (1870-1965), whose stock market speculating made him a multi-millionaire by the early 1900's, and whose foreign and domestic policy expertise led Presidents from Wilson to Kennedy to seek his advice; were the two who were relied on heavily by Schiff to carry out his plans. Herbert Lehman was also a close aide to Schiff.

President Woodrow Wilson wrote about House (published in *The Intimate Papers of Col.House*): "Mr. House is my second personality. He is my independent self. His thoughts and mine are one. If I were in his place, I would do just as he suggested ... If anyone thinks he is reflecting my opinion, by whatever action he takes, they are welcome to the conclusion." George Sylvester Viereck wrote in *The Strangest Friendship in History: Woodrow Wilson and Colonel House*: "When the Federal Reserve legislation at last assumed definite shape, House was the intermediary between the White House and the financiers." Schiff, who was known as the "unseen guardian angel" of the Federal Reserve Act, said that the U.S. Constitution was the product of 18th century minds, was outdated, and should be "scrapped and rewritten."

In 1908, Sen. Nelson W. Aldrich (father-in-law of John D. Rockefeller, Jr. and grandfather of Nelson and David Rockefeller) proposed a bill, in which banks, in an emergency situation, would issue currency backed by federal, state, and local government bonds, and railroad bonds, which would be equal to 75% of the cash value of the bonds. It was harshly criticized because it didn't provide a monetary system that would respond to the seasonal demand, and fluctuate with the volume of trade. Aldrich was the most powerful man in Congress, and the Illuminati's head man in the Senate. A member of Congress for 40 years, 36 of them in the Senate, he was Chairman of the powerful Senate Finance Committee.

In the House of Representatives, Rep. E. B. Vreeland of New York, proposed the Vreeland Bill. After making some compromises with Aldrich, and Speaker of the House Joseph Cannon, at a meeting in a hotel room at the Arlington House, his bill became known as the Vreeland Substitute. It called for the acceptance of asset currency, but only in cases of emergency, and the currency would be based on commercial paper rather than bonds. It passed in the House, 184-145; but when it got to the Senate, Aldrich moved against it, and pushed for further compromises. The Aldrich-Vreeland Bill, called the Emergency Currency Act, was passed on May 30, 1908, and led to the creation of the National Monetary Commission, which was made up of members of Congress. Now, any monetary legislation sent to Congress, would have to go through this group first.

The Bill approved by the National Monetary Commission was known as the Aldrich Bill, and formed the legislative base for the Federal Reserve Act. It was introduced as an amendment to the Republican sponsored Payne-Aldrich Tariff Bill, in order to have Republican support. It was based on Warburg's plan, except it would only have 15 districts; half of the directors on the district level would be chosen by the banks, a third by the stockholders, and a sixth by the other directors. On the National Board: two chosen by each district; nine chosen by the stockholders; and seven ex-officio members to be the Governor, Chairman of the Board, two Deputy Governors, Secretary of the Treasury, Secretary of Commerce and Labor, Secretary of Agriculture, and Comptroller of the Currency. Most people were against the Bill, because it finally identified the banking institution as a central bank, and the Democratic Party opposed it in the 1912 Party platform.

Aldrich was appointed as head of the National Monetary Commission, and from 1908-10, at a cost of $300,000, this 16-man committee traveled around Europe to study the central banking system.

In 1910, Warburg gave a speech entitled, "A United Reserve Bank of the United States," which called for a United Reserve Bank to be located in Washington, D.C., having the capital of $100 million. The country would be divided into 20 districts, and the system would be controlled by a Board of Directors, which would be chosen by the banking associations, the stockholders, and the government. Warburg said that the U.S. monetary system wasn't flexible, and it was unable to compensate for the rise and fall of business demand. As an example, he said, that when wheat was harvested, and merchants didn't have the cash on hand to buy and store a large supply of grain, the farmers would sell the grain for whatever they could get. This would cause the price of wheat to greatly fluctuate, forcing the farmer to take a loss. Warburg called for the development of commercial paper (paper money) to circulate as currency, which would be issued in standard denominations of uniform sizes. They would be declared by law to be legal tender for the payment of debts and taxes.

President Theodore Roosevelt said, concerning the criticism of finding capable men to head the formation of a central bank: "Why not give Mr. (Paul) Warburg the job? He would be the financial boss, and I would be the political boss, and we could run the country together."

After a conference was held at Columbia University on November 12, 1910, the National Monetary Commission published their plan in the December, 1910 issue of their *Journal of Political Economy* in an article called "Bank Notes and Lending Power."

On November 22, 1910, Aldrich called a meeting of the banking establishment and members of the National Monetary Commission, which was proposed by Henry P. Davison (a partner of J. P. Morgan). Aldrich said that he intended to keep them isolated until they had developed a "scientific currency for the United States."

All those summoned to the secret meeting, were members of the Illuminati. They met on a railroad platform in Hoboken, New Jersey, where they chartered a private railroad car owned by Aldrich to Georgia. They were taken by boat, to Jekyll Island, off the coast of Brunswick, Georgia. Jekyll Island is in a group of ten islands, including St. Simons, Tybee, Cumberland, Wassau, Wolf, Blackbeard, Sapelo, Ossabow, and Sea Islands. Jekyll Island was a 'hideaway resort of the rich,' purchased in 1888 by J. P. Morgan, Henry Goodyear, Joseph Pulitzer, Edwin and George Gould, Cyrus McCormick, William Rockefeller (John D. Rockefeller's brother), William K. Vanderbilt, and George F. Baker (who founded Harvard Business School with a gift of $5 million) for $125,000 from Eugene du Bignon, whose family owned it for a century. Up until the time it was converted into a public resort, no uninvited foot ever stepped on its shores. It was said, that when all 100 members of the Jekyll Island Hunting Club sat down for dinner at the clubhouse, it represented a sixth of the world's wealth. St. Simons Island, a short distance away, to the north, was also owned by Illuminati interests.

Those attending the meeting at the private hunting lodge were said to be on a duck-hunting expedition. They were sworn to secrecy, even addressing each other by code names or just by their first names. Details are very sketchy, concerning who attended the meeting, but most scenarios agree that the following people were present: Sen. Aldrich, Frank A. Vanderlip (Vice-President of the Rockefeller owned National City Bank), Henry P. Davison (of the J. P. Morgan and Co.), Abram Piatt Andrew (Assistant Secretary of the Treasury, an Assistant Professor at Harvard, and Special Assistant to the National Monetary Commission during their European tour), Paul Moritz Warburg (of Kuhn, Loeb and Co.), Benjamin Strong (Vice-President of Morgan's Bankers Trust Co.), Eugene Meyer (a former partner of Bernard Baruch, and the son of a partner in the Rothschild-owned Lazard Freres, who was the head of the War Finances Corporation, and later gained control of the *Washington Post*), J. P. Morgan, John D. Rockefeller, Col. House, Jacob Schiff, Herbert Lehman (of Lehman Brothers), Bernard Baruch (appointed by President Wilson to be the Chairman of the War Industries Board, which gave him control of all domestic contacts for Allied war materials, which enabled him to make $200 million for himself while working for the government), Joseph Seligman (a leading Jewish financier, who founded J. & W. Seligman and Co., who had helped to float bonds during the Civil War, and were known as 'World Bankers,' then later declined President Grant's offer to serve as the Secretary of Treasury), and Charles D. Norton (President of the First National Bank of New York).

About ten days later, they emerged with the groundwork for a central banking system, in the form of, not one, but two versions, to confuse the opposition. The final draft was written by Frank Vanderlip, from Warburg's notes, and was incorporated into Aldrich's Bill, in the form of a completed Monetary Commission report, which Aldrich railroaded through Congress by avoiding the term 'central bank.' No information was available on this meeting until 1933, when the book *The Federal Reserve Act: It's Origins and Problems*, by James L. Laughlin, appeared; and other information, which was supplied by B. C. Forbes, the editor of *Forbes Magazine*. In 1935, Frank Vanderlip wrote in the *Saturday Evening Post*: "I do not feel it is any exaggeration to speak of our secret expedition to Jekyll Island as the occasion of the actual conception of what eventually became the Federal Reserve System."

The banker-initiated mini-depressions, the last of which had occurred in 1907, helped get Congressional support for the Bill, and on May 11, 1911, the National Citizens League for the Promotion of a Sound Banking System, an Illuminati front-organization, publicly announced their support for Aldrich's Bill. However, the Aldrich Bill was destined for failure, because he was so closely identified with J. P. Morgan. So, the Illuminati went to Plan B, which was the second version hammered out at the Jekyll Island summit. The National Citizens League publicly withdrew their support of the Aldrich Bill, and the move was on to disguise it, so that it could get through Congress.

Once the new version was ready, they were a little apprehensive about introducing it in Congress, because even if it would be passed by Congress, President Taft would veto it, so they had to wait until they could get their own man elected. That man was Woodrow Wilson.

The Democrats, with the exception of Grover Cleveland's election, had been out of power since 1869. Being a 'hungry' Party, the Illuminati found them easier to infiltrate. During the late 1800's, they began the process of changing the Democrats from conservative to liberal, and the Republicans, from liberal to conservative.

Wilson graduated from Princeton University in 1879, studied law at the University of Virginia, and received his doctorate degree from Johns Hopkins in 1886. He taught Political Science and History at Bryn Mawr and Wesleyan, and in 1902, became President of Princeton. Because of his support of Aldrich's Bill, when it was first announced, he was supported by the Illuminati in his successful bid as Governor of New Jersey in 1910. The deal was made through Vanderlip agents, William Rockefeller and James Stillman, at Vanderlip's West Chester estate. The liaison between the Illuminati and Wilson, would be his prospective son-in-law, William G. McAdoo.

Rabbi Stephen Wise, a leading Jewish activist, told an audience at the Y.M.C.A. in Trenton, New Jersey: "On Tuesday the President of Princeton University will be elected Governor of your state. He will not complete his term of office as Governor. In November, 1912, he will be elected President of the United States. In March,

1917, he will be inaugurated for the second time as President. He will be one of the greatest Presidents in American history." Wise, who made this prophetic statement in 1910, later became a close advisor to Wilson. He had good reason to believe what he said, because the deal had already been struck. Wilson wasn't viewed as being pro-banking, and the Democratic Party Platform opposed a Central Bank, which was now linked to the Republicans and the bankers.

The main problem for the Democrats, was the Republican voting edge, and their lack of money. After the Illuminati made the decision to support Wilson, money was no problem. Records showed that the biggest contributors to Wilson's campaign were Jacob Schiff, Bernard Baruch, Henry Morgenthau, Sr., Thomas Fortune Ryan (mining magnate), Samuel Untermyer, Cleveland H. Dodge (of the National City Bank), Col. George B. M. Harvey (an associate of J. P. Morgan, and editor of the Morgan-controlled *Harper's Weekly*, and President of the Harper and Brothers publishing firm), William Laffan (editor of the *New York Sun*), Adolph Ochs (publisher of the *New York Times*), and the financiers that owned the *New York Times*, Charles R. Flint, Gen. Sam Thomas, J. P. Morgan, and August Belmont. All of these men were Illuminati members.

The problem of the voter registration edge was a bit more difficult, but that was a project that the Illuminati had already been working on. The Russian pogroms of 1881 and 1882, in which thousands of Russians were killed; and religious persecution and anti-Semitism in Poland, Romania, and Bulgaria in the early 1890's, began three decades of immigration into the United States by thousands of Jews. By the turn of the century, a half-million Jews had arrived to the port cities of New York, Baltimore, and Boston. It was the Democrats who initiated a program to get them registered to vote. Humanitarian committees were set up by Schiff and the Rothschilds, such as the Hebrew Immigration Aid Society, and the B'nai B'rith, so when the Jews arrived, they were made naturalized citizens, registered Democrat, then shuffled off to other large cities, such as Chicago, Philadelphia, Detroit and Los Angeles, where they were given financial help to find a place to live, food, and clothing. This is how the Jews became a solid Democratic voting bloc, and it was these votes that would be needed to elect Wilson to the Presidency.

In 1912, with President William Howard Taft running for re-election against Wilson, the Illuminati needed some insurance. They got it by urging another Republican, former President, Theodore Roosevelt (1901-09) to run on the Progressive ticket. Taft had served as Roosevelt's Secretary of War (1905-09), and was chosen by Roosevelt to succeed him as President. Now, Roosevelt was running again. Advocating the 'New Nationalism,' Roosevelt said: "My hat is in the ring ... the fight is on and I am stripped to the buff." Identified as 'anti-business' because of his stand against corporations and trusts, his proposals for reorganizing the government were attacked by the Illuminati-controlled *New York Times* as "super-socialism." His 'Bull Moose' Platform said: "We are opposed to the so-called Aldrich Currency Bill because its provisions would place our currency and credit system in private hands, not subject to effective public control." Frank Munsey and George Perkins, of the J. P. Morgan and Co. organized, ran, and financed Roosevelt's campaign. A recent example of the same plan that pulled votes away from Taft, in order to get Wilson elected, occurred in the 1992 Presidential election. In a 1994 interview, Barbara Bush told ABC-TV news correspondent Barbara Walters, that the third-party candidacy of independent H. Ross Perot was the reason that Bill Clinton was able to defeat the re-election bid of President George Bush.

The Illuminati was able to get the support of perennial Democratic Presidential candidate, William Jennings Bryan, by letting him write the plank of the Party Platform which opposed the Aldrich Bill. Remember, the second version of the Bill prepared at Jekyll Island was to be an alternative, so public attention was turned against the Aldrich Bill. Wilson, an aristocrat, having socialistic views, was in favor of an independent reserve system, because he didn't trust the 'common men' which made up Congress. However, publicly, he promised to "free the poor people of America from control by the rich," and to have a money system that wouldn't be under the control of Wall Street's International Bankers. In fact, in the summer of 1912, when he accepted the nomination as the Democratic candidate for the Presidency, he said: "A concentration of the control of credit ... may at any time become infinitely dangerous to free enterprise." According to the Federal Reserve's historical narrative, the shift in Wilson's point of view was "a combination of political realities and his own lack of knowledge about banking and finance (and) after his election to the Presidency, Wilson relied on others for more expert advice on the currency question."

Because of the voting split in the Republican Party, not only was Woodrow Wilson able to win the Presidency, but the Democrats gained control of both houses in Congress.

```
DEMOCRAT (Wilson)        435 electoral votes 6,286,214 popular votes
PROGRESSIVE (Roosevelt)   88 electoral votes 4,126,020 popular votes
REPUBLICAN (Taft)          8 electoral votes 3,483,922 popular votes
```

Rep. Carter Glass of Virginia, Chairman of the Banking and Currency Committee, met with Wilson after his election, along with H. Parker Willis (who was Dean of Political Science at George Washington University) of the National Citizens League, to prepare a Bill, known as the Glass Bill, which began taking form in January, 1913. Now Plan B was set into motion. Remember, the National Citizens League, headquartered in Chicago, had already announced their opposition to the Aldrich Bill, now the Wall Street banking interests had come out against the Glass Bill, which was actually the Aldrich Bill in disguise.

The Wall Street crowd was generally referred to as the 'money trust.' However, a 1912 Wall Street Journal editorial said that the term 'money trust' was just a reference to J. P. Morgan. The suspicion of the 'money trust' peaked in 1912, during an investigation by a House banking subcommittee which revealed that twelve banks in New York, Boston, and Chicago, had 746 interlocking directorships in 134 corporations. Rep. Robert L. Henry of Texas said that for the past five years, the nation's financial resources had been "concentrated in the city of New York (where they) now dominate more than 75 percent of the moneyed interests of America..." George McC. Reynolds, the President of the Continental Bank of Chicago, said to a group of other bankers: "The money power now lies in the hands of a dozen men..." The threat from this powerful private banking system was to be ended with the establishment of a central bank.

To avoid the mention of central banking, Wilson himself suggested that the regional banks be called 'Federal Reserve Banks,' and proposed a special session of the 63rd Congress to be convened to vote on the Federal Reserve Act. On June 23, 1913, he addressed the Congress on the subject of the Federal Reserve, threatening to keep them in session until they passed it. Wilson got Bryan's support by making him Secretary of State, and in October, 1913, Bryan said he would assist the President in "securing the passage of the Bill at the earliest possible moment."

The Glass Bill (HR7837) was introduced in the House of Representatives on June 26, 1913. The revision mentioned nothing about central banking, which was what the people feared. It was believed that Willis had written the Bill, but it was later discovered that Professor James L. Laughlin, at the Political Science Department of Columbia University, had written it, taking special precaution not to clash with the Bryan plank of the Democratic Party Platform. It was referred to the Banking and Currency Committee, reported back to the House on September 9th, and passed on September 18th.

Sen. Robert Latham Owen of Oklahoma, Chairman of the Senate Banking and Finance Committee, along with five of his colleagues, drafted a Bill which was more open-minded to the suggestions of the bankers. A Bill drafted by Sen. Gilbert M. Hitchcock, a Democrat from Nebraska, called for the elimination of the 'lawful money' provision, and stipulated that note redemption must be made in gold. It also provided for public ownership of the regional reserve banks, which would be controlled by the government.

In the Senate, the Glass Bill was referred to the Senate Banking Committee, and reported back to the Senate on November 22, 1913. The Bill was now known as the Glass-Owen Bill. Sen. Owen, who opposed the Aldrich Bill, made some additional revisions, in an attempt to keep them from completely dominating our monetary system. Sen. Elihu Root of New York criticized some of these revisions, and some points were modified. It was passed by the Senate on December 19th.

Since different versions had been passed by both Houses, a Conference Committee was established, which was stacked with six Democrats and only two Republicans, to insure that certain portions of the original Bill would remain intact. It was hastily prepared without any public hearings, and on December 23, 1913, two days before Christmas, when many Congressmen, and three particular Senators, were away from Washington; the Bill was sent to the House of Representatives, where it passed 298-60, and then sent to the Senate, where it passed with a vote of 43-25 (with 27 absent or abstaining). An hour after the Senate vote, Wilson signed the Federal Reserve Act into law, and the Illuminati had taken control of the American economy. The gold and silver in the nation's vaults were now owned by the Federal Reserve. Baron Alfred Charles Rothschild (1842-1918), who masterminded the entire scheme, then made plans to further weaken our country's financial structure.

Although Wilson, and Rep. Carter Glass were given the credit for getting the Federal Reserve Act through Congress, William Jennings Bryan played a major role in gaining support to pass it. Bryan later wrote: "That is the one thing in my public career that I regret- my work to secure the enactment of the Federal Reserve Law." Rep. Glass would later write: "I had never thought the Federal Bank System would prove such a failure. The country is in a state of irretrievable bankruptcy."

Eustace Mullins, in his book *The Federal Reserve Conspiracy*, wrote: "The money and credit resources of the United States were now in complete control of the banker's alliance between J. P. Morgan's First National Bank, and Kuhn & Loeb's National City Bank, whose principal loyalties were to the international banking interests, then quartered in London, and which moved to New York during the First World War."

The Reserve Bank Organization Committee, controlled by Secretary of the Treasury, William Gibbs McAdoo, and Secretary of Agriculture David F. Houston (who along with Glass, later became Treasury Secretaries under Wilson), was given $100,000 to find locations for the regional Reserve Banks. With over 200 cities requesting this status, hearings were held in 18 cities, as they traveled the country in a special railroad car.

On October 25, 1914, the formal establishment of the Federal Reserve System was announced, and it began operating in 1915.

Col. House, who Wilson called his "alter ego," because he was his closest friend and most trusted advisor, anonymously wrote a novel in 1912 called *Philip Dru: Administrator*, which revealed the manner in which Wilson was controlled. House, who lobbied for the implementation of central banking, would now turn his attention towards a graduated income tax. Incidentally, a central bank, providing inflatable currency; and a graduated income tax, were two of the ten points in the *Communist Manifesto* for socializing a country.

It was House who hand-picked the first Federal Reserve Board. He named Benjamin Strong as its first Chairman. In 1914, Paul M. Warburg quit his $500,000 a year job at Kuhn, Loeb and Co. to be on the Board, later resigning in 1918, during World War I, because of his German connections.

The Banking Act of 1935 amended the Federal Reserve Act, changing its name to the Federal Reserve System, and reorganizing it, in respect to the number of directors and length of term.

Headed by a seven member Board of Governors, appointed by the President, and confirmed by the Senate for a 14 year term, the Board acts as an overseer to the nation's money supply and banking system,

The Board of Governors, the President of the Federal Reserve Bank in New York, and four other Reserve Bank Presidents, who serve on a rotating basis, make up the Federal Open Market Committee. This group decides whether or not to buy and sell government securities on the open market. The Government buys and sells government securities, mostly through 21 Wall Street bond dealers, to create reserves to make the money needed to run the government. The Committee also determines the supply of money available to the nation's banks and consumers.

There are twelve Federal Reserve Banks, in twelve districts: Boston (MA), Cleveland (OH), New York (NY), Philadelphia (PA), Richmond (VA), Atlanta (GA), Chicago (IL), St. Louis (MO), Minneapolis (MN), Kansas City (KS), San Francisco (CA), and Dallas (TX). The twelve regional banks were set up so that the people wouldn't think that the Federal Reserve was controlled from New York. Each of the Banks has nine men on the Board of Directors; six are elected by member Banks, and three are appointed by the Board of Governors.

They have 25 branch Banks, and many member Banks. All Federal Banks are members, and four out of every ten commercial banks are members. In whole, the

Federal Reserve System controls about 70% of the country's bank deposits. Ohio Senator, Warren G. Harding, who was elected to the Presidency in 1920, said in a 1921 Congressional inquiry, that the Reserve was a private banking monopoly. He said: "The Federal Reserve Bank is an institution owned by the stockholding member banks. The Government has not a dollar's worth of stock in it." His term was cut short in 1923, when he mysteriously died, leading to rumors that he was poisoned. This claim was never substantiated, because his wife would not allow an autopsy.

Three years after the initiation of the Federal Reserve, Woodrow Wilson said: "The growth of the nation ... and all our activities are in the hands of a few men ... We have come to be one of the worst ruled; one of the most completely controlled and dominated governments in the civilized world ... no longer a government of free opinion, no longer a government by conviction and the free vote of the majority, but a government by the opinion and duress of a small group of dominant men."

In 1919, John Maynard Keynes, later an advisor to Franklin D. Roosevelt, wrote in his book *The Economic Consequences of Peace*: "Lenin is to have declared that the best way to destroy the capitalist system was to debauch the currency ... By a continuing process of inflation, governments can confiscate secretly and unobserved, an important part of the wealth of their citizens ... As the inflation proceeds and the real value of the currency fluctuates wildly from month to month, all permanent relations between debtors and creditors, which form the ultimate foundation of capitalism, become so utterly disordered as to be almost meaningless..."

Congressman Charles August Lindbergh, Sr., father of the historic aviator, said on the floor of the Congress: "This Act establishes the most gigantic trust on Earth ... When the President signs this Act, the invisible government by the Money Power, proven to exist by the Money Trust investigation, will be legalized ... This is the Aldrich Bill in disguise ... The new law will create inflation whenever the Trusts want inflation ... From now on, depressions will be scientifically created ... The worst legislative crime of the ages is perpetrated by this banking and currency bill." Lindbergh supposedly paid for his opposition to the Illuminati. When there appeared to be growing support for his son Charles to run for the Presidency, his grandson was kidnapped, and apparently killed.

Rep. Henry Cabot Lodge, Sr. said of the Bill (*Congressional Record*, June 10, 1932): "The Bill as it stands, seems to me to open the way to vast expansion of the currency ... I do not like to think that any law can be passed which will make it possible to submerge the gold standard in a flood of irredeemable paper currency."

On December 15, 1931, Rep. Louis T. McFadden, who for more than ten years served as Chairman of the Banking and Currency Committee in the House of Representatives, said: "The Federal Reserve Board and banks are the duly appointed agents of the foreign central banks of issue and they are more concerned with their foreign customers than they are with the people of the United States. The only thing that is American about the Federal Reserve Board and banks is the money they use..." On June 10, 1932, McFadden, said in an address to the Congress:

"We have in this country one of the most corrupt institutions the world has ever known. I refer to the Federal Reserve Board and the Federal Reserve Banks ... Some people think the Federal Reserve Banks are United States Government institutions. They are not Government institutions. They are private credit monopolies which prey upon the people of the United States for the benefit of themselves and their foreign customers ... The Federal Reserve Banks are the agents of the foreign central banks ... In that dark crew of financial pirates, there are those who would cut a man's throat to get a dollar out of his pocket ... Every effort has been made by the Federal Reserve Board to conceal its powers, but the truth is the FED has usurped the government. It controls everything here (in Congress) and controls all our foreign relations. It makes and breaks governments at will ... When the FED was passed, the people of the United States did not perceive that a world system was being set up here ... A super-state controlled by international bankers, and international industrialists acting together to enslave the world for their own pleasure!"

On May 23, 1933, McFadden brought impeachment charges against the members of the Federal Reserve:

"Whereas I charge them jointly and severally with having brought about a repudiation of the national currency of the United States in order that the gold value of said currency might be given to private interests...

I charge them ... with having arbitrarily and unlawfully taken over $80,000,000,000 from the United States Government in the year 1928...

I charge them ... with having arbitrarily and unlawfully raised and lowered the rates on money ... increased and diminished the volume of currency in circulation for the benefit of private interests...

I charge them ... with having brought about the decline of prices on the New York Stock Exchange...

I charge them ... with having conspired to transfer to foreigners and international money lenders, title to and control of the financial resources of the United States...

I charge them ... with having published false and misleading propaganda intended to deceive the American people and to cause the United States to lose its independence...

I charge them ... with the crime of having treasonably conspired and acted against the peace and security of the United States, and with having treasonably conspired to destroy the constitutional government of the United States."

In 1933, Vice-President John Garner, when referring to the international bankers, said: "You see, gentlemen, who owns the United States."

Sen. Barry Goldwater wrote in his book *With No Apologies*: "Does it not seem strange to you that these men just happened to be CFR (Council on Foreign Relations) and just happened to be on the Board of Governors of the Federal Reserve, that absolutely controls the money and interest rates of this great country. A privately owned organization ... which has absolutely nothing to do with the United States of America!"

Plain and simple, the Federal Reserve is not part of the Federal Government. It is a privately held corporation owned by stockholders. That is why the Federal Reserve Bank of New York (and all the others) is listed in the Dun and Bradstreet Reference Book of American Business (Northeast, Region 1, Manhattan/Bronx). According to Article I, Section 8 of the U.S. Constitution, only Congress has the right to issue money and regulate its value, so it is illegal for private interests to do so. Yet, it happened, and because of a provision in the Act, the Class A stockholders were to be kept a secret, and not to be revealed. R. F. McMaster, who published a newsletter called *The Reaper*, through his Swiss and Saudi Arabian contacts, was able to find out which banks held a controlling interest in the Reserve: the Rothschild Banks of London and Berlin; Lazard Brothers Bank of Paris; Israel Moses Seif Bank of Italy; Warburg Bank of Hamburg and Amsterdam; Lehman Brothers Bank of New York; Kuhn, Loeb, and Co. of New York; Chase Manhattan Bank of New York; and Goldman, Sachs of New York. These interests control the Reserve through about 300 stockholders.

Because of the way the Reserve was organized, whoever controls the Federal Reserve Bank of New York, controls the system, About 90 of the 100 largest banks are in this district. Of the reportedly 203,053 shares of the New York bank: Rockefeller's National City Bank had 30,000 shares; Morgan's First National Bank had 15,000 shares; Chase National, 6,000 shares; and the National Bank of Commerce (Morgan Guaranty Trust), 21,000 shares.

A June 15, 1978 Senate Report called "Interlocking Directorates Among the Major U.S. Corporations" revealed that five New York banks had 470 interlocking directorates with 130 major U.S. corporations: Citicorp (97), J. P. Morgan Co. (99), Chase Manhattan (89), Manufacturers Hanover (89), and Chemical Bank (96). According to Eustace Mullins, these banks are major stock holders in the FED. In his book *World Order*, he said that these five banks are "controlled from London." Mullins said: "Besides its controlling interest in the Federal Reserve Bank of New York, the Rothschilds had developed important financial interests in other parts of the United States ... The entire Rockefeller empire was financed by the Rothschilds."

A May, 1976 report of the House Banking and Currency Committee indicated: "The Rothschild banks are affiliated with Manufacturers Hanover of London in which they hold 20 percent ... and Manufacturers Hanover Trust of New York." The Report also revealed that Rothschild Intercontinental Bank, Ltd., which consisted of Rothschild banks in London, France, Belgium, New York, and Amsterdam, had three American subsidiaries: National City Bank of Cleveland, First City National Bank of Houston, and Seattle First National Bank. It is believed, that the Rothschilds hold 53% of the stock of the U.S. Federal Reserve.

Each year, billions of dollars are 'earned' by Class A stockholders, from U.S. tax dollars which go to the FED to pay interest on bank loans.

How Our Gold Reserves Have Been Manipulated

The Coinage Act of 1792 established a dollar consisting of 371.25 grains of pure silver, but was later replaced with a gold dollar consisting of 25.8 grains of gold. In 1873, the Coinage Act was passed, prohibiting the use of Silver as a form of currency, because the quantity being discovered was driving the value down. In 1875, after temporarily suspending gold convertibility during the Civil War greenback period, the U.S. was put more firmly on the gold standard by the Gold Standard Act of 1900. From 1900 to 1933, gold was coined by the U.S. Mint, and our paper currency was tied into the amount of gold held in the U.S. Treasury reserves.

In July, 1927, the directors of the Bank of England, the New York Federal Reserve Bank, and the German Reichsbank, met to plan a way to get the gold moved out of the United States, and it was this movement of gold which helped trigger the depression. By 1928, nearly $500 million in gold was transferred to Europe.

President Franklin D. Roosevelt accepted the advice of England's leading economist, John Maynard Keynes (1883-1946), a member of the Illuminati, who said that deficit spending would be a shot in the arm to the economy. Most of the New Deal spending programs to fight economic depression, were based on Keynes theories on deficit spending, and financed by borrowing against future taxes. In 1910, Lenin said: "The surest way to overthrow an established social order is to debauch its currency." Nine years later, Keynes wrote: "Lenin was certainly right, there is no more positive, or subtler, no surer means of overturning the existing basis of society than to debauch the currency ... The process engages all of the hidden forces of economic law on the side of destruction, and does it in a manner that not one man in a million is able to diagnose."

A Presidential Executive Order by Roosevelt on April 5, 1933, required all the people to exchange their gold coins, gold bullion, and gold-backed currency, for money that was not redeemable in precious metals. The Gold Reserve Act of 1934, known as the Thomas Amendment, which amended the Act of May 12, 1933, made it illegal to possess any gold currency (which was rescinded December 31, 1974). Gold coinage was withdrawn from circulation, and kept in the form of bullion. Just as the public was to return all their gold to the U.S. Government, so was the Federal Reserve. However, while the people received $20.67 an ounce in paper money issued by the Federal Reserve, the Reserve was paid in Gold Certificates. Now the Federal Reserve, and the Illuminati, had control of all the gold in the country.

In 1934, the value of gold increased to $35 an ounce, which produced a $3 billion profit for the Government. But when the price of gold increases, the value of the dollar decreases. Our dollar has not been worth 100 cents since 1933, when we were taken off of the Gold Standard. In 1974, our dollar was worth 22-1/2 cents, and in 1983 it was only worth 38 cents. In 2002, it took $13.88 to buy what cost $1.00 in 1933. Since our money supply had been limited to the amount of gold in Treasury reserves, when the value of the dollar decreased, more money was printed.

The first United Nations Monetary and Financial Conference, held in Bretton Woods, New Hampshire, from July 1 to July 22, 1944, which was under the direction of Harry Dexter White (CFR member, and undercover Russian spy), established the policies of the International Monetary Fund. Its goals were to strip the United States of its gold reserves by giving it to other nations; and to merge with their industrial capabilities; as well as their economic, social, educational and religious policies; to facilitate a one-world government.

Because of paying off foreign obligations and strengthening foreign economies, between 1958 and 1968, the amount of gold bullion in the possession of the U.S. Treasury dropped by 52%. Of the amount remaining, $12 billion was reserved by law for backing the paper money in circulation. Our money had been backed by a 25% gold reserve in accordance to a law that was passed in 1945, but it was rescinded in 1968. The amount of gold slipped from 653.1 million troy ounces in 1957, to 311.2 million ounces in 1968, which according to the Treasury Department, was due to sales to foreign banking institutions, sales to domestic producers, and the buying and selling of gold on the world market to stabilize prices. This was a loss of 341.9 million troy ounces. In August, 1971, gold was used only for world trade, because foreign countries wouldn't accept U.S. dollars. As of November, 1981, sources had indicated that the gold reserve had dropped to 264.1 million troy ounces.

Title 31 of the U.S. Code, requires an annual physical inventory of our gold supply, but a complete audit was never done, so officially, nobody knows what has occurred. After World War II, America had 70% of the World's supply of loose gold, but today, we may have less than 7%. Sen. Jesse Helms seemed to think that the OPEC nations have our gold, while others believe that 70% of the world's gold supply is being held by the World Bank, which is dominated by the financial grip of the Rothschilds and the Rockefellers.

Some years ago, I had been contacted by a gentleman in Michigan, whose research indicated that counterfeit $5,000 and $10,000 Federal Reserve Notes had been used to steal U.S. gold reserves. Illegal to own, these notes are actually checks which are used to transfer ownership of large amounts of gold without actually moving the gold itself. Using public records, he found the serial numbers of the bills which were originally printed, and discovered that there are now more in existence.

It has been reported that 40% (13,000 tons) of the world's gold is five levels below street level, in a sub-basement of the New York Federal Reserve Bank, behind a 90-ton revolving door. Some of it is American-owned, but most is owned by the central banks of other countries. It is stored in separate cubicles, and from time to time, is moved from one cubicle to another to satisfy international transactions.

The Destructive Measures of the Federal Reserve

After March, 1964, Silver certificates were no longer convertible to Silver dollars; and in March, 1968, near the conclusion of the Johnson Administration, Silver backing of the dollar was removed. On the 1929 series of notes, it read: "Redeemable in gold on demand at the United States Treasury, or in gold or lawful money at any Federal Reserve Bank." This was just like the Silver Certificate, which was guaranteed by a dollar in silver that was on deposit. On the 1934 series of notes, it read: "This note is legal tender for all debts, public and private, and is redeemable in lawful money at the United States Treasury, or at any Federal Reserve Bank." The 1950 series bore the same information, but reduced it to three lines, and reduced the size of the type. In the 1953 series, the wording was totally removed, although the bottom portion contained a promise to "pay the bearer on demand." However, in 1963, even that message was removed, and our dollars became nothing more than worthless pieces of paper because they no longer met the legal requirements of a note, which meant it had to list an issuing bank, and amount payable, a payee or 'bearer,' and a time for payment, which was 'on demand.'

Since 1933, the Reserve has been printing too much money, compared to the declining Gross National Product (GNP). The GNP is the accumulated values of services and goods produced in the country. If the GNP is 4%, then the money produced should only be about 5-6%, thus insuring enough money to keep the goods produced by the GNP in circulation. Additional social services, which are promised during election year rhetoric to gain votes, increase the Federal Budget, so more money is printed. Then the Government will cut the Budget, establish wage and price controls. The extra money in circulation decreases the value of the dollar, and prices go up. Simply put, too much money in circulation causes inflation, and that is what the Reserve is doing, purposely printing too much money in order to destroy the economy. On the other hand, if they would stop printing money, our economy would collapse.

The Reserve is responsible for setting the interest rate that member banks can borrow from the Reserve, thus controlling the interest rates of the entire country. So, what it boils down to, is that the Federal Reserve determines the amount of money needed, which is created by the International Bankers out of nothing. Besides the face value, they charge the government 3¢ to produce each bill. The Federal government pays the Reserve in bonds (which are also printed by the Reserve), and then pay the bonds off at a high rate of interest. That interest will very soon become the largest item in the Federal Budget.

William McChesney Martin, a member of the Council on Foreign Relations (CFR), and Chairman of the Federal Reserve (FED) during the 'New Frontier' years of the Kennedy Administration, testified to the Federal Banking Committee, that the value of the dollar was being scientifically brought down each year by 3-3-1/2%, in order to allow wages to go up. The reasoning behind this, was that the people were being made to think that they were getting more, when in fact they were actually getting less.

The Congress has also contributed to this process, by approving Federal Budgets, year after year, which requires the printing of more money to finance the debt, which, by the end of 2003, was over $6,900,000,000,000 ($6.9 trillion). When Wilson was President, the debt was about $1 billion, and in 1974, the debt was about $1 trillion.

In 1937, Rep. Charles G. Binderup of Nebraska, realizing the consequences of the Federal Reserve System, called for the Government to buy all the stock, and to create a new Board controlled by Congress to regulate the value of the currency and the volume of bank deposits, thus eliminating the FED's independence. He was defeated for re-election. Others have also tried to introduce various Bills to control the Federal Reserve: Rep. Goldborough (1935), Rep. Jerry Voorhis of California (1940, 1943), Sen. M. M. Logan of Kentucky, and Rep. Usher L. Burdick of North Dakota.

Rep. Wright Patman of Texas (who was the House Banking Chairman until 1975), said in 1952: "In fact there has never been an independent audit of either the twelve banks of the Federal Reserve Board that has been filed with the Congress ... For 40 years the system, while freely using the money of the government, has not made a proper accounting." Patman, said that the Federal Open Market Committee (who, in addition to the Board of Governors, decide the country's monetary policy) is "one of the most secret societies. These twelve men decide what happens in the economy ... In making decisions they check with no one— not the President, not the Congress, not the people."

Patman also said: "In the United States we have, in effect, two governments ... We have the duly constituted Government ... Then we have an independent, uncontrolled and uncoordinated government in the Federal Reserve System, operating the money powers which are reserved to Congress by the Constitution." During his career, Patman has sought to force the FED to allow an independent audit, lessen the influence of the large banks, shorten the terms of the FED Governors, expose it to regular Congressional review just like any other Federal agency, and to have only officials nominated by the President and confirmed by Congress to be on the Federal Open Market Committee. In 1967, Patman tried to have them audited, and on January 22, 1971, introduced HR11, which would have altered its organization, diminishing much of its power. He was later removed from the Chairmanship of the House Banking and Currency Committee, which he held for years.

On January 22, 1971, Rep. John R. Rarick of Louisiana introduced HR351: "To vest in the Government of the United States the full, absolute, complete, and unconditional ownership of the twelve Federal Reserve Banks." He said: "The Federal Reserve is not an agency of government. It is a private banking monopoly." He was later defeated for re-election. During the 1980's, Rep. Phil Crane of Illinois introduced House Resolution HR70 that called for an annual audit of the FED (which never came to a full vote); and Rep. Henry Gonzales of Texas introduced HR1470, that called for the repeal of the Federal Reserve Act.

The Federal Reserve System has never been audited, and their meetings, and minutes of those meetings, are not open to the public. They have repelled all attempts to be audited. In 1967, Arthur Burns, the Chairman of the Federal Reserve, said that an audit would threaten the independence of the Reserve.

In 1979, after dismissing Secretary of Treasury, Michael Blumenthal, President Jimmy Carter offered the position to American Illuminati chief, David Rockefeller, the CEO of Chase-Manhattan Bank, as did Nixon, but he turned it down. He also turned down the nomination for the Chairmanship of the Federal Reserve Board. Carter then appointed Paul Volcker as Chairman. Volcker graduated from Princeton with a degree in Economics, and from Harvard, with a degree in Public Administration. He was an economist with the Federal Reserve Bank of New York (1952-57), worked at the Chase Manhattan Bank (1957-61), was with the U.S. Treasury Department (1961-65), Deputy Under Secretary for Monetary Affairs (1963-65), Under Secretary for Monetary Affairs (1969-74), and President of the New York Federal Reserve Bank (1975-79).

In the Nixon Administration, as the Under Secretary for Monetary Policy and International Affairs, the executive branch official who works most closely with the Federal Reserve, he and Treasury Secretary John Connally helped formulate the policy that took us off the gold standard in 1971, because of the dwindling gold reserves at Fort Knox. Volcker was chosen because he was the "candidate of Wall Street." He was a member of the Trilateral Commission, and a major Rockefeller supporter. Bert Lance, the Georgia banker and political advisor to Carter who became his Budget Director, and was later forced to resign, contacted Gerald Rafshoon, a Carter aide, and said that if Volcker would be appointed, he would be "mortgaging his re-election to the Federal Reserve." Lance predicted that he would bring high interest rates and high unemployment. He was confirmed by the Senate Banking Committee in August, 1979, replacing Arthur Burns, an Austrian-born economist who was a CFR member with close ties to the Rockefellers. Volcker was against a gold-back dollar, and gold being used as a form of currency. He attempted to tighten the money situation in order to curb the 10% annual growth in the money supply, and to ease the pressure of loan demand. The result was a dramatic increase in interest rates, which climbed to 13-1/2% by September, 1979, and then soared to 21-1/2% by December, 1980.

Conjecture could dictate that this economic decline was purposely engineered to cause the political decline of Carter. In response to the rising interest rates, Carter said: "As you well know, I don't have control over the FED, none at all. It's carefully isolated from any influence by the President or the Congress. This has been done for many generations and I think it's a wise thing to do." Even though inflation had skyrocketed to all-time highs, Reagan kept Volcker on. It was Volcker who started the collapse of the U.S. economy.

During the 1970's, many banks had left the Federal Reserve, and in December, 1979, Volcker told the House Banking Committee that "300 banks with deposits of $18.4 billion have quit the FED within the past 4-1/2 years," and that another 575 of the remaining 5,480 member banks, with deposits of $70 billion, had indicated that they intended to withdraw. He said that this would curtail their control over the money supply, and that led Congress, in 1980, to pass the Monetary Control Act, which gave the Federal Reserve control of all banking institutions, regardless if they are members or not.

Alan Greenspan, who became the Chairman of the Federal Reserve Board in 1987, is a member of the Council of Foreign Relations. He has a bachelor's and master's degree, and a doctorate in Economics from New York University. He met Ayn Rand, the author of *Atlas Shrugged*, in 1952, and they became friends. It is from her that he learned that capitalism "is not only efficient and practical, but also moral." In February, 1995, the seventh increase in the interest rate, within the period of a year, took place. This put Greenspan in the limelight, as well as the Federal Reserve. It was very interesting how the media spin doctors churned out information that totally skirted the issue concerning the FED's actual role in controlling our economy.

In the mid-1970's, Paper 447, Article 3, from the World Bank, said that the

World economy would be fairly stable until 1980, when it would begin falling, in domino fashion. On October 29, 1975, the *Wall Street Journal* printed a comment by H. Johannes Witteveen, Managing Director of the United Nation's International Monetary Fund, that the IMF "ought to evolve into a World Central Bank ... to prevent inflation." Dr. H. A. Murkline, Director of the International Institute University in Irving, Texas, wrote in *World Oil: 1976* that he projected that the Federal Government could only hold out till the end of 1981. Dow Theory Letters, Inc. reported that by 1982, the cost of dealing with the national debt "would eat up all the government tax money available."

The *Robbins Report* of January 15, 1978, said: "If Carter introduces Bancor, which will be the yielding of our dollar to the ECU (European Currency Unit), this is what will happen: look for hyperinflation and collapse of all the world's paper money before 1985." Julian Snyder said in the *International Money Line* of February, 1978: "The United States is trying to solve its problem through currency depreciation (debasement) ... it will not work. If the crash does not occur this year, it could be postponed until 1982."

On March 13, 1979, while meeting at Strasbourg, France, the Parliament of Europe, which governs the European Economic Community (Common Market), oversaw the establishment of a new European money system. Known as the ECU, it was backed by 20% of the participating countries' gold reserves (about 3,150 tons). What little strength our dollar had, came from the fact that all nations buying oil from OPEC, had to use U.S. dollars. Then came the word in March, 1980, from Arab diplomatic sources at the United Nations that the Chase Manhattan Bank was making plans to drop the dollar in lieu of the ECU.

Dr. Franz Pick, a well known authority on world currency, said in December, 1979, in the *Silver and Gold Report*: "The most serious problem we face today is the debasement of our currency by the government. The government will continue to debase the dollar until ... within 12-24, months it will shrink to 1 cent ... at which time Washington will be forced to create the new hard currency ... A currency reform is nothing but a fancy name for state bankruptcy ... A currency reform completes the expropriation of all kinds of savings ... it will wipe out all public and private bonds, most pensions; all annuities, and all endowments."

Against all odds, our economy has continued to hang on, even though financial analysts have continued to forecast disastrous conditions.

In 1993, Sen. Bob Kerrey (Democrat, NE) promised to support President Bill Clinton's Budget Plan, if Clinton would appoint a Committee to study the condition of the American economy. The President established a 32-member bipartisan committee and in August, 1994, they issued their report. According to the committee's findings, by the year 2012, unless drastic changes are made, we won't even be able to pay the interest on the national debt. Knowing this, the federal government has allowed the trend to continue, almost as if they're trying to run our economy into the ground. It seems obvious that the destruction of the American economy has been part of a deliberate plot to financially enslave our nation.

FINAL WARNING

The New Money

Dr. Pick said that late 1983 or early 1984 was the target date for the 'new money.' Carl Mintz, a staff member of the House Banking Committee, had said: "I believe it's in the billions of dollars, and it's buried in lots of places." In the late 1970's, it was believed to have already been printed, and stored at the Federal Reserve Emergency Relocation Facility in Culpepper, Virginia, which is built into the side of a mountain, and would be able to continue functioning during the aftermath of a nuclear or natural disaster; and the 200,000 sq. ft. Federal Reserve underground facility in Mt. Weather, Virginia (near Berryville), which is the primary relocation area for the President, Cabinet Secretaries, Supreme Court Justices, and several thousand federal employees (Congress would be relocated to an underground facility in White Sulphur Springs, West Virginia). It is believed, that when our monetary system is finally destroyed, a reorganization will occur within the confines of a world government, and new money will be issued.

Rep. Ron Paul, Republican from Texas, who was on the Committee on Banking, Finance and Urban Affairs, wrote about the new money in a letter to Charles T. Roberts, Executive Vice-President of the Hull State Bank in Texas: "In a closed briefing for the members of the House Banking Committee on November 2nd, representatives of the Bureau of Engraving and Printing, the Federal Reserve, and the Secret Service described plans for making changes in Federal Reserve Notes beginning in 1985 (although the long range target is 1988) ... These changes, which will probably include taggents, security threads, and colors, and may include holograms, diffraction gratings, or watermarks, will be made in coordination with six other nations: Canada, Britain, Japan, Australia, West Germany and Switzerland. Japan, for example, will begin recalling its present currency in November, 1984, and have it nearly completed within six months ... According to the government, the only reason for the currency changes is to deter counterfeiting. Although it was admitted by one spokesman in the group that there would have to be a call-in of our present currency for new currency to work, the spokesmen for the government were adamant in saying that there was no other motive for a currency change..." According to law, only the Treasury Secretary has the authority to change the currency.

Over $3 million had been spent under 'counterfeit prevention' authority for the development of the new money, which according to the Currency Design Act (HR6005) hearings would be issued by the Federal Reserve Board. It was first reported by the Patterson Organization in Cincinnati, Ohio, that in a July, 1983 market survey in Buena Park, California, people were shown proposed designs for "new U.S. dollar bills." The variations shown, consisted of each denomination being a different color; Federal Reserve seals replaced with a design utilizing reflective ink; and other optical devices like holograms (a process which produces a three-dimensional image which can change color depending on the angle it is viewed), and multilayer diffraction gratings (similar to a hologram); as well as bills containing metal security threads, and planchettes (red and blue colored discs incorporated into the paper, similar to threads) to trigger scanning equipment which would detect its presence, and to sort cash faster. A consumer research firm from

Illinois was hired by the Treasury Department to gauge the public's reactions to the various designs.

It was shown that a drastic change would not be accepted, so a process of incrementalism was adopted. It was decided that the Bureau of Printing and Engraving would have a fine metallic strip running through the currency, leaving the basic design intact; however, they later decided to use a clear imprinted polyester strip, woven into the paper, running vertically on the left side of the Federal Reserve Seal. The length of the translucent polyester filament reads "USA100" for $100 bills, "USA50" for $50 bills, and so on; and can only be read if held up to direct light. It was reported that a company called Checkmate Electronics, Inc., which manufactures the equipment needed to scan checks, scanned the new money, and found the strip to contain "machine detectable" aluminum. Their scan produced an indecipherable bar code.

Though the basic design did not change, there was microscopic type printed around the picture which reads, "The United States of America," but appeared to only be a line. This currency with oversized, off-center portraits, was introduced in 1996 with the $100 bills, then $50 bills and $20 bills (1998), and culminated with $10's and $5's in 2000. The Government discontinued printing any of the old money, and began emptying their vaults to get rid of the old bills. The old money was never recalled, and continued to be circulated.

Then in June, 2002, only a few years after the last makeover, the rumors of colored money became a fact, as the Bureau of Engraving and Printing announced that further changes were being made to our money for security reasons. In October, 2003, the new, colored $20 bill (the most counterfeited note), was introduced. The new bill retained the security thread, color-shifting ink, and watermark; but also had the colors of green and peach added to its background, as well as small yellow "20's" printed on the back. The new $50 and $100 bills will be coming in 2004 and 2005.

Some financial experts have theorized that when every denomination is changed over, that the business sector may not want to accept old bills, which would then become worthless, and could create a financial emergency. But Federal officials have said that the old money would be accepted, but scrutinized. It has been suggested that the government could really take advantage of the situation, that in order for people to exchange their old money for new, an exchange rate may be determined which would benefit the economy. For example, it may take two old dollars to exchange for a new one. It is possible that we may be experiencing the final transition to the "new money."

This transitional currency may be just another step in testing the public's willingness to accept economic change. The Reserve formally had about seven currency sorting machines which counted up to 55,000 bills per minute, but by the end of 1983, they had received 110 new machines which could count up to 72,000 bills per minute. Jane Kettleson, an economic consultant to the U.S. Paper Exchange, said that, "the FED will have the capability to physically replace the entire U.S. currency in circulation in just four days time."

The International Monetary Fund has been responsible for the decline of our dollar, and our present economic situation. The first step to initiating this 'crash' was the Monetary Control Act of 1980, which instead of a 6:1 ratio, mandated the

Federal Reserve to only have one dollar on deposit for every twelve they create. Further plans were made during a meeting of Western leaders at Williamsburg, Virginia, on May 28-30, 1983.

International cooperation has been intense to coordinate currency changes among its member governments. In 1985, officials from the Morgan Bank in New York met with the Credit Lyonnais Bank in France. They established the European Currency Unit Banking Association (ECUBA), to get world cooperation for a unified currency, and had support from bankers in Europe, Japan, and the United States. It was an offshoot of the Banking Federation of the European Community (BFEC), which has been engaged in shutting down small banks in order to develop a conglomerate of a few huge banks. In October, 1987, the Association for the Monetary Union of Europe (AMUE), secretly met and recommended that the ECU (European Currency Unit) replace existing national currencies; and that all European Central Banks be combined into one and issue the ECU as the official unified currency (which is scheduled to occur in the year 2000). It is believed that the plan is to have only three central banks in the world: The Federal Reserve Bank, the European Central Bank, and the Central Bank of Japan. In a June, 1989 hearing of the Senate Banking Securities Subcommittee, Alan Greenspan, Chairman of the Federal Reserve, said that exchange rates could be fixed in order to solve the problem of uniformity between the currencies of various nations.

Many countries have issued new money, such as Switzerland, the United Kingdom, Japan, Canada, France, Germany, Australia, and Brazil. Of the countries that already had, most currencies had a common 1" square, usually on the left side of the bill. Held over a light, a hologram appears on the spot, barely visible to the naked eye, which cannot be reproduced on a copier. It is believed that this spot is being reserved for a central World Bank overprint. They also contain metallic strips that can be detected when they pass through scanners at airports and international borders.

On May 10, 1994, when *USA Today* carried a page one article concerning major changes in the design of the paper currency, which was expected to take place by the end of the year, it was accompanied with a picture of the new $100 bill, featuring a larger portrait of Benjamin Franklin which had been pushed to the right side of the bill, and the Eagle in the center. The line "United States of America" appeared along the top right, and the line "One Hundred Dollars" appeared on the lower left, with the serial number being placed over that. There was a conspicuous open spot on the left side of the bill, very similar to the new currency in other countries, which some researchers feared was being reserved for some future use.

The institution of a common world-wide currency may be delayed because of the possibility of moving right to a cashless system, making paper money obsolete. The Visa MagiCard was the first step towards a national debit card. With this card, you could make purchases at any of the 10 million merchants who accepted Visa, and have the amount electronically deducted from your checking account. Financial experts said at the time, that within only a few years, there would be more debit cards than credit cards. Since then, there has been a massive campaign to promote debit cards, and a move to accommodate their use in all areas of life.

More and more banks have decided not to return people's cancelled checks, because of the expense to do so; and it seems likely that there is a plan underway to gradually move away from the use of paper checks. With the existence of debit cards, and the fact that credit cards are so easily attainable, there's no doubt that we're being pushed into an electronic economy of Direct Deposit and Automatic Withdrawal. When total saturation has been achieved, then the stage will be set. Sure, it's really convenient to whip out a piece of plastic to buy things, and to have all your financial affairs handled through the bank's computer system. But do you realize, that when their plan is complete, you will be nothing more than a number in a computer. Everything you do can be tracked; and with a click of a mouse, or the press of a button, you could be denied access to your own money.

In a letter to Edward M. House (President Wilson's closest aide), dated November 23, 1933, Franklin D. Roosevelt said: "The real truth of the matter is, and you and I know, that a financial element in the large centers has owned the government of the U.S. since the days of Andrew Jackson." Henry Ford, founder of the Ford Motor Company, said: "It is well enough that the people of the nation do not understand our banking and monetary system, for if they did, I believe there would be a revolution before tomorrow morning." In 1957, Sen. George W. Malone of Nevada said before Congress about the Federal Reserve: "I believe that if the people of this nation fully understood what Congress has done to them over the past 49 years, they would move on Washington: they would not wait for an election ... It adds up to a preconceived plan to destroy the economic and social independence of the United States."

THE FEDERAL INCOME TAX

With the Illuminati in complete control of our monetary system, they were ready for the next step. They couldn't touch the money of the people, because the Constitution did not contain any provision for the taxing of income; so they now set into motion a plan to accomplish this, in order to oppress the middle class, and increase the lower class, who would have to depend on the government for their survival.

From 1862-72, to support the Civil War effort, Congress enacted the nation's first income tax: 3% on incomes from $600 to $10,000, and 5% for incomes above that, which was later deemed to be insufficient, and it was increased twice, till it reached a high of 10% on all incomes over $5,000. The tax was criticized because it wasn't apportioned among the states according to population. The Act of 1862 also provided for a sales tax, excise tax, and inheritance tax; and established the office of Commissioner of Internal Revenue, who was given the power to assess, levy, and collect taxes, and was given the authority to enforce tax laws. In 1868, tobacco and alcoholic beverages were taxed.

The income tax was discontinued in 1872, but after heavy lobbying by the Populist Party, it was reinstated in 1894, as part of the Wilson-German Tariff Bill, when Congress enacted a 2% tax on all incomes over $4,000 a year. On May 20, 1895, the U.S. Supreme Court ruled that the tax was unconstitutional, because it was not distributed among the states in accordance with the Constitution. Newspapers controlled by the Illuminati denounced the Court's decision.

When the income tax legislation was introduced in the Senate in 1894, Sen. Aldrich had come out against it, saying it was "communistic and socialistic," but in 1909, he proposed the 16th Amendment to the Constitution, with the support of President Taft, which called for the creation of a progressive graduated income tax. It was ratified in February, 1913, and levied a 1% tax on all incomes over $3,000, and a progressive surtax on incomes over $20,000. Although praised by reformers, conservatives said it was "a first step toward complete confiscation of private property."

According to a 2-volume investigative report called *The Law That Never Was*, by William J. Benson (who had been a special agent with the Illinois Department of revenue for 10 years) and M. J. Beckman, on February 25, 1913, shortly before the end of his term, Secretary of State Philander C. Knox ignored various irregularities, and fraudulently declared that the 16th Amendment had been ratified by three-fourths (or 36) of the 48 states. Benson traveled to all the states' archives, and to the National Archives in Washington, DC, obtaining more than 17,000 pages of documents, all properly notarized and certified by state officials, that proved that the 16th Amendment was never ratified.

A 16-page memo dated February 15, 1913, to Knox, from his solicitor, stated that only four states had "correctly" ratified the amendment, that Minnesota had not forwarded their copy yet, and that the resolutions from 33 states contained punctuation, capitalization, or wording different than the Resolution that was approved by Congress. The memo read:

> "In the certified copies of the resolutions passed by the legislatures of the several states ratifying the proposed 16th amendment, it appears that only four of these resolutions (those submitted by Arizona, North Dakota, Tennessee and New Mexico) have quoted absolutely accurately and correctly the 16th amendment as proposed by Congress. The other thirty-three resolutions all contain errors either of punctuation, capitalization, or wording. Minnesota, it is to be remembered, did not transmit to the Department a copy of the resolution passed by the legislature of the state. The resolutions passed by twenty-two states contain errors only of capitalization or punctuation, or both, while those of eleven states contain errors in the wording..."

Benson discovered that some word changes and misplaced commas were done by legislative intent. State Legislatures voting to ratify a proposed Constitutional amendment, must use a certified, exact copy, as passed by the Congress. Since this was not done, legally, the Government can only collect an income tax within the guidelines set forth by the Supreme Court in Pollock v. Farmers Loan & Trust Co., 157 U.S. 429 (1895), and all sections of the Internal Revenue Code, based on the 16th Amendment, are not valid.

So, of the 48 states:

> Eight states (Rhode Island, Utah, Connecticut, New Hampshire, Kentucky, Florida, Virginia, and Pennsylvania) did not approve or ratify the

amendment.

Texas and Louisiana were forbidden by their own state constitution to empower the federal government to tax their citizens.

Vermont and Massachusetts rejected the amendment with a recorded vote count, but later declared it passed without a recorded vote only after the amendment had been declared ratified by Knox.

Tennessee, Ohio, Mississippi, California, and Washington violated their own state constitutions during their ratification procedures.

Minnesota had not sent any copy of its resolution to Knox, let alone a signed and sealed copy, as was required by law.

Oklahoma, Georgia, and Illinois had made unacceptable changes in the wording, as did some of the above states (in addition to the other unacceptable procedures).

When you deduct these 21 states, you only had a proper ratification by only 27 states, far less than the Constitutionally-mandated 36.

Because of his diligence, Benson was arrested and imprisoned on income tax charges, but later released.

Why the Federal Government Doesn't Have Jurisdiction Over States

According to Article I, Section 8 of the Constitution of the United States: "The Congress shall have power ... to exclusive legislation in all cases whatsoever, over such district (not exceeding ten miles square) as may, by cession of particular States and the acceptance of Congress, become the seat of the Government of the United States, and to exercise like authority over all places purchased by the consent of the legislature of the State in which the same shall be, for the erection of forts, magazines, arsenals, dockyards, and other needful building..."

This passage reveals the true intention of our forefathers, which was for the Federal Government to coordinate the efforts of all the States in order to combine their resources when it came to things like trade and defense, since the States were actually like separate countries. Therefore, the Congress only had jurisdiction over the area of Washington, D.C., and non-state territories like Alaska, and Hawaii (before they became states); and the present countries of Puerto Rico, Virgin Islands, Guam, American Samoa, and others; and Federal property such as military bases. This area will be hereinafter referred to as the District (as in the District of Columbia), as it is in the United States Code (see 26 USC 7701(a) (1), and 26 USC 3121(e) (1)).

Since America is a Republic, and not a democracy, the Government has a responsibility to protect the inalienable rights of its citizens, as granted by the Constitution, rather than to grant privileges, known as civil rights, which are decided by the will of the majority. When the sovereign state citizen gave power to the State Constitution, which created State Government; this in turn gave power to the U.S. Constitution, which created the Federal Government; which has, in a sense, incorporated and gave power to the United States Government; which has turned the U.S. citizen into a subject of the U.S. Government. Therefore, the Federal Government has been able to wield its influence over the entire country, rather than just the area referred to as the District.

This is possible, because, for all intents and purposes, there are two of every state. For example, the official name of Pennsylvania is the Commonwealth of Pennsylvania; but to the U.S. Government, it is known as the State of Pennsylvania. There are even two state flags. One with a gold fringe, which represents the State of Pennsylvania, and martial law under the U.S. Government; and one without the fringe, which represents the Commonwealth of Pennsylvania. The gold-fringed flag was reserved for use by the General of the Army, where it was present at military headquarters and displayed at court martials. Its use elsewhere, as a government battle flag, was only to be done at the discretion of the President, within his role as the Commander-in-Chief of the military, to establish the jurisdiction of the military presence. This gold-fringed flag, which is common in many public places, such as courthouses, and schools, is not the national flag which represents our constitutional republic. It is a symbol of federal government jurisdiction.

When Franklin D. Roosevelt was inaugurated on March 4, 1933, he called for an emergency session of Congress on March 9th, where the Emergency Banking Relief Act (also known as the War Powers Act, which seized all the country's constitutional gold and silver coinage) was passed, which gave FDR the power to issue any order, and do anything he felt was necessary to run the country, without restriction, by authority of the Trading with the Enemy Act of October 6, 1917 (which placed all German citizens under the authority of the President, because they were enemies of the U.S.).

In 1917, Chapter 106, Section 2, subdivision (c), of the Trading with the Enemy Act, defined the Enemy as someone "other than citizens of the United States..." and in 1933, according to Chapter 106, Section 5, subdivision (b), the Act designated as the Enemy "any person within the United States."

America was under the authority of an emergency war government. According to the book *Constitution: Fact or Fiction* by Dr. Eugene Schroder (with Micki Nellis), our Constitution was actually nullified on March 9, 1933, when President Franklin Roosevelt declared a national emergency. As recorded in *Congressional Record* in 1933, Rep. James Buck said: "... the doctrine of emergency is the worst. It means that when Congress declares an emergency, there is no Constitution. This means it's dead." Senate Report 93-549 (Senate Resolution 9, 93rd Congress, 1st Session) in 1973 said that since 1933 "the United States has been in a state of declared national emergency ... A majority of the people of the United States have lived all their lives under emergency rule. For 40 years freedoms and governmental procedures guaranteed by the Constitution have, in varying degrees, been abridged by laws brought into force by states of national emergency..." The Act was never repealed after the World War II, because Roosevelt died; and Truman used the extraordinary powers he gained through the rewriting of the War Powers Act to establish the National Security infrastructure, which included the C.I.A.

The "national emergency" technically ended on September 14, 1976, when the 93rd Congress passed H.R. 3884, the National Emergencies Termination Act (50 USC 1601, Public Law 94-412) in response to President Richard Nixon's abuse of the Trading with the Enemy Act (which was part of Roosevelt's emergency legislation). Though he had promised an end to the U.S. involvement in the Vietnam War, he actually escalated the war by authorizing the secret bombing of Cambodia. And then later, in December, 1972, Nixon ordered American B-52's to drop over 36,000 tons of bombs over Haiphong and Hanoi. Congress then appointed the Special Committee on the Termination of the National Emergency, headed by Sen. Frank Church (D-ID), who began having hearings in July, 1973. Even though it appeared that the emergency legislation was repealed, the last paragraph said that it didn't apply to any "authorities under the act of October 6, 1917, as amended."

Chuck Morse wrote in his article "Is the 'National Emergency of FDR' Still In Place?" that: "This was a classic example of sleight of hand. In fact, Congress exempted all laws, based on the emergency of 1933 that were already in place. Rather than being based on the authority of the President under a 'national emergency' these federal laws would now be codified as a permanent part of the U.S. Federal Code. Included among the codified laws would be Section 5(b) of the Trading with the Enemy Act, which classifies the American citizen as an enemy of the government."

The declaration of a National Emergency can legally empower the President to suspend the Constitution. According to Senate Report 93-549, the "President may: Seize property, organize commodities, assign military forces abroad, institute Martial Law, seize and control transportation and communication, regulate operation of private enterprise, restrict travel, and in a plethora of particular ways, control the lives of all American citizens."

President Carter declared a new national emergency in 1979 during the Iranian hostage crisis, and Bill Clinton, during his two terms in office, declared 12 National Emergencies.

A 1976 Senate report noted that there were 470 extraordinary grants of power to the President, during times of National Emergency.

However, because of Executive Orders 6073, 6102 (gold confiscation), 6111, 6260 and 6262 by President Franklin D. Roosevelt, it is believed that the District went bankrupt in 1933, and since then, has undergone various "reorganizations." The Secretary of Treasury was appointed "receiver" in the bankruptcy (Reorganization Plan, No. 26, 5 U.S.C.A. 903; Public Law 94-564; Legislative History, pg. 5967). Representative James A. Traficant, Jr. of Ohio, according to the *Congressional Record* (pg. H1303), on March 17, 1993, said: "Mr. Speaker, we are now in Chapter 11. Members of Congress are official Trustees presiding over the greatest reorganization of any bankrupt entity in world history, the United States government..."

It was in 1933 that FDR enacted the Social Security Act, which effectively redefined the word "employee" to indicate "government worker." Then came the Public Salary Tax Act in 1939, which gave the U.S. Government the power to levy a tax on those people who were either government employees, or who lived and worked in a "Federal Area." A year later, the Buck Act was passed, which gave the U.S. Government the power to create a "Federal Area" so they could levy the

FINAL WARNING

Public Salary Tax. Since it was unconstitutional to tax anyone outside of the jurisdiction of the District, this Act, in Section 110(d) and (e), made the land within the territorial boundaries of a State, a "Federal Area." This, in effect, created a paper state, known as a Federal Area, for the purposes of the U.S. Government; and those people who were sovereign state citizens, now found themselves also living in this Federal Area. Now the U.S. Government had to make that citizen one of their subjects by bringing them under the jurisdiction of the District.

This was accomplished by deceiving the citizen into entering an adhesion contract with the U.S. Government, such as a Social Security application, an Income Tax form, a Driver's License application, a Bank Account application, and other similar things. Contrary to what most people believe, it is not mandatory to apply for a Social Security number; however, in order for a sovereign state citizen to be eligible for Social Security benefits, they have to waive the rights given to them under our Republic.

Probably, the most incredible example of the adhesion contract is the Income Tax system. In 1884, it was accepted that the "property which every man has is his own labor (and) as it is the original foundation of all other property, so it is the most sacred and inviolable." Therefore, since 'wages' are received as compensation for labor, it can not be legally taxed. 'Income,' however, is the process of profiting from a business (someone else's labor) or investments, and is taxable, as in a Corporation, which is an artificial entity which is given the right to exist by the State. The Constitution only allows the Congress to collect taxes, and that is limited to a uniform excise tax on gasoline, alcohol, tobacco, telephone bills, firearms, and tires, things revolving in one way or another around interstate commerce. The payment of these taxes are voluntary, because they are based on consumption. These funds go directly to the U.S. Treasury to pay the expenses of the country.

Because we live in a Republic, the Internal Revenue Service Code, Title 26 USC, could not be passed into law by the Congress, and instead, was passed only as a Resolution, which is a formal expression of intent that was to pertain only to citizens of the District. So, how do they make you a citizen of the District? In the upper left-hand corner of the 1040 Federal Income Tax form is a place to put your preprinted address label, which is designated with the words "label here." However, to the left of that is the word "label," which seemingly identifies the entire section as a whole. However, the word "label" actually has another legal meaning that has nothing to do with your name and address. According to *Black's Law Dictionary*, "label" is defined as: "A slip of ribbon, parchment, or paper, attached as a codicil to a deed or other writing to hold the appended seal." Since your "seal" is your signature, the "label" is actually a codicil which indicates you are waiving your constitutional right as a sovereign state citizen to become a citizen of the District and its Federal Area.

Although the Internal Revenue Service is considered to be a Bureau of the Department of Treasury, like the Federal Reserve, they are not part of the Federal Government (Diversified Metal Products v. IRS et al. CV-93-405E-EJE U.S.D.C.D.I.; Public Law 94-564; Senate Report 94-1148, pg. 5967; Reorganization Plan No. 26; Public Law 102-391), and in fact were incorporated in Delaware in 1933. It is pointed out that all official Federal Government mail is sent postage-free because of the franking privilege, however, the IRS has to pay their own postage, which indicates that they are not a government entity. They are in fact a collection agency for the Federal Reserve, because they do not collect any taxes for the U.S. Treasury. All funds collected are turned over to the Federal Reserve. If you have ever sent a check to the IRS, you will find that it was endorsed over to the Federal Reserve. The Federal Reserve, in turn, deposits the money with the International Monetary Fund, an agency of the United Nations (Black's Law Dictionary, 6th edition, pg. 816), where it is filtered down to the International Development Association (see Treasury Delegation Order No. 91), which is part of the International Bank for Reconstruction and Development, commonly known as the World Bank. Therefore, it is now clear, that the American people are unknowingly contributing to the coming World Government.

The Secretary of the Treasury is the "Governor" of the International Monetary Fund (Public Law 94-564, supra, pg. 5942; U.S. Government Manual 1990/91, pgs. 480-81; 26 U.S.C.A. 7701(a)(11); Treasury Delegation Order No. 150-10); the United States has not had a Treasury since 1921 (41 Stat. Ch. 214, pg. 654); and for all intents and purposes the U.S. Treasury is the IMF (Presidential Documents, Volume 29, No. 4, pg. 113; 22 U.S.C. 285-288).

Chief Justice John Marshall said: "The power to tax involves the power to destroy." Alan Keyes, the former ambassador to the UN, who ran for President in 2000 said:

> "We ought to have realized that the income tax is utterly incompatible with liberty. It is actually a form of slavery. A slave is someone the fruit of whose labor is controlled by somebody else. A slave is not somebody with nothing. Rather, he has only what the master lets him have ... Under the income tax, the government takes whatever percentage of the earner's income it wants. The income tax, therefore, represents our national surrender to the government of control over all the money we earn. There are, in principle, no restrictions to the pre-emptive claim the government has."

The income tax was intended to rob the earnings of the low and middle class; or as the saying goes, "the more you make, the more they take." However, the tax didn't touch the huge fortunes of Illuminati members. The tax was an indication that the U.S. was heading for a planned war, because they couldn't go into a war without money. Since the tax provided less than 5% of total Federal revenues, increases were later made to accommodate World War I, FDR's New Deal, and World War II. In July, 1943, workers in this country were subject to a payroll withholding tax in the form of a "victory tax" that was touted as a temporary tax to boost the economy because of the War, and would later be discontinued. However, the deduction remained because it forced compliance.

FOUNDATIONS

Under the guise of philanthropy, the Illuminati avoided taxation by transferring their wealth to tax-free foundations.

Foundations are either state or federally chartered. The first was chartered by Benjamin Franklin in 1790, in Philadelphia and Boston, from a $4,444.49 fund, to make loans "to young married artificers (artisans) of good character." In 1800, the Magdalen Society was established in Philadelphia, "to ameliorate that distressed condition of those unhappy females who have been seduced from the paths of virtue, and are desirous of returning to a life of rectitude." In 1846, the Smithsonian Institution was established by the bequest of English scientist James Smithson "for the increase and diffusion of knowledge among men." The Peabody Education Fund was initiated in 1867 by banker George Peabody, to promote education in the South.

Before 1900, there were only 18 foundations; from 1910-19, there were 76; during the 1920's, 173; the 1930's, 288; the 1940's, 1,638; and during the 1950's, there were 2,839 foundations.

United Press International (UPI) reported on July 19, 1969, that the top 596 foundations had an income that was twice the net earnings of the country's 50 largest commercial banking institutions.

According to Rep. Wright Patman, in a report to the 87th Congress, it is because of the existence of foundations, that "only one-third of the income of the nation is actually taxed."

Some of the important foundations are: Ford Foundation (Ford Motor Co.), Rockefeller Foundation (Standard Oil), Duke Endowment (Duke family fortune), John A. Hartford Foundation (Great Atlantic and Pacific Tea), W. K. Kellogg Foundation (the Kellogg Cereals), Carnegie Corp. (Carnegie Steel), Alfred P. Sloan Foundation (General Motors), Moody Foundation (W. L. Moody's oil, realty, newspapers, and bank holdings), Lilly Endowment (Eli Lilly Pharmaceuticals), Pew Memorial Trust (Sun Oil Co. or Sunoco), and the Danforth Foundation (Purina Cereals), which all have assets of well over $100 million.

The first Congressional Committee to investigate the tax-free foundations was the Cox Committee in 1952, led by Rep. Eugene E. Cox, a Democrat from Georgia. Its purpose was to find out which "foundations and organizations are using their resources for purposes other than the purposes for which they were established, and especially to determine which such foundations and organizations are using their resources for un-American and subversive activities or for purposes not in the interest of tradition of the United States."

Cox discovered that officers and trustees of some foundations were Communists, and that these foundations had given grants to Communists or Communist-controlled organizations. A former Communist official, Maurice Malkin, testified that in 1919 they were trying "to penetrate these organizations (foundations), if necessary take control of them and their treasuries ... that they should be able to finance the Communist Party propaganda in the United States." During the investigation, Cox died, and the facts were glossed over in a cover-up.

Another member of the Committee, Rep. Carroll Reece of Tennessee, the former Chairman of the Republican National Committee, forced another investigation in 1953, to see if foundations were being used "for political purposes, propaganda, or attempts to influence legislation." *The Washington Post* called the investigation "unnecessary," and that it was "stupidly wasteful of public funds." Reece even referred to a "conspiracy."

The Eisenhower Administration was clearly against the probe. Three of the four who were selected for the Committee, with Reece, were House members who had voted against the investigation. Rep. Wayne Hays of Ohio worked from the inside to stall the investigation. During one 3-hour session, he interrupted the same witness 246 times. He prohibited evidence discovered by two of its investigators from being used. Rene A. Wormser, legal counsel to the Committee, revealed why, in his 1958 book *Foundations: Their Power and Influence*: "Mr. Hays told us one day that 'the White House' had been in touch with him and asked him if he would cooperate to kill the Committee." Wormser also revealed that the Committee had discovered that these foundations were using their wealth to attack the basic structure of our Constitution and Judeo-Christian ethics; and that the influence of major foundations had "reached far into government, into the policy-making circles of Congress and into the State Department."

Reece's Special Committee to Investigate Tax Exempt Foundations discovered that many foundations were financing civil rights groups, liberal political groups, political extremist groups, and supporting revolutionary activities throughout the world. The Committee reported:

> "Substantial evidence indicates there is more than a mere close working together among some foundations operating in the international field. There is here, as in the general realm of social sciences, a close interlock. The Carnegie Corporation, the Carnegie Endowment for International Peace, the Rockefeller Foundation and, recently, the Ford Foundation, joined by some others, have commonly cross-financed, to a tune of many millions ... organizations concerned with internationalists, among them, the Institute of Pacific Relations, the Foreign Policy Association (which was "virtually a creature of the Carnegie Endowment"), the Council on Foreign Relations, the Royal Institute of International Affairs and others ... and that it happened by sheer coincidence stretches credulity."

On August 19, 1954, Reece summed up his investigation: "It has been said that the foundations are a power second only to that of the Federal Government itself ... Perhaps the Congress should now admit that the foundations have become more powerful, in some areas, at least, than the legislative branch of the Government." The investigation ended in 1955, when funding was withheld.

The Rockefeller Foundation

The Rockefeller Family

John Davison Rockefeller, Sr. (1839-1937)
|
John Davison Rockefeller, Jr. (1874-1960)
|
John Davison Rockefeller, III (1906-78)
Nelson Rockefeller (1908-79)

Laurance Rockefeller (1910-)
Winthrop Rockefeller (1912-73)
David Rockefeller (1915-)

John Davison Rockefeller (1839-1937), grandfather of former Vice-President Nelson Aldrich Rockefeller, and David Rockefeller (head of the Chase Manhattan Bank) was the richest man of his time. He started out in 1859 as a produce merchant, turning to oil in 1865, at the age of 26. In 1870, when Standard Oil of Ohio was incorporated, Rockefeller controlled 21 out of 26 refineries in Cleveland. By 1871, Standard Oil was the largest refining company in the world. In 1879, he controlled over 90% of all refined oil sold in the country, with 20,000 producing wells, and 100,000 employees. In 1884, he moved his main office to New York City; and by 1885, Standard Oil virtually controlled the entire oil industry in the United States, and had set up branches in Western Europe and China.

The Rockefellers and Rothschilds have been partners ever since the 1880's, when Rockefeller was able to get a rebate on each barrel of oil he shipped over the Pennsylvania, Baltimore and Ohio railroads, which were owned by Kuhn, Loeb and Co.

In 1888, details concerning the Rockefeller Oil Trust began to leak out in the newspapers. In Ohio, at the time, a company within the state could not own stock in a company in another state, which occurred when Rockefeller bought out smaller companies. Using the secret Trust, which was established in 1879, the trustees for the companies that had been taken over, the 37 Standard Oil stockholders, and Standard Oil of Ohio, relayed all out-of-state subsidiary stock to three clerks from Standard Oil. In 1882, the three "dummy" trustees, 42 Standard Oil stockholders, and Standard Oil of Ohio, transferred all its stock to nine trustees, who were controlled by Rockefeller. In March, 1892, the Ohio Supreme Court ordered Standard Oil to withdraw from the Trust, after Ohio and other states outlawed trusts. Rockefeller countered by moving Standard Oil to New Jersey, who allowed their corporations to hold stock in out-of-state companies, thus, Standard Oil of New Jersey became that holding Company.

In 1889, Rockefeller helped establish, with a grant of $600,000, the University of Chicago. He promised to support the school for ten years, which he did, donating $34,708,375. In 1901, he incorporated the Rockefeller Institute for Medical Research (now Rockefeller University), with a grant of $200,000. In 1903, he established the Rockefeller General Education Board, which he donated $42 million to, within a two-year period (and $129 million in total). The Board was organized by Fred Gates, the front man for the Pillsbury flour company. In 1909, the Rockefeller Sanitation Commission was established, to which he gave $1 million.

Rockefeller's goal was for Standard Oil to be the world's only refining company, and to that end, it was alleged that he blew up a competitor's refinery in Buffalo, New York. He owned large blocks of stock in quite a few newspapers, including the *Buffalo People's Journal*, the *Oil City Derrick* (in Pennsylvania), the *Cleveland Herald*, and the *Cleveland News Leader*. He had contracts with over 100 newspapers in Ohio, to print news releases and editorials furnished by a Standard Oil-controlled agency, in return for advertisement.

He 'owned' several New Jersey and Ohio state legislators. Rep. Joseph Sibley, of Pennsylvania, was President of the Rockefeller-controlled Galena Signal Oil

Co.; and in 1898, Rep. John P. Elkins, also of Pennsylvania, accepted a $5,000 bribe from Standard Oil. In 1904, Sen. Bois Penrose of Pennsylvania received a $25,000 bribe from Rockefeller, and Sen. Cornelius Bliss received $100,000. Others who received Standard Oil bribes: Sen. Matthew Quay (PA), Sen. Joseph B. Foraker (OH), Sen. Joseph Bailey (TX), Sen. Nathan B. Scott, Sen. Mark Hanna (OH), Sen. Stephen B. Elkins (WV), Rep. W. C. Stone (PA), and Sen. McLaurin (SC). President William McKinley, through Sen. Mark Hanna, was a pawn of Standard Oil and the bankers.

The 'rebates' Rockefeller received from various railroads, were actually kickbacks. These rebates made it possible for him to keep his prices lower so he could bankrupt his competition. He said: "Competition is a sin." Standard Oil also made kickbacks, in the form of stock, to railroad people, such as William H. Vanderbilt, who received stock without contributing any capital, as did various bankers who lent money freely to Standard Oil.

Willie Winkfield, a Rockefeller messenger, sold evidence of Rockefeller's bribery to William Randolph Hearst's *New York American*, for $20,500, and Hearst revealed the information at election time, in an attempt to get the Rockefeller stooges out of office. In 1905, an exposé by Ida M. Tarbell, called *The History of Standard Oil Co.*, which came on the heels of an 1894 book by Henry Demarest Lloyd, called *Wealth Against Commonwealth*, began to turn public opinion against Standard Oil.

Robert M. LaFollette, Sr., in a speech to the Senate in March, 1908, said that fewer than 100 men controlled the business interests of the country. However, a few years later, through an analysis of the Directory of Directors, it was discovered that through interlocking directorates, less than a dozen men controlled the country's business interests. Most notable were Rockefeller and Morgan. On December 13, 1911, George M. Reynolds of the Continental and Commercial Bank of Chicago, said to a group of other bankers: "I believe the money power now lies in the hands of a dozen men."

In March, 1910, Sen. Nelson Aldrich of Rhode Island, introduced a Bill of Incorporation for the Rockefeller Foundation, but it came at a time when there was an antitrust suit against Standard Oil, and the Bill was withdrawn. On May 15, 1911, Standard Oil was found to be in violation of the Sherman Antitrust Act of 1890, and the U.S. Supreme Court ordered, in a 20,000 word decision, the breakup of Standard Oil of New Jersey. The Court said that Standard Oil wanted to establish a monopoly in order "to drive others from the field and exclude them from their right to trade," and that "seven men and a corporate machine have conspired against their fellow citizens. For the safety of the Republic, we now decree that the dangerous conspiracy must be ended..."

Standard Oil was forced to dissolve into 38 separate companies, including Standard Oil of Indiana (Amoco), Standard Oil of Ohio (Sohio), Standard Oil of Louisiana, Standard Oil of New Jersey (Exxon, which is one of the largest corporations in the world, controlling 321 other companies, including Humble Oil and Venezuela's Creole Oil), Standard Oil of New York (Socony or Mobil); and others such as Continental Oil (Conoco), Atlantic-Richfield (Arco), Gulf, Phillips 66, Texaco, and Marathon Oil, which were also Rockefeller-controlled companies. Rockefeller owned 25% of Standard Oil of New Jersey, which meant that he now owned 25% of all 38 Standard Oil subsidiaries. In 1914, the *Congressional Record* referred to Standard Oil as the "shadow government" and as the extent of its holdings became known, its value tripled.

In May, 1913, after three years of Congressional opposition, the New York State Legislature voted to establish the Rockefeller Foundation (which was located in the *Time-Life* Building), "to promote the well-being of mankind throughout the world." However, a 1946 report stated that the "challenge of the future is to make this one world." The endowment to establish the Foundation totaled $182,851,000, and was given in securities, enabling the foundation to disperse over $1 billion, even though it is only third in total assets compared to the Ford and Johnson Foundations.

In 1899, with an estimated wealth of $200,000,000, Rockefeller "retired." But, only in regard to being involved in the day-to-day operation of the company. He didn't officially retire until 1911, when he resigned as President of Standard Oil. He had become America's first billionaire, yet when he died, he only left a taxable estate of $26,410,837.10, which after Federal and State taxes were levied, left about $16 million. The remainder of his fortune had been left to surviving relatives ($240 million), his sons ($465 million), and his foundations.

Rockefeller, said to own 20% of American industry, between 1855 and his death in 1937, gave away nearly $550 million. In 1855, when he was 16, he gave $2.77 of his meager earnings to charity, 1856 ($19.31), 1857 ($28.37), 1858 ($43.85), 1859 ($72.22), 1860 ($107.35), 1861 ($259.97), 1865 ($1,012), 1869 ($5,000), 1871 ($6,860), 1879 ($29,000), 1880 ($32,865), 1884 ($119,000), 1891 ($500,000), 1892 ($1,500,000), 1893 ($1,472,122), 1907 ($39,170,480), 1909 ($71,453,231), 1913 ($45,499,367), 1914 ($67,627,095), and 1919 ($138,624,574). He gave $182,851,480 to the Rockefeller Foundation, $129,209,167 to the General Education Board, $73,985,313 to the Laura Spelman and Rockefeller Memorial Fund, and $60,673,409 to the Rockefeller Institute for Medical Research.

John D. Rockefeller, Jr. (1874-1960), who was married to Abby Aldrich, daughter of Sen. Nelson Aldrich, according to a February, 1905 *McClure's* magazine article, was part of a corrupt political machine. He continued the charitable tradition of his father. He spent over $40 million to buy up land and convert it to National Parks, donating it to the public. The most prominent of these parks is the Jackson Hole Preserve at the Grand Teton National Park in northeastern Wyoming. In 1926, he reconstructed the colonial town of Williamsburg, Virginia, spending $52.6 million to restore 81 colonial buildings, and rebuild 404 others from original plans, on their original foundations. Over 700 modern homes were torn down in the 83 acre area to bring the 18th century town back to life. He also built 45 other buildings, including three hotels to serve the public, and planted gardens.

In 1929, he began building the Rockefeller Center in New York City, a complex of 14 buildings, at a cost of $125 million, which was to surpass the stature of the Dupont's Empire State Building. The Rockefeller empire is run from the 55th and 56th floors of the RCA building, at 30 Rockefeller Plaza.

Rockefeller was quoted to have said: "So it may come to pass that someday ... no one will speak of 'my country,' but all will speak of 'our world'."

He pushed his sons into five different areas of influence: John III, into philanthropy; Nelson, into government (4-term Governor of New York, and Vice-President under Ford); Laurance, into business; Winthrop, into oil (also 2-term Governor of Arkansas); and David, into banking (Chairman of the Chase Manhattan Bank and Director of the Federal Reserve Bank of New York).

The Rockefellers, undeniably the richest family in America, increased their fortune by marrying into other wealthy and influential families. By 1937, there existed "an almost unbroken line of biological relationships from the Rockefellers through one-half of the wealthiest sixty families in the nation."

Percy Rockefeller (John, Jr.'s cousin), married Isabel Stillman, daughter of James A. Stillman, President of National City Bank, and William G. Rockefeller (another cousin), married S. Elsie Stillman.

Ethel Geraldine Rockefeller married Marcellus Hartley Dodge, which linked Standard Oil and National City Bank, to the $50,000,000 fortune of the Remington Arms Company and the Phelps Dodge Corp.

J. Stillman Rockefeller (grand nephew of John, Sr.) married Nancy C. S. Carnegie, the grand niece of Andrew Carnegie. Their son was named Andrew Carnegie Rockefeller.

Edith Rockefeller (John, Jr.'s sister), married Harold F. McCormick, an heir to the International Harvester Co. fortune. Their son, Fowler, grandson to John, Sr. and Cyrus McCormick (who invented the Reaper), married Fifi Stillman, the divorced wife of James Stillman.

Nelson Aldrich Rockefeller, was married to Mary Todhunter Clark, the granddaughter of the President of the Pennsylvania Railroad. They were later divorced.

Winthrop Rockefeller married Jeanette Edris, a hotel and theater heiress; and John (Jay) D. Rockefeller IV (one of John, Jr.'s grandsons), the family's only Democrat (2-term Governor, and later U.S. Senator, of West Virginia), married Sharon Percy, the daughter of Sen. Charles Percy, who had been one of the Senate's most influential members.

All together, the Rockefeller family had been joined in marriage to the Stillman, Dodge, McAlpin, McCormick, Carnegie, and Aldrich family fortunes, and its wealth has been estimated to be well over $2 billion. Some estimates even claim it to be as high as $20 billion. To compare, John Paul Getty, Howard Hughes, and H. L. Hunt, had fortunes between $2-$4 billion; and the Duponts and Mellons had fortunes between $3-$5 billion.

Ever since the TNEC hearings in 1937, which convened for the purpose of finding out who was controlling the American economy, the Rockefellers had been able to avoid any sort of accounting in regard to their vast assets and holdings. That ended in December, 1974, when Nelson Rockefeller was nominated to be Vice-President. Two University of California professors, Charles Schwartz and William Domhoff, circulated a report called "Probing the Rockefeller Fortune" which indicated that 15 employees working out of room 5600 of the RCA building had positions on the boards of almost 100 corporations that had total assets of $70 billion. This was denied by the family, and in an unprecedented event, a family spokesman, J. Richardson Dilworth, appeared before the U.S. House of Representatives' Judiciary Committee during the 1975 'Hearings into the Nomination of Nelson Rockefeller to be Vice-President of the United States' to document the family's wealth, which he said only amounted to $1.3 billion.

Part of the Rockefeller's financial holdings consists of real estate, foremost being the 4,180 acre family estate at Pocantico Hills, north of New York City, which has 70 miles of private roads, 75 buildings, an underground archives, and close to 500 servants, guards, gardeners and chauffeurs. They also maintain over 100 residences in all parts of the world. Besides investments held in personal trusts, the family also holds stock in numerous companies.

Some of their major holdings: Chase Manhattan Bank, American Telephone & Telegraph (AT & T), Eastman Kodak, IBM, General Electric, Texas Instruments, Xerox, Minnesota Mining and Manufacturing, Monsanto Chemical, Aluminum Co. of America (Alcoa), Armour, Bethlehem Steel, Chrysler, DuPont, General Motors, International Paper, Polaroid, Sears and Roebuck, Standard Oil of California (Chevron), Standard Oil of New York (Mobil), Standard Oil of Indiana, U.S. Steel, International Basic Economy Corp., International Harvester, Quaker Oats, Wheeling-Pittsburgh Steel, Itek, Federated Department Stores, Walgreen Stores, Transcontinental Gas Pipeline, Consolidated Edison, Anaconda Copper Co., General Foods, Pan American World Airways, Colgate-Palmolive, E. I. du Pont de Nemours, W. R. Grace, Inc., Corning Glass Works, Owens Corning Fiberglass, Cummins Engine, Hewlett-Packard, R. R. Donnelly and Son, Dow Chemical, Teledyne, Inc., Warner-Lambert, Westinghouse, International Telephone and Telegraph (IT & T), Motorola, S. S. Kresge, Texaco, National Cash Register, Avon, American Home Products, Delta Airlines, Braniff Airlines, Northwest Airlines, United Airlines, and Burlington Industries.

The financial core of the family fortune included the Chase Manhattan Bank, Citicorp (which grew out of the Rockefeller-controlled First National City Bank), the Chemical Bank of New York, First National Bank of Chicago, Metropolitan Equitable, and New York Mutual Life Insurance. By the 1970's, Rockefeller-controlled banks accounted for about 25% of all assets of the 50 largest commercial banks in the country, and about 30% of all assets of the 50 largest life insurance companies.

The Chase Manhattan Bank, however, remains the supreme symbol of Rockefeller domination. Founded in 1877 by John Thompson, the Chase National Bank was named after Salomon P. Chase (Lincoln's Secretary of Treasury). It was taken over by the Rockefellers in a merger with their Equitable Trust Co., whose President was Winthrop Aldrich, son of Sen. Nelson Aldrich. In 1955, it merged with the Bank of Manhattan (which had been controlled by Warburg; and Kuhn, Loeb and Co), the oldest banking operation in America (founded in 1799 by Alexander Hamilton and Aaron Burr), which had 67 branches in New York, and $1.6 billion in assets. Although it was only the sixth largest bank (over $98,000,000 in assets), it was the most powerful.

In 1961, the Chase Manhattan Bank Plaza was built in downtown Manhattan, at a cost of $125,000,000. It is 64 stories high, with five basement floors, the lowest of which contains the largest bank vault in the world.

They had 28 foreign branches, and over 50,000 banking offices in more than 50 countries, and had a controlling interest in many of the largest corporations in America. Some of those that were listed in the *Patman Report*: American National Bank and Trust, Safeway Stores, Reynolds Metals, White Cross Stores, J. C. Penney, Northwest Airlines, Eastern Airlines, TWA, Pan American World Airways, Western Airlines, Consolidated Freightways, Roadway Express, Ryder, Wyandotte

Chemicals, Armstrong Rubber, A. H. Robins, G. D. Searle, Sunbeam, Beckman Instruments, Texas Instruments, Sperry Rand, Boeing, Diebold, Cummins Engine, Bausch and Lomb, CBS-TV, International Basic Economy Corp., Addressograph-Multigraph, Aetna Life, American General Insurance Co., Allegheny-Ludlum Steel, National Steel.

Men from the Chase Manhattan's Board of Directors have also sat on the Boards of many of the largest corporations, which have created a system of interlocking directorates. Some of these have been: Allegheny-Ludlum Steel, U.S. Steel, Metropolitan Life, Travelers Insurance, Continental Insurance, Equitable Life Assurance, General Foods, Chrysler Corp., Standard Oil of Indiana, *New York Times*, Cummins Engine, Burlington Industries, ABC-TV, Standard Oil of New Jersey, R. J. Reynolds Tobacco, Scott Paper, International Paper, International Basic Economy Corp., International Telephone & Telegraph, Goodyear Tire & Rubber, Anaconda Copper, Allied Stores, Federated Department Stores, R. H. Macy, Colgate-Palmolive, Bell Telephone of Pennsylvania, Consolidated Edison of New York, DuPont, Monsanto, Borden, Shell Oil, Gulf Oil, Union Oil, Dow Chemical, Continental Oil, Union Carbide, and S. S. Kresge.

Chase also owned or controlled the Banco del Commerce (with over 100 branches in Columbia and Peru), Banco Continental (with about 40 branches in Peru), Banco Atlantida (with 20 branches in the Honduras), Nederlandsche Crediet (with over 60 branches in the Netherlands), and Standard Bank Group (with over 1,200 branches in 17 African countries).

Through a subsidiary, the Chase Investment Corp., they owned a sheep and cattle raising operation in Australia, hotels in Puerto Rico and Liberia, a ready-mix concrete facility in Brazil, a cotton textile mill in Nigeria, a paint factory in Venezuela, a steel mill in Turkey, a petrochemical plant in Argentina, a bus line in the Virgin Islands, and bowling alleys in England.

Our tax dollars, through the Export-Import Bank, International Monetary Fund, Cooperation for Overseas Investment, and the International Stabilization Fund, are used to give aid to other countries, some who were communist. Millions of dollars were given to Yugoslavia, including hundreds of jets, many of which ended up being given to Castro in Cuba.

Chase, and the Export-Import Bank financed 90% of the $2 billion loan to build the Kama River truck complex in Russia, which was equipped with the world's largest industrial computer system, with the capability of producing up to 200,000 ten-ton trucks a year. A U.S. Government official who toured the facility, reported that V-12 diesel engines were being produced there, and said: "There is only one vehicle in Russia that uses that type of engine, and that's a Russian battle tank." Besides the production of trucks, they also have the capability of producing jeeps, military transports and rocket launchers. The repayment period for the loan was twelve years, with a 4-1/2 year grace period. The loan repayment was guaranteed by the U.S. taxpayers through government agencies like the Overseas Private Investment Corp., and the Foreign Credit Insurance Association.

Chase Manhattan and the Bank of America lent about $36 million for the Bechtel Corp. to build and equip an international Trade Center in Moscow, which had been arranged by Armand Hammer of Occidental Petroleum, a personal friend of Lenin, and son of one of the founders of the U.S. Communist Party.

The Export-Import Bank, and other private American banks also put up all but $40 million for a $400 million fertilizer plant in Russia.

In 1967, the International Basic Economy Corp. (with 140 subsidiaries and affiliates), owned by all five Rockefeller Brothers, run by Richard Aldrich (grandson of Sen. Nelson Aldrich), and Rodman Rockefeller (son of Nelson Rockefeller, and a CFR member); and Tower International, Inc., headed by Cyrus S. Eaton, Jr., a Cleveland financier (who was the son of a man who started his career as secretary to John D. Rockefeller, later making his own fortune), joined to promote trade among the Iron Curtain countries. In 1969 the IBEC announced that N. M. Rothschild and Sons of London had become a partner. This partnership built a $50 million aluminum production center in Russia, and announced a multi-million plan for Russia and other Eastern European countries, which included the building of large hotels in Bucharest, Sofia, Budapest, Belgrade, Prague, and Warsaw; rubber plants, and a glass plant in Romania. In addition, Tower International made an agreement with the Soviet patent and licensing organization, Licensintorg, to promote Soviet-American trade, which up to that time, was done by Amtorg Trading Corp., the official Soviet agency in America. This gave the Rockefellers and Eatons complete control over what technology was sent to Russia.

David Rockefeller, the head of the Chase Manhattan, and the family patriarch, controls many secondary interlocks which contribute to the family's power and influence. Some of these have been: Firestone Tire & Rubber Co., Honeywell, Inc., Northwest Airlines, Minnesota Mining and Manufacturing Co., Allied Chemical Corp., General Motors, Chrysler Corp., International Basic Economy Corp., R. H. Macy and Co., Mutual Benefit Life Insurance Co. of New York, American Express Co., Hewlett-Packard, Exxon, Equitable Life Assurance Society of the U.S., Federated Department Stores, General Electric, Scott Paper, AT & T, Burlington Industries, Wachovia Corp., R. J. Reynolds Industries, U.S. Steel Corp., Metropolitan Life Insurance Co., May Department Stores, Sperry Rand Corp., and Standard Oil of Indiana.

On July 9, 1968, the *New York Times* reported on a study by a House Banking Subcommittee, headed by Rep. Wright Patman of Texas, which said: "A few banking institutions are in a position to exercise significant influence, and perhaps even control, over some of the largest business enterprises in the nation." Just as the Rockefellers have these extensive interlocking connections, other leading bankers, the other 107 directors of the 12 Federal Reserve Banks, and members of the Council on Foreign Relations, Trilateral Commission, and Bilderbergers, also have similar connections to these and hundreds of other major corporations. Now you can see how these like-minded individuals have been able to control American industry and business.

Though the Rockefeller Foundation is the primary foundation of the family, there are many others operated by them, such as the Rockefeller Family Fund, Rockefeller Brothers Fund, Martha Baird Rockefeller Fund for Music, Laura Spelman Rockefeller Memorial Fund, John D. Rockefeller III Fund, Rockefeller Institute, Standard Oil (Indiana) Foundation, Esso Education Foundation, American International Foundation for Economic and Social Development, China Medical Board, Agricultural Development Council, Government Affairs Foundation, Sealantic Fund (oversees contributions to religious charities "to strengthen and develop Protestant education" to which John Rockefeller, Jr. contributed $23 million), Jackson Preserve, Inc., Council on Economic and Cultural Development, and the Chase Manhattan Bank Foundation. There are some who believe that the Rockefellers may run close to 200 trusts and foundations.

Prior to their appointments, Cyrus Vance (Secretary of State under Carter) and Dean Rusk (Secretary of State under Kennedy) were both Presidents of the Rockefeller Foundation.

You have seen how powerful the Rockefeller family is, now let's look at how the Rockefeller Foundation has used its money.

Through interlocking directorates, the Foundation controls the Carnegie Endowment, and the Ford Foundation. While the Carnegie Endowment deals with education, as it relates to international matters; the Rockefeller Foundation concentrates on education, as it relates to domestic issues. It financed and influenced seven major policy-making agencies: Social Science Research Council (who explored the means of controlling people through scientific methods, such as mass media), Russian Institute of Columbia University (who developed methods of conditioning Americans into accepting a merging of the Soviet Union and America under a one-world government), Council on Foreign Relations, National Bureau of Economic Research (who worked closely with the Federal Reserve Board), Public Administration Clearing House (in Chicago), Brookings Institution, and the Institute of Pacific Relations (who was responsible for planning the communist subversion of America).

The Rockefeller Foundation provided over $50,000 to fund the Building America textbook series, which played up Marxism, and sought to destroy "traditional concepts of American government." Over 100 communist organizations contributed material, including the writings of over 50 communist writers. The California Legislature said that the books contained "purposely distorted references favoring Communism..." The Foundation contributed money to the pro-communist New School for Social Research in New York City, and funded projects for the communist-staffed Southern Christian Leadership Conference, led by Rev. Martin Luther King, Jr. Rep. Cox said that the Rockefeller Foundation has "been used to finance individuals and organizations whose business it has been to get communism into private and public schools of the country, to talk down to America, and play up Russia..." The Foundation also funded the *Kinsey Report*, which heralded a new era of sexual immorality.

The purpose of the Rockefeller Brothers Fund, is the "support of efforts in the U.S. and abroad that contribute ideas, develop leaders, and encourage institutions in the transition to global interdependence." In 1974, the Rockefeller Brothers Fund gave grants to: A.C.L.U. Foundation ($45,000); Atlantic Institute for International Affairs, in Paris ($10,000); Carnegie Endowment for International Peace ($60,000); Columbia University ($9,500); Council on Foreign Relations ($125,000), Foreign Policy Association ($20,000); International Institute for Strategic Studies, in London ($5000); NAACP ($145,000); National Council of Churches of Christ in the U.S.A. ($10,000); National Urban League ($100,000); Trilateral Commission ($50,000); U.N. Association of the U.S.A., Inc. ($25,000); United Negro College Fund, Inc. ($10,000); and the U.S. Conference for the World Council of Churches, Inc. ($2,500).

The Carnegie Endowment

Andrew Carnegie (1835-1919) came to the United States as a poor immigrant from Scotland in 1848, and never became an American citizen. He built the Carnegie Steel Corporation, which he sold to J. P. Morgan for $500 million, who incorporated the company into the United States Steel Corporation in 1901, enabling Carnegie to retire and concentrate on his philanthropic activities.

In 1889, William Torrey Harris, the U.S. Commissioner of Education, told a high-ranking railroad official that the schools were being scientifically designed not to overeducate children. He believed that the schools should alienate children from their parents and religion. In 1890, Carnegie wrote eleven essays which were published under the title *The Gospel of Wealth*. The underlying premise was that the free-enterprise system had been locked-up by men such as himself, J.P. Morgan, and John D. Rockefeller, and that they not only owned everything, but also controlled the government. His worry, was that subsequent generations would realize this, and work against them. His solution was to control the education system, and to create a direct relationship between the amount of education a person had, and how good of a job they could get. Therefore, this created a motivation for children to attend school, where they would be taught only what the social engineers of this country wanted them to know.

This was to be accomplished by instituting the educational system developed by Prussia between 1808 and 1819. German Philosopher Johann Gottlieb Fichte (1762-1814) in his "Addresses to the German Nation" (1807-08) said that he did not trust parental influence and preferred education to be carried out in a "separate and independent" environment controlled by the state. Prussia became the first government to have compulsory education, setting up a three-tiered system. The children of the elite, about one-half of one percent, went to schools called academies, and were taught to think and be independent. About 5-1/2% went to Realschulen, where they were partially taught how to think. The other 94% went to Volkschulen, where the idea of being a follower and a good citizen was stressed.

This system of education was brought to the United States through the effort of a coalition of big business led by Carnegie, J.P. Morgan, and Rockefeller; major universities like Columbia, Johns Hopkins, the University of Wisconsin, the University of Michigan, and the University of Chicago; and large foundations like Carnegie, Rockefeller, Ford, Mellon, Peabody, Sage, and Whitney. The success in creating an organized compulsory educational system in this country has allowed the elite of this country to prevent each generation from truly understanding how this country is actually run, thus keeping them from doing anything about it. This 'dumbing-down' has enabled the government to more easily assimilate the people of this country into a population which can be easily deceived and controlled.

John Dewey, known as the "Father of American Education," was a Socialist, and a founding member of the Intercollegiate Socialist Society (who changed their name to League for Industrial Democracy, which he became the President of), and one of the 34 signers of the *Humanist Manifesto* in 1933. In his *My Pedagogic Creed* (1897) and *The School and Society* (1899), he expressed his belief at how the schools should be instrumental in developing a socialist society in America."

His system of 'progressive education' would deemphasize academics, and use psychology to do that. The July, 1908 *Hibbert Journal* quoted him as saying: "Our schools ... are performing an infinite significant religious work. They are promoting the social unity out of which in the end genuine religious unity must grow."

With a grant of $27,000,000, Carnegie established the Carnegie Institute of Technology in Pittsburgh, in 1900, which became the Carnegie-Mellon University in 1967, when it merged with the Mellon Institute, which had been founded in 1913. In 1905, he established the Carnegie Foundation for the Advancement of Teaching, which, within a 20 year period, gave over $20 million to retiring teachers (and widows) at universities and technical schools in the United States and Canada to support the profession and encourage higher education. In 1904, in the U.S., and 1908 in the United Kingdom, he set up the Carnegie Hero Fund to reward heroic deeds by civilian citizens, and gave out close to $500,000,000. He also established the world renowned Carnegie Hall, and over 2,000 public libraries. He was also a major supporter of the Tuskogee Institute in Alabama, which was founded by Booker T. Washington.

The Carnegie Endowment for International Peace was established in 1910, to promote international peace and bring about the abolition of war; and the Carnegie Corporation of New York in 1911 (with a grant of $125,000,000), was set up "to promote the advancement and diffusion of knowledge and understanding among the people of the United States by aiding technical schools, institutions of higher learning, libraries, scientific research, hero funds, useful publications, and by such other agencies and means as shall time to time be found appropriate therefore."

With such a history of philanthropic contributions, the Carnegie Endowment, on its face, appeared to be innocent. However, its goal of promoting international peace, was just a ruse to disguise its true purpose to promote one-world government.

The first three Presidents of the group were: Elihu Root, socialist and former Secretary of State under President Theodore Roosevelt, who was a leading advocate of the League of Nations; he was succeeded in 1925 by Nicholas Murray Butler, the former President of Columbia University; and then Alger Hiss, the communist who helped found the United Nations. Their President during the 1960's, was Joseph E. Johnson (a member of the CFR), a close friend of Hiss, who was known as the "permanent unofficial Secretary of State." He worked closely with the Donner Foundation, which financed the Temple of Understanding, an occult organization connected to the Lucis Trust in England (a group of Satan worshipers with ties to the Theosophical Society). Members of the Temple met at the Endowment headquarters in the United Nations Plaza. Among their members: Robert McNamara (Secretary of Defense under Kennedy and Johnson), Eleanor Roosevelt, Thomas Watson (President of IBM), Max Lerner, James Linen (of *Time-Life*), Norman Thomas, James A. Pike, Ellsworth Bunker, and John D. Rockefeller IV.

The 1934 Yearbook of the Carnegie Endowment, said that they were "an unofficial instrument of international policy, taking up here and there the ends of international problems and questions which the governments find it difficult to handle, and ... reaching conclusions ... which officially find their way into the policies of government."

The 1947 Yearbook recommended:

"...that the Endowment work for the establishment of the United Nations headquarters in New York ... that the Endowment construct its programs primarily for the support of the United Nations ... that the Endowment's programs should be broadly educational in order to encourage public understanding and support of the United Nations at home and abroad ... that Endowment supported organizations such as International Relations Clubs in colleges, the Foreign Policy Association, the Institute of Pacific Relations, the Council on Foreign Relations, and local community groups be utilized to achieve these goals, of achieving broader understanding and support for the United Nations."

The Carnegie Endowment and Rockefeller Foundation gave over $3,000,000 to the Institute of Pacific Relations, who used the media to convince the American people that the Communists in China were agricultural reformers. The Endowment has also given money to the Council on Foreign Relations, the Aspen Institute for Humanistic Studies, the United Nations Association of the U.S., and the American Civil Liberties Union Foundation.

Norman Dodd, who in July, 1953, was appointed as the research director of the Special Congressional Committee to Investigate Tax-Exempt Foundations, said he discovered that the oldest tax exempt foundations were established before the initiation of income taxes, therefore they existed for a different purpose. He examined minutes of the Board of Trustees, and found that for the first year, the members concentrated on whether there was any means more effective than war to alter the life of the people of a nation. They concluded that to get America into an upcoming war, they had to control the diplomatic machinery of the State Department.

Dodd discovered that all high-level appointments in the State Department took place only after they had been cleared through a group called the Council of Learned Societies, which was established by the Carnegie Endowment. He saw in the minutes of the Carnegie Board, record of a note to President Wilson, requesting that he "see to it that the War does not end too quickly."

Syndicated columnist Joseph Kraft, writing in *Harper's* in July, 1958, said that records indicated that the Carnegie trustees hoped to involve the U.S. in a world war to set the stage for world government. Dodd said they wanted "to bring the idea of 'one-world' (government) to the point where it is acceptable to the people of this country. That is the primary aim, and everything that has happened since then is a means to that one end." Their memos indicated that they believed their efforts were successful, because the war "had brought about a change in the American psyche."

In the archives of the Endowment, Dodd discovered that they felt that the "only way to maintain control of the population was to obtain control of education in the U.S. They realized this was a prodigious task so they approached the Rockefeller Foundation with the suggestion that they go in tandem and that portion of education which could be considered as domestically oriented be taken over by the Rockefeller Foundation and that portion which was oriented to international matters be taken over by the Carnegie Endowment." Dodd said that "they decided that the success of this program lay in an alteration in the matter in which

American history was to be presented."

The Guggenheim Foundation agreed to award fellowships to historians recommended by the Carnegie Endowment, and a group of 20 were assembled, and sent to London, where they were briefed and became founding members of the American History Association. In 1928, the A.H.A. was given a grant of $400,000 by Carnegie to write a 7-volume study on the direction the nation was to take. The secret of its success would be that it would be done gradually.

Rene Wormser, legal counsel to Reece's Committee, said that the Carnegie Endowment was attempting to mold the minds of our children by deciding "what should be read in our schools and colleges." He also described how the Rockefeller Foundation, the Ford Foundation, the Carnegie Endowment, and the Carnegie Corporation jointly sponsor conferences to push the goals of the United Nations.

The investigation by Reece's Special House Committee, found that the Carnegie Corporation financed the writing and publication of the *Proper Study of Mankind* by Stuart Chase, the book praised by the communist agents Harry Dexter White and Lauchlin Currie, which outlined an "ideal" society in which the individual is suppressed. Over 50,000 copies of the book were distributed by the foundation to libraries and scholars. They also gave a $340,000 grant to print a 17-volume study on American education by Dr. George Counts, which was later called "an educational program for a socialist America."

The Ford Foundation

In 1903, Henry Ford, Sr. (1863-1947) founded the Ford Motor Company, and in 1907, he bought out all of his partners, so his family would control the entire company. In 1924, he was so popular, that various polls indicated that he would be elected President if he ran.

Henry Ford said: "It is well enough that the people of the nation do not understand our banking and monetary system, for if they did, I believe there would be a revolution before tomorrow morning." In 1936, with his son Edsel, he established the Ford Foundation as an inheritance tax dodge, which he saw as a plot to take money away from Americans; and for his family to retain control after his death. An enemy of the establishment, Ford wanted American hero Charles A. Lindbergh (who supported the conservative 'America First' movement) to be the Director of his Foundation, but Lindbergh refused. Ford, and his son Edsel, died before the Foundation's leadership could be placed in safe hands, and control passed to Edsel's widow, and grandson Henry Ford II (who later married into the Rothschild family), who brought in such 'insiders' as William Benton, Dr. Robert M. Hutchins (who became Associate Director), and Paul G. Hoffman (who became the Chief Administrator).

The Ford Foundation, with assets of $4 billion, is the world's largest endowment. They own 90% of Ford Motor's stock. Ford also established the Edison Institute; and the Henry Ford Hospital, which gave two-thirds of its grants to education, and one-third to communications, public health, economic development, science, engineering, senior citizens, the humanities and the arts.

The Foundation financed a Black voter registration drive in Cleveland, which helped elect the city's first Black mayor ($175,000); financed the pro-Castro Mexican-American Youth Organization in Texas; gave grants to the Marxist Black group known as C.O.R.E. ($475,000); the leftist National Students Association ($315,000); the socialist Citizens Crusade Against Poverty ($508,500); the communist-controlled Southern Christian Leadership Conference ($230,000); the leftist Urban League ($1,600,000); the pro-Vietcong American Friends Service Committee, which encouraged pacifism, resistance to military service and preparedness, and conscientious objectors ($100,000); National Council of Churches ($108,000); Anti-Defamation League ($35,000); National Catholic Conference for Interracial Justice ($552,000); American Jewish Congress ($100,000); American Council for Nationalities Service ($200,000); National Committee Against Discrimination in Housing ($162,000); Council on Foreign Relations ($1,000,000); Adlai E. Stevenson Institute of International Affairs ($1,000,000); UNESCO ($200,000); United Nations Association ($150,000); Institute for International Education ($1,625,000); American Assembly ($166,000); World Affairs Council ($102,000); Congress for Cultural Freedom ($1,500,000); the Committee for Economic Development's Foreign Policy Research ($275,000); National Committee on U.S.-China Relations ($250,000); the communist-staffed Southern Regional Council ($648,000); the leftist National Educational Television and Radio Center ($6,000,000); and the Public Broadcast Laboratory ($7,900,000).

In November, 1953, Norman Dodd, Director of Research for the House Special Committee investigating the tax-exempt foundations, was told by Roman Gaither, President of the Ford Foundation, "that most of the men who are now running the foundations, formerly worked for the State Department, the United Nations Relief and Rehabilitation Association, the Marshall Plan or other foreign relief agencies, and that in those capacities, they were working under instructions from the White House to bring about such sociological, economic, and political changes, as would make union with communist Russia easy and comfortable for the American people. Now, in the foundations, we are working toward the same objectives." He said that the Ford Foundation operated under directives which "emanate from the White House," and that the "substance of the directives under which we operate is that we shall use our grant-making power so to alter life in the United States that we can be comfortably merged with the Soviet Union."

The Fund for the Republic (one of the six other Ford-controlled foundations), founded in 1953 under the direction of Robert G. Hoffman and Robert M. Hutchins, are known for their attacks on the internal security program of America, and criticism towards the FBI and Congressional committees investigating communism. They were responsible for ending the anti-communist fervor that was sweeping the country. They were also responsible for the establishment of the Center for the Study of Democratic Institutions, in Santa Barbara, California, who developed a Constitution for one-world government.

Robert McNamara, an executive with the Ford Motor Co., became the Foundation's President in 1960, later resigning to serve as the Secretary of Defense (1961-68) in the Kennedy and Johnson Administration. He helped lay the foundation for the SALT treaty. In 1968, he became President of the World Bank. McGeorge Bundy, a CFR member, the Chief Advisor for Foreign Affairs for

Kennedy and Johnson, became President of the Foundation in 1966. He ushered in an era of social unrest by announcing that the Negro movement, "the first of the nation's problems," would be his top priority.

THE STOCK MARKET CRASH AND DEPRESSION

The Federal Reserve Board held a secret meeting on May 18, 1920, to plan a depression. Large banks began calling in loans, causing stocks to drop from a high of 138.12 in 1919, to a low of 66.24 in 1921. When the value of government bonds plummeted, they were forced to call in even more loans. When thousands of the banks' customers could not pay their notes, the banks seized their assets.

After 1922, profits rose, and with the Federal Reserve's ability to lend ten times more than their reserves, credit was easily obtained. From 1923 to 1929, $8 billion was sliced off of the deficit. The Reserve expanded the money supply by 62%, and this excess money was used to bid the stock market up to fantastic heights. The media began publicizing that there was an enormous profit to be made from the stock market. This push was planned at a meeting of the International Bankers in 1926, who made the boom possible, and who was going to bring about financial disaster later.

In 1928, the House hearings on the Stabilization of the Purchasing Power of the Dollar, revealed that the Federal Reserve Board had met with the heads of various European central banks at a secret luncheon in 1927 to plan what they believed may be a major crash. On February 6, 1929, after Montagu Norman, Chairman of the Bank of England, came to the United States to meet with Andrew Mellon, the Secretary of Treasury, the Reserve reversed its monetary policy by raising the discount rate, and during the next few months, after Paul Warburg had issued a tip in March, 1929, Illuminati members, who knew what the future held, got their money out of the stock market, reinvesting it in gold and silver. In the year before the crash, 500 banks failed.

On October 24, 1929, the New York banking establishment began calling in their loans, forcing their customers to sell stock at ridiculously low prices in order to pay off the loans. Stock prices fell by 90%, and U.S. Securities lost $26 billion. Thousands of smaller banks and insurance companies went bankrupt, and people who had been millionaires, were now broke. To prolong the depression after the crash, from 1929 to 1933, the Reserve began to reduce the money flow by one-third.

The Great Depression, as it became known, was engineered by the Illuminati to take money from the people, and to make them dependent on the Government through the subsequent New Deal programs of Roosevelt. Congressman Louis T. McFadden, Chairman of the House Banking and Currency Committee said: "It was no accident. It was a carefully contrived occurrence ... The International Bankers sought to bring about a condition of despair here so they might emerge as the rulers of us all."

To a limited extent, this same method was used to create minor 'depressions' in 1937, 1948, 1953, 1956, 1960, 1966, 1970, and 1979.

In his book, *My Exploited Father-in-Law* by Curtis Dall (son-in-law of Franklin D. Roosevelt) wrote: "The depression was the calculated 'shearing' of the public by the World Money powers, triggered by the planned sudden shortage of supply of call money in the New York money market ... The One World Government leaders and their ever close bankers have now acquired full control of the money and credit machinery of the U.S. via the creation of the privately owned Federal Reserve Bank."

CHAPTER THREE

BRINGING THE WORLD TOGETHER

WORLD WAR I

World War I began in 1914, and in 1915, the United States, who were not yet involved, lent France and Great Britain $500 million through American banks. In 1916, a single French loan totaled $750 million. In all, the total amount of the loans to these allied countries amounted to $3 billion, plus another $6 billion for exports, none of which were repaid. This was just one of the reasons for America's entry into the war. Had Germany won, those bonds held by American bankers would have been worthless. J. P. Morgan (who served as England's financial agent in the U.S.), Rockefeller (who made more than $200,000,000 on the war), Warburg, and Schiff, were instrumental in pushing America into the war, so they could protect their loans to Europe.

The Illuminati-controlled newspapers publicized, and played-up the sinking of the British auxiliary cruiser, the Lusitania, which was torpedoed by a German U-Boat on May 7, 1915. The Germans said they had the right to attack an allied ship, even though the United States, up to that time, had been neutral. The Lusitania, which had been converted into an ammunition war ship early in the war, was armed with guns, and was carrying six million pounds of ammunition, which were to be sold to England and France for use in the war against Germany. It was illegal for American passengers to be on board a ship carrying munitions, and on May 1, 1915, the German embassy in Washington, D.C., ran ads in the New York papers, in addition to verbal announcements, warning Americans that the ship would be attacked. Three months earlier, Germany had issued a proclamation that the waters around the British Isles were part of the war zone, In addition, it was later revealed, that on December 14, 1914, British Intelligence broke the German war code, which meant that the First Lord of the Admiralty, Winston Churchill, knew the location of every U-Boat in the English Channel area.

When the ship was sunk off the coast of Ireland, 1201 people were killed, including 128 Americans. The Illuminati used the incident to create a war fever, portraying the Germans as being barbaric. Because of President Wilson's handling of the Lusitania affair, William Jennings Bryan, his Secretary of State, resigned.

Colonel House was already in England, making firm commitments that America would enter the war; and on April 6, 1917, Congress declared war, selling it as a "war to end all wars," and a war "to make the world safe for democracy."

When the war was finally over, over 63,000 American soldiers had been killed in the fighting. A year later, in 1919, Lenin offered four-fifths of Soviet territory, in exchange for the formal recognition of his communist government, and economic aid from the United States. He offered to accept the creation of allied-sponsored non-communist states in the Baltic region, in the area of Archangel, Western Byelorussia, half of the Ukraine, Crimea, the Caucasus, the Ural Mountains, and all of Siberia. Wilson rejected the offer for "patriotic reasons," because the Illuminati had big plans for that country. Had he accepted the offer, Russia would have never have become a world power.

THE LEAGUE OF NATIONS

Before World War I, the Illuminati, using various influential groups in the United States and Great Britain, urged the creation of an organization to promote world peace, even though George Washington warned against involvement with foreign nations. President Wilson favored the idea, and echoed those sentiments in his famous "Peace Without Victory" speech before the Senate. He proposed his idea of a League of Nations to the Senate in 1917, seeing it as a means of preventing another World War. It would provide "collective security," or in other words, an attack on one, would be considered an attack on all. The League would also help in the arbitration of international disputes, the reduction of armaments, and the development of open diplomacy.

The armistice ending World War I on November 11, 1918, was negotiated on the basis of Wilson's "Fourteen Points" and on June 28, 1919, was included in the Treaty of Versailles, a 20-year truce which divided up Europe, setting the stage for World War II. It demanded that Germany pay war reparations to the victorious countries. The Allies maintained that "since Germany was responsible for the War she was liable for the costs and damages incurred by the victors." This amount was set at $32 billion, plus interest; which called for annual payments of $500 million, plus a 26% surcharge on exports. The agreement forced Germany to forfeit some of her prime provinces, colonies, and natural resources. They signed away their rights, had to make trade concessions, and lost what property they had in those foreign countries.

The Treaty was widely criticized. David Lloyd George, the Prime Minister of England, said: "We have written a document that guarantees war in 20 years ... When you place conditions on a people (Germany) that it cannot possibly keep, you force it to either breech the agreement or to war. Either we modify that agreement, and make it tolerable to the German people, or when the new generation comes along they will try again." Lord Curzon, the British Foreign Secretary, said: "This is no peace, this is only a truce for twenty years!" Even President Wilson was reported to have said: "If I were a German, I think I should never sign it."

The League of Nations was signed and sealed at the Paris Peace Conference. Even though the United States was represented by Wilson, Col. House was calling the shots. Bernard Baruch, who, as head of the War Industries Board made about $200,000,000 for himself, was also in the American delegation at the Paris Conference; as well as, Waiter Lippman (who later became a syndicated newspaper columnist), Allen Dulles (who was appointed Director of the CIA in 1951), John Foster Dulles (brother of Allen, who later became the Secretary of State under Eisenhower), and Christian Herter (who became Secretary of State after the death of Dulles). English Prime Minister George was accompanied by Sir Philip Sassoon, a member of the British Privy Council and a direct descendant of Amschel Rothschild. Georges Clemenceau, the French Prime Minister, had at his side, his advisor, Georges Mandel, also known as Jeroboam Rothschild.

The citizens of the United States refused to accept the League of Nations, because they felt it would draw them into future European conflicts. Frank B. Kellogg (who in 1925 became Secretary of State under Coolidge), inspired by the American "outlawry of war" movement, and supported by those who were disappointed at the failure of the United States to enter the League, proposed a pact to the French Foreign Minister, Aristide Briand in the spring of 1927. Its purpose was to create alliances directed against a possible resurgence of German aggression. This Pact of Paris was signed on August 27, 1928, by 65 nations, who promised to settle all international disputes by peaceful means.

Because of the efforts of Sen. Henry Cabot Lodge, who saw through Wilson's plan, the United States didn't join the League, and in 1921, made a separate peace treaty with Germany and Austria.

The League of Nations, headquartered in Geneva, Switzerland, throughout the 1920's, gained new members, and helped settle minor international disputes. However, weakened by the failure of the United States to join, and the restlessness of nations who were not satisfied, such as Japan, Italy and Germany, the Illuminati's second attempt at establishing a one-world government failed. The League had little impact on international affairs, and ceased to exist in 1946 when the United Nations was established.

What the League of Nations did do, was allow the Illuminati to get more of a grip on world finances. Countries which belonged to the League, sought financial aid from the United States, wherein Rockefeller said that no country could get a loan unless the International Bankers controlled the bank. If they had no bank, they were able to set one up. Through the Bank for International Settlement, established in 1930, the Illuminati was able to control more of the world's money.

SYMBOL OF THE ILLUMINATI

When Weishaupt founded the Order of the Illuminati, he adopted the All-Seeing Eye symbol of Masonry, to be the symbol of the organization. It is the Great Pyramid of Cheops, with the capstone missing, and replaced with an eye. The All-Seeing Eye can be traced back to Chaldea as the Solar Eye, the Eye of Jupiter or Apollo, or the Eye of Providence. Hieroglyphics in ancient Egypt identified the name of the chief Sun God Osiris with a human eye.

On July 4, 1776, Thomas Jefferson (a Mason and Illuminist), John Adams (a Mason), and Ben Franklin (a Mason and Rosicrucian), were appointed by a Committee of the Continental Congress to prepare the Great Seal of the United States to signify that the 13 states had united in an act of independence. After some preliminary work by another, William Barton submitted an Eagle on the pinnacle of a Doric column, the All-Seeing Eye, and the stars (representing a new constellation, or new empire). Barton's second design pushed the All-Seeing Eye to the reverse side, and moved the eagle up to the crest, and placed a phoenix (a mythical bird that would be consumed with fire of its own volition, then be resurrected out of its own ashes, which was the Egyptian symbol of regeneration used by the Rosicrucians) rising from the flames at the column's summit, which was to indicate the revival of the new (America) out of the old (England).

This design was accepted on May 9, 1782 and referred to Charles Thompson (a Mason), the Secretary of Congress on June 13th. The final version, approved and adopted by an act of Congress on June 20, 1782, was the result of a series of committee meetings which combined ideas from Barton, Thompson and Jefferson, who placed a triangle around the eye, added the year '1776,' 'E Pluribus Unum,' the olive branch on the front, stars above the eagle, and other things. Within weeks, a brass plate of the face of the Great Seal was produced, but not the reverse side.

Although the design of the seal was not to deviate from the one approved, when the original wore out, and a second engraving in 1841 was ordered by Secretary of State Daniel Webster. The design by French artist R. P. Lamplier and cut by John V. N. Throop had many subtle differences, such as six, rather than thirteen arrows, and the phoenix clearly became an eagle. Referred to as the Websterian Great Seal, it was used until 1885.

The third engraving was prepared in 1885 under Secretary of State F. T. Frelinghuysen and cut by Tiffany and Co.; and the fourth engraving, under Secretary of State John Hay, engraved by Max Zeiler, and cut by Baily, Banks & Biddle; were both consistent with the design passed by law in 1782.

A committee appointed by Frelinghuysen, consisting of Theodore F. Dwight (Chief of the Bureau of Rolls and Library of the State Department), Justin Winsor (historian), Charles Eliot Norton (Harvard professor), William H. Whitmore (genealogist), John Denison Chaplin, Jr. (associate editor of *American Cyclopedia*) and James Horton Whitehouse (designer for Tiffany and Co. in New York City) decided that a die for the reverse side of the seal would not be produced and used as an official seal. Norton called it a "dull emblem of a Masonic fraternity." However, a 1957 pamphlet by the U.S. Government Printing Office, called *The Seal of the United States*, indicated that in 1885 "a die may have been cut," but never used.

Celestia Root Lang (editor and publisher of *Divine Life* magazine from the Independent Theosophical Society of America) wrote in 1917: "The reverse side must have been designed by a mystic, one versed in symbolism ... The time will come ... when the white stone (pyramid capstone) will become the headstone of the corner of our government ... in proclaiming a new religion in which all spiritual currents flowing from every religion shall meet in the perfection of the white stone ... having neither dogma nor doctrine ... We see in Mr. Barton only the facade of the instrument; that if he himself was not a mystic or seer, then, a Master (thought to have been Thomas Paine) stood behind him."

Arthur M. Schlesinger, Jr. wrote in his book *The Coming of the New Deal*, that Vice President Henry A. Wallace (a Mason) was "fascinated" by the occult, and was impressed enough with the significance of the reverse side of the Great Seal to lobby Treasury Secretary Morganthau to have it put on the back of the one dollar bill in 1935. Wallace later ran for President as a Socialist. What this gesture meant, was that the Illuminati had finally reached the point where they could set into motion their plans for the New World Order by initiating the destruction of our Constitution.

The front side of the Great Seal, or the Eagle, is well known. It is used to seal all governmental documents. The reverse side displays a pyramid, with an eye in the capstone and a Latin inscription around it. This seems to be a continuation of the Masonic symbolism found on the front. The number thirteen is displayed prominently, and was thought to have referred to the thirteen colonies. However, the number thirteen was a mystical number to the Egyptians and Babylonians, and also the Masons.

There are:

13 stars in the crest
13 stripes and bars in the shield
13 olive leaves
13 olives
13 arrows in the right claw
13 feathers in the arrows
13 letters in "Annuit Coeptis"
13 letters in "E Pluribus Unum"
13 courses of stone in the pyramid
13 X 9 dots in the divisions around the crest

It has been said that the cluster of 13 five-pointed stars above the head of the eagle is actually a representation of a hexagram, which is the most evil of all occult symbols, and is used to invoke Satan.

This is not to be confused with the Star of David, Mogen David, or Seal of Solomon, which consists of two interlaced equilateral triangles, which symbolize the union of God and man.

There are 32 long feathers on the right wing which represent the 32 degrees in Scottish Rite Masonry, and there are 33 feathers on the left, which represent the 33 degrees of York Rite Freemasonry. The pyramid has thirteen levels, said to represent the 13 bloodlines; and within the capstone is an eye. It is not the eye of God, as we have been taught to believe. It stems from Masonic tradition, where it is known as the 'Eye of Horus' (the Sun God), or the 'All-Seeing Eye,' which refers to the protection of Providence, "whose eye never slumbers nor sleeps," alluding to the 'Big Brother' system of constant surveillance. To the Illuminati, it represents the eye of Satan, who its members worship.

The pyramid represents the organizational structure of the Illuminati, and the capstone containing the eye, represents the House of Rothschild, who control the group, and have perpetuated the goal of one-world government. Some sources claim that on the top level, the 1st block represents the Council of 13 (the 13 most powerful witches), the 2nd block represents the Council of 33 (33 highest ranking Masons in the world), and the 3rd block is the Council of 500 (500 richest people and corporations in the world).

According to the original Treasury Department press release of August 15, 1935, which gave details of the symbol being put on the back of the one dollar bill, said the following: "The eye and triangular glory symbolize an all-seeing Deity. The pyramid is the symbol of strength and its unfinished condition denoted the belief of the designers of the Great Seal that there was still work to be done." Notice they said "Deity," and not "God."

The news release indicated that the Latin phrase "Annuit Coeptis" is translated as "he (God) favored our undertakings," and comes from Virgil's 'audacibus annue coeptis' or "favor my daring undertaking," which refers to the 'golden' age during which the 'Saturnian' (Saturn was the father of Osiris) kingdom shall return. "Novus Ordo Seclorum" is translated as 'a new order of the ages,' which is taken from Virgil's 'magnus ab integro seclorum nascitur ordo' or "the great series of ages begins anew." To the Illuminati, the combination of these two Latin phrases is translated as: "Announcing the Birth of a New Secular Order."

The date 1776, found at the base of the pyramid in Roman numerals, doesn't refer to July 4th, the date of the country's independence; but May 1st, when the Illuminati was founded. May 1st is also an international holiday for all workers, known as May Day, which was established in 1889 at the International Socialist Congress.

Now, take a pen, and on the seal on the left side of the bill, find the word "Annuit" and draw a circle around the first letter 'A.' Find the word "Coeptis" and draw a circle around the last letter 'S.' Find the word "Novus" and draw a circle around the first letter 'N.' Find the word "Ordo" and draw a circle around the last letter 'O.' Find the word 'Seclorum' and draw a circle around the last letter 'M.' Now, take your pen, and starting from 'N' to the top of the capstone, back down to 'M' and back over to 'N' (utilizing the entire pyramid as one triangle). Then draw a line from 'A' to 'S' then down to 'O' and then back up to 'A' which is the second triangle. Not only will you will see a representation of the six-pointed star, but you will also an anagram that spells the word M-A-S-O-N.

The reverse side of the Great Seal, which can be found in the Meditation Room of the United Nations, has never been used to seal one document in this country's history, and it never will, because it is the seal of the Illuminati.

CHAPTER FOUR

DOMESTIC TAMPERING

THE ILLUMINATI CREATES RACIAL TENSION

In the book *A Racial Program for the Twentieth Century*, published in 1913 by Israel Cohen of the Fabian Society (a follow-up to Zangwill's *Melting Pot*), he wrote:

> "We must realize that our Party's most powerful weapon is racial tension. By propounding into the consciousness of the dark races, that for centuries have been oppressed by the Whites, we can mold them to the program of the Communist Party ... In America, we will aim for subtle victory. While enflaming the Negro minority against the Whites, we will instill in the Whites, a guilt complex for the exploitation of the Negroes. We will aid the Negroes to rise to prominence in every walk of life, in the professions, and in the world of sports and entertainment. With this prestige, the Negroes will be able to intermarry with the Whites, and begin a process which will deliver America to our cause."

On June 17, 1957, this passage was read into the *Congressional Record* by Rep. Thomas G. Abernathy.

In 1922, the Russian Comintern provided $300,000 for the spreading of communist propaganda among Negroes. In 1925, the Communist Party, U.S.A., told its members:

> "The aim of our Party in our work among the Negro masses is to create a powerful proletarian movement which will fight and lead the struggle of the Negro race against the exploitation and oppression in every form and which will be a militant part of the revolutionary movement of the whole American working class ... and connect them with the struggles of national minorities and colonial peoples of all the world and thereby the cause of world revolution and the dictatorship of the proletariat."

In 1925, a dozen Blacks were recruited for propaganda training in Russia. That same year, the American Negro Labor Congress was established. In 1930, they changed their name to the League of Struggle for Negro Rights. They merged with the United Negro Congress when it was founded in 1936, in Washington, D.C. By 1940, communists made up two-thirds of its membership. In 1947, they united with the Civil Rights Congress, a communist front group.

In a 1928 pamphlet by John Pepper (alias for Joseph Pogany) called *American Negro Problems*, a move was being made by Stalin to ferment revolution and stir the Blacks into creating a separate Republic for the Negro. Another pamphlet put out by the New York Communist Party in 1935, called *The Negroes in a Soviet America*, urged the Blacks to rise up and form a Soviet State in the South by applying for admission to the Comintern. It contained a firm pledge that a revolt would be supported by all American communists and liberals. On page 48, it said that the Soviet Government would give the Blacks more benefits than they would give to the Whites, and "any act of discrimination or prejudice against the Negro would become a crime under the revolutionary law."

In *The Communist Party: A Manual On Organization* by J. Peters, he writes:

"The other important ally of the American proletariat is their mass of 13,000,000 Negro people in their struggle against national oppression. The Communist Party, as the revolutionary party of the proletariat, is the only party which is courageously and resolutely carrying on a struggle against the double exploitation and national oppression of the Negro people, becoming intense with the developing crisis, can win over the great masses of the Negro people as allies of the Proletariat against the American bourgeosie."

In James Cannon's *America's Road to Socialism*, he says that the Negroes "will play a great and decisive role in the revolution ... And why shouldn't they be? They have nothing to lose but their property and discrimination, and a whole world of prosperity, freedom, and equality to gain. You can bet your boots the Negro will join the Revolution to fight for that— once it becomes clear to them that it cannot be gained except by revolution."

The former FBI Director, J. Edgar Hoover, said of the Communists goals: "Communists seek to advance the cause of communism by injecting themselves into racial situations and in exploiting them, (1) to intensify the frictions between Negroes and Whites to 'prove' that discrimination against the minorities is an inherent defect of the capitalistic system, (2) to foster domestic disunity by dividing Negroes and Whites into antagonistic, warring factions, (3) to undermine and destroy established authority, (4) to incite racial strife and riotous activity, and (6) to portray the Communist movement as the 'champion' of social protest and the only force capable of ameliorating the conditions of the Negro and the oppressed."

In light of all this, you can see why the Supreme Court, under elitist Earl Warren, issued the desegregation law in 1954, and why Eisenhower and Kennedy enforced it by using Federal troops. It was to create more tension between Blacks and Whites. Incidentally, it was the Warren Court who prohibited prayer and the singing of Christmas carols in the schools. This was intended to weaken Christianity.

Jacob Schiff, the Rothschild's man in America, decided that the best way to create racial tension was to establish leadership among the Blacks. In 1909, he laid out plans for the National Association for the Advancement of Colored People (NAACP). It was the merging of the communist-controlled Niagara Movement, a group of Blacks led by W. E. B. DuBois; and a group of White social activists. In the beginning, the top leaders of the NAACP were a group of Jews appointed by Schiff. Their goal was to fight segregation and discrimination. They are the largest Black organization in the country, with well over 1500 chapters, and about a half-million members.

Communist Party members were told to join the NAACP, in order to infiltrate them. The Communist Party platform stated: "The Negro race must understand that capitalism means racial oppression, and communism means social and racial equality." Manning Johnson, who held the highest position a Black could have in the Communist Party, said in his 1958 book *Color, Communism and Common Sense*, that he quit, because he felt Russia was attempting to involve them in a bloody revolution where as many as five million Blacks would die. Another Negro Communist, Leonard Patterson, testified on November 18, 1950: "I left the Communist Party because I became convinced ... that the Communist Party was only interested in promoting among the Negro people a national liberational movement that would aid the Communist Party in its efforts to create a proletarian revolution in the United States that would overthrow the government by force and violence through bloody full-time revolution, and substitute it with a Soviet form of government with a dictatorship of the proletariat."

The May, 1968 issue of *Political Affairs*, the voice of the Communist Party, wrote after the death of Rev. Martin Luther King, Jr.: "The Reverend Martin Luther King, Jr., the voice, inspiration and symbol of the Negro people's struggle for freedom and equality, is dead ... The man who, more than anyone else, personified the heroic determination of the Black people to win their liberation now. One of humanity's great leaders has been silenced forever ... We must see that his memory not be desecrated. We must not fail to do all in our power to realize the dream for which he died."

King, the most powerful Black leader in the country, was a pawn of the Illuminati. He supported North Vietnam during the War, and was photographed in 1957 at the Highlander Folk School, a communist training school in Tennessee, with Abner Berry, who held a post on the Central Committee of the Communist Party. The Joint Legislative Committee on Un-American Activities reported that his Southern Christian Leadership Conference was "substantially under the control of the Communist Party through the influence of the Southern Conference Educational Fund and the communists who manage it." King had connections with over 60 communist front organizations. Nine of his closest aides were high-ranking communist activists and one of those later became an aide to Rev. Jesse Jackson. Stanley Levison, who had been a King advisor since 1956, had been involved with the Communist Party up to 1955, and brought other known communists onto King's staff.

Rev. Uriah J. Fields, King's secretary during the early years, wrote about him: "King helps to advance Communism. He is surrounded with Communists. This is the major reason I severed my relationship with him during the fifties. He is soft on Communism." Karl Prussion, an FBI agent who infiltrated the Communist Party, and for five years attended meetings in California, testified in 1963: "I further swear and attest that at each and everyone of the aforementioned meetings, one Reverend Martin Luther King was always set forth as the individual to whom Communists should look and rally around in the Communist struggle on many racial issues." Julia Brown, a former Communist, said: "We were told to promote Martin Luther King to unite Negroes and also Whites behind him ... He was taking directions from Communists. I know for a fact the Communists would never have promoted him, financed him, and supported him if they couldn't trust him. I am certain as I can be that he knew what he was doing."

Although a 1977 court order sealed the FBI's extensive surveillance records on King in the National Archives for 50 years, a book by Sen. Jesse Helms in 1998 called *The King Holiday and Its Meaning* said that Charles D. Brennan, an Assistant Director of the FBI who was personally involved in the surveillance, characterized his activities as "orgiastic and adulterous escapades," in which he could be "bestial in his sexual abuse of women." He also observed that "King frequently drank to excess." The 1981 book by David Garrow, called *The FBI and Martin Luther King, Jr.* told of King's liaisons with prostitutes and the misappropriation of Southern Christian Leadership Conference funds. The FBI investigation had led J. Edgar Hoover to say that "King is a tom cat with obsessive degenerate sexual urges," and President Lyndon Johnson to call him a "hypocrite preacher."

The oldest Jewish service organization, known as the B'nai B'rith (which means 'Son of the Covenant'), was a secret Masonic order founded by twelve wealthy American Jews in New York in 1843. In 1913, Schiff, along with Chicago author and attorney Sigmund Livingston, reorganized the group, and established the Anti-Defamation League of the B'nai B'rith (ADL) to fight anti-Semetism and religious prejudice. They have been used as an instrument to convince people that an attack on the Rothschilds and the Illuminati is a direct attack on the Jewish people. They are the most powerful Jewish organization in the world, with chapters in 44 countries. In the United States, they have over 2,000 agencies, about 25 regional offices, and a membership of a half-million. Its leaders had controlled the NAACP, the Urban League, and other Black organizations, and often worked closely with the ACLU. Their influence on advertising with some major department stores, hotel chains, and major corporations, has been able to slant the media toward Blacks. Nearly half of their annual budget comes through donations from non-Jews.

The American League to Limit Armaments was established on December 18, 1914, a spin-off of the Emergency Peace Federation, led by communist Louis Lochner. The League was organized by Jane Addams, John Haynes Holmes, George Foster Peabody, Stephen Wise, L. Hollingsworth Wood, and Morris Hillquit, all communists and socialists. In 1915, they changed their name to the American Union Against Militarism, establishing a Civil Liberties Bureau to oppose draft laws, The director of the Bureau, socialist Roger Baldwin, reorganized it into the National Civil Liberties Bureau, and in 1920, with the help of Jane Addams, Clarence Darrow, Norman Thomas, Felix Frankfurter, and Arthur Garfield Hays, founded the American Civil Liberties Union (ACLU). Their goal was to fight for "the rights of man (as) set forth in the Declaration of Independence and the Constitution."

The original National Committee of the ACLU included, Elizabeth Gurley Flynn and William Z. Foster, who both later became Chairmen of the Communist Party; communist Scott Nearing; and Norman Thomas, Socialist Party Chairman.

Since the 1920's, 80% of its National Committee members had Communist connections. In 1935, Baldwin said: "I am for socialism, disarmament, and ultimately for abolishing the State itself as an instrument of violence and compulsion. I seek the social ownership of property, the abolition of the propertied class and social control of those who produce wealth. Communism is the goal."

In 1920, a Joint Committee of the New York State Legislature reported that the ACLU "in the last analysis is a supporter of all subversive movements; and its propaganda is detrimental to the interests of the State. It attempts not only to protect crime, but to encourage attacks upon our institutions in every form." A September, 1923 report by the United Mine Workers of America, said that the group "is working in harmony and unity with the Communist Superstructure in America ... conducting a nationwide campaign for the liberation of Bolshevik agents and disloyal agitators who have been convicted under the wartime laws or the syndicalist laws of different States for unpatriotic or revolutionary activities."

A January, 1931 report by the Special House Committee to Investigate Communist Activities in the United States, said: "The American Civil Liberties Union is closely affiliated with the Communist movement in the United States ... it is quite apparent that the main function of the ACLU is to attempt to protect Communists in their advocacy of force and violence to overthrow the government..." The California Fact-Finding Committee on Un-American Activities reported in 1943: "The American Civil Liberties Union may be definitely classed as a Communist front..." Dr. J. B. Matthews, Chief Investigator for the House Special Committee on Un-American Activities, said in January, 1955: "In 37 years of history of the Communist movement in the United States, the Communist Party has never been able to do as much for itself as the American Civil Liberties Union has done for it."

The ACLU is made up of about 200,000 members, with an army of 3,000 unpaid volunteer attorneys, and chapters in 47 states. They are a finger organization of the Illuminati, and are most noted for their cases involving the separation of church and state. They have defended the rights of Jehovah Witnesses to refrain from saluting the flag, and to protect the rights of the Nazis and KKK to organize and speak freely. They have become the most powerful weapon against the Church, and Christian tradition, in this country.

THE ELECTORAL COLLEGE

Another contributing factor to Wilson's election to the Presidency, and how the Illuminati controls the American electorate today, is accomplished through a process known as the Electoral College.

Because delegates to the Constitutional Convention, which met in Philadelphia in 1787, thought that the general public lacked the insight and the judgment necessary to elect a President, and could be easily misled by irresponsible candidates, they enacted the Electoral College to do the job.

The President and Vice-President are the only public officials in the country who are not elected through a direct vote of the people. Each party, in every state, has a slate of electoral candidates, based on the number of representatives it has in

Congress. They are known as the Electoral College. Presently, there are 100 Senators and 435 Representatives in the United States, for a total of 538 (includes 3 votes from the District of Columbia) electoral votes.

The electors of the Party receiving the highest vote are elected and meet on the first Monday, after the second Wednesday in December, to vote for their party's nominees. Even though the members of the Electoral College are pledged to vote for the presidential candidate of their Party, they are not constitutionally bound to do so, and can change their mind at any time. Technically, however, a candidate wins all of the state's electoral votes, if he wins a majority of the popular votes. If a presidential candidate has the largest popular vote, but doesn't obtain the necessary electoral votes, he doesn't win the Presidency. This happened in 1824, 1876, 1888, and 2000. If no candidate has a majority, then the House of Representatives chooses a President from the three highest candidates, with all the Representatives from each state combining to cast one vote for each state. If a Vice-Presidential candidate receives no clear majority, then the Senate chooses from the top two, with each Senator casting an individual vote.

Therefore, the candidate's objective is not to win a majority of the popular vote, but a majority of the electoral votes, which is 270. Thus, if a candidate could be guaranteed just eleven states (leaving 267 remaining electoral votes in 39 states, and the District of Columbia), he could be guaranteed the Presidency: California (55), Texas (34), New York (31), Florida (27), Pennsylvania (21), Illinois (21), Ohio (20), Michigan (17), New Jersey (15), Georgia (15), and North Carolina (15). Combined, these states have 271 electoral votes.

That is why you see a concentration of effort in these states at election time. With the Illuminati controlling the media in these large population centers, it is not a difficult task to alter public opinion and sway votes to the candidate they choose. With these states in line, the rest of the country generally follows. The bottom line is, that the people's right to choose a President has practically been taken away, and without the financial resources necessary to fight it, there is very little that can be done.

CHAPTER FIVE

THE COUNCIL ON FOREIGN RELATIONS

THE BRITISH EAST INDIA COMPANY

The British East India Company was a British commercial and political organization established in India in the late 1600's, which was known as the Governor and Company of Merchants of London. A forerunner of this group was the London Mercers Company, and earlier than that, the London Staplers. The organization traced their lineage back to the ancient commercial groups involved in trading between the Mediterranean and India. They were closely related to the Levant Company, and the Anglo-Muscovy Company, and spawned the London Company, which was chartered in 1606 by King James I, to establish the Virginia Plantation on a communistic basis, and the Plymouth Colony in 1621.

It was mainly organized for trading, but soon became an agent for British imperialism. Bending to government pressure, they reorganized in 1702. Every year, 24 Directors were elected by the Court of Proprietors (or shareholders, a majority of which were English Masons). They traded in cotton, tea, silk, and salt peter; and were accused of dealing with opium and participating in the slave trade. They virtually monopolized all trade from South India, the Persian Gulf, Southeast Asia and East Asia.

Indian policy was influenced by the company from 1757 to 1773, when their power was broken by the 1773 Regulatory Act, and Pitt's India Act of 1784, finally ending their monopoly in 1813. When they ceased to exist in 1873, many of its shareholders were major financiers. The principals of this group perpetuated their elitist goals by establishing the Fabian Society.

In 1606, King James also chartered the Virginia Company, a joint stock corporation made up of a group of London entrepreneurs, charged with establishing Jamestown, in the Chesapeake region of North America known as Virginia. It had the authority to appoint the Council of Virginia, the Governor, and other officials; and also had the responsibility to provide settlers, supplies, and ships for the venture. Although initially favorable, as the mortality rate rose, and the prospect for profit faded, the support for it began to decline. They resorted to lotteries, searching for gold, and silkworm production to increase their chances of making a profit. Although Great Britain controlled the colony through this company, because of the Indian Massacre of 1622, the Charter was revoked in 1624, and Virginia became a Crown colony.

THE FABIAN SOCIETY

On October 24, 1883, in London, a group of 17 wealthy Socialists gathered to discuss a 'Fellowship of the New Life,' which was based on the writings of scholar Thomas Davidson, who hoped to start some sort of monastic order. The group included: George Bernard Shaw (1864-1926), a free-thinking Marxist-atheist writer whose plays contained socialistic references, an ideology he pursued after hearing a speech by American economist Henry George in 1882, and reading Marx's *Das Kapital*; Graham Wallas, a classical scholar; Sidney James Webb (1859-1947), a civil servant who was the most influential socialist in the country; Edward Pease; Havelock Ellis; Frank Podmore; Annie Besant; John Galsworthy; R. H. Tawney; G. D. H. Cole; Harold Laski; Israel Zangwill (1864-1926), a Jewish playwright and novelist, who in 1910, wrote the play *The Melting Pot*, which was a propaganda play showing how Americans discriminated against Blacks and Jews; and Israel Cohen, a Jewish writer. Some of these people were also members of the Society for Physical Research, an organization dedicated to spiritualism research, which was founded in 1882.

Sidney Webb later founded the London School of Economics in 1895, which became a branch of the University of London. Among its major contributors: the Rockefeller Foundation, the Carnegie United Kingdom Trust, and Mrs. Ernest Elmhirst, the widow of J. P. Morgan partner Willard Straight, who founded the socialist magazine *New Republic*. In 1912, Webb established an independent journal called *The New Statesman*, and later became a leader in the Labor Party, writing *Labor and the Social Order* in 1918. He held several political offices, and was a disciple of John Stuart Mill, who served as the Secretary of the British East India Company.

On November 7, 1883, this group met to discuss the establishment of an organization "whose ultimate aim shall be the reconstruction of Society in accordance with the highest moral possibilities." However, they split into two factions, and on January 4, 1884, one of the factions established a group known as the Fabian Society. On January 25th, one member, J. G. Stapleton, delivered their first lecture, called "Social Conditions in England, With a View to Social Reconstruction or Development." At a time when there were 30,000 Socialist voters, after a few weeks, they only had 20 members.

In April, 1884, their first publication was distributed, a four-page pamphlet called *Why Are We Poor?* In May, journalist George Bernard Shaw (who would win the Nobel Prize for Literature in 1925) joined, and soon became the leading figure of the Fabians. In March, 1885, Sidney Webb, then a clerk from the Colonial Office, joined; and in 1886, so did Graham Wallas. Shaw, Webb, Wallas, and Sidney Olivier became known as the 'Big Four.'

The other faction, known as 'The Fellowship,' continued for 15 years under Davidson, with members such J. Ramsey MacDonald (who later became Prime Minister), Edward Carpenter, and Havelock Ellis.

Their pamphlet *Facts for Socialists* in 1887, maintained that any person who knew the facts of Socialism, had no other choice but to be one. It was their best selling piece of propaganda.

In 1884, John W. Martin and Rev. W. D. P. Bliss moved to Boston (MA), and established a magazine known as *The American Fabian*. The move was an unsuccessful effort to bring the Fabian's socialistic movement to New York, Philadelphia, San Francisco, and Chicago.

By 1889, 6500 tracts had been distributed, and 31 speakers had delivered 721 lectures. From 1891-92, there had been 3,339 lectures given by 117 Fabian members. Their membership rose to 400 by 1892, 681 in 1894, and 881 in 1899. They had 74 local chapters in Canada, Australia, New Zealand, India, South Africa, Spain, Denmark, and Germany.

In 1899, *The Fabian Essays*, the most noted work on socialism, was written by seven influential members of the Society, and edited by Shaw. It became the blueprint for socialistic legislation, and was later reprinted in 1908, 1920, 1931, and 1952.

Fabian leaders were drawn to Herbert George Wells (1866-1946), and his ideas of the 'New Republic' which he described as "a sort of outspoken Secret Society ... an informal and open freemasonry," made up of the educated class, whose common goals would lead to the creation of a new World State, thus saving the human race from disaster. Known as the 'Prophet of Our Time' because of writing about many things before they came to be, in books like *The Time Machine* and *War of the Worlds*; Wells would give the Fabians the notoriety they needed. Edward Pease, Secretary of the Fabians, wrote to H. G. Wells on January 10, 1902, to say that Webb and his wife Beatrice, were the "pioneers of your New Republic."

Sponsored by Wallas and Shaw, Wells joined them in February, 1903. In his first lecture after joining, he said that the World State was a necessity. In his 1905 book, *A Modern Utopia*, he wrote of the World State taking control and creating a "sane order," and how they maintained a central records system in Paris, which they used to keep track of every person on Earth, and aided the state to eliminate the unfit.

Wells was unimpressed with the Fabians, and called for expansion, by raising money, getting new offices, appointing a new staff, and relaxing the guidelines for membership. He wanted to initiate an all-out propaganda campaign, and outlined his views in a paper called *The Faults of the Fabians*, which dealt with the need for reorganization, and why he wanted to change their name to the 'British Socialist Society.' His views were not shared by the Fabian inner circle, and in September, 1908, he resigned.

Wells maintained his socialistic views, and in 1928, wrote *The Open Conspiracy: Blueprints for a World Revolution*, which was an elaboration of ideas from his 1926 book *The World of William Clissold*, which gave a seven-point program for the development of the "new human community," and was inspired by the rise of communism. These ideas had been fleshed out in his 1897 short story *A Story of the Days to Come*, and his 1901 book, *Anticipations of the Reaction to Mechanical and Scientific Progress Upon Human Life and Thought*.

The character, Clissold, had called his project for world revolution, the "open conspiracy," which meant:

> "...the establishment of the economic world-state by the deliberate invitation, explicit discussion, and cooperation of the men most interested in economic organization, men chosen by their work, called to it by a natu-

ral disposition and aptitude for it, fully aware of its importance and working with the support of an increasing general understanding ... It is not a project to overthrow existing governments by insurrectionary attacks, but to supersede them by disregard. It does not want to destroy them or alter their forms but to make them negligible by replacing their functions. It will respect them as far as it must. What is useful of them it will use; what is useless it will efface by its stronger reality; it will join issue only with what is plainly antagonistic and actively troublesome."

His plan was to be accomplished by "an intelligent minority ... without the support of the crowd and possibly in spite of its dissent..."

The Open Conspiracy was Wells' perspective of his New Republic, which represented a classless World State that controlled everything. Its establishment would be accomplished by "functional men, men of high natural intelligence and professional competence, who performed the creative and managerial work of the world." They were recruited from "the men and women whose knowledge, skill, creative gifts made them indispensable to modern society" who would "gradually have the reins of power into their hands." The revolution was to begin through the "formation of small groups of friends, family groups, groups of students and employees or other sorts of people meeting and conversing frequently in the course of normal occupations." They were to "enlarge themselves and attempt to establish communications with kindred groups for common ends."

He further elaborated: "The Open Conspiracy will appear first, I believe, as a conscious organization of intelligent, and in some cases wealthy men, as a movement having distinct social and political aims, confessedly ignoring most of the existing apparatus of political control, or using it only as an incidental implement in the stages, a mere movement of a number of people in a certain direction, who will presently discover, with a sort of surprise, the common object toward which they are all moving. In all sorts of ways, they will be influencing and controlling the ostensible government."

He also wrote: "From the outset, the Open Conspiracy will set its face against militarism," in the sense that they will encourage "refusal to serve in any war (as conscientious objectors) ... For the furtherance of its aims, the Open Conspiracy may work in alliance with all sorts of movements and people ... (and) restricted movements will attend only to a portion of its program."

According to Wells, expansion would occur through:

"branching and development ... (with) the Open Conspiracy as consisting of a great multitude and variety of overlapping groups, but now all organized for collective political, social and educational as well as propagandist action. They will recognize each other much more clearly than they did at first and they will have acquired a common name ... The character of the Open Conspiracy will now be plainly displayed. It will have become a great world movement as widespread and evident as socialism and communism. It will largely have taken the place of these movements. It will be more, it will be a world-religion. This large loose assimilatory mass of groups and societies will be definitely and obviously attempting to swallow up the entire population of the world and become the new human community."

Two years later, in a published article titled "The Banker," Wells even included the international banking houses in Clissold's "open conspiracy" through a three-point program that would by-pass governments by negotiating agreements stabilizing the currency, adjusting credit availability to control the fluctuation of business, and the withdrawal of credit to governments or armament industries who instigate an arms race.

It is obvious that Wells either based his writings on the actual plans of the Fabian elitists, or used his knowledge of what they had already done in order to formulate a theory of what they were going to do in the future. Since he did quit, were these writings meant to be an exposé or a warning; or was he just stating facts, daring people to try and stop them. We don't know his intent, but what we do know, was that he was incredibly prophetic in his description of their methods. It would indeed be a 'blueprint' for the manner in which the Illuminati would entrench itself in our governmental affairs.

Edward Bernays, former head of CBS-TV, and a friend of H. G. Wells, wrote in his 1928 book, *Propaganda:* "As civilization becomes more complex, and as the need for invisible government has been increasingly demonstrated, the technical means have been invented and developed by which public opinion may be regimented. With printing press and newspaper, the telephone, telegraph, radio and airplanes, ideas can be spread rapidly, and even instantaneously, across the whole of America." These tools would be fully utilized to begin the destruction of America.

The secret goal of the Fabian Society was to create a godless, classless, socialistic society that was dedicated to the ultimate victory of Socialism, which really meant— Communism. In 1891, they became affiliated with the Second Socialist International (established in 1889), and helped establish a Democratic Socialist state in Great Britain.

The aims of the Fabian Society was developed by Webb, from what Englishman John Ruskin (1819-1900) taught at Oxford University. Ruskin, a teacher at the Working Men's College (founded in 1854 by Christian-Socialist philosopher J. F. D. Maurice), a professor of Fine Arts at Oxford, an artist and writer, based his views on those of Socialist Robert Owen. He advocated a utopian society, and espoused theories developed from the teachings of Plato (428-347 BC), who had studied under Socrates, and became the greatest philosopher in history. Plato established an academy which operated for 800 years, producing many great men, including Aristotle. In his work, *The Republic*, he outlined his ideal society, which was an aristocratic society ruled by the elite. It included the elimination of marriage and the family, and introduced selective breeding by the government, who would destroy all inferior offspring. In Plato's utopia, sexual equality dictated that women would fight alongside the men in times of war.

The Fabians were working towards a new world, by indoctrinating young scholars who would eventually rise to power in various policy-making positions throughout the world; by infiltrating educational institutions, government agencies, and political parties. Their strategy was called the "doctrine of inevitability of gradualism," which meant that their goals would be gradually achieved. So gradual, that nobody would notice, or "without breach of continuity or abrupt change of the entire social issue." The secret was evolution, not revolution, or what Webb called "permeation." Shaw (whose mistress, Florence Farr, was a witch in the Order of the Golden Dawn), revealed that their goal was to be achieved by "stealth, intrigue, subversion, and the deception of never calling socialism by its right name."

In fact, that's how they got their name. The name originated from the Roman Consul, General Quintus Fabius Maximus, the Cunctator ('Delayer'), who through patient, cautious, delaying and elusive tactics, during the early phases of the Second Punic War (218-201 BC), enabled the Roman army to regroup and defeat Hannibal's stronger Carthaginian army.

One good example of this concept is television. Ever since Bible reading and prayer have been taken out of schools, the entertainment industry has been slowly and methodically taking bolder steps in the content of their programming. We are seeing things being televised, which would have never been considered thirty and forty years ago. Nudity done in 'good taste,' or done to be culturally or historically accurate, is acceptable. Obscene language is tolerated (especially on the radio), if it is an essential part of the plot. Even though the level of sex and violence is increasing, the rate of complaints to the television networks is decreasing. This shows a gradual acceptance on the part of the public, or what the network bosses call the "relaxing of moral standards." This was done to brainwash our children to constantly bombard them with trash that would influence them, and turn them away from God. This is so evident with the concept of music videos, which have been able to combine sex and violence along with a hard driving musical composition that has been shown to ferment rebellion in young people.

In 1905, American Fabians established the Rand School of Economics in New York City. On September 12, 1905, five of the Fabians met at Peck's Restaurant in New York's Lower Manhattan: Upton Sinclair (well-known author and socialist), Jack London (well-known fiction writer), Rev. Thomas Wentworth Higginson (a Unitarian minister), J.G. Phelps Stokes, and Clarence Darrow (legendary lawyer). They incorporated the Intercollegiate Socialist Society, for the purpose of promoting "an intelligent interest in socialism among college men and women," and established chapters at Harvard, Princeton, Columbia, New York University, and the University of Pennsylvania. Their true purpose was to begin de-Christianizing America. One of its founding members was John Dewey, the father of progressive education, whose philosophy consisted of "atheism, socialism and evolution." In 1921, they changed their name to the League for Industrial Democracy, whose purpose was "education for a new social order based on production for use and not for profit." They established a network of 125 chapters. Dewey would later serve as its Vice-President, and in 1941, became its President.

The Fabians had broken away from the Liberal Party in the 1890's and contributed to the founding of the Labor Representation Committee, which in 1906, became the Labor Party. Shaw called for "wire-pulling" the government in order to get Socialist measures passed. In 1918, the Labor Party adopted a program which implemented the ideas of Fabianism.

In 1931, the New Fabian Research Bureau was organized, joining the Fabian Society in 1938 to form a reorganized group. In 1940, the Colonial Bureau of the

Fabian Society was established; and in 1941, the Fabian International Bureau was formed, which catered to international issues.

In December, 1942, the Fabians published the *Beveridge Report*, written by Sir William Beveridge (later made a Lord), who made a long list of promises to Britons, if they would accept his package of social reforms. In 1945, Fabian Socialists took control of the House of Commons, on the strength of the Report, and the *Parliamentary Reforms*, which had been published eleven years earlier by Sir Ivor Jennings. Within a few years, British industries and services were nationalized and put under government control, which now meant that the Rothschilds were able to control more, because all the banks were forced to use Bank of England notes, instead of their own.

At its peak in 1946, the Fabian Society had 8,400 members in 80 local chapters. Among their members: Bertrand Russell (philologist, mathematician and philosopher), (Pandit) Motilal Nehru (father of India's first Prime Minister, Jawaharial Nehru, and leader of the Independence movement who founded the Swaraj, or 'self-rule' Party), and Ramsey MacDonald (Prime Minister of England in 1924, 1929-35). Nearly half of all Labor Party representatives of the Parliament in the House of Commons were members, along with most Party leaders.

Today, from their headquarters at 11 Dartmouth Street, in London, they spread their ideas among teachers, civil servants, politicians, union officials, and other influential people. They publish the *Fabian Review* magazine. They also hold meetings, lectures, conferences, and seminars; do research in political, economic, and social problems; and publish their findings and views in magazines, books and pamphlets. Their concentration has been mainly on reforms to social services and the nationalization of industry.

THE ROUND TABLE

Cecil Rhodes (1853-1902, South African financier, British statesman and industrialist, who wanted to make Africa a "British dominion from the Cape to Cairo"), with the financial support of Nathaniel Mayer Rothschild (1840-1915) and Alfred Beit, was able to control the diamond mines of South Africa with his DeBeers Consolidated Mines Limited, by buying out the French Diamond Co. and then merging with the Barnato Diamond Mining Company. He eventually controlled the production of diamonds throughout the world. His Consolidated Gold Fields was also a prosperous gold mining operation. He made $5 million annually.

In 1877, while still studying at Oxford (it took him 8 years because of having to run the diamond mines), he wrote the first of seven wills, in which each became a separate and legally binding document. It called for the establishment of a "secret society with but one object— the furtherance of the British Empire and the bringing of the whole uncivilized world under British rule, for the recovery of the United States, (and) for ... making the Anglo-Saxon race but one Empire." Frank Aydelotte, a founding member of the Council on Foreign Relations, and the American Secretary to the Rhodes Trustees, wrote in his book, *American Rhodes Scholarships*: "In his first will Rhodes states his aim still more specifically: 'The extension of British rule throughout the world ... the foundation of so great a power as to hereafter render wars impossible and promote the interests of humanity'." When he died, his third will, drafted in 1888, called for the establishment of a trust, run by his son-in-law Lord Rosebury, a Rothschild agent, to administer his fortune. His seventh and last will, named Rothschild the administrator of his estate, and established an educational grant known as the Rhodes Scholarships at Oxford University (which was controlled by the Fabians). The Scholarships provided a two-year program for young men, and later, women, from the United States, United Kingdom and Germany, to carry on the Illuminati conspiracy.

Among the Rhodes Scholars: Dean Rusk (CFR, Secretary of State, 1961-69), Walt Whitman Rostow (Special Assistant for National Security Affairs, 1966-69), Sen. James William Fulbright (AR, 1945-74), Harlan Cleveland (Assistant Secretary of State for International Organization Affairs in the Kennedy administration, Ambassador to NATO under Presidents Johnson and Nixon), Nicholas Katzenbach (CFR, U.S. Attorney General, 1965-66), Sen. Frank Church (ID.1956-81), Sen. Bill Bradley (NJ, 1979-97), Sen. David Boren (OK, 1979-94, CFR), Sen. Richard D. Lugar (IN, 1976-present), Sen. Larry Pressler (SD, 1979-97, CFR, Phi-Beta-Kappa), Sen. Paul Sarbanes (MD, 1977-present), Rep. Elliot H. Levitas (GA, 1975-85), Gov. Bill Clinton (AR, 1979-81, 1983-92; President, 1993-2001; CFR, Trilateral Commission— he didn't graduate), Gov. Richard Celeste (OH, 1983-91), Supreme Court Justice Byron 'Whizzer' White (1962-93, also Phi Beta Kappa), Charles Collingwood (TV commentator), Howard K. Smith (TV commentator), George Jerome Goodman (writer known as 'Adam Smith'), Brig. Gen. Pete Dawkins, Pat Haden (former quarterback of the Los Angeles Rams), Kris Kristofferson (songwriter/singer/actor), Rep. Carl Albert (OH, 1947-77, Speaker of the House from 1971-77), Hedley Donovan (former Editor-in-Chief of *Time* magazine, later a senior advisor to President Carter), R. James Woolsey (CFR, CIA Director, 1993-95), Rep. John Brademas (IN, 1959-81, later New York University President), Gen. Bernard W. Rogers (Supreme Commander of the NATO forces in Europe, 1979-87), Gen. Wesley Clark (Supreme Commander of the NATO forces in Europe, 1997-2000), Stansfield Turner (CIA Director, 1977-81), Robert Penn Warren (Pulitzer Prize-winning poet and novelist, best known for his book *All the King's Men*).

The Rhodes fortune, through the Rhodes Scholarship Fund, has been used to promote the concept of globalism and one-world government. Up to 1953, out of 1,372 American Rhodes Scholars, 431 had positions in teaching and educational administration, 31 were college presidents, 113 had government positions, 70 held positions in the media, and 14 were executives in foundations.

Rhodes began developing his philosophy after hearing a speech by John Ruskin (1819-1900) at Christ Church at Oxford University, which espoused an opinion, which by extension, furthered the teaching found in Plato's *Republic*. Plato called for "...a ruling class with a powerful army to keep it in power and a society completely subordinate to the monolithic authority of the rulers." Rhodes was also greatly influenced by Windom Reade's book *The Martyrdom of Man*, published in 1872, which advocated Darwinism and the tremendous suffering that man must undergo, which was epitomized in the phrase "the survival of the fittest." The book said that the "inevitable progress of man (was) to perfection." Rhodes incorporated this rationalization into his thinking.

Rhodes talked about starting an organization to preserve and extend the British Empire. He said in 1877: "It is our duty to seize every opportunity of acquiring more territory ... more territory simply means more of the Anglo-Saxon race, more of the best, the most human, most honorable race the world possesses ... the absorption of the greater portion of the world under our rule simply means the end of all wars." It was this mentality that fueled his desire to unite the world under one form of government. Using the Jesuits and the Masons as organizational models, Rhodes, Rothschild agent Lord Alfred Milner (1854-1925); other Ruskin associates at Oxford such as Arnold Toynbee, Arthur Glazebrook, Sir George Parkin, Philip Lyttleton Gell, Sir Henry Birchenough; and a similar group at Cambridge, led by social reformer and journalist William T. Stead, which included, Lord Reginald Baliol Brett, Sir John B. Seeley, Lord Albert Grey, and Edmund Garrett; joined together to form a secret group, on February 5, 1891.

There was an Inner Circle, known as the 'Circle of Initiates,' led by Rhodes, and included an Executive Committee with Stead, Brett, and Milner, the chief Rhodes Trustee; and other members like Lord Arthur Balfour (British Foreign Secretary who wrote to Rothschild promising his support for the establishment of a Jewish homeland in Palestine), Lord Lionel Walter Rothschild, Sir Harry Johnston, and Lord Albert Grey. The Outer Circle was known as the 'Association of Helpers,' but was not implemented until 1909-1913, when Milner established it as the Round Table organization. Their goal was to eventually establish a one-world government, which would be controlled by the international banking community, under the cloak of socialism. They saw England, not as a European power, but as an Atlantic power, and wanted to have a federation of the English-speaking world, which would be controlled by them.

In 1897, British and American elitists met in order to come up with ways to accomplish Rhodes' plan to consolidate their respective governments, which would pave the way for a one-world government. On July 24, 1902, a secret organization known as the Pilgrim Society was started in London. Six months later, an American branch was established in New York. Funded by the Rhodes Foundation, they were instrumental in taking control of the Democratic Party in the United States.

While he was Governor-General and High Commissioner of South Africa from 1897-1905, Milner (one of the most influential men in the political and financial circles in England) began to recruit young men, mostly from Oxford and Toynbee Hall, to help run his Administration. They became known as Milner's Kindergarten. With his backing, they were able to get jobs in influential positions in government and finance, where they became a dominant force in England's domestic and foreign policy. Between 1909-1913, Milner, Lionel Curtis, Philip H. Kerr (Lord Lothian), and Sir William S. Marris used this group to establish semi-secret discussion and lobbying groups, known as Round Table Groups, in England; the main British dependencies, South Africa, Canada, Australia, New Zealand, and India; and the United States. They were all controlled from England, and maintained contact through personal correspondence, frequent trips, and a quarterly journal begun in 1910, called *The Round Table*. The membership consisted of men who not only had a vast amount of political clout, but some who served in the highest levels of the British government.

Though they are still generally referred to as the Illuminati, from this point on, the Round Table would be the group responsible for perpetuating the conspiracy to establish a one-world government. Members of the Round Table have also been referred to as the 'Committee of 300,' or the 'Olympians.'

Most members had private fortunes, or were known financiers, however, it was the fortunes of Rhodes, Alfred Beit (1853-1906, the German financier from Frankfurt), Sir Abe Bailey (1864-1940), and the Astor Family, that formed the core of their financial support. Since 1925, substantial contributions have come from the Carnegie United Kingdom Trust, J. P. Morgan, the Rockefeller and Whitney families, and associates of Lazard Brothers Bank and Morgan, Grenfell and Company (the London affiliate of Morgan).

The Round Table controlled the *London Times* newspaper, which was owned by the Astor Family, as well as publications in other countries.

Milner led the group until his death in 1925, when the leadership was taken over by Lionel Curtis, and then by Lord Robert H. Brand (brother-in-law of Lady Astor) until he died in 1963, when the leadership was passed to Adam D. Marris, the son of Sir William, who was promoted to succeed Brand as managing director of Lazard Brothers Bank.

Lionel George Curtis (1872-1955), the British High Commissioner to South Africa and Secretary to Sir Alfred Milner, advocated British imperialism, and the establishment of a World State. He believed that "men should strive to build the Kingdom of Heaven here upon this earth, and that the leadership in that task must fall first and foremost upon the English-speaking peoples." In 1919, he established a front organization for the Round Table, known as the Royal Institute of International Affairs, which, after 1923, was headquartered at Chatham House (and is sometimes referred to as the Chatham House Study Group) at 10 St. James' Square in London.

From 1919-1927, there was an Institute of International Affairs started to cover all the Round Table Groups in the British dependencies, and the United States (where it is known as the Council on Foreign Relations), which was a front for J. P. Morgan and Company who controlled a small American Round Table Group. They were funded by Sir Abe Bailey and the Astor Family. Today you'll find the Institut des Relations Internationales in Belgium, the Institute for International Affairs in the Netherlands, the Institute for International Affairs in Rome, the Norwegian Institute for Foreign Affairs, the French Institute of International Relations, the Australian Institute of International Affairs, and many others.

In June, 2002, the former royal butler, Paul Burrell, revealed to the *Daily Mirror* in London, that Queen Elizabeth II told him: "There are powers at work in this country about which we have no knowledge."

THE COUNCIL ON FOREIGN RELATIONS

In the spring of 1918, a group of people met at the Metropolitan Club in New York City to form the Council on Foreign Relations. The group was made up of "high-ranking officers of banking, manufacturing, trading, and finance companies, together with many lawyers ... concerned primarily with the effect that the war and the treaty of peace might have on post-war business." The honorary Chairman was Elihu Root, a Wall Street lawyer, former New York Senator, former Secretary of War under McKinley, former Secretary of State under Theodore Roosevelt, member of the Carnegie Endowment for International Peace (who won the Nobel Peace Prize in 1912), and the most recognized Republican of his time. From June, 1918 to April, 1919, they held a series of dinner meetings on a variety of international matters, but soon disbanded.

In the fall of 1917, a group called 'The Inquiry' was assembled by Col. Edward M. House to negotiate solutions for the Paris Peace Conference in Versailles. They worked out of the American Geographical Society doing historical research, and writing position papers. The Inquiry was formed around the inner circle of the Intercollegiate Socialist Society, which was a group of American socialist-oriented intellectuals.

House, President Wilson's most trusted advisor, who was an admirer of Marx, in 1912, anonymously wrote the book *Philip Dru: Administrator* (published by Fabian B. W. Huebsch), which was a novel that detailed the plans for the takeover of America, by establishing "socialism as dreamed by Karl Marx," and the creation of a one-world totalitarian government. This was to be done by electing an American President through "deception regarding his real opinions and intentions." The book also discussed the graduated income tax, and tax-free foundations. The novel became fact, and Philip Dru was actually House himself.

On May 30, 1919, Baron Edmond de Rothschild of France hosted a meeting at the Majestic Hotel in Paris, between The Inquiry, which was dominated by J. P. Morgan's people, and included members such as— historian George Louis Beers (who later became the U.S. representative for the Round Table), Walter Lippman, Frank Aydelotte, Whitney H. Shepardson, Thomas W. Lamont, Jerome D. Greene, Col. Edward House, Dr. James T. Shotwell, Professor Archibald Coolidge, Gen. Tasker H. Bliss (the U.S. Army Chief of Staff), Erwin D. Canham (of the *Christian Science Monitor*), and Herbert Hoover (who, when he was elected to the Presidency in 1928, chose CFR member Henry L. Stimson to be his Secretary of State); and the Round Table, including members— Lord Alfred Milner, Lord Robert Cecil, Lord Eustace Percy, Lionel Curtis, and Harold Temperley; to discuss a merger. They met again on June 5, 1919, and decided to have separate organizations, each cooperating with the other.

On July 17, 1919, House formed the Institute of International Affairs in New York City, and The Inquiry became the American branch of the Round Table. Their secret aims were "to coordinate the international activities and outlooks of all the English-speaking world into one ... to work to maintain peace; to help backward, colonial, and underdeveloped areas to advance towards stability, law and order, and prosperity, along the lines somehow similar to those taught at Oxford and the University of London..."

The Council on Foreign Relations, and the Institute of International Affairs, both supporters of Wilson, strongly supported the League of Nations. However, the Round Table wanted to weaken the League by eliminating the possibility of collective security in order to strengthen Germany, and isolate England from Europe so an Atlantic power could be established, consisting of England, the British

Dominions, and the United States. In 1921, when it became apparent that the United States wasn't going to join the League, the Council on Foreign Relations was incorporated on July 21st, consisting of members from both groups, and others who had participated in the 1919 Paris Peace Talks. The name change was made so that the American branch of the Round Table would appear to be a separate entity, and not connected to the organization in England.

The Council on Foreign Relations (CFR) became the American headquarters for the Illuminati. Led by House, who wrote the Charter, they were financed by Paul Warburg, Jacob Schiff, William Averell Harriman, Frank Vanderlip, Bernard Baruch, Nelson Aldrich, J. P. Morgan, Otto Kahn, Albert H. Wiggin, Herbert H. Lehman, and John Rockefeller.

The membership of the CFR was mainly made up from the 150 members of House's task force which worked on the Peace Treaty. Many were associates of the J. P. Morgan Bank. The first Board consisted of the seven who were on the Merger Committee: Whitney H. Shepardson (Executive Secretary), George W. Wickersham (Chairman, Wall Street lawyer, Attorney General for President Taft), Frank L. Polk (Wall Street banker, Under Secretary of State), Paul Warburg, William R. Shepherd (president of Columbia University), Edwin F. Gay (Secretary-Treasurer, who later became the editor of the *New York Evening Post* which was owned by CFR member Thomas Lamont, who was a senior partner of J. P. Morgan and a financial advisor to President Wilson), and Stephen P. Duggan (director of the International Education Board); plus nine others: John W. Davis (President, former Ambassador to Great Britain, former Democratic Congressman from West Virginia, who later became chief counsel for J. P. Morgan & Co., Rockefeller Foundation trustee, and also a Democratic candidate for the Presidency in 1924), Elihu Root (Honorary President), Paul D. Cravath (Vice President, NY lawyer), Archibald Cary Coolidge (Harvard historian), Isaiah Bowman (director of the American Geographical Society), Norman H. Davis (NY banker, former Under Secretary of State), John H. Finley (associate editor at the *New York Times*), David F. Houston (former Secretary of Treasury), and Otto Kahn (NY banker). Other members included: J. P. Morgan, John D. Rockefeller, Edward M. House, Christian Herter, Jacob Schiff, Averell Harriman, Nelson Aldrich, Bernard Baruch, Owen D. Young, Russell C. Leffingwell, John Dulles, Allen Dulles, James T. Shotwell, Professor Charles Seymour, Joseph Chamberlain, Philip Jessup, Philip Moseley, Grayson Kirk, Henry M. Wriston, Arthur H. Dean, Philip D. Reed, John J. McCloy, and Walter Lippman (founder of the Intercollegiate Socialist Society).

Where All Souls College at Oxford University was the base for Round Table operations in England; the Institute for Advanced Study at Princeton University, established by Abraham Flexner of the Carnegie Foundation and Rockefeller's General Education Board, was the center of activities for the American branch.

Their membership grew from 97 in 1921, to 210 in 1922. In 1927, they began to receive funding from the Rockefeller Foundation, and later the Carnegie Endowment and Ford Foundation; in addition to the financial support they got from J. P. Morgan and the Wall Street banking interests. By 1936, their membership reached 250, and they already had a lot of influence on five American newspapers: *The New York Times*, *New York Herald Tribune*, *Christian Science Monitor*, *The Washington Post*, and the *Boston Evening Transcript*. This gave them the ability to slant the news in a way which would reflect their views, and thus begin the process of molding America to suit their needs.

In 1937, the CFR came up with the idea for 'Committees on Foreign Relations,' which would be established in various major cities around the country, for the "serious discussion of international affairs by leading citizens in widely separated communities." Between 1938 and 1940, Francis P. Miller organized these mini-Councils with funding from the Carnegie Corporation, to better influence thinking across the country. John W. Davis said after World War II that these committees had "provided an avenue for extending the Council to every part of the country." These CFR subsidiaries were established in 38 cities: Albuquerque, Atlanta, Billings, Birmingham, Boise, Boston, Casper, Charlottesville, Chicago (the most prominent), Cleveland, Denver, Des Moines, Detroit, Houston, Indianapolis, Little Rock, Los Angeles, Louisville, Miami, Nashville, Omaha, Philadelphia, Phoenix, Portland (ME), Portland (OR), Providence, Rochester, St. Louis, St. Paul-Minneapolis, Salt Lake City, San Francisco, Santa Barbara, Seattle, Tampa Bay, Tucson, Tulsa, Wichita, and Worcester.

The CFR has always claimed to be a private organization that doesn't formulate any government policy, in fact, the following disclaimer appears on their books: "The Council on Foreign Relations is a non-profit institution devoted to the study of the international aspects of American political, economic, and strategic problems. It takes no stand, expressed or implied, on American policy." From the beginning, their goal was to infiltrate the government, and that was done. Actually, they were so successful, that today, the CFR practically controls, and dictates, both domestic and foreign policy.

President Franklin D. Roosevelt had Henry Wallace (Secretary of Agriculture) and Louis Douglas (Director of the Budget Bureau) work with a CFR study group on national self-sufficiency, out of which came the Export-Import Bank and the Trade Agreements Act of 1934.

On September 12, 1939, after the start of World War II, CFR members Hamilton Fish Armstrong (editor of the CFR magazine *Foreign Affairs*) and Walter H. Mallory (Executive Director), went to the State Department and met with Assistant Secretary of State George S. Messersmith (CFR member), to offer the services of the Council by establishing a CFR study group concerning the war and a plan for peace, which would make recommendations to the State Department. They proposed to do research, and make informal recommendations in areas regarding national security and economics. Secretary of State Cordell Hull, and Under Secretary of State Sumner Welles (CFR member) liked the idea, and the War and Peace Studies Project was initiated with funding from the Rockefeller Foundation, who gave grants totaling $300,000 over a 6 year period.

Under that umbrella, there were 5 study groups, each with 10-15 men and a full-time paid secretary. All together, between 1940 and 1945, there were 100 people involved, with 362 meetings, producing 682 documents, and meets regularly with State Department officials.

War and Peace Studies Project—
    Norman H. Davis (Chairman)
    Waiter H. Mallory (Secretary)

Peace Aims: Hamilton Fish Armstrong
Territorial: Isaiah Bowman (President of Johns Hopkins University, geography expert)
Armaments: Allen W. Dulles (international corporate lawyer), Hanson W. Baldwin (military correspondent for *New York Times*)
Political: Whitney H. Shepardson (corporate executive who was House's secretary at the 1919 Versailles Peace Conference)
Economic & Financial: Alvin H. Hansen (professor of political economy at Harvard), Jacob Viner (professor of economics at University of Chicago)

In December, 1941, at the urging of the CFR, the State Department created the 14-member Advisory Committee on Post-War Foreign Policy, in which the CFR was represented by eight of its members (2 more became members later). The core of the group was Cordell Hull, Sumner Welles, Norman H. Davis, Myron C. Taylor (corporate executive), Isaiah Bowman and Leo Pasvolsky (economist), all of whom were CFR members, with the exception of Hull, and were known as the 'Informal Political Agenda Group' which Roosevelt called his "post-war advisers." They controlled the Committee, and were assisted by a research staff financed and controlled by the CFR. In order to formulate a closer liaison between the CFR and the Advisory Committee, the Research Secretaries from the War and Peace Studies were brought into the State Department as consultants to the corresponding subcommittee of the Advisory Committee. The Committee had their last general meeting in May, 1942, and all work from then on occurred at the subcommittee level.

As World War II came to an end, CFR study groups planned the reconstruction of Germany and Japan, the establishment of the United Nations, the initiation of the International Monetary Fund, and the World Bank (the UN International Bank for Reconstruction and Development). In December, 1943, the CFR began to outline their proposal for the United Nations, which was presented at the Dumbarton Oaks Conference. Historian Ruth B. Russell wrote in her 1958 book, *A History of the United Nations Charter: The Role of the United States, 1940-1945*, that "the substance of the provisions finally written into the (UN) Charter in many cases reflected conclusions reached at much earlier stages by the United States Government."

In 1945, the CFR moved into their present headquarters, which was largely financed by Rockefeller; and the study groups disbanded, with the men in those groups taking their place in the forefront of national affairs. For instance, Allen Dulles, former President of the CFR, was appointed director of the CIA; and John Foster Dulles, became Eisenhower's Secretary of State. Senator Barry Goldwater would later say: "From that day forward the Council on Foreign Relations had placed its members in policy-making positions with the federal government, not limited to the State Department."

In 1945, Sen. Arthur K. Vandenberg, a leading Republican, and a CFR member, traveled around the country to drum up support for the creation of the United Nations. He was also instrumental in getting the Republican-controlled Congress to go along with Truman's CFR-controlled foreign policy. When the UN Conference met in San Francisco in 1945, there were 47 CFR members in the U.S. delegation, including Alger Hiss (a State Department official and communist spy, who in 1950 was convicted of perjury after denying he had passed secret documents to the Russians, and was sentenced to five years in prison), Harry Dexter White (a communist agent), Owen Lattimore (who was called by the Senate Internal Security Subcommittee, a "conscious articulate instrument of the Soviet conspiracy"), Nelson Rockefeller, John Foster Dulles, Dean Acheson, Harold Stassen, Ralph Bunche, John J. McCloy, Adlai Stevenson, Philip Jessup, John Carter Vincent (identified as a "security risk"), Edward R. Stettinius (Secretary of State), Leo Pasvolsky, Joseph E. Johnson, Clark M. Eichelberger, and Thomas K. Finletter.

In 1925, Lionel Curtis, established the Institute of Pacific Relations (IPR) in 12 countries, in order to steer America towards Communism. The Round Table finger organization was financed by the Rockefeller Foundation, the Carnegie Corporation, the Carnegie Endowment for International Peace, and the Ford Foundation. The American branch received funding from Standard Oil, Vacuum Oil, Shell Oil, International General Electric, Bank of America, National City Bank, Chase National Bank, International Business Machines (IBM), International Telephone and Telegraph (IT & T), *Time* Magazine, and J. P. Morgan.

The IPR was led by Professor Owen Lattimore, head of Johns Hopkins University School of Diplomacy, who, during a 1951-52 investigation of the IPR, was identified as a Soviet operative. The Senate found the group to be "a vehicle toward Communist objectives." Men from the IPR (who were all communist or procommunist) were placed in important teaching positions, and dominated the Asian Affairs section of the State Department. After a four-year battle, their tax exempt status was revoked from 1955-1960.

Their publications were used by the armed forces, colleges, and close to 1,300 public school systems. They published a magazine called *Amerasia*, whose offices had been raided by the FBI, who found 1,700 secret documents from various government agencies, including the Army and Navy, that were either stolen, or given to them by traitors within the State Department. The Senate Internal Subcommittee concluded that the American policy decision which helped establish Communist control in China (by threatening to cut-off aid to Chiang Kai-shek unless he went communist), was made by IPR officials acting on behalf of the Soviet Union. Besides Lattimore, they also names Laughlin Curry (an Administrative Assistant to the President, who was identified as a Soviet agent by J. Edgar Hoover), Alger Hiss, Joseph Barnes, Philip Jessup, and Harry Dexter White, as Communist sympathizers. While he was Assistant Secretary of Treasury, Harry Dexter White provided Russia with the means of printing currency. He became Director of the International Monetary Fund in 1946, but resigned in 1947, when Whittaker Chambers accused him of being pro-communist, which he denied. In November, 1948, after White's death, Whittaker produced five rolls of microfilmed documents, which included eight pages of U.S. military secrets which had been written by White.

After World War II, the CFR was able to expand its study programs with grants of $1.5 million from the Ford Foundation, $500,000 from the Rockefeller Foundation, and $500,000 from the Carnegie Endowment.

Pro-communist Cyrus Eaton, Sr., a recipient of the Lenin Peace Prize, established the 'Joint Conferences on Science and World Affairs,' also known as the 'Pugwash Conferences,' in 1945, to gather intellectuals from across the world, and to exchange information on ways to push America towards disarmament. The group was financed by the CFR, the Rockefeller Foundation and the Ford Foundation. In 1959, a disarmament proposal developed by the CFR, and discussed at the Conference, became the basis for Kennedy's disarmament policy in September, 1961.

In Study No. 7 ('Basic Aim of U.S. Foreign Policy'), published by the CFR in November, 1959, they revealed their plans for the country: "The U.S. must strive to build a new international order ... (which) must be responsive to world aspirations for peace ... (and) for social and economic change...including states labeling themselves as 'Socialist' ... (and to) gradually increase the authority of the UN." They also advocated secret negotiations with Russia concerning disarmament, and increased foreign aid to China. The foreign policy of the CFR seemed to mirror that of the U.S. Communist Party, only because a change to a socialistic form of government would bring them that much closer to a one-world government.

THE CFR ELECTS NIXON

The career of Richard M. Nixon began in 1946, when, backed by Eastern Establishment money, he came out of obscurity to defeat incumbent Congressman Jerry Voorhis in California, who was anti-Federal Reserve. Voorhis wrote in a pamphlet called *Dollars and Sense*: "...the representatives of the American people in Congress should speedily proceed to transfer the ownership of the 12 Federal Reserve Banks from the private ownership of the member banks to the ownership of the nation itself."

In 1952, Nixon and Earl Warren, then the Governor of California, helped create an Eisenhower majority within a California delegation that had been leaning towards Robert Taft, an anti-communist. Nixon was rewarded by being selected as the Vice-President, while Warren was named to the Supreme Court.

During the 1960 Republican Convention, Nixon, the Republican nominee, left Chicago and flew to New York, where he secretly met with Nelson Rockefeller. A subsequent news release indicated that Rockefeller had requested the meeting, when in fact Nixon had. The result of the meeting was the Fourteen Points of the "Compact of Fifth Avenue," which injected Rockefeller's socialistic plans into the Platform of the Republican Party.

After losing to Kennedy, Nixon ran for Governor in California, but lost to Pat Brown in 1962. He left his law practice, and moved to New York, where he worked as a partner in the law firm of John Mitchell, who was Rockefeller's personal attorney. He lived in an apartment at 810 Fifth Avenue, a building owned by Rockefeller. He was a CFR member from 1961-65, and it was during this time that Nixon rebuilt his political career.

On November 22, 1963, the citizens of Dallas, Texas, found in their *Dallas Morning News* an unsigned leaflet titled "Wanted for Treason." At the top appeared John F. Kennedy's picture, and a list of reasons for the accusation. It was later discovered that it had been drafted at a Pepsi-Cola 'convention' in Dallas, by lawyers of the Rockefeller law firm of Nixon, Mudge, Rose, Guthrie, and Alexander, to be used as an attack on Kennedy during the 1963 Presidential campaign. There is more than one Kennedy Assassination researcher who feels that Nixon had prior knowledge of Kennedy's shooting, though no hard evidence has ever come to light.

While it is widely accepted that there was a conspiracy behind Kennedy's death, as the volumes of evidence prove, there has never been a single group pinpointed as the mastermind of such a plan. The complexities involved in such a cover-up, certainly point to the Illuminati, because they are the only group in the world, operating behind the scenes, able to influence and control all the elements necessary to pull off something like this. His murder was carried out publicly, because they wanted the political leaders in this country to know who was in control.

Ten days before he was shot in Dallas, it has been reported that President Kennedy said in a speech at Columbia University: "The high office of President has been used to foment a plot to destroy the American's freedom, and before I leave office I must inform the citizen of this plight."

There has been a phenomenal amount of research done on the case of President Kennedy's murder, and it almost seems that when he died, the tide changed in this country. The forces behind the assassination of Kennedy were able to change the course of history at will, and with the new-found confidence at their success, the power they gained, literally allowed them to exert complete control over American government.

One fact that linked the Illuminati to the Kennedy conspiracy was the oil connection. Huge oil fields had been discovered off the coast of Vietnam in 1950, and Rockefeller was able to use oil as a ploy to ferment a fear that Vietnam would be lost to Communism, the way Cuba was. However, Kennedy wanted to end American involvement in the war, and in October, 1963, he recalled 1,000 so-called advisers. He planned to bring home all American soldiers by 1965. After Kennedy was eliminated, the U.S. government escalated the war in Vietnam. Billions of dollars was being made from the war, because war is good business. This money source would have ended.

Though the Office of Strategic Services (OSS), an offshoot of the Coordinator of Information, was initiated in 1942 by President Roosevelt, President Harry Truman was the one responsible for its evolution into the Central Intelligence Agency in 1947. He also began to see its growing power. In a column that appeared in the *Washington Post* on December 21, 1963, he revealed his feelings about the agency: "For some time I have been disturbed by the way the CIA has been diverted from its original assignment. It has become an operational and at times a policy-making arm of the government..." On January 16, 1961, in his

'Farewell to the Nation,' President Eisenhower said: "In the councils of government, we must guard against the acquisition of unwarranted influence, whether sought or unsought, by the military-industrial complex. The potential for the disastrous rise of misplaced power exists and will persist. We must never let the weight of this combination endanger our liberties or democratic processes." Kennedy's hatred of the CIA was well-known. After the Bay of Pigs disaster, he fired CIA Director Allen Dulles (who had secretly developed plans to expand the Vietnam War), and said he wanted "to splinter the CIA in a thousand pieces and scatter it to the winds." Using a federal statute, Kennedy was going to force J. Edgar Hoover, the aging Director of the FBI, to retire, because he wanted somebody who better represented his New Frontier.

Conservative in his economics, it was his intention to circumvent the Federal Reserve, by returning the authority to "coin and regulate money" back to the Congress, rather than have it manipulated by the international bankers who print the money and then loan in back to the federal government— with interest. On June 4, 1963, he signed Executive Order #11110 which called for the issuance of $4.3 billion in United States Notes through the U.S. Treasury, rather than the Federal Reserve, very similar to what Abraham Lincoln did. The Order also provided for the issuance of "silver certificates against any silver bullion, silver, or standard silver dollars in the Treasury not then held for redemption of any outstanding silver certificates, to prescribe the denominations of such silver certificates, and to coin standard silver dollars and subsidiary silver currency for their redemption..." This meant that for every ounce of silver in the U.S. Treasury's vault, the government could issue money against it. This resulted in the introduction of more than $4 billion worth of U.S. Notes into circulation, consisting of $2.00 and $5.00 bills; and although they were never issued, $10.00 and $20.00 notes were in the process of being printed when Kennedy was killed. On Monday, November 25, 1963, the day of Kennedy's funeral, President Johnson signed an executive order to recall the U.S. Notes that had been issued by Kennedy's earlier directive; and five months later, the Series 1958 Silver Certificate was no longer issued, and was subsequently removed from circulation.

And to top matters off, he advocated a strong West Germany; and after winning the showdown with Russia over Cuba, signed a limited nuclear test ban treaty with the Soviets. Needless to say, Kennedy's agenda was contrary to the plans for a New World Order. As Jacqueline Kennedy was getting ready to leave Air Force One when it arrived in Washington, still wearing the bloodstained clothing from Dallas, she said: "I want them to see what they have done." A very strange comment to make since Oswald was already in custody.

In 1968, Sen. Robert F. Kennedy promised an honorable end to the Vietnam War, and with Martin Luther King, Jr. delivering the Black support, Kennedy most likely would have been elected President. However, that did not fit into the plans of the Illuminati, who wanted to prolong the war, and wanted Nixon to be President, because he represented the instrument that would perpetuate their goals. Again, there is plenty of evidence that points to a conspiracy in the assassinations of Bobby Kennedy, as well as King. The likelihood that the same forces were involved is evident, because again, the course of the nation was altered to fit into their plans.

The Illuminati didn't want Nixon elected in 1960, and to insure that he wasn't, Eisenhower told the country that he couldn't think of a single thing that Nixon had done to help, during the eight years of his Administration. That comment and his haggard appearance during the debates, were the two main things that kept him from being elected. However, in 1968, the responsibility of moving the country closer to socialism, and towards a one-world government, was put upon his shoulders. Former Secretary of the Navy, William Mittendorf, Finance Chairman of Nixon's 1968 campaign, said that at 5:30 AM on the morning after Nixon's election victory, Nelson Rockefeller and William Rogers went to Nixon's room to help select his Cabinet.

He appointed Mitchell, his campaign manager, to be his Attorney General. He appointed Henry Kissinger to be his Secretary of State, even though Kissinger's views were the complete opposite of his own. In reality, the Kissinger appointment was urged by Nelson Rockefeller, so the Illuminati could control U.S. foreign policy. At the beginning of each of his terms, Nixon offered the post of Treasury Secretary to David Rockefeller, but he refused it. It was Nixon who chose George Bush, the former Texas Congressman, to be the Chairman of the Republican Party, after Bush lost the Senate race to Democrat Lloyd Bentsen in Texas; and later appointed him to be the Ambassador to the UN, the Ambassador to China, and the Director of the CIA.

In his 1971 State of the Union Address, Nixon said: "We in Washington will at last be able to provide government that is truly for the people. I realize that what I am asking, is that not only the Executive Branch, but even the Congress will have to change by giving up some of its power." Three days later, he announced that the country was being divided up into ten federal districts, and in February, 1972, he signed Executive Order #11647, which gave the government the power to accomplish that division. The Ten Regional Councils, a direct extension of the Executive Branch, since then, have been getting control of local, county, and state governmental functions, through federal loans.

Nixon told ABC news correspondent Howard K. Smith, that he was "Keynesian in economics." This was a reference to John Maynard Keynes, the English economist and Fabian socialist, who said he was promoting the "euthanasia of capitalism." Even though his policies had already indicated it, Nixon was basically saying that he was a Socialist.

Nixon had resigned from the CFR in 1962, when it became an issue in the California gubernatorial primary campaign, but later rejoined. In his book, *Six Crises*, he wrote: "Admitting Red China to the United Nations would be a mockery of the provision of the Charter which limits its membership to 'peace-loving nations'..." Yet he wrote in the October, 1967 edition of *Foreign Affairs* about how he would have a new policy towards Red China. Even after a July 15, 1971 statement on Radio Peking in China that called for the "people of the world, (to) unite and defeat the U.S. aggressors and all their running dogs," Nixon accepted an invitation by Premier Chou En Lai to go to China, where the groundwork for trade relations was established.

In the early 1970's, things began to go sour for Nixon. It was the establishment newspapers, the *Washington Post* and the *New York Times* who forced a third-rate burglary onto the front pages, and turned Watergate into a major media event, which forced President Nixon to resign from office. As more and more facts came out, it was quite obvious that Watergate was a move by the Illuminati to get rid of an uncooperative President.

Watergate can actually be traced back to 1956, when Nixon's brother, Donald, received a secret loan from Howard Hughes. It proved to be embarrassing when it surfaced during the 1960 Presidential election. Nixon vowed revenge against the Democrats, and later discovered that Democratic Party Chairman Lawrence F. O'Brien had been secretly retained by Hughes. Nixon sent a memo to Chief of Staff H. R. Haldeman, in January, 1971, to get his Special Counsel Charles Colson to get the proof so that they could expose him. It was believed that the second break-in at the Democratic National Committee on June 16-17, 1972, was to retrieve any derogatory information the Democrats had on the Republicans, but it was later revealed that the main goal was to place a bug on the frequently used phone that was in the area of the DNC that housed the offices of R. Spencer Oliver, his secretary, and the Chairman of the State Democratic Governors organization.

In March, 1974, financier Robert Vesco told CBS's Walter Cronkite in an interview, that six months before Watergate, a group had come to him who "were going to attempt to get initial indictments of some high officials using this as a launching board to get public opinion in their favor and using the press media to a great degree. The objective was to reverse the outcome of the public election." There had been an article in the *Washington Post* pertaining to a secret contribution to the Republican Party, and this group of Democrats had went to him, seeking more information to use against Nixon. The three people that Vesco dealt with, "were names that everyone would recognize (who) held extremely high posts in past Administrations." Vesco told *New York Times* writer Neil Cullinan, that Watergate was intentionally created to stop Nixon.

Nixon aide Bruce Herschenson said that the Watergate plot was deliberately sabotaged "by a non-elected coalition of power groups." Former CIA agent, James W. McCord, Jr., the security chief for the Committee to Re-Elect the President, has been accused of being a double agent, and used to bring Nixon down by sabotaging the break-in at the Watergate Hotel.

There is evidence to believe that the police had been tipped off on the night of the break-in. Detective Lt. Carl Shoffler, and three other officers, who usually went off duty at midnight, just happened to stay on for the next shift, and was parked just a minute away from the hotel complex. When the security guard, Frank Wills, found the tape on the door, and called the police, it was those officers who came immediately to arrest the White House 'plumbers' (Special Investigations Unit). To top it off, McCord and Shoffler were friends.

McCord had entered the Watergate while it was still open, and put some tape on one of the doors so it wouldn't lock. The tape was put on horizontally, so that it could be seen between the doors. When the 'plumbers' arrived hours later, instead of the doors being open, they were locked, which indicated that the piece of tape had been discovered. They left, since there was no longer any assurance of a successful operation. McCord told them to go back and pick the lock, since the police had not been called. E. Howard Hunt and his Cuban accomplices, did this, and left tape on the door for McCord to get in. About five minutes later, he joined them. He was supposed to remove the tape from the door, but he didn't; however, he told the other 'plumbers' that he did. He also instructed them to shut-off their walkie-talkies, so the static wouldn't be heard, which means they were inside the office without being able to hear any outside communications taking place. They were caught, when Wills discovered the door taped for a second time.

Afterward, on March 19, 1973, McCord wrote a letter to Judge John J. Sirica, which turned the Watergate affair into a national crisis, by saying that Attorney General John Mitchell was involved, that campaign money was used to pay the 'plumbers,' and that the White House was trying to blame the CIA; when in fact the White House had engineered the entire operation, and Nixon covered it up. This came after Nixon held a press conference to say: "There is no involvement by the White House."

In the years since Watergate occurred, one simple fact seems to have emerged, and that is, that Nixon probably had no prior knowledge of the break-in. White House Counsel John Dean III ordered it and "deceived the President of the United States into joining a conspiracy to obstruct justice in order to cover up a crime that Nixon had not committed."

If it wouldn't have been for the discovery of the Watergate tapes, Nixon may very well have survived the scandal. Gen. Alexander M. Haig, Jr., an aide to National Security Adviser Henry Kissinger, who later became Nixon's Chief of Staff, controlled the vault where the tapes were kept, and secretly made copies of the transcripts available.

Haig became Cyrus Vance's (CFR member, Secretary of the Army, later Deputy Secretary of Defense under Robert McNamara, who was also a CFR member) assistant in 1962. After a short tour of duty in Vietnam in 1966, where he was decorated for bravery, he was made a full colonel in 1968. He transferred to West Point to assist Commandant Gen. Andrew Goodpaster (CFR) for two years, after which Goodpaster recommended Haig to Kissinger in 1969, and Haig was put on the National Security Council. In less than a year, he was promoted to general, and in two more years, to major-general. Although he had served only four months as a battalion commander, and one month as a brigade commander, in 1972 he was given four stars, and nominated for Army Vice Chief of Staff. It was said, that 183 other generals, who were more deserving, were passed over. Ford would later promote him to Supreme Allied Commander in Europe. He resigned in 1979 because he was critical of Carter's defense and foreign policies. He became the chief operating officer of United Technologies, only to return to government for 18 months as Reagan's Secretary of State. Haig was a member of the Council on Foreign Relations.

John Dean claimed that 'Deep Throat,' the man who leaked information to Bob Woodward of the *Washington Post*, was Alexander Haig. Haig denied it. Woodward had claimed that he didn't meet Haig until 1973, however, it has since been revealed that prior to Woodward becoming a reporter, he was a lieutenant in the Navy, and as a special briefing officer, and had contact with Haig at the National Security Office in the White House. It now appears that Haig had a huge role in bringing Nixon down.

So why did the Illuminati turn against Nixon? In addition to the previously mentioned economical changes, he infuriated Kissinger by bombing North Vietnam without consulting anyone. It was even rumored that Nixon was planning to get rid of Kissinger. However, Kissinger was the Illuminati's man in the White House, and his job was to control Nixon, so he was the one running the show.

Some very interesting information surfaced about Henry Kissinger. In 1961, Col. Gen. Michael Goleniewski, of Polish Intelligence (GZI), defected to the United States, bringing with him 5,000 pages of secret documents, 160 microfilms of secret reports, 800 pages of Russian intelligence reports, plus the names of hundreds of Soviet agents in American and Europe. State Department Security Officer, John Norpel, Jr., testified before the Senate Internal Security Subcommittee that the information provided by Goleniewski was never proven to be inaccurate, and Goleniewski was honored by the 88th Congress for his efforts.

The documents indicated that after World War II, Russia established an ODRA spy ring in Poland to infiltrate British and American intelligence. The GZI, discovered that one communist agent, code-named 'Bor,' had worked with another agent, Ernst Bosenhard (a clerk at the U.S. Intelligence Headquarters in Oberammergau, Germany), who had been sending secret documents to Moscow. Bosenhard was convicted of espionage in 1951. 'Bor' returned to the United States, and was secretly working with the CIA, while teaching at Harvard University. 'Bor' was identified as Sgt. Henry Alfred Kissinger.

Kissinger became a consultant on security matters during the Administrations of Eisenhower, Kennedy, and Johnson; and served as Nelson Rockefeller's chief advisor on foreign affairs. In his book *White House Years*, he called Rockefeller, "the single most influential person in my life." His book, *Nuclear Weapons and Foreign Policy*, in 1957, established him as the leading authority on U.S. strategic policy, and he was the one who initiated the Strategic Arms Limitation Talks (SALT). There should be little doubt where his allegiances are in regard to his support of one-world government.

This story took on additional meaning, when in 1965, former CIA Chief of Research and Analysis, Herman E. Kimsey, used fingerprint, dental and medical records, handwriting analysis, blood tests, and interviews with childhood friends and relatives to reach a conclusion that Goleniewski was actually Aleksei Romanoff, the son of Nicholas II, who survived the alleged Communist massacre of the Russian Royal family.

The Bolshevik government had claimed, that in the middle of the night, July 16, 1918, they had captured the seven members of the Russian Imperial family, which included the Czar Nicholas, his wife (Alexandra), son (Aleksei), and four daughters (Olga, Tatiana, Maria, and Anastasia); as well as Dr. Eugene Botkin, the imperial physician, and three servants; and murdered them in the basement of the Ipatiev house in Ekaterinburg (now Sverdlovsk). They took their bodies fourteen miles away to the abandoned Four Brothers Mine, soaked the bodies with gasoline, attempted to burn them, and buried them in the swamp. They were only successful in burning the two youngest ones, Aleksei and Anastasia. Their personal belongings were thrown down a mine shaft. Fearing that they would be discovered, two days later, the bodies were retrieved. Those remaining were buried in the middle of a dirt road, where in 1979, they were discovered by a local historian and

Soviet television personality, who excavated two skulls, analyzed them, and then reburied them. The discovery was finally announced in 1989.

In 1991, the final resting place of the Romanov's was "reopened for the last time," and the remains, a box of bones purported to be five of the seven Romanov's, were removed for DNA analysis. In 1995, the tests results were released, which indicated that the remains were that of the Royal family. However, many Russians doubted the claims, and in 1998, when a funeral was finally held, the head of the Russian Orthodox Church ordered the officiating priest not to refer to Romanov's by name, but instead, as the "victims of the Revolution." The priest said before the funeral: "The truth is I don't know who I am burying."

According to the official report, there were a total of 23 people in the cellar, which measured 17 feet by 14 feet. One of the first investigator's on the scene, Captain Malinovsky, of the Officer's Commission, concluded: "As a result of my work on this case I became convinced that the imperial family was alive. It appeared to me that the Bolsheviks had shot someone in the room in order to simulate the murder of the imperial family…" Some have suggested that it was only Dr. Botkin and the servants who were shot.

In December, 1970, documents released by the British Government revealed that President Wilson backed a secret mission to Russia that resulted in the rescue of the Czar and his family, who were smuggled out of Russia in the back of trucks, and then taken by ship to Europe where they have lived since 1918. The Report said that, "Sir William Wiseman, a partner in the New York banking house of Kuhn, Loeb & Co.," received $75,000 from the U.S. government as part of a "scheme" for a secret mission to rescue the Czar and his family.

Prince Kuli-Mirza, commander of the 'White Russian' forces, believed that the Royal family survived, and showed Gleb Botkin, the son of the Czar's doctor, documents which said that "the imperial family had first been taken to a monastery in the province of Perm, and later to Denmark." A 1919 book called *Rescuing the Czar*, by James P. Smyth, who identified himself as an American secret agent, revealed how he led the Romanovs through a secret tunnel to the British Consulate in Ekaterinburg, and from there they were secretly taken to Tibet.

The remains of the two youngest of the Romanov children, Aleksei and Maria, have never officially been located; and through the years, there has been some evidence to suggest that Aleksei and Anastasia may have survived the execution. An entry in the diary of Richard Meinertzhagen, a former British intelligence agent, suggested that one of the Czar's daughters escaped; and in the 1993 book *The Romanov Conspiracies*, British writer, Michael Occleshaw, also claimed that one of the Czar's daughters survived.

The Treaty of Brest-Litovsk between Russia and Germany, which was signed on March 3, 1918 to end the hostilities between them, was said to also contain a codicil that guaranteed that the Romanov's would not be harmed. The Russian people were to continue believing that they were dead, so the communists could replace the monarchy. It had been hoped that the Bolshevik government wouldn't survive, so they could return, but it never happened.

On June 11, 1971, the *New York Daily Mirror* announced the exclusive publication of "Reminiscences of Observations" by 'His Imperial Highness Aleksei Nicholaevich Romanoff, Tsarevich and Grand Duke of Russia.' The U.S. Government never officially recognized Goleniewski as a Romanov, because history reported that prince had suffered from hemophilia, an incurable genetic disease—but Goleniewski didn't.

The Czar left millions in American and European banks, which today is worth billions, and some researchers have made the claim, that the respective governments wanted to keep the Romanovs "dead," because without the existence of a surviving heir, the money that had been left behind probably had already been 'taken' by the international bankers. Goleniewski pledged that as the Czar's heir, if he would be granted his rightful inheritance, he would use the money to destroy Communism.

Nixon also angered the Illuminati because of his choice of Vice Presidents. After Vice President Spiro Agnew resigned because of income tax evasion charges, Establishment insiders had urged Nixon to appoint Nelson Rockefeller. However, Nixon instead, appointed Gerald Ford to be his Vice President (who, when he became President, did appoint Rockefeller to be his VP). If Rockefeller would have been appointed, he would have become President after Nixon was destroyed. So, Nixon ruined their plans, and may have known that, because after he resigned, he was having problem with a swollen leg, and said that if he would have gone to Bethesda Naval Hospital to get it taken care of, he would have "never come out alive."

Later, Lynette "Squeaky" Fromme would attempt to shoot Ford on September 5, 1975; and on September 22, 1975, Sara Jane Moore would also attempt to shoot Ford. Moore said she was trying to expose the nation's "phony system of government" by elevating "Nelson Rockefeller to the Presidency." In a June, 1976, *Playboy* interview, she said that there was a "part that I don't think I can talk about. I just haven't figured out a way to talk about it and protect everyone. I'm not saying that anyone helped me plan it. I'm not just saying that there are other things—which means there are other people, though not in terms of a conspiracy. There are areas I'm not willing to talk about for a lot of reasons." The article also said that U.S. District Judge Samuel Conti, "added to the air of mystery surrounding her case (and) sealed all the trial evidence." This certainly gives some serious overtones to the attempts on Ford's life, and if they were actually intended to elevate Rockefeller to the Presidency.

The bottom line seems to be, that Nixon got cocky. With the Illuminati hoping to have world control by 1976 (it was "rescheduled" for the mid-eighties), Nixon was hoping to follow in the steps of Woodrow Wilson and Franklin D. Roosevelt who were virtual dictators, and began acting on his own to bring about change, so he could head the world government. On May 21, 1971, James Reston (CFR) wrote in an article that appeared in the *New York Times*: "Mr. Nixon would obviously like to preside over the creation of a new world order, and believes he sees an opportunity to do so in the last twenty months of his first term." It is likely that the plan to get rid of Nixon was beginning to take shape at that time.

In the summer of 1973, Republicans partial to Nixon had announced to the Washington media that they wanted Nixon to be elected to a third term and had organized a group known as 'The Committee to Repeal the Twenty-Second Amendment.' The movement sort of died within a couple of weeks. Then in October, came the rumor that Nixon may be considering a military coup to stay in office. Gen. Alexander Haig told the Congress during his confirmation hearings for the position of Secretary of State on January, 1981, that some people in Washington were "flirting with solutions which would have been extra-Constitutional." Watergate Special Prosecutor Leon Jaworski warned the grand jury, that if they decided to indict Nixon, he may use force to remain in office. In June, 1982, Harold Evans, Watergate grand juror, appearing on a segment of the ABC-TV news show "20/20." said that Jaworski told them, that if they indicted Nixon, he might "surround the White House with armed forces."

On October 26, 1973, in a *Washington Star* article called "Has President Nixon Gone Crazy?" syndicated columnist Carl Rowan wrote: "…in the face of a vote to impeach he might try, as 'commander-in-chief' to use military forces to keep himself in power." In another article called "The Pardon," in the August, 1983 edition of the *Atlantic Monthly*, Seymour Hersh, one of Nixon's Joint Chiefs of Staff, wrote that in a December 22, 1973 meeting:

> "He kept on referring to the fact that he may be the last hope, (that) the eastern elite was out to get him. He kept saying, 'This is our last and best hope. The last chance to resist the fascists' (of the left). His words brought me straight up out of my chair. I felt the President, without the words having been said, was trying to sound us out to see if we would support him in some extra-constitutional action ... (Secretary of Defense James) Schlesinger began to investigate what forces could be assembled at his order as a counterweight to the Marines, if Nixon— in a crisis— chose to subvert the Constitution. The notion that Nixon could at any time resort to extraordinary steps to preserve his presidency was far more widespread in the government than the public perceived..."

He felt it would be led by General Robert Cushman, the Marine Representative on the Joint Chiefs of Staff, who had been loyal to Nixon ever since he had been his military aide while he was the Vice President under Eisenhower. Schlesinger, in July, 1974, believing the Washington contingent of Marines to be the probable force used in a coup attempt, began developing a strategy to bring in the Army's 82nd Airborne Division from Fort Bragg, North Carolina.

On August 2, 1974, Secretary of State Henry Kissinger admitted that General Haig had informed him that Nixon was considering the idea of surrounding the White House with troops. In an August 27, 1974. article in the *Washington Post*, called "Military Coup Fears Denied," the fact was revealed that: "Defense Secretary James Schlesinger requested a tight watch in the military chain of command to ensure that no extraordinary orders went out from the White House during the period of uncertainty (and) that no commanders of any forces should carry out orders which came from the White House, or elsewhere, outside the normal military channels."

Tantamount to a military coup, and contrary to the Constitution, the Joint Chiefs of Staff sent a secret communiqué to all Commanders of the U.S. military forces around the world: "Upon receipt of this message you will no longer carry out any orders from the White House. Acknowledge receipt."

Rather than a plot by the Illuminati to militarily take over the government, it seemed to be more of an attempt by Nixon to keep from getting pushed out of office by the powers that actually run this country. In the end, he knew what kind of power he was dealing with, and resigned his office on August 9th, rather than risk what remaining credibility he had, by trying to grab what he could not hold. His resignation also prevented an impeachment trial, which may have allowed secret information to come to light.

THE CFR AND THEIR GOALS

The CFR's "1980's Project," evolved from a Council Study Group on International Order, which had met from 1971-73. They sought to duplicate the success they had achieved with the War & Peace Studies, and their concentration was to be on creating a new political and economic system that would have global emphasis. Miriam Camps, former Vice-Chairperson of the State Department's Policy Planning Council, recorded the group's discussion in a report called *The Management of Independence*, which called for "the kind of international system which we should be seeking to nudge things."

In the fall of 1973, the 1980's Project was initiated, and to accommodate it, the CFR staff was expanded, and additional funds raised, including $1.3 million in grants from the Ford, Lilly, Mellon and Rockefeller Foundations. The Coordinating Committee had 14 men, with a full-time staff; plus 12 groups, each with 20 members; in addition to other experts and advisors who acted as consultants to the project. Some of the reports produced: Reducing *Global Inequities*, *Sharing Global Resources*, and *Enhancing Global Human Rights*.

Stanley Hoffman, a chief participant of the Project, wrote a book in 1978, called *Primacy or World Order*, which he said was an "illegitimate offspring" of the Project. Basically, it was a summary of the Project's work, and concluded that the best chance for foreign policy success, was to adopt a "world order policy."

When Jimmy Carter was elected to the Presidency in 1976, some of the Project's strongest supporters, such as Cyrus Vance, Michael Blumenthal, Marshall Shulman, and Paul Warnke, went to the White House to serve in the new Administration.

In 1979, the Project was discontinued for being too unrealistic, which meant it was too soon for that kind of talk.

The CFR headquarters and library is located in the five-story Howard Pratt mansion (a gift from Pratt's widow, who was an heir to the Standard Oil fortune) at 58 E. 68th Street, in New York City (on the corner of Park Ave. and 68th Street), on the opposite corner of the Soviet Embassy to the United Nations. They are considered a semi-secret organization whose 1966 Annual Report stated that members who do not adhere to its strict secrecy, can be dropped from their membership. On the national level, the Business Advisory Council and the Pilgrim Society are groups which form the inner circle of the CFR, while on the international level, it's the Bilderbergers.

James P. Warburg (banker, economist, a member of FDR's brain trust, and son of Paul M. Warburg) of the CFR, told a Senate Foreign Relations Committee on February 17, 1950: "We shall have world government whether or not we like it. The only question is whether world government will be achieved by conquest or consent."

The *Chicago Tribune* printed an editorial on December 9, 1950 which said: "The members of the Council are persons of much more than average influence in the community. They have used the prestige that their wealth, their social position, and their education have given them to lead their country towards bankruptcy and military debacle. They should look at their hands. There is blood on them— the dried blood of the last war and the fresh blood of the present one."

They have only been investigated once, and that was in 1954, by the Special House Committee to Investigate Tax-Exempt Foundations (the Reece Committee), who said that the CFR was "in essence an agency of the United States Government." The Committee discovered that their directives were aimed "overwhelmingly at promoting the globalistic concept."

A July, 1958 *Harper's* magazine article said: "The most powerful clique in these (CFR) groups have one objective in common: they want to bring about the surrender of the sovereignty and the national independence of the U.S. They want to end national boundaries and racial and ethnic loyalties supposedly in increase business and ensure world peace. What they strive for would inevitably lead to dictatorship and loss of freedoms by the people. The CFR was founded for 'the purpose of promoting disarmament and submergence of U.S. sovereignty and national independence into an all-powerful one-world government'."

On September 1, 1961, *The Christian Science Monitor* printed the following statement: "The directors of the CFR make up a sort of Presidium for that part of the Establishment that guides our destiny as a nation."

On December 23, 1961, columnist Edith Kermit Roosevelt (granddaughter of President Theodore Roosevelt) wrote in the *Indianapolis News* that CFR policies "favor ... gradual surrender of United States sovereignty to the United Nations." Researcher Dan Smoot, a former FBI employee, said their goal was "to create a one-world socialist system and make the United States an official part of it."

Rep. John R. Rarick of Louisiana said in 1971:

"The CFR, dedicated to one-world government, financed by a number of the largest tax-exempt foundations, and wielding such power and influence over our lives in the areas of finance, business, labor, military, education and mass communication-media, should be familiar to every American concerned with good government and with preserving and defending the U.S. Constitution and our free-enterprise system. Yet, the nation's right-to-know machinery, the news media, usually so aggressive in exposures to inform our people, remain conspicuously silent when it comes to the CFR, its members and their activities. The CFR is the establishment. Not only does it have influence and power in key decision-making positions at the highest levels of government to apply pressure from above, but it also finances and uses individuals and groups to bring pressure from below, to justify the high level decisions for converting the U.S.

from a sovereign Constitutional Republic into a servile member state of a one-world dictatorship."

Phyllis Schlafly and Rear Admiral Chester Ward (former Judge Advocate General of the Navy from 1956-60), who was a member of the CFR for 16 years, wrote in their 1975 book *Kissinger on the Couch* that the CFR's "purpose of promoting disarmament and submergence of U.S. sovereignty and national independence into an all-powerful one-world government is the only objective revealed to about 95 percent of 1,551 members (1975 figures). There are two other ulterior purposes that CFR influence is being used to promote; but it is improbable that they are known to more than 75 members, or that these purposes ever have even been identified in writing." The book went on to say that the "most powerful clique in these elitist groups have one objective in common— they want to bring about the surrender of the sovereignty and the national independence of the United States." Ward's indictment of the group revealed their methods: "Once the ruling members of the CFR have decided that the U.S. Government should adopt a particular policy, the very substantial research facilities of CFR are put to work to develop arguments, intellectual and emotional, to support the new policy, and to confound and discredit, intellectually and politically, any opposition."

The published accounts of CFR activities greatly understate their power and influence on national and foreign policy. They have been called the "invisible government" or a front for the intellectual leaders who hope to control the world through the Fabian technique of "gradualism." Besides their involvement in the government, they hold key positions in all branches of the media, including the control or ownership of major newspapers, magazines, publishing companies, television, and radio stations.

The *New York Times* wrote: "The Council's membership includes some of the most influential men in government, business, education and the press (and) for nearly half a century has made substantial contributions to the basic concepts of American foreign policy." *Newsweek* called the Council's leadership the "foreign policy establishment of the U.S." Well-known political observer and writer Theodore White said: "The Council counts among its members probably more important names in American life than any other private group in the country." In 1971, J. Anthony Lukas wrote in the *New York Times Magazine*: "If you want to make foreign policy, there's no better fraternity to belong to than the Council."

From 1928-72, nine out of twelve Republican Presidential nominees were CFR members. From 1952-72, CFR members were elected four out of six times. During three separate campaigns, both the Republican and Democratic nominee were, or had been a member. Since World War II, practically every Presidential candidate, with the exception of Johnson, Goldwater, and Reagan, has been members.

The position of Supreme Allied Commander has usually been held by CFR members, like Gen. Dwight D. Eisenhower, Gen. Matthew B. Ridgeway, Gen. Alfred M. Groenther, Gen. Lauris Norstad, Gen. Lyman L. Lemnitzer, Gen. Andrew J. Goodpaster, and Alexander M. Haig, Jr. Most of the superintendents at the U.S. Military Academy at West Point have been members.

In Sen. Barry Goldwater's 1979 memoir, *With No Apologies*, he wrote: "When a new President comes on board, there is a great turnover in personnel but no change in policy." That's because CFR members have held almost every key position, in every Administration, from Franklin D. Roosevelt to Bill Clinton. During that period, every Secretary of State, with the exception of Cordell Hull, James F. Byrnes, and William Rogers, has been members. Every Secretary of Defense, from the Truman Administration, up to the Clinton Administration, with the exception of Melvin Laird, has been members. Since 1920, most of the Treasury Secretaries have been members; and since the Eisenhower Administration, nearly all of the National Security Advisors have been members.

Curtis Dall wrote in his book, *FDR: My Exploited Father-in-Law*: "For a long time I felt that FDR had developed many thoughts and ideas that were his own to benefit this country, the USA. But, he didn't. Most of his thoughts, his political 'ammunition' as it were, were carefully manufactured for him in advance by the CFR-One World money group."

CFR Members

Harry S. Truman Administration

Dean Acheson (Secretary of State), Robert Lovett (Secretary of State, and later Secretary of Defense), W. Averill Harriman (Marshall Plan Administrator), John McCloy (High Commissioner to Germany) , George Kennan (State Department advisor) , Charles Bohlen (State Department advisor).

Dwight Eisenhower Administration

When CFR member Dwight Eisenhower became President, he appointed six CFR members to his Cabinet, and twelve to positions of 'Under Secretary':

John Foster Dulles (Secretary of State, an in-law to the Rockefellers who was a founding member of the CFR, past Chairman of the Rockefeller Foundation and Carnegie Endowment for International Peace), Robert B. Anderson (Secretary of the Treasury), Lewis Straus (Secretary of Commerce), Allen Dulles (head of the OSS operation in Switzerland during World War II who became Director of the CIA, and President of the CFR).

John F. Kennedy Administration

When CFR member John F. Kennedy became President, 63 of the 82 names on his list of prospective State Department officials, were CFR members. John Kenneth Galbraith said: "Those of us who had worked for the Kennedy election were tolerated in the government for that reason and had a say, but foreign policy was still with the Council on Foreign Relations people." Among the more notable members in his Administration:

Dean Rusk (Secretary of State), C. Douglas Dillon (Secretary of the Treasury), Adlai Stevenson (UN Ambassador), John McCone (CIA Director), W. Averell Harriman (Ambassador-at-Large), John J. McCloy (Disarmament Administrator), Gen. Lyman L. Lemnitzer (Chairman of the Joint Chiefs of Staff), John Kenneth

Galbraith (Ambassador to India), Edward R. Murrow (head of the U.S. Information Agency), Arthur H. Dean (head of the U.S. Delegation to the Geneva Disarmament Conference), Arthur M. Schlesinger, Jr. (Special White House Assistant and noted historian), Thomas K. Finletter (Ambassador to NATO and the Organization for Economic Cooperation and Development), George Ball (Under Secretary of State for Economic Affairs), McGeorge Bundy (Special Assistant for National Security, who went on to head the Ford Foundation), Robert McNamara (Secretary of Defense), Robert F. Kennedy (Attorney General), Paul H. Nitze (Assistant Secretary of Defense), Charles E. Bohlen (Assistant Secretary of State), Walt W. Restow (Deputy National Security Advisor), Roswell Gilpatrick (Deputy Secretary of Defense), Henry Fowler (Under Secretary of State), Jerome Wiesner (Special Assistant to the President), Angier Duke (Chief of Protocol).

Lyndon B. Johnson Administration

Roswell Gilpatrick (Deputy Secretary of Defense), Walt W. Rostow (Special Assistant to the President), Hubert H. Humphrey (Vice-President), Dean Rusk (Secretary of State), Henry Fowler (Secretary of the Treasury), George Ball (Under Secretary of State), Robert McNamara (Secretary of Defense), Paul H. Nitze (Deputy Secretary of Defense), Alexander B. Trowbridge (Secretary of Commerce), William McChesney Martin (Chairman of the Federal Reserve Board), and Gen. Maxwell D. Taylor (Chairman of the Foreign Intelligence Board).

Richard M. Nixon Administration

Nixon appointed over 100 CFR members to serve in his Administration:

George Ball (Foreign Policy Consultant to the State Department), Dr. Harold Brown (General Advisory Committee of the U.S. Committee of the U.S. Arms Control and Disarmament Agency, and the senior member of the U.S. delegation for talks with Russia on SALT), Dr. Arthur Burns (Chairman of the Federal Reserve), C. Fred Bergsten (Operations Staff of the National Security Council), C. Douglas Dillon (General Advisory Committee of the U.S. Arms Control and Disarmament Agency), Richard N. Cooper (Operations Staff of the National Security Council), Gen. Andrew I. Goodpaster (Supreme Allied Commander in Europe), John W. Gardner (Board of Directors, National Center for Volunteer Action), Elliot L. Richardson (Under Secretary of State, Secretary of Defense, Attorney General; and Secretary of Health, Education and Welfare), David Rockefeller (Task Force on International Development), Nelson A. Rockefeller (head of the Presidential Mission to Ascertain the Views of Leaders in the Latin America Countries), Rodman Rockefeller (Member, Advisory Council for Minority Enterprise), Dean Rusk (General Advisory Committee of the U.S. Arms Control and Disarmament Agency), Gerald Smith (Director, Arms Control and Disarmament Agency), Cyrus Vance (General Advisory Committee of the U.S. Arms Control and Disarmament Agency), Richard Gardner (member of the Commission on International Trade and Investment Policy), Sen. Jacob K. Javits (Representative to the 24th Session of the General Assembly of the UN), Henry A. Kissinger (Secretary of State, Harvard professor who was Rockefeller's personal advisor on foreign affairs, openly advocating a "New World Order"), Henry Cabot Lodge (Chief Negotiator of the Paris Peace

Talks), Douglas MacArthur II (Ambassador to Iran), John J. McCloy (Chairman of the General Advisory Committee of the U.S. Arms Control and Disarmament Agency), Paul H. Nitze (senior member of the U.S. delegation for the talks with Russia on SALT), John Hay Whitney (member of the Board of Directors for the Corporation for Public Broadcasting), George P. Shultz (Secretary of the Treasury), William Simon (Secretary of Treasury), Stanley R. Resor (Secretary of the Army), William E. Colby (Director of the CIA), Peter G. Peterson (Secretary of Commerce), James Lynn (Housing Secretary), Paul McCracken (chief economic aide), Charles Yost (UN Ambassador), Harlan Cleveland (NATO Ambassador), Jacob Beam (USSR Ambassador), David Kennedy (Secretary of Treasury).

Gerald R. Ford Administration

When CFR member Gerald Ford became President, among some of the other CFR members:

William Simon (Secretary of Treasury), Nelson Rockefeller (Vice-President).

Jimmy Carter Administration

President Carter (who became a member in 1983) appointed over 60 CFR members to serve in his Administration:

Walter Mondale (Vice-President), Zbigniew Brzeznski (National Security Advisor), Cyrus R. Vance (Secretary of State), W. Michael Blumenthal (Secretary of Treasury), Harold Brown (Secretary of Defense), Stansfield Turner (Director of the CIA), Gen. David Jones (Chairman of the Joint Chiefs of Staff).

Ronald Reagan Administration

There were 75 CFR and Trilateral Commission members under President Reagan:

Alexander Haig (Secretary of State), George Shultz (Secretary of State), Donald Regan (Secretary of Treasury), William Casey (CIA Director), Malcolm Baldridge (Secretary of Commerce), Jeanne J. Kirkpatrick (UN Ambassador), Frank C. Carlucci (Deputy Secretary of Defense), William E. Brock (Special Trade Representative).

George H. W. Bush Administration

During his 1964 campaign for the U.S. Senate in Texas, George Bush said: "If Red China should be admitted to the UN, then the UN is hopeless and we should withdraw." In 1970, as Ambassador to the UN, he pushed for Red China to be seated in the General Assembly. When Bush was elected, the CFR member became the first President to publicly mention the "New World Order," and had in his Administration, nearly 350 CFR and Trilateral Commission members:

Brent Scowcroft (National Security Advisor), Richard B. Cheney (Secretary of Defense), Colin L. Powell (Chairman of the Joint Chiefs of Staff), William Webster (Director of the CIA), Richard Thornburgh (Attorney General), Nicholas F. Brady (Secretary of Treasury), Lawrence S. Eagleburger (Deputy Secretary of State), Horace G. Dawson, Jr. (U.S. Information Agency and Director of the Office of Equal Opportunity and Civil Rights), Alan Greenspan (Chairman of the Federal Reserve Board).

Bill Clinton Administration

When CFR member Bill Clinton was elected, *Newsweek* magazine would later refer to him as the "New Age President." In October, 1993, Richard Harwood, a *Washington Post* writer, in describing the Clinton Administration, said its CFR membership was "the nearest thing we have to a ruling establishment in the United States".

Al Gore (Vice-President), Donna E. Shalala (Secretary of Health and Human Services), Laura D. Tyson (Chairman of the Council of Economic Advisors), Alice M. Rivlin (Deputy Director of the Office of Management and Budget), Madeleine K. Albright (U.S. Ambassador to the UN), Warren Christopher (Secretary of State), Clifton R. Wharton, Jr. (Deputy Secretary of State and former Chairman of the Rockefeller Foundation), Les Aspin (Secretary of Defense), Colin Powell (Chairman, Joint Chiefs of Staff), W. Anthony Lake (National Security Advisor), George Stephanopoulos (Senior Advisor), Samuel R. Berger (Deputy National Security Advisor), R. James Woolsey (CIA Director), William J. Crowe, Jr. (Chairman of the Foreign Intelligence Advisory Board), Lloyd Bentsen (former member, Secretary of Treasury), Roger C. Altman (Deputy Secretary of Treasury), Henry G. Cisneros (Secretary of Housing and Urban Development), Bruce Babbit (Secretary of the Interior), Peter Tarnoff (Under Secretary of State for International Security of Affairs), Winston Lord (Assistant Secretary of State for East Asian and Pacific Affairs), Strobe Talbott (Aid Coordinator to the Commonwealth of Independent States), Alan Greenspan (Chairman of the Federal Reserve System), Walter Mondale (U.S. Ambassador to Japan), Ronald H. Brown (Secretary of Commerce), Franklin D. Raines (Economics and International Trade).

George W. Bush Administration

Richard Cheney (Vice President, former Secretary of Defense under President Bush), Colin Powell (Secretary of State, former Chairman of the Joint Chiefs of Staff under Presidents Bush and Clinton), Condoleeza Rice (National Security Advisor, former member of President Bush's National Security Council), Robert B. Zoellick (U.S. Trade Representative, former Under Secretary of State in the Bush administration), Elaine Chao (Secretary of Labor), Brent Scowcroft (Chairman of the Foreign Intelligence Advisory Board, former National Security Advisor to President Bush), Richard Haass (Director of Policy Planning at the State Department and Ambassador at Large), Henry Kissinger (Pentagon Defense Policy Board, former Secretary of State under Presidents Nixon and Ford), Robert Blackwill (U.S. Ambassador to India, former member of President Bush's National Security Council), Stephen Friedman (Sr. White House Economic Advisor), Stephen Hadley (Deputy National Security Advisor, former Assistant Secretary of Defense under Cheney), Richard Perle (Chairman of Pentagon Defense Policy Board, former Assistant Secretary of Defense in the Reagan administration), Paul Wolfowitz (Assistant Secretary of Defense, former Assistant Secretary of State in the Reagan administration and former Under Secretary of Defense in the Bush administration), Dov S. Zakheim (Under Secretary of Defense, Comptroller, former Under Secretary of Defense in the Reagan administration), I. Lewis Libby (Chief of Staff for the Vice President, former Deputy Under Secretary of Defense).

The *Christian Science Monitor* said that "almost half of the Council members have been invited to assume official government positions or to act as consultants at one time or another."

The Council accepts only American citizens, and has a membership of about 3,600, including influential bankers, corporate officers, and leading government officials who have been significantly affecting domestic and foreign policy for the past 30 years. Every member had been handpicked by David Rockefeller, who heads the inner circle of the CFR. It is believed that the hierarchy of their inner circle includes descendants of the original Illuminati conspirators, who have Americanized their original family names in order to conceal that fact.

Some of the CFR directors have been: Walter Lippman (1932-37), Adlai Stevenson (1958-62), Cyrus Vance (1968-76, 1981-87), Zbigniew Brzezinski (1972-77), Robert O. Anderson (1974-80), Paul Volcker (1975-79), Theodore M. Hesburgh (1926-85), Lane Kirkland (1976-86), George H. W. Bush (1977-79), Henry Kissinger (1977-81), David Rockefeller (1949-85), George Shultz (1980-88), Alan Greenspan (1982-88), Brent Scowcroft (1983-89), Jeane J. Kirkpatrick (1985-), Warren M. Christopher (1982-91), and Richard Cheney (1987-89).

Among the members of the media who have been in the CFR: William Paley (CBS), Dan Rather (CBS), Harry Reasoner (CBS), Roone Arledge (ABC), Bill Moyers (NBC), Tom Brokaw (NBC), John Chancellor (NBC), Marvin Kalb (CBS), Irving Levine, David Brinkley (ABC), John Scali, Barbara Walters (ABC), William Buckley (PBS), George Stephanopoulos, Daniel Schorr (CBS), Robert McNeil (PBS), Jim Lehrer (PBS), Diane Sawyer, and Hodding Carter III.

Some of the College Presidents that have been CFR members: Michael I. Sovern (Columbia University), Frank H. T. Rhodes (Cornell University), John Brademus (New York University), Alice S. Ilchman (Sarah Lawrence College), Theodore M. Hesburgh (Notre Dame University), Donald Kennedy (Stanford University), Benno J. Schmidt, Jr. (Yale University), Hanna Holborn Gray (University of Chicago), Stephen Muller (Johns Hopkins University), Howard R. Swearer (Brown University), Donna E. Shalala (University of Wisconsin), and John P. Wilson (Washington and Lee University).

Some of the major newspapers, news services and media groups that have been controlled or influenced by the CFR: *New York Times* (Sulzbergers, James Reston, Max Frankel, Harrison Salisbury), *Washington Post* (Frederick S. Beebe, Katherine Graham, Osborne Elliott), *Wall Street Journal, Boston Globe, Baltimore Sun, Chicago Sun-Times, L.A. Times Syndicate, Houston Post, Minneapolis Star-Tribune, Arkansas Gazette, Des Moines Register & Tribune, Louisville Courier*, Associated Press, United Press International, Reuters News Service, and Gannett Co. (publisher of *USA Today*, and 90 other daily papers, plus 40 weeklies; and also owns 15 radio stations, 8 TV stations, and 40,000 billboards).

In 1896, Alfred Ochs bought the *New York Times*, with the financial backing of J. P. Morgan (CFR), August Belmont (Rothschild agent), and Jacob Schiff (Kuhn, Loeb). It later passed to the control of Arthur Ochs Sulzberger, who was also a CFR member. Eugene Meyer, a CFR member, bought the *Washington Post* in 1933. Today it is run by his daughter, Katherine Graham, also a member of the CFR.

Some of the magazines that have been controlled or influenced by the CFR: *Time* (founded by CFR member Henry Luce, who also published *Fortune, Life,*

Money, People, Entertainment Weekly, and *Sports Illustrated;* and Hedley Donovan), *Newsweek* (owned by the *Washington Post,* W. Averell Harriman, Roland Harriman, and Lewis W. Douglas), *Business Week, U.S. News & World Report, Saturday Review, National Review, Reader's Digest, Atlantic Monthly, McCall's, Forbes, Look,* and *Harper's Magazine.*

Some of the publishers that have been controlled or influenced by the CFR: Macmillan, Random House, Simon & Schuster, McGraw-Hill, Harper Brothers, Harper & Row, Yale University Press, Little Brown & Co., Viking Press, and Cowles Publishing.

G. Gordon Liddy, former Nixon staffer, who later became a talk show pundit, laughed off the idea of a New World Order, saying that there are so many different organizations working toward their own goals of a one-world government, that they cancel each other out. Not the case. You have seen that their tentacles are very far reaching, as far as the government and the media. However, as outlined below, you will see that the CFR has a heavy cross membership with many groups; as well as a cross membership among the directorship of many corporate boards, and this is a good indication that their efforts are concerted.

Some of the organizations and think-tanks that have been controlled or influenced by the CFR: Brookings Institute, RAND Corporation, American Assembly, Foreign Policy Association (a more open sister to the CFR, which CFR member Raymond Fosdick, Under Secretary of General to the League of Nations, helped create), World Affairs Council, Business Advisory Council, Committee for Economic Development, National Foreign Trade Council, National Bureau of Economic Research, National Association of Manufacturers, National Industrial Conference Board, Americans for Democratic Action, Hudson Institute, Carnegie Endowment for International Peace, Institute for Defense Analysis, World Peace Foundation, United Nations Association, National Planning Association, Center for Inter-American Relations, Free Europe Committee, Atlantic Council of the U.S. (founded in 1961 by CFR member Christian Herter), Council for Latin America, National Committee on U.S.-China Relations, African-American Institute, and the Middle East Institute.

Some of the many companies that have been controlled or influenced by the CFR: Morgan, Stanley; Kuhn, Loeb; Lehman Brothers; Bank of America; Chase Manhattan Bank; J. P. Morgan and Co.; First National City Bank; Brown Brothers, Harriman and Co.; Bank of New York; CitiBank/Citicorp; Chemical Bank; Bankers Trust of New York; Manufacturers Hanover; Morgan Guaranty; Merrill Lynch; Equitable Life; New York Life; Metropolitan Life; Mutual of New York; Prudential Insurance; Phillips Petroleum; Chevron; Exxon; Mobil; Atlantic-Richfield (Arco); Texaco; IBM; Xerox Corporation; AT & T; General Electric; ITT Corporation; Dow Chemical; E. I. du Pont; BMW of North America; Mitsubishi; Toyota Motor Corporation; General Motors; Ford Motor Company; Chrysler; U.S. Steel; Proctor & Gamble; Johnson & Johnson; Estee Lauder; Avon Products; R. J. R. Nabisco; R. H. Macy; Federated Department Stores; Gimbel Brothers; J. C. Penney Company; Sears, Roebuck & Company; May Department Stores; Allied Stores; American Express; PepsiCo; Coca Cola; Pfizer; Bristol-Myers Squibb; Hilton Hotels; and American Airlines.

In September, 1922, when the CFR began publishing its quarterly magazine, *Foreign Affairs*, the editorial stated that its purpose was "to guide American opinion." By 1924, it had "established itself as the most authoritative American review dealing with international relations." This highly influential magazine has been the leading publication of its kind, and has a circulation of over 75,000. Reading this publication can be highly informative as to the views of its members. For instance, the Spring, 1991 issue, called for a UN standing army, consisting of military personnel from all the member nations, directly under the control of the UN Security Council.

A major source of their funding (since 1953), stems from providing a "corporate service" to over 100 companies for a minimum fee of $1,000, that furnishes subscribers with inside information on what is going on politically and financially, both internationally and domestically; by providing free consultation, use of their extensive library, a subscription to *Foreign Affairs*, and by holding seminars on reports and research done for the Executive branch. They also publish books and pamphlets, and have regular dinner meetings to allow speakers and members to present positions, award study fellowships to scholars, promote regional meetings and stage round-table discussion meetings.

Being that the Council on Foreign Relations was able to infiltrate our government, it is no wonder that our country has been traveling on the course that it has. The moral, educational and financial decline of this nation has been no accident. It has been due to a carefully contrived plot on behalf of these conspirators, who will be satisfied with nothing less than a one-world government. And it is coming to that. As each year goes by, the momentum is picking up, and it is becoming increasingly clear, what road our government is taking. The proponents of one-world government are becoming less secretive, as evidenced by George Bush's talk of a "New World Order." The reason for that is that they feel it is too late for their plans to be stopped. They have become so entrenched in our government, our financial structure, and our commerce, that they probably do control this country, if not the world. In light of this, it seems that it will be only a matter of time before their plans are fully implemented.

THE BROOKINGS INSTITUTION

The Brookings Institution was established by St. Louis tycoon and philanthropist, Robert Somers Brookings (1850-1932). At the age of 21, Brookings had become a partner in Cupples and Marston (a manufacturer of woodenware and cordage), which, ten years later, under his leadership, expanded and flourished. In 1896, at the age of 46, he retired to devote his duties towards higher education, and became President of Washington University's Board of Trustees, which, through the next twenty years, turned into a major university. He was one of the original Trustees of the Carnegie Endowment for International Peace, and a consultant to the Commission on Economy and Efficiency during the Taft Administration. In 1917, he was appointed to President Wilson's War Industries Board (which had the responsibility of receiving and distributing the supplies needed by the military), later becoming Chairman of its Price Fixing Committee (responsible for negotiating prices for all goods purchased by the Allied governments), which gave him a key role in the Wilson Administration.

At the age of 70, he took over the leadership of the Institute for Government Research (IGR, founded by lawyer and economist Frederick A. Cleveland in 1916), and raised $750,000 from 92 corporations and a dozen private citizens, to get it moving. Their first project was to push for legislation creating a federal budget, which was successful. The first U.S. Budget Director, under President Harding, was Charles G. Dawes, who relied heavily on the IGR's staff. The Institute was also involved in civil service reform legislation in the 1920's. Among their members: Supreme Court Chief Justice William Howard Taft (who was Chief Justice from 1921-30, after his Presidential term), Herbert Hoover (President, 1929-32), and Elihu Root.

Brookings decided that economics was the biggest issue, and not the administrative aspects that the Institute was covering, so in June, 1922, with a $1,650,000 grant from the Carnegie Corporation, he established the Institute of Economics to represent the interests of the labor unions and the general public. In 1924, he established the Robert S. Brookings School of Economics and Government (an outgrowth of Washington University in St. Louis), to allow doctoral students to spend time in Washington, D.C. to work on the staffs of the IGR and the Institute of Economics.

In 1927, he merged all three organizations to form the Brookings Institution, whose purpose was to train future government officials. He put $6 million, and 36 years of his life, into the nonpartisan, nonprofit center, which analyze government problems, and issue statistical reports. They produce an annual report, *Setting National Priorities*, which analyze the President's Budget.

Their headquarters is an eight story building, eight blocks from the White House, at 1775 Massachusetts Avenue, NW. They have a staff of about 250, including about 45 senior fellows and 19 research associates. Salaries go as high a $40,000 a year.

After serving close to ten years in the State Department, Leo Pasvolsky returned to the Brookings Institution in 1946, along with six other members of the State Department. With the financial backing of the Rockefeller Foundation, the Carnegie Corporation, and the Mellon Trust, Pasvolsky initiated an International Studies Group, which developed the basis for the Marshall Plan, to aid the European war recovery efforts.

In 1951, the Chicago Tribune said that the Brookings Institution had created an "elaborate program of training and indoctrination in global thinking," and that most of its scholars wind up as policy makers in the State Department. Truman was the first President to turn to them for help. In 1941, he named Brookings Vice President Edwin Nouse as the first Chairman of the President's Council of Economic Advisors. Kennedy and Johnson appointed many of their members to key posts. Carter's foreign policy became a resting place for the many of the group's recommendations.

President Johnson said that the purpose of his 'Great Society' legislation was to "try to take all of the money that we think is unnecessarily being spent and take it from the 'haves' and give it to the 'have-nots' that need it so much." Ralph Epperson, author of *The Unseen Hand*, one of the best books about the Master Conspiracy, said that Johnson was a "closet Communist." Another well-known researcher, John Coleman, said that the Brookings Institute had developed and drafted the Great Society programs which were "in every detail, simply lifted from Fabian Socialist papers drawn up in England. In some instances, Brookings did not even bother to change the titles of the Fabian Society papers. Once such instance was using 'Great Society,' which was taken directly from a Fabian Socialist paper from the same title." After Socialist leader Eugene Debs died in 1926, Socialist Norman Thomas, who graduated from and was ordained by the Union Theological Seminary, became the leader of the Socialist Party, running for President six times. Thomas was happy with Johnson's vision and said: "I ought to rejoice and I do. I rub my eyes in amazement and surprise. His war on poverty is a Socialistic approach…"

Republican's regard the Institution as the "Democratic government-in-exile," yet, Nixon appointed Herbert Stein, a Brookings scholar, to be Chairman of the Council of Economic Advisors. The Nixon Administration, who at one time had considered bombing the Brookings Institution, in order to allow the FBI to seize their documents, had considered the idea of a "Brookings Institution for Republicans," to offset the liberalism of Brookings. They thought of calling it the Institute for an Informed America, or the Silent Majority Institute. E. Howard Hunt, of Watergate fame, was to be its first Director, but he wanted to turn it into a center for covert political activity.

The role of the "conservative Brookings" was taken by an existing research center called the American Enterprise Institute for Public Policy Research, which was founded in 1943 by Louis H. Brown (Chairman of the Board at Johns-Manville Corporation), to promote free enterprise ideas. During the early sixties, they shortened their name to the American Enterprise Institute, and later received a lot of financial support during the Nixon and Ford Administrations, when the organization became a pool from which they drew their advisors. When Carter was elected, the AEI became a haven for many Republican officials, including President Gerald Ford, and William E. Simon, the Secretary of Treasury.

THE COMMITTEE FOR ECONOMIC DEVELOPMENT

In 1941, Paul Gray Hoffman, President of the Studebaker Company, and a Trustee of the University of Chicago; along with Robert Maynard Hutchins, and William Benton, the University's President and Vice President; organized the American Policy Commission to apply the work of the University's scholars and economists to government policy. They later merged with an organization established in 1939 by *Fortune* magazine, called Fortune Round Table.

Starting out as a group of business, labor, agricultural, and religious leaders, they soon evolved into an Establishment organization, with such members as: Ralph

McCabe (head of Scott Paper Co.), Henry Luce (Editor-in-Chief and co-founder of *Time*, *Life*, and *Fortune* magazines), Ralph Flanders (a Boston banker), Marshall Field (Chicago newspaper publisher), Clarence Francis (head of General Foods), Ray Rubicam (an advertising representative), and Beardsley Ruml (treasurer of Macy's Department Store in New York City, former Dean of Social Sciences at the University of Chicago, and Chairman of the New York Federal Reserve Bank, whose idea it was to deduct taxes from your paycheck).

At the beginning of World War II, Hoffman and Benton approached Jesse Jones, the Secretary of Commerce, with an idea for an 'American Policy Commission' to "analyze, criticize, and challenge the thinking and policies of business, labor, agriculture, and government," which Jones accepted, and began to organize, with their help. On September 3, 1942, the Committee for Economic Development was incorporated in Washington, D.C. (2000 L Street NW, Suite 700) to:

> "to foster, promote, conduct, encourage, and finance scientific research, education, training, and publication in the broad field of economics in order that industry and commerce may be in a position, in the postwar period, to make their full contribution to high and secure standards of living for people in all walks of life through maximum employment and high productivity in our domestic economy; to promote and carry out these objects, purposes, and principles in a free society without regard to, and independently of the special interests of any group in the body politic, either political, social, or economic."

Basically, their work centered around how to prepare the U.S. economy for a smooth transition from a wartime to a peacetime environment without the occurrence of a major depression or recession. A 1944 CED Report, *International Trade and Domestic Employment*, by Duke University Professor Calvin B. Hoover, helped push the United States into the International Monetary Fund, which was laid out at the Bretton Woods Conference in June, 1944, by chief negotiators Harry Dexter White (of the CFR) and John Maynard Keynes (of the Fabian Society); and the International Bank for Reconstruction and Development (World Bank); which both became part of the United Nations. It also helped motivate Establishment backing for what later emerged as the General Agreement on Trade and Tariffs. About three years later, their report on *An American Program of European Economic Cooperation* was eventually developed into the strategy for European recovery that became part of the Marshall Plan. In fact, Hoffman, who became the first CED Chairman, later headed the Federal agency that administered the Marshall Plan.

After the War, while Hoover was on leave from Duke, he worked with Hoffman to develop what eventually became known as the Marshall Plan. The group's later work laid the groundwork for regional government in the United States.

CHAPTER SIX

SETTING THE STAGE FOR WORLD WAR II

THE PROTOCOLS OF THE LEARNED ELDERS OF ZION

The *Protocols of the Learned Elders of Zion* is a 25,000 word document, which contains 24 'Protocols' by a member of a secret group of Jews, known as the Elders of Zion. It purported to be an outline for the control of the world by the Jews, with the help of the Masons. The document has been used to prove that the Illuminati is an exclusively Jewish plan for world domination, and has put the Jewish race in a bad light. In the course of some very intense research, I have not found any concrete evidence to prove this accusation. There is no "Jewish" conspiracy. Even though the Illuminati's founders were Jewish, and many influential Jews were part of the inner circle, that is no reason to indict the entire Jewish race.

The Bible identifies the Jews as God's chosen people, so it is highly unlikely that, as a race, they are behind such a Satanic plot. It has even been said that the people in Israel are not true Jews. One only has to look at the history of Israel, and see how they have been able to miraculously survive, to see that this is nothing but anti-Semitic rhetoric. It is not race, which is the common denominator here; it is money and greed. For the most part, the conspiracy has been dominated by the Europeans, and perpetuated by the English-speaking countries of the world.

No one is quite sure about this notorious document, and how it fits into the puzzle of the one-world government conspiracy. We know that its influence was taken advantage of, by the Illuminati, however, as to the actual origin and its purpose, we may never know for sure, because portions of it are highly accurate in its revelations. It is either true, or a clever forgery. If it is true, how much of it is true? If it is a forgery, it most certainly was based upon a factual document. Whatever the case, it is included in this book because it may contain some clues about the early stages of the Illuminati conspiracy, and the people behind it.

French Jesuit, the Abbé Barruel, who in 1797 wrote the five-volume *Memoire pou servir á l'histoire du Jacobinisme*, received a copy of a letter in 1806, from J. B. Simonini, an army officer in Florence. In it was a statement that the Jews "promised themselves that in less than a century, they would be the masters of the world." This letter had been widely circulated in France. It was later revealed that the letter had been fabricated by the French police to turn Napoleon against the Jews.

In 1848, Hermann Goedsche, a German postal official, forged letters indicating that Benedic Waldeck was conspiring to assassinate Frederick William IV, the

King of Prussia. After it became known that they were forgeries, he was removed from his job, and he began writing under the pseudonym, Sir John Retcliffe. One of those novels, *Biarritz*, written in 1868, contained a chapter titled, "In the Jewish Cemetery in Prague," in which the heads of the twelve tribes of Israel met with Satan to tell him of their plans to control the world. However, the covert proceeding was witnessed by two men, who then dedicated their lives to fighting the Satanic Jewish plot. In 1872, Russian anti-Semites printed the chapter in a pamphlet, as fiction based on fact. It was reprinted in 1876 and 1880. In July, 1881, the story was published in the French paper *Le Contemporain* as fact, and all of the speeches by each tribal head were consolidated into a single speech, supposedly made by a chief rabbi in a secret meeting of influential Jews. To substantiate the claim, it was said to have been taken from a forthcoming book by English diplomat, Sir John Readclif (a take-off on Goedsche's pen name), called *Annals of the Political and Historic Events of the Last Ten Years*.

In 1891, the story appeared in the Russian newspaper *Novorossiysky Telegraf*, which established that the speech was made in 1869 by a rabbi to a secret Sanhedrin (possibly referring to the First Congress of Reformed Judaism, held in Leipzig). Its authenticity, again, was supported by the fictional Sir John Readclif. Later, in the October 21, 1920 issue of *La Vielle France*, the newspaper said there was a striking analogy between the *Protocols of the Elders of Zion* and the discourse of Rabbi Reichhorn, presented in Prague in 1869, over the tomb of the Grand Rabbi Simeon-ben-Ihuda.

Early in 1900, this fictional speech was used to instigate pogroms against the Jews, and became known as "The Rabbi's Speech." An anti-Semite, P. A. Khrushevan, used the speech to provoke a pogrom at Kishinev, in the Ukraine, in 1903, in which 45 Jews were killed, and 400 injured, in an incident that destroyed 1,300 Jewish homes and shops. The speech is now used to prove the authenticity of the Protocols.

The document known as the *Protocols of the Learned Elders of Zion*, seems to be a conglomeration of many anti-Jewish publications during that period. In 1869, Gougenot de Mousseaux wrote a book that said that the world was being taken over by a group of Satan-worshipping Jews, out of which a man would emerge that the Jews would worship as their returned Messiah. In 1881, Abbé Chabauty wrote a 600-page book that said Satan was using the Jews to prepare the way for the Antichrist. His second book, published in 1882, included two letters that were allegedly written in 1489 by a Jewish leader who spoke of the Jews rising up to "dominate the world." These letters have come to be known as the *Letter of the Jews of Constantinople*. They were actually satirical comments on the Spanish Jews.

In 1893, Monsignor Meurin, the Archbishop of Port Louis, Mauritius, said: "Freemasonry is fundamentally Jewish, exclusively Jewish, passionately Jewish, from the beginning to the end," and that "someday history will tell how all the revolutions of recent centuries originated in the Masonic sect under the supreme command of the Jews." He said that the Masons of the 33rd degree were the leaders of the conspiracy, and indeed the Protocols are signed: "...by the representatives of Zion, of the 33rd degree." In *World Conquest by the Jews*, Osman-Bey wrote, that in 1840, a meeting of eminent Jewish leaders was held in Cracow,

Poland, to discuss the expansion of Judaism over the entire world. This book became the framework for the Protocols.

Victor E. Marsden, the Russian correspondent for *The Morning Post* of London, wrote in his 1934 English translation of the Protocols, that in 1884, Joseph Schorst, a Jew who was a member of the Mizraim Lodge, stole the document and sold it for 2,500 francs to Justine Glinka, the daughter of a Russian General. She in turn gave the French document, and a Russian translation to Gen. Orgevskii in St. Petersburg, who gave it to his superior, Gen. Cherevin, who filed it. Glinka was later arrested, returned to Russia, and exiled to her estate in Orel; while Schorst was killed in Egypt. It had also been reported that Glinka had given a copy to Alexis Sukhotin, a law enforcement official in Orel, who then showed them to two friends, Stepanov, and Professor Sergei Nilus, a religious mystic.

Nilus showed them to the Czar in 1903, who believed them to be fraudulent, and ordered that all copies were to be destroyed. After Nilus was banned from the Court, it is believed that he may have altered the text to be more intense then they originally were. However, as far as the mysterious references to the "representatives of Sion, of the 33rd degree," he would not have any idea what this meant, and probably would not have altered this and any other in-kind references.

The Protocols of the Learned Elders of Zion first appeared, in a shortened form, in an August, 1903 edition of the Kishinev newspaper, in the Ukraine; then in 1905, in the appendix of the third edition of a book by Nilus called *The Great in the Small*, which was about the coming of the Antichrist. Nilus said that the Protocols were translated from the French text of a speech made to 300 influential Jews. A prostitute allegedly stole the document from a leading Jew. A copy was received by the British Museum in London, in August, 1906, where it was translated by English journalist Victor Marsden, who published it in 1921. Marsden said that he couldn't work on the translation for more than an hour at a time, because of the evil he felt while reading it. In 1917, Nilus revised and expanded his book, which he called, *He is Near, At the Door: Here Comes the Antichrist and the Reign of the Devil on Earth*. Nilus wrote: "These Protocols are nothing else than a strategic plan for the conquest of the world ... presented to the Council of the Elders by ... Theodor Herzl, at the time of the first Zionist Congress (held by the World Zionist Organization in 1897, at Basel, Switzerland)." However, in his 1905 edition, he said that the Protocols had been given in 1902-03. In fact, with each subsequent edition that appeared in different countries, the origin of the document was different.

On August 16, 17, and 18, 1921, the *New York Times* ran editorials by Phillip Graves, a *London Times* correspondent, who said that the Protocols had been copied from a rare 1864 French political satire called *Dialogues in Hell Between Machiavelli and Montesquieu* (also referred to as the *Dialogues of Geneva* by the *London Times* because Geneva had been identified as a center of revolutionary activities) by lawyer Maurice Joly (1831-1878). It was a pamphlet containing a conversation between Montesquieu (presenting a case for liberalism) and Machiavelli (who represented autocracy) which criticized the government of Napoleon III (who was deposed in 1871). Being illegal to criticize the Monarchy, he fictionalized it, making Napoleon the character of Machiavelli, to explain the Emperor's underlying motives. Joly had it printed in Belgium, then attempted to have it smuggled over the French border. It was seized by the police, who confiscated as many copies as they could, then banned the book. The police traced the book to Joly, who was then tried on April 25, 1865, and sentenced to fifteen months in prison. At the Berne trials, a witness for the prosecution tried to prove that Joly was a Jew, and that his book was a coded version of the Jewish plan for world domination. Another writer, Victor Hugo (1802-1885), a Grand Master of the Prieuré de Sion (1844-1885) who in 1849 made a reference to the 'United States of Europe,' wrote satirical poetry against Napoleon III.

As it turns out, over 160 passages from the Protocols are similar to Joly's book, which is about half the text. Some sections are almost word for word. The only major change is that it was altered from the past, to the future.

Some researchers believe that either, Joly was given the minutes to a Masonic meeting by Adolphe Cremieux (a Mason and Rosicrucian), who urged Joly to write the book, which he did under the pseudonym of "Mr. X"; or that the minutes were from a Marxist meeting which took place in a Masonic lodge in Geneva, and had been stored in the archives of the Mizraim Masonic Lodge in Paris, where Cremieux, who sat on the Supreme Council, discovered them.

Who could have forged the Protocols isn't known, if in fact it is a forgery. Some researchers claim it was done in Russia, in 1904, by agents of the Czar. However, the general consensus is that it was probably done by Elie de Cyon (Ilya Tsion), a Russian journalist living in Paris, who was an opponent of Sergey Witte, the Russian Minister of Finance.

When Witte took office in 1892, he began to modernize Russia by doubling steel, iron, and coal production; and constructing railroads. He was disliked by those who had their money tied up in agriculture. He caused inflation by abandoning the gold standard in 1898 because of an economic slump. The Protocols say that such economic depressions are caused by the Elders to gain control of the money; and that the gold standard has ruined every country that has adopted it. Researchers say that the economic and financial data could have been extracted from Joly's book, and applied to Witte, in order to present him as a tool of the Elders of Zion.

So, Cyon allegedly forged and translated the Protocols, expanding them as a satire on Witte. His writings resembled the style used in the Protocols; and he was known to have used another French satire on a dead statesman, by changing the names. In 1897, Gen. Pyotr Ivanovich Rachkovsky, head of the Russian Secret Police in Paris, on instructions from Witte, broke into Cyon's villa at Territet, Switzerland, to look for additional written attacks on Witte. It is believed that Rachkovsky discovered the Protocols there, and used it for a dual purpose. He could use it against the Jews, claiming it was part of a Jewish conspiracy; and he could reveal that it was written by a Jew, which Cyon was, thus destroying Cyon. It was kind of ironic, that the Russian translation for Cyon's name, 'Tsion', means 'Zion.'

In 1921, Count Alexandru du Chayla said that Nilus revealed to him in 1909 that the Protocols were fraudulent, and had been sent to him by Gen. Rachkovsky.

During the 1934 trial of two Swiss Nazis in Berne, brought by a group of Jews who accused them of distributing the Protocols, the historian Vladimir Burtsev and a professor, Sergey Svatikov, testified that Rachkovsky and other Czarist officials had a hand in the fabrication of the Protocols. In 1891, Rachkovsky sent a letter to the Police, and announced his intentions to oppose the Jews. This was followed up by a book that stated his views about the Jews, and how, as a result of the French Revolution, they controlled Europe. It is quite possible that he added to Cyon's manuscript to produce the Protocols, and then gave it to Sergei Nilus to publish in his book. Czar Nicholas II even identified the Protocols as being fraudulent. On May 14, 1935, the Court of Berne ruled that the Protocols were not of Jewish origin.

To complicate matters even more, a book by Jacob Venedey, called *Machiavelli: Montesquieu and Rousseau*, which was published in Berlin, in 1850, also contained passages very similar to the Protocols.

Standard Oil allegedly had the Protocols distributed in Russia to create a tense situation between the Czarist Russian government, and the Jewish-owned Royal Dutch Co., who had oil distribution rights in Russia. The document was also used in the late 1800's to instigate pogroms against the Jews so they would migrate to the United States. Once they were in America, they were registered to vote Democratic, and greatly contributed to Wilson's election in 1912. During the Russian Civil War from 1918-20, Bolsheviks distributed the Protocols, and in the subsequent pogroms, over 100,000 Jews were killed. During World War II, the document gave Hitler an excuse to exterminate the Jews, and there is evidence which indicates that he was financed and controlled by the Illuminati.

Eventually the Protocols were distributed all over the world, and it gave the anti-Semitic people of various countries an excuse to persecute the Jews. In 1920, U.S. industrialist Henry Ford supported them in a series of articles in his newspaper *The Dearborn Independent* and eventually in his book *The International Jew*, which he published in 1921. On February 17, 1921, in *New York World*, Ford said: "The only statement I care to make about the Protocols is that they fit in with what is going on. They are sixteen years old, and they have fitted the world situation up to this time. They fit it now." The German translation was known as *The Eternal Jew*. Ford supported Hitler, who was seen as fighting against the international Jewish conspiracy. In 1927, he renounced his belief in them after his car was sideswiped, forcing it over a steep embankment. He interpreted this as an attempt on his life by elitist Jews.

In 1938, Father Charles E. Coughlin printed them in his weekly paper *Social Justice*, and various other semi-religious organizations followed suit.

Those researchers who believe in the authenticity of the Protocols, trace them back to 1785, when the Illuminati courier was struck by lightning on the way to Paris, and their plans for world control was discovered. The Illuminati had drafted a master plan that was worded in such a way, that it diverted attention away from the Illuminati, and directed it towards the Jewish Revolutionary movement in Russia. Their plan would appear to be a Jewish plot to achieve world control through political Zionism, when in fact it represented the future plans of the international bankers of the Illuminati. The fact that the document was anti-Semitic, would help suppress it.

One inescapable fact is that the Protocols do reflect some of the views of Weishaupt, and the writings of various Socialists on Bolshevism; and because of that, they were not easily dismissed. Even though they were written so long ago, they have become an accurate barometer of events during this century, and seem to parallel the goals of the Illuminati, as you can see in these excerpts from the Victor Marsden translation:

"Out of the temporary evil we are now compelled to commit, will emerge the good of an unshakable rule, which will restore the regular course of the machinery of the national life, brought to naught by liberalism. The result justifies the means. Let us, however, in our plans, direct our attention not to what is good and moral, as to what is necessary and useful. Our power in the present tottering condition of all forms of power will be more invisible than any other, because it will remain invisible until the moment when it has gained such strength that no cunning can any longer undermine it. Before us is a plan in which is laid down strategically the line from which we cannot deviate without running the risk of seeing the labor of many centuries brought to naught..."

"Only force conquers in political affairs, especially if it be concealed in the talents essential to statesmen ... This evil is the one and only means to attain the end, the good. Therefore we must not stop at bribery, deceit, and treachery, when they should serve towards the attainment of our end. In politics one must know how to seize the property of others without hesitation if by it we secure submission and sovereignty."

"Our international rights will then wipe out national rights, in the proper sense of right, and will rule the nations precisely as the civil law of States rules the relations of their subjects among themselves. The administrators, whom we shall choose from among the public, with strict regard to their capacities for servile obedience, will not be persons trained in the art of government, and will therefore easily become pawns in our game in the hands of men of learning and genius who will be their advisors, specialists bred and reared from early childhood to rule the affairs of the whole world."

"Do not suppose for a moment that those statements are empty words: think carefully of the successes we arranged for Darwinism, Marxism, Nietzcheism. To us, at any rate, it should be plain to see what a disintegrating importance these directives have had upon the minds of the goyim (a slur against those who were not Jewish)."

"Through the Press we have gained the power to influence while remaining ourselves in the shade; thanks to the Press we have got the gold in our hands, notwithstanding that we have had to gather it out of the oceans of blood and tears."

"To this end we have stirred up every form of enterprise, we have armed all parties, we have set up authority as a target for every ambition ... disorders and bankruptcy will be universal."

"We appear on the scene as alleged saviors of the worker from this oppression when we propose to him to enter the ranks of our fighting forces— Socialists, Anarchists, Communists— to whom we will always give support."

"Our power is in the chronic shortness of food ... Hunger creates the right of capital to rule the worker more surely than it was given to the aristocracy by the legal authority of kings."

"By want and the envy and hatred which it engenders we shall move the mobs and with their hands we shall wipe out all those who hinder us ... When the hour strikes for our Sovereign Lord of all the World to be crowned it is these same hands which will sweep away everything that might be a hindrance thereto."

"This hatred will be still further magnified by the effects of an economic crisis, which will stop dealings on the exchanges and bring industry to a standstill. We shall create by all the secret subterranean methods open to us and with the aid of gold, which is all in our hands, a universal economic crisis whereby we shall throw upon the streets whole mobs of workers simultaneously in all the countries of Europe."

"Remember the French Revolution, to which it was we who gave the name of 'Great': the secrets of its preparations are well known to us, for it was wholly the work of our hands..."

"We shall create an intensified centralization of government in order to grip in our hands all the forces of the community. We shall regulate mechanically all the actions of the political life of our subjects by new laws ... These laws will withdraw one by one all the indulgences and liberties which have been permitted ... to wipe out any unenlightened who oppose us by deed or word."

"We have set one against another the personal and national reckonings of the goyim religious and race hatred, which we have fostered into a huge growth in the course of the past twenty centuries. This is the reason why there is one State which would anywhere receive support if it were to raise its arm, for every one of them must bear in mind that any agreement against us would be unprofitable to itself. We are too strong— there is no evading our power. The nations cannot come to even an inconsiderable private agreement without our secretly having a hand in it..."

"Nowadays it is more important to disarm the peoples then to lead them into war..."

"In order to put public opinion into our hands we must bring it into a state of bewilderment by giving expression from all sides to so many contradictory opinions and for such length of time as will suffice to make the goyim lose their heads in the labyrinth and come to see that the best thing is to have no opinion of any kind in matters political, which it is not given to the public to understand, because they are understood only by him who guides the public. This is the final secret."

"By all these means we shall so wear down the goyim that they will be compelled to offer us international power of a nature that by its position will enable us, without any violence, gradually to absorb all the State forces of the world and to form a Super-Government ... Its hands will reach out in all directions like nippers and its organization will be of such colossal dimensions that it cannot fail to subdue all the nations of the world."

"We shall raise the rate of wages, which, however, will not bring any advantage to the workers, for at the same time, we shall produce a rise in prices ... We shall further undermine artfully and deeply sources of production, by accustoming the workers to anarchy and to drunkenness ... In order that the true meaning of things may not strike the unenlightened before the proper time we shall mask it under an alleged ardent desire to serve the working classes and the great principles of political economy about which our economic theories are carrying on an energetic propaganda."

"The intensification of armaments, the increase of police forces— are all essential for the completion of the aforementioned plans. What we have to get at is that there should be in all the States of the world, besides ourselves, only the masses of the proletariat, a few millionaires devoted to our interests, police and soldiers."

"In a word, to sum up our system of keeping the governments of the goyim in Europe in check, we shall show our strength to one of them by terrorist attempts and to all, if we allow the possibility of general rising against us, we shall respond with the guns of America or China or Japan."

"Our directorate must surround itself with all these forces of civilization among which it will have to work. It will surround itself with publicists, practical jurists, administrators, diplomats and, finally, with persons prepared by a special super-educational training in our special schools."

We have in our service persons of all opinions, of all doctrines, restoring monarchists, demagogues, socialists, communists, and utopian dreamers of every kind. We have harnessed them all to one task: each one of them on his own account is boring away at the last remnants of authority, is striving to overthrow all established forms of order."

"We have fooled, bemused and corrupted the youth of the goyim by rearing them in principles and theories which are known to us to be false although it is by us that they have been inculcated."

"Above the existing laws without altering them, and by merely twisting them into contradictions of interpretations, we have erected something grandiose in the way of results. These results found expression first in the fact that the interpretations masked the laws: afterwards they entirely hid them from the eyes of the government owing to the impossibility of making anything out of the tangled web of legislation."

"The chamber of deputies will provide cover for, will protect, will elect presidents, but we shall take from it the right to propose new, or make changes in existing laws, for this right will be given by us to the responsible president, a puppet in our hands ... We shall invest the president with the right of declaring a state of war..."

"Not a single announcement will reach the public without our control. Even now this is already attained by us inasmuch as all news items are received by a few agencies, in whose offices they are focused from all parts of the world. These agencies will then be already entirely ours and will give publicity only to what we dictate to them."

"Our wise men, trained to become leaders of the goyim, will compose speeches, projects, memoirs, articles, which will be used by us to influence the minds of the goyim, directing them towards such understanding and forms of knowledge as have been determined by us."

"Economic crises have been produced by us for the goyim by no other means than the withdrawal of money from circulation ... You are aware that the gold standard has been the ruin of the States which adopted it, for it has not been able to satisfy the demands for money, the more so that we have removed gold from circulation as far as possible."

"Thanks to such methods (paying interest on loans), allowed by the carelessness of the goy States, their treasuries are empty. The period of loan supervenes, and that has swallowed up remainders and brought all the goy states to bankruptcy."

"...any form of taxation per head, the State is baling out the last coppers of the poor taxpayers in order to settle accounts with wealthy foreigners, from whom it borrowed money from the pockets of the poor to those of the rich..."

"We have got our hands into the administration of the law, into the conduct of elections, into the press, into the liberty of the person, but principally into education and training as being the corner-stones of a free existence."

"...it is indispensable for us to undermine all faith, to tear of minds out of the unenlightened the very principle of Godhead and the spirit, and to put in its place arithmetical calculations and material needs."

"When we come into our kingdom it will be undesirable for us that there should exist any other religion but ours of the 'One God' with whom our destiny is bound up by our position as the Chosen People and through whom our same destiny is united with the destinies of the world. We must therefore sweep away all other forms of belief."

After reading these words, you may also have a feeling of uneasiness. Seemingly, the Protocols do elaborate on the Illuminati program for world takeover that would not have pertained to the world at the time the Protocols were alleged to have been written. Because of the depth of information given on the various aspects of the plan, I believe that they were written by, or based on the writings of someone who had an intimate knowledge of the future plans and inner workings of the international bankers. From that standpoint, I consider the information to be authentic. However, because the document identifies the Jews as being responsible for carrying out this insidious plot, I consider the Protocols as a whole, to be a fraudulent rendering of an earlier document, which has since been lost.

A few years ago, another theory came to light in regard to the Protocols. If the document was forged with the intent of being an indictment against all Jews, it would not just pinpoint a small group of individuals. It speaks of a "King of the blood of Sion" who will preside over a "Masonic kingdom" and that this king will be of "the dynastic roots of King David." It claims that the "King of the Jews will be the real Pope" and "the patriarch of an international church."

Eliphas Levi (Alphonse Louis Constant), who had joined a Martinist-affiliated Masonic lodge, which later merged with the Memphis and Mizraim Lodges, had assisted Charles Nodier (Grandmaster of the Prieuré de Sion 1801-1844) to sift through the Vatican documents taken by Napoleon. Before he died in 1875, he said that "in 1879 a new political and religious 'universal Kingdom' would be established, and that it would be possessed by 'him who would have the keys of the East'." This unusual comment has lead researchers to believe that he had access to the original Protocol document which was kept at the Mizraim Lodge.

Protocol number 3 states: "When the hour strikes for our Sovereign Lord of all the World to be crowned it is these hands which will sweep away everything that might be a hinderance thereto. 'Ours' they will not touch, because the moment of the attack will be known to us and we shall take measures to protect our own. Ever since that time we have been leading the peoples from one disenchantment to another, so that in the end they should turn also from us in favor of that King-Despot of the blood of Sion, whom we are preparing for the world."

Protocol number 15 states: "When the King of Israel sets upon his sacred head the crown offered to him by Europe he will become the patriarch of the world." Number 17 says: "The King of the Jews will be the real Pope of the Universe, the patriarch of an international church." And number 24 reads: "I pass now to the method of confirming the dynastic roots of King David to the last strata of the earth. The prop of humanity in the person of the supreme lord of all the world of the holy seed of David must sacrifice to his people all personal inclinations."

It concludes by saying that "certain members of the Seed of David will prepare the Kings and their heirs ... Only the King and the three who stood sponsor for him will know what is coming." It is signed "...by the representatives of Sion, of the 33rd degree." These strange references have been linked to a little known organization known as the Prieuré de Sion, which will be discussed in a later chapter. It is possible that the original text of the Protocols was based on a document taken from this organization, which was altered by Sergei Nilus, to make the entire Jewish race look bad.

WORLD WAR II AND THE RISE OF HITLER

As a youth, Adolf Hitler (1889-1945) fled Austria, and went to Germany to escape the draft. He was arrested, and in February, 1914, a report was put in his file, which read in part: "Unfit for military or auxiliary service; too weak; incapable of bearing arms." This was the man that the Illuminati would choose to further their goals.

As a puppet of the Illuminati, he was used to set the stage for the conflict which would eventually lead to the establishment of the United Nations, a major step towards one-world government; and to shame the world into allowing the State of Israel to be established.

Edward George Bulwer-Lytton (1803-73), a graduate of Cambridge University, and a Mason, who became a member of the British Parliament, wrote a novel in 1871 called *Vril: The Power of the Coming Race*, about a super-race of white Aryans that took control of the world. Researchers consider him responsible for the birth of the Nazi movement, because Hitler was said to have been influenced by this book, and another novel, *Rienzi: The Last of the Roman Tribunes*, which was adapted into a major opera by German composer Richard Wagner. After seeing *Rienzi* for the first time in November, 1906, Hitler talked about a "mandate which, one day, he would receive from the people, to lead them out of servitude to the heights of freedom." He believed that he would be entrusted with a special mission. He later told Frau Wagner, the composer's widow: "In that hour it began (the Nazi movement known as National Socialism)."

History shows that Hitler ordered the death of six million Jews during the Holocaust in Europe. Why he did, has become a mystery, since it really hasn't been established that he had an intense hatred for Jews.

A U.S. Office of Strategic Services psychological report by Walter C. Langer, later published as *The Mind of Adolf Hitler*, says that the young Hitler was befriended by Jewish art dealers who "paid generously for his mediocre watercolors." Because of his financial situation, a Jewish landlady charged him only a nominal rent, and even moved out of her apartment on one occasion so that Hitler and a friend could have more room. A Jewish used-clothing dealer gave him a long black overcoat, which he wore constantly. When he was a lance-corporal during World War I, Hitler was awarded the Iron Cross (First and Second Class), a rare honor for a soldier of such low rank, who hadn't really done anything to deserve such a distinction. He learned later, that the commendation was the result of the "efforts of the regimental adjutant, Hugo Gutmann, a Jew."

When he became Fuhrer, Hitler hired a Jewish maid to do his cooking. On one occasion, when it was suggested that he get rid of her, he became furious. Dr. Eduard Bloch, a Jewish physician, had been the Hitler family doctor since Hitler was a child. Bloch had treated Hitler's mother when she was dying of cancer. After her funeral, Hitler accompanied his sisters to thank him, and said: "I shall be grateful to you forever." He sent the doctor two postcards, one that he handpainted. Both of them said: "From your ever grateful patient, Adolf Hitler."

Hitler had even wondered if he himself was Jewish. This idea stemmed from the fact that Hitler's father, Alois, was illegitimate, and the identity of his grandfather had never been established. During Hitler's rise to power, his half-brother's son threatened to reveal that Hitler was of Jewish ancestry. One investigation discovered that Hitler's grandfather had been the son of a Jewish family called Frankenburger, in Gratz, who employed Hitler's grandmother, Maria Anna Schicklgruber, as a maid. She had become pregnant by their son, while she was working in their home. The family sent her money for a year and a half to help support the child. Another investigation said that Alois was conceived in Vienna, where Hitler's grandfather was employed as a servant in the home of Baron

Rothschild. Maria was sent home to Spital, where Hitler's father was born.

In *Hitler's War*, written in 1977 by British author and historical revisionist, David Irving, he revealed that Hitler didn't order the Jewish massacres, and didn't find out about it until late in the war. There is no record of Hitler ever visiting a concentration camp, although he did watch films and see photographs.

So what turned Hitler against the Jews, if indeed he was; or was there someone else making decisions for him.

As early as 1919, he spoke of removing Jews altogether; and in his book *Mein Kampf*, written while he was in prison in 1924, for the 'Beer Hall Putsch,' spoke of the overthrow of "world Jewry": "I believe that I am today acting according to the purposes of the almighty Creator. In resisting the Jew, I am fighting the Lord's battle." On January 30, 1939, he said in a speech to the Reichstag: "Today I want to be a prophet once more: if international finance Jewry inside and outside of Europe should succeed once more in plunging nations into another world war, the consequence will not be the bolshevization of the earth and thereby the victory of Jewry, but the annihilation of the Jewish race in Europe." In a public speech in Munich, on November 8, 1942, he said that "International Jewry will be recognized in its full demonic peril; we National Socialists would see to that."

Hitler had read the *Protocols of the Learned Elders of Zion*, and in 1942, was told by Himmler, that they were forged, however, Hitler disregarded that fact and said: "We shall regain our health only by eliminating the Jew." He attributed the weakness of the German economy to the Jews, and considered the Treaty of Versailles, a Jewish document. He even accused the Jews of spreading communism; yet in a speech on February 5, 1941, said that "basically, National Socialism (Naziism) and Communism are the same."

Why does the life of Hitler seem to be a series of contradictions? One clue was revealed in *The Secret Diaries of Hitler's Doctors*, written in 1983 by David Irving, which revealed that Hitler had taken 75 different medications. He was given strychnine and belladonna (for gas), cocaine and adrenalin (for conjunctivitis), amphetamines, painkillers, and sedatives, including Eukodal, a synthetic morphine derivative. One has to wonder if Hitler was even aware of what he was being given. Were they being given to him for the sole purpose of making him mentally unstable, so he could be controlled by advisors, who were acting on behalf of the forces that Hitler wrongly identified as the Jewish bankers.

There may also be a more sinister reason which contributed to Hitler's state of mind. Hitler and some of his officers had been linked to various occult groups and the use of the swastika gave evidence of that. In its normal usage, it is a sign of the power of light; but in its reverse form, as used by the Nazis, it represents the power of darkness. According to writer Joseph Carr: "We know that Hitler and his top luminaries were either dabblers in the occult, or, outright Satanists." As a youth, Hitler had been influenced by George Lanz von Liebenfels, an Austrian magician who in 1907 founded "The Order of the New Templars," which used the swastika as its emblem. He wrote in a 1932 letter that Hitler was one of his pupils and that one day he would "develop a movement that will make the world tremble."

Hitler joined a secret group in 1919, called the Thule Society, which practiced black magic and worshipped Satan. They wanted to form a political party to rally the people against communism. Its members were drawn from the upper echelon of Society. The founder, Dietrich Eckart, was one of the seven founding members of the Nazi Party, and said on his deathbed: "Follow Hitler. He will dance, but it is I who have called the tune! I have initiated him into the 'Secret Doctrine,' opened his centres in vision and given him the means to communicate with the Powers. Do not mourn for me: I shall have influenced history more than any other German." Hitler grew to fear those around him who practiced the black arts, and it was discovered that along with the Jews, Masons and occult practitioners were also killed and imprisoned in the concentration camps. Some of the reported book burnings were actually the confiscation and destruction of Masonic libraries.

Karl Ernst Haushofer (who created the Vril Society, which made up the inner circle of the Nazi Party), also of the Thule Society, was the University professor who schooled Hitler on geopolitics. Hitler was also influenced by the writings of Friedrich Nietzsche, from whose name came the word Nazi. In 1943, Hitler's birthday gift to Mussolini, was *The Collected Works of Nietzche*.

In the fall of 1919, Hitler joined the German Workers' Party, and soon became one of its leaders. In the summer of 1920, it was renamed the National Socialist German Workers' Party, and then in 1923, it became known as the Nazi Party.

Because of Hitler's failed November revolt, he was jailed on April 1, 1924, sentenced to five years, but was released after eight months, so he could be built up to national prominence. Though *Mein Kampf* was published as a work of Adolf Hitler while he was in prison, it was discovered later that it was actually written by Nazi politicians Rudolf Hess and Hermann Wilhelm Goerring (and possibly Haushofer), as a follow-up to the Karl Marx book *A World Without Jews*. The Illuminati made sure the book was well circulated, and it became the springboard for Hitler's political career.

In 1925, Dr. Karl Duisberg, I. G. Farben's first Chairman, and founder of the Bayer Co. in the United States, said: "Be united, united, united. This should be the uninterrupted call to the parties of the Reichstag. We hope that our words of today will work, and will find the strong man who will finally bring everyone under one umbrella ... for he is always necessary for us Germans, as we have seen in the case of Bismarck." The depressive economic situation in Germany at the time, created by the Versailles Treaty, made it possible for Hitler's leadership to take root, and he became Chancellor in January, 1933.

Since 1924, the Dawes Plan flooded Germany with a tremendous amount of American capital, which enabled Germany to build its war machine. The three largest loans went into the development of industries, such as I. G. Farben Co. (the German company which became the largest corporation in Europe, and the largest chemical company in the world, after a $30 million loan from the Rockefeller's National City Bank after World War I, and who created a process of making high grade fuel from low quality coals) and Vereinigte Stahlwerke (who produced about 95% of Germany's explosives). In 1939, Standard Oil of New Jersey sold I. G. Farben $20,000 worth of high quality aviation fuel. I. G. Farben's assets in the United States were controlled by a holding company called American I. G. Farben Chemical Corp. On the Board of Directors of this corporation was Edsel Ford (President of the Ford Motor Co.), Charles E. Mitchell (President of National City Bank in New York City), Walter C. Teagle (President of Standard Oil of New York), Paul Warburg (Chairman of the Federal Reserve), and Herman Metz (Director of the Warburg's Bank of Manhattan). Several Germans on this Board were found guilty of war crimes at Nuremburg. A U.S. War Department investigation revealed that without Farben's support, "Germany's prosecution of the war would have been unthinkable and impossible."

Hitler received support and financing from the aristocracy and elite of Germany, including Gustav Krupp (industrialist), Carl Duisberg (founder of I.G. Farben), Ernst Tengelmann (director of the Ruhr coal mining operation), Dr. Hjalmar Schacht (prominent banker), and Fritz Thyssen (Chairman of the Board of United Steel Works, Germany's largest company). Hitler maintained that the Nazi Party would continue "only until the German people had been freed from the threat of Marxism and could reach a decision as to whether the final form of government would be a republic or a monarchy." Thyssen told the Kaiser that Hitler was made Chancellor only as "a transitional stage leading to the reintroduction of the German monarchy."

America's Ambassador to Germany, William Dodd, reported to President Roosevelt in August, 1936: "At the present moment, more than a hundred American corporations have subsidiaries here or cooperative understandings. The du Ponts have their allies in Germany that are aiding in the armament business. Their chief ally is the I. G. Farben Company (the primary supporter of Hitler) ... Standard Oil Company (of New York) sent $2,000,000 here in December, 1933, and has made $500,000 a year helping Germans make Ersatz gas for war purposes; but Standard Oil cannot take any of its earnings out of the country except in goods ... The International Harvester Company President told me their business here rose 33% a year but they could take nothing out. Even our airplane people have secret arrangements with Krupps. General Motors Company and Ford do enormous business here through subsidiaries and take no profits out. I mention these facts because they complicate things and add to war dangers."

Germany's two largest tank producers were Opel, a subsidiary of General Motors (controlled by J. P. Morgan and the du Ponts), and Ford A. G., a subsidiary of the Ford Motor Company. International Telephone and Telegraph (ITT) held a substantial interest in Focke-Wolfe, an airplane manufacturer who produced German fighter aircraft.

Prior to World War II, the Round Table organization, through various means, made sure Hitler wasn't stopped in Austria, the Rhineland, or Sudentenland. His financing was done through the Warburg-controlled Mendelsohn Bank of Amsterdam; and the J. Henry Shroeder Bank (financial agent for the Nazi government), which had branches in Frankfurt, London, and New York. The Chief Legal Counsel for the Shroeder Bank, was the firm of Sullivan and Cromwell, whose senior partners included CFR members John Foster Dulles (who was the top policy-making director for the International Nickel Co. who helped negotiate an agreement with Farben which helped the Nazis to stockpile nickel for war purposes) and his brother Allen Dulles (who was a Director on the Board of the Henry Shroeder Bank, and later became the head of the CIA). They were cousins to the Rockefellers (who later got a controlling interest in Farben).

Hitler indirectly received financing from the Krupps, Kennedys, and the Rothschilds. The liaison between Hitler and Wall Street was Hjalmar Horace Greely Schact, the President of Reichsbank, who aided in the rebuilding of Germany. His father worked in the Berlin office of the Morgan-controlled Equitable Trust Co. of New York. Without a shadow of a doubt, Hitler was controlled by the Illuminati.

The Holocaust had begun with the Jews being stripped of their German citizenship; and from 1939-45, Hitler's death camps claimed the lives of six million Jews, or about 1/3 of the entire Jewish race. The world turned against him, and his actions instigated World War II, which had actually been planned years before.

Another reason for World War II, was to make it possible for Russia, our ally at the time, to gain strength and receive recognition as a world power. Although they were our ally, they were still a Communist nation, with growing designs on world domination. There is an incredible amount of evidence that indicates the willingness of our government to allow the spread of Communism, because of the efforts of Communists who had been employed and were acting on behalf of the Illuminati.

In May, 1943 the Allies had pushed the Germans out of Africa, invading Sicily in June, and in September, pushed their way through Italy, on the way to Southern Germany, their weakest point. However, the U.S. withdrew troops from the invasion force so they could be used in a later invasion of France. In his 1950 book *Calculated Risk*, Gen. Mark Clark said that this decision was "made at high level and for reasons beyond my field and knowledge." Churchill had wanted the attack to "bring the Central European and Balkan countries under Allied control, before they were allowed to slip into Red slavery." But instead, under the leadership of Gen. Dwight David Eisenhower, the German advance was spread out, which allowed the Russian forces to advance. Was this an intentional move on the part of the United States to allow the Russians an opportunity to pursue their ulterior motives. It certainly seems so.

In the spring of 1943, a faction within the German Secret Service was prepared to assassinate Hitler, and surrender, on one condition— that the Soviets would not be allowed to advance into Central Europe. Roosevelt refused to accept, and postponed a planned European invasion, in order to give the Russians more time to advance, and occupy more land. According to military documents released in 1970, Gen. Eisenhower allowed the Russians to get to Berlin first, before the Americans, which eventually allowed part of the city to fall under Communist control.

Russia was able to come away from 1945 Conference in Yalta with so much, because Roosevelt believed that the Russians were "perfectly friendly. They aren't trying to gobble up the rest of Europe. These fears that have been expressed by a lot of people here that the Russians are going to try and dominate Europe, I personally don't think there is anything do it ... I have just a hunch that Stalin ... doesn't want anything but security for his country, and I think that if I give him everything I possibly can, and ask nothing in return, he won't try to annex anything and will work for a world of democracy and peace." Russia walked away from the bargaining table with Latvia, Estonia, Lithuania, eastern Poland, east and central Europe, N. Korea, the Kuril Islands, and the northern part of Sakhalin.

An American General, Albert C. Wademeyer, was convinced that Russia was the only winner of World War II. He said: "Stalin was intent on creating favorable conditions for the realization of Communist aims throughout the Balkans and Western Europe. He emerged as the only winner of the War. We insured the emergence of a more hostile, menacing predatory power than Nazi Germany, one which has enslaved more people than we liberated."

Gen. George S. Patton wanted to retire because he planned on being able to speak his mind about America being "soft on Communism." However, before resigning his Commission, he died after an automobile accident forced him to be hospitalized. In 1979, Douglas Bazata, a former Secret Service agent for the Office of Strategic Services (OSS, the predecessor of the CIA) revealed that he was ordered by the Director 'Wild Bill' Donovan to kill Patton in 1944. Although he didn't, he knows who did, and said that Patton was killed with cyanide at the hospital he was taken to after the accident.

Frank Murphy, appointed by Roosevelt to the post of Attorney General in 1938, and later, as a Supreme Court Justice, told Congressman Martin Dies: "We're doomed! The United States is doomed! The Communists have control completely ... They've got control of Roosevelt and his wife as well." In 1949, upon waiting to be released from a Detroit hospital, he died of a heart attack.

James Forrestal, a partner and President of Dillon, Read and Company, was appointed Secretary of the Navy in 1944, then the Secretary of Defense in 1947, till Truman asked him to resign in 1949. After the War, he became dedicated to destroying Communism, because it seemed as though the United States was constantly yielding to them. Truman believed Forrestal was under a lot of mental stress, and had him admitted to the U.S. Naval Hospital at Bethesda, Maryland.

His personal diaries, consisting of 15 loose-leaf binders, about 3,000 pages, were removed from his office at the Pentagon, and held at the White House. Forrestal had told a friend that he was being followed, and that his phone was tapped. He noticed the beginnings of the Korean War, fifteen months before it actually started.

Once he was in the hospital, he was allowed no visitors. On May 22, 1949, his brother, Henry Forrestal, decided to take his brother for a ride into the country. That same day, James Forrestal, jumped from the 16th floor of the hospital. Found on a third floor projection, the cord of his bathrobe was tied around his neck, and the hospital released a statement that he committed suicide, even though there was not enough evidence to prove that he had.

In 1951, his diaries were published by Viking Press, but they were heavily censored by the White House, the Pentagon, and Walter Millis, of the *New York Tribune*, so the full story could never be known. His family priest, Monsignor Maurice S. Sheehy said: "Many, many times in his letters to me, Jim Forrestal wrote anxiously and fearfully and bitterly of the enormous harm that had been; and was unceasingly being done, by men in high office in the United States government, who he was convinced were Communists or under the influence of Communists, and who he said were shaping the policies of the United States government to aid Soviet Russia and harm the United States."

To this day, Forrestal continues to be labeled as being insane, and the cause of his death remains unknown.

Towards the end of 1949, three men visited the office of Sen. Joseph McCarthy to show him an FBI report detailing the Communist penetration of the State Department and other government spy networks. On February 9, 1950, in a speech before the Ohio County Women's Republican Club of Wheeling, West Virginia, he said: "I have in my hand 57 cases of individuals who would appear to be either card-carrying members or certainly loyal to the Communist Party, but who nevertheless are still helping to shape our foreign policy." A Special Subcommittee of the Senate Foreign Relations Committee was established to investigate where there were disloyal people employed at the State Department. However, instead of investigating the accusations, they investigated McCarthy, and a wave of anti-McCarthy sentiment swept the country. On September 23, 1950, McCarthy revealed what would happen because of the Yalta Conference in 1945: "Here was signed the death warrant of the young men who were dying today in the hills and valleys of Korea. Here was signed the death warrant of the young men who will die tomorrow in the jungles of Indochina (Vietnam)."

McCarthy was accused of smearing the reputation of innocent people, and on July 30, 1954, Sen. Ralph Flanders introduced a resolution condemning him for "conduct unbecoming a member." The speech by Flanders was written by the National Committee for an Effective Congress, which had been created by Arthur Goldsmith, who compiled the charges against McCarthy. He was originally charged with 46 counts, but after the hearings, only two remained, and the Senate voted only to "censure" him, which is a milder punishment than "condemning" him.

McCarthy died on May 2, 1957 at the Bethesda Naval Hospital of "acute hepatic failure." No autopsy was ever performed, leading many to believe that he was killed because he was closer to the truth the most people ever dreamed. Of the 81 security risks that McCarthy said was in the State Department, by November, 1954, they had all been removed, either by dismissal or resignation. Over a year later, the Senate Internal Security Subcommittee revealed that they had a list of 847 security risks in the State Department.

Louis Budenz, a former Communist, said: "The destruction of Joe McCarthy leaves the way open to intimidate any person of consequence who moves against the Conspiracy. The Communists made him their chief target because they wanted him a symbol to remind political leaders in America not to harm the Conspiracy or its world conquest designs."

All of this information should proves the contention, that the invisible forces at work within our government used World War II as a means of promoting the Russian goal of conquest, and allowed the spread of Communist propaganda.

THE DECEPTION OF PEARL HARBOR

In the Pacific Theater, the stirrings of World War II actually began years before. China had allowed Japan to drill for oil in several provinces, because Standard Oil's price for kerosene was too high. Through contacts in the Chinese government, Standard Oil had been able to keep anyone from drilling, until the Japanese came and developed huge fields. Standard Oil pushed them out, but the Japanese vowed to return, even going as far as saying that they would seize China to recover their oil investments.

When the Japanese invaded China in the 1930's, one of their first acts was to destroy Standard Oil property, because they had been responsible for their ouster.

In 1931, Henry L. Stimson, the Secretary of State (a Rockefeller lawyer and agent), met with President Herbert Hoover, on behalf of the Illuminati, to make a deal. The international bankers promised to end the Depression if Hoover would declare war on Japan, and send in the military to protect Standard Oil property. Even though Hoover accommodated the bankers in many cases, this was one deal that he refused.

So Stimson pitched the idea to Governor Franklin Delano Roosevelt (who has a dozen U. S. Presidents in his family tree), who was indebted to them because of his philanthropic operation at Georgia's Warm Springs.

Roosevelt was born at Hyde Park, New York, in 1882. He graduated from Harvard, received a law degree from Columbia Law School, and in 1910, was elected to the New York State Senate (re-elected in 1912). He was appointed Assistant Secretary of the Navy by Wilson in 1913, on orders from Col. House. According to House biographer Arthur D. Howden Smith, Col. House "picked Roosevelt as a natural candidate for the Presidency long before any other responsible politician." In the 1920 Presidential election, Roosevelt was James Cox's running mate, but the Democratic team suffered from the mistakes of the Wilson Administration, and lost miserably to the Harding-Coolidge ticket. Roosevelt later became a two-term governor of New York. After the 1932 Democratic convention in Chicago, where Roosevelt became the Party's nominee, he met with Col. House at his Massachusetts home. House told another biographer, Charles Seymour, in 1938: "I was close to the movement that nominated Roosevelt ... He has given me a free hand in advising (Secretary of State, Cordell) Hull. All the Ambassadors have reported to me frequently."

The Illuminati put all their political power behind Roosevelt to get him elected, and in 1940, Roosevelt appointed Stimson (a CFR member) to the post of Secretary of War, even though he was a Republican. House, who was 75 years old, didn't become Roosevelt's 'alter ego.' That role was filled by another Wilson advisor, Bernard Baruch, who became the liaison between Roosevelt and the bankers. FDR's uncle, Frederic Delano, was a member of the Federal Reserve Board, and in 1925, became the Chairman of the League of Nations Committee. In 1934, he was appointed as Chairman of the National Resources Planning Board, and in 1936, became Chairman of the Federal Reserve Bank in Richmond, Virginia.

Roosevelt was a 32nd degree Mason, a Knight Templar, and a member of the Shrine. He is a direct descendent of socialist Clinton B. Roosevelt, the New York assemblyman who wrote *The Science of Government Founded in Natural Law*, where he revealed a plan for world government. Clinton Roosevelt and Horace Greeley (founder and owner of the *New York Tribune* and *New Yorker* magazine) were the pioneers of social engineering research. In the February, 1953 edition of the *Empire State Mason*, the official publication of the Grand Lodge of New York, the claim was made that if one-world government ever came about, FDR should get much of the credit.

In 1932, Major General Smedley Butler of the U. S. Marine Corps was approached by Grayson Mallet-Provost Murphy (a director of Guaranty Trust), Robert S. Clark (a banker who inherited a fortune from the founder of the Singer Sewing Machine Co.), and John W. Davis (a 1924 Presidential candidate, who was an attorney for J. P. Morgan), with a plan to lead a revolution to overthrow the government and establish a Fascist dictatorship, Butler was to "seize the White House with a private army (of 500,000 veterans), hold Franklin Roosevelt prisoner, and get rid of him if he refused to serve as their puppet in a dictatorship they planned to impose and control." Butler chose to expose the plot, rather than lead it, supposedly because of his patriotism. Or was it because he recognized their true aim, which was for Roosevelt to impose a dictatorship during a national emergency, so the government could take complete control. Butler is on record as having said: "War was largely a matter of money. Bankers lend money to foreign countries and when they cannot repay, the President sends Marines to get it."

When the planned revolt didn't materialize, other plans were developed. Frances Perkins, Secretary of Labor, reported: "At the first meeting of the Cabinet after the President took office in 1933, the financier and advisor to Roosevelt, Bernard Baruch, and Baruch's friend, General Hugh Johnson, who was to become the head of the National Recovery Administration, came in with a copy of a book by Gentile, the Italian Fascist theoretician, for each member of the Cabinet, and we all read it with care." Future plans called for the government to be moved towards Fascism, and government control without a revolution. They decided that the best method was through war, and Jim Farley, Roosevelt's Postmaster General, said that during the second Cabinet meeting in 1933: "The new President again turned to the possibility of war in Japan." Gen. Johnson wrote: "I know of no well informed Washington observer who isn't convinced that, if Mr. Roosevelt is elected (in 1940), he will drag us into war at the first opportunity, and that, if none presents itself, he will make one."

Roosevelt wanted Japan to withdraw, not only from Indo-China, but also China (Manchuria). To enforce his demands, he froze all Japanese assets in this country, and cancelled a 1911 commercial treaty. He had their fuel supplies cut and placed an embargo on 11 raw materials which were necessary for their military. In December, 1939, this was extended to light steel. In England, Winston Churchill, and later the Dutch government, followed suit. Former President Herbert Hoover observed the various political manipulations, and said in August, 1941: "The American people should insistently demand that Congress put a stop to step-by-step projection of the United States into undeclared war..."

On September 28, 1940, Japan, Germany, and Italy signed the Tripartite Treaty, which declared that if any of the three were attacked, all three had to respond. So if Japan attacked the U.S., and the U.S. would declare war against Japan, they would also be at war with Germany and Italy.

In October, 1940, part of FDR's strategy to push Japan into committing an overt act of war, was to move America's Pacific fleet out of California, and have it anchored at Pearl Harbor. Admiral James Richardson, the commander of the Pacific Fleet, expressed to Roosevelt his strong opposition to putting the fleet in harm's way. He was relieved of his command. Richardson later quoted Roosevelt as saying: "Sooner or later the Japanese will commit an overt act against the United States and the nation will be willing to enter the war."

Roosevelt and Churchill had already been working on a plan to get America to enter the war in Europe. After the German ship Bismarck sank the British ship, known as the Hood, Churchill suggested in April, 1941, "that an American warship should find the Prinz Eugen (the Bismarck's escort ship) then draw her fire, 'thus providing the incident for which the United States would be so thankful' i.e.,

FINAL WARNING

bring her into war." While Roosevelt planned for such a provocation in the Atlantic, Hitler told his naval commanders in July, 1941, to avoid confrontation with the United States while his Russian campaign was in progress.

Joseph C. Grew used his post as the U.S. Ambassador to Japan to encourage the Japanese to enter a state of military preparedness. They were shipped steel scrap from the entire 6th Avenue Elevator Railroad of New York. The Institute of Pacific Relations, through a $2 million grant, funded communist spies who were to help induce the Japanese to strike back at the United States.

Since then, it has become common knowledge that the attack was not the surprise it was claimed to be. On January 27, 1941, Grew sent a telegram to the Secretary of State to report the following: "The Peruvian minister has informed a member of my staff that he heard from many sources, including a Japanese source, that, in the event of trouble breaking out between the United States and Japan, the Japanese intended to make a surprise attack against Pearl Harbor." (Source: U.S., Department of State, Publication 1983, *Peace and War: United States Foreign Policy, 1931-1941*, Washington, D.C.: U.S., Government Printing Office, 1943, pp. 617-618)

In August, 1941, Congressman Martin Dies, Chairman of the House Committee on Un-American Activities, collected evidence that the Japanese were planning to attack Pearl Harbor. The Committee was in possession of a strategic map, prepared by the Japanese Imperial Military Intelligence Department that clearly indicated their plans to attack Pearl Harbor. Dies was told not to go public with his information. An Army Intelligence officer in the Far East discovered the plan for the Pearl Harbor attack, and prior to the attack, sent three separate messages to Washington detailing the plan.

Soviet agent Richard Sorge told the Russian Government in October, 1941 that "the Japanese intend to attack Pearl Harbor in the next 60 days," and received a response from his superiors that the information had been passed onto President Roosevelt. Dusko Popov, a British double agent, received information from Germany about Japan's plans, and passed the information onto Washington. It was never acted on.

As early as 1944, Presidential candidate, New York Governor Thomas E. Dewey, said that Roosevelt knew about the attack on Pearl Harbor, before it happened. In documents declassified by the National Security Agency in 1981, America had broken the Blue (diplomatic) and Purple (naval) secret codes of the Japanese, knew all the details of the attack, and the whereabouts of the Japanese fleet. From September, 1941, until the attack itself, all Japanese communications had been intercepted and decoded by American intelligence, and indicated an impending attack on Pearl Harbor.

One transmission, from a fake weather report broadcast on a Japanese shortwave station contained the words "higashi no kaze ame," which means "east wind, rain," which the Americans already knew was the Japanese code for war with the United States. Top military officials denied that the "winds" message existed and attempted to destroy all traces of its receipt.

Late in November, 1941, the following order was sent out to all U.S. military commanders: "The United States desires that Japan commit the first overt act." According to Secretary of War Stimson, this order came directly from Roosevelt.

According to Stimson's diary, 9 people in the war cabinet, all the military people, knew about FDR's plan of provocation.

The State Department knew on November 20th, that a naval force, which included four of the largest Japanese aircraft carriers were heading towards Hawaii, and this information was passed on to Pearl Harbor on November 27th. However, the American base in Hawaii was not given this information. Three days before the attack, Australian Intelligence spotted the Japanese fleet heading for Hawaii. They sent a warning to Washington, but it was dismissed by Roosevelt who said it was a politically motivated rumor circulated by the Republicans.

On December 1, 1941, the head of the Far East Division of U.S. Naval Intelligence wrote in his report to head of the Pacific Fleet: "War between the United States and Japan will begin in the nearest future." The Report never made it to the commander's desk, because it had been 'accidentally' detained by his superiors. Early in December, Army Intelligence knew that the diplomats at the Japanese Embassy in Washington had been ordered to destroy all codes, and to return to Japan. Washington also knew that Japan had ordered all of its merchant ships home, because they would be needed to transport soldiers and supplies for the war. On December 5, Col. Sadtler from U.S. Military Communications transmitted the following telegram to his superiors, based on information he had received: "War with Japan will begin immediately; exclude all possibility of a second Port Arthur." This telegram never got to its destination.

In 1932, the U.S. Navy had conducted tests at Pearl Harbor which indicated that it was vulnerable to an attack from sixty miles away without being able to detect it. Admiral J. O. Richardson, Commander-in-Chief of the Pacific fleet, wanted the fleet withdrawn to the west coast of the United States, because they were inadequately manned for war, and because the area was too exposed. It was not done. In January, 1941, Richardson was relieved of his command. It was later revealed that Roosevelt wanted him to create a naval blockade around Japan, to provoke them into a response, so the United States could declare war. He refused to do it, saying it was an act of war.

Besides knowing about the security weaknesses at the base in Pearl Harbor, and having previous knowledge about the impending attack, Roosevelt guaranteed a slaughter by ordering that the planes be grouped in circles, with their propellers facing inward, because he claimed that he wanted to protect them against 'acts of sabotage.' Rear Admiral Robert A. Theobold, USN, Retired, author of *The Final Secret of Pearl Harbor*, and Col. Curtis B. Dall, the son-in-law of FDR, in an interview with Anthony Hilder for his book *Warlords of Washington*, admitted that they knew about the Pearl Harbor attack before it occurred. Theobold, the Commander of all the destroyers at Pearl Harbor, said in his book, that Roosevelt knew about the attack 21 hours before it happened. So the result of this positioning of the aircraft, made it difficult for them to get out of the circle, and up in the air, because they didn't have a reverse gear. Theobold wrote: "An incontestable fact in the true history of Pearl Harbor is the repeated withholding from Admiral Kimmel and General Walter C. Short (Navy and Army Command in Pearl Harbor) of supremely important military information ... There's never been a case in history when a commander was not informed that his country will be at war within a few hours and that his forces will most likely become the first object of attack at sunrise."

FINAL WARNING

Theobold also cited the testimony of Admiral Harold Stark (head of Navy Headquarters in Washington) who did not reveal Japan's de facto declaration of war to Admiral Kimmel, and said he was acting on orders from a "higher authority," referring to Roosevelt, because Marshall did not outrank Stark. Marshall merely passed on the Roosevelt directive of December 4th, which said that no communications could be sent to Pearl Harbor, unless it was cleared by Marshall. On November 26, 1941, Roosevelt had sent an ultimatum, insisting that the Japanese withdraw all their troops. He refused any negotiations with Prince Kenoye, the Japanese Prime Minister, even though Joseph Grew (CFR member, and Rockefeller agent), the Ambassador to Japan, said that such a meeting would prevent war with the Japanese. The Japanese response from Tokyo to the Japanese embassy, encrypted in the "purple code," was intercepted by the Navy, decoded, and given to Roosevelt on the evening of December 6th. The thirteen-point communiqué revealed, that because of the intense pressure of the economic sanctions, diplomatic relations with the United States were being terminated at 1:00 PM Eastern time on Sunday, December 7th. For all intents and purposes, this was a declaration of war, and upon reading it, Roosevelt said: "This means war." It was not passed onto Pearl Harbor command, and it was at that time that the attack began.

While FDR was pushing Japan into drawing first blood, he told the American public in his famous campaign statement of 1940: "While I am talking to you mothers and fathers, I give you one more assurance. I have said this before, and I shall say it again and again and again: Your boys are not going to be sent into any foreign wars." Then he said later that he wouldn't send our boys to war unless we were attacked.

Lieutenant Commander Arthur McCollum worked for Naval Intelligence in Washington and was the communications routing officer for FDR. All the intercepted Japanese messages would go to McCollum, who would then route them to Roosevelt. In October, 1940, he wrote a memo which contained the basis for FDR's plan for provoking the Japanese into attacking at Pearl Harbor. It was given to two of Roosevelt's closest advisors. The memorandum revealed his sentiments that it was inevitable that Japan and America were going to war, and that Germany was going to be a threat to America's security. He said that American had to go to war, but he also understood that public opinion was against that. So public opinion had to be swayed, and Japan had to be provoked into attacking America. He named eight specific suggestions for things that America should do to make Japan more hostile towards us, ultimately pushing them into attacking us. That would rally the country behind the war effort. Because he was born and raised in Japan, he said that he understood the Japanese mentality, and knew how they would react. This included moving the Pacific fleet to Hawaii, and decimating Japan's economy with an embargo. McCollum said: "If you adopt these policies the Japan will commit an overt act of war." Although there is no proof that FDR actually saw this memo, he ended up implementing all eight of McCollum's points.

The Administration discovered that in 1941 a Japanese naval officer was working at the Japanese consulate in Honolulu under an assumed name. They followed him, and began to intercept his messages to Japan, which enabled the Japanese to develop a timetable for the attack, and even bomb plots. They never stopped him, and it enabled the Japanese to prepare themselves for an attack against us.

Fleet Admiral Halsey wrote: "Our intelligence data spoke of a likely attack by Japan on the Philippines or the Dutch East Indies. Although Pearl Harbor wasn't excluded from discussion, everything relayed to us pointed to other objects of attack. If we had known that the Japanese were continually collecting detailed information about the exact location and movements of our warships in Pearl Harbor (which is made clear by intercepted reports), we naturally would have concentrated our efforts on preparations to repel an attack on Pearl Harbor."

Secretary of War Henry L. Stimson, after meeting with the Roosevelt administration on November 25, 1941, wrote in his diary: "The discussion was about how we should maneuver to force the Japanese to fire the first shot, while not exposing ourselves to too great a danger; this will be a difficult task."

Admiral Husband E. Kimmel wrote in his memoirs: "It was part of Roosevelt's plan that no warning be sent to the Hawaiian Islands. Our leaders in Washington, who deliberately didn't inform our forces in Pearl Harbor, cannot be justified in any way. The Pearl Harbor Command wasn't informed at all about ... the American note of November 26, 1941, delivered to the Japanese ambassador, which practically excluded further negotiations and made war in the Pacific inevitable. The Army and Navy Command in the Hawaiian Islands received not even a hint about intercepted and deciphered Japanese telegrams which were forwarded to concerned parties in Washington on the 6th and 7th of December, 1941."

The Pacific fleet had consisted of nine battleships, three aircraft cruisers, and some smaller ships. The aircraft carriers, and the smaller, more mobile ships, were moved prior to the attack, because Roosevelt knew they would be needed for a war at sea. On November 28th Fleet Admiral William F. Halsey (under Kimmel's command) sailed to Wake Island with the carrier Enterprise, three heavy destroyers and nine small destroyers; and on December 5th, the Lexington, three heavy cruisers and five destroyers were sent to Midway, and the Saratoga went to the Pacific Coast. The other battleships were considered dispensable, because they had been produced during and prior to World War I, and were viewed as old and obsolete. They were to be sacrificed.

On December 7, 1941, the Japanese attacked the U.S. fleet at Pearl Harbor, instead of attacking Russia, as they originally intended to do. The 'sneak attack' gave Roosevelt a reason to direct the full force of America's military might against Japan. The next day, Roosevelt asked Congress to declare war on Japan: "We don't like it— and we didn't want to get in it— but we are in it and we're going to fight it with everything we've got." On January 1, 1942, the 25 allied nations who went to war against Germany and Japan, signed a "Declaration by the United Nations," which indicated that no one nation would sign a separate armistice, and Gen. Douglas MacArthur was appointed as the 'United Nations Commander of the South Pacific,' becoming the Commander-in-Chief of all armed forces in the Pacific Theater.

The attack on Pearl Harbor resulted in the deaths of 2,341 American soldiers, and 2,233 more were injured or missing. Eighteen ships, including eight battleships, two destroyers, two squadron minesweepers, were sunk or heavily damaged; and 177 planes were destroyed. All of this, just to create an anti-Japanese sentiment in the country, and justify American action against Japan.

General George C. Marshall (Supreme Commander of the U.S. Army), and

Admiral Harold R. Stark (Supreme Commander of the U.S. Navy) in Washington, testified that the message about the attack was not forwarded to Kimmel and Short because the Hawaiian base had received so many intercepted Japanese messages that another one would have confused them. In truth, Marshall sat on the information for 15 hours because he didn't want anything to interfere with attack. The message was sent after the attack started. Internal Army and Navy inquiries in 1944 found Kimmel and Short derelict of duty, but the truth was not revealed to the public.

Two weeks before the attack, on November 23rd, Kimmel had sent nearly 100 warships from the Pacific fleet to, what turned out to be, the exact location where Japan planned to launch their attack. Unquestionably, he was looking to prevent the possibility of a sneak attack. When the Administration learned of his actions, he was criticized for "complicating the situation."

Eleven days after the attack, the Roberts Commission, headed by Supreme Court Justice Owen Roberts, made scapegoats of Kimmel and Short, who were denied open hearings, publicly ruined, and forced to retire. Short died in 1949, and Kimmel died in 1968.

The most incredible of the eight investigations was a joint House-Senate investigation that echoed the Roberts Commission. Both Marshall and Stark testified that they couldn't remember where they were the night the declaration of war had come in. A close friend of Frank Knox, Secretary of the Navy, later said that Knox, Stark, and Marshall spent most of that night with Roosevelt in the White House, waiting for the bombing to begin, so they could enter the war.

According to historian John Toland, Marshall told his top officers: "Gentlemen, this goes to the grave with us."

In 1995, a Department of Defense study concluded that "Army and Navy officials in Washington were privy to intercepted Japanese diplomatic communications ... which provided crucial confirmation of the imminence of war."

The full extent of the deception came to the forefront with the publishing of the book *Day of Deceit: The Truth About FDR and Pearl Harbor* by Robert B. Stinnett, a retired *Oakland Tribune* photographer who served in the Pacific during World War II. After retirement, he began his investigation by interviewing former American military communications personnel, and filing Freedom of Information requests with the National Security Agency. For 17 years he gleaned through volumes of previously classified messages which had been intercepted from the Japanese.

Stinnett discovered that on November 25, 1941, Japan's Admiral Yamamoto dispatched a radio message to the group of warships that would be used to attack Pearl Harbor. It read, in part: "...the task force, keeping its movements strictly secret and maintaining close guard against submarines and aircraft, shall advance into Hawaiian waters, and upon the very opening of hostilities shall attack the main force of the United States fleet in Hawaii and deal it a mortal blow." From November 17th to 25th, the U.S. Navy intercepted 83 messages that Yamamoto sent to his carriers.

This Pearl Harbor scenario was a repeat of the American battleship 'Maine,' which was 'sunk' by a Spanish mine in the port of Havana in 1898. The rallying cry of "Remember the Maine," was used to stir up anti-Spanish hysteria in America to justify us declaring war on Spain. Years later, when the ship was examined, it was established that the hull had been blown out by an explosion from inside the ship.

So what did World War II accomplish for the Illuminati? With the Japanese prepared to surrender in February, 1945, the war was prolonged in order to destroy much of the industrial areas of Japan with a devastating air attack of incendiary atomic bombs. This allowed the ground to be cleared for the Illuminati to rebuild Japan with new industries so they could use cheap labor to flood the American market with cheaply manufactured goods. This would turn the United States into a nation that consumed more than it produced, creating unemployment and financial instability.

As stated previously, on the European front, the War enabled the Russians to gain control of Eastern Europe, promoted Communism, paved the way for the United Nations, and the creation of the nation of Israel.

At a cost of about $400 billion, the War raised our National Debt to $220 billion, and pushed us deeper into the clutches of the Illuminati's international bankers. Because of all the intricate angles involved in this conflict, it would not be an understatement to say that World War II was probably the most costly event in American history. We may have won, but, in the long run, we lost.

CHAPTER SEVEN

THE COMMUNIST AGENDA

THE ORIGIN OF COMMUNISM

In a previous chapter, we found out how the Illuminati created Communism to be used as an adversary against liberty. An indication of that fact came from a statement by Dr. Bella Dodd, who was a member of the National Committee of the U.S. Communist Party. She indicated that when their Board could not reach a decision, one of their members would go to the Waldorf Towers in New York City to consult with Arthur Goldsmith. Goldsmith's decision would later be confirmed by Communist officials in Russia. Goldsmith was not a Communist, but was a wealthy 'capitalist.' The Communist movement was created out of the roots of Socialism, in fact, President Hoover said: "Socialism is the forerunner of communism."

Socialistic ideas can be traced back to Plato's (427-347 BC) *Republic*, and English Statesman Sir Thomas More's (1478-1535) *Utopia* in 1516. Plato envisioned a society where marriage would be eliminated, all women would belong to all men, and all men would belong to all women. Women would be equal to men, working and fighting wars side by side. All children would be raised by the state. There would be a tri-level society consisting of the ruling class, the military class, and the working class. Private property would be eliminated, and the intellectuals would determine what was best for the lower classes.

Indian settlements were communistic. The Pilgrims and Virginia colonists tried them, but failed. Captain John Smith of Virginia said: "When our people were fed out of the common store, and labored jointly together, glad was he who could slip from his labor and sleep over his task..."

The Mennonites, who came to Pennsylvania from Germany, in 1683, established communes. As they moved westward, they left behind a splinter group, called the Amish, who gradually developed a society based on the private ownership of property. Also in 1683 followers of a Frenchman, Jean de Labadie (former Jesuit, turned Protestant) immigrated to Maryland. They held property in common, but broke up within a couple of years.

In 1774, Englishwoman Ann Lee, leading a group called the Shakers (United Society of Believers in Christ's Second Appearing), which was a splinter group of the Quaker movement, established a celibate communal society near Albany, New York, in an area known as Watervliet. Religious persecution had forced them to

America, where they practiced celibacy, equality of sexes, common ownership of property, and the public confession of sins. In 1787, two of Lee's followers, Joseph Meacham and Lucy Wright, established a similar colony in New Lebanon, NY. By 1840, they had 6,000 members in 19 communes, from New York, to Indiana and Kentucky. Their numbers declined after the Civil War, and they finally broke up in the 1940's.

Francois Emile Babeuf (1760-97), was a member of the Illuminati (his pseudonym was 'Gracchus'), and as such, his social views reflected those of Weishaupt's. He formed a Masonic-like association of disciples called Babouvistes, who advocated violence as a means of achieving reform. They met at the dining hall of the Abbey, and sometimes in the crypt. The location of the building, which was near the Pantheon, led to the name of the Order, which was known as the Pantheonistes. The group, at its peak, had about 2,000 members.

Babeuf wrote: "In my system of Common Happiness, I desire that no individual property shall exist. The land is God's and its fruits belong to all men in general." One of his disciples, the Marquis de Antonelle, a former member of the Revolutionary Tribunal, wrote: "The state of communism is the only just, the only good one; without this state of things, no peaceful and really happy societies can exist."

In April, 1796, Babeuf wrote his *Manifesto of the Equals*, which was published under the title *Analysis of the Doctrine of Babeuf*. In it he wrote:

> "No more private property in land, the land belongs to no one ... the fruits of the earth belong to everyone ... Vanish at last, revolting distinctions of rich and poor, of great and small, of masters and servants, of governors and governed. Let there be no difference between men than that of age and sex. Since all have the same needs and the same faculties, let there be only one education, one kind of food. They content themselves with one sun and air for all; why should not the same portion and the same quality of food suffice for each of them..."

Under his plan, workers wouldn't be paid in money, since the owning of personal property would be abolished. Instead, payment would be made through the distribution of products. These products, stored in communal warehouses, would be equally handed out. Another notable aspect of his plan was that children would not be allowed to bear the name of their father, unless he was a man of great importance.

Knowing that people would never allow such a communistic system, they never fully revealed their plans. Instead, their propaganda centered on "equality among men" and "justice of the people," while they criticized the "greed" of the government. The working men didn't fully understand Babeuf's doctrines, nevertheless, they praised his ideas.

In August, 1796, Babeuf and 45 leaders of his movement were arrested after the government found out they were making preparations to lead a revolt of the people against them. They were put on trial in a proceeding that lasted from February to May, 1797. The Illuminati was secretly directing the Babouviste movement, and Babeuf testified that he was just an agent of the conspiracy: "I attest they do for me too much honor in decorating me with the title of head of this affair. I declare that I had only a secondary and limited part in it ... The heads and the leaders needed a director of public opinion. I was in the position to enlist this opinion." On May 28, 1797, Babeuf was hung, and many of his followers were deported.

Those who have studied the Russian Revolution have observed that there is little difference between Babouvism and Bolshevism. The Third Internationale of Moscow in 1919, in its first Manifesto, traced its descent from Babeuf. The Russian Revolution may have been the ultimate goal of Babeuf, who wrote: "The French Revolution is only the forerunner of another revolution, very much greater, very much more solemn, and which will be the last!"

The earliest advocate of the movement, later to be known as Socialism, was the English mill owner Robert Owen (1771-1858). He was a student of spiritualism and published his views in the *Rational Quarterly Review*. At his Scotland textile factory, he was known as a model employer because of the reforms he instituted, even enacting child labor laws. He felt production could be increased if competition was eliminated. Many of his principles were derived from the writings of Weishaupt. For instance, Weishaupt wrote that the aim of the Illuminati, was "to make the human race, without any distinction of nation, condition or profession, one good and happy family." Owen said that the "new state of existence upon the earth, which, when understood and applied rationally to practice, will cordially unite all as one good and enlightened family." Many of Owen's philosophies were parallel to those of the Illuminati.

Owen's long term goal was to "cut the world into villages of 300 to 2,000 souls," in which, "the dwellings for the 200 or 300 families should be placed together in the form of a parallelogram." According to his philosophy, "individualism was to be disallowed," and "each was to work for the benefit of all." A colony established along those lines in Ireland failed, so in 1824, Owen sailed to America, where he bought several thousand acres from George Rapp's pietistic Harmony Society, in Posey County, Indiana. In 1825, with 1,000 settlers, he started his "New Harmony Community of Equality." It was a model town of non- profit making stores.

Other settlements like this were started in America and Scotland, and communism was born. However, Owen was a weak leader, had few skilled workmen, and had to put additional duties on the few competent workers that he had, in an attempt to insure success. In 1826, he adopted a Constitution that condemned private property and organized religion.

However, Owen had failed to take into account human nature, something he had fought so hard for in earlier years, when he advocated better housing for workers, better education for children, and the elimination of unhealthy living conditions. Even though he failed in an attempt to merge all the trade unions into a "Great Trades Union," his reforms completely transformed the town of New Lanark, Scotland. In 1827, Owen resigned as manager, and dissolved the colony, because he was forced to change his thinking. He wrote: "No societies with common property and equality could prosper. In order to succeed it was needful to exclude the intemperate, the idle, the careless, the quarrelsome, the avaricious, the selfish..."

His son, Robert Dale Owen (1801-77), was a leader in the Workingman's

Party in 1829, which evolved down through the years into the U.S. Communist Party.

In 1817, a group of German separatists, led by Joseph M. Bimeler, settled near the Tuscarawas River in Ohio, naming their society after one of the few Biblical plain cities that escaped the destruction of Sodom and Gomorrah. In 1819, they were incorporated as the Society of Separatists of Zoar. All property was held in common; factories and shops were managed by an elected Board of Trustees. They prospered during the 1850's, establishing the town of Zoar, having over 10,000 acres, and $1 million worth of assets. After Bimeler's death in 1853, interest declined, and the town dissolved in 1898.

There were other communistic settlements, such as Harmony, PA (1805); Nashoba, Tennessee (1825); the Cooperative Store at Toad Street (1844); and the Cooperative Society of Oldham (1850), set up by the Rochdale Pioneers, which also failed.

Some groups today can trace their roots to the 19th century communes. In the 1830's, Joseph Smith, who founded the Church of Jesus Christ of the Latter Day Saints (the Mormons), moved his followers from New York, to Ohio, then to Missouri, and finally to Utah, because of religious persecution. He believed that a form of communal Christianity existed during the time of the Apostles.

John Humphrey Noyes ("Father Noyes"), after establishing a colony at Putney, Virginia, in 1846, set up another in Oneida, New York, in 1848, which featured common property ownership and child rearing, selective 'breeding' of babies, and a society in which every woman was considered to be the wife of each man, and every man the husband of each woman. By 1874, there were 300 members. Noyes went to Canada in 1879 after threats of prosecution, and the colony discontinued their unusual sexual practices. They reorganized as a joint stock company, which is still operating today.

Christian Metz, head of the 17th century German Protestant sect known as the Community of True Inspiration, settled on a farm near Buffalo, New York, in 1842, where they established a Christian commune where all property was commonly owned. Work and worship was combined. In 1855, they moved to an 18,000 acre area in Iowa, forming the community of Amana. It eventually expanded into seven villages, with farms, stores, sheds and factories. The commune still exists today, with its factories producing various appliances. Its stock was held by about 1400 members.

Comte Henri de Saint-Simon (1776-1825), French nobleman, philosopher and socialist, was the grandson of the author of King Louis XIV's memoirs. He was considered by some to be mentally unbalanced, because of an infliction inherited from his insane mother. Others believed him to be a genius. His philosophy, known as the "New Christianity," advocated the placing of all property and people under the State's control, to insure that the exploitation of the poor would end. He declared that the existing social system was dead and should be done away with. He called for the merging of scientific and technological knowledge towards industrialism, in order to have the elite rule. He said that all men were not created equal. His followers, known as "The Family" instituted a political program, calling for the public control of industrial production, abolition of inheritance, and equal rights for women. They even tried to start a Saint-Simonian Church.

In 1836, one of Simon's disciples, Philippe Joseph Benjamin Buchez, attempted to combine Socialism with Catholicism, with something called Christian Socialism. This was a continuation of Weishaupt's efforts to identify Christianity with the Illuminati, in order to draw members. Peaceful revolution was to be carried out through the principles of Christian love and brotherhood, with Jesus being represented as a Socialist. The group published a labor newspaper called *L'Atelier* ("*The Workshop*"), which was written and edited by the workers themselves. They warned against the use of violence to obtain social change, and barred the workers from belonging to secret organizations. Small co-op communities were established. They started the Council for Promoting Working Men's Associations, and in 1854, started the Working Men's College in London.

As Christian Socialism developed, it was promoted by saying that Socialism was the ultimate goal of Christianity. In America, prominent Protestant clergymen, such as Washington Gladden, Walter Rauschenbush, Lyman Abbott, Josiah Strong, and Charles M. Sheldon, through sermons, books, magazine and newspaper articles, called for better working conditions for women, the elimination of child labor, a six-day work week, and a decent working wage. These principles were later adopted by the Federal Council of Churches of Christ in America in 1908. The aforementioned ministers, and economist Richard T. Ely, in 1889, organized the Society of Christian Socialists, which advocated a cooperative society based on the teachings of Christ. Rev. Endicott Peabody, founder of the Grotan School, spoke of such reform to the capitalist system. One of his young students was Franklin D. Roosevelt.

Buchez' followers soon grew dissatisfied with the equal payment plan, and the organization split into several factions, one professing Christianity (setting up several Christian Socialist organizations), and the other, calling for revolution.

Francois Marie Charles Fourier (1772-1837), a French philosopher, planned out model communities, in which people would live in a pleasurable atmosphere, and work at their own pace, at jobs they like. Everyone would know what to do and when to do it. There would be no need for regulations. In his communities, called 'phalanxes' (or 'phalansteries'), everyone was to live in the same building. Jobs were assigned, and workers received a nominal wage. In 1832, he failed in an attempt to set up such a commune at Versailles. However, his followers founded about 30 communal settlements in the United States, such as the Brook Farm (1841-47).

In 1841, George Ripley, Nathaniel Hawthorne, and Charles A. Dana, all advocates of Transcendentalism, established a 192-acre settlement in West Roxbury, Massachusetts. In 1844, they instituted a constitution, making it a co-op based on the scientific division of labor advocated by Fourier. They published a journal, *The Harbinger* (1845-49), which was edited by Ripley, and featured such writers as James Russell Lowell and John Greenleaf. Ralph Waldo Emerson, Horace Greeley, and Henry David Thoreau, established another Fourier commune at Red Bank, New Jersey in 1843, where members picked their jobs and were paid according to the repulsiveness of their work. The dirtier the job, the more it paid. They had about 1200 members, and operated for about ten years. Fourier disciples, Elizabeth Peabody, Parke Goodwin, and William Henry Channing, also began communes.

Louis Blanc, a Mason, developed a Workingman's Association, but his was to be under State control. He called for the establishment of labor organizations in the form of national workshops, with the workers electing their management. He despised all religion, and eliminated the idea of Christianity, criticizing Buchez for being too sentimental.

In France, during the 1840's, Louis-Auguste Blanqui espoused a form of radical socialism that was based on democratic populism. He said that capitalism was unstable and would be replaced by cooperative institutions.

Etienne Cabet, the son of a barrelmaker, went to England in 1834, where he became a convert of Robert Owen. When he returned to France in 1839, he laid out a plan for a communistic settlement, which he established in the Red River region of Texas in 1847. His 69 followers were called "Icarians," after his 1840 novel *Voyage en Icaria*, which portrayed a society where all property was held in common, and products of the community were distributed according to need. Later that year, he wrote a book on the French Revolution, and traced the course of communistic theories starting with Plato, Pythagoras (a 6th century BC philosopher), the Essenes of Judea, More, Campanella, Locke, Montesquieu, Mably, Rousseau, and other 18th century philosophers. He claimed that the communists were the disciples, the imitators, and continuers of the philosophy of Jesus.

In 1849, he took 280 of his followers to Nauvoo, Illinois, after the Texas commune failed because of poor soil, crooked land agents, and an attack of malaria. This Hancock County area had been a Mormon community of about 15,000 people, who after the death of Joseph Smith in 1844, went to Salt Lake City, Utah, with Brigham Young. By 1855, Nauvoo had farms, a running mill, a distillery, a theater, a printing press, and a school. Soon there were over 500 people in the town.

They eventually grew restless because of Cabet's autocratic leadership, since they didn't have a voice in their own affairs. They threw him out in 1856, and he took 200 of his followers with him. As time went on, only a few diehards remained, until the commune finally broke up in 1888. Meanwhile, Cabet started a "true Icaria" in Cheltinham, Missouri (near St. Louis), but soon after, died of apoplexy. The commune lasted until 1864. Some followers of Cabet also started communes at Corning, Iowa (1860-84), and Cloverdale, California (1881-87).

THE RISE OF KARL MARX

Heinrich Karl Marx (Moses Mordecai Marx Levy, 1818-83) was born of wealthy parents (his father was a lawyer), and much of his personal life has never been revealed. Professor M. Mtchedlov, Vice-Director of the Marx Institute, said that there were 100 volumes in his collection, but only thirteen have ever been reprinted for the public. When he was six, his family converted to Christianity, and although he was once a believer in God, after attending the Universities of Bonn and Berlin, Marx wrote that he wanted to avenge himself "against the One who rules above." He joined the Satanist Church run by Joana Southcott, who was said to be in contact with the demon Shiloh. His early writings mentioned the name "Oulanem," which was a ritualistic name for Satan. A friend of Marx wrote in

1841, that "Marx calls the Christian religion one of the most immoral of religions." His published attacks against the German government caused him to be ejected from the country.

He received a Doctorate in Philosophy in 1841, but was turned down for a teaching position, because of his revolutionary activities. In 1843, he studied Economics in Paris, where he learned about French communism. Again he was expelled for revolutionary activities. In 1844, he wrote the book *A World Without Jews* even though he was Jewish. In 1845, he moved to Brussels, where, with German philosopher, Friedrich Engels (the son of a wealthy textile manufacturer, 1820-95), who he met in Paris in 1844, they reorganized the Communist League.

Engels had joined the 'Young Germany' group (which had been established by Giuseppe Mazzini) in Switzerland in 1835. He later became a 32nd degree Mason (as did Marx). In 1842 he was sent to England to manage the family's mill in Manchester. A journalism student, in 1843 he published a treatise on economics called *Outlines of a Critique of Political Economy*; and in 1844, wrote a review of Thomas Carlyle's *Past and Present,* and also a booklet called *The Condition of the Working Class in England in 1844.* It was Engel's philosophy that established the basis for the ideas which were developed by Marx.

In 1848, Marx published his *Communist Manifesto* (which he was working on from 1830-47), from an Engel's draft (which was an extension of Engel's *Confessions of a Communist*), which also borrowed heavily from Clinton Roosevelt's book, *The Science of Government Founded on Natural Law* which echoed the philosophies of Weishaupt. It had been commissioned by the Communist League in London. The League, formerly known as the League of the Just (or the League of Just Men), which was an off-shoot of the Parisian Outlaws League (which evolved from the Jacobin movement), was founded by Illuminati members who fled from Germany. The League was made up of rich and powerful men from different countries that were behind much of the turmoil that engulfed Europe in 1848. Many researchers consider them either a finger organization of the Illuminati, or an inner circle. Originally introduced as the *Manifesto of the Communist Party* in London, on February 1, 1848, the name was changed to the *Communist Manifesto*, and the name of Karl Marx was added as its author twenty years later, after a series of small revolutions failed.

Marx wrote in 1848: "The coming world war will cause not only reactionary classes and dynasties, but entire reactionary peoples, to disappear from the face of the earth." Friedrich Engels, that same year, wrote: "The next world war will make whole reactionary peoples disappear from the face of the earth."

The Manifesto was described by Marxians as "The Charter of Freedom of the Workers of the World," and it was the platform of the Communist League. It advocated the abolition of property in land, and the application of all land rent to public purposes; a heavy progressive or graduated income tax; abolition of all rights of inheritance; the confiscation of all the property of immigrants and rebels; centralization of credit in the hands of the State with a national bank; centralization and State control of all communication and transportation; expansion of factories to cultivate waste lands, and create industrial armies, especially for agriculture; gradual abolition of the distinction between town and country to have a more equitable distribution of the population over the country; the elimination of child factory labor and free education for all children in public schools.

This revolutionary plan for socialism, which included the abolition of all religion, was reminiscent of the doctrines of Weishaupt. It was basically a program for establishing a 'perfect' state, and it called for the workers (proletariat) to revolt and overthrow capitalism (the private ownership of industry), and for the government to own all property. Marx, felt, that by controlling all production, the ruling power could politically control a country. After the communist regime would take over, the dictatorship would gradually "wither away" and the result would be a non-government. The final stage of communism is when the goods are distributed on the basis of need. Leonid Brezhnev, when celebrating the 50th anniversary of the U.S.S.R., said: "Now the Soviet Union is marching onward. The Soviet Union is moving towards communism."

Meanwhile, Professor Carl Ritter (1779-1859), of the University of Berlin, a co-founder of modern geographical science, was writing a contrasting view, under the direction of another group of Illuminists. The purpose of this was to divide the people of the world into opposing camps with differing ideologies. The work started by Ritter, was finished after he died, by German philosopher Friedrich Wilhelm Nietzsche (1844-1900), who founded Nietzscheism, which later developed into Fascism, and then into Nazism, which was later used to ferment World War II. Although the Nazis, in quoting from Nietzsche, considered themselves to be the Master Race, Nietzsche did not. Nietzsche tried to stir things up at the top of the social order, while Marx hammered away at the bottom, concentrating on the lower class and working people. Nietzsche wanted to keep the uneducated in a state of slavery, while Marx wanted to neutralize the elite, and pushed for the rights of the people.

Marx worked as a correspondent for the *New York Tribune* (whose Editor was Horace Greeley, 1852-61), covering the 1848 European revolutions. One source has reported that even these articles were written by Engels. In 1857 and 1858, Marx wrote a few articles for the *New American Cyclopedia*.

On September 28, 1864, Marx and Engels founded the International Workingmen's Association at St. Martin's Hall in London, which consisted of English, French, German, Italian, Swiss, and Polish Socialists, who were dedicated to destroying the "prevailing economic system." It later became known as the First Socialist International, which eight years later spread to New York and merged with the Socialist Party. The statutes they adopted were similar to Mazzini's, and in fact, a man named Wolff, the personal secretary of Mazzini, was a member, and pushed Mazzini's views. Marx wrote to Engels: "I was present, only as a dumb personage on the platform." James Guillaume, a Swiss member, wrote: "It is not true that the Internationale was the creation of Karl Marx. He remained completely outside the preparatory work that took place from 1862 to 1864..." Again, we find evidence that the Illuminati did in fact control the growing communist movement, but not to deal with the problems of workers and industry, rather it was to instigate riot and revolution. The Marxist doctrine produced by the Association was accepted and advocated by the emerging labor movement, and soon the organization grew to 800,000 dues-paying members.

Even though Marx publicly urged the working class to overthrow the capitalists (the wealthy who profited from the Stock Exchange), in June, 1864, "in a letter to his uncle, Leon Phillips, Marx announced that he had made 400 pounds on the Stock Exchange." It is obvious that Marx didn't practice what he preached, and therefore didn't really believe in the movement he was giving birth to. He was an employee, doing a job for his Illuminati bosses.

Nathan Rothschild had given Marx two checks for several thousand pounds to finance the cause of Socialism. The checks were put on display in the British Museum, after Lord Lionel Walter Rothschild, a trustee, had willed his museum and library to them.

In 1867, Marx wrote the first volume of *Das Kapital*, which became known as the "Bible of the Working Class." Marx felt, that as the workers achieved various reforms, there would be a possibility for the peaceful evolution towards socialism. A little known fact, is that Marx' beliefs were gleaned from the writings of Weishaupt, Babeuf, Blanc, Cabet, Owen, Ogilvie, Hodgkin, Gray, Robert Thompson, William Carpenter, and Clinton Roosevelt; which he discovered from his hours of research in the Reading Room of the British Museum. The second volume appeared after Marx' death, edited by Engels from Marx' notes, in 1885; and volume three appeared in 1894.

When Marx died in March 14, 1883, only six people attended his funeral. He never supported his family, which had produced six children. Three of them died of starvation in infancy and two others committed suicide. Actually, Engels supported Marx with income from his father's cotton mills in England. Marx was buried in London, at Highgate Cemetery.

The Social Democratic Party in Germany, in 1869, was the first Marxist aligned political Party. They favored an independent working class. It grew rapidly, despite the effort of Chancellor Otto von Bismarck to break it up through the enactment of anti-socialist legislation. In 1877, they elected a dozen members to the Reichstag. In 1881, they had 312,000 members; and by 1891, 1,427,000. In 1891, they eliminated their earlier leanings toward State-aid for co-ops, and aligned themselves with the Marxist goal of "the abolition of class rule and of classes themselves."

Some of the early Socialist Parties were: Danish Social Democratic Party (1870's), Swedish Socialist Party (1889), Norwegian Labor Party (1887), Austrian Social Democratic Party (1888), Belgian Labor Party (1885), Dutch Socialist-Democratic Workers Party (1894), Spanish Social Labor Party (1879), Italian Socialist Party (1892), and the Social Democratic Federation of Great Britain (1880's).

In 1889, the Second International was formed, with their headquarters in Brussels, Belgium. Their main responsibility was to create some sort of unity within its ranks. It was totally organized along Marxist philosophies.

LENIN TAKES CONTROL

Nikolai Lenin (Vladimir Ilyich Ulyanov, 1870-1924) was a Russian revolutionary and student of Marx, who was out for revenge, after his older brother, Alexander, was hung in 1887, along with four comrades, for conspiring to assassinate Czar Alexander II, the grandfather of Nicholas II.

During his teenage years, he admired Mikhail Bakunin (1814-1876), a follower of Weishaupt's principles, and a Satanist, who was the driving force behind the initial effort to organize Communism. In 1887, Lenin entered Kazan University, and in 1889, he became a Mason, and soon began advocating the philosophies of Marx. He said: "We must combat religion. This is the ABC's of all materialism and consequently of Marxism." In 1891, he passed his law exam. In the early 1900's, he said that socialism could only be achieved by mobilizing workers and peasants through revolution, since trade unions were not able to bring about any change.

In 1903, in London, he initiated a split in the Russian Social-Democratic Workers Party, which was completed in 1912, and became known as the All Russian Communist Party in 1918. His left-wing faction became known as the Bolsheviks, or "bolshinstvo," which meant "majority" (the Menshevicks, or "menshinstvo," meant "minority"). The movement was slow to catch on, and by 1907, he only had 17 members, but he would soon have over 40,000. He received financial support from the Fabians, including a $15,000 contribution from Joseph Fels, an American soap manufacturer and a Fabian.

George Bernard Shaw, one of the Fabian's founders, called Lenin, the "greatest Fabian of them all," and in a speech he made in Moscow in 1931, said: "It is a real comfort to me, an old man, to be able to step into my grave with the knowledge that the civilization of the world will be saved ... it is here in Russia that I have actually been convinced that the new Communist system is capable of leading mankind out of its present crisis, and saving it from complete anarchy and ruin."

Lenin was an advocate of the Populist doctrine, which had been developed by author Aleksandr Herzen during the 1860's. He felt that the peasant communes could be the socialist society of the future, and called for Russian Socialism to be based on the ancient peasant tradition. The peasant revolt later developed into all-out revolution. In 1881, they succeeded in assassinating Czar Alexander II, and continued to function as a conspiratorial organization. Many Populists began advocating Marxist doctrine, and in 1883, led by Georgy Plekhanov, established the Marxist "Liberation of Labor Group."

Lenin wanted to use the Populists to overthrow the government and introduce socialism. He added two Marxist elements to the Populist theory: the notion of a class struggle, and the need for Russia to pass through a stage of capitalism. He led the people to believe that the purpose of his movement was to help the working class. In America during the 1800's, an alliance of various farming groups produced the Populist Party in 1892, which came to be known as the National People's Party. With their slogan, "The people against the tycoons," they fought for an increase in currency circulation, free silver, labor reform, a graduated income tax, government ownership of the railroads, and the direct election of U.S. Senators. By 1896, they were almost fully integrated into the Democratic Party, while their principles were later embraced by the Progressive Party.

The Progressive Party was a coalition of socialists, labor leaders and farmers, organized by Republican Senator Robert M. LaFollette of Wisconsin in 1911 to oppose the conservatism of the Republican Party, and to fight for an aggressive program of social legislation. They later reunited with the Republican Party until

1924, when a coalition of liberals, farmers, Republican progressives, socialists, and left-wing labor leaders reorganized the Progressive Party, as LaFollette promised to sweep conservatism out of the Federal government. He wanted to "end control of government and industry by private monopoly," to have public control of natural resources, public ownership of railroads, and a reduction in taxes.

When he died in 1925, the Party broke up, but was revived in 1948 by Communist Party leaders and left-wing labor leaders. Their platform included civil rights legislation, and called for negotiations with the Russians. The Party's credibility was damaged when it was revealed that their leadership was communist dominated. The Progressive Party was able to wield enough influence to help pass the Federal Reserve Act, the Federal Income Tax, and the 17th Constitutional Amendment, which provided for the direct election of U.S. Senators, rather than being appointed by the state legislators. They also provided support for the effort which eventually gave women the right to vote. Many of their goals were achieved during the Administration of President Franklin D. Roosevelt.

THE RUSSIAN REVOLUTION

In 1905, while Russia was engaged in the Russo-Japanese War, the communists tried to get the farmers to revolt against the Czar, but they refused. After this aborted attempt, the Czar deposited $400,000,000 in the Chase Bank, National City Bank, Guaranty Trust Bank, the Hanover Trust Bank, and Manufacturers Trust Bank; and $80,000,000 in the Rothschild Bank in Paris, because he knew who was behind the growing revolutionary movement, and hoped to end it.

In 1917, the revolt began. Grand Duke Nicholas said: "It is on God himself that the Bolshevicks are waging war." Czar Nicholas II (who succeeded Alexander III, 1881-94) was dethroned in March after a series of riots, and a provincial government was set up by Prince George Lvov, a liberal progressive reformer who wanted to set up a democracy. He made an effort to strengthen the Russian Army to prevent any future revolts, but ended up resigning, which allowed Kerensky, a democratic Socialist, to take over and form a coalition government. He kept the war with Germany going, and issued an amnesty order for the communists who had been exiles after the aborted Red Revolution in 1905. Nearly 250,000 revolutionaries returned to Russia.

The Rothschilds, through Milner, planned the Russian Revolution, and along with Schiff (who gave $20 million), Sir George Buchanan, the Warburgs, the Rockefellers, the partners of J. P. Morgan (who gave at least $1 million), Olaf Aschberg (of the Nye Bank of Stockholm, Sweden), the Rhine Westphalian Syndicate, a financier named Jovotovsky (whose daughter later married Leon Trotsky), William Boyce Thompson (a director of Chase National Bank, who contributed $1 million), and Albert H. Wiggin (President of Chase National Bank), helped finance it.

The Rockefellers had given their financial support after the Czar refused to give them access to the Russian oil fields, which was already being pumped by the Royal Dutch Co. (owned by the Rothschilds and the Nobel brothers), who was giving Standard Oil plenty of competition on the international market. Even though John D. Rockefeller possessed $15,000,000 in bonds from the Royal Dutch Co. and Shell, rather than purchase stock to get his foot in the door and indirectly profit, he helped to finance the Revolution so that he would be able to get Standard Oil firmly established in the country of Russia.

As the Congress of Vienna had shown, the Illuminati had never been able to control the affairs of Russia, so they had to get rid of the Czar, so he couldn't interfere with their plans.

Leon Trotsky (whose real name was Lev Davidovich Bronstein, 1879-1940, the son of wealthy Jewish parents), who was exiled from Russia because of his part in the aborted revolution in 1905, was a reporter for *Novy Mir*, a communist paper in New York, from 1916-17. He had an expensive apartment and traveled around town in a chauffeur-driven limousine. He sometimes stayed at the Krupp mansion, and had been seen going in and out of Schiff's New York mansion. Trotsky was given $20 million in Jacob Schiff gold to help finance the revolution, which was deposited in a Warburg bank, then transferred to the Nya Banken in Stockholm, Sweden. According to the Knickerbocker Column in the *New York Journal American* on February 3, 1949: "Today it is estimated by Jacob's grandson, John Schiff, that the old man sank about $20,000,000 for the final triumph of Bolshevism in Russia."

Trotsky left New York aboard the S. S. Kristianiafjord (S. S. Christiania), which had been chartered by Schiff and Warburg, on March 27, 1917, with communist revolutionaries. At Halifax, Nova Scotia, on April 3rd, the first port they docked at, the Canadians, under orders from the British Admiralty, seized Trotsky, and his men, taking them to the prison at Amherst; and impounded his gold.

Official records, later declassified by the Canadian government, indicate that they knew Trotsky and his small army were "socialists leaving for the purposes of starting revolution against present Russian government..." The Canadians were concerned that if Lenin would take over Russia, he would sign a Peace Treaty and stop the fighting between Russia and Germany, so that the Germany Army could be diverted to possibly mount an offensive against the United States and Canada. The British government (through intelligence officer Sir William Wiseman, who later became a partner with Kuhn, Loeb and Co.) and American government (through Col. House) urged them to let Trotsky go. Wilson said that if they didn't comply, the U.S. wouldn't enter the War. Trotsky was released, given an American passport, a British transport visa, and a Russian entry permit. It is obvious that Wilson knew what was going on, because accompanying Trotsky, was Charles Crane of the Westinghouse Company, who was the Chairman of the Democratic Finance Committee. The U.S. entered the war on April 6th. Trotsky arrived in Petrograd on May 17.

Meanwhile, Lenin had been able to infiltrate the Democratic Socialist Republic established by Kerensky. In October, 1917, when the Revolution started, Lenin, who was in Switzerland (also exiled because of the 1905 Bolshevik Revolution), negotiated with the German High Command, with the help of Max Warburg (head of the Rothschild-affiliated Warburg bank in Frankfurt), to allow him, his wife, and 32 other Bolsheviks, to travel across Germany, to Sweden, where he was to pick up the money being held for him in the Swedish bank, then go on to Petrograd.

He promised to make peace with Germany, if he was able to overthrow the new Russian government. He was put in a sealed railway car, with over $5 million in gold from the German government, and upon reaching Petrograd, was joined by Stalin and Trotsky. He told the people that he could no longer work within the government to effect change, that they had to strike immediately, in force, to end the war, and end the hunger conditions of the peasants. His war cry was: "All power to the Soviets."

He led the revolution, and after seizing the reins of power from Kerensky on November 7, 1917, replaced the democratic republic with a communist Soviet state. He kept his word and made peace with Germany in February, 1918, and was able to get out of World War I. While most members of the Provisional Government were killed, Kerensky was allowed to live, possibly because of the general amnesty he extended to the communists exiled in 1905. Kerensky later admitted to receiving private support from American industry, which led some historians to believe that the Kerensky government was a temporary front for the Bolsheviks.

Elections were held on November 25, 1917, with close to 42 million votes being cast, and the Bolshevik Communists only received 24% of the vote. On July 18, 1918, the People's Congress convened, having a majority of anti-Bolsheviks, which indicated that communism wasn't the mass movement that Lenin was claiming. The next day he used an armed force to disband the body.

In a speech to the House of Commons on November 5, 1919, Winston Churchill said: "...Lenin was sent into Russia ... in the same way that you might send a vial containing a culture of typhoid or of cholera to be poured into the water supply of a great city, and it worked with amazing accuracy. No sooner did Lenin arrive than he began beckoning a finger here and a finger there to obscure persons in sheltered retreats in New York, Glasgow, in Berne, and other countries, and he gathered together the leading spirits of a formidable sect, the most formidable sect in the world ... With these spirits around him he set to work with demoniacal ability to tear to pieces every institution on which the Russian State depended."

In a February 8, 1920 article for the *Illustrated Sunday Herald*, Churchill wrote:

> "(From) the days of Spartacus Weishaupt to those of Karl Marx, to those of Trotsky, Bela-Kuhn, Rosa Luxembourg and Emma Goldman, this world-wide conspiracy ... has been steadily growing. This conspiracy played a definitely recognizable role in the tragedy of the French Revolution. It has been the mainspring of every subversive movement during the nineteenth century; and now at last this band of extraordinary personalities from the underworld of the great cities of Europe and America have gripped the Russian people by the hair of their heads, and have become practically the undisputed masters of that enormous empire. There is no need to exaggerate the part played in the creation of Bolshevism and in the bringing about of the Russian revolution by these international and for the most part atheistical Jews. It is certainly a very great one; it probably outweighs all others. With the notable exception of Lenin, the majority of the leading figures are Jews."

Russian General Arsene DeGoulevitch wrote in *Czarism and the Revolution* that the "main purveyors of funds for the revolution, however, were neither crackpot Russian millionaires nor armed bandits on Lenin. The 'real' money primarily came from certain British and American circles which for a long time past had lent their support to the Russian revolutionary cause..." DeGoulevitch, who received the information from another Russian general, said that the revolution was "engineered by the English, more precisely by Sir George Buchanan and Lord (Alfred) Milner (of the Round Table) ... In private conversations I have been told that over 21 million rubles were spent by Lord Milner in financing the Russian Revolution."

Frank Vanderlip, President of the Rockefeller-controlled First National Bank, compared Lenin to George Washington. The Rockefeller's public relations man, Ivy Lee, was used to inform Americans that the Communists were "misunderstood idealists who were actually kind benefactors of mankind."

Lenin even knew that he wasn't really in control, and wrote: "The state does not function as we desired. How does it function? The car does not obey. A man is at the wheel and seems to lead it, but the car does not drive in the desired direction. It moves as another force wishes."

In March, 1918, on orders from Schiff, which were relayed by Col. House, the Bolshevik's Second Congress adopted the name "Communist Party." That same year, Lenin organized the Red Army (Red Army-Red Shield-Rothschild?) to control the population, and a secret police to keep track of the communists.

The Third International (or Comintern) had its first Congress in 1919 in Moscow, where they established that Russia would control all of the world's communist movements. They met again in 1920 to lay the foundation for the new Communist Party. Hopes of world revolution ran high, as they hoped to 'liberate' the working class and enable them to break away from the reformist democracy they sprung from. Lenin said that the "victory of the world communist revolution is assured." But, he added, that the revolutionary activities had to be discontinued so they could develop trade relations with capitalist countries, to strengthen their own. The name of the country was officially changed to the Union of Soviet Socialist Republics (U.S.S.R.). Their aims, were to create a single world-wide Communist Party and to overthrow the "international bougeoisie" by force to create "an international Soviet Republic."

From 1916-21, famine swept through Russia (perhaps due to crop tampering), with close to five million dying, because industry was shut down. On September 21, 1921, American relief services began in Russia, after President Herbert Hoover received a plea from famous Russian writer Maxim Gorky. The United States appropriated $20 million for the country, with $8 million spent for medical supplies. Over 700,000 tons of goods were sent to feed 18,000,000 people. As it turned out, the U.S. was actually supporting the Communist Civil War, which ended in 1922.

American and European industrialists rushed to the aid of the Russians. The International Barnsdale Corporation and Standard Oil got drilling rights; Stuart, James and Cook, Inc. reorganized the coal mines; General Electric sold them electrical equipment; and other major firms like Westinghouse, DuPont and RCA, also aided the Communists. Standard Oil of New Jersey bought 50% of their huge Caucasus oil fields, and in 1927, built a large refinery in Russia. Standard Oil, with their subsidiary, Vacuum Oil Co., made a deal to sell Soviet oil to European countries, and even arranged to get them a $75 million loan. Today, Russia is the world's largest petroleum producer, and some researchers believe that the Rockefellers still own the oil production facilities in Russia, withdrawing the profits through Switzerland.

Rockefeller's Chase National Bank (later known as Chase Manhattan Bank) helped establish the American-Russian Chamber of Commerce in 1922, and its first President was Reeve Schley, a Chase Vice-President. In 1925, Chase National and PromBank (a German bank) developed a complete program to finance the Soviets raw material exports to the United States, and imports of U.S. cotton and machinery. Chase National and Equitable Trust Co. were the dominant forces in Soviet credit dealings. In 1928, Chase sold the Bolsheviks bonds in America, and was severely criticized by various patriotic groups who called them "a disgrace to America."

America sent Russia vast quantities of food and other relief supplies. Lenin had said that the capitalists would do business with anyone, and when Russia was through with them, the Communists would take over the world. That is what the Russian Communists have been led to believe. In reality, the Illuminati was completely financing the entire country of Russia, in order to transform them into a world power with principles completely opposite to that of the United States.

In May, 1922, Lenin suffered the first of a series of strokes. When he died in 1924, supposedly from syphilis, the country's leadership was taken over by Joseph Stalin (1879-1953, Iosif Visarionovich Dzhugashvili), after a bitter fight with Trotsky. Lenin said on his deathbed: "I committed a great error. My nightmare is to have the feeling that I'm lost in an ocean of blood from the innumerable victims. It is too late to return. To save our country, Russia, we would have needed men like Francis of Assisi. With ten men like him we would have saved Russia." Trotsky was expelled from the Party in 1927, and then exiled from the country in 1929. He attempted to mobilize other communist groups against Stalin.

In 1924, Stalin wrote *The Foundations of Leninism*, hoping that Lenin would pass the torch of leadership to him. However, in a December, 1922 letter to the Party Congress, Lenin said of Stalin: "After taking over the position of Secretary-General, Comrade Stalin accumulated in his hands immeasurable power and I am not certain whether he will be always able to use this power with the required care." Lenin wrote in January, 1923: "Stalin is excessively rude, and this defect, which can be freely tolerated in our midst and in contacts among U.S. communists, becomes a defect which cannot be tolerated in one holding the position of Secretary-General. Because of this, I propose that the comrades consider the method by which Stalin would be removed from this position and by which another man would be selected for it; a man, who above all, would differ from Stalin, in only one quality, namely, greater tolerance, greater loyalty, greater kindness, and more considerate attitude toward the comrades, a less capricious temper, etc."

Financed by Kuhn, Loeb and Co., Stalin implemented a new economic policy for rapid industrialization, known as the "First Five Year Plan." Even though the U.S. Government was sending over food, Stalin was using the food as a weapon to finish communizing the country. Those who refused to cooperate with the communist government were starved to death. Between 1932-33, it is estimated that between three and seven million people died as a result of Stalin's tactics.

Stalin later admitted that two-thirds of Russia's industrial capability was due to the assistance of the United States.

Just as Lenin said: "Down with religion! Long live atheism!" Stalin said: "God must be out of Russia in five years." He eventually did away with the "withering away" concept, and developed a fanatical, rigid, and powerful police state. Stalin said that the goals of Communism was to create chaos throughout the world, institute a single world economic system, prod the advanced countries to consistently give aid to underdeveloped countries, and to divide the world into regional groups, which would be a transitional stage to a one-world government. The Communists have not deviated from this blueprint.

In 1933, the Illuminati urged FDR to recognize the country of Russia in order to save them from financial ruin, as a number of European countries had already done. On November 17, 1933, the U.S. granted diplomatic recognition to Russia. In return, Russia promised not to interfere in our internal affairs. A promise they never kept. They became a member of the League of Nations in 1934, but were thrown out in 1939 because of their aggressive actions toward Finland.

Meanwhile, the U.S. continued to send them aid. The Cleveland firm of Arthur G. Mackee provided equipment for a huge steel plant at Magnitogorski; John Clader of Detroit, equipped and installed a tractor plant at Chelyabinski; Henry Ford and the Austin Co. provided equipment for an automobile production center at Gorki; and Col. Hugh Cooper, creator of the Mussel Shoals Dam, planned and built the giant hydroelectric plant at Dniepostrol.

On August 23, 1939, Hitler signed a non-aggression pact with Stalin, and together they attacked Poland in a blitzkrieg war, which led to World War II. Because of a treaty with Poland, France and England were forced to declare war on Germany. Hitler had said publicly, that he didn't want war with England, but now was forced into battle with them. By the end of May, the Netherlands and Belgium had fallen, and France followed in June. In 1940, Russia moved against Latvia, Lithuania, Estonia, Bessarabia (now Moldova), northern Bukovina (NE Romania), and part of Poland. This sort of worried Hitler.

In England, the Illuminati-controlled press attacked Prime Minister Chamberlain, because they felt their war against Germany was too mild. The International Bankers wanted a major war. Chamberlain was pressured into resigning, and Winston Churchill replaced him, and immediately stepped up the war with an air attack on Germany.

A year later, the German High Command, unknown by Hitler, sent Rudolph Hess to England to meet with Lord Hamilton and Churchill to negotiate a Peace Treaty. Hess, next to Hitler, was Germany's highest ranking officer (credited for writing down and editing Hitler's dictation for *Mein Kampf* and also contributing to its content). The German generals offered to eliminate Hitler, so they could join forces to attack Communist Russia. Churchill refused, and had Hess jailed. He was later tried and convicted at the Nuremberg war crime trials, and was given a life sentence, which was served out at the Spandau prison in Spain.

Shortly after their failure, the German High Command convinced Hitler to attack Russia, which he did. After overrunning Europe, 121 German divisions, 19 armored divisions, and three air fleets, invaded Russia on June 22, 1941. American communists urged the world to mount an immediate united effort to help Russia.

The Nazi advance was swift and savage, with the German army barreling deep into the Ukraine with one victory after another. Foreign Policy experts predicted the defeat and collapse of the country. In October, Kiev fell, and Hitler announced there would be a final effort to take Moscow and end the war. On October 24, with his army 37 miles from Moscow, Hitler planned on waiting until the winter was over before he made his final attack. But then, Japan attacked Pearl Harbor, and the U.S. entered the War.

Through a lend-lease agreement, America responded by sending $11 billion in raw materials, machinery, tools, complete industrial plants, spare parts, textiles, clothing, canned meat, sugar, flour, weapons, tanks, trucks, aircraft, and gasoline to aid the Russians, which turned the tide against the Germans. Some of the material which was sent: 6,430 aircraft; 121 merchant ships; 1,285 locomotives; 3,734 tanks; 206,000 trucks, buses, tractors, and cars; 82 torpedo boats and small destroyers; 2 billion tons of steel; 22,400,000 rounds of ammunition; 87,900 tons of explosives; 245,000 telephones; 5,500,000 pairs of boots; 2,500,000 automobile inner tubes; and two million tons of food. In dollars, it broke down this way:

1942 - $1,422,853,332
1943 - $2,955,811,271
1944 - $3,459,274,155
1945 - $1,838,281,501

The Russians were to pay for all supplies, and return all usable equipment after the war. It didn't happen. For instance, they kept 84 cargo ships, some of which were used to supply North Vietnam with equipment during the Vietnam War. What we sent to the Russians, after the War, became the foundation upon which the Soviet industrial machine was built. Through an agreement negotiated years later by Henry Kissinger, the Russians agreed to pay back $722 million of the $11 billion, which amounted to about 7 cents on the dollar. In 1975, after paying back $32 million, they announced they were not going to pay the remainder of the Lend-Lease debt.

After the War, in 1946, America turned over two-thirds of Germany's aircraft manufacturing capabilities to Russia, who dismantled the installations, and rebuilt them in their country, forming the initial stage of their jet aircraft industry.

Even though Congress had passed legislation forbidding shipments of non-war materials, various pro-Soviet officials and Communist traitors in key positions openly defied the law and made shipments. In 1944, Harry Hopkins, Henry Morgenthau (Secretary of the Treasury), Averell Harriman (U.S. Ambassador to Russia), and Harry Dexter White (Assistant Secretary of Treasury), supplied the material needed for Russia to print occupation currency. Printing plates, colored inks, varnish, tint blocks, and paper were sent from Great Falls, Montana, in two shipments of five C-47's each, which had been loaded at the National Airport near Washington, DC.

The Russians then set up a printing facility in a Nazi printing plant in Leipzig and began to print currency which the U.S. couldn't account for. Russia refused to redeem the currency with rubles, therefore the U.S. Treasury had to back the currency. The Russians were using these newly printed Marks to sap the German economy, and take advantage of the United States, who, by the end of 1946, had lost $250,000,000 because of redeeming, in U.S. dollars, marks which were issued in excess of the total amount of marks issued by the Finance Office, who was officially printing occupation money for the Germans. In addition, the $18,102 charge for the plates and printing material was never paid.

In 1943, a Congressional investigation revealed, that even before the U.S. had built its first atomic bomb, half of all the uranium and technical information needed to construct such a bomb, was secretly sent to Russia. This included chemicals, metals, and minerals instrumental in creating an atomic bomb, and manufacturing a hydrogen bomb. In 1980, James Roosevelt, the son of President Franklin Roosevelt, wrote a novel, *A Family Matter*, which detailed how his father made "a bold secret decision— to share the results of the Manhattan Project with the Soviet Union," in 1943 and 1944.

Air Force Major Racey Jordan, was a Land-Lease expediter and liaison officer for the Russians in Great Falls, which was the primary staging area for the massive Lend-Lease supply operation to the Soviet Union. In his diaries, which were published in 1952, he said that the U.S. built the Soviet war machine by shipping all the materials needed to construct an atomic pile, including graphite, cadmium metal, thorium, and uranium. In March, 1943, a number of black leather suitcases wrapped in white window sash cord, and sealed with red wax, said to be of a diplomatic nature, were to be sent to Moscow. One night the Russians had taken them out for dinner, and suspicious of their friendliness, Jordan decided to sneak away, and went back to the base with an armed sentry. He discovered that two Russian couriers from Washington had arrived and had procured a plane bound for Russia, to take about 50 of these cases.

He detained the flight, and discovered that the shipment was being sent to the "Director, Institute of Technical and Economic Information" in Moscow. He opened eighteen of the cases, and discovered a collection of maps that identified the names and locations of all the industrial plants in the U.S., along with classified military sites. One case contained a folder of military documents marked, "from Hiss," and another case which contained a White House memo from "H.H." (Harry Hopkins, former Secretary of Commerce and head of the Lend-Lease Program) to Al Mikoyan (Russia's number three man, after Stalin and Foreign Commissar Molotov), which accompanied a map of Oak Ridge and the Manhattan Engineering District, and a report from Oak Ridge, which contained phrases like: "energy produced by fission," and "walls five feet thick, of lead and water, to control flying neutrons."

In short, traitors within the Administration of Roosevelt were giving the Soviets the instructions and the material to build nuclear weapons, even before the United States had fully developed the technology for use by our country. Jordan reported all of this to Air Force Intelligence, but nothing ever happened.

The Russian's ability to establish their space program was also provided by America. When General Patton was moving eastward through Germany, he captured the towns of Peenemunde and Nordhausen, where German scientists had developed the V-1 and V-2 rockets. Gen. Dwight Eisenhower ordered him to turn the two towns over the Russians, who dismantled the facilities and shipped them to Russia, along with the scientists. One of the German scientists, Dr. Werner von

Braun, led a group of 100 other scientists, who surrendered to the Americans. He later became head of the American space program.

Braun was prepared to launch history's first satellite, long before Russia developed one, but Eisenhower would not authorize it, because it was to be made to appear that Russian technology was superior to ours, when it wasn't. It would add to the facade being developed that Russia was stronger than we were, and therefore should be feared.

As recently as 1978, it was believed that Russia still had not been able to construct a single-stage rocket capable of placing large payloads in orbit. American researcher, Lloyd Mallan, called the Soviet's 'Lunik' moon landing a hoax, since no tracking station picked up its signals, and that Alexie Leonov's spacewalk on March 18, 1965 was also staged. Concerning the film of the spacewalk, Mallan said:

> "Four months of solid research interviewing experts in the fields of photo-optics, photo-chemistry and electro-optics, all of whom carefully studied the motion picture film and still photographs officially released by the Soviet Government ... (indicate them to be) double-printed. The foreground (Leonov) was superimposed on the background (Earth below). The Russian film showed reflections from the glass plate under which a double plate is made ... Leonov was suspended from wire or cables ... In several episodes of the Russian film, light was reflected from a small portion of wire (or cable) attached to Leonov's space suit ... One camera angle was impossible of achievement. This showed Leonov crawling out of his hatch into space. It was a head-on shot, so the camera would have had to have been located out in space beyond the space ship."

The U.S. donated two food production factories ($6,924,000), a petroleum refinery ($29,050,000), a repair plant for precision instruments ($550,000), 17 steam and three hydroelectric plants ($273,289,000).

Later, Dressler Industries built a $146 million plant at Kuibyshov, to produce high quality drill bits for oil exploration. The C. E. Lummus Co. of New Jersey built a $105 million petrochemical plant in the Ukraine ($45 million would be put up by Lummus through financing from Eximbank and other private banks, which was guaranteed by the O.P.I.C.). Allis-Chalmers built a $35 million iron ore pelletizing plant in Russia, which is one of the world's four largest. The Aluminum Co. of America (ALCOA) built an aluminum plant, which consumed "half the world's supply of bauxite." We sent the Russians computer systems, oil drilling equipment, pipes, and other supplies. The ball-bearings used by Russia to improve the guidance systems on their rockets and missiles, such as their SS-18 intercontinental ballistic missies, were purchased in 1972 from the Bryant Grinder Co. in Springfield, Vermont.

All of this financial aid to Russia was advocated by Henry Kissinger and the U.S. Government. The reasoning behind it was to allow Russia to increase their industrial and agricultural output to match ours, because by bringing the two countries closer together, hostilities would be eased. They were not. The Illuminati, through the U.S. Government, had allowed the Soviet Union to have a technology equal to our own. Congressman Otto Passman, who was the Chairman of the Appropriations Subcommittee, said: "The United States cannot survive as a strong nation if we continue to dissipate our resources and give away our wealth to the world."

CHINA GOES COMMUNIST

Russia, as early as 1920, was conspiring against China. Shortly after the Bolshevik revolution ended in 1918, the Communists announced: "We are marching to free ... the people of China." In 1921, a Russian agent was sent to Peking, then to Shanghai, to make plans for the First Congress of the Chinese Communist Party, which would become the world's largest. They began to infiltrate the government in 1922, and by 1924, the Chinese armed forces were reorganized along the same lines as the Soviet army. Chiang Kai-shek (1887-1975) was the Commandant, and Chou En-lai was in charge of Political Affairs.

With the use of Soviet troops commanded by Gen. Michael Borodin, Chiang attacked Shanghai, robbing the Rothschild-affiliated Soong Bank. President Coolidge refused to send U.S. troops against the Chinese forces, and T.V. Soong negotiated with Chiang, offering him $3 million, his sister May-ling as a wife (even though Chiang had a wife and family), and the presidency of China for life, if he would change sides. He agreed, and began to rule China as a British ally. In December, 1927, he married the sister of Soong. Seeing the Russians as a threat to his country, he had them ejected, and had many communist advisors arrested. Mao Tse-tung fled, and hid out in the northern provinces, where he began training rebels for a future insurrection.

In 1937, Japan attacked Shanghai, and coupled with the growing Communist insurgency, created a two-front war. China needed help, and sent the following telegram to Roosevelt on December 8, 1941: "To our new common battle, we offer all we are and all we have to stand with you until the Pacific and the world are freed from the curse of brute force and endless perfidy." China's plea was brushed off, and they were the last country to get military aid, which came in the form of a $250 million loan in gold to stabilize their economy. Assistant Secretary of the Treasury, Harry Dexter White, the Soviet spy, was in charge of making sure China got the money, and over a period of 3 years, he only sent them $27 million. In 1945, Congress voted a second loan of $500 million, and Dexter made sure they didn't get any of that, which resulted in the collapse of their economy.

After World War II, special envoys Gen. George C. Marshall (Army Chief of Staff, and CFR member, who served as Secretary of State 1947-49, and Secretary of Defense 1950-51; who had knowledge of the impending attack on Pearl Harbor, but didn't inform the commanders in the Pacific) and Patrick J. Hurley were sent to China to meet with Chiang Kai-shek. They urged him to give the Communists representation in the Chinese Government, and for the Nationalists (Kuomintang) to have a coalition government, since they felt that the Russians weren't influencing the Chinese Communists. However, Chiang would not accept any kind of Communist influence in his government, so Marshall recommended that all American aid be stopped, and an embargo enforced. There was no fuel for Chinese tanks and planes, or ammunition for weapons. Russia gave the Chinese Communists military supplies they had captured from Japan, and also diverted some of the American Lend-Lease material to them. Soon, Mao began making his final preparations to take over the government.

High level State Department officials, such as Harry Dexter White and Owen Lattimore, who were members of the Institute of Pacific Relations, besides planning the destruction of the Chinese economy, also falsified documents to indicate that the Chinese Communists were actually farmers who were pushing for agricultural reform. Thus, from 1943-49, magazines like the *Saturday Evening Post* (who ran over 60 articles) and *Colliers*, advocated and promoted the Communist movement. While Mao Tse-tung was made to appear as an "agrarian reformer," Chiang was blasted for being a corrupt dictator. In 1945, Lattimore sent President Truman a memorandum suggesting a coalition government between the Communists and the National Government. John Carter Vincent of the IPR elaborated upon that memo, and it became the basis upon which Truman based his China policy, which was announced on December 15, 1945.

It was alleged by some researchers, that Russia sent China a telegram, saying that if they didn't surrender, they would be destroyed. They were requested to send ten technicians to see the bomb that would be used, and when they went, they saw an atomic bomb with the capability of destroying a large city. As the story goes, Chiang sent a telegram to President Truman, asking for help. Truman refused. In 1948, Congress voted to send China $125 million in military aid, but again the money was held up until Chiang was defeated. In October, 1949, 450 million people were turned over to the Communist movement.

Chiang fled to the island of Taiwan, 110 miles off the east coast of China, where he governed that country under a democracy. Mao Tse-tung, who announced in 1921 that he was a Marxist, after reading the *Communist Manifesto*, took over as China's leader, and Peking was established as the new capital. On February 14, 1950, a thirty-year treaty of friendship was signed with Russia.

In March, 1953, Mao proposed to the Soviet Union, a plan for world conquest, in which every country, except the United States, would be communist-controlled by 1973. It was called a "Memorandum on a New Program for World Revolution," and was taken to Moscow by the Chinese Foreign Minister, Chou En-lai. The first phase was to be completed by 1960, and called for Korea, Formosa, and Indochina to be under Chinese control.

On July 15, 1971, Chairman Mao appealed to the world to, "unite and defeat the U.S. aggressors and all their running dogs."

While campaigning in 1968, Richard Nixon said: "I would not recognize Red China now, and I would not agree to admitting it to the United Nations." In his book *Six Crises*, he said that "admitting Red China to the United Nations would be a mockery of the provision of the Charter which limits its membership to 'peace-loving nations.' And what was most disturbing, was that it would give respectability to the Communist regime which would immediately increase its power and prestige in Asia, and probably irreparably weaken the non-Communist governments in that area." Yet it was Nixon who opened the dialogue with China, and in 1971, Communist China was seated as a member country of the United Nations, while the Republic of China (Taiwan) was thrown out. With the visits to China by Nixon and Kissinger in 1971, on up to Reagan in 1984, relations between the two countries were almost as good as they were when they were allies in 1937. In 1978, President Carter approved the sending of U.S. technology to China, and the American government recognized the Communists as the official government of China. On January 1, 1979, Carter severed diplomatic ties with Taiwan, saying that "there is but one China, and Taiwan is part of China."

KOREA FALLS

From 1910, until 1945, Korea was part of the Japanese empire. The victorious World War II allies agreed that Korea should be made an independent country, but until negotiations could take place, the U.S. took charge of the area south of the 38th parallel, while the Soviets occupied the northern half. Plans to establish a unified Korean government failed, and in 1948, rival governments were established: the Communist government of Kim Il Sung in the North, and the pro-Western government under Syngman Rhee in the South.

An officers training school, and a small arms plant was set up by the United States. They gave the country $100,000,000 worth of military hardware to arm the 96,000 soldiers of the South Korean armed forces. On July 17, 1949, Owen Lattimore said: "The thing to do is let South Korea fall, but not to let it look as if we pushed it." In a memo to the State Department, he wrote: "The United States should disembarrass itself as quickly as possible from its entanglements in South Korea." In 1949, the American troops were withdrawn from South Korea, and in a January 12, 1950 speech, U.S. Secretary of State, Dean G. Acheson publicly stated that South Korea was "outside of (the U.S.) defense perimeter."

The North Koreans, heavily equipped by the Russians, considered Acheson's statement an invitation to attack, in order to unify the country under communism. Gen. Douglas MacArthur had received military intelligence reports from Gen. Charles A. Willoughby, that North Korea was preparing for an invasion, and John Foster Dulles of the State Department went to 'investigate,' and covered up the activity he viewed at the 38th parallel.

On June 24, 1950, the North Koreans swarmed across the 38th parallel, and proceeded to overrun the country. Rhee appealed to the United States, and the United Nations for help, as the communists closed in on the South Korean capital of Seoul.

Truman called for an immediate meeting of the United Nations Security Council, who convened the next day, and called the attack a "breach of the peace," ordering the North Koreans to withdraw to the border. Two days later, the Security Council called upon the UN members to furnish assistance. Immediately the U.S. sent in ground troops and began air strikes. On July 7, the Security Council urged 15 of the countries to put their troops at the disposal of the United States, under the UN command of Gen. Douglas MacArthur.

With the UN being involved in the war, all U.S. battle plans had to be submitted for approval, in advance, to the Under Secretary for Political and Security

Council Affairs. Due to a secret agreement made by Secretary of State Edward Stettinius in 1945, this position was to always be filled by a Communist from an eastern European country. During the war, it was filled by Russia's General Constantine Zinchenko. It was later revealed, that Russian military advisors were actually directing the North Korean war effort, and one of those advisors, Lt. Gen. Alexandre Vasiliev, actually gave the order to attack. Vasiliev was the Chairman of the UN Military Staff Committee, who along with the Under Secretary for Political and Security Council Affairs, was responsible for all UN military action. Vasliliev had to take a leave of absence from his position, to command the communist troops. So, what it boiled down to, was that the Communists were controlling both sides of the war, and Russia was able to receive vital information concerning all troop movements within the UN forces in Korea, which was passed on to the North Koreans and Chinese.

General MacArthur realized what was happening and planned one of the most daring military assaults in the history of modern warfare. To execute the engagement he hand-picked a group of trusted and loyal officers so the initial stages would be kept a secret. MacArthur did not submit the strategy to General Zinchenko. The resulting amphibious assault on September 15, 1950, at Inchon Bay, turned the tide of the war by enabling UN forces to recapture Seoul, destroyed large supply dumps, and began to push the North Koreans back across the border. In October, they captured the North Korean capital of Pyongyang, and many communists retreated into Manchuria and Russia.

The Taiwan government was planning to move against China, and Truman warned Chiang Kai-shek not to make an attempt to recapture his homeland. Truman ordered the American Seventh Fleet into the Strait of Formosa to prevent any type of invasion. This freed the Red China army to enter the Korean War. The Chinese, with the excuse that they were protecting the security of their country, stormed across the border on November 26, 1950, and stopped the UN army at the Yalu River. Chiang then offered to send an advance force of 33,000 troops into North Korea, but the State Department refused. They were a member of the UN, yet the United States would not let them fight.

The Korean War, Korean Conflict, or Police Action, as it is sometimes called, developed into a stalemate of broken cease-fire agreements, and MacArthur made plans for a massive retaliation against China. He wanted to bomb the ammunition and fuel dumps, the supply bases, and communication lines to China (bridges across the Yalu River), and to post a blockade around the Chinese coast. However, on December 5, 1950, Truman and other Administration officials decided that this sort of action would bring Russia into the conflict, and possibly initiate World War III. MacArthur was ordered not to proceed with any of his plans. The Joint Chiefs of Staff said: "We felt the action urged by Gen. MacArthur would hazard this safety (of the U.S.) without promising any certain proportionate gain." A letter written to a Congressman, by MacArthur, was read on the floor of the House, giving them the full story of how much the Red Chinese were involved. Still, nothing was done. Gen. Lin Piao, the Red Chinese commander, said later: "I would never have made the attack and risked my men and military reputation if I had not been assured that Washington would restrain General MacArthur from taking adequate retaliatory measures against my lines of supply and communication."

With MacArthur insisting that there was no substitute for victory and that the war against Communism would be either won or lost in Korea, he was relieved of his command, on April 11, 1951, by Gen. Matthew B. Ridgeway, a member of the CFR.

Air Force Commander, Gen. George Stratemeyer said: "We had sufficient air bombardment, fighters, reconnaissance so that I could have taken out all those supplies, those airdromes on the other side of the Yalu; I could have bombed the devils between there and Mukden, stopped the railroad operating and the people of China that were fighting could not have been supplied ... But we weren't permitted to do it. As a result, a lot of American blood was spilled over there in Korea."

Gen. Stratemeyer testified before the Congress: "You get in war to win it. You do not get in war to stand still and lose it and we were required to lose it. We were not permitted to win." Gen. Matt Clark told them: "I was not allowed to bomb the numerous bridges across the Yalu River over which the enemy constantly poured his trucks, and his munitions, and his killers."

MacArthur would later write:

"I was ... worried by a series of directives from Washington which were greatly decreasing the potential of my air force. First I was forbidden 'hot' pursuit of enemy planes that attacked our own. Manchuria and Siberia were sanctuaries of inviolate protection for all enemy forces and for all enemy purposes, no matter what depredations or assaults might come from there. Then I was denied the right to bomb the hydroelectric plants along the Yalu River. This order was broadened to include every plant in North Korea which was capable of furnishing electric power to Manchuria and Siberia ... Most incomprehensible of all was the refusal to let me bomb the important supply center at Racin, which was not in Manchuria or Siberia, but many miles from the border ... (where) the Soviet Union forwarded supplies from Vladivostok for the North Korean Army. I felt that step-by-step my weapons were being taken away from me..."

"That there was some leak in intelligence was evident to everyone. (Brig. Gen. Walton) Walker continually complained to me that operations were known to the enemy in advance through sources in Washington ... information must have been relayed to them assuring that the Yalu River bridges would continue to enjoy sanctuary and that their bases would be left intact. They knew they could swarm down across the Yalu River without having to worry about bombers hitting their Manchurian supply lines ... I realized for the first time that I had actually been denied the use of my full military power to safeguard the lives of my soldiers and the safety of my army."

Gen. Douglas MacArthur also said: "I am concerned for the security of our great nation, not so much because of any threat from without, but because of the insidious forces working from within."

Over 33,000 American lives were lost in a war that they were not allowed to win. Instead, a truce was signed on July 27, 1953.

However, the Communists weren't giving up on Korea. With North Korea being supported by China, Russia and the Eastern Europe communist bloc countries, they built up their military strength, and made enormous economic gains. During the late 1960's, they began a dialogue for the reunification of Korea, and bilateral talks were held in 1972, which further improved their relations, as the Communists attempted to take over with diplomacy. A nonaggression pact was signed in December, 1991; and in 2000 a summit meeting was held to explore the possibility of a reconciliation.

As information about communist agents occupying high cabinet posts surfaced, the American people took out their frustrations at the polls. Eisenhower's slogan was: "Let's clean up the mess in Washington." He had promised "peace with honor" in Korea, however, the truce allowed 400 soldiers to remain in communist prisons. Even though the 1952 Republican Platform called the Truman Plan "ignominious bartering with our enemies," in reality, Eisenhower's plan made even more concessions.

Eisenhower's tough rhetoric on communism ushered in a renewed patriotism in America. People behind the Iron Curtain were inspired, and in the fall of 1956, Hungarian freedom fighters forced the Russians to leave their homeland, ending Soviet occupation. So what did the United States do? According to the *Congressional Record* of August 31, 1960, the U.S. State Department sent the Soviet Union a telegram which read: "The Government of the United States does not look with favor upon governments unfriendly to the Soviet Union on the borders of the Soviet Union." Hours after receiving the telegram on November 4, 1956, Khrushchev sent Russian troops back into Hungary to retake the country.

Soon Eisenhower initiated foreign aid programs to the communist governments in Poland and Yugoslavia, who by 1961 received almost $3 billion in food, industrial machinery, jets, and other military equipment.

In June, 1956, John Foster Dulles said that if the U.S. discontinued their aid to Marshal Tito, Yugoslavia would be driven into the Soviet fold. However, two weeks before, Tito said: "In peace as in war, Yugoslavia must march shoulder to shoulder with the Soviet Union." On September 17, Tito announced his full support of the Soviet foreign policy. Meanwhile, U.S. aid continued, even after 1961, when Yugoslavia began their own foreign aid programs to spread communism among the world's underdeveloped nations.

When Eisenhower's two terms came to an end, the amount of economic and military aid to communist and 'neutralist' countries came to $7 billion. In the February 25, 1961 edition of *People's World*, and the March 10, 1961 issue of *Time*, Robert Welch, founder of the anti-communist John Birch Society, charged that the Eisenhower Administration was a tool of the communists.

THE VIETNAM CONQUEST

As the communists moved forward with their plan for world domination, Southeast Asia was to be the next target. In July, 1954, Indo-China fell. William Zane

Foster, Chairman of the U.S. Communist Party, said in February, 1956, that they "constitute the beginning of a new socialist world."

They moved on to Vietnam, where the U.S. was pulled into a conflict, which was to become the longest in U.S. history. American intervention actually began in 1954 with economic and technical assistance, after the Geneva Accords ended the Indo-Chinese War.

Kennedy increased the military budget, and escalated the War just for the purposes of impressing the Russians after being embarrassed and humiliated by the failed Bay of Pigs invasion of Cuba. Later, Kennedy planned to begin scaling back.

Vietnam escalated into a major war by 1964, with casualties peaking in 1969. In 1964, with a possibility that ultra-conservative Barry Goldwater might win the presidency, a coalition of liberal forces, under the guidance of Illuminati advisors, worked for the election of former Vice President Lyndon B. Johnson, who had taken over after Kennedy's assassination in 1963. Johnson was urged to pursue "peace at any price," but the Illuminati didn't want peace, and Johnson further escalated the War. At the height of the war, there were about 543,000 American soldiers in Vietnam.

On July 25, 1965, President Johnson told an American television audience that the military build-up was to administer "death and desolation" to the communists, yet he made agreements to provide the Soviet Union, and her communist satellite countries, with millions of dollars worth of food, computers, industrial plants, oil refinery equipment, jet engines, military rifles, and machine tools for an $800 million automobile production facility. At the same time, our Supreme Court ruled that communists could teach in our schools, and work in our defense plants; and the Senate and State Department allowed them to open diplomatic offices in major American cities, even though FBI Director J. Edgar Hoover warned that their embassies were part of an espionage network.

Johnson's war policies severely damaged his chances for re-election, and he was forced to drop out of the 1968 Primary race.

In 1966, after Averill Harriman had made a 22-day, 12 nation peace tour for Johnson, he was asked by a television reporter how the Russians felt about the Vietnam War, and Harriman said they were "embarrassed by the war. They don't like it and they would like to see it stopped." A brilliant piece of propaganda, considering the fact that the Russians were shipping guns, ammunition, missiles, and MiG fighters to the North Vietnamese.

In 1968, the Congress increased 'foreign aid' of war materials to communist bloc countries by over 80% from the previous year, and this 'aid' was then redirected by railroad, to North Vietnam, who used it to manufacture military equipment.

A peace treaty was signed on January 23, 1973, by the U.S., North and South Vietnam, and the Vietcong (National Liberation Front, later referred to as the Provisional Revolutionary Government). The treaty specified that the Vietcong was to have equal recognition with the South Vietnamese capital of Saigon. Thieu agreed to sign after Nixon and Kissinger promised that the U.S. would "respond vigorously" to any Communist violations of the agreement.

The cease-fire didn't hold, and after the American pullout, which left over $5 billion worth of military equipment, the communists were given a free hand in Southeast Asia. On April 30, 1975, the government of South Vietnam fell to the communist regime, and on July 2, 1976, the country of Vietnam was officially unified as a Communist state.

It is estimated that 57,000 Americans died during the Vietnam conflict.

THE CUBAN COVER-UP

Fulgencio Batista, in 1934, had overthrown the government of Cuba, which hampered the social reform that had been begun by four separate Presidents. In 1952, he established a dictatorship. Fidel Castro, who had become a communist in 1947, during his second year in law school; and Argentinian revolutionary Ernesto Guevara, rebuilt the guerrilla forces that Castro had used in an unsuccessful revolt in 1953 (in which Castro had been captured and arrested, but later paroled).

With financial backing from Russia, Castro bribed many military leaders. He got a substantial amount of support from the intellectual and working class, who knew nothing of his communist intentions.

In April, 1957, Herbert L. Matthews, a correspondent for the *New York Times* and CFR member, interviewed Castro at his mountain retreat, for three successive front page articles. He compared Castro to Lincoln, and presented him as a "peasant patriot," "a strong anti-communist," a "Robin Hood," and a "defender of the people." Earlier, in a February 25, 1957 article, Matthews reported: "There is no communism to speak of in Fidel Castro's movement."

On CBS-TV, Edward R. Murrow portrayed him as a national hero. President Kennedy in a speech compared him to South American patriot Simon Bolivar. Ed Sullivan interviewed Castro for a film clip, which was seen by about 30 million people, in which he said: "The people of the United States have great admiration for you and your men because you are in the real American spirit of George Washington." He retracted the statement 18 months later, but it was too late.

In 1958, in an interview with Jules DuBois, Castro said: "I have never been nor am I a Communist..." The American Ambassador to Cuba declared that Batista was no longer supported by the American government, and that he should leave. Roy Rubottom, the Assistant Secretary for Latin American Affairs, said in December, 1958: "There was no evidence of any organized Communist elements within the Castro movement or that Senor Castro himself was under Communist influence." In April, 1959, Castro visited the U.S., and the State Department welcomed him as a "distinguished leader."

A member of the Intelligence section of the Cuban army hand-carried Castro's dossier to Washington in 1957, delivering it to Allen Dulles, head of the CIA, which revealed that Castro was a Communist. Dulles 'buried' the file. In July, 1959, Major Pedro Diaz Lanz, of the Cuban Air Force, toured the United States, and revealed that he had first-hand knowledge that Castro was a Communist. This fact, for the most part, was kept out of the media. The truth of the matter, was that the State Department was purposely covering up Castro's communist connections, the fact that his supporters were trained by Russia, and that he was carrying out a communist revolution.

Arthur Gardner, the American Ambassador to Cuba, referred to Castro as a communist terrorist, and he was replaced by Earl E. T. Smith, who, instead of being briefed by Gardner, was briefed by Herbert Matthews. A Senate Committee investigation of William A. Wieland, who in 1957 became the State Department's Caribbean representative, said that he "regularly disregarded, sidetracked or denounced FBI, State Department and military intelligence sources which branded Castro as a Communist." Robert Hill, Ambassador to Mexico, said under oath in a Senate hearing: "Individuals in the State Department, and individuals in the *New York Times*, put Castro in power." These individuals included Robert McNamara, Theodore C. Sorenson, Arthur M. Schlesinger, Jr., Roy Rubottom, McGeorge Bundy, William J. Fulbright, and Roger Hilsman.

After being asked to abdicate, by Eisenhower, Batista left office on December 31, 1958; and Castro took control of the country in January, 1959. Later that year, he addressed a meeting of the CFR at their New York headquarters.

Soon, Castro revealed his alliance with Russia, nationalized all business and industry. On October 20, 1960, Kennedy said: "We must attempt to strengthen the non-Batista democratic anti-Castro forces in exile, and in Cuba itself who offer eventual hope of overthrowing Castro." After the U.S. broke diplomatic ties with Cuba on January 3, 1961, an invasion force was organized, financed, and trained in Florida and Guatemala, by the State Department and the Central Intelligence Agency, who recruited from the thousands of Cubans who had fled to the U.S. to get away from Castro.

On April 17, 1961, an anti-Castro force of 1,400 landed at the Bay of Pigs in Cuba to begin the invasion. Within striking distance, were two U.S. carriers, five World War II Liberty ships, and other support vessels, whose decks were loaded with planes. About 500 miles away, a group of B-26's waited. Kennedy had promised air support, but it never came.

Years later, after it was revealed that both John and Bobby Kennedy had sexual relationships with Marilyn Monroe, it was reported that she had threatened to expose them, and referred to her "diary of secrets."

According to an August 3, 1962 C.I.A. memo that was released under the Freedom of Information Act, information procured from phone taps of conversations with reporter Dorothy Kilgallen and her close friend, Howard Rothberg; as well as with Marilyn Monroe and Attorney General Robert Kennedy, revealed the following:

1. Rothberg discussed the apparent comeback of subject with Kilgallen and the break up with the Kennedys. Rothberg told Kilgallen that she was attending Hollywood parties hosted by the "inner circle" among Hollywood's elite and was becoming the talk of the town again. Rothberg indicated in so many words, that she had secrets to tell, no doubt arising from her trists with the President and the Attorney General. One such "???" mentions the visit by the President at a secret air base for the purpose of inspecting things from outer space. Kilgallen replied that she knew what might be the source of the visit. In the mid-fifties Kilgallen

learned of secret effort by US and UK governments to identify the origins of crashed spacecraft and dead bodies, from a British government official. Kilgallen believed the story may have come from the ??? in the late forties. Kilgallen said that if the story is true, it could cause terrible embarrassment to Jack and his plans to have NASA put men on the moon.
2. Subject repeatedly called the Attorney General and complained about the way she was being ignored by the President and his brother.
3. Subject threatened to hold a press conference and would tell all.
4. Subject made references to "bases" in Cuba and knew of the President's plan to kill Castro.
5. Subject made reference to her "diary of secrets" and what the newspapers would do with such disclosures.

After her suicide (or murder, as some researchers believe), Lionel Grandison, the Los Angeles County Coroner sent a driver to Marilyn's house to get an address book, so that Monroe's relatives could be contacted. Her housekeeper, Eunice Murray, gave him the address book and a little red diary. Grandison was the last person to examine the diary and said that there were references to the Kennedys, as well as other people, such as Fidel Castro. It was locked in the office safe. The next day, when the safe was opened, the diary was gone, and never seen again. One of the bits of information that was purported to be in the diary, was that on the day of the Bay of Pigs invasion, President Kennedy was incapacitated because of excruciating pain in his back, and Bobby Kennedy was actually running the country. It was alleged that he made the decision not to provide air support.

The invasion failed, because it was not able to launch the attack at the alternate site which had an airfield nearby and was more suitable for the unloading of troops and supplies, plus, there were nearby mountains to hide in. Besides the fact that the U.S. didn't provide the needed air support, it wasn't even a surprise attack, because the *New York Times* carried an article on January 10, 1961 with this headline: "U.S. Helps Train Anti-Castro Force At Secret Guatemalan Air-Ground Base," thus, the complete communist domination of Cuba was insured.

Russia, in May of 1962, realizing the potential of Cuba's location, tried to build missile sites on the island, but the U.S., considering them to be a threat to our national security, threatened Russia with possible military action if they weren't removed. After a blockade was imposed, the missiles were removed; however, the Soviets were still able to bolster the Cuban military by providing advisors, troops, aircraft, submarines, and military bases.

There are some researchers who believe that there were never any missiles on the island. The objects identified as "missiles" in government photos were no larger than pencil dots, and it was impossible to concretely label them as ballistic missiles. It is believed that the incident was created by the Russians, and that empty crates were removed from Cuba, in exchange for an agreement by the United States to remove missiles from Russia's borders, and for a guarantee that the U.S. would not support an anti-Castro invasion.

According to *The Nuclear Deception: Nikita Khrushchev and the Cuban Missile Crisis* (Spook Books, 2002, an imprint of InteliBooks) by Servando González (who was a political officer in the Cuban Army at the time), the presence of missiles in Cuba was never proven. The CIA maintained that there were never nuclear warheads in Cuba, and American planes flying over "missile sites" and Soviet ships had never detected any radiation.

In a 1996 article called "Fidel Castro: Supermole," González said that Cuba had turned into an economic embarrassment. He wrote: "Cuba, which was intended to be a showcase of the Soviet model of development in America, was in fact quickly turning into a showcase of Soviet inefficiency, mainly due to the Cuban leader's inability (and the) propagation of Fidel's 'heretical' ideas." Because Castro was perceived as being "unpredictable, volatile, undisciplined," he was being blamed for the Soviet's failure in Cuba, and Khrushchev decided he had to cut his losses and withdraw from the country. However, leaving voluntarily would give the impression that they were admitting failure, so the scheme was hatched to get rid of Castro "as a result of American aggression."

Initially, an uprising was planned that would have unseated Castro and replaced him with Aníbal Escalante, a trusted Party ally. However, Castro discovered the plan and neutralized it by expelling the ringleader, Soviet ambassador Mikhailovich Kudryavtsev. A frustrated Khrushchev then hit on the idea of provoking Kennedy to invade Cuba. The idea was that Castro would be overthrown, and when no missiles would be found, the American government would be embarrassed. According to González: "Khrushchev's carefully conceived plans had not counted on the unexpected and apparently irrational behavior of President Kennedy." González writes:

"... Finally, Soviet developments in Cuba were so blatant and political pressures in the U.S. so strong, that Kennedy was forced to act. But, when he announced the blockade of the island, he unexpectedly stated that the American actions were not directed against Cuba, but against the Soviet Union. Kennedy's behavior was so surprising that Khrushchev was caught completely off balance and panicked before the possibility of a nuclear confrontation which he had not anticipated and for which he was not prepared ... Fortunately for the world, Khrushchev was enough of a political realist to recognize when a gambit had been lost ... Khrushchev never understood why Kennedy had acted in such an irrational and foolish way, by not attacking Cuba and, thereby, allowing Castro to stay in power."

On December 2, 1961, Castro proclaimed: "I have been a Communist since my teens." On December 11, 1963, the *New York Times* printed one of President Kennedy's last interviews, in which he said: "I think we have spawned, constructed, entirely fabricated without knowing it, the Castro movement." In 1979, the *New York Times* published a letter from the former U.S. Ambassador to Cuba, Earl E. T. Smith, in which he said: "Castro could not have seized power in Cuba without the aid of the United States. American government agencies and the United States press played a major role in bringing Castro to power ... The State Department consistently intervened ... to bring about the downfall of Batiste, thereby making it possible for Fidel Castro to take over the government of Cuba."

COMMUNISTS FIGHT AMONG THEMSELVES

At the meeting of the 22nd Party Congress in the fall of 1961, the rivalry between Russia and China came out in the open. It centered around two issues: the place of Stalin in communist history, and relations with the country of Albania. Khrushchev (1894-1971), the Soviet premier from 1958-64, made verbal attacks on Stalin constantly, and even had his body removed from the mausoleum on Red Square. Mao Tse-tung, and the Chinese Communists went out of their way to proclaim their loyalty to the dead leader. When Enver Hoxha, the Communist ruler of Albania refused to follow Khrushchev's lead in condemning Stalin, Russia canceled all economic and technical aid, and recalled all Soviet personnel. China then sent in their own advisors, praising Albania for their stand.

China was upset because Russia failed to support them during a recent military action, and was suspicious of Khrushchev's policy of 'peaceful coexistence' with the United States. Since 1961, world communists have split into either pro-Soviet or pro-China factions. China began advocating Maoism, rather than Marxist-Leninism.

Stalin had said: "The object of Soviet Communism is victory of Communism throughout the world ... by peace or war." Russia boasted that within a generation, the whole world would be communist. Meanwhile, China also insisted that war was inevitable. Chou En-lai, the Chinese premier from 1949-76, said publicly: "The white race constitutes about one-tenth of the world's population. Let us completely annihilate the White man. Then we shall be free of him once and for all."

Because China had their own thoughts of world domination, a major rift developed between the two communist giants. China became angry over Russia's refusal to give them nuclear weapons, so after 14 years, Russia ceased all aid to China.

THE SPREAD OF COMMUNISM

George Washington, during the winter of 1777 at Valley Forge, had a vision that showed a red light moving towards America, The account was given in 1859 by an old soldier, to writer Wesley Bradshaw, who had it published in the American War Veteran's paper, the *National Tribune*, in December, 1880 (reprinted in *Stars and Stripes*, on December 21, 1950):

> "I do not know whether it is owing to the anxiety of my mind, or what, but this afternoon, as I was sitting at this table engaged in preparing a dispatch, something in the apartment seemed to disturb me. Looking up, I beheld standing opposite me a singularly beautiful being. So astonished was I, for I had given strict orders not to be disturbed, that it was some moments before I had found language to inquire the cause of the visit. A second, a third, and even a fourth time did I repeat my question, but received no answer from my mysterious visitor except a slight raising of the eyes.

By this time I felt strange sensations spreading through me. I would have risen but the riveted gaze of the being before me rendered volition impossible. I assayed once more to speak, but my tongue had become useless, as if paralyzed. A new influence, mysterious, potent, irresistible, took possession of me. All I could do was to gaze steadily, vacantly at my unknown visitor.

Gradually the surrounding atmosphere seemed to fill with sensations, and grew luminous. Everything about me seemed to rarefy, the mysterious visitor also becoming more airy and yet more distinct to my sight than before. I began to feel as one dying, or rather to experience the sensations which I have sometimes imagined accompany death. I did not think, I did not reason, I did not move. All were alike impossible. I was only conscious of gazing fixedly, vacantly at my companion.

Presently I heard a voice saying, 'Son of the Republic, look and learn,' while at the same time my visitor extended an arm eastward. I now beheld a heavy white vapor at some distance rising fold upon fold. This gradually dissipated, and I looked upon a strange scene. Before me lay, spread out in one vast plain, all the countries of the world— Europe, Asia, Africa, and America. I saw rolling and tossing between Europe and America the billows of the Atlantic and between Asia and America lay the Pacific. 'Son of the Republic,' said the same mysterious voice as before, 'look and learn.'

At that moment I beheld a dark, shadowy being, like an angel, standing, or rather floating in mid-air, between Europe and America. Dipping water out of the ocean in the hollow of each hand, he sprinkled some upon America with his right hand, while with his left he cast some over Europe. Immediately a cloud arose from these countries, and joined in mid-ocean. For awhile it seemed stationary, and then it moved slowly westward, until it enveloped America in its murky folds. Sharp flashes of lightning gleamed through it at intervals, and I heard the smothered groans and cries of the American people (the American Revolution, which was in progress).

A second time the angel dipped water from the ocean and sprinkled it out as before. The dark cloud was then drawn back to the ocean, in whose heaving billows it sank from view.

A third time I heard the mysterious voice saying, 'Son of the Republic, look and learn.' I cast my eyes upon America, and beheld villages and towns and cities springing up one after another until the whole land from the Atlantic to the Pacific was dotted with them. Again, I heard the mysterious voice say, 'Son of the Republic, the end of the century cometh, look and learn.'

And this time the dark shadowy angel turned his face southward. From Africa I saw an ill-omened specter approach our land. It flitted slowly and heavily over every town and city of the latter. The inhabitants presently set themselves in battle array against each other. As I continued looking I saw a bright angel on whose brow rested a crown of light, on which was traced the word 'Union.' He was bearing the American flag.

He placed the flag between the divided nation and said, 'Remember, ye are brethren (referred to the Civil War).

Instantly, the inhabitants, casting down their weapons, became friends once more and united around the National Standard.

Again I heard the mysterious voice saying, 'Son of the Republic, look and learn.' At this the dark, shadowy angel placed a trumpet to his mouth, and blew three distinct blasts; and taking water from the ocean, he sprinkled it upon Europe, Asia, and Africa.

Then my eyes beheld a fearful scene. From each of these continents arose thick black clouds that were soon joined into one. And throughout this mass there gleamed a dark red light by which I saw hordes of armed men. These men, moving with the cloud, marched by land and sailed by sea to America, which country was enveloped in the volume of the cloud. And I dimly saw these vast armies devastate the whole country and burn the villages, towns and cities which I had seen spring up.

As my ears listened to the thundering of the cannon, clashing of swords, and the shouts and cries of millions in mortal combat, I again heard the mysterious voice saying, 'Son of the Republic, look and learn.' When this voice had ceased, the dark shadowy angel placed his trumpet once more to his mouth, and blew a long and fearful blast.

Instantly a light as of a thousand suns shone down from above me, and pierced and broke into fragments the dark cloud which enveloped America. At the same moment the angel upon whose head still shown the word 'Union,' and who bore our national flag in one hand and a sword in the other, descended from the heavens attended by legions of white spirits. These immediately joined the inhabitants of America, who I perceived were well-nigh overcome, but who immediately taking courage again, closed up their broken ranks and renewed the battle.

Again amid the fearful noise of the conflict, I heard the mysterious voice saying, 'Son of the Republic, look and learn.' As the voice ceased, the shadowy angel for the last time dipped water from the ocean and sprinkled it upon America. Instantly the dark cloud rolled back, together with the armies it had brought, leaving the inhabitants of the land victorious.

Then once more, I beheld villages, towns, and cities springing up where I had seen them before, while the bright angel, planting the azure standard he had brought in the midst of them, cried with a loud voice: 'While the stars remain, and the heavens send down dew upon the earth, so long shall the Union last.' And taking from his brow the crown on which blazened the word 'Union,' he placed it upon the standard while the people, kneeling down said, 'Amen.'

The scene instantly began to fade and dissolve, and I, at last saw nothing but the rising, curling vapor I at first beheld. This also disappeared, and I found myself once more gazing upon the mysterious visitor, who, in the same voice I had heard before, said, 'Son of the Republic, what you have seen is thus interpreted. Three great perils will come upon the Republic. The most fearful for her is the third. But the whole world united shall not prevail against her. Let every child of the Republic learn to live for his God, his land and Union.' With these words the vision vanished, and I started from my seat and felt that I had seen a vision wherein had been shown me the birth, the progress, and the destiny of the United States."

A red light was indeed moving towards America, and it was communism, which at its peak, controlled 14,000,000 square miles of territory, or about 1/4 of the inhabited land in the world; and close to 1,500,000,000 people, or about a third of the world's population. The communist menace swept through Russia (1917), Mongolia (1924), Estonia (1940), Latvia (1940), Lithuania (1940), Bessarabia (1940), Bukovina (1940), Albania (1944), Tannu-Tuva (1945), Ukraine (1945), Yugoslavia (1945), Outer Mongolia (1945), Manchuria (1945), Karafuto (1945), Kurile Islands (1945), Bulgaria (1946), Poland (1947), Romania (1947), East Germany (1948), Hungary (1948), North Korea (1948), Czechoslovakia (1948), China (1949), Sinkiang (1950), Tibet (1951), North Vietnam (1954), Guinea (1958), Cuba (1960), Libya (1969), South Yemen (1969), Guyana (1970), Benin (1974), Burma (1974), Laos (1975), South Vietnam (1975), Madagascar (1975), Angola (1976), Somalia (1976), Seychelles (1977), Mozambique (1977), Ethiopia (1977), Cambodia (1979), Grenada (1979), Congo (1979), and Afghanistan (1980).

On January 10, 1963, the *Congressional Record* published a list of 45 goals of the Communists, which included: 1) for the U.S. to co-exist with communism; 2) further disarmament; 3) to establish the United Nations as a one-world government, with an independent military force; 4) to infiltrate the media; 5) to overthrow all colonial governments before self-rule can be instituted. There were 90 Communist Parties worldwide, recognized by the Comintern, who were working toward those goals.

The communist conquest has claimed well over 145,300,000 lives: Soviet Union (1917-59), 66,700,000; Soviet Union (1959-78), 5,000,000; Red China, 64,000,000; Katyn Massacre, 14,242; expelled Germans (1945-46), 2,923,700; Cambodia (1975-78), 2,500,000; repression in eastern Europe, 500,000; Malaya, Burma, Philippines, Cuba, Black Africa, Latin and Central America, 3,600,000.

Retired Air Force General G. J. Keegan, Jr. said that our government had been covering up the evidence of an imminent Soviet attack on the United States. Keegan, a former Assistant Chief of Staff for the Air Force Intelligence Unit, said that Russia had been going through extensive preparations to mobilize their forces against the free world. He said: "After sixty years of aggression by the Soviets, only 17% of the remaining world population, lives in what could be termed a free society."

Dimitri Manvilski, a professor at the Lenin School of Political Warfare in Moscow, said in 1930: "War to the hilt between communism and capitalism is inevitable. Today, of course, we are not strong enough to attack. Our time will come in thirty or forty years. To win, we shall need the element of surprise. The western world will have to be put to sleep. So we shall begin by launching the most spectacular peace movement on record. There shall be electrifying overtures and unheard of concessions. The capitalist countries, stupid and decadent, will rejoice to cooperate with their own destruction. They will leap at another chance to be friends. As soon as their guard is down, we shall smash them with our clenched fist."

Lenin said: "First, we will take eastern Europe, then the masses of Asia, then we will encircle the United States which will be the last bastion of capitalism. We will not have to attack. It will fall into our hands like an overripe fruit." William C. Bullitt, our first Ambassador to Russia, wrote: "...it must be recognized the communists are agents of a foreign power whose aim is not only to destroy the institutions and liberties of our country, but also to kill millions of Americans."

In 1955, Khrushchev made this statement to the Warsaw Pact countries: "We must realize that we cannot coexist eternally, for a long time. One of us must go to his grave. We do not want to go to the grave. They (America) do not want to go to their grave, either. So what must be done? We must push them to the grave." In July, 1957, he said: "...I can prophecy that your grandchildren in America will live under socialism. And please do not be afraid of that. Your grandchildren will ... not understand how their grandparents did not understand the progressive nature of a socialist society." Khrushchev said, while banging his shoe on a table at the United Nations: "Our firm conviction is that sooner or later Capitalism will give way to Socialism. Whether you like it or not, history is on our side. We will bury you." On July 19, 1962, Khrushchev said: "The United States will eventually fly the Communist red flag ... The American people will hoist it themselves."

According to the June 26, 1974 edition of the *Congressional Record*, Soviet President Leonid Brezhnev is quoted as saying: "We Communists have got to string along with the capitalists for awhile. We need their credits, their agriculture, and their technology. But we are going to continue massive military programs and by the middle 1980's we will be in a position to return to a much more aggressive foreign policy designed to gain the upper hand in our relationship with the West." In a 1973 speech to the Warsaw Pact leaders in Prague, Brezhnev said: "Trust us, comrades, for by 1985, as a consequence of what we are now achieving with detente, we will have achieved most of our objectives in Western Europe. We will have consolidated our position. We will have improved our economy. And a decisive shift in the correlation of forces will be such that come 1985, we will be able to exert our will wherever we need to."

In a 1961 speech by FBI Director J. Edgar Hoover: "We are at war with the communists, and the sooner every red-blooded American realizes this, the safer we will be." He later wrote: "Communists want to control everything: where you live, where you work, what you are paid, what you think ... how your children are educated, what you may not and must read and write ... Remember, always, that 'it could happen here' and that there are thousands of people in this country now working in secret to make it happen here."

U.S. Communist Party members pledged "to defend the Soviet Union ... (and) to remain at all times a vigilant and firm defender of the Leninist line of the Party, the only line that insures the triumph of Soviet power in the U.S." How loyal are Communist Party members? Gus Hall, a prominent official of the U.S. Communist Party, said at the February, 1961 funeral of Eugene Dennis, National Chairman of the U.S. Communist Party: "I dream of the hour when the last Congressman is strangled to death on the guts of the last preacher— and since Christians love to sing about the blood, why not give them a little of it."

During the 1980's, statements coming out of Russia, continued to be of a threatening nature. Janos Kadar, Hungary's Communist leader, told 5,000 delegates to the Soviet Party Congress: "There is no force on earth that can stop the Soviet Union's advance and the triumph of Communism." Anatoly P. Alexandrov, President of the Soviet Union's Academy of Sciences, and one of Russia's top scientists, said: "The Soviet Union was never as strong as it is today." A UPI report stated: "Top ranking party officials declared today that the Soviet Union is mightier than it has ever been and is no longer threatened by force— making the triumph of communism inevitable."

Russia has been at war with us for years in an effort to destroy us. Former Czech Communist official J. Bernard Hutton wrote in his book *The Subverters*:

> "Today thousands of highly trained Russian and Red China undercover master-subverters live under respectable 'cover' occupations and professions in all countries of the western democracies. International security officers estimate that at least thirty thousand undercover subverters, paid by Moscow and Peking, and continually undermining the Western democracies. They are aided by specially trained Communist Party members and fellow travelers. The conservative estimate by Western security experts is that at least half a million men and women are at work all over the world, bringing about the downfall of the profit-making economic system."

In 1920, Lenin talked about their plans: "The communists in Western Europe and America must ... strive everywhere to awaken the masses, and draw them into the struggle ... It is difficult to do this in Western Europe and America, but it can be done and must be done. Propaganda, agitation and organization inside the armed movements and among the oppressed must be coordinated in a new way." In 1921, he came up with the idea of spreading communism through trade unions, youth organizations, cooperatives, and other associations. This idea was taken even further by Otto Kuusinen, a Finland Communist, who at a meeting of the Comintern Executive Committee in March, 1926, advocated the creation of a "whole solar system of organizations and smaller committees around the Communist Party ... actually working under the influence of the Party, but not under its mechanical control." The organizations were developed by Willi Munzenberg, a German communist. Their aim was to further the cause of Soviet communism, and act as a cover, if communism was illegal, in order to spread propaganda.

Stalin said, during a secret meeting of the Kremlin's Inner Circle, in March, 1948:

> "Comrades, it is imperative that we create an entirely new type of fighting force. It will operate first in the most advanced capitalist countries, and later in other countries. This fighting force will consist of devoted and trained comrades who will have no connection with the Communist Party whatsoever. These comrades will operate undercover, as do our intelligence officers and spies who are working abroad. This special force will control networks of other undercover comrades, who will also have

no outward connection with the Communist Party of their country ... The objective of this fighting force is to speed up the development of revolutionary situations and spread awareness of how unrest, public disturbance, disorders and industrial dissatisfaction can bring about a breakdown of the capitalist system. This will lead to the revolutionary overthrow of governments, and the establishment of Soviet states."

In another secret meeting in April, 1948, Stalin said:

"The way to assure success is for us to create not one, but two undercover subverter networks. They will operate simultaneously in all the countries of the capitalist world. The undercover subverters of the first network will operate quite independently of the second ... In each capitalistic country one undercover subverter network will be composed of tried and trusted communists who are nationals of that country. Their activities will be directed by Comrade Suslov who will be responsible to the Politburo. This network of undercover subverters will comprise of men and women of ability and intelligence, especially selected for these qualities. As soon as they undertake the undercover subverter work, they will sever all contact with the Communist Party— and dedicate themselves to working for the Party by indirect methods. They will be called upon to join and operate within organizations and societies that are bourgeois and opposed to communism and the Soviet Union. They will engage in undercover subverter activities within these organizations and societies on behalf of the Communist Party. It will be necessary for them to conceal their previous and present connection with the Communist Party. They will create the impression they are opposed to the ideology of communism ... The second network of undercover subverters will consist of operators of Soviet nationality. These comrades will be under direct orders from our Secret Service Headquarters (KGB). A new department of Secret Service Headquarters will be created forthwith, to be named 'Special Division for Subversion.' The directors of this Special Division will select and train recruits of Soviet nationality for this professional undercover master-subverters network, in the same way that they select and train Soviet comrades for work abroad as Secret Service Network Operators..."

Mikhail Suslov's undercover subverter network was referred to as Institute 631's Subversive Cadres, and later that year, they sent a coded directive to the world's Communist Party leaders: "The leaders of all Communist Parties must select completely trustworthy comrades who will take up undercover subverters work outside the Communist Party. Their activity will be revolutionary and subversive. It is essential that these chosen comrades sever all connections with the Party. It is desirable that they become regarded as antagonistic to the Party, and in conflict with its policy."

Thus, the Red 'fifth column' was instituted in order to infiltrate the West, While appearing to be anti-communist, by going to church, getting involved in charities, and voting conservatively; they were secretly attending training centers to learn techniques of sabotage, terrorism and subversion in order to instigate strikes, provoke riots and stage demonstrations.

Inside the Soviet Union, candidates were chosen to attend the Marx-Engels School near Moscow, for what they were told would be training for a career within the Party. The recruits would then be sent to the Lenin Technical School at Verkhovnoye, which is a complex spread out of over seven square miles in a desolate area. During the time they were here, their family, and friends, did not know their whereabouts. The training lasted 12 months, and consisted of military-like training, such as survival techniques, various methods of hand-to-hand combat, handling firearms and heavy combat equipment, how to make and deactivate explosives, methods of electronic surveillance, and the use of poisons. If the recruit passed, they would be sent on a vacation, during which they would be arrested by the Secret Police as a foreign agent. This final test subjected the candidate to brainwashing, torture and interrogation, to see if they would break under the pressure. If they passed, they would be sent to one of the Soviet Ace Spy Schools, where the training could last for up to ten years.

The Prakhovka Ace Spy School was located near Minsk, within a 220 square mile area along the border of the Latvian Soviet Republic. The northern sector was for Norway, Sweden, Denmark, and Finland; the southwestern sector was for the Netherlands; the southern area was for Austria and Switzerland; and the southeastern area was for Germany. At the Stiepnaya Ace Spy School, near Chkalov, along the northern border of the Kazakh Soviet Republic, the northwestern section was for France; the northern area for the Spanish countries; the northeastern section for Italy; and the southern end for Portugal, Brazil, Argentina and Mexico. The Vostocznaya Ace Spy School near Khabarovsk, was for Asian and Middle East countries; and the Novaya Ace Spy School, near Tashkent, was for the African countries.

Another Soviet Spy School was located in Gaczyna, in a 425 square mile area along the southern border of the Tarter Autonomous Soviet Republic, and continuing to the Bashkir Autonomous Soviet Republic. It was sealed off for a radius of thirty miles by State Security, and the location was so secret, that it was not shown on any map. It was known to only the highest officers of the Secret Service. The School was developed for those selected to work in the English-speaking world, and was divided into three sections: the northern section was for North America and Canada; the northeastern section was for the United Kingdom; and the southern area was for Australia, New Zealand, India, and South Africa. There was no communication between the different areas.

In the United Kingdom section, the candidate would live in actual British-style homes, hotels, and apartments, which were full-size replicas of actual English buildings, on actual streets. There were British banks, restaurants, theaters, and a Post Office, all in a sixty square mile area. Here the recruit ate British food, wore British clothes, rode London buses, and received a weekly salary dispensed in British currency, read English papers and magazines, and watched English television shows. The recruits were given English names, and were ordered to speak only English, which they were given five years to master. They had to learn all necessary British customs.

During the second five years, they memorized unbreakable codes, and were taught how to assemble and dismantle radio receivers and transmitters; and were taught how to use photographic equipment to reduce blueprints, records, and documents into microdots. They were given further instruction in guerrilla warfare.

After this intensive training, the recruit was, in almost every way, British. Each agent was smuggled into the country of their training, which in this case was England. They would never again see their families. They would be given actual identification and 'cover' documents from people who were dead or missing, so that a background check couldn't reveal their true identities. Within their new identity, they became involved in public life, working to undermine the government as a representative of the communist government of the Soviet Union.

China had similar schools, but their training period was only ten months, because spies were recruited mainly for Chiang Kai-shek's Nationalist China, and other countries within Asia, where they would fit in. To infiltrate the West, the Chinese recruited people from all over the world, and smuggled them into China to undergo training. The school in the Honan province was for France, Italy, and Spain; the school in the Chekiang province was for West Germany; and the school in the Shantung province was for Austria, Switzerland, and the Arab countries.

At the start of World War II, Roosevelt made Gen. William Donovan the head of the Office of Strategic Services (OSS). Donovan didn't see anything wrong with Communists, and recruited OSS personnel from Communist ranks. When the FBI discovered this, and informed him, he said: "I know they're Communists. That's why I hired them." After the war, the OSS became known as the Central Intelligence Agency (CIA), and in 1952, the head of the CIA, Gen. Walter Bedell Smith, said that he was sure there were Communists working inside the CIA. Three high-level Soviet KGB defectors, Anatoli Golitsin, Yuri Nosenko, and Michael Goleniewski, acknowledged their belief that there were Communist spies in the U.S. intelligence community. Retired Air Force Major General Follette Bradley, wrote a letter, published by the *New York Times*, on August 31, 1951, that Russian representatives and military personnel came into our country, and were "free to move about without restraint or check, and in order to visit our arsenals, depots, factories, and proving grounds, they had only to make known their desires ... I personally know that scores of Russians were permitted to enter American territory in 1942 without visa."

A year before Russian Premier Nikita Khrushchev visited the United States, he told Communist leaders in the Kremlin: "It is of vital importance to cripple the armaments industry and all other important industries of all capitalist enemies. It is of still greater importance to accomplish this within that cradle of aggression—war hungry America! The Americans are feverishly preparing for war against the peace-loving bloc of the Soviet Union and other People's Democracies..." Then referring to the orders by the Institute 631, he told the leaders: "Because the United States of America is our Enemy Number One, even more ruthless action is called for in that country."

When Khrushchev came to America, he referred to Americans as "peace-loving," and his "true and loved friends," and after being presented with a gavel made from the wood of one of California's Redwood trees, said: "I will use it for the first time when I strike it, in triumph, on the table, the day we sign a Pact of Nonaggression and Eternal Love between the Soviet Union and America; and a second time when we sign a Treaty of Disarmament with all the nations of the world. I await with impatience my talks with your President (Eisenhower), hoping that our two hearts will be prompted to reach agreement and establish conditions of peace and friendship."

The Special Committee of Investigation for the United Mine Workers of America, said in a Report:

> "The major points in this revolutionary program of the Communists are:
> 1) Overthrow and destruction of the Federal, State, and Provincial governments, with the elimination of existing constitutional forms and foundations.
> 2) Establishment of a Soviet dictatorship, absolute in its exercise of power, owing allegiance to, and conceding the authority only of the Communist, or Third Internationale, at Moscow, as a 'governmental' substitute.
> 3) Destruction of all social, economic, and political institutions as they exist at this time.
> 4) Seizure of all labor unions through a process of 'boring from within' them, and utilizing them as a strategic instrument in fulfillment of their revolutionary designs upon organized and constitutional government."

In 1960, American subversives received a new directive from Moscow:

> "1) Comrades working in telegraph, teleprinter, and telephone services must organize an effective monitoring system to intercept important communications, and enable the Party to learn what is going on inside the U.S. Government, the Security forces, industry, and in all other important establishments.
> 2) Comrades working in armament factories or in nuclear establishments must memorize all charts, blueprints, production lists, etc. that they come upon through their employment. If it is possible to photograph such documents without the risk of detection, this is preferable.
> 3) Comrades must make a determined effort to infiltrate all sections of the U.S. Armed Forces ... He should be converted into a determined opponent of war between the United States and the Soviet Union ... Acts of sabotage at nuclear bases are invaluable. If the well publicized launchings of a space rocket results in a failure, this is of tremendous propaganda value.
> 4) In addition to the above special tasks, everyday life in all parts of the U.S. must be disrupted as often, and as effectively, as possible ... Racial riots are the most easily provoked disorders. If they are brought about in a way which makes it seem that the ruling class has precipitated the riots, this is valuable propaganda ... The class enemy must be discredited, hit often, and where it hurts the most."

In his book *The Conscience of a Conservative*, Arizona Senator Barry Goldwater wrote:

> "The exchange program in the Soviet eyes, is simply another operation in Communist political warfare. The people that the Kremlin sends over

here are, to a man, trained agents of Soviet policy. Some of them are spies, seeking information; all of them are trusted carriers of Communist propaganda. Their mission is not cultural, but political. Their aim is not to inform, but to mislead. Their assignment is not to convey a true image of the Soviet Union, but a false image. The Kremlin's hope is that they will persuade the American people to forget the ugly aspects of Soviet life, and the danger that the Soviet system poses to American freedom ... But the Kremlin's aim is not to make American's approve of Communism, much as they would like that; it is to make us tolerant of Communism ... They know that if Americans regard the Soviet Union as a dangerous implacable enemy, Communism will not be able to conquer the world."

During the Johnson Administration, 66 Senators voted for the Consulate Treaty, despite the tremendous public criticism of it, which opened up the country to spies and saboteurs, who would be protected with the mantle of diplomatic immunity.

In 1905, Lenin wrote his *Instructions to Revolutionaries*, which indicated how important it was to concentrate on young people. He wrote:

"Go to the youth. Form fighting squads everywhere at three, ten, and thirty persons. Let them arm themselves at once as best they can, be it with a revolver, a knife, a rag soaked in kerosene to start fires ... Some may undertake to kill a spy or blow up a police station, others to raid a bank ... for insurrection ... let every group learn, if only by beating up a policeman; this will train hundreds of experienced fighters who tomorrow will be leading hundreds of thousands..."

In 1919, a pamphlet called *Communist Rules for Revolution* was aimed at hooking young people: "Get the youth corrupted, get them away from religion. Get them interested in sex ... Destroy their ruggedness ... Get control of all publicity ... Divide the people into hostile groups by constantly harping on controversial matters ... Destroy the people's faith in their leaders ... Always preach true democracy, but seize power as fact and us ruthlessly as possible ... Encourage government extravagance ... Destroy its credit ... Incite unnecessary strikes and civil disobedience ... Cause the registration of firearms on some pretext, with view to confiscate them, leaving the population helpless."

In the mid-1960's, Moscow and Peking told their armies of subversives to "concentrate upon the young, the most malleable and most gullible section of the population." A directive from the Special Division for Subversion, in April, 1968, which was sent to West Germany, said:

"Action must be taken at once to create disruptive situations that will rock the very foundations of the capitalist system. The disturbances must occur on such a large scale that they cause deep concern to the population ... lightning strikes of key workers in important industrial centers must be encouraged. The objective is to bring the maximum of factories to a complete standstill ... Demonstrations must be instigated on every possible occasion. Demonstrations are a symptom of public discontent ... Revolutionary action by students must be stepped up. Every effort must be made now to encourage students to demonstrate, and if possible, to riot on the largest possible scale. Students are susceptible to an idealistic approach. They should be tackled on the lines laid down in our previous directives ... When known Communist Party members are persuading others to take military action, our undercover subverters must oppose this communist inspired action. It is vitally important for them to safeguard their established undercover positions."

A similar directive was sent to France in 1968:

"The student population must be induced to demonstrate publicly and fight vigorously for their rights. Subtle undercover tactics must be adopted to ensure these demonstrations culminate in rioting and street fighting. The objective is to create a dangerous, revolutionary situation in which law and order is discredited ... Simultaneously our undercover cadres in industry, commerce, the trade unions, religious organizations and political parties, must propagate the idea that the working population should give full support to any students' strike actions."

While the Soviets were calling for more "grievance strikes, more wildcat strikes, and more trade union obstruction to smooth working of industry; more racial riots, and more sabotage to industrial plants," Red China's agents were instructed to "seize every opportunity to speed drug addiction," and all sorts of drugs were smuggled into the West. Russia later adopted the same strategy. Chou En-lai told Egyptian President Nassar, in 1966, of his plans to turn our American soldiers into drug addicts: "The more troops they (America) send to Vietnam, the happier we shall be. We shall then have them in our power and can have their blood."

In addition to the undercover subversion, there are various Communist Parties established in various countries. If the Party is outlawed, they function under the name of the "Worker's Party" or the "Socialist Party." Over 80 countries had Parties that were officially recognized by the Comintern in Moscow. The leaders of these Parties were sent to Moscow for training in communist theory and revolutionary tactics, so they could return to spread propaganda in order to recruit members.

Organized communism began in the United States when Socialist Eugene V. Debs ran for the Presidency in 1900, 1904, and 1908. When he ran in 1912, he garnered over 6% of the vote. The U.S. Communist Party was organized in 1919, having sprung from ideas gleaned from books and pamphlets smuggled in from Europe, and nurtured by members of the Illuminati. They joined the Comintern, which is the world Communist organization run by the Soviet Union.

To aid the local parties, there were hundreds of 'front' organizations established to defend Soviet policies and attack its opponents. They functioned through the media, local Communist parties, and other small organizations. Among the organizations controlled by Russia: International Institute for Peace (Vienna), World Council of Peace (Prague), International Union of Students (Prague), Women's

International Democratic Federation (E. Berlin), International Association of Democratic Lawyers (Brussels), World Federation of Scientific Workers (London), International Organization of Journalists (Prague), World Federation of Trade Unions (Prague), World Federation of Teachers Unions (Prague), International Radio and Television Organization, and the International Medical Association (formerly known as the World Congress of Doctors).

Some of the groups operating in the United States and Canada: American Friends Service Committee, Arms Control Association, Center for Defense Information, Coalition for a New Foreign and Military Policy, Council on Economic Priorities, National Lawyers Guild, Citizens Committee for a Sane World, War Register League, Women for Racial and Economic Equality, and the Center for International Policy.

There were also a number of bilateral organizations, known as 'Friendship Societies' which also work under Soviet direction, some of these were: British-Soviet Friendship Society, Britain-China Friendship Society, Soviet-India Friendship Society, and the Society for Friendship with the Peoples of Africa.

On top of all of this support, Communism also had its apologists and representatives in our government, such as Sen. J. William Fulbright (a CFR member), Chairman of the Senate Foreign Relations Committee, who said in a speech on the floor of the Senate, on June 29, 1961, concerning world Communism: "We can hope to do little more than mitigate our problems as best we can and learn how to live with them." He believed that once Russia caught up to the United States in technology, relations would improve between the two countries. He advocated increased aid, and compromises to avoid direct confrontation. He felt that the presence of Soviet missiles in Cuba did not endanger our national security. When Tito, the Yugoslavia dictator, joined with Russia to provide "all necessary aid to North Vietnam," Fulbright said that Yugoslavia had "proven itself a reliable and stalwart associate in the advancement of certain interests on which our interests coincide." Later, the Johnson Administration sent them 700,000 tons of American wheat, 92,000 bales of cotton, and gave them a loan for $175 million to aid their economy and industry.

Jimmy Carter said in 1980: "Being confident of our own future, we are now free of that inordinate fear of communism." Walter Mondale said in 1981: I'm very worried about U.S.-Soviet relations. I cannot understand— it just baffles me why the Soviets these last few years have behaved as they have. Maybe we have made some mistakes..." Sen. John Glenn, a member of the Foreign Relations Committee, said in 1983: "I don't think you want to involve American troops even if El Salvador was about to fall to communist-backed guerrillas." Many of our country's leaders have become soft on communism, because they are no longer perceived as a threat.

In his last book, *With No Apologies*, Sen. Barry Goldwater wrote: "The Russians are determined to conquer the world. They will employ force, murder, lies, flattery, subversion, bribery, extortion, and treachery. Everything they stand for and believe in is a contradiction of our understandings of the nature of men. Their artful use of propaganda has anesthetized the free world. Our will to resist is being steadily eroded..."

In an effort to appear that they were embracing democracy, Mikhail Gorbachev introduced 'glasnost' ('openness') and 'perestroika' ('economic restructuring') in the Soviet Union in 1985, and the Russian people began to experience a degree of freedom never before seen. However, these reforms failed, and communism as a form of government ended when the Soviet Union collapsed in 1991.

DISARMING AMERICA

The campaign for nuclear disarmament was directly linked to the International Department of Specific Activities in the Kremlin, when after World War II, the "Ban the Bomb" movement was born, because the U.S. was the only country to have nuclear capabilities. The Soviet Union organized and financed the World Peace Council, a well-known 'freeze' group, to influence public opinion and government policy in non-Communist countries. Their international headquarters was in Helsinki, Finland, and local chapters had been established in 100 countries. The American branch was called the U.S. Peace Council, and had offices in Washington, DC and New York City, They once sent a KGB colonel to meet with a group of Congressmen in Washington, then boasted about it.

On September 20, 1961, the United States and the Soviet Union announced an agreement for general disarmament that included the disbanding of military forces, dismantling of military bases, ceasing weapon production, and eliminating all weapon stockpiles. However, no treaty was signed, because they could never agree on all points. For instance, Russia wanted the U.S. to dismantle all foreign bases and destroy nuclear weapons, but this would have given Russia an edge in conventional weapons. The Disarmament Committee of the United Nations, composed of 18 members, also failed to come up with an adequate agreement between the two countries.

President John F. Kennedy had promised to close the missile gap in order to reestablish our military strength, but his Secretary of Defense, Robert McNamara, wanted to allow our defense program to decline until Russia was equal to us. In a speech on September 18, 1967, McNamara said that our inventory of nuclear warheads was "greater than we had originally planned and in fact more than we require." The move towards unilateral disarmament began when McNamara announced that Russia wouldn't sign an arms limitation agreement until they caught up to the United States in strategic offensive weapons.

The Strategic Arms Limitation Talks (SALT) originated from the discussions between President Lyndon B. Johnson and Soviet Prime Minister Aleksei N. Kosygin, in 1967. These conferences developed into the SALT I Agreement, which was signed by President Richard M. Nixon and Soviet Premier Leonid I. Brezhnev in 1972. While the number of U.S. strategic missiles had been frozen at the 1967 level, the Soviets had continued to build, matching that amount in 1970. By 1972, Russia had a 3-2 advantage in the number of intercontinental ballistic missiles (ICBM's).

SALT I was actually two agreements. The first was a treaty of indefinite duration, restricting defensive anti-ballistic missiles (ABM's) to 200 on each side (reduced to 100 in a 1974 agreement). It also froze the number of offensive missiles at the 1972 level for five years. With Russia having 2,358 land and sea-based missiles, and the U.S. only 1,710, the Soviets were certainly getting the best part of that deal. Submarine-based missiles were restricted by a complicated formula which gave the Russians a numerical advantage, but was balanced by permitting the U.S. more warheads for its reliable and more accurate missiles.

The second part of the agreement was a five-year pact limiting some offensive strategic weapons, and the number of launchers for ICBM's carrying nuclear warheads. It limited each side to 2 ABM installations, totaling 200 missile launchers; one at the nation's capitol, and the other would protect an offensive missile site (Grand Forks, North Dakota). This stipulation was amended in 1974 to only one site in each country.

SALT I was ratified by an 88-2 vote in the Senate, but the Jackson Amendment stipulated that the next agreement was to be more equal. The Agreement was to remain in effect until October 3, 1977.

On November 24, 1974, President Gerald R. Ford and Brezhnev reached an agreement to limit the number of all offensive strategic weapons and delivery systems until December 31, 1985.

SALT II was a treaty that resulted from a second round of talks, and was signed by President Jimmy Carter and Brezhnev on June 18, 1979, and was to remain in effect until 1985. It limited each side to 2,400 ICBM launchers and long range bombers, within six months of ratification (by the end of 1981, a new limit of 2,250 was to take effect). It would allow each country to develop one new missile, and to modernize their existing weaponry, with certain limitations. Each side would be expected to verify the other's compliance by its own surveillance methods. Regardless of the many stipulations, it still did not meet the requirements of the Jackson Equality Amendment. The numbers were manipulated to make them appear equal. For example, in the count of U.S. Strategic Weapons, 100 B-52's (a heavy bomber capable of hitting speeds of 650 mph, altitudes of 50,000 ft., and has air-launched missiles and bombs which can hit several targets hundreds of miles apart) that were mothballed in a graveyard in Arizona, were included, even though it would take more than a year to get them all flying again. However, 150 of the new Russian 'Backfire' bombers were not counted.

A prominent general stated: "If SALT II is passed, we are in the final 1000 days of history."

The Senate never ratified SALT II, because the Soviet Union invaded Afghanistan; however, the U.S. adhered to it, but not Russia.

Assistant to the Chairman of the Joint Chiefs of Staff, Air Force Lieutenant General John S. Pustay said that the Russians, for years, have continued to "out-man, out-gun, out-build ... us in most meaningful military categories." The Soviets had outspent us in a display of armament and mobilization that had not occurred since Hitler's preparations for World War II. According to 1991 statistics, Russia's defense spending was 8% (down from 11-13% in the late 1970's) of their Gross National Product, while ours was only 5.7% (down from 6.1% in the late 1970's).

If their military escalation wasn't an indication of their intentions, then the capabilities of their civil defense program should have been. Retired Air Force General G. J. Keegan, Jr. said: "The Soviets have deployed and developed the most intensive system of nuclear shelter for its military leadership, its civilian leadership, its industrial factory workers, and its civilian population ever deployed or built in history." New housing construction included mandatory underground shelters. They have built 1,575 huge underground command posts, each the size of the White House, embedded in the earth up to 400 feet deep, and covered by 75 feet of reinforced concrete. They have protected water, power generators, and communications systems. The Pentagon estimated that each post cost about $500 million. In the event of a nuclear exchange, it is believed that a large part of the Russian population would survive.

Meanwhile, the United States Government has literally abandoned its civil defense program, in lieu of the "Continuity of Government" plan developed by the Federal Emergency Management Administration (FEMA). There are said to be as many as 96 underground facilities throughout Maryland, West Virginia, Virginia, Pennsylvania, and North Carolina that will house government officials in case of an impending nuclear incident. The most prolific is a highly classified underground city, with a subterranean lake for drinking water, 40 miles east of Washington, DC, in the Appalachian foothills, known as Mount Weather. It has streets, sidewalks, offices, houses, and a medical facility. It will house federal government officials, and contain all records on its computers, such as census, Social Security, and IRS information. Civilians will be left to seek out the 235,000 buildings designated as fall-out shelters. In addition, the Defense Department's Civil Defense Preparedness Agency (DCPA) indicates that there is the potential for sheltering 50 million people in mines. Nevertheless, if a nuclear exchange were to occur today, the best estimates are that 160,000,000 Americans would die, but only 5,000,000 Russians.

The Russians have 100 times as many radar detectors than we have, and on top of that, Air Force experts once said that the U.S. Radar System is so inferior, that Russia could sneak in as many as 50 bombers through its holes, in a surprise attack.

Phyllis Schlafly and Chester Ward wrote in *Kissinger on the Couch*: "Every single key provision of both SALT agreements originated with Soviet strategic experts and planners in the Kremlin, approved by Leonid Brezhnev and his closest associates in the Politburo, and was passed by Soviet Ambassador Anatoly F. Dobrynin to Henry Kissinger, who then provided the rationalization for it and 'sold' it to President Nixon."

In the book, *An Analysis of SALT II*, compiled by Congress, it states: "In short, the Soviets will soon have a 'first strike capability' authorized by SALT. And when that capability is in hand, Soviet leaders may logically presume that the U.S. would not retaliate after a first strike ... Soviet leaders could reason that a U.S. President would not order a retaliation, knowing that his few surviving weapons could not annihilate Soviet society; and that a counterstrike by Soviet second-strike weapons would, in fact, utterly destroy the U.S. as a viable society ... The fact is that after a first strike, the Soviets would have more missiles and bombers in reserve for the second strike that the U.S. had to start with."

Despite this knowledge, disarmament has continued. Carter canceled plans for the production of the B-1 Strategic bomber, which was to be built by Rockwell International, General Electric, and the Boeing Co. The B-1 was to replace the obsolete B-52, and would have the capability of evading Soviet radar detection because of its ability to fly at high speeds, at low altitudes; and twice the speed of sound at higher altitudes. They would be able to carry a weapons payload twice the amount of the B-52, including 24 SRAM's (short-range attack missiles) inside its body, and eight on its wings. Internally, it can carry 75,000 pounds of conventional bombs, in addition to 40,000 externally. Its take-off distance is half that of the B-52, giving it access to more areas.

Since 1961, about 1,000 of our B-57 strategic bombers have been phased out, and the supersonic B-58's were deactivated in 1970.

The Russians, however, produced their delta-wing supersonic 'Backfire' bomber, which has a maximum range of over 5,000 miles, and can travel 1,500 mph. This means that they can be launched from bases in the Siberia, can cross the United States to refuel in Cuba, or somewhere else in Latin America. They were not covered by SALT.

Also, not included in SALT, were Russia's mobilized ICBM's. They can be hidden, and there is no way to keep track of how many they have, The U.S. had planned to have 200 MX missiles, each armed with ten nuclear warheads, hidden throughout 4,600 shelters in the obscure valleys of Nevada and Utah, which could be moved periodically, so that Russian spy satellites couldn't pinpoint their exact location. It would have taken two Russian missiles at each site to be sure of neutralizing it, which is more than they have. This would give the U.S. time to retaliate with stationery missile silos. The MX system, with its 2,000 warheads, would have the capability of devastating the Soviet Union. The idea for the MX was opposed, and dropped from consideration.

Soviet fixed silos are designed to refire, ours are not; and they have at least 1,000 extra missiles for refiring. They also have larger missiles, giving them a 6-1 advantage in firepower.

The Soviet's SS-9 Scarp Rocket can lift five times the load that the U.S.'s LGM-30 G Minuteman missile (which has 3 MIRV warheads) can, and hurl a 35-kiloton multiple warhead close to 6,600 miles, enabling it to destroy a group of U.S. ICBM silos. The SS-18 is so accurate, that at the most, it would miss by only 400 yards. It can carry a 20-megaton warhead, or three smaller warheads, each independently aimed. It can even carry 14 one-megaton warheads, all of which could directed to different locations, delivering enough explosive power to destroy a large city. With a single warhead, the missile can travel 5,700 miles, but only 4,700 with a multiple warhead. The SS-19, which is smaller, can only carry six warheads. With their increased number of warheads, and improved accuracies, the Pentagon indicated that Russia's SS-18 and SS-19 missiles could destroy America's land-based missile force of 1,000 Minuteman and 54 Titans in a single barrage, giving them a first-strike capability. Russia's biggest missile can carry 30 warheads, while our largest can only carry three 1-megaton warheads. Keep in mind, Russia also has many small missiles, such as the SS-20, a mobile multiple warhead missile, with a range of over 5,000 miles, that would be effective in taking out NATO ports and airfields, and with the addition of a rocket booster, could reach the United States. It was not covered by SALT. The Russians also developed the SS-24, a rail-mobile missile, and the SS-25, a road-mobile missile.

In 1977, Brezhnev called for a joint renunciation of neutron weapons, and in 1978, Carter said they wouldn't be produced. However, in 1981, President Reagan made the decision to begin production of the Neutron bomb, and Russia's edge in strategic weapons didn't seem that important after this addition to our nuclear arsenal. The Lance missile, and eight-inch artillery shells in the U.S. were furnished with a radiation enhanced warhead, which contained a radioactive isotope known as tritium, that produces far more radiation, and far less explosion and heat than conventional nuclear weapons. The result is that they kill people, without that much damage to surrounding buildings. It was designed to stop Russian tanks in Europe. The Tass News Agency in Russia responded by saying: "It seems that the same cannibalistic instincts prevail now in the White House by which in 1945 the then President Truman was guided when ordering the use of atomic weapons."

America had an edge with the Navy's nuclear-powered, nuclear-armed Polaris submarines. While at sea, they can't be detected, yet they can track Russian subs because of their ultra-sensitive electronic surveillance system. Knowing this, Russia stepped up the development of their long-range missiles. The Polaris subs can fire 16 missiles (each having ten warheads), in eight minutes to hit 160 targets, hundreds of miles apart, from a location almost 3,000 miles away, The Soviets began producing their larger Delta-class submarine, the Typhoon, which at 25,000-30,000 tons, is the world's largest. It carries 20 SLBM SS-N-20 intercontinental nuclear missiles, which have a range of 4,800 miles, farther than ours. It is capable of striking any target in the United States from protected Soviet waters. The Typhoon subs, built at Severodvinsk, the world's largest submarine production yard, are designed to operate under the Arctic Ocean ice cap. They also began producing the Soviet submarines with torpedo-proof titanium hulls,

Even though Russia had more tanks than we did, the NATO force tanks, for example, had about 193,000 anti-tank missiles, which was nine times the number that was in the arsenal of the Warsaw Pact. They are accurate from distances up to two miles away, which is outside the range of Russia's tanks. However, Russia developed the T-80 tank, which has an armor consisting of a honeycomb process which combines steel, ceramics, and aluminum to create a substance that is three times stronger, yet weighs little more.

In testimony before the Senate Armed Services Committee, Harold Brown, Carter's Secretary of Defense, said: "The United States is not now inferior to the Soviet Union in overall military strength." Yet, the figures available during the SALT talks, indicated that Russia was outspending us 3-1 for strategic arms, had a 2-1 advantage over us in manpower, 2-1 advantage over us in offensive strategic weapons, 2-1 in major surface combat ships and subs, 2-1 advantage in helicopter production, a 3-1 advantage in nuclear-powered subs, a 4-1 advantage in tanks and artillery, a 5-1 advantage in naval ships, a 5-1 edge in the production of tanks and combat vehicles, a 6-1 edge in nuclear firepower (megatonage), a 7-1 advantage in artillery, a 10-1 advantage in fighter bombers, a 47-1 advantage in defensive strategic weapons, and a 100-1 advantage in regular ammunition. Brown did admit, later, in January, 1979, that the Russian military was "potentially very dangerous to us."

The Soviet nuclear war plan, called the Red Integrated Strategic Operations Plant (RISOP) by the Pentagon, is believed to include over 2,500 targets: 1,000 Minuteman and ICBM silos, 100 ICBM launch control centers, and 50 command and control facilities and nuclear weapons storage depots; 54 nuclear bomber and bomber dispersal bases and 3 naval bases that service missile-firing submarines;

475 naval bases, airfields, ports, terminals, camps, depots and other military installations; 150 industrial production facilities that have Defense Department contracts for $1 million or more a year in military equipment; close to 325 electric power plants that generate nearly 70% of the nation's electricity; about 150 oil refineries that produce about 70% of the country's petroleum products; about 200 'soft' targets including economic communications, transportation, chemical, and civilian leadership targets.

The propaganda put out by our government, painted this scenario: After a massive surprise first strike by the Russians, at least 120 bombers, 17 Poseidon submarines, and 700 land-based ICBM's, totaling some 5,000 nuclear weapons would survive, and have the capability of destroying 80% of Russia's industrial base and 90% of its military installations, other than missile silos, killing between 20 and 95 million people, depending on their civil defense preparedness. For some reason, the United States government tried to disguise, and hide the fact, that we may no longer be the most powerful nation on Earth. Not only are they hiding it, but continue to make it worse with further plans for disarmament.

On December 8, 1987, Russian leader Mikhail Gorbachev and President Reagan signed the Intermediate-Range Nuclear Forces (INF) Treaty, which was to eliminate all medium and short range nuclear missiles. It was ratified, with conditions, by the Senate, on May 27, 1988.

At the time of SALT, out of 27 Summit Agreements with Russia, they had broken or cheated on all but one, and that includes the Nuclear Test Ban Treaty of 1962, the ABM Treaty of 1972, SALT I, and SALT II. They cheated on the INF Treaty of 1989, and did not fully comply with the Conventional Forces in Europe (CFE) Treaty of 1991. Many wars or confrontations since SALT I, had been started by, or influenced by Russia in one way or another. They have been fought by their proxies, satellite allies, or agents; countries protected by friendship treaties; or they have used their veto power in the United Nations.

George Washington said: "The best way to insure peace is to be prepared for war." At that time, we were not ready for war. Admiral Elmo R. Zumwalt, former Navy Chief of Operations, said at the Australian Naval Institute Seminar in February, 1979: "It is the professional judgment of senior officials in the United States that our Navy has only a 35% probability of winning a conventional naval war against the Soviet Union. Our military knows this, and so does theirs. About the only people who do not know it are the general public in the United States and Australia. Nor do they know that a nuclear exchange in 1981 on present trends would result in about 160 million dead in the United States." England's Winston Spencer Churchill (nephew of the former Prime Minister) said in a 1977 speech to a meeting of the National Association of Freedom: "The Soviet build-up is far beyond any requirements of self-defense, indeed the Soviets are building the greatest war machine the world has ever seen. This is more than a challenge to the West—it is the most deadly threat to freedom and to peace any generation has ever known."

In December, 1979, over 50,000 Soviet soldiers moved into the country of Afghanistan with tanks and helicopters; and by January, there were close to 100,000 Russian troops in positions throughout the country. There were reports that Soviet Army officers were arming and training Baluchi tribesmen in southern Afghanistan, who had long sought their own homeland. They live in the region covering parts of Afghanistan, Iran and Pakistan, along the strategic coasts of the Arabia Sea and the Gulf of Oman. Afghan Minister for Foreign Affairs, Lieutenant Colonel Faiz Mohammed Khan, a member of the pro-Moscow faction of the Afghan Communist Party, said that Russia would take over the Baluchistan section of Iran and Pakistan, which is all that separated them from the Indian Ocean. It was believed that the intent of the Soviets, was to gain access to the Ocean, where they would be able to control the Strait of Hormuz, in the Arabian Sea, where much of the world's oil supply is shipped from. Khan hinted, that since more than half of the students that held our hostages in Iran were pro-Soviet Communists, the Russians may have instigated the incident, hoping that it would escalate into a full-blown confrontation, so that the Soviet Union could invoke a 1921 treaty with Iran that would give them a right to send in troops if their southern border was threatened.

During the years when Hitler came to power in Nazi Germany, Russia made the prediction: "We will take Iran. Not by direct intervention, but it will fall into our hands like an overripe piece of fruit." An issue of *World Crisis* (published by Kilbrittain Newspapers Ltd. of Dublin, Ireland) reported during the early 1970's: "...Russia is planning a new offensive in the Middle East. Our precise and categorical information is that Russia plans to have totally taken over Southern Africa, all the Middle East, and Western Europe by January 8-9, 1984." Alexander Ginzburg, the exiled Russian human rights activist, said that America is threatened by "expansionist Russian ambitions," but won't recognize the danger until "it comes to Mexico or Canada." Thomas J. Watson, Jr., the American Ambassador to Russia, told President Reagan: "I perceive the world to be more dangerous than it has ever been in its history." The January, 1981, *Bulletin* of the Atomic Scientists said: "We feel impelled to record and emphasize the accelerating drift toward a disaster in almost all realms of social activity, Accordingly, we have decided to move the hands of the Bulletin's clock-symbol of the world's approach to nuclear doomsday— from seven to four minutes (each minute represents a year) before midnight (nuclear disaster)."

THE END OF COMMUNISM?

Mikhail Gorbachev, the youngest member of the Soviet Politburo, was chosen to be the General Secretary of the Communist Party. He participated in four Summit meetings with Reagan, and in 1987, initiated a program of reforms to bring democracy to their political process. The reforms were denounced by some Eastern bloc countries and old-line communists. A decline in the economy, the worst since World War II, developed an atmosphere of unrest. This is the same Gorbachev, who made the following statement, which was printed by *Pravda* on December 11, 1984: "In the struggle for peace and social progress the Communist Party of the Soviet Union pursues a consistent policy of rallying the forces of the international communist and working-class movement in every possible way. We uphold the historical justness of the great ideas of Marxism-Leninism, and along with all the revolutionary and peace loving forces of mankind, stand for social progress, and peace and security for all nations. This is what should determine the resolute nature of our propaganda."

Gorbachev said in November, 1987: "In our work and worries, we are motivated by those Leninist ideals and noble endeavors and goals which mobilized the workers of Russian seven decades ago to fight for the new and happy world of socialism. Perestroika (restructuring) is a continuation of the October Revolution." He also said: "Gentlemen, Comrades, do not be concerned about all you hear about glasnost and perestroika and democracy in the coming years. These are primarily for outward consumption. There will be no significant internal change within the Soviet Union, other than for cosmetic purposes. Our purpose is to disarm the Americans and let them fall asleep." On another occasion he said: "We are moving toward a new world, the world of Communism. We shall never turn off that road."

In February, 1989, after a futile eight year guerrilla war against government rebels in Afghanistan, the Soviets pulled their troops out of the country. The Communist super-power had lost a lot of the prestige that years of propaganda had built up, and the embarrassing defeat signaled the beginning of the end.

Gorbachev said: "We are not going to change Soviet power, of course, or abandon its fundamental principles, but we acknowledge the need for changes that will strengthen socialism." In October, 1989, Gorbachev said: "The concept, the main idea, lies in the fact that we want to give a new lease on life to socialism through perestroika and to reveal the potential of the socialist system." Also in 1989, he said: "Through perestroika we want to give Socialism a second wind. To achieve this, the Communist Party of the Soviet Union returns to the origins and principles of the Bolshevik Revolution, to the Leninist ideas about the construction of a new society." He said in December, 1989: "Today we have perestroika, the salvation of socialism, giving it a second breath, revealing everything good which is in the system." He also said: "I am a Communist, a convinced Communist. For some that may be a fantasy. But for me, it is my main goal." In June, 1990, he said: "I am now, just as I've always been, a convinced Communist. It's useless to deny the enormous and unique contribution of Marx, Engels and Lenin to the history of social thought and to modern civilization as a whole."

On August 19, 1991, a report from Russia indicated that Gorbechev had become ill, and the Vice-President had taken over the country, imposing a state of emergency. In reality, the military, the KGB, and communist hardliners had initiated a coup to take over the government. Or at least that is what they wanted us to think. It is the belief of Donald S. McAlvany, who publishes the *McAlvany Intelligence Advisor*, that the coup was a hoax. He reported that all eight coup leaders were Gorbachev appointees, and coup leader, Gennady Yanayev, referred to himself as the "acting President," saying that Gorbachev would return to power after he recovered from his "illness." In all past coups and revolutions, the KGB would have killed Gorbachev, and other reform leaders; but they weren't even arrested. Only a minimal amount of troops participated in the coup, the internal or international lines of communication were not cut, the press was not controlled, and the airports were not closed. A very strange "coup" indeed.

Boris Yeltsin, the President of the Russian Republic, denounced the coup, and called for a show of force, which produced about 50,000 demonstrators at the

Russian parliament. The picture of him on top of a Soviet tank, in open defiance of the Communist hardliners, was an indelible image in the hearts of the Soviet people, and the world. This Russian "John Wayne" had joined the Communist Party in 1961, at the age of 30, and by December, 1985, had been appointed head of the 1.2 million member Moscow City Party Committee, the largest Communist organization in the Soviet Union. However, he resigned from the Communist Party in July, 1990, and was now known as a "non-Communist reformer."

By August 21, 1991, the coup had failed, and Gorbachev was restored as President. Of the eight coup leaders, one was said to have committed suicide, and may have been murdered; the other seven were tried and imprisoned. In the past, such men would have just been shot, which gives credibility to the theory that the coup was a hoax. They were later released from prison.

Shortly after the coup, the President of Soviet Georgia accused Gorbachev of masterminding the coup. Eduard Shevardnadze, Gorbachev's former foreign minister, even said that he may have been behind it. Private polls indicated that 62% of the Soviet people believed the coup to be staged. So what did the coup accomplish? In light of the sagging economy, the coup was to give Gorbachev the appearance of grabbing control back from the old-guard Communists, which would boost his popularity with the Soviet people, and make the West think that there was a potential for widespread democratic reforms in Russia.

On August 24th, Gorbachev resigned as the leader of the Communist Party, and recommended that its central committee be discontinued. On August 29th, the Soviet parliament voted to suspend all activities of the Communist Party. Political insiders believe that the Communist Party has not discontinued, but has undergone a massive restructuring to streamline it, which will be reborn with a new image and a new name, but with the same old goals. The Communist Party in Italy became known as the Democratic Party; in Poland, it became known as the Social Democratic Party; and in Romania, it was called the New Salvation Front.

On September 2nd, Gorbachev announced that his country was "on the brink of catastrophe," and that all authority was to be transferred to himself, the Presidents of the ten independent republics, and an appointed legislative council, which would be the basis for a new Soviet Union. However, Gorbachev would not be the one to lead it. The coup was not able to rally the support that he needed, and on December 25th, 1991, he resigned, and said: "I hereby discontinue my activities at the post of president of the Union of Soviet Socialist Republics. We're now living in a New World!" The next day, the Soviet Union officially broke up, ending the domination of the Communist Party.

Yeltsin became President of a Russian Federation known as the Union of Soviet Sovereign Republics. His first actions were to eliminate state subsidies on most goods and services, which caused prices to rise; and initiated a program to privatize thousands of large and medium-sized state-owned businesses.

The Strategic Arms Reduction Treaty (START I) had been signed July 31, 1991, in Moscow, by Gorbachev and President Bush, and it was to reduce the amount of strategic offensive arms by about 30%, in three phases, over the next seven years. It was approved by the Senate on October 1, 1992, and the Russian Supreme Soviet on November 4, 1992, but because of the negotiations with the four former Soviet republics, which are now independent, the transfer of all nuclear weapons to the Russian Republic had not been completed. The republics of Belarus and Kazakhstan have each ratified START, and have acceded to the Nuclear Non-proliferation Treaty as non-nuclear nations; but not the Ukraine, which was still negotiating with Russia to transfer their weapons. Meanwhile, On January 3, 1993, President Bush and Boris Yeltsin signed START II, which became the biggest disarmament pact in history. It called for both sides to reduce their long-range nuclear arsenals to about a third of their current levels within ten years, and totally eliminating all land-based multiple warhead missiles. It was intended to eliminated those weapons that would be used in a first-strike situation.

President Clinton and Yeltsin signed the Comprehensive Nuclear Test Ban Treaty (CTB) in 1996, with some other nations, which banned the testing of nuclear weapons. The U.S. Senate refused to ratify this Treaty in 1999.

In 2001 Russian President Putin, and President George W. Bush discussed the possibility of limiting the number of warheads to about 1/3 of what was called for in START II, and it was signed in May, 2002.

Eleina Bonner, the widow of Sakharov, said: "The point is that the Communist goal is fixed and changeless it never varies one iota from their objective of world domination, but if we judge them only by the direction in which they seem to be going, we shall be deceived." Former NATO Supreme Allied Commander Bernard W. Rogers said: "The Soviet goal remains world domination." In 1981, Anatoly Golitsyn, a former major in the KGB, who defected to the West, wrote a book called *New Lies For Old: The Communist Strategy of Deception and Disinformation*, which was published in 1984. He outlined virtually everything that had taken place in Russia, such as the tearing down of the Berlin Wall and the reunification of East and West Germany; the partial relinquishing of their control of Eastern Europe; and the declaration that communism is dead. He wrote that their plan was to deceive the West into believing that the Soviet Union was falling apart, their satellites splintering, and its economy in shambles. The facade of weakness and instability would be part of a massive deception staged by the Kremlin to extort aid from the West, and to get the United States to withdraw troops out of Western Europe. It was Lenin who said: "We advance through retreat." He also said: "When we are weak, boast of strength ... when we are strong, feign weakness."

At various times during the history of the Soviet Union, they have appealed to the U.S. for help, and have gotten it, mostly through deception, and the efforts of apologists and traitors in our government. But this is the first time that Russia has made this kind of concession. They have made it appear that communism is dead, that democracy is sweeping the former Soviet Union and its satellite countries, and that they want to be part of the new family of nations known as the New World Order. But, with their record, can they be trusted? If you consider all the evidence that was put forth, it just seems to be another ploy by the Soviets to undermine America. A respected Sovietologist has stated his belief that the motive behind the Russian's actions, and their plea for financial aid, is not so much need, but an attempt to destroy the U.S. economy by defaulting on an international loan that could be as much as $100 billion, which could precipitate a financial collapse.

Yeltsin ended up addressing a joint session of Congress to appeal for economic aid. The Bush Administration shut down Clark Air Force Base in the Philippines, and announced in September, 1991, that it was also closing the Subic Bay Naval Base, and would completely withdraw from the island. They have also pulled out of, and are closing 79 military bases in Western Europe; and have withdrawn U.S. nuclear missiles, tanks, planes, and troops. The U.S. also announced the withdrawal of troops from South Korea. In September, 1993, Congress approved the recommendation of the Base Closure and Realignment Commission to close 130 domestic military bases, and scale down 45 others. Between 1990 and 1992, the total number of military personnel has decreased by over 8%, and the trend to scale down our military was continuing. The U.S. is virtually shutting down our tank, submarine (only producing one a year, compared to one every six weeks for the Russians), and F-16 production lines. On June 7, 1991, the House of Representatives voted to discontinue U.S. bomber production. The House also voted to slash production of submarine launched ballistic missiles (SLBM's), to coincide with the decrease of our submarine fleet, even though the Soviets have consistently outproduced us. Our government had set a goal of spending only 3.6% of GNP on defense by 1996.

Lenin said: "They disarm, we build." Nikita Krushchev said in a January 14, 1969 speech to the Supreme Soviet: "The Soviets intend to conceal vast reserves of missiles and warheads, hiding them in places throughout the expansive Soviet Union where the imperialists could not spot them. Later, they could be launched in a nuclear war." An official in the Soviet Council of Ministers said in 1987: "Perestroika is expressly designed to enhance Soviet military capability and combat readiness."

With military actions in Bosnia and Kosovo in Yugoslavia, Afghanistan, and now Iraq, our military has become stretched around the world; and it has become preoccupied domestically with the "War on Terrorism." Bush's growing interaction with Putin seems to indicate that our government has continued to fall for the massive deception being put forth by the Russian Federation, and continues to make our country vulnerable, while it looks for ways to continue dismantling our military in the name of creating a leaner, meaner more modern fighting force. Meanwhile, the Soviets are watching, and waiting, preparing to implement the next stage of their master plan.

THE ULTIMATE GOAL OF COMMUNISM

Remember how communism started? It was a created, nurtured, and supported by the Illuminati as an opposing political ideology in order to achieve their goals. There is certainly enough evidence to indicate massive collusion, but as far as being controlled by the Illuminati, here is what Gary Allen wrote in his book *None Dare Call It Conspiracy*: "Indicative of this strange event which occurred in October of 1964. David Rockefeller, president of the Chase Manhattan Bank and Chairman of the Board of the Council on Foreign Relations, took a vacation in the Soviet Union. This is a peculiar place for the world's greatest 'imperialist' to take his vacation, since much of the communist propaganda deals with taking all of David's wealth away from him and distributing it to 'the people.' A few days after

Rockefeller ended his 'vacation' in the Kremlin, Nikita Khrushchev was recalled from a vacation at a Black Sea resort to learn that he had been fired. How strange! As far as the world knew, Khrushchev was the absolute dictator of the Soviet government and, more important, head of the Communist Party which runs the USSR. Who has the power to fire the man who was supposedly the absolute dictator? Did David Rockefeller journey to the Soviet Union to fire an employee? Obviously the position of Premier in the Soviet Union is a figurehead with the true power residing elsewhere. Perhaps in New York."

Rockefeller had just opened a Hong Kong branch of the Chase Manhattan, for trade with China, but since trade relations had broken off between Russia and China, because of an overbearing Khrushchev, Rockefeller got rid of the problem in order to stabilize the situation. He later formed the National Council for U.S./Red China Trade, with Gabriel Hauge (Manufacturers Hanover Trust), W. M. Blumenthal (Bendix Corp.), John W. Hanley (Monsanto Chemicals), Donald Burnham (Westinghouse Electric), Thornton Wilson (Boeing Aircraft), William Hewitt (Deere & Co.), and Lucien Pye (Massachusetts Institute of Technology).

In the *Communist Manifesto*, Karl Marx wrote about the abolition of private property, a progressive income tax, a central bank, and state control of the family, religion, and education, which are all aspects of a Socialist government, the prelude to the utopian goal of Communism. Yet, they are part of our own political system, which has lead to the 'convergence theory.' The theory is, that while the Soviets would slowly move to the political right, the United States would be pushed to the left, with the two meeting in the middle as Social Democrats. And from there, it would only a small step to a socialist one-world government, or the New World Order. Norman Thomas (1884-1968), known as the "conscience of America," who ran for President six times as a candidate of the Socialist Party, said: "The American people will never knowingly adopt socialism. But, under the name of 'liberalism,' they will adopt every fragment of the socialist program, until one day America will be a socialist nation, without knowing how it happened." In a February 6, 1994 speech to leaders of the group United We Stand, H. Ross Perot said: "I think we may be the only great country in the world moving toward great socialism."

It is apparent that the Russian Federation will continue to abolish the use of the word 'Communism' in lieu of the word 'socialism,' in order to gain the acceptance of Western Europe. The 1990 Communist Congress stated: "...the USSR is in a transition from a unitary state to a friendship of nations." They will be brought into future 'collective-security' agreements, as protection against Third World dictators and terrorism. The amplification of these agreements are what the United Nations has long sought, a global reactionary force made up of American, Russian, European and Third World troops.

CHAPTER EIGHT

THE ILLUMINATI INFLUENCE ON INTERNATIONAL AFFAIRS

THE UNITED NATIONS

Jan Tinbergen (from the Netherlands), the winner of the 1969 Nobel Prize for Economics, has said: "Mankind's problems can no longer be solved by national governments; what is needed is a world government." Although this mentality is becoming more pronounced, getting to that point has taken many years.

In 1939, Dr. James T. Shotwell organized a group known as the Commission to Study the Organization of Peace, which was made up of a number of small subcommittees. One of these, the Subcommittee on International Organization was chaired by Sumner Wells, the Under Secretary of State, and its purpose was to plan postwar policy. Shotwell and Isaiah Bowman, members of the subcommittee, were also members of the League of Nations Association, and had been on Col. House's staff at the Paris Peace Conference in 1918, where plans for the League of Nations had been laid out. This established a direct link between the League of Nations and the United Nations. The subcommittee's work formed the basis for the Charter of the United Nations, and was the means by which the Council on Foreign Relations was able to condition the Congress, and the people of the country to accept the United Nations.

Two weeks after the attack on Pearl Harbor, Cordell Hull, the Secretary of State, sent a letter to President Roosevelt recommending the establishment of a Presidential Advisory Committee on Post War Foreign Policy, which actually became a planning group for the United Nations. Ten of the Fourteen Committee members came from the CFR. Roosevelt's "Four Freedoms Speech" planted the seed for the United Nations. A conference held in Washington, D.C between the representatives of the 26 nations that had banded together against the axis powers, gave momentum to the movement by issuing the "Declaration of the Twenty-Six United Nations" on January 1, 1942. In February, 1942, the State Department's Advisory Committee on Post-War Foreign Policy secretly worked out more details. One of their reports said: "Its discussions throughout were founded upon belief in the unqualified victory by the United Nations. It predicted, as an absolute prerequisite for world peace, the continuing strength of the United Nations through unbroken cooperation after the war."

In 1942, *Free World*, a periodical published by the International Free World Association (organized in 1941), they stated that their objective was to create the "machinery for a world government in which the United Nations will serve as a nucleus ... in order to prepare in time the foundations for a future world order."

Leading diplomats from the United States, Russia, England, and China, attended preliminary meetings in October, 1943, at a conference in Moscow. In November, Cordell Hull "secured the consent of Stalin to establish a general organization ... for the maintenance of international peace and security," and in proposing it to Roosevelt, made it appear as though it was an American project. Among the leading U.S. figures who were involved in the planning of the United Nations: Alger Hiss, Harry Dexter White, Virginius Frank Coe, Noel Field, Laurance Duggan, Henry Julian Wadleigh, John Carter Vincent, David Weintraub, Nathan Gregory Silvermaster, Harold Glasser, Victor Perlo, Irving Kaplan, Solomon Adler, Abraham George Silverman, William L. Ullman, William H. Taylor, and Dean Acheson. All of these men, were either communists, or had pro-communist sympathies.

The idea for the United Nations was officially proposed in 1944, at the secret Dumbarton Oaks Conference, where the framework was developed, and the final plans laid out. The conference was attended by representatives from the U.S., England, and Russia, and it was all coordinated by Alger Hiss. Hiss was a Trustee of the Woodrow Wilson Foundation, a director of the Executive Committee of the American Association for the United Nations, a director of the American Peace Society, a Trustee of the World Peace Foundation, a director of the American Institute of Pacific Relations, and President of the Carnegie Endowment for International Peace. In 1950, he was convicted of perjury, and sent to prison. Exposed as a Soviet spy, his communist activities extended back to 1939. Other Americans who attended: Harry Dexter White, Virginius Coe, Noel Field, Laurance Duggan, Harry Wadleigh, John Carter Vincent, David Weintraub, Nathan Silvermaster, Harold Glasser, Victor Perlo, Irving Kaplan, Solomon Adler, Abraham Silverman, William Ullman, William Taylor, and John Foster Dulles (who had been hired by Joseph Stalin to be the Soviet Union's legal counsel in the United States).

In February, 1945, at the Yalta Conference, President Roosevelt, Winston Churchill, and Joseph Stalin agreed to the plans proposing the establishment of the United Nations.

The April, 1945 issue of *Political Affairs*, the official publication of the U.S. Communist Party, said: "Great popular support and enthusiasm for the United Nations policies should be built up, well organized and fully articulated ... The opposition must be rendered so impotent that it will be unable to gather any significant support in the Senate against the United Nations Charter and the treaties which will follow."

On June 26, 1945, the San Francisco Conference, attended by 50 nations, established the United Nations, and adopted the Charter which had been drafted. The General Assembly held their first meeting in London, on January 10, 1946. The U.S. Senate ratified the UN Charter with only two dissenting votes; and in December, 1946, John D. Rockefeller, Jr. donated an 18-acre tract of land in Manhattan (which he had purchased for $8,500,000, with New York City contributing the remaining $4,250,000), to provide the organization with a permanent headquarters, which is located between First Avenue and Roosevelt Drive, and East 42nd and East 48th Streets.

The United World Federalists were established on February 22, 1947, by two CFR members, Norman Cousins and James P. Warburg, when the Americans United for World Government, World Federalists, Massachusetts Committee for World Federation, Student Federalists, World Citizens of Georgia, and World Republic, all merged. Their goal was to endorse "the efforts of the United Nations to bring about a world community favorable to peace ... (and) to strengthen the United Nations into a world government of limited powers adequate to prevent a war and having direct jurisdiction over the individual." Nixon said of them: "Your organization can perform an important service by continuing to emphasize that world peace can only come through world law. Our goal is world peace." Ronald Reagan was associated with them before he became a conservative. Various other left-wing organizations have also defended and supported this international organization.

The United Nations, "open to all peace-loving nations as sovereign equals," is made up of 191 member nations, and exists primarily to maintain peace and security; develop international cooperation in solving the political, economic, social, cultural, and humanitarian problems of the world; and ensure the existence of friendly relations. Many of the countries are non-democratic, being ruled by dictators, royal families, military officers, or one-party governments.

As you have read, there was a strong communist influence during the establishment of the organization, and all indications are that it has maintained a socialistic slant to its affairs. Earl Browder, a former leader in the U.S. Communist Party, said in his book *Victory and After*: "The American Communists worked energetically and tirelessly to lay the foundations for the United Nations, which we were sure would come into existence." Alger Hiss, who was later convicted as a communist traitor, became the acting Secretary-General after the establishment of the UN. The April 16, 1945 issue of *Time* magazine called him "one of the State Department's brighter young men." It was Hiss, and Joseph E. Johnson (who later became Secretary of the Bilderbergers) who wrote much of the UN Charter, patterning it after the Constitution of Russia, and the *Communist Manifesto*. An Associated Press dispatch from April 7, 1970 which appeared in the *Los Angeles Times* said: "Secretary-General U Thant praised Vladimir I. Lenin, founder of the Soviet Union, as a political leader, whose ideals were reflected in the UN Charter." It contained self-granted powers for a one-world government. Even their official seal, which was similar to Russia's, was designed by Aldo Marzani, a socialist.

Trygve Lie, the first official UN Secretary-General, was a high-ranking member of Norway's Social Democratic Labor Party, which was an offshoot of the Third Communist International. Dag Hammarskjold, the second Secretary-General, was a Swedish socialist who openly pushed communist policies, and U Thant, the third Secretary, was a Marxist.

In 1978, Arkady Shevchenko, an ex-KGB agent, and Under Secretary for Political and Security Council Affairs, who defected, said that many Soviet UN delegates worked for the KGB.

With the United States having only one vote within the socialist-dominated organization, we were powerless to prevent the socialists from using diplomacy to achieve their goals. Nonaligned nations, a majority of the delegates, voted with the communists 85% of the time in the General Assembly; and in 1987, member nations voted with the U.S. only 18.7% of the time. In fact, on key issues, the UN has voted against the United States nearly 85% of the time.

The Constitutional right of Congress to declare war has been completely transferred to the UN Military Committee, and as such, they can order us into war at any time, without our consent, as they did in Korea. The United States didn't make the treaty with Japan to end World War II, it was made with the UN. The UN refused to come to the aid of China in 1949, ignored the Hungarian freedom fighters in 1956, shunned the Tibetans when they were attacked by Chinese Communists, and in the early 1960's, supported the communist attempt to overthrow the African country of Katanga. They even criticized the American invasion of Grenada, which sought to stem communist activity in the Caribbean. Remember, the Under Secretary for Political and Security Council Affairs had always been a Russian, who along with the Chairman of the UN Military Staff Committee was responsible for all UN military action. Prior to the Korean War, the Chairman was Lt. Gen. Alexandre Vasiliev, who took a leave of absence from the position to command the communist troops, and actually gave the orders to attack. He continued to get valuable information about the UN's military plans from his handpicked successor, Gen. Ivan A. Skliaro.

In 1915, in No. 40 of the Russian document *The Socialist Democrat*, Lenin called for a "United States of the World." The Communist International in 1936, said that a world dictatorship "can be established only by victory of socialism in different countries or groups of countries, after which the Proletariat Republics would unite on federal lines with those already in existence, and this system would expand ... at length forming the World Union of Soviet Socialist Republics." In the November, 1946 issue of the communist publication *Bolshevik*, it said: "The masses know that peace is possible only on the basis of cooperation among the existing states ... The Soviet Union is fighting to have the United Nations as effective as possible." On October 7, 1961 *People's World*, a West Coast Communist Party newspaper, published an editorial, "Save the UN," which said: "The UN commands a great reservoir of support in our country ... People should write President Kennedy, telling him— do not withdraw from the UN, restore the UN to the Grand Design of Franklin Roosevelt— the design for peaceful coexistence." The Preamble to the Constitution of the U.S. Communist Party, urges the "strengthening of the United Nations as a universal instrument of peace."

The Preamble of the UN Charter says: "We the people of the United Nations, determined to save succeeding generations from the scourge of war..." In light of this, you should be aware of what Albert Einstein said after the first atomic bomb was dropped on Hiroshima on August 6, 1945: "The secret of the bomb should be committed to a World Government and the U.S.A. should announce its readiness to give it to a World Government."

According to the *Congressional Record* of June 7, 1949, on pages 7356 and 7357, this was the wording for HCR64, a joint resolution (corresponds to Senate Concurrent Resolution 56, the Tobey or 'World Federalist' Resolution) that was introduced in the House of Representatives: "Resolved by the House of Representatives (the Senate concurring) that it is the sense of the Congress that it should be a fundamental objective of the foreign policy of the United States to support and strengthen the United Nations and to seek its development into a world federation, open to all nations, with defined and limited powers adequate to preserve peace and prevent aggression through the enactment, interpretation and enforcement of world law." Concerning this Resolution, Cord Meyer, chairman of the National Executive Committee of the United World Federalists, said at a hearing before the Senate Subcommittee on the United Nations Charter: "We in the United States would be declaring our willingness to join with other nations in transferring to the UN constitutional authority to administer and enforce law that was binding on national governments and their individual citizens."

By February, 1950, after the public expressed their outrage over the Resolution, the Liberals who sponsored it turned their backs on it in an attempt to salvage their political reputations. Rep. Bernard W. Kearney (R-New York) said: "We signed the Resolution believing we were sponsoring a movement to set up a stronger power within the United Nations for world peace ... Then we learned that various organizations were working on state legislatures and on peace movements for world government action under which the entire U.S. Government would be submerged in a super world government ... Perhaps we should have read the fine print in the first place. We do not intend to continue in the role of sponsors of any movement which undermine U.S. sovereignty. Many Congressmen feel as I do. We will make our position thoroughly clear." Within two years, 18 of the 23 states which had passed the Resolution eventually rescinded it.

Information about HCR64 / SCR56 can be found in the infamous Document No. 87, *Review of the United Nations Charter: A Collection of Documents*, by the Senate Subcommittee on the United Nations Charter, and published by the Government Printing Office in 1954. It was reportedly given to each of the Senators at the time, and only two copies now remain in existence. This report blows the lid off of the U.S. Government's determination for one-world government. Also discussed are Senate Resolution 133, introduced July 8, 1949 by Sen. Sparkman (Democrat from Alabama) who said: "We can create now, with Russia if possible, without Russia if necessary an overwhelming collective front open to all nations under a law just to all." The report urged (p. 846): "American atomic, military, and economic superiority is only temporary. It is essential before that superiority is lost that there be created an international organization with strength to enforce the peace." Senate Concurrent Resolution 57, introduced July 26, 1949 by Sen. Kefauver (D-Tennessee) called for an Atlantic Union of Canada, England, France, the Netherlands, Belgium, Luxembourg, and the United States. The report said (p. 848): "The establishment of a federal union ... would involve not only basic economic and social changes but also important changes in the structure of the United States Government. It is very doubtful if the American people are ready to amend the Constitution to the extent necessary to give an Atlantic Union the powers it would need to be effective."

Senate Concurrent Resolution 66, introduced September 13, 1949 by Sen. Taylor (D-Idaho) called for the Charter of the United Nations to "be changed to provide a true world government constitution." He claimed: "Only a true world government can achieve everlasting peace." The report stated (p. 850): "Anything less than world government would be merely a stopgap." The existence of Document No. 87 proves that the government of the United States and the political leaders of this country are working behind the scenes to strengthen the United Nations and to move towards one-world government.

In 1953, during the World Federal Government Conference in Copenhagen, Denmark, UN supporters revealed plans to push for a revision of the UN Charter, which would provide for the UN to become a World Federal Government with a world legislature and court, mandatory universal membership with no right of secession; and a full and immediate disarmament which would be militarily supported by the UN. Another conference, in London, in 1954, by the World Movement for World Federation, also proposed similar ideas.

This movement to remove the sovereignty of the United States and member countries, convinced Senator John Bricker to propose his "Bricker Amendment" which would have placed in the U.S. Constitution, a safeguard against the possibility of a treaty which could result in a world government: "A provision of a Treaty or other international agreement which conflicts with this Constitution, or which is not made in pursuance thereof, shall not be supreme law of the land nor be of any force or effect." During debate on the Bill, Sen. Pat McCarren (D-Nevada) said of the powers provided to the UN by Articles 55 and 56 of the UN Charter: "The Congress of the United States, because of the power granted to it by treaty, could enact laws ... taking over all private and parochial schools, destroying all local school boards ... and substitute a federal system ... Congress could by law provide for censoring all press telegrams ... Congress could utilize this power to put into effect a complete system of socialized medicine, from cradle to grave ... even legislate compulsory labor, if it found that the goal of full employment required such legislation or would be served by it."

The Bricker Amendment was opposed by all the "one-world" organizations and internationalists like U.S. Supreme Court Justice William O. Douglas; Sen. Ralph Flanders (R-Vermont), Sen. Hubert Humphrey (D-Minnesota), John J. McCloy (former Assistant Secretary of Defense and former High Commissioner to Germany), Paul Hoffman (of the State Department), Thomas K. Finletter, John Foster Dulles (Secretary of State), and President Eisenhower, who said it would curtail the power of the Presidency. After a long, bitter fight, the Amendment failed by a vote of 60-31, just one vote short of the necessary two-thirds majority of the U.S. Senate.

H. G. Wells wrote in his 1933 book *The Shape of Things to Come*: "When the existing governments and ruling theories of life, the decaying religious and the decaying political forms of today, have sufficiently lost prestige through failure and catastrophe, then and then only will world-wide reconstruction be possible."

Robert M. Hutchins (former President of Rockefeller's University of Chicago) was the Chairman of the Committee to Form a World Government, who had drafted a new Constitution. On August 12, 1945, they said on a Round Table broadcast, that they wanted to turn control of our nation over to a Socialist world government. In Hutchin's 1947 book, *The Constitutional Foundations for World Order* (published for the Foundation for World Order), he says: "Tinkering with the United Nations will not help us, if we agree with the *New York Times* that our only hope is in the ultimate abolition of war through an ultimate world government." President Dwight D. Eisenhower said on October 31, 1956: "I am more deeply convinced that the United Nations represents the soundest hope for peace in the world."

A State Department document, #7277, called *Freedom From War: The United States' Program for General and Complete Disarmament in a Peaceful World*, revealed a plan to disarm the U.S. military, shut down bases, and to give the UN control of our Armed Forces, and nuclear weapons. The UN military arm would then be the world's police force to act as "peacekeepers." The document, which on September 1, 1961, was sent by courier to the UN Secretary General, suggested a "progressive reduction of the war-making capability of the nations and the simultaneous strengthening of international institutions to settle disputes and maintain the peace..." It was to be done through a three-step program:

> "The first stage would significantly reduce the capabilities of nations to wage war by reducing the armed forced of the nations ... nuclear capabilities would be reduced by treaties ... and UN peace-keeping powers would be strengthened ... The second stage would provide further substantial reductions in the armed forces and the establishment of a permanent international peace force within the United Nations ... The third stage would have the nations retaining only those forces required for maintaining internal order, but the United States would provide manpower for the United Nations Peace Force."

The plan called for "all weapons of mass destruction" to be eliminated, except for "those required for a United Nations Peace Force" (page 12, 1st paragraph); and (on page 16, 8th paragraph) to "keep the peace, all states will reaffirm their obligations under the UN Charter to refrain from the threat of use of any type armed force." I'm sure that this includes the disarming of American citizens. Sarah Brady, one of the leading proponents in this country against handguns, said: "Our task of creating a socialist America can only succeed when those who would resist us have been totally disarmed." Sen. Joseph S. Clark of Pennsylvania said during a March 1, 1962 debate on the Senate floor, that the program is "the fixed, determined, and approved policy of the government of the United States." The Program was later revised in *The Blueprint for the Peace Race*, which said on page 33: "...the Parties to the Treaty would progressively strengthen the United Nations Police Force ... until it had sufficient armed forces and armaments so that no state could challenge it." The Program was again revised by the present *Outline of Basic Provisions of a Treaty on General and Complete Disarmament in a Peaceful World*.

In 1961, during the Kennedy administration, Robert McNamara, McGeorge Bundy and Dean Rusk (all CFR members), initiated a secret study to study the direct and indirect ramifications of war, and how they could control the economy during peace-time. They wanted to know what situations the United States would be exposed to in the world if it moved from a period of war to a time of permanent peace, or as the Report said, "to consider the problems involved in the contingency of a transition to a general condition of peace, and to recommend procedures for dealing with this contingency." Conceivably, it would look for ways to slowly move this country into the New World Order. By 1963, fifteen experts (known as the SSG or Special Study Group) from various academic fields: psychology, anthropology, international law, biochemistry, physics, astronomy, mathematics, literature, history, military, economy, sociology, and industry. Their first and last meeting had taken place at Iron Mountain in Hudson, New York, the first secure underground records storage center designed to protect vital corporate records in case of a nuclear disaster.

There was some speculation that the think-tank known as the Hudson Institute actually conducted the study. The Institute was started in 1961, "to help determine the entire future of the U.S.— and, time permitting, much of the world beyond. Many of their fellows and members belonged to the CFR.

The long-term plan to control the population was said to have been completed in 1966. It was reported that President Johnson ordered the Report to be sealed, because with the knowledge it contained, the American people could have used it to prevent the takeover of their country during the early stages. The cover letter of the Report said: "Because of the unusual circumstances surrounding the establishment of this Group, and in view of the nature of its finding, we do not recommend that this Report be released for publication ... such actions would not be in the public interest ... a lay reader, unexposed to the exigencies of higher political or military responsibility, will misconstrue the purposed of this project, and the intent ...We urge that the circulation of the Report be closely restricted to those who's responsibilities require that they be apprised of its contents..."

The Report, in fact, appeared to be a blueprint for the future of this country, and contained recommendations that included plans for governmental control and manipulation, depopulation, gun control and disarmament, an international police force, and concentration camps.

One man, calling himself John Doe, who was involved in the Report, decided to release its contents, it was published in 1967 by Dial Press (a division of Simon and Schuster) as the *Report From Iron Mountain on the Possibility and Desirability of Peace*. Even though it was publicly denounced by the Establishment as a hoax, it was translated into fifteen languages.

The SSG concluded that peace "would almost certainly not be in the best interest of stable society," because War, was too much a part of the world economy, and therefore it was necessary to continue a state of war indefinitely:

"War has provided both ancient and modern societies with a dependable system for stabilizing and controlling national economies. No alternate method of control has yet been tested in a complex modern economy that has shown itself remotely comparable in scope or effectiveness. War fills certain functions essential to the stability of our society; until other ways of filling them are developed, the war system must be maintained, and improved in effectiveness."

It also said that war, "provides anti-social elements with an acceptable role in the social structure ... the younger, and more dangerous, of these hostile social groupings have been kept under control by the Selective Service System ... man destroys surplus members of his own species by organized warfare ... enables the physically deteriorating older generation to maintain control of the younger, destroying it if necessary."

The report also argued that the authority that the government exercised over the people came from its ability to wage war, and that without war the government might cease to exist: "War is virtually synonymous with nationhood. The elimination of war implies the inevitable elimination of national sovereignty and the traditional nation-state."

The Report covered a number of recommendations that the Federal government should do in the event that they were thrust into an era of peace:

> "(a) A comprehensive social-welfare program, directed toward maximum improvement of general conditions of human life; (b) A giant open-end space research program, aimed at unreachable targets; (c) A permanent, ritualized, ultra-elaborate disarmament inspection system, and variant of such a system."

It also recommended the invention of "alternate enemies."

Then in 1972, in a *New York Times* article, Leonard C. Lewin, a New York free lance writer and editor (*A Treasury of American Political Humor*), who wrote the introduction to the book, confessed to being the author of the Report, and said he wrote it "to caricature the bankruptcy of the think-tank mentality by pursuing its style of scientific thinking to its logical ends."

In 1996 Simon & Schuster reprinted the Report with a new introduction. Evidently the germination of the Report took place in 1966 when Victor Navasky (Publisher and Editorial Director of *The Nation*), who was editor of the *Monacle* a political satire magazine, read a *New York Times* article about the stock market declining because of a 'peace scare.' Navasky said something to Lewin who then wrote the report, and they presented the Report to E.L. Doctorow, Editor-in-Chief (and co-conspirator) of Dial Press, who agreed to publish it as nonfiction. Navasky said the purpose of the hoax was "to provoke thinking about the unthinkable— the conversion to a peacetime economy and the absurdity of the arms race."

However, some still believe the Report to be authentic because a large portion of it has come to pass.

At the Conference on Conditions of World Order, which met from June 12-19, 1965 (which no doubt led to the establishment of the Club of Rome), at the Villa Serbelloni (facilities obtained through the Rockefeller Foundation) in Bellagio, Italy, which was sponsored by the Congress for Cultural Freedom (with a grant from the Ford Foundation and the American Academy of Arts and Sciences), 21 scholars, writers and scientists from all over the world met to define the concepts of world order. A segment of their report, by Helio Jaguaribe said:

> "The establishment of world order depends not only on its intrinsic desirability and viability, but also on the support of men and groups who decide to dedicate themselves to the completion of such a goal. As increasing sectors of developed and underdeveloped societies begin to realize the urgent necessity of world order, the viability of its establishment, and the fact that it can be achieved by adopting measures which are reason-

able in themselves, none of the governments will be able to escape public pressure for establishing world order ... It is incumbent upon the intellectuals to play the decisive role in the formation of pressure groups in favor of world order ... the establishment of world order demands the mobilization of groups dedicated to international pressure for the gradual implantation of that world order ... the negotiated establishment of world order is theoretically possible and practically feasible since, in the last analysis, the probable effects of nuclear conflagration have made way an impractical alternative to the peaceful solution of contemporary problems."

On May 18, 1972, Roy Ash of the Office of Management and Budget during the Nixon Administration, said: "Within two decades the institutional framework for a World Economic Community will be in place ... (when) aspects of individual sovereignty will be given over to a supernational authority."

ABC-TV's Harry Reasoner (who later went to CBS) said on June 18, 1974: "The only eventual answer is some kind of World Government ... whether it is capitalist or communist."

President Ford called for the development of a global strategy and a policy concerning food and oil; and President Carter, in what he called an organization for the "world structure of peace," tried to persuade the Chinese to take part.

The *Borger New Herald* in Texas reported: "A meeting was held May 24, 1976 through July 4, 1976, in Valley Forge Park, King of Prussia, PA, to formulate a new World Constitution, elaborating a Bill of Human Rights for the world and setting up a permanent Secretariat of Human Rights there to superintend the Government of the World..." The World Constitution and Parliament Association (WCPA, located at 1480 Hoyt Street, Suite 31, Lakewood, CO) was established in 1959 by Philip Isely who had emerged during the 1940's as a leader in the one-world movement; as an organizer for the Action for World Federation from 1946-50 and the North American Council for the People's World Convention from 1954-58. The WCPA have assumed the task of trying to establish a New World Order, and have assembled a Provisional World Parliament. Their original "Agreement to Call a World Constitutional Convention" was first circulated from 1958-61, where it was signed by several thousand dignitaries. In 1965, work began on a world constitution, and a meeting was held in the City Hall of Wolfach, West Germany, in June, 1968. A second meeting, known as the World Constituent Assembly was held at Innsbruck, Austria, from June 16-29, 1977, to draft a "Constitution for the Federation of Earth," which was adopted by participants from 25 countries. It was revised in 1991. Reinhart Ruge, President of the WCPA said: "Only a full-scale world government will save the world from nuclear holocaust."

The Preamble of the Constitution began: "Realizing that Humanity today has come to a turning point in history and that we are on the threshold of a new world order, which promises to usher in an era of peace, prosperity, justice and harmony ... We, the citizens of the world, hereby resolve to establish a world federation to be governed in accordance with this Constitution for the Federation of Earth."

A third session was held in January, 1979, in Colombo, Sri Lanka, where a strategy was discussed on how to get the Constitution ratified by national parliaments and governments. There were four later meetings of the Provisional World

Parliament: 1982, in Brighten, England; 1985, in New Delhi, India; 1987, in Miami, Florida; and 1996, in Innsbruck, Austria. A timetable announced in 1984, called for a world government to be instituted by 1990, which obviously didn't happen. They announced that when the Provisional World Parliament met for the fifth time, a world government would emerge. Well, they met on the island of Malta in 2000, and there is still no world government. So far, they have released 11 World Legislative Acts.

They sent out a letter, dated December 12, 1990, "To All Presidents, Prime Ministers, Kings, Queens, and Other Heads of Governments and National Parliaments": "We who sign this appeal to you, are ready for a Democratic Federal World Government, under a ratified World Constitution ... Will you support this move for a federal world government? ... Will you appoint official delegates to the world constituent assembly ... Now is the time to assure the dawn and full blooming of a new era for humanity on Planet Earth."

Not satisfied with how long it is taking the UN, the WCPA has been organizing for the time when they feel they can usurp existing sovereign governments. And they're pretty cocky about it too, because as far as the UN, they say: "Viable agencies of the UN, are transferred to the World Government."

The directorship of the WCPA is closely linked with the United World Federalists, the American Civil Liberties Union, Global Education Associates, Friends of the Earth, Planetary Society, Worldwatch Institute, Planetary Citizens (founded in 1974 by UN executive Robert Mueller, author Norman Cousins, and activist Donald Keyes, to push for a one-world government by the year 2000), World Future Society, Planetary Initiative, American Movement for World Government, Rainbow Coalition, World Citizens Assembly, and others. Nearly 20% of their members are affiliated with the UN in various capacities.

It is quite clear, that America has become preoccupied with the goal of achieving peace in the world, and would do anything to accomplish that. President Truman said in 1948: "I would rather have peace in the world than be President." On another occasion he said: "Our goal must be, not peace in our time, but peace for all time." U Thant, the third UN Secretary-General said in 1969:

> "I do not wish to seem overdramatic, but I can only conclude from the information that is available to me as Secretary-General that the members of the United Nations have perhaps ten years left in which to subordinate their ancient quarrels and launch a global partnership to curb the arms race, to improve the human environment, to diffuse the population explosion, and supply the required momentum to world development efforts. If such a global partnership is not forged within the next decade, then I very much fear the problems I mentioned will have reached staggering proportions that they will be beyond our capacity to control."

In the quest for that peace, the United States has allowed itself to become weaker, and has ignored all the signs, that along with world peace, will be a new world order dominated by a socialist form of government. In 1983, Elliot Roosevelt, the son of FDR, published a book called *The Conservators*, calling world government "an immediate necessity."

The United Nations is the root of that one-world government, and since its inception, seventeen of their agencies have been working toward that goal: International Bank for Reconstruction and Development (World Bank), which will place the financial power of the entire world in the hands of the UN; World Health Organization, to internationalize medical treatment; International Labor Organization, to standardize labor practices; International Monetary Fund, to promote international trade and commerce; World Meteorological Association; Universal Postal Union; International Civil Aviation Organization; World Intellectual Property Organization; United Nations' Educational, Scientific, and Cultural Organization (UNESCO); International Telecommunication Union; International Fund for Agricultural Development; International Finance Corporation; International Development Association; Inter-Government Maritime Consultive Organization; General Agreement on Tariffs and Trade; Food and Agriculture Organization of the United Nations; and the International Atomic Energy Agency.

Brock Chisholm, the first director of the UN World Health Organization said: "To achieve one world government it is necessary to remove from the minds of men their individualism, their loyalty to family traditions and national identification." When he accepted an award from the World Federalist Association, CBS newscaster Walter Cronkite said: "We must strengthen the United Nations as a first step toward a world government ... We Americans will have to yield up some of our sovereignty."

The Ditchley Group, which first met in May, 1982, at Ditchley Park in London, is engineering a plan by Harold Lever (a director on the Board of the UNILEVER conglomerate) to control the fiscal and the monetary policies of the United States and called for the International Monetary Fund to control the central banks of all nations. Representatives of 36 of the world's biggest banks met at the Vista Hotel in New York in January, 1982, to lay the groundwork; then met again in October, where it was reported that plans were underway to bring legislation before the U.S. Senate that would designate the IMF as the Controller of U.S. fiscal policy by the year 2000.

On January 8, 1983, Hans Vogel of the Club of Rome, met at the White House with President Reagan, Secretary of State George Schultz, Secretary of Defense Caspar Weinberger, George Kennan, and Lane Kirkland (President of the AFL-CIO), to discuss the objectives of the Ditchley Group. The Group met on January 10-11, 1983 in Washington to discuss the IMF takeover; and later in the year, in Williamsburg, Virginia, with a group of international bankers, to discuss a disintegration of the U.S. banking system which would force the Senate into accepting IMF control. Dennis Weatherstone of Morgan Guaranty said that this was the only way for the U.S. to save itself.

The propaganda of world peace propels the United Nations further into the control of this world, and what negative publicity has emerged, has done little to slow its momentum. Originally the UN wanted the United States to pay 50% of their budget, but eventually, negotiations lowered the amount to 39.89%. Later it was lowered further to 25%, or about $3.9 billion. At one point, the Soviet Union was only paying 13%; Japan, 10%; West Germany, 8%; Great Britain, 4%; and Saudi Arabia, .5%. The 100+ Third World-non-aligned countries were only paying 9%, yet controlled 3/4 of the voting power in the General Assembly; and the 80 poorest countries were contributing less than 1% of the UN budget. In September, 1983, the Senate introduced legislation that sought to cut the U.S.'s contribution by 21% for 1983-84, and 10% more for each of the following three years, which would make America's portion of the UN budget less than 15%.

The United States further showed their displeasure with the United Nations, when in December, 1983, the Reagan Administration announced it was withdrawing from UNESCO, because the UN agency had "increasingly placed an overfed bureaucracy at the service of a coalition of Soviet bloc and Third World countries," which was to be effective January 1, 1985, unless reforms were made. UNESCO was labeled by newsman Paul Harvey as "communism's trap for our youth." Another area which demonstrated the UN's communist leanings was revealed by the McGraw Edison Committee for Public Affairs: "The United Nations' International Children's Emergency Fund (UNICEF) ... appropriated $59,000,000 between 1947 and 1958 to Communist countries. In a ratio not unlike that of other UN ventures, the United States has furnished $42,000,000 of the money ... As with other aid programs, the assistance does not go to the needy but it is administered through governments."

Since the establishment of the UN, up to 1991, there were 157 wars. J. Reuben Clark, Jr., Ambassador to Mexico, and Under Secretary of State, in his August, 1945, analysis of the UN Charter, wrote: "The Charter is built to prepare for war, not to promote peace ... The Charter is a war document, not a peace document..." He is quoted (pg. 27) in the book *The United Nations Today* as saying: "Not only does the Charter Organization (UN) not prevent future wars, but it makes it practically certain that we shall have future wars; and as to such wars, it takes from us (U.S.) the power to declare them, to choose the side on which we shall fight, and to determine what forces and military equipment we shall use in the war, and to control and command our sons who do the fighting."

Former President Herbert Hoover said in an August 10, 1962 speech: "I urged the ratification of the United Nations Charter by the Senate. But I stated at that time 'The American people should be under no illusions that the Charter assures lasting peace.' But now we must realize that the United Nations has failed to give us even a remote hope of lasting peace. Instead, it adds the dangers of wars which now surround us." An article about the UN in the March 2, 1964 edition of the *Santa Ana Register* made this comment: "The whole purpose and, indeed, the method of the UN is to use armed might against any nation presumed to be an aggressor. Its function is to make war..."

Rep. John E. Rankin (D-MS, 1921-53) said: "The United Nations is the greatest fraud in all history. Its purpose is to destroy the United States." According to the March 9, 2003 edition of the *Washington Times*, Rep. Ron Paul (R-TX) said: "I think the United Nations is dangerous to our republic and therefore we ought not to participate."

As long as prominent members of our government and our uninformed elected representatives continue to tout the United Nations as being the only way for lasting peace, then the propaganda will continue to grow, and we will become more desensitized to the campaign that continues to slowly take away the freedoms that our forefathers fought and died for.

While campaigning for the Presidency, Bill Clinton said: "My vision is that we would become an instrument working as much as possible through the United Nations for freedom and democracy and human rights and global economic growth." In a speech to the World Affairs Council in Los Angeles, Clinton called for a permanent UN "rapid deployment force." Richard Gardner, a Clinton advisor on the UN, and a professor of international law, has outlined a plan for a world army of 30,000 men. The five member nations of the Security Council would provide 2,000 men, and 30 other nations would add up to 750 each. This would create a military force that the Security Council could deploy within 48 hours to maintain the peace.

In a February 1, 1992 speech to the UN General Assembly, President George Bush said: "It is the sacred principles enshrined in the United Nations charter to which the American people will henceforth pledge their allegiance."

In 1993, the UN became financially stretched to the limit, because of all the peace-keeping operations throughout the world (numbering about 70,000, they pay each country $988 per soldier every month, and more for specialized troops), which forced it to cutback on travel, meetings, and the use of consultants. While the U.S. is still paying about 25% of its annual budget of over $1 billion, and about 30% of all peace-keeping costs, a move was on to force member nations to contribute a portion of their defense budgets to the UN. According to the January 16, 1996 *Washington Times* it was announced that "Secretary General Boutros Boutros-Ghali ... urged the (UN) to consider imposing its own taxes to become less dependent on the United States…"

We can expect one of two things to happen in the future. Either the UN will steadily grow in power, until it evolves into a one-world government; or if perceptions continue that it has not lived up to expectations, it could be disbanded (perhaps if the United States would drop out), and replaced by an already burgeoning alliance, such as the WCPA. Walter Hoffman, the executive Vice President of the World Federalist Association, wrote in a letter to a national news magazine, that we need "a new, more effective UN, one that will have the power to stop wars and arbitrate disputes between national groups." It seems likely, that the strength of our economy may determine how soon our country agrees to become part of a one world government. If it continues to decline due to government mismanagement and manipulation by the Illuminati, it may not be long till we have to be 'saved' in order to survive, even if it is, as part of a new world order dominated by a socialistic political ideology.

THE EUROPEAN UNION

The European Union, formerly known as the European Communities (EC), or European Economic Community (Common Market), is a movement to unite Western Europe. For hundreds of years, there has been an ongoing effort to unify Europe. Prior to World War II, because of intermarriage between Royal families, all crowned heads were closely related.

French philosopher Montesquieu said in the 18th century: "Whenever in the past Europe has been united by force, the unity lasted no longer than the space of a single reign." He went on to predict the peaceful unification of Europe. In 1871,

Victor Hugo, the French novelist, said: "Let us have the United States of Europe; let us have continental federation; let us have European freedom."

In 1922, Count Richard Coudenhove-Kalergi founded the Pan European Union. He fled Austria in 1940, and came to the United States, where he continued to work towards European unity. In 1941, Andre Malraux called for a "European New Deal, a federal Europe excluding the USSR." In an October, 1942 letter to the British War Cabinet, Winston Churchill wrote: "Hard as it is to say now, I trust that the European family may act unitedly as one under a Council of Europe. I look forward to a United States of Europe." He also said in a September 19, 1946 speech at the University of Zurich: "We must build a kind of United States of Europe." Churchill made the United Europe Movement a cohesive group, by merging the Union of European Federalists, the Economic League for European Cooperation, and the French Council for a United Europe, into an organization known as the International Committee of Movements for European Unity.

Late in 1947, various people and groups formed a committee to coordinate their efforts, and by May, 1948, organized the Congress of Europe, which convened at the Hague in the Netherlands. Nearly 1000 prominent Europeans from 16 countries called for the establishment of a United Europe. Dr. Joseph Retinger, who had helped organized the meeting at the Hague, came to the United States in July, 1948, along with Winston Churchill, Duncan Sandys, and former Belgian Prime Minister Henri-Paul Spaak, to raise money for the movement. This led to the establishment of the American Committee on a United Europe (ACUE) on March 29, 1949. Their first Chairman was William Donovan, the first Director of the Office of Strategic Services (OSS, the forerunner of the CIA); the Vice-Chairman was Allen Dulles, who later became the Director of the CIA; and the Secretary was George S. Franklin, who was a Director in the Council on Foreign Relations, and later a coordinator with the Trilateral Commission.

Lord James Edward Salisbury, the conservative British statesman, said: "Federation is the only hope of the world." The historic address on June 5, 1947, by Gen. George C. Marshall, the Secretary of State, which made proposals for European aid known as the Marshall Plan, also called for the unification of Europe.

On March 17, 1948, a 50 year treaty was signed for "collaboration in economic, social, and cultural matters and for collective self defense," in Brussels, by England, France, the Netherlands, Belgium, and Luxembourg. In 1950, its functions were transferred to NATO, and in May, 1955, a military alliance, known as the Council of Western European Union was established, made up of the foreign ministers from Belgium, France, West Germany, Italy, the Netherlands, Luxembourg, and England, who met every three months. There was also a Western European Union Assembly made up of delegates to the Consultive Assembly of the Council of Europe in Paris.

The Western European Coalition began on June 8, 1948, with the signing of the Benelux Agreement by Luxembourg, Belgium, and the Netherlands, to unite their economic and domestic policies.

On May 5, 1949, Foreign Ministers from ten European countries signed a Treaty in London, for the purpose of working for "greater European unity, to improve the conditions of life and principle human value in Europe and to uphold the principles of parliamentary democracy, the rule of law and human rights." The

Treaty sought to promote unity, both socially and economically, among its first members were: Belgium (1949), Denmark (1949), France (1949), Ireland (1949), Italy (1949), Luxembourg (1949), Netherlands (1949), Norway (1949), Sweden (1949), England (1949), Greece (1949), Turkey (1949), and Iceland (1949). It now has 45 member states. The Council of Europe, led by a Secretary-General, is open to all European States which accepted the "principles of the rule of law and of the enjoyment by all persons within (their) jurisdiction of human rights and fundamental freedoms." They are headquartered in Strasbourg, France (Avenue de l'Europe).

The North Atlantic Treaty Organization (NATO), the father of the Common Market, was a defense alliance developed to implement the North Atlantic Treaty in 1949, and to apply counter pressure against the growing Soviet military presence in Europe. Article V states: "The Parties agree that an armed attack against one or more of them in Europe shall be considered an attack against them all and consequently they agree that, if such an attack occurs, each of them ... will assist the Party or Parties so attacked ... to restore and maintain the security of the North Atlantic Area." Belgium, France, the Netherlands, Italy, West Germany, Spain, Luxembourg, United Kingdom, Canada, Denmark, Greece, Iceland, Norway, Portugal, Turkey, and the United States, all joined to oppose the growing threat of communism. Soon afterwards, the Russians, recognizing NATO as a stumbling block to their plans, emulated the group by uniting their communist satellites in 1955 with the Warsaw Treaty Organization. The Warsaw Pact alliance included the countries of Albania, Czechoslovakia, East Germany, Hungary, Poland, Romania, and Russia.

In 1950, Robert Schuman, the French Foreign Minister, came up with an idea to integrate all the coal and steel industries of the western European nations; and in 1951, the European Coal and Steel Community (ECSC) was set up with six member countries: Belgium, West Germany, Luxembourg, France, Italy, and the Netherlands. An independent body known as the 'High Authority' was able to make decisions in regard to the industries in those countries. Their first President was the French economist and diplomat, Jean Monnet, called the 'Father of Europe.'

On May 27, 1952, the European Defense Community Treaty was signed in Paris, and provided for the armies of West Germany, France, Italy, Belgium, the Netherlands, and Luxembourg, to become closely aligned with England's. On October 23, 1954, it was replaced with the Western European Union, who merged their armies into a multi-national armed force.

Jean Monnet said: "As long as Europe remains divided, it is no match for the Soviet Union. Europe must unite." He established a pressure group in 1955 called the Action Committee for the United States of Europe. He also said: "Once a Common Market interest has been created, then political union will come naturally."

On March 25, 1957, the European Atomic Energy Community (EURATOM) and the European Economic Community (EEC) was established with a 378-page Declaration of Intent, called the Treaty of Rome, to facilitate the removal of barriers, so trade could be accomplished among member nations; eventual coordination of transportation systems, agricultural and economic policies; the removal of all measures restricting free competition; and the assurance of the mobility of labor, capital, and entrepreneurship. The partnership began with six countries: France,

West Germany, Italy, Belgium, the Netherlands, and Luxembourg. George McGhee, the former U.S. ambassador to West Germany, said that "the Treaty of Rome, which brought the Common Market into being, was nurtured at the Bilderberg meetings." In 1967, the ECSC, EURATOM, and EEC were brought together into a single group that was known as the European Community.

In 1973, Henry Kissinger, Nixon's Secretary of State (known to favor one-world government) urged the Common Market to include four more nations: Norway, United Kingdom, Denmark, and Ireland. Norway eventually backed out, but on May 28, 1979, in Athens, Greece became the tenth nation to join the Common Market. When they officially became a member in January, 1981, Europe was as unified as it was in 814, when Charlemagne, founder of the Roman Empire, died.

A French foreign minister said: "The Europe of the future, when it finally unites politically as well as economically, will be the mightiest force on earth." Walter Hallstein said: "Make no mistake about it, we are not in business, we are in politics. We are building the United States of Europe." *Time* magazine wrote: "If the Europe of tomorrow could muster the political will, it could become a co-equal of the other two superpowers, the United States and Russia..." Another publication said: "The European Common Market is emerging to shake the world economically and politically." England's former Prime Minister, Edward Heath, said: "Europe must unite or perish."

Another huge step was taken toward a united Europe when a direct-election was held June 7-9, 1979 that elected a 410 member European Parliament, the first in over 1,000 years. It was made up of members from the countries of Great Britain, France, West Germany, Italy, the Netherlands, Belgium, Denmark, Ireland, and Luxembourg. With the Maastricht Treaty in 1992, and the Amsterdam Treaty in 1997, they now possess actual legislative authority. Now with 626 members, the body includes the United Kingdom and Germany, as well as Greece, Spain, Portugal, Finland, Sweden, and Austria. They are headquartered in Strasbourg, France, but are also known to work in Brussels, Belgium and Luxembourg. They are the parliamentary body of the European Union.

On March 17, 1979, the Common Market initiated a new monetary system to encourage trade and investment by stabilizing their currency values in relation to each other. The main feature of this link-up was a $33 billion fund made up of each other's gold and currency reserves. Members could borrow against this fund to support their own currencies. The value of each of the participating currencies was set against "European Currency Units" established by the fund.

On January 1, 1986, Spain and Portugal became the 11th and 12th members of the European Community. On November 11, 1991, Jeane Kirkpatrick, former U.S. Ambassador to the UN, wrote: "If the Bush Administration has a vision of the New World Order, it is time to share it with the Europeans and Americans, because a New World Order is precisely what is emerging on the continent of Europe today." On December 9-11, 1991, at a meeting in Maastricht, in the Netherlands, a serious effort was made to establish a common currency, and discussions were held concerning a common foreign policy, and a common defense policy. After the 1992 Treaty of Maastricht, the Common Market became known as the European Union.

On December 31, 1992, the "Single Europe Act" went into effect, uniting the

12 nations into a federation and lifting the restrictions on the movement of goods, services, capital, workers and tourists within the Community. They also adopted common agricultural, fisheries, and nuclear research policies. Jacques Delors, in the *Delors Report*, a blueprint for EC unification, called for a "transfer of decision-making power from member states to the community."

On January 1, 1995, Austria became the 13th nation.

The European Union (located at Rue de la Loi, Brussels, Belgium) is now made up of Austria, Belgium, Denmark, Finland, France, Germany, Greece, Irish Republic, Italy, Luxembourg, Netherlands, Portugal, Spain, Sweden, and the United Kingdom. It had been reported that the EU was looking to have a total of 20 member nations, yet in 2004 they are adding Cyprus, the Czech Republic, Estonia, Hungary, Latvia, Lithuania, Malta, Poland, Slovakia, and Slovenia.

After deciding in 1992 to move towards a single European currency controlled by a European Central Bank; that currency, known as the 'euro,' emerged in 2002, when euro notes and coins replaced the national currencies of 12 of the 15 countries of the European Union.

The industrial capability of the European Union is nearly equal to that of the United States. Western Europe also accounts for about 25% of the world's production, and 35% of its trade. When the time comes, and it surely will, that the people of the European Union finally allow themselves to become a single political entity, they will be a world power, and a force to be reckoned with.

THE BILDERBERGER GROUP

Dr. Joseph H. Retinger (who died in 1960), economist, political philosopher, communist Poland's Charge d'Affaires, and a major proponent of a united Europe; along with Prince Bernhard (of Lippe-Biesterfeld) of the Netherlands, Colin Gubbins (former director of the British SOE, Special Operations Executive), and Gen. Walter Bedell Smith (former American Ambassador to Moscow, and director of the CIA, who said when he took over the CIA: "We can't lick world communism— no counterinsurgency plans will work. We must compromise and co-exist with communism." He later became an Under Secretary of State in the Eisenhower Administration); joined together in 1954 to organize this secret group. Created under the direction of Alastair Buchan, son of Lord Tweedsmuir, and Chairman of the Royal Institute of International Affairs; its governing council was made up of Robert Ellsworth (Lazard Freres), John Loudon (N. M. Rothschild), Paul Nitze (Shroeder Bank), C. L. Sulzberger (*New York Times*), Stansfield Turner (who later became CIA Director), Peter Calvocoressi (Penguin Books), Andrew Schoenberg (RIIA), Daniel Ellsburg, and Henry Kissinger.

Bernhard said: "It is difficult to reeducate the people who have been brought up on nationalism to the idea of relinquishing part of their sovereignty to a supranational body..."

Lord Rothschild and Laurance Rockefeller handpicked 100 of the world's elite, and they have a heavy cross membership with the Council on Foreign Relations (which they control), the English Speaking Union, the Pilgrims Society, the

Round Table, and the Trilateral Commission. Their purpose was to regionalize Europe, according to Giovanni Agnelli, the head of Fiat, who said: "European integration is our goal and where the politicians have failed, we industrialists hope to succeed." In Alden Hatch's biography of Bernhard, he stated that the Bilderberg Group gave birth to the European Community (now the European Union). Their ultimate goal is to have a one-world government.

Their first meeting was held at the Hotel de Bilderberg (hence the name of the group, even though they have referred to themselves as 'The Alliance') in Oosterbeek, Holland, from May 29-31, in 1954. Charles Douglas Jackson (Vice President of *Time* magazine, delegate to the United Nations, Special Assistant to the President, and later publisher of *Life* magazine), spokesman for the American delegation, led by David Rockefeller, promised those present: "Whether he (Sen. Joseph McCarthy) dies by an assassin's bullet, or is eliminated in the normal American way of getting rid of boils on the body politic, I prophecy that by the time we hold our next meeting, he will be gone from the American scene." McCarthy was the crusading Senator who revealed that communists had infiltrated high level posts within the U.S. Government. He didn't die until 1957.

The Bilderbergers hold annual meetings in locations all over the world. In Europe, the Rothschilds have hosted some of the meetings, while the meetings in 1962 and 1973, in Saltsjobaden, Sweden, were hosted by the Wallenbergs (who had an estimated fortune of $10 billion). The meetings were chaired by the German-born Prince Bernhard, the husband of Queen Juliana of the Netherlands, said to be the richest woman in the world (because of her partnership with Baron Victor Rothschild in the Royal Dutch Shell Oil Co., owning 5% of the stock, which in 1978 was worth $425 million; and also holds stock in Exxon), until he was forced to resign in August, 1976, because of his involvement in the Lockheed Aircraft bribery scandal, and his extramarital affairs. Bernhard wrote: "Here comes our greatest difficulty. For the governments of the free nations are elected by the people, and if they do something the people don't like they are thrown out. It is difficult to reeducate the people who have been brought up on nationalism to the idea of relinquishing part of their sovereignty to a supernational body..." Walter Scheel of Germany took over as Chairman, and then it was Britain's Lord Carrington, who is on the Board of the Hambros Bank.

There are about 120 participants that are invited to the Bilderberg meetings, of whom about two-thirds come from Europe and the rest are from North America; and about one-third are from government and politics, and the other two-thirds are from the fields of finance, industry, labor, education, communications. The meetings are closed to the public and the press, although a brief press conference is usually held at the conclusion of each meeting, to reveal, in general terms, some of the topics which were discussed. The resort areas and hotels where they meet, are cleared of residents and visitors, and surrounded by soldiers, armed guards, the Secret Service, State and local police. All conference and meeting rooms are scanned for bugging devices before every single meeting.

Among those who have attended their meetings: Owen Lattimore (CFR, former Director of Planning and Coordination for the State Department), Winston Lord (CFR, Clinton's Assistant Secretary of State), Allen Dulles (CIA), Sen. William J. Fulbright (from Arkansas, a Rhodes Scholar), Dean Acheson (Secretary of State under Truman), Gabriel Hauge (Assistant to President Eisenhower, who according to the *Wall Street Journal*, "helped teach Ike what to think"; and later became Chairman of Manufacturers Hanover Trust Co.), George Ball (CFR, Johnson's Under Secretary of State from 1961-66, and foreign policy consultant to Nixon), Philip Jessup (representative to the International Court), Henry A. Kissinger (Chairman, Kissinger Associates), David Rockefeller (Member, JP Morgan International Council), Nelson Rockefeller, Laurance Rockefeller, Dean Rusk (Kennedy's Secretary of State and former President of the Rockefeller Foundation), Gerald Ford, Henry J. Heinz II (Chairman of the H. J. Heinz Co.), Sen. Henry M. Jackson, Sen. Jacob J. Javits (NY), Prince Phillip of Great Britain, Lord Louis Mountbatten, Denis Healy (former British Defense Minister), Manlio Brosio (Secretary of NATO), Wilfred S. Baumgartner (Bank of France), Guido Carli (Bank of Italy), Thomas L. Hughes (President of the Carnegie Endowment for International Peace), Robert S. McNamara (Kennedy's Secretary of Defense and former President of the World Bank), Margaret Thatcher (Prime Minister of England), Valery Giscard D'Estang (President of France), Harold Wilson (Prime Minister of England), Edward Heath (Prime Minister of England), William P. Bundy (former President of the Ford Foundation, and editor of the CFR's *Foreign Affairs* journal), John J. McCloy former President of the Chase Manhattan Bank), Christian Herter (Secretary of State under Eisenhower), Lester Pearson (former Prime Minister of Canada), Shepard Stone (Director of International Affairs for the Ford Foundation), Dirk U. Stikker (Secretary-General of NATO), Gardner Cowles (Editor-in-Chief and Publisher of *Look* magazine), Paul G. Hoffman (of the Ford Foundation, U.S. Chief of Foreign Aid, and head of the UN Special Fund), Donald H. Rumsfeld (President Ford's and George W. Bush's Secretary of Defense), Father Theodore M. Hesburgh (former President of Notre Dame University), Helmut Schmidt (Chancellor of West Germany), George F. Kennan (former U.S. Ambassador to the Soviet Union), Paul H. Nitze, Robert O. Anderson (Chairman of Atlantic-Richfield Co. and head of the Aspen Institute for Humanisitic Studies), Donald S. MacDonald (Canadian Minister of National Defense), Prince Claus of the Netherlands, Marcus Wallenberg (Chairman of Stockholm's Enskilda Bank), Nuri M. Birgi (Turkish Ambassador to NATO), Bill Moyers (journalist), William F. Buckley (editor of *National Review*), John D. Rockefeller IV (Governor of West Virginia, now U.S. Senator), Cyrus Vance (Secretary of State under Carter), Rep. Donald F. Fraser, Rep. Peter Frelinghuysen, Rep. Henry S. Reuss, Rep. Donald W. Riegle, Sen. Adlai Stevenson III, Sen. Charles Mathias (MD), Lt. Gen. John W. Vogt (former Director of the Joint Chiefs of Staff), Eugene Black (former President of the World Bank), Joseph Johnson (President of the Carnegie Endowment for International Peace), Hannes Androsch (Austrian Minister of Finance), David J. McDonald (President of the United Steelworkers Union), Paul van Zeeland (Prime Minister of Belgium), Pierre Commin (Secretary of the French Socialist Party), Imbriani Longo (Director-General of the Banco Nationale del Lavoro in Italy), Vimcomte Davignon (Belgium Minister of Foreign Affairs), Walter Leisler Kiep (member of the German Parliament), Ole Myrvoll (member of Norway's Parliament), Krister Wickman (former Swedish Minister of Foreign Affairs, and Governor of the Bank of Sweden), Sen. Walter Mondale (MN, later Vice President under Carter), Rep. Thomas S. Foley (former Speaker of the House), Henry Ford III (head of the Ford Motor Co.), Gen.

Walter Bedell Smith, Gen. Andrew J. Goodpaster (former Supreme Allied Commander in Europe, and later superintendent of the West Point Academy), Zbigniew Brzezinski, Gen. Alexander Haig (European NATO Commander, former assistant to Kissinger, later became Secretary of State under Reagan), Alan Greenspan (Chairman, Federal Reserve System), C. Douglas Dillon (Secretary of Treasury in the Kennedy and Johnson Administrations, from Dillon, Read and Co.), Baron Edmond de Rothschild, Pierce Paul Schweitzer (Managing Director of the UN's International Monetary Fund), Paul B. Finney (editor of Fortune magazine), James Rockefeller (Chairman, First National City Bank), Giovanni Agnelli (Chairman of Fiat in Italy), Otto Wolff (German industrialist), Theo Sommer (German newspaper columnist), Arthur Taylor (former Chairman of CBS-TV), Neil Norlund (Editor-in-Chief of *Berlingske Tindende* in Denmark), and Sen. Lloyd Bentsen (TX, Chairman of the Senate Finance Committee, candidate for Vice President in 1988 with Michael Dukakis, and now the Secretary of Treasury under Bill Clinton).

Although this list is a bit tedious to go through, you have probably started to see how the same names keep showing up over and over.

Bilderberg policy is carried out by a 35 member Bilderberg Steering Committee, including an inner circle known as an Advisory Committee, which is said to be made up of Giovanni Agnelli (Italy), David Rockefeller (U.S.), Eric Roll (Great Britain), and Otto Wolff von Amerongen (Germany). Some of the Steering Committee members are: Henry Kissinger, Jessica T. Mathews (President, Carnegie Endowment for International Peace), James D. Wolfensohn (President, World Bank), Marie-Josee Kravis (Senior Fellow, Hudson Institute), and Jorma Ollila (Chairman of the Board and CEO of Nokia Corp.). All American members of the Steering Committee are members of the CFR.

A few of the Bilderberg permanent U.S. members are: George W. Ball, Gabriel Hauge, Richard C. Holbrooke, Winston Lord, Bill Moyers, and Paul Wolfowitz

The permanent Bilderberg Secretariat is located at: 1 Smidswater, the Hague, the Netherlands (though another address is sometimes reported at 2301 Da Leiden, in the Netherlands) Their address in America was at 345 E. 46th Street, in New York City (which was also the location of the Trilateral Commission, and the Carnegie Endowment for International Peace). The American Friends of Bilderbergs, with offices at 477 Madison Avenue (6th floor) in New York City, is an IRS-approved charitable organization that received regular contributions from the likes of Exxon, Arco, and IBM; while their meetings are funded by the Ford Foundation, Rockefeller Foundation, and the Carnegie Endowment Fund.

The Goals 2000 program, developed during the presidency of George Bush to revamp the nation's public school system, was born at the April, 1970, Bilderberger meeting in Bad Ragaz, Switzerland. The purpose of the new educational philosophy was the "subordination of national ambitions to the idea of the international community." Because our schools are "too nationalistic," children, in the future, will be indoctrinated to consider themselves "world citizens."

Prior to the 1971 meeting in Woodstock, Virginia, Prince Bernhard said that the subject of the meeting was the "change in the world role of the United States." After the weekend conference, Kissinger was sent to Red China to open up trade relations, and an international monetary crisis developed, which prompted the devaluing of the dollar by 8.57% (which made a tremendous profit for those who converted to the European Currency).

In 1976, fifteen representatives from the Soviet Union attended the meeting which was held in the Arizona desert, and it was believed, that at that time, the plans were formulated for the "break-up of communism in the Soviet Union." At the 1978 meeting, they predicted that a depression would hit the world in 1979, and that the dollar would die. Their solution was to replace the dollar with an international 'bancor' system (international bank note) of currency that would be universally acceptable as a medium of exchange. The 'bancor' system would have the international gold reserve deposited in a neutral country. It is an offshoot of the same Keynesian system developed at Bretton Woods in 1944 from the idea by German economist Julius Wolf in 1892. This system would protect the Illuminati when they spring their trap, and the world economy would crumble.

At their 1990 meeting at Glen Cove, Long Island in New York, they decided that taxes had to be raised to pay more towards the debt owed to the International Bankers. And George Bush, who pledged during the campaign, "Read my lips— no new taxes!" found himself signing one of the biggest tax increases in history on November 15, 1990, a move which was a contributing factor to his defeat when he ran for re-election.

At their 1991 meeting at the Black Forest resort in Baden Baden, Germany, they discussed plans for a common European currency, and European central banking; and reviewed Middle Eastern events and developments in the Soviet Union. David Rockefeller, said during the meeting:

> "We are grateful to the *Washington Post*, the *New York Times*, *Time* magazine, and other great publications whose directors have attended our meetings and respected their promises of discretion for almost forty years ... It would have been impossible for us to develop our plan for the world if we had been subject to the bright lights of publicity during these years. But, the world is now more sophisticated and prepared to march towards a world government. The supernational sovereignty of an intellectual elite and world bankers is surely preferable to the national auto-determination practiced in past centuries."

Then Governor of Arkansas, Bill Clinton (a Rhodes Scholar, who attended Oxford University in England), was invited to speak, and a decision was made to endorse his candidacy (according to Jim Tucker, a *Spotlight* reporter, who had a source within the group, code-named 'Pipeline'). No wonder Clinton was able to survive all the media attacks regarding his personal life and lack of experience. One of his top money men was investor and international banker Jackson Stephens, who also donated $100,000 to the Bush campaign. His wife was the Co-Chairwoman of the national "Bush for President" organization in 1988. Also in attendance, were Michael Boskin, Chairman of Bush's Council of Economic Advisors, who was a speaker; Nicholas Brady, U.S. Treasury Secretary; and Vice President Dan Quayle, who impressed the group enough, that there was talk of supporting him for the Republican nomination in 1996. In fact, after the meeting, Bilderberger member Katherine Graham, head of the *Washington Post*, published a series of positive articles on Quayle.

At their 1992 meeting, the group discussed the possibility of "conditioning the public to accept the idea of a UN army that could, by force, impose its will on the internal affairs of any nation." Henry Kissinger, who attended the meeting, said: "Today, Americans would be outraged if UN forces entered Los Angeles to restore order. Tomorrow, they will be grateful."

The official press release for their 2002 Conference said: "Bilderberg's only activity is its annual Conference. At the meetings, no resolutions are proposed, no votes taken, and no policy statements issued." They are just "a small flexible, informal and off-the-record international forum in which different viewpoints can be expressed and mutual understanding enhanced." However, Phyllis Schlafly wrote in *A Choice Not An Echo*, that the Bilderbergers are a "little clique of powerful men who meet secretly and plan events that appear to 'just happen'."

ATLAS SHRUGGED

In 1957, a 1,168 page book by Ayn Rand, called *Atlas Shrugged*, was published. According to one source, Rand was alleged to be a mistress to Philippe Rothschild, who instructed her to write the book in order to show that through the raising of oil prices, then destroying the oil fields and shutting down the coal mines, the Illuminati would take over the world. It also related how they would blow up grain mills, derail trains, bankrupt and destroy their own companies, till they had destroyed the economy of the entire world; and yet, they would be so wealthy, that it would not substantially affect their vast holdings. The novel is about a man who stops the motor of the world, of what happens when "the men of the mind, the intellectuals of the world, the originators and innovators in every line of industry go on strike; when the men of creative ability in every profession, in protest against regulation, quit and disappear."

If we are to believe that the book represents the Illuminati's plans for the future, then the following excerpts may provide some insight to the mentality of the elitists who are preparing us for one-world government.

One of the characters, Francisco d'Anconia, a copper industrialist and heir to a great fortune, the first to join the strike, says:

> "I am destroying d'Anconia Copper, consciously, deliberately, by plan and by my own hand. I have to plan it carefully and work as hard as if I were producing a fortune— in order not to let them notice it and stop me, in order not to let them seize the mines until it is too late ... I shall destroy every last bit of it and every last penny of my fortune and every ounce of copper that could feed the looters. I shall not leave it as I found it— I shall leave it as Sebastian d'Anconia found it— then let them try to exist without him or me!"

A bit later, d'Anconia says: "We produced the wealth of the world— but we let our enemies write its moral code." Still later, he says: "We'll survive without it. They won't."

Dagney Taggart, the main character of the book, is the head of the Taggart

Transcontinental Railroad. Her goal was to find out who John Galt was. She discovered that he was a young inventor with the Twentieth Century Motor Company, who said he would put an end to the regulations which bound a man to his job indefinitely. Before disappearing, he said: "I will stop the motor of the world." He told her:

> "Dagney, we who've been called 'materialists' ... we're the only ones who know how little value or meaning there is in material objects ... we're the ones who create their value and meaning. We can afford to give them up ... We are the soul, of which railroads, copper mines, steel mines, and oil wells are the body— and they are living entities that beat day and night, like our hearts, in the sacred function of supporting human life, but only so long as they remain our body, only so long as they remain the expression, the reward and the property of achievement. Without us, they are corpses and their sole product is poison, not wealth or food, the poison of disintegration that turns men into hordes of scavengers ... You do not have to depend on any material possessions, they depend on you, you create them, you own the one and only tool of production ... leave them the carcass of that railroad, leave them all the rusted nails and rotted ties and gutted engines— but don't leave them your mind."

Later in the book, Galt says:

> "And the same will be happening in every other industry, wherever machines are used— the machines which they thought could replace our minds. Plane crashes, oil tank explosions, blast furnace breakouts, high tension wire electrocutions, subway cave-ins, and trestle collapses— they'll see them all. The very machines that made their life so safe— will now make it a continuous peril ... You know that the cities will be hit worst of all. The cities were made by the railroads and will go with them ... When the rails are cut, the city of New York will starve in two days. That's all the supply of food its got. It's fed by a continent three thousand miles long. How will they carry food to New York? By directive and oxcart? But first, before it happens, they'll go through the whole of the agony— through the shrinking, the shortages, the hunger riots, the stampeding violence in the midst of the growing stillness ... They'll lose the airplanes first, then their automobiles, then their trucks, then their horsecarts ... Their factories will stop, then their furnaces and their radios. Then their electric light system will go."

Francisco d'Anconia, who blew up all the copper mines in the world, said of Galt:

> "He had quit the Twentieth Century. He was living in a garret in a slum neighborhood. He stepped to the window and pointed at the skyscrapers of the city. He said that we had to extinguish the lights of the world, and when we would see the lights of New York go out, we would know that our job was done."

Galt led the men of the mind, on strike, and they retired to a self-supporting valley, where a character, Midas Mulligan, says that "the world is falling apart so fast that it will soon be starving. But we will be able to support ourselves in this valley." Galt said: "There is only one kind of men who have never been on strike in human history ... the men who have carried the world on their shoulders, have kept it alive, have endured torture as sole payment ... Well, their turn has come. Let the world discover who they are, what they do and what happens when they refuse to function. This is the strike of the men of the mind."

The book describes what resulted from the strike: "But years later, when we saw the lights going out, one after another, in the great factories that had stood like mountains for generations, when we saw the gates closing and the conveyer belts turning still, when we saw the roads growing empty and the streams of cars draining off, when it began to look as if some silent power were stopping the generators of the world and the world was crumbling quietly..." And the culmination of their efforts: "The plane was above the peaks of the skyscrapers when suddenly, with the abruptness of a shudder, as if the ground had parted to engulf it, the city had disappeared from the face of the earth. It took them a moment to realize that the panic had reached the power stations— and the lights of New York had gone out." The men of the mind had taken over the world.

Ayn Rand, author of *Atlas Shrugged*, which was a bestseller; had previously written *We the Living* (1936); *The Fountainhead* (1943), which became a 1949 movie starring Gary Cooper as an architect willing to blow up his own work, rather than see it perverted by public housing bureaucrats; and *Anthem* (1946). She later wrote *For the New Intellectual* (1961), *Capitalism: The Unknown Ideal* (1966), and *The New Left: The Anti-Industrial Revolution* (1970). She also published a monthly journal (with Nathaniel Branden, a psychological theorist) called *The Objectivist*.

Rand based her novel on her philosophy which she calls Objectivism. As she puts it: "We are the radicals for capitalism ... because it is the only system geared to the life of a rational being ... The method of capitalism's destruction rests on never letting the world discover what it is that is being destroyed." She also said about the book: "I trust that no one will tell me that men such as I write about don't exist. That this book has been written— and published— is proof that they do."

In the book *Capitalism: The Unknown Ideal*, in a chapter titled "Is Atlas Shrugging" she wrote that "the purpose of this book is to prevent itself from being prophetic." She also quoted several news stories which seemed to indicate that the world was indeed being depleted of its brains and intellectuals.

Is *Atlas Shrugged* a coded blueprint for the Illuminati's plans of bringing this world to a point where they can institute a one world government? It certainly is thought provoking, and it is included only for the sake of conjecture. Being that the Illuminati is destroying our economy, and they do control the corporate structure of the United States, if not the world, there just may be something to this book, and maybe we should consider it a warning.

THE SEVEN SISTERS

One oil cartel is the Organization of Petroleum Exporting Countries, known as OPEC, which is made up of Iran, Iraq, Venezuela, Kuwait, Saudi Arabia, Algeria, Indonesia, Libya, Nigeria, Qatar, and the United Arab Emirates. The group was created on September 14, 1960, for the purpose of setting oil prices by controlling oil production. They were originally thought to be primarily Arabian, in ownership, however, it is actually an international group, which includes Americans. The cartel was established from an agreement signed on September 17, 1920, by Royal Dutch Shell, Anglo-Iranian, and Standard Oil, for the purpose of fixing oil prices. By 1949, the cartel was made up of Anglo-Iranian, Socony-Vacuum, Royal Dutch Shell, Gulf, Esso, Texaco, and Calso. In the early 1950's, revelations surfaced that the oil companies would pump the oil from the Middle East, then split the profits with the government of the country where the oil was produced. OPEC was formed to make people believe that the Arabian oil reserves were not owned by non-Arabian oil companies.

Those non-Arabian oil companies are another cartel, which had been informally called "The Seven Sisters," and control what is shipped to the United States, and how much is refined into gas and heating oil. Originally, it was made up of the Rockefeller-controlled Exxon (previously known as Standard Oil of New Jersey, or Esso), Mobil (Socony or Standard Oil of New York, which merged with Vacuum Oil), and Chevron (Socal or Standard Oil of California); the Mellon's Gulf Oil; Shell (Royal Dutch Petroleum), Texaco, and British Petroleum (Anglo-Iranian). They controlled 90% of crude exports to world markets by controlling every important pipeline in the world, such as the 753-mile TransArabian Pipeline, from Qaisuma in Saudi Arabia to the Mediterranean Sea, which was owned by Exxon, Chevron, Texaco, and Mobil. Exxon owned the 100-mile Interprovincial Pipeline in Canada; and also the 143-mile pipeline in Venezuela. The 799-mile Alaskan Pipeline was owned by British Petroleum and Exxon. By controlling these, and other vital arteries, they can restrict the flow of oil, limiting supplies to refineries.

You could also see their link, through the joint ownership of the major crude oil production companies:

Abu Dhabi Marine Areas (British Petroleum)— 66-2/3%
Compagnie Francaise de Petroles— 33-1/3%
Kuwait Oil Co. (British Petroleum)— 50%
Gulf— 50%
Iran Consortium (Gulf)— 7%
Shell— 14%
Exxon— 7%
Chevron— 7%
Compagnie Francaise des Petroles— 6%
Texaco— 7%
British Petroleum— 40%
Mobil— 7%
other— 5%

Abu Dhabi Petroleum Co. (Shell)— 23.75%
Exxon— 11.875%
Compagnie Francaise des Petroles— 23.75%
British Petroleum— 23.75%
Mobil— 11.875%
other— 5%

Iraq Petroleum (Compagnie Francaise des Petroles)— 23.75%
British Petroleum— 23.75%
Mobil— 11.875%
Shell— 23.75%
Exxon— 11.875%
other— 5%

Aramco Saudi Arabia (Exxon)— 30%
Chevron— 30%
Mobil— 10%
Texaco— 30%

Bahrain Petroleum Co. (Chevron)— 50%
Texaco— 50%

The Sisters were also interlocked with eight of the largest banks in the country, and with each other: Exxon had ties to Mobil, Chevron, and Texaco; and Mobil had ties to Exxon, Shell, and Texaco. When six of the nation's major commercial banks held their Executive Board meetings, the directors of the top eight oil companies, with the exception of Gulf and Chevron, met with them. When the Bank of America had a Board meeting, the directors of Chevron and Getty Oil met with them. Chevron also had ties with Western Bancorp. Shell and Mobil directors were present at the Board meetings of First National City Bank. Mobil also had ties with Bankers Trust, and Chemical Bank. Exxon was tied in with the Chase Manhattan Bank (a holding company for hundreds of smaller oil companies, including Humble Oil and Creole Petroleum), Morgan Guaranty, and Chemical Bank. Amoco (Standard Oil of Indiana) was tied in with Chase Manhattan, Continental Illinois, and National Bank and Trust.

Some of the oil executives who were members of the Council on Foreign Relations: Lawrence G. Rawl (Chairman of Exxon), Lee R. Raymond (President of Exxon, and Trilateral Commission member), Jack G. Clark, Sr. (Vice President of Exxon); Alfred C. Decrane, Jr. (Chairman of Texaco), John Brademas (a Director of Texaco, and Trilateral Commission member), William J. Crowe, Jr. (a Director of Texaco, and Trilateral Commission member); Allan E. Murray (Chairman & President of Mobil, and Trilateral Commission member), Lewis M. Branscomb (a Director of Mobil), and Helene L. Kaplan (a Director of Mobil).

The Seven Sisters also controlled 70% of the U.S. coal supply, which during World War II, the Germans used to make pollution-free synthetic fuel. Their philosophy was "to mine it now, it's coal; to mine it later, it will be like gold."

These seven companies announced their alliance with the statement: "We have formed a very exclusive club ... And we are now united. We are making history." Remember, in 1914, Congress referred to Standard Oil as "the invisible government." The oil companies are powerful, and their power was never more apparent, then it was during the manufactured crisis of 1973.

On October 6, 1973, as synagogues in Israel observed Yom Kippur, the Jewish Day of Atonement, Syrian MiG-21's attacked a group of Israeli jets. Egypt, Syria, Jordan, and eight other Arab nations had mobilized against Israel. Egypt attacked the Sinai Peninsula with 4,000 tanks, knocking out many Israeli tanks; while Syria attacked the Golan Heights with 1,200. New Soviet-made SAM-6 missiles plucked Israeli planes out of the sky with ease. However, within a few days, the tide was turned. Israel regained control of the Heights, and took a large part of Syria. On October 12, they were only 18 miles from Damascus. With 12,000 soldiers, and 200 tanks, they swept across the Suez Canal in two directions to surround the Egyptian Third Army, which had been caught on the east side, and came within 12 miles of Cairo.

Since the first day of the war, Russia had been airlifting supplies to the Arabs, so to counter that move, the United States said they intended to supply Israel "with whatever it needs." Once Israel began smashing their way to victory, Russia sent a Naval force of 71 ships, including 16 submarines, to the Mediterranean, and put their seven airborne divisions on full alert.

On October 12th, the Chairmen of Exxon, Texaco, Mobil, and Chevron (who made up the production company of Aramco in Saudi Arabia), sent Chief of Staff Gen. Alexander Haig (who later became Reagan's Secretary of State) a memo warning against any increased aid to Israel, by saying it would "have a critical and adverse effect on our relations with the moderate Arab producing countries." On October 17th, Omar Saqqaf, the Foreign Minister of Saudi Arabia, gave President Nixon a letter from King Faisal, which said that if the U.S. did not discontinue their shipment of military supplies to Israel within two days, there would be an embargo. Nixon stated that he was committed to supporting Israel. The U.S. Sixth Fleet of 49 ships, including 2 aircraft carriers, was sent to the Mediterranean, where they maintained a state of combat readiness.

OPEC met and decided to raise the price of oil to $5.12 a barrel, which was 70% higher than they had agreed to before the Arab-Israeli War. The next day, the Arab countries met, and decided to cut oil production by 5%, however, the Saudis later decided to cut back production by more than 20%, and by October 20th, had embargoed all oil shipments to the U.S., and countries that were partial to Israel.

As the Israeli counterattack continued, Egypt and Syria were in serious trouble, and Russia urged the UN to call a ceasefire. Jim Akins, the ambassador to Saudi Arabia sent a message to Aramco that the oil embargo would not be lifted "unless the political struggle is settled in a manner satisfactory to the Arabs." Two days later, the Saudis requested from the Aramco directors, information concerning the amount of oil used by the U.S. military, which they supplied. The Saudis then instructed them to stop all supplies to the military. In December, OPEC announced a price of $11.65 a barrel, and the result was economic chaos in the United States and Western Europe.

Though Aramco claimed that they had no choice in what they did, and that they weren't acting as agents of a foreign government against the United States, the cry went out that the oil industry was putting "profits before patriotism." Before the embargo, America was importing 1.2 million barrels oil a day; and by February, only 18,000 barrels, which was a drop of 98%. The rush was on to reallocate other sources of oil (Venezuela and Iran had not joined the boycott), and to distribute it throughout the world. The global emphasis of the American oil companies were revealed, when they refused to favor the U.S. at the expense of the other countries, causing us to lose a higher percentage of the available oil supply.

In Egypt, Sadat's terms for a ceasefire, was that Israel had to withdraw from all territories that it had won during the 1967 war; thus pressure from the United States and the Soviets, forced Israel to turn their victory into a negotiated compromise.

To add insult to injury, when the winter was at its worst during the shortage, the announcement that oil companies were experiencing record profits, left a very sour taste in the mouths of Americans. Exxon announced that their third quarter profits were up 80% over the previous year, while Gulf was up 91%. Exxon ended up the year with a profit that was an all-time record for any company, in any industry.

By March, 1974, the embargo was lifted from the U.S., and the oil companies scrambled to salvage their shattered reputations. However, the incident would never be forgotten, because it shocked the American people back to the reality of just how much control a foreign government, and multinational corporations could exert over our nation. The price of oil never went down to their pre-embargo levels, and the threat of another shortage would always remain as the Arabs realized that they could achieve political leverage by using oil to blackmail the world.

There have been many changes in the oil industry since the inception of the Seven Sisters. In 1984, Chevron (Standard Oil of California) bought, and merged with Gulf Oil; and then in 2001, merged with Texaco (who in 1984 had bought Getty Oil), to become ChevronTexaco, the 2nd largest oil company in the country, and 5th largest in the world. In 2002, Shell Oil acquired a couple of Texaco's interests. In 1998, Exxon (Esso, Standard Oil of New Jersey) merged with Mobil (Socony, Standard Oil of New York) to become ExxonMobil, the biggest oil company in the country, and third largest company in the U.S. In 1987 British Petroleum purchased the remaining 45% of Sohio (Standard Oil of Ohio) that they didn't already own, then in 1998, merged with Amoco (Standard Oil of Indiana), and in 2000 merged with Arco (Atlantic Richfield).

The Seven Sisters are now the Four Sisters, so what you have now is an expanded amount of power and influence that is concentrated in less hands, as oil companies have sought to consolidate their interests because of economic concerns. It's uncanny in that it has happened in less than 20 years. It's almost as if the old Standard Oil Company was coming back together. In 2001, Conoco (Continental Oil) and Phillips Petroleum (Phillips 66) merged, to make ConocoPhillips, the 3rd largest oil company, the 12th largest company, and the 6th largest oil company in the world. If this trend continues, it will make it all the more easier for oil companies to manipulate and control a crucial commodity like gasoline and oil.

CLUB OF ROME

This think-tank of Anglo-American financiers, scientists, economists, politicians, heads of state, and industrialists from ten different countries, met in April, 1968 at Rockefeller's private estate in Bellagio, Italy, at the request of Aurelio Peccei, the Italian industrialist who had close ties to Fiat and the Olivetti Corporation. He claimed to have solutions for world peace and prosperity, which could be accomplished through world government. The Club of Rome (COR) was established with a membership of 75 prominent scientists, industrialists, and economists from 25 countries, which along with the Bilderbergers, have become one of the most important foreign policy arms of the Roundtable group.

Many of the COR executives were drawn from NATO, and they have been able to formulate a lot of what NATO claims are its policies. Through Lord Carrington, they were able to split NATO into two factions, a left-wing political group (whose doctrine was formed on the basis of Peccei's book *Human Quality*), and its former military alliance.

The first Club of Rome conference in the U.S. was in 1969, where the American branch was organized as the "American Association of the Club of Rome." Among its members were: Norman Cousins (honorary Chairman of Planetary Citizens), John Naisbitt (author of *Megatrends*), Amory Lovins (a speaker at Windstar, John Denver's New Age center in Snowmass, Colorado), Betty Friedan (founding President of NOW, the National Organization of Women), Jean Houston and Hazel Henderson (New Age authors and speakers), Robert O. Anderson and Harlan B. Cleveland (CFR members and part of the Aspen Institute for Humanistic Studies), Sen. Claiborne Pell (D-RI), and Rep. Frank M. Potter (staff director of the House Subcommittee on Energy).

Their first book, called *The Limits to Growth*, was published in 1972, and described their vision for the world:

> "We believe in fact that the need will quickly become evident for social innovation to match technical change, for radical reform of the institutions and political processes at all levels, including the highest, that of world polity. And since intellectual enlightenment is without effect if it is not also political, The Club of Rome also will encourage the creation of a world forum where statesmen, policy-makers, and scientists can discuss the dangers and hopes for the future global system without the constraints of formal intergovernmental negotiation."

For the most part, the Club (main office at 193 Rissener Landstr. In Hamburg, Germany) functions as a research institute on economic, political, and social problems, and claim that "there is no other viable alternative to the future survival of civilization than a new global community under a common leadership." Their website claims:

> "The Club of Rome's mission is to act as a global catalyst of change that is free of any political, ideological or business interest. The Club of Rome contributes to the solution of what it calls the world problematique, the complex set of the most crucial problems— political, social, economic,

technological, environmental, psychological and cultural— facing humanity. It does so taking a global, long term and interdisciplinary prospective aware of the increasing interdependence of nations and the globalization of problems that pose predicaments beyond the capacity of individual countries."

It almost sounds like the Club of Rome is the A-Team of internationalist groups. Just like how the proposals suggested by the Bilderbergers seem to gain acceptance, we have to worry that the same thing will happen with the COR.

On September 17, 1973, they released a Report called the "Regionalized and Adaptive Model of the Global World System," which was prepared by Directors Mihajlo Mesarovic and Eduard Pestel (part of the "Strategy for Survival Project"), which revealed the Club's goal of dividing the world into ten political/economic regions (which have been equated to the 10 "Kingdoms" of Bible prophecy), which would unite the entire world under a single form of government. These regions are: North America, Western Europe, Eastern Europe, Japan, Rest of Developed World, Latin America, Middle East, Rest of Africa, South and Southeast Asia, and China. The same plan was published in a Club of Rome book called *Mankind at the Turning Point*, which said: "The solution of these crises can be developed only in a global context with full and explicit recognition of the emerging world system and on a long-term basis. This would necessitate, among other changes, a new world economic order and a global resources allocation system..."

In 1976, they published *RIO: Reshaping the International Order* which called for a new international order, including an economic redistribution of wealth.

Howard T. Odum, a marine biologist at the University of Florida, who is a member of the Club of Rome, was quoted in the August, 1980 edition of *Fusion* magazine, as saying: "It is necessary that the United States cut its population by two-thirds within the next 50 years." He didn't say how this would be accomplished. Their 1972 book, *The Limits to Growth* (which sold 12 million copies in 27 languages), dealt with the problem of worldwide overpopulation, and stated that "if the world's consumption patterns and population growth continued at the same high rates of the time, the earth would strike its limits within a century."

During the Carter Administration, a task force was appointed to expand upon this report, and on July 24, 1980, a two-volume document called "Global 2000 Report," which had been written by former Secretary of State Cyrus R. Vance, was presented to President Carter, and then Secretary of State Edward S. Muskie. It attempted to project global economic trends for the next twenty years, and indicated that the resources of the planet were not sufficient enough to support the expect dramatic increase in the world population. The report called for the population of the U.S. to be reduced by 100 million people by the year 2050.

About six months later, the Council on Environmental Quality made recommendations based on the Report, called "Global Future: A Time to Act." They suggested an aggressive program of population control which included sterilization, contraception and abortion. In August, 1982, the *Executive Intelligence Review* published a report called "Global 2000: Blueprint for Genocide" which said that the two aforementioned Presidential reports "are correctly understood as political statements of intent— the intent on the part of such policy centers as the

Council on Foreign Relations, the Trilateral Commission, and the International Monetary Fund, to pursue policies that will result not only in the death of the 120 million cited in the reports, but in the death of upwards of two billion people by the year 2000."

Peccei wrote (based on a report by COR member Harland Cleveland, U.S. Ambassador to NATO, who believed that Third World countries should decide for themselves who should be eliminated):

> "Damaged by conflicting policies of three major countries and blocs, roughly patched up here and there, the existing international economic order is visibly coming apart at the seams ... The prospect of the necessity of the recourse to triage deciding who must be saved is a very grim one indeed. But, if lamentably, events should come to such a pass, the right to make such decisions cannot be left to just a few nations because it would lend themselves to ominous power over life of the world's hungry."

Throughout the world, the Club of Rome has indicated that genocide should be used to eliminate people who they refer to as "useless eaters."

This would be accomplished by using limited wars in advanced countries, and even a limited nuclear strike at a strategic location; as well as starvation through created famines and diseases in Third World countries.

In the 1976 novel *Ceremony of the Innocent* by Taylor Caldwell, she effectively explains the rationale behind their actions: "...there will be no peace in the tormented world, only a programmed and systematic series of wars and calamities— until the plotters have gained their objective: an exhausted world willing to submit to a planned Marxist economy and total and meek enslavement— in the name of peace."

Have their plans for genocide already started? AIDS (Acquired Immunodeficiency Syndrome) has become a plague in our society, spreading to 91 nations. In the early 1990's the *U.S. News and World Report* stated: "If there is not a cure for AIDS within the next thirteen years, tens of millions will die." Even though there has been a lot of talk about AIDS awareness and prevention, the full danger of it has been covered-up by the Center for Disease Control, and the media, which has increasingly shown its pro-homosexual bias.

In 1969, at a House Appropriations hearing, the Defense Department's Biological Warfare unit requested funds to develop, through gene-splicing, a new disease that would be resistant to treatment, and break down a victim's immune system. They received $10 million (H.B. 15090), to produce "a synthetic biological agent, an agent that does not naturally exist and for which no natural immunity could have been acquired."

In the 1972 Bulletin of the UN's World Health Organization (WHO), volume 47, page 251, it says: "An attempt should be made to see if viruses can in fact exert selective effects on immune function. The possibility should be looked into that the immune response to the virus itself may be impaired if the inflicting virus damages, more or less selectively, the cell responding to the virus." This sounds like the AIDS virus, so why is it being discussed by a health organization?

Derivatives from sheep and cattle have been commonly used to manufacture vaccines, however, certain viruses common to these animals can interact indefinitely, forming a new strain of deadly viruses called retro-viruses. In 1974, the National Academy of Sciences recommended that "Scientists throughout the world join with members of this committee in voluntarily deferring experiments (linking) animal viruses." Dr. Robert Strecker, a practicing gastroenterologist, with a Ph.D. in pharmacology, who was hired as a consultant to work on a health-care proposal for Security Pacific Bank, said: "I don't think there is any doubt that AIDS is a man-made problem. The question is whether it was created either accidentally or intentionally. I believe the AIDS virus was requested, predicted, produced, and deployed."

The most common theory about the origin of AIDS was that it came from green monkeys in Africa. Yet several virologists have said that the AIDS virus does not occur naturally in any animal. Besides, it would have been statistically impossible to reach the point we are at now, just from a single episode. If the AIDS virus had originated with the monkeys, then the disease would have surfaced with the Pygmies, who are closer to them, and use them as a food source, yet, it appeared first in the cities. Further damaging evidence comes from the fact that AIDS practically occurred simultaneously in the United States, Haiti, Brazil, and Central Africa.

Strecker's research indicated that the AIDS virus (code-named 'MKNAOMI') was developed by the Frederick Cancer Research Facility of the National Cancer Institute, in cooperation with the WHO, in their laboratories at Fort Detrick, Maryland (which until 1969 was part of the U.S. Army's germ warfare unit, known as the Army Infectious Disease Unit, or Special Operations Division); by combining bovine (cow) leukemia virus and visna (sheep) virus, and injecting them into human tissue cultures. The bovine leukemia virus is lethal to cows, but not to humans; and the visna virus is deadly to sheep, but not to man. However, when combined, they produce a retro-virus that can change the genetic composition of the cells that they enter. He said:

> "If one analyzes the genes of the human AIDS virus and the genes of the bovine leukemia virus of cattle and the visna virus of sheep, and compares them, the genes appear related. How is it possible that the bovine visna virus— which looks like AIDS and produces an AIDS-like disease, and which produced pneumocystis carinii pneumonia in chimpanzees in 1972— has not been analyzed and compared with AIDS ... until 1987 when 'Characterization and Molecular Cloning of Bovine Lente (Latin for 'slow') Virus Related to Human Immunodeficiency Virus' was published in *Nature* magazine. Matthew Gonda, the author, described a virus that looks like AIDS, named bovine visna virus, and suggested that it was most closely related to AIDS and may well be its precursor."

On August 11, 1988, Ted Strecker, Dr. Strecker's brother was found shot to death in his home in Springfield, Missouri. His death was ruled a suicide. On September 22, 1988, Illinois State Representative Douglas Huff of Chicago was found dead in his home. The autopsy revealed that he died of a stroke as a result of an overdose of cocaine and heroin. Rep. Huff just happened to be a very vocal supporter of Dr. Strecker's work to publicize the AIDS cover-up. Coincidence or conspiracy?

There was a vaccination program for Smallpox in Africa by the WHO. Some researchers believe that the Smallpox vaccination program in 1972 was used to introduce the virus into the population. On May 11, 1987, the *London Times* ran an article called "Smallpox Vaccine 'Triggered AIDS Virus'," written by Science Editor Pearce Wright, who linked the mass vaccination program of the World Health Organization in the 1970's to the outbreak of AIDS, because Central Africa was the focus of the program, and they have become the most affected area in the world.

Though in Africa, AIDS is generally regarded as a heterosexual disease, in the United States, it has the stigma of being a 'gay' disease. Prior to 1978, there was no sign of the AIDS virus here, yet in 1978, the killer disease struck with a vengeance within the homosexual community. The evidence points to the introduction of an experimental Hepatitis B vaccine. In 1969, Dr. W. Schmugner, a Polish physician, who was educated in Russia, came to the United States, where he became head of the New York City Blood Bank. He set up guidelines for a Hepatitis vaccine study, and only promiscuous males between the ages of 20 and 40 were included in the study, which has led some to believe that this was how the virus was introduced into the gay population.

In 1978, more than 1,000 non-monogamous gay adult males received an experimental vaccination against Hepatitis B, which was sponsored by the National Institute of Health and the Center for Disease Control. With the Hepatitis vaccine, which is not produced from a human tissue culture, it is impossible to have an accidental contamination, which seems to indicate that the AIDS virus was intentionally put in the vaccine. In 1981, the Center for Disease Control reported that 6% of those receiving the Hepatitis vaccine were infected with AIDS, but in 1984, they admitted that it was actually 64%. These Hepatitis vaccine studies are now in the possession of the Justice Department in Washington, DC.

To allow the disease to become entrenched within the population, various facts were covered-up and glossed-over. A great deal of emphasis had been put on the prime cause of AIDS infection, being the exchange of body fluid, through sexual activity and intravenous drug use, which has brought a campaign for the importance of using clean, unused needles, and condoms. The use of a condom does not guarantee protection against the transmission of the AIDS virus. All it takes is one AIDS virion (a complete virus particle with its outer coat intact), and the smallest sperm is 500 times larger that one such virion. In addition, the quality of condoms have become highly suspect, since failure rates of 30-50% have been reported.

The risk of casual contact has been played down when in fact AIDS is a highly contagious disease which demands that a quarantine be placed on those who suffer from the disease. Rather than treat the disease as the epidemic it is, the government has concerned itself with giving AIDS carriers more rights and more exposure to the general population. There is concrete medical evidence that indicates that the virus can survive up to 7 days on a dry petri dish, and up to 15 days, in an aqueous (wet) environment. This raises the question, what would happen if an AIDS carrier would sneeze into a punch bowl or a salad bowl. It can incubate 10-15 years before causing any noticeable signs of illness, which means that sexual relations exposes you to every sexual contact your partner has had in that period of time.

A February, 1985 report in the British medical journal *Lancet*, said: "There is little evidence for homosexual activity among African AIDS patients (and it) appears to be transmitted through heterosexual contact or exposure to blood through insect bites..." On September 9, 1985, a research team of researchers from the National Cancer Institute, the Laboratory of Tumor Cell Biology and the Institute of Tropical Medicine, said that "human retroviruses could be transmitted by mosquitoes or within the parasite itself." In a report published in the October, 1981, issue of *Science*, Boston hematologist Dr. Jerome Groopman, and researchers with the National Institute of Health said that recovery of the AIDS virus "from saliva suggests that direct contact with this body fluid should be avoided..."

On January 11, 1985, the Center for Disease Control reported: "There is a risk of infecting others by ... exposure of others through oral-genital contact or intimate kissing ('french' kissing)." Dr. Richard Restak, a Washington neurologist, made this statement:

> "At this point live AIDS virus has been isolated from blood, semen, serum, saliva, urine and now tears. If the virus exists in these fluids, the better part of wisdom dictates that we assume the possibility that it can also be transmitted by these routes. It seems reasonable, therefore, that AIDS victims should not donate blood or blood products, should not contribute to semen banks, should not donate tissues or organs to organ banks, should not work as dental or medical technicians, and should probably not be employed as food handlers."

Professor William Haseltine of the Harvard Medical School, in a presentation to a University audience, said that anyone "who tells you categorically that AIDS is not contracted by saliva is not telling you the truth. AIDS may in fact be transmissible by tears, saliva, bodily fluids, and mosquito bites."

AIDS is an epidemic that will not be stopped. The scientists that created this deadly virus, have created a virus that multiplies 100 times faster than influenza. There are more than 180 different AIDS viruses, and 300 strains, which makes blood testing meaningless. The virus is constantly mutating, which makes it impossible to develop a general vaccine that would be effective with everyone. Quite simply, AIDS is a world-wide, modern-day plague, and every year, the number of those affected increases drastically. In the March, 1987 issue of *Vanity Fair*, Dr. William Grace, chief of Oncology at St. Vincent's Hospital in New York, is quoted as saying: "I think AIDS is going to devastate the American medical system." Besides not being able to combat it medically, the disease will progress to being an economic drain, especially if national health care is instituted."

If its purpose was to glean out the population, it certainly will be successful. It must be assumed that the progenitors of this disease must have a measure of protection to prevent themselves from being exposed. The elite have already segregated themselves from the general population by virtue of their position, so from that aspect, there is little risk from being contaminated. In the event of medical treatment, they have access to the best medical treatment that money can buy, and most likely possess a private, untainted blood supply. Somehow, I just can't help thinking, that when their goal of limits to the population have been reached, how will they end the scourge which they have placed upon the earth. Just as the saying goes, that a lawyer in court doesn't ask the witness a question that he doesn't already have the answer for; the same reasoning would seem to apply here, that the Illuminati would not unleash a disease that they didn't already have a cure for.

Bro. R. G. Stair, a well-known radio evangelist, had received an anonymous letter which seemed to confirm this theory. The writer claimed to be a molecular biologist who worked in the same laboratory with Dr. Robert C. Gallo (the molecular biologist noted for his involvement in the co-discovery of the AIDS virus). The writer claimed that there is an AIDS vaccine that is now available, and that 500,000,000 doses have been produced and is now available. Now the bombshell. The writer accidentally discovered that Gallo had actually created the AIDS virus, and found a couple letters in his office, from high government officials which mentioned the New World Order.

In 1961, in a Litton Bionetics laboratory (who was working with the Navy's Biomedical Research Laboratory, in association with the Univeristy of California), retroviral experiments with African Green Monkeys and Human T-Cell Leukemia were being conducted under the auspices of the National Institute of Health (contract # SVCP PR#8 NIH #71-2025). It consisted of taking monkey viruses that were harmless to humans, recombined them with DNA, RNA and enzymes from other animal viruses that were known to cause leukemias, lymphomas, and sarcomas; then got them to jump species, and cultured the new mutant viruses into human white blood cells in some studies, and in other studies— human fetal tissues, which produced an "immune-system destroying, cancer-causing viruses" for which "no natural immunity could have been acquired, and no cure exists." The scientist who was directing the tests was Dr. Robert Gallo.

In 1975, Gallo and eight other scientists (working at the Bethesda Cancer Research Center in Maryland) had been working to modify the genetic structure of the virus so that it can be more easily transmitted. That same year, after Fort Detrick had become demilitarized, the newly established Frederick Cancer Research Facility was placed under the direction of the Bethesda Cancer Research Center, where Gallo was the Director. One investigation revealed that in March, 1976, a special federal government virus development program began producing the AIDS virus, and it was headed by Dr. Gallo and Dr. Novakhatskiy of the Ivanosku Institute in Russia. Gallo would later be investigated and found guilty of scientific misconduct, but President Clinton pardoned him.

In response to the charges that AIDS was developed as a military biological warfare weapon, in February, 1987, Army Col. David Huxsoll said: "Studies at army laboratories have shown that the AIDS virus would be an extremely poor biological warfare agent." He later denied saying it.

Whether AIDS is the vehicle of elimination, that the Club of Rome has referred to, or a precursor, just like Gulf War Syndrome, Ebola, and SARS, is undoubtedly open to speculation, even in light of all the questions raised. However, you can't deny how neatly this little piece of the puzzle fits into the entire picture of preparing the world for a one-world government.

INDEPENDENT COMMISSION ON INTERNATIONAL DEVELOPMENT ISSUES

The Toronto Globe and Mail, on April 7, 1980, reported the story of a conference to be hosted by Canadian Prime Minister Trudeau, that fall, which would "reshape global structures." The Summit, known as the "North-South Dialogue," which would "make recommendations on ways of breaking through existing international political impasse in North-South negotiations for global development," was sponsored by the Independent Commission on International Development Issues, and was to include President Jimmy Carter, *Newsweek* and *Washington* Post publisher Kathryn Graham, Robert McNamara, former British Prime Minister Edward Heath, and West German Chancelor Helmut Schmidt.

On January 14, 1977, Robert McNamara, President of the World Bank, proposed the establishment of an international commission of politicians and economists who would meet, not as government representatives, but independently to discuss "basic proposals on which global agreement is both essential and possible." Willy Brandt, the former West German Chancellor was asked to chair the commission.

On September 28, 1977, Brandt announced his intention to launch the Independent Commission on International Development Issues, and said that it "would not interfere with ongoing international negotiations, and would make recommendations to help improve the climate of North-South relations." Brandt wanted the Commission, consisting of 18 members, to represent many views, and to be politically and regionally balanced, with a majority coming from developed countries. Their initial meeting was in December, 1977.

There was two phases to what is more commonly referred to as Brandt's Commission. The funding for the first ($750,000) in 1980, producing *North-South: A Program for Survival*, was provided by the Dutch Government, as well as Denmark, Finland, India, Japan, Republic of Korea, Norway, Saudi Arabia, Sweden, United Kingdom, the Commission of the European Communities, OPEC Special Fund, German Marshall Fund of the United States, the Ford Foundation, Friedrich-Ebert and Friedrich-Naumann Foundations of the Federal Republic of Germany, and the International Development Research Center of Canada.

Subsequent funding was provided by the governments of Denmark, the Netherlands, Norway, Sweden, United Kingdom, and the OPEC Special Fund.

The funding for the second phase ($350,000), which produced the 1983 report *Common Crisis: North-South Cooperation for World Recovery*, came from the governments of Canada, the Federal Republic of Germany, the Netherlands, Kuwait, the Commission of the European Communities, and the German Marshall Fund of the United States.

In short, the Brandt Reports "called for a full-scale restructuring of the global economy," and the purpose of the Commission was "to influence public opinion to help change government attitudes, as well as to make proposals for revitalizing North-South negotiations."

In the 380-page report called *North-South*, which called for the "instant" redistribution of wealth from the richer, to poorer nations, and a stepping up of world disarmament. They wanted "greater power for the International Monetary Fund and the World Bank." Their rationale was that the "transfer of wealth must be tackled, not out of charity, but to ward off economic collapse ... Hence, the global super summit now. Worldwide security is not achieved by granting more aid, but by reshaping global structures, by greater regionalized planning and development." In *Common Crisis* they recommended that a supernational authority be established to regulate world commerce and industry, international currency, and an international police force, under the direction of the UN Security Council.

CHAPTER NINE

READY TO SPRING THE TRAP

THE TRILATERAL COMMISSION

In July, 1944, during World War II, economist John Maynard Keynes of England, and Harry Dexter White of the United States, organized the United Nation's Monetary and Financial Conference (or Bretton Woods Conference) in Bretton Woods, New Hampshire, to lay out a plan for stabilizing the world economy. The General Agreement on Tariffs and Trade was signed; and the International Bank for Reconstruction and Development (World Bank) and International Monetary Fund were established. In the early 1960's, the American economy began declining, and the international situation became unbalanced again. On August 15, 1971, President Nixon announced a new economic policy. The dollar was devalued, and its convertibility to gold was suspended. He initiated a 90-day wage price freeze, stimulative tax and spending cuts, and placed a temporary 10% tariff on most U.S. imports. Japan and Western Europe were pressured into relaxing their trade barriers, in order to give the United States more access to them; and Japan, South Korea, Hong Kong, and Taiwan were requested to decrease the flow of goods and textiles into the country. These moves offered relief to the country's economic woes, but was an indication that Nixon was retreating from the global policies which were formulated during the 1960's.

This series of drastic changes in the U.S. international policy motivated David Rockefeller (a Director of the Federal Reserve Bank of New York, and head of the Illuminati in the U.S.), who, after attending the Bilderberg Conference and consulting with Zbigniew Brzezinski, wanted to "bring the best brains in the world to bear on problems of the future." Speaking at the Chase Manhattan International Financial Forums in London, Brussels, Montreal, and Paris, he proposed the creation of an International Commission of Peace and Prosperity (which would later become the Trilateral Commission) in early 1972. At the 1972 Bilderberger meeting, the idea was widely accepted, but elsewhere, it got a cool reception. According to Rockefeller, the organization could "be of help to government by providing measured judgment."

Zbigniew Brzezinski, a professor at Columbia University, and a Rockefeller advisor, who was a specialist on international affairs, left his post to organize the group with Henry Owen (a Foreign Policy Studies Director with the Brookings Institution), George S. Franklin, Robert Bowie (of the Foreign Policy Association and Director of the Harvard Center for International Affairs), Gerard Smith (Salt I negotiator, Rockefeller in-law, and its first North American Chairman), Marshall Hornblower, William Scranton (former Governor of Pennsylvania), Edwin Reischauer (a professor at Harvard), and Max Kohnstamn. Brzezinski was the author of the book *Between Two Ages*, which was published in 1970, in which he called for a new international monetary system, and it was considered to be the 'Bible' of the Trilateralists. On page 72, he said: "Marxism is simultaneously a victory of the external, active man over the inner, passive man and a victory of reason over belief." He called for "deliberate management of the American future (pg. 260)," a "community of nations (pg. 296)," and a "world government (pg. 308)." He became its first Director (1973-76), drafted its Charter, and became its driving force.

Funding for the group came from David Rockefeller, the Charles F. Kettering Foundation, and the Ford Foundation.

Journalist Bill Moyers (a CFR member), wrote about the power of David Rockefeller in 1980: "David Rockefeller is the most conspicuous representative today of the ruling class, a multinational fraternity of men who shape the global economy and manage the flow of its capital ... Private citizen David Rockefeller is accorded privileges of a head of state ... He is untouched by customs or passport offices and hardly pauses for traffic lights." In his 1979 book *Who's Running America?*, Thomas Dye said that Rockefeller was the most powerful man in America.

In July, 1972, Rockefeller called his first meeting, which was held at Rockefeller's Pocantico compound in New York's Hudson Valley. It was attended by about 250 individuals who were carefully selected and screened by Rockefeller and represented the very elite of finance and industry.

Within a year, after their first full meeting of the Executive Committee in Tokyo, the Trilateral Commission, considered to be an off-shoot of the Bilderberger group, was officially initiated, holding biannual meetings. Because of a heavy cross-membership, some researchers have said that they appear to be an inner circle of the Council on Foreign Relations (and also have ties to the Atlantic Institute for International Affairs, which was established in 1961 as "a sort of public arm of NATO"), and represent a union of experts and transnational elite from the three noncommunist industrial regions of the world: North America, Japan, and Western Europe (excluding Austria, Greece, and Sweden). Rockefeller saw the need for such a private consultation among these three democratic areas. With the demise of the Bretton Woods system, they believed an overhaul was needed. The theory was, that America's role should be diminished, and made equal to the Common Market and Japan, because together, the three represented 70% of the world's trade.

In 1973, David Rockefeller met with 27 heads of state, including representatives from the Soviet Union and China; and in 1974, had a meeting with Pope Paul VI, who afterward called for the nations to form a world government.

A Trilateral Commission Task Force Report, presented at the 1975 meeting in Kyoto, Japan, called *An Outline for Remaking World Trade and Finance*, said: "Close Trilateral cooperation in keeping the peace, in managing the world economy, and in fostering economic development and in alleviating world poverty, will improve the chances of a smooth and peaceful evolution of the global system." Another Commission document read: "The overriding goal is to make the world safe for interdependence by protecting the benefits which it provides for each country against external and internal threats which will constantly emerge from those willing to pay a price for more national autonomy. This may sometimes require slowing the pace at which interdependence proceeds, and checking some aspects of it. More frequently however, it will call for checking the intrusion of national government into the international exchange of both economic and non-economic goods." In other words, they were promoting world government by encouraging economic interdependence among the superpowers.

This little-known organization is actually controlled by the Rockefellers, who oversee its activities and provide guidance for their policies. Their membership consists of over 300 members (with membership ceilings of 107 from North America, 150 from Western Europe, and 117 from Pacific-Asian), is made up of top bankers, industrialists, businessmen, labor leaders, scholars, politicians, senators, and governors. They only consider people interested in promoting close international cooperation, especially among non-communist industrial nations, which actually means they advocate a one-world government. Many Cabinet level officers, and advisors, from the Kennedy Administration to the Clinton Administration have served on the Commission.

There is a Chairman (former Speaker of the House Thomas S. Foley is the current North American Chairman), Deputy Chairman, and Director for each of the three areas, as well as a 44 member Executive Committee, with such recognizable names as: C. Fred Bergsten (former U.S. Assistant Secretary of the Treasury for International Affairs), Zbigniew Brzezinski, Joseph S. Nye, Jr. (Dean of the John F. Kennedy School of Government at Harvard University, and former U.S. Assistant Secretary of Defense for International Security Affairs), and Paul Volcker (former Chairman of the Federal Reserve, and a former North American Chairman of the Trilateral Commission, 1991-2001).

An analysis of one of their three-year budgets of $1.67 million, indicated that $644,000 came from foundations, $530,000 from corporations, $220,000 from individual contributors, $180,000 from the Rockefeller Brothers Fund, $150,000 from David Rockefeller's personal account, $100,000 from the Rockefeller Foundation, and $84,000 from investment income.

The Commission holds an annual three-day meeting, rotated among the three areas, to discuss the world monetary situation, and other economic and military issues; and sometimes have regional meetings. The meetings are closed to the public, and the media is denied access.

There are three headquarters, Washington, D.C. (1156 Fifteenth Street, NW), Paris (5, rue de Téhéran), and Tokyo (Japan Center for International Exchange, 4-19-17 Minami-Azabu, Minato-ku). Each branch has a small full-time staff.

The organization had published a quarterly magazine, called the *Trialogue*. The first three issues of the year were devoted to significant international matters, while the fourth, covered in detail, their annual meeting. It was discontinued in 1985 to help lower expenses. However, they do still publish a report about their annual meeting. Their Task Force Reports usually take up to a year to prepare, and they are always written by at least three experts, representing each region.

The Commission has been served by internationalists drawn from firms like: Wachovia Bank and Trust Co., Chase Manhattan, Citicorp, Morgan Guaranty, Bank of America, Lloyds of London, Bank of Tokyo, Barclays Bank, Compagnie Financiere Holding, Brown Brothers, Harriman and Co., Fuji Bank, Banque de Paris, Provincial Bank of Canada, Toronto-Dominion Bank, First City Bancorp, Bank of Italy, Industrial Bank of Japan, Mitsui Bank, Chemical Bank, Mitsubishi Bank, and the Continental Illinois National Bank and Trust Co.

The Commission has been served by corporate officers from companies like: Boeing, Coca-Cola, Japan Air Lines, Volkswagenwerk, Ford Motor Co., Deere, Caterpillar Tractor, Cargill, Cummins Engine, Xerox, Sony, Toyota, Johnson & Johnson, Fiat, Dunlop, Rolls-Royce, Thyssen, Bendix, Texas Instruments, Exxon, Texaco, Mobil, Arco, Pepsico, Rand Corp., RJR Nabisco, Levi Strauss, Archer Midland Daniels, Coca-Cola, American Express, ITT Corp, Hewlett-Packard, Kaisar Resources, Shell, Mitsubishi, Hitachi, Nippon Steel, Sears and Roebuck, Weyerhaeuser, and General Motors.

They have been served by such Union leaders as: Lane Kirkland (President of the AFL-CIO), I. W. Abel (President of the United Steel Workers of America), Leonard Woodcock (United Auto Workers), Sol Chaikin (President of the International Ladies Garment Workers Union), Albert Shanker (American Federation Of Teachers), Jay Mazur (Union of Needletrades, Industrial and Textile Employees), and Glenn Watts (President of the Communications Workers of America).

The Commission has some of its members in such branches of the media as: *New York Times*, *Washington Post*, *Wall Street Journal*, *Minneapolis Star and Tribune*, *Los Angeles Times*, *Chicago Sun Times*, Kyodo News Service, *Japan Times*, *La Stampa*, *Die Ziet*, *Financial Times*, Columbia Broadcasting (CBS-TV), *The Economist*, Japan Broadcasting Corp., *Time*, Associated Press, and United Press International.

A good example of how the Trilateral Commission influences the media, could be seen in the January 15, 1981 episode of the ABC-TV show "Barney Miller." A man was arrested for breaking into the offices of the Commission, and when he was taken to the 12th Precinct, he began ranting and raving about how the Commission was attempting to set up an "international community" and how they eventually wanted to take over the world. The character, William Klein (played by Jeffrey Tambor) was made to look like a fool, and upon leaving the squad room, Detective Sgt. Arthur Dietrich (played by Steve Landesberg) said: "Well, I think you have some very valid criticisms of the Commission, and I'm certainly gonna bring them up at the next meeting." After Dietrich tells the man he was a Trilateral member, which he wasn't, the man reacted: "Oh God, no..." The character was made to look like a paranoid maniac, reminiscent of the McCarthy era. This was only one of the many propaganda pieces that was used to make the Commission look just like any other organization. This is the principle that the Illuminati has used for years to slant the news, so that the public will accept their views.

In the late 1800's, at an annual dinner of the American Press Association, John Swinton, an editor at the *New York Times*, said:

"There is no such thing, at this date, of the world's history, in America, as an independent press. You know it and I know it. There is not one of you who dares to write your honest opinions, and if you did, you know beforehand that it would never appear in print. I am paid weekly for keeping my honest opinions out of the paper I am connected with. Others of you are paid similar salaries for similar things, and any of you who would be so foolish as to write honest opinions would be out on the streets looking for another job. If I allowed my honest opinions to appear in one issue of my paper, before twenty-four hours my occupation would be gone. The business of the journalist is to destroy truth; to lie outright; to pervert; to vilify; to fawn at the feet of mammon, and to sell his country and his race for his daily bread. You know it and I know it and what folly is this toasting an independent press? We are the tools and vassals for rich men behind the scenes. We are the jumping jacks, they pull the strings and we dance. Our talents, our possibilities, and our lives are all the property of other men. We are intellectual prostitutes."

David Rockefeller said in a *Saturday Evening Post* article he wrote to defend his group: "My point is that far from being a coterie of international conspirators with designs on covertly ruling the world, the Trilateral Commission is, in reality, a group of concerned citizens interested in fostering greater understanding and cooperation among international allies." However, those who have penetrated the inner workings of the organization, say the real purpose of the Commission is to take over all key policy-making positions in the government. Antony Sutton wrote in the *Trilateral Observer* that the Trilateralists have rejected the U.S. Constitution and the democratic political process; and their objective is to obtain the wealth of the world for their own use, under the guise of "public service," and to have, ultimately, a one-world socialist government, with them in control.

Conservative critics claim the "Commission constitutes a conspiracy seeking to gain control of the U.S. Government to create a new world order." Mike Thompson, Chairman of the Florida Conservative Union, said: "It puts emphasis on interdependence, which is a nice euphemism for one-world government." The John Birch Society suspects them of being radical infiltrators of the government. Sen. Barry Goldwater wrote that the Commission was "intended to be the vehicle for multinational consolidation of the commercial and banking interests by seizing control of the political government of the United States. Goldwater wrote in his book *With No Apologies*:

"In my view, the Trilateral Commission represents a skillful, coordinated effort to seize control and consolidate the four centers of power: political, monetary, intellectual, and ecclesiastical. All this is to be done in the interest of creating a more, peaceful, more productive world community. What the Trilateralists truly intend is the creation of a worldwide economic power superior to the political governments of the nation-states involved. They believe the abundant materialism they propose to create will overwhelm existing differences. As managers and creators of the system they will rule the future."

On the left, the U.S. Labor Party alleges that the Commission was created by multinational companies in order to dominate American foreign policy. Upon analysis, their economic plans leaned toward the controlling of energy sources, food production, and the international monetary system, so was there any reason to doubt that there were ulterior motives to their agenda.

The July, 1977 issue of *Atlantic Monthly* reported: "Although the Commission's primary concern is economic, the Trilateralists pinpointed a vital political objective: to gain control of the American Presidency." The author of the article, Jeremiah Novak, said: "For the third time in this century, a group of American schools, businessmen, and government officials is planning to fashion a new world order…" and that they had achieved one of their objectives, which was to "gain control of the American Presidency." Craig S. Karpel wrote in his book *Cartergate: The Death of Democracy*:

> "The presidency of the United States and the key cabinet departments of the federal government have been taken over by a private organization dedicated to the subordination of the domestic interests of the United States to the international interests of the multi-national banks and corporations. It would be unfair to say that the Trilateral Commission dominates the Carter Administration. The Trilateral Commission is the Carter Administration."

Late in 1972, W. Averell Harriman (known at that time as the "grand old man of the Democrats"), Establishment strategist and CFR member, told Milton Katz (also a CFR member), Director of International Studies at Harvard: "We've got to get off our high horses and look at some of those southern governors." Carter was mentioned, and Katz informed Rockefeller, who had actually met with Carter in 1971, when they had lunch in the Chase Manhattan's Board of Director's dining room, and he was impressed with the fact that Carter had opened trade offices for the state of Georgia in Tokyo.

In February, 1973, while former Secretary of State Dean Rusk (a Bilderberger) was having dinner with Gerald Smith (U.S. Ambassador-at-Large for Non-Proliferation Matters), Rusk suggested that Carter would be a good candidate for the Commission. In April, while Robert Bowie (former professor of International Affairs at Harvard, who later became Deputy Director of the CIA), George S. Franklin (Rockefeller assistant, CFR member, and Coordinator for the Commission), and Smith were discussing the recruitment of candidates, it was decided that they needed better representation from the South. Franklin went to Atlanta to talk to Carter, and then proposed his name for membership. It had been a choice between Carter, and Gov. Reuben Askew of Florida.

In the fall of 1973, after having dinner with David Rockefeller in London, Carter's political momentum began. From that point on, he was groomed for the Presidency by Zbigniew Brzezinski, and the Trilateralists. Just to be on the safe side, they also brought in Minnesota Senator Walter Mondale (a protege of Hubert Humphrey, whose eventual withdrawal from the Presidential race guaranteed the Democratic nomination for Carter), and Rep. Elliot Richardson (former U.S. Attorney General; Secretary of Health, Education, and Welfare and Secretary of Defense, and Under Secretary of State under Nixon; former Secretary of Commerce under Ford; and former Ambassador to Great Britain) as possible candidates, and even considered Sen. Ted Kennedy of Massachusetts.

Brzezinski said in an October, 1973 speech: "The Democratic candidate will have to emphasize work, family, religion, and increasingly, patriotism, if he has any desire to be elected." Carter campaigned by stressing those very virtues, as he asked America to elect him, an "outsider," to clean up the mess in Washington.

In December, 1975, seven months before the Democratic National Convention, the Gallop Poll indicated that only 4% of the country's Democrats wanted Carter. Even the *Atlantic Constitution* in his own state, ran a headline which said: "Jimmy Carter Running For What?" Within six months, the nomination was his because of the most elaborate media campaign in history. Carter was glorified as the new hope of America as the media misrepresented his record as Governor in Georgia. This led former Georgia Governor Lester Maddox to say: "Based on false, misleading and deceiving statements and actions ... Jimmy Carter in my opinion, neither deserves or should expect one vote from the American people." According to the Dektor Psychological Stress Evaluator, a lie detector which measures voice stress with an oscillograph, there was no stress in Carter's voice when he lied, which would seem to indicate that he is a pathological liar.

Even though Carter later resigned from the Commission, he was hardly an "outsider." He was supported by the Trilateral Commission, the Rockefellers, and *Time* magazine. Early contributions came from Dean Rusk, C. Douglas Dillon, Henry Luce, and Cyrus Eaton. Leonard Woodcock of the United Auto Workers Union, and Henry Ford II, both of whom are CFR members, endorsed Carter on the same day. Carter's two major foreign policy speeches during the primary campaign were made to the Chicago Council on Foreign Relations and the Foreign Policy Association. He used terms like "a just and peaceful world order," and "a new international order." In another primary campaign speech, Carter talked about "world-order politics." A *Los Angeles Times* article in June, 1976, identified the advisors that helped Carter prepare his first major speech on foreign policy: Zbigniew Brzezinski, Richard Cooper, Richard Gardner, Henry Owen, Edwin O. Reischauer, Averill Harriman, Anthony Lake, Robert Bowie, Milton Katz, Abram Chayes, George Ball, and Cyrus Vance; who were all members of the CFR (and most were also members of the Trilateral Commission).

Carter's religious convictions became a big part of his campaign, but things weren't really what they seemed. Carter claimed that his favorite theologian was Reinhold Niebuhr (a pro-communist), former professor at the Union Theological Seminary (which had been funded by the Rockefellers), who founded the Americans for Democratic Action. He denied the virgin birth, and the resurrection of Christ. Carter also admired Karl Barth (who said the Bible was "fallible," and filled with "historic and scientific blunders," and "theological contradictions"), Paul Tillich, and Soren Kierkegaad, all liberals who led the 'God is Dead' movement during the 1960's.

Carter told his sister, evangelist Ruth Carter Stapleton, that he wouldn't give up politics for Christ. He admitted he wasn't "born-again" until 1967, yet he joined a Southern Baptist Church when he was 10, taught Sunday School at 16, and became a deacon in the church in his twenties. In the infamous *Playboy* magazine interview, Carter said: "I've looked on a lot of women with lust. I've committed adultery in my heart many times." When he found out that California Governor

Jerry Brown was throwing his hat in the ring for a run at the presidency, a supporter said that Carter "used expletives which I didn't know he knew." In the 1980 campaign, Massachusetts Senator Ted Kennedy accused Carter of not being more specific on the issues, to which Carter responded: "I don't have to kiss his ass."

During his acceptance speech, after winning the nomination at the Democratic National Convention, Carter attacked the "unholy, self-perpetuating alliances (that) have been formed between money and politics ... a political and economic elite who have shaped decisions and never had to account for mistakes nor to suffer from injustice. When unemployment prevails, they never stand in line for a job. When deprivations results from a confused welfare system, they never do without food, or clothing or a place to sleep. When public schools are inferior or torn by strife, their children go to exclusive private schools. And when bureaucracy is bloated and confused, the powerful always manage to discover and occupy niches of special influence and privilege." Now the trap was set, and America fell for it, hook, line, and sinker.

After Carter beat Ford, Hamilton Jordan, his chief aide, said: "If, after the inauguration, you find Cy Vance (former President of the Rockefeller Foundation) as Secretary of State and Zbigniew Brzezinski as head of National Security, then I would say we have failed." In an interview with *Playboy* magazine, Jordan said he would quit if they were appointed. They were— he didn't.

Brzezinski had become Carter's biggest influence. Henry Kissinger had called Brzezinski his "distinguished presumptive successor." It was Brzezinski who said: "The approaching two-hundredth anniversary of the Declaration of Independence could justify the call for a national constitutional convention to re-examine the nation's formal institutional framework. Either 1976 or 1989— the two-hundredth anniversary of the Constitution— could serve as a suitable target date culminating a national dialogue on the relevance of existing arrangements..."

When James Earl Carter took the oath of office, he said that the "United States will help erect ... a world order." This self-proclaimed "outsider" filled many of his administrative posts with establishment insiders from the Rockefeller Foundation, the Brookings Institution, and Coca Cola. Extracted from Coke, were George Ball, Clark Clifford, Samuel P. Huntingdon, Marshall Shulman, Richard Gardner, Henry Owen, Robert Roosa, and J. Paul Austin. Because of the extent to which he used the company when he was governor, he called the Coca-Cola company, his "own State Department."

The Trilateral Commission had accomplished its goal of controlling the Presidency, and it heralded that fact by making Jimmy Carter *Time* magazine's Man of the Year in January, 1977. The Editor-in Chief for *Time* was Hedley Donovan, a Rhodes Scholar, and member of the Commission.

Commission members must resign when they accept positions in the Executive branch, but they remain loyal, and usually rejoin the group when their service is complete. About 40% of the American Trilateral members joined the Carter Administration. In all, 291 members of the Trilateral Commission and the Council on Foreign Relations joined the Administration. Among the Carter Administration officials who have been members:

Jimmy Carter (President), Walter F. Mondale (Vice President), Cyrus Vance (Secretary of State, nephew of John W. Davis, of the J. P. Morgan bank who was the first President of the CFR), W. Michael Blumenthal (Secretary of Treasury), Harold Brown (Secretary of Defense), Zbigniew Brzezinski (National Security Advisor), Andrew Young (Ambassador to the United Nations), Paul A. Volcker (Chairman of the Federal Reserve Board), Sol Linowita (Chief Negotiator on the Panama Canal Treaties/ Mid-East Envoy), John C. Sawhill (Deputy Secretary of Energy/Head of the Synthetic Fuels Corp.), Hedley Donovan (Special Assistant to the President), Lloyd N. Cutler (Counsel to the President), Gerald C. Smith (Ambassador at Large for Nuclear Power Negotiations), Richard N. Gardner (Ambassador to Italy), Elliot L. Richardson (Delegate to the UN Law of the Sea Conference), Henry Owen (Special Representative of the President for Economic Summits/Economic Advisor), Warren Christopher (Deputy Secretary of State), Paul C. Warnke (Director of the Arms Control and Disarmament Agency), Richard N. Cooper (Under Secretary of State for Economic Affairs), Lucy Wilson Benson (Under Secretary of State for Security Affairs), Anthony Solomon (Deputy Secretary of State for Monetary Affairs), Robert R. Bowie (Deputy Director of Intelligence for National Estimates), W. Anthony Lake (Under Secretary of State for Policy Planning), Richard Holbrooke (Assistant Secretary of State for East Asian and Pacific Affairs), C. Fred Bergsten (Assistant Secretary of Treasury for International Affairs), Leslie Gelb (Director of the Bureau of Politico-Military Affairs), Theordore C. Sorenson (Director of the Central Intelligence Agency), Richard Moose (Assistant Secretary of State for African Affairs), Brock Adams (Secretary of Transportation), Leonard Woodcock (U.S. Ambassador to Peking), and Joseph Califano (Secretary of Health, Education and Welfare)

U.S. News and World Report reported: "The Trilateralists have taken charge of foreign policy-making in the Carter Administration, and already the immense power they wield is sparking some controversy. Active or former members of the Trilateral Commission now head every key agency involved in mapping U.S. strategy for dealing with the rest of the world." Being dominated by the chief advisors of the Commission, almost every aspect of Carter's foreign policy reflected a Trilateral viewpoint. They took advantage of Carter's ignorance of foreign policy, which became a series of concessions to Cuba, Panama, Red China, and Russia:

1) The Panama Canal was given away by the Carter Administration in a treaty negotiated by Sol Linowitz of the Commission. The reason— Marxist Panamanian leader Omar Torrijos owed the International Bankers $2 billion in loan payments, so income received from the Canal could help pay them back. The U.S. also guaranteed a 5-year program of loans and credits, which amounted to $295 million; and a 10 year, $50 million arms sale agreement to bolster the defense of the Canal.

2) Carter's withdrawal of a large number of troops from South Korea opened the area up for possible communist aggression from North Korea.

3) The Carter Administration granted full diplomatic relations with Red China, so American industry could begin trade with the communist government. When Carter broke off diplomatic relations with the government of Taiwan, Sen.

Goldwater said at a news conference: "I have no idea what motivated him other than the Trilateral Commission, composed of bankers in this country and others, want to expand big business ... He did it for the big banks of the world— Chase Manhattan and the French bankers and for companies like Coca-Cola." In May, 1989, George Bush would bestow favored-nation trade status to China.

4) In Africa, the Carter Administration was soft on the spread of Marxism.

5) Carter pledged his support for communist-dominated Hungary, and gave its dictator, Janos Kadar, the priceless Crown of St. Stephen (the founder and patron saint of Hungary) which the U.S. had in its possession since 1945.

In a 1978 meeting with 200 Trilateralists at the White House, Carter said that if the Commission had been in existence after World War I, they would have prevented World War II. However, we know that they were in existence after World War I, and precipitated World War II. In his book *Why Not the Best*, Carter said: "Membership on this Commission has provided me with a splendid learning opportunity, and many other members have helped me in my study of foreign affairs." Carter's membership in the organization was the only foreign policy experience he had, and that was limited to attending a couple of conferences in Europe and Japan. Congressman John Anderson, himself a member, said that Carter became a member just to improve his image. Carter's indoctrination made him a willing pawn in furthering the goals of the Trilateral Commission. In a personal letter to the Commission, who was meeting in Tokyo, Japan, in January, 1977, he wrote: "We share economic, political, and security concerns that make it logical we should seek ever increasing cooperation and understanding. And this cooperation is essential not only for our three regions, but in the global search for a more just and equitable world order."

The Commission, which operates in literal secrecy, made news in the fall of 1979, when David Rockefeller, Henry Kissinger, and John J. McCloy (former President of the Ford Foundation, former President of the World Bank, Chairman of the Chase Manhattan Bank, former High Commissioner to Germany, and on the Advisory Board of *Foreign Affairs* magazine) pressured Carter into allowing the deposed Shah of Iran (who had financial dealings with the Chase Manhattan) into the country for medical treatment. The move caused the Iranian government, under the leadership of the Ayatollah Khomeini, to storm the American Embassy, and hold 52 American hostages for nearly 1-1/2 years. Carter's inadequacy in dealing with this situation certainly cost him the election.

The Presidential election of 1980 saw two other former Trilateralists running for President. Jimmy Carter was running for re-election, and Illinois Republican, Rep. John Anderson, was running as an Independent. Republican George Bush had resigned his post on the Council on Foreign Relations because they were "too liberal," however, he didn't resign his seat on the Commission. The son of Sen. Prescott Sheldon Bush (R-CT, who during the 1930's was on the Board of Directors of Union Banking Corporation of New York, who helped finance the Nazis), had been born in Maine, raised in Connecticut, and was a two-term Republican Representative from Houston, Texas; became Ambassador to the UN in 1971; Chairman of the Republican National Committee; and from 1976-77, served as Director of the CIA. George Bush was associated with the international banking firm of Brown Brothers, Harriman and Company (who helped finance the growth of the Soviet Union); and attended Yale, where he was a member of the secret organization known as "The Order" (or "Skull and Bones"). This group also had as members: William F. Buckley, Jr., McGeorge Bundy, Winston Lord (former Chairman of the CFR), and other CFR members, who allegedly make up a powerful inner circle that controls the CFR.

On March 17, 1980, during the campaign, Ronald Reagan was asked if he would allow Trilateral Commission members to serve in his cabinet, and he responded by saying: "I don't believe that the Trilateral Commission is a conspiratorial group, but I do think its interests are devoted to international banking, multinational corporations, and so forth. I don't think that any Administration of the U.S. Government should have the top nineteen positions filled by people from any one group or organization representing one viewpoint. No, I would go in a different direction."

After a bitter Primary fight between the two, Reagan chose Bush to be his Vice Presidential running mate, over the likes of Rep. Philip Crane from Illinois, and Sen. Jack Kemp from New York. Reagan had originally wanted former President Ford to be his Vice-President, however, Ford wanted the power to appoint people to the National Security Council and the Cabinet. He also wanted to prepare "position papers" on foreign policy matters. This situation would have been almost like a co-Presidency, making Reagan more of a figurehead, which he refused to be, so his only other option was Bush.

Manchester Union Leader publisher William Loeb made the Commission a campaign issue during the New Hampshire Primary by saying: "It is quite clear that this group of extremely powerful men is out to control the world." He accused them of advocating a "world order in which multinational corporations ... can thrive without worrying about so-called national interests." During the campaign, Reagan attacked Carter's ties to David Rockefeller, and other Trilateral financiers; while Edwin Meese, a Reagan advisor, said that Trilateral influence was responsible for a "softening of defense."

Although Reagan appeared to be anti-Commission, it was only a front. Reagan's Campaign Manager, William J. Casey (former Chairman of the Securities and Exchange Commission, who Reagan later appointed as Director of the CIA) was a Trilateralist. His campaign was controlled by such Trilateralists as David Packard, George H. Weyerhaeuser, Bill Brock, Anne Armstrong, Philip M. Hawley, William A. Hewitt, Caspar Weinberger, and others who were CFR members. Reagan had the personal support of David Rockefeller, and belonged to the elitist Bohemian Grove Club in Northern California.

The Bohemian Grove is the site of an annual two-week (3 weekends) summer retreat on a 2,700 acre redwood estate about 75 miles north of San Francisco (near the town of Monte Rio), along the Russian River. It was established in 1872 by five reporters of the *San Francisco Examiner* as a social club "to help elevate journalism to that place in the popular estimation to which it is entitled." By 1878, when the first Grove-fest took place, reporters were being pushed out. *Newsweek* (August 2, 1982) called it "...the world's most prestigious summer camp." There is a $2,500 initiation fee, and annual dues of $600. Nearly every Republican President since Calvin Coolidge has been a member of this conservative clan. President Herbert Hoover called it the "greatest men's party on Earth." Among its 2,000 members are other high level government officials, and the very elite of America's corporate power, who sit on a variety of organizations such as the Trilateral Commission, CFR, and the Committee for Economic Development.

Among their members: Alexander Haig, Caspar Weinberger, Richard Nixon, Henry Kissinger, George P. Shultz, Newt Gingrich, Stephen Bechtel, Jr., Alan Greenspan, Gerald R. Ford, Jack Kemp, Dwight D. Eisenhower, Colin Powell, William F. Buckley, Jr., Merv Griffin, Joseph Coors, Edward Teller, Malcolm Forbes, Ronald Reagan, A. W. Clausen, George H. W. Bush, William French Smith, Richard Cheney, and William E. Simon.

They "own 25-30% of all privately held wealth in America, own 60-70% of the privately held corporate wealth ... direct the large corporations and foundations, and dominate the federal government in Washington." The bottom line, is that it is "one of the most influential meetings of the powers-that-be," and a setting for policy-making on specific issues; and not the all-male social club they purport to be.

It has been said that the Manhattan Project (which created the first atomic bomb) was first discussed at the Grove. One of the few stories to emerge was about a 1967 agreement by Ronald Reagan, over a drink with Nixon, to stay out of the upcoming Presidential primaries. However, after Alex Jones, a patriot talk show host, snuck onto the grounds and secretly videotaped a ritualistic ceremony in front of a 40 foot high concrete owl that they were worshiping, and a mock burning of a human being; rumors began circulating that the owl represented the pagan god Moloch, and that human sacrifices were actually being performed in remote areas. An investigation in the 1980's regarding the allegations turned up nothing.

In June of 1993, the *Washington Times* reported: "Presidential counselor David Gergen resigned yesterday from the all-male Bohemian Club, three days after saying he would not run around naked at its annual Bohemian Grove encampment and insisting he would not quit. White House spokeswoman Dee Dee Myers announced the resignation along with Mr. Gergen's departure from 17 other interest groups, charities and public boards ranging from the Trilateral Commission, the Bilderberg Group and Council on Foreign Relations."

Reagan received a great deal of support by such Christian political action groups as the Moral Majority, Round Table, and Christian Voice; and on November 6, 1980, said: "I think there is an elite in this country and they are the very ones who run an elitist government. They want a government by a handful of people because they don't believe the people themselves can run their lives ... Are we going to have an elitist government that makes decisions for people's lives, or are we going to believe as we have for so many decades, that the people can make these decisions for themselves?" Sounds a lot like what Carter said. Maybe Reagan was still acting- just on a far bigger stage. The November 24th issue of the *U.S. News and World Report* revealed: "Top officials of the Reagan team have sent a message to the Moral Majority: 'It isn't your Administration' ... 'Hell with them,' Vice-President-elect George Bush declared on November 10th in Houston, referring to right-wing groups that supported the President-elect."

Reagan's 59-member "transition team" who would pick, screen, and propose appointees for major administrative posts, consisted of 28 CFR members, 10

Bilderbergers, and 10 Trilateralists, including CFR members William Simon (former Secretary of Treasury under Nixon and Ford), Alexander Haig, George P. Shultz (former Secretary of Treasury under Nixon), Donald Rumsfeld (former Secretary of Defense under Ford), Alan Greenspan (former Chairman of the Council of Economic Advisors), and Henry Kissinger; and Trilateralists, William Casey and Anne Armstrong.

A note about George Pratt Shultz— his father was Dr. Birl Earl Shultz, who from 1918-23 was Personnel Director of the American International Corporation in New York, which was located in the same building as the Federal Reserve Bank of New York. They had offered $1,000,000 in credits to the Bolsheviks during the Russian Revolution. Shultz was a close friend of Armand Hammer's father, Julius Hammer, co-founder of the U.S. Communist Party. George was a member of the Pratt family, who were related to the Rockefellers, and who donated the Pratt mansion to the CFR. According to *The Oregonian* (1/3/87), George Shultz was quoted as saying: "The New Age has already dawned, and a new financial World Order is fast taking shape."

Reagan had 287 CFR and Trilateral Commission members in his Administration. Trilateral member, Caspar W. Weinberger (Reagan's Finance Director when he was Governor of California, former Vice President of Bechtel Corp., and former Secretary of Health, Education and Welfare under Nixon and Ford), became Secretary of Defense. Weinberger said: "The Trilateral Commission is performing a very valuable service in strengthening the ties between the United States and our natural allies."

Other members who joined the Administration: Alexander Haig (Secretary of State, also a CFR member), George Shultz (Secretary of State, also a CFR member), Nicholas Brady (Secretary of Treasury), Donald Regan (Secretary of Treasury, also a CFR member), John C. Whitehead (Deputy Secretary of State, also a CFR member), Caspar Weinberger (Secretary of Defense, also a CFR member), Frank Carlucci (Deputy Secretary of Defense, also a CFR member), Winston Lord (Ambassador to China, also a CFR member), Malcolm Baldridge (Secretary of Commerce, also a CFR member), William Brock (Secretary of Labor, also a CFR member), Alan Greenspan (Chairman of the Federal Reserve, also a CFR member).

Seemingly, Reagan was the Establishment's candidate all along, because he played ball with them. Republican Presidential candidate (during the 1980 Primary) John Connally, said that if he was elected, he wouldn't appoint any Trilateralists to his Administration. His campaign quickly ran out of steam— and money.

The 1984 Presidential campaign had Trilateralists Walter Mondale, Sen. John Glenn from Ohio, and Sen. Alan Cranston from California, fighting for the Democratic nomination among a slate of seven. Cranston had been the President of the United World Federalists. After World War II, he traveled the country saying that disarmament "must be done by an international army and a world court." However, he changed his tune when he became a Presidential candidate, and said: "I do not feel that world federalism is a realistic objective," and that disarmament "does not require world government." When asked about his membership with the United World Federalists, he said: "I would point out that at the time I was national president of the United Federalists, one of its more noted members was one Ronald Reagan."

Among the Trilateralists in the George H. W. Bush Administration, were Brent Scowcroft (National Security Advisor), and Nicholas F. Brady (Secretary of Treasury). Bush later rejoined.

Trilateralists in the Bill Clinton (who was a member) Administration was: Al Gore (Vice President), Donna E. Shalala (Secretary of Health and Human Services), Alice M. Rivlin (Deputy Budget Director), Madeleine Albright (UN Ambassador), Peter Tarnoff (Under Secretary of State for International Security of Affairs), Warren M. Christopher (Secretary of State), Ronald H. Brown (Secretary of Commerce), Henry G. Cisneros (Secretary of Housing and Urban Development), Bruce Babbitt (Secretary of Interior), Walter Mondale (U.S. Ambassador to Japan), William J. Crowe (Chairman of the Foreign Intelligence Advisory Board), William S. Cohen (Secretary of Defense), William J. Perry (Secretary of Defense) and Lloyd N. Cutler (Counsel to the President).

The following Trilateralists in the George W. Bush Administration, are also members of the CFR: Richard B. Cheney, Robert B. Zoellick, Brent Scowcroft (past member), Richard N. Haass, Henry A. Kissinger, Stephen J. Friedman, and Richard N. Perle. Other Trilateralists are Colin L. Powell (Secretary of State), and Donald H. Rumsfeld (Secretary of Defense).

In the 1964 book *With No Apologies*, by Sen. Barry M. Goldwater, he said:

"The Trilateral Commission is intended to be the vehicle for multinational consolidation of the commercial and banking interests by seizing control of the political government of the United States. The Trilateral Commission represents a skillful, coordinated effort to seize control and consolidate the four centers of power, political, monetary, intellectual, and ecclesiastical. What the Trilateralists intend is the creation of a worldwide economic power superior to the political governments of the nation states. In other words, what they are driving, orchestrating, meshing and gearing to accomplish is the New World Order, the one-world government."

Despite propaganda, the goal of the Commission is to "shape public policy, not through overt mass mobilization, but through pressure on select arenas of world power and appeals to a small, attentive public of elite world decision makers."

The Commission had suggested that Iran, Saudi Arabia, Brazil, and Mexico (did become a member in 1994) be brought into the Organization for Economic Cooperation and Development (OECD), an association of 24 (now 30) rich industrial nations (including all 15 countries of the European Community) founded in 1961 to encourage world trade, economic progress, and to aid underdeveloped nations. The move was considered by one Brazilian diplomat, as "an attempt to buy us out," and not an "attempt to build new understanding."

Their long range goals had included joint policy making in regard to economic and political relations with the Third World and the former communist bloc countries. Their policy for maintaining peace, involved the decrease of military forces, and nuclear disarmament; and to avoid confrontation at all costs, even if it means knuckling under to their threats, by abandoning allies (as had been done with Taiwan), and reducing America to a second-rate power. The Commission has pushed for the restructuring of the International Monetary Fund, so that they would be able to create new money, and restrict its use, by issuing a form of currency that had been initially called Bancor (or SDR, Special Drawing Rights), which would replace our dollar, gold, silver, and all other forms of currency— even Travelers Checks.

Winston Lord, U.S. Ambassador to China during the Reagan Administration and Assistant Secretary of State for Asian and Pacific Affairs under Clinton— a CFR member, is reported to have said: "The Trilateral Commission doesn't run the world, the Council on Foreign Relations does that!"

REGIONAL GOVERNMENT

On April 21, 1935, the *New York Times* magazine published a plan in which the states would merge into new units called Federal Regions that would be controlled from Washington, DC. In 1959, Nelson Rockefeller called for an Advisory Commission on Intergovernmental Relations (ACIR), which became a federally-funded Rockefeller think-tank within Congress to prepare a working formula for the concept. The ACIR analyzed information produced by the Public Administration Clearing House (also known as the "1313") and translated it into legislation to develop regional government, which would usurp the power of the local government. The Clearing House, located at the Rockefeller-controlled University of Chicago, represented a group of 26 private organizations which had been infiltrating local government agencies to usurp their power and authority. Some of these organizations are: National Association of Counties, National League of Cities, U.S. Conference of Mayors, American Public Works Association, Public Personnel Association, National Association of Attorney Generals, and the National Governors Conference. Their purpose was to train and place a "new administrative class" in every level of government, which would replace elected officials.

On March 27, 1969, as published in the *Federal Register*, under the direction of his Illuminati advisers, President Nixon announced the "Restructuring of Government Service Systems," which called for the merging of states into eight federally-controlled regions.

An Executive Order, when decreed by the President, is printed in the *Federal Register*, and then becomes law 15 days later. After Bill Clinton signed Executive Order #13083, Presidential Aide Paul Begala was overheard saying: "Stroke of a pen, law of the land. Kinda cool."

Executive Order #11647 was signed by Nixon on February 10, 1972, establishing Federal Regional Councils for the "development of closer working relationships between major Federal grant-making agencies of State and local government." In each of the ten standard Federal Regions, there was to be a council made up of the directors of the regional offices of: Dept. of Labor; Dept. of Health, Education, and Welfare; Dept. of Housing and Urban Development; Secretarial Representative of the Dept. of Transportation; Office of Economic Opportunity;

Environmental Protection Agency; and the Law Enforcement Assistance Administration. The President was to designate one member of each Council as the Chairman.

This Executive Order was unconstitutional because Article IV of the U.S. Constitution prohibited the merging of the states, and guaranteed a government represented by elected officials. However, regional government was accepted, because it brought with it, revenue-sharing funds.

Here is how the Ten Regions are organized (regional office in parenthesis):

1) Maine, Vermont, New Hampshire, Massachusetts (Boston), Connecticut, Rhode Island
2) New York (New York), New Jersey, Virgin Islands, Puerto Rico
3) Pennsylvania (Philadelphia), Maryland, Delaware, West Virginia, Virginia, District of Columbia
4) Kentucky, Tennessee, North Carolina, Mississippi, Alabama, Georgia (Atlanta), South Carolina, Florida
5) Minnesota, Wisconsin, Michigan, Illinois (Chicago), Indiana, Ohio
6) New Mexico, Oklahoma, Texas (Dallas-Ft. Worth), Arkansas, Louisiana
7) Nebraska, Iowa, Kansas (Kansas City), Missouri
8) Montana, North Dakota, South Dakota, Wyoming, Utah, Colorado (Denver)
9) Arizona, Nevada, Hawaii, California (San Francisco), American Samoa, Guam, N. Mariana Islands, Marshall Islands, Micronesia
10) Idaho, Washington (Seattle), Oregon, Alaska

In October, 1976, Jimmy Carter said before the National Association of Regional Councils (NARC): "I believe that regional organizations should be strengthened. If elected President, I intend first to upgrade the role of regional councils representing the federal government to assist State and local officials, as well as private citizens, in dealing with federal agencies ... I also intend to encourage the development of regional councils representing State and local governments."

Carter expanded the Federal Regional System on July 20, 1979, with Executive Order #12149, to "provide a structure for interagency and intergovernmental cooperation ... to establish practical and appropriate liaison functions with State, tribal, regional and local officials." Each of the Ten Councils were made up of a representative from each of the following agencies: Dept. of the Interior; Dept. of Agriculture; Dept. of Commerce; Dept. of Labor; Dept. of Health, Education, and Welfare; Dept. of Housing and Urban Development; Dept. of Transportation; Dept. of Energy; Environmental Protection Agency; Community Services Administration; Office of Personnel Management; General Services Administration; ACTION (Peace Corp., VISTA, senior citizen programs, and other special volunteer programs); Small Business Administration; Federal Emergency Management Agency; U.S. Army Corps of Engineers; and the Regional Action Planning Commission. It included over 550 aid programs and block grants. The Department of Education was added later, after it separated from the Dept. of Health, Education and Welfare (which became the Dept. of Health and Human Services).

On the same day, he signed Executive Order #12148— "Federal Emergency Management," which created the Federal Emergency Management Agency (FEMA), an agency within the Department of Justice, which oversees all of the federal agencies that have specific duties during times of emergency, such as the Federal Disaster Assistance Agency, and the Federal Emergency Broadcast System. It seems that only about 10% of its personnel are actually involved in disaster assistance. Being that it has the capability to assume government control if necessary, they have been given police powers which some researchers believe will be used as the enforcement branch of the Regional Government. In other words, a national police force. Its purpose was to merge every community's police force, transferring control of them to a central government. This was to be done through revenue-sharing funds providing special training programs to the local police, special communications equipment, and other things. The National Guard began receiving SWAT (Special Weapons and Tactical Team) training to be part of this national police force. Located at the National Security Agency building in Fort Meade, MD, it has been reported that FEMA has been actively engaged in developing a computer database, for CAPS (Crisis Action Programs), to collect records on millions of Americans.

In addition to dividing the country into Ten Federal Regions, the government has also been making plans for the establishment of a literal dictatorship, which among other things, will freeze prices and wages, close the Stock Exchange, and regulate the amount of money you can withdraw from your checking and savings account. The following Presidential Executive Orders will accomplish this:

#10312 (12-10-51) Gives Government the power to take over all radio stations.

#10346 (04-17-52) All Federal Departments and Agencies are required to prepare civil defense plans.

#10995 (02-16-62) Gives Government the power to take over all communications and media.

#10997 (02-16-62) Gives Government the power to take over all energy and power sources such as electricity, petroleum and natural gas.

#10998 (02-16-62) Gives Government the power to take over farms, farm machinery, and food sources; including production, manufacturing, processing, distribution, and retailing.

#10999 (02-16-62) Gives Government the power to take over all modes of transportation, seaports, highways, etc.

#11000 (02-16-62) Gives Government the authority to mobilize citizens into work forces under Government supervision.

#11001 (02-16-62) Gives Government the power to take over all health, welfare and educational functions.

#11002 (02-16-62) The Postmaster General will be responsible for registering all Americans.

#11003 (02-16-62) Gives Government the power to take over all airports and aircraft.

#11004 (02-16-62) Gives Government the power to take over housing and financial institutions, to relocate communities, to erect new housing with public funds, to declare areas to be abandoned because they are unsafe, and to establish new locations for the population.

#11005 (02-16-62) Gives Government the power to take over all railroads, inland waterways, and public storage facilities.

#11051 (09-27-62) Authorization for Executives Orders to be put into effect during times of international, economic, or financial crisis, and for the Office of Emergency Planning to carry them out.

#11310 (10-11-66) Gives Government the power to use all prisons to administer medical treatment, for mass feeding, and housing.

#11490 (10-28-69) was amended by the 36-page Executive Order #11921(6-11-76), which consolidated the following Executive Orders: #10312, #10346, #10997-#11005, #11087-#11095, and #11310. It assigned emergency preparedness functions to most Federal Departments and Agencies to assure the "continuity of the Federal Government."

On the heels of these provisions that would initiate martial law, a meeting arranged by Nelson Rockefeller, was held from April 5-8, 1976 in Philadelphia with representatives from the Center for the Study of Democratic Institutions, the League of Women Voters, the National Council of Churches, National Urban League, NAACP, United Auto Workers, Common Cause, and various other University professors and governmental experts, to study our present Constitution to see if it could be modernized and improved.

On January 30, 1976, came the announcement of "A Declaration of Interdependence," a document which endorsed a one-world government. The announcement was made at a meeting held at Philadelphia's Independence Hall, which was sponsored by the World Affairs Council (and had stemmed from a five point program they had announced in September, 1975). The meeting was funded with a $100,000 grant from the Pennsylvania Bicentennial Committee. The document, written by CFR member Henry Steele Comsmager began with this sentence: "Two centuries ago our forefathers brought forth a new nation; now we must join with others to bring forth a new world order." It was signed by 24 U.S. Senators and 80 U.S. Representatives, such as: Sen. Alan Cranston (D-CA, CFR), Sen. Jacob Javits (R-NY), Sen. Hubert Humphrey D-MN), Sen. George McGovern (D-SD), Sen. William Proxmire (D-WI), Sen. Charles Mathias (CFR), Sen. Clairborne Pell (CFR), Rep. Paul Simon, Rep, Patricia Shroeder, Rep. Louis Stokes, Rep. Les Aspin (Secretary of Defense under Clinton), Rep. John B. Anderson (R-IL), and Rep. Morris K. Udall (D-AZ).

This document went through further drafts, and in 1984, it was presented by the Committee on a Constitutional System (CCS) as an alternative to the existing Constitution. One of the group's Board members, James MacGregor Burns, a history professor, said: "If we are to turn the founders upside down ... we must directly confront the constitutional structure they erected." About a third of the CCS Board members belonged to the CFR, including Chairman C. Douglas Dillon (former Secretary of Treasury), Lloyd Cutler (former legal council to President Carter, and council to President Clinton), and Sen. Nancy Kassebaum. Some of the other members were: Robert McNamara (former Secretary of Defense under Kennedy and Johnson), Sen. Daniel Patrick Moynihan, Sen. Charles Mathias, Sen.

William J. Fulbright, and others who were associated with the Brookings Institute, Rockefeller Foundation, and Woodrow Wilson Center.

In October, 1970, the Center for the Study of Democratic Institutions, a tax-exempt foundation in Santa Barbara, California (financed by the Ford and Rockefeller Foundations with up to $2-1/2 million annually), published in their magazine *Center*, an article called the "Constitution for the United Republics of America," which emanated from a concept that was initially drafted in 1964, and was the forerunner for a later version. The principle author of this document was Rexford Guy Tugwell (who was the Assistant Secretary of Agriculture under President Franklin Roosevelt), who directed a team of close to 100 socialist educators who contributed to the project.

In Tugwell's 1974 book, *The Emerging Constitution*, the 40th version of the original draft was published as "A Constitution for the Newstates of America," which the Ford Foundation spent $25 million to produce and promote. Tugwell claimed that our Constitution was too cumbersome and needed to be changed. He believed that it was possible to get this new "Constitution" adopted, and said: "...it could happen that the present system of government would prove so obstructive and would fail so abysmally to meet the needs of a continental people and a great power that general recognition of the crisis would occur. There might then be a redrafting of the basic law, and, if so, then it might be that this model we have worked out over a number of years might be taken into account." The new Constitution calls for the States to be divided into Ten Federal Regions, called Republics, which would be "subservient departments of the national government."

The document contains no guarantees of freedoms that we now have under the Bill of Rights (Article I, Part A, Section 1: "Freedom of expression shall not be abridged except in declared emergency"). In an emergency, the government will have the power to curtail communication, movement, and the right to assemble. It calls for public education, and gun control (Article I, Part B, Section 8 "The bearing of arms or the possession of lethal weapons shall be confined to police, members of the armed forces, and those licensed under the law"). The President will serve one 9-year term (Article VI, Part B, Section 9, Subsection 8: "To assist in the maintenance of world order and, for this purpose, when the President shall recommend, to vest jurisdiction in international legislative, judicial and administrative agencies."), and there will be two Vice-Presidents. A hundred Senators will be appointed by the President for lifetime terms, not elected; and there would be 400 members in the House of Representatives. Each of the 100 Congressional Districts will elect three for a three year term; and 100 will be elected by the entire country, to serve a nine year term, and only they can become Committee Chairmen.

With the completion of the proposed Newstates Constitution, Vice President Nelson Rockefeller, president of the U.S. Senate, developed support for the introduction of HCR 28, which called for an unlimited Constitutional Convention in 1976. Swift public opposition soundly defeated this attempt, so the Convention supporters then went to the states promoting a "limited convention for the purpose of adding a balanced budget amendment." They were able to convince 32 of the required 34 states to pass resolutions calling for a convention. The last state to sign on was Missouri in 1983, but after that, the legislatures in three states (Alabama, Florida and Louisiana) realized the consequences of their actions and rescinded their call.

It is ironic, but organizations claiming to be "conservative," seem to be the strongest supporters for a convention. Most notable are: American Legislative Exchange Council (ALEC), National Taxpayers' Union (NTU), Republican National Committee (RNC), and the Committee on the Constitutional System (CCS).

In 1992, Ross Perot, who had become a political force to be reckoned with, publicly called for a Constitutional Convention. In guest appearances with Barbara Walters, Phil Donahue and Larry King he stated that we needed a Parliamentary Government, and pledged that "his people" could get the remaining states needed for a Constitutional Convention call "in their sleep."

Another threat to our Constitution was the Conference of States (COS). It was being peddled as a movement for the states to come together and discuss the need to balance the relationship between the states, and the federal government, in a "co-equal partnership," even though our original Constitution intended for the States to be sovereign, and for the federal government to only have limited powers.

Their first meeting was to be held in Annapolis (MD), July 6-9, 1995, with a historical reenactment of the 1786 Annapolis convention; and the second had been planned for October 24-26, 1995 (which, ironically, was the 50th anniversary of the establishment of the UN), in Philadelphia (PA), a reenactment of the 1787 convention. It was being funded by three private organizations which are associated with the Advisory Commission on Intergovernmental Relations (ACIR): Council of State Governments (CSG, established in 1930 with funding from a Rockefeller Grant), National Governors Association (NGA), and the National Conference of State Legislatures (NCSL, established in 1933 with funding from a Rockefeller Grant).

In December of 1994 the NCSL had a meeting in North Carolina where state legislators were told the Conference of States was a way for States to keep the federal government from encroaching on their sovereignty. So this COS resolution was taken back to their respective state legislatures and the first 12 states to ratify it was able to accomplish it through deceit by having legislative leaders introduce it, bypassing any committees so there would be no hearings, and bringing it to the floor for a quick vote. According to Michael Leavitt, the Republican governor of Utah, the goal of the Resolution's proponents was to have 26 states pass it, although Governor Nelson of Nebraska was pressing for 34, which was the exact number of States needed to call for a Constitutional Convention.

Leavitt, a member of the ACIR, told the *Salt Lake City Tribune* in 1994, that he wanted a constitutional convention. In a May, 1994 Position Paper, he said that our government was "...outdated and old fashioned ... not suited for the fast-paced, high-tech, global-marketplace we are entering. There is a better way," The "better way" he suggested, seemed to be an end-run around the Constitution; because the COS literature indicated their interest in passing Constitutional amendments. He indicated his high expectations for what the meeting could accomplish:

> "Congress tried to limit the convention's authority by stating it would meet 'for the sole and express purpose of revising the Articles of Confederation ... As we all know, the delegates to the great Constitutional Convention in 1787 in Philadelphia did much more than that. They threw out the Articles of Confederation and drafted a new constitution."

Though Article V of the Constitution indicates that two-thirds of the States must vote for a constitutional convention before Congress could call one, the COS was planning to use the same method the delegates did at the Annapolis convention in 1786. Within ten years, the Constitution that was originally drafted on June 12, 1776 (and fully ratified by 1781), was no longer able to meet the needs of a growing nation. The delegates of Virginia, New York, Delaware, New Jersey, and Pennsylvania, meeting in Annapolis were charged with the task of amending the Articles of Confederation, and were to meet in Philadelphia "for the sole and express purpose of revising" them. The need for a stronger central government was expressed, one that didn't limit States rights. However, upon meeting in Philadelphia in May, 1787, they locked all the doors, and posted armed guards; and even closed all the windows, so they could deliberate in secret while they actually set up a new national government. Neither the Congress or the people could stop them. Their work was finished on September 17, 1787 (and was fully ratified on May 29, 1790), and the Constitution of the United States was born, and is still in existence today.

Many people were worried about this Conference of States, because nobody was really sure what could happen. Charles Duke, the Republican state senator from Colorado, said that the COS would be the "edge of the sword that knocks the head off the Constitution."

Case law mandates that members of a constitutional convention must be directly elected by the people, so they can act as their representatives to exercise the sovereign power of the state. Each state delegation to the COS would consist of the governor, and two leaders from each party in the state legislature (plus two alternates, one from each party), and therefore could be empowered with the necessary legal status as representatives of the people, should the decision be made to turn the meeting into a constitutional convention.

Speaker of the House Newt Gingrich (R-GA), and 33rd Degree Mason Bob Dole (R-KS) openly supported the COS, and on March 24, 1995, Republican senators Hank Brown (CO) and Jesse Helms (NC) sponsored a Senate Resolution which would give Congressional authorization to transform the COS into a bonafide Constitutional Convention. They maintained that without this Congressional approval, it would be in conflict with Article 1, Section 10 of the Constitution, which does not allow any agreements between States.

Ultimately, because only 14 state legislatures passed resolutions calling for their participation in the COS, which was short of the 26 needed, their organizational meeting scheduled for July, 1995 was canceled. However, the same forces behind this movement planned to have a "federalism summit" in Cincinnati on October 22 with the support of the Council of State Governments, National Governors Association and the National Conference of State Legislators.

It is obvious that the Illuminati had taken a two-prong approach to regional government. They have been working within the confines of the Executive Branch to get various Executive Orders passed; and they have also used their various finger organizations to study our existing constitution, and recommend changes. All of their efforts may eventually culminate in a call for a Constitutional Convention that will spell the end of democracy as we know it in this country.

CREATING A CRISIS

Certain questions raised during the 1973 Oil Embargo, seem to point to the fact that the crisis was created by the Illuminati, as a test, to see what it would be like without gasoline for automobiles, and fuel for heating homes.

During the Embargo, Maine's Governor, Democrat Kenneth M. Curtis, accused the Nixon Administration of "creating a managed oil shortage to force support of its energy programs." A 1973 study by *Philadelphia Inquirer* reporters Donald Bartlett and James B. Steele, revealed, that while American oil companies were telling the U.S. to curtail oil consumption, through a massive advertising campaign, the five largest oil companies (Exxon, Mobil, Texaco, Gulf, and Standard Oil of California) were selling close to two barrels overseas, for every barrel (42 gallons) of oil sold here. They accused the oil companies and the Federal government of creating the crisis. In 1974, Lloyd's of London, the leading maritime insurance company in the world, said that during the three months before the Embargo, 474 tankers left the Middle East, with oil for the world. During the three months at the height of the crisis, 492 tankers left those same ports. During the Embargo, Atlantic Richfield (ARCO, whose President, Thornton Bradshaw was a member of the CFR) drivers were hauling excess fuel to storage facilities in the Mojave desert. All of this evidence points to the conclusion that there was no oil shortage in 1973.

Antony C. Sutton wrote in *Energy: The Created Crisis*: "Our mythical energy shortage can be dismissed with a few statistics. The U.S. consumes about 71 quads (a 'quad' is one quadrillion BTU's, or 10 to the 15th power British Thermal Units) of energy per year. There is available now in the U.S., excluding solar sources and without oil and gas imports, about 151,000 quads. Consequently, we have sufficient energy resources to keep us functioning at our present rate of consumption for about 2,000 to 3,000 years— without discovering new reserves. Even at higher consumption rates there will be no problem in the next millennium"

In 1977, independent petroleum companies discovered 88% of the new oil fields, drilling on 81% of those. They have been hampered by the large corporations, referred to earlier as the Seven Sisters, who wanted to avoid adding to our national supply so they can profit from the higher prices. Carter's Department of Energy was established to perpetuate the propaganda of the existence of an energy crisis.

In 1975, an anonymous ARCO official told Hugh M. Chance, a former State Senator from Colorado, that the Government had allowed only one pool of oil in a 100 square mile area on Alaska's North Slope, to be developed, even though the entire area north of Brooks Range has so much oil, that if it were drilled, "in five years the United States could be totally energy free, and totally independent from the rest of the world as far as energy is concerned." The Prudhoe Bay oil field is one of the richest oil fields on earth, able to produce an oil flow for at least 20 years, without the need of a pump; and a natural gas supply which could supply the entire country for 200 years. However, the Government wouldn't allow it to be pumped out, and it is funneled back into the ground. The Gull Island find had a different chemical structure, as did the Kuparuk oil field, west of there, which meant that the three different chemical compositions indicated the existence of separate pools of oil on the North Slope in an area of 50,000 square miles. Needless to say, this seems to be an almost unlimited supply of domestic oil.

Another ARCO official told Lindsey Williams, a chaplain for the work camps on the Trans-Alaska Oil pipeline, that "there will never be an energy crisis (because) we have as much oil here as in all Saudi Arabia." Williams had witnessed a huge oil discovery at Gull Island (5 miles north of Prudhoe Bay in the Beaufort Sea) that could have produced so much oil, that the official said that another pipeline could be built "and in another year's time we can flood America with oil- Alaskan oil ... and we won't have to worry about the Arabs." However, a few days after the find, the Federal Government ordered the documents and technical reports locked up, the well capped, and the rig withdrawn. Their excuse was that an oil spill in that part of the Arctic Ocean would kill various micro-organisms. Williams felt that the U.S. Government was deliberately creating an oil crisis, and delaying the flow of oil, in order to bankrupt the oil companies, which would lead to the nationalization of oil and gas.

William Brown, Director of Technological Studies at the Hudson Institute, said: "The President (Carter) said there is no chance of us becoming independent in our oil supplies. That is just wrong. We have at least 100 years of petroleum resources in this country." In 1976, proven resources were set at 37 billion barrels and the estimated recoverable resources were set at 150 billion barrels. This is about a 50-year supply at current usage levels. The American Petroleum Institute said in their 1977 Annual report, that recoverable crude was set at 30.9 billion barrels, and with today's technology, the amount of recoverable crude was 303.5 billion barrels, which is about an 80-year supply. The 1968 U.S. Geological Survey reported that the crude oil potential of the Atlantic Ocean continental shelf area is 224 billion barrels, the Gulf of Mexico has 575 billion barrels, the Pacific Coast has 275 billion barrels, and Alaska has 502 billion barrels, which is a grand total of 1,576 billion barrels. Only about 2% of these areas have been leased, which at the time of the report, had yielded 615 million barrels of oil, and 3.8 TCF (trillion cubic feet) of natural gas yearly.

The *Wall Street Journal* said that we possessed "1001 years of natural gas." Only about 2% of the Outer Continental Shelf has been leased, even though it may contain over half of our potential natural gas reserves. Along the Atlantic Coast, there is a potential of 67 TCF of gas, yet only about a dozen wells had been drilled in those areas. The Potential Gas Committee said in 1972, that we had 1412 TCF in reserve; in 1973, Mobil said we had 758 TCF; Exxon said we had 660-1380 TCF; the U.S. Geological Survey reported in 1974, that we had 761-1094 TCF in reserve; the National Academy of Sciences said in 1974, that we had 885 TCF; and there were other reports which indicated that we had over 700 TCF. These sources did not include the unconventional sources of coalbeds, shale formations, "tight sand" formations, and deep underground water areas.

From conventional sources, our known reserves were estimated to be about 237 TCF, and underground reserves were estimated to be about 530 TCF. An analysis of unconventional resources indicated the following yield: tight sand (600 TCF), coal (250 TCF), shale (500 TCF), underground water zones in the Gulf (200 TCF), and synthetic gas from peat (1443 TCF). This all adds up to a total of 3,800 TCF of natural gas, and with the U.S. using an average of 21 TCF a year, that would be enough to provide us with another 100 years worth of energy. That doesn't take into account the synthetic gas obtainable from growing marine bio-mass, such as the California Giant Kelp (Macrocystis Pyrifera), which grows two feet per day, and could be a renewable source for the production of synthetic gas.

It is also estimated that the United States could have up to half of the world's known recoverable coal reserves, which could be about 200 billion tons— 45 billion of which is near the surface. At the time of this report, maximum production up to 1985 would have only used 10% of this reserve, even if no new reserves were discovered. In 1979, Herbert Foster, Vice-President of the National Coal Association, said: "America has three trillion tons of coal out there, ready to be mined ... all we produced last year was 590 million tons. That's only one pound of coal for every 2-1/2 tons still in the ground. The U.S. Geological Survey has estimated our coal reserves will last us well into the next century." One reason coal development has been held up, is that 40% of all reserves are on land owned by the Federal Government, and environmentally-minded citizens.

The book *The Next 200 Years* by Herman Kahn and the Hudson Institute said: "Allowing for the growth of energy demand ... we conclude that the proven reserves of these five major fossil fuels (oil, natural gas, coal, shale, and tar sands) alone could provide the world's total energy requirements for about 100 years, and only one-fifth of the estimated potential reserves sources could provide for more than 200 years of the projected energy needs." The Hudson Institute said in 1974: "There is no shortage of energy fuels." Antony Sutton wrote: "The energy 'crisis' is a phony, a rip-off, a political con game designed to perpetuate a 'crisis' that can be 'managed' for political power purposes."

Conservative estimates indicate that we have 100 years of energy sources available, while evidence of other undeveloped finds show that we have adequate reserves that would last long beyond that. The Illuminati has a firm grip on the oil supply, and after their 'test' in 1973, its obvious that oil will be used as a weapon of control. One can only wonder what would happen to this country if a large-scale oil crisis occurred. Needless to say, it would be a disaster of unbelievable proportions that most likely would cause an economic collapse. Law and order would not exist in this scenario, as the population would fight among themselves for the limited resources that would be available, thus making the perfect situation for a World Government to step in.

RIOT AND REVOLUTION

Revolution has always been the method used to facilitate change, and it would seem likely that an environment could be created that would ultimately lead to a revolt by the citizens of this country. As our economy continues to decline, and it becomes harder for people to get by, there may be a ground swell of revolt across the country against the government, Of course, the Illuminati has already planted these seeds.

As you have read, the Illuminati controls the leadership of the labor unions, and the corporate structure of America. Thus, a major strike could cripple this country. For instance, a strike by the Longshoremen would prevent anything from being unloaded off the ships. A strike by the Teamsters would prevent anything from being shipped on trucks. A strike by the Air Traffic Controllers would prevent all flights, except for military planes. Basically, with a major labor strike, nothing would move, and there would be no way to get food and other products of necessities to the cities. Again, this would be a crucial blow to the economy. On top of that, and history has shown this, a major strike would most likely be accompanied with acts of violence and sabotage. Indeed, this situation would make it possible for the initiation of martial law, and a World Government to step in to maintain control.

It is a known fact that revolution has been fermenting in this country for a long time, and riots could be instigated through the many terrorist groups that exist here. Riots, bank robberies, racial confrontations, skyjackings, strikes, demonstrations, assassinations, and kidnappings, are not just unrelated events, according to J. Bernard Hutton, who wrote in his 1972 book *The Subverters* that the "increasing violence and terrorism is a direct result of an organized world-wide plot to destroy the Western democracies."

The first hint of revolution came from the Communists. Prominent U.S. Communist Gus Hall said at the 1961 funeral of Eugene Dennis, National Chairman of the U.S. Communist Party: "...slit the throats of Christian children and drag them over the mourner's bench and the pulpit and allow them to drown in their own blood." As much as the Government would like us to believe it, Communism is not dead— only sleeping. When it awakes, most likely under the banner of Socialism, it will be a force to be reckoned with. The Communists, through their subversive agents in this country, have maps of all strategic locations, such as military firearm storage, police stations, fire stations, water hydrants, railroads and other transportation centers, communication centers, and water reservoirs and supplies. It wasn't too long ago, that we discovered that Russia still has spies working within the CIA. Despite their overtures toward democracy, they are clearly continuing to follow an agenda to undermine the United States.

The riots could be racially motivated. Percy E. Sutton, a former Borough President of Manhattan in New York City, who is Black, said in his keynote address before the National Conference of Anti-Poverty Agencies at Columbia University's Teachers College on February 22, 1968, that there was a plan to use thousands of Black Veterans from the Vietnam War to wage war on Whites. He said: "I am afraid that the greatest battle of the era— of the Vietnam War— will not be fought in the demilitarized zone north of Da Nang, but will be fought in the streets of America." In April and May of 1992, after four policemen were acquitted in the beating of a Black man, Rodney King, massive riots swept across south-central Los Angeles, and the military had to be sent in to restore order. It was reported that 600 buildings were burned, and 52 people killed. Damage estimates ran as high as $1 billion. Incidents were also reported in Atlanta, Las Vegas, San Francisco, Miami, and Seattle. Even though the Blacks in this country have achieved quite a bit in the past 30 years, the fight against oppression has hardened them, and has created a generation that thinks nothing of using the political power of violence and demonstration to make their views known. This powder keg could be ignited again in the future, on a wider scale, in order to create a nationwide crisis.

FINAL WARNING

The riots could be radically motivated. Jerry Rubin, who was a member of the Students for a Democratic Society (SDS) at Kent State University, said on July 20, 1970: "The first part of the Yippie program is to kill your parents. And I mean that quite literally, because until you're prepared to kill your parents, you're not ready to change the country. Our parents are our first oppressors." In his book *Do It*, he wrote:

> "We've got Amerika (sic) on the run. We've combined youth, music, sex, drugs, rebellion with treason— and that's a combination hard to beat ... High school students will seize radio, TV, and newspaper offices across the land ... Police stations will blow up ... Revolutionaries will break into jails and free all prisoners ... The Youth International Revolution will begin with mass breakdown of authority, mass rebellion, total anarchy in every institution in the Western World..."

Jerry Kirk, a student at the University of Chicago, who was active in the Communist Party up to 1969, told the House and Senate Internal Security Committees:

> "Young people have no conception of the conspiracy's strategy of pressure from above and pressure from below, so well outlined in Jan Kozak's *And Not A Shot Is Fired*. They have no idea they are playing into the hands of the Establishment they claim to hate. The radicals think they are fighting the forces of the super-rich, like Rockefeller and Ford, and don't realize that it is precisely such forces which are behind their own revolution, financing it, and using it for their own purposes."

In his book, *The Strawberry Statement: Notes of a College Revolutionary*, James S. Kunen (who in April, 1968, was one of the students who took over Columbia University) wrote:

> "In the evening we went up to the U. to check out a strategy meeting. A kid was giving a report on the SDS Convention. He said that ... at the Convention men from Business International Roundtables ... tried to buy up a few radicals ... These men are the world's leading industrialists and they convene to decide how our lives are going to go. These are the guys who wrote the Alliance for Progress. They are the left wing of the ruling class ... They offered to finance our demonstrations in Chicago (1968). We were offered Esso (Standard Oil of New Jersey, Exxon— Rockefeller) money. They want us to make a lot of radical commotion so they can look more in the center as they move to the left."

Another radical threat has come from militant homosexuals. On September 19, 1993, at the Sunday evening service of the Hamilton Square Baptist Church in San Francisco, California, Rev. Lou Sheldon of the Traditional Values Coalition was to be the scheduled speaker. Around 5:00 PM, homosexual demonstrators began arriving, and by the time of the service at 6:00 PM, so many had shown up, that they completely controlled the area outside of the church and they attempted to prevent people from entering the church, including the pastor and his wife. The protesters took down the Christian flag, and hoisted the Gay flag. Even though the police were there, they did nothing, claiming that the situation was under control. When the riot police finally were called in to force the gays out of the church courtyard, the rioters moved to the emergency exit doors on the west side of the church where they "pounded and kicked the doors, seeking to break them down." The noise was so disturbing that the service had to be temporarily stopped. I heard a recording of this on a radio show, and needless to say, it was very unnerving.

As the churchgoers left, they were shouted and cursed at; and the speaker had debris thrown at him. A group of gay demonstrators were heard yelling: "We want your children! Give us your children!" Through it all, not one arrest was made, because the police were told that this was "an open public meeting and not a worship service" and therefore "were not allowed to enforce the law regarding the disturbance of church worship services." Just like the civil rights movement of the 1960's, this may have very well been the beginning of gays exercising militant action to gain rights to carry out their perverse lifestyle, especially now that inroads are being made in regard to gay marriages.

In a 1987 edition of *Gay Community News* this interesting bit of information was published:

> "We shall sodomize your sons ... We shall seduce them in your schools, in your dormitories, in your gymnasiums, in your locker rooms, in your sports arenas, in your seminaries, in your youth groups, in your movie theater bathrooms, in your army bunkhouses, in your truck stops, in your all-male clubs, in your houses of Congress, wherever men are with men together. Your sons shall become our minions and do our bidding. They will be recast in our image. They will come to crave and adore us ... All laws banning homosexual activity will be revoked ... All homosexuals must stand together as brothers ... We will triumph only when we present a common face to the vicious heterosexual enemy ... We will unmask the powerful homosexuals who masquerade as heterosexuals ... We are everywhere; we have infiltrated your ranks ... We shall conquer the world because warriors inspired by and banded together by homosexual love and honor are invincible as were the ancient Greek soldiers. The family unit will be abolished ... All churches who condemn us will be closed ... We too are capable of firing guns and manning barricades of the ultimate revolution."

Regardless of who is involved in these riots, the police and the military will be mobilized to bring order. In 1965, the Department of Justice established the Office of Law Enforcement Assistance to help the local police fight crime. In 1968, as part of the Crime Control Act, it became known as the Law Enforcement Assistance Agency (LEAA). Charles H. Rogovin, an administrator of the LEAA, said in an October 1, 1969 speech to the International Association of Chiefs of Police, meeting in Miami: "If local law enforcement fails, then something else will replace it. I do not raise the spectre of a federal police force merely to frighten you. Look at the organized crime field. We now see a substantial federal effort there—

and not simply because organized crime is interstate in nature. It is also because law enforcement has failed to do its job." The LEAA originally discussed the possibility of a National Police Force to be used in the event of a civil disturbance, for crowd dispersal and to neutralize revolutionary leadership. However, an article in the January 15, 1973 edition of the *Boston Herald American* talked about the "plans for reorganization, regionalization and consolidation of police departments."

The Deputy Attorney General of California had said during a conference on Civil Emergency Management that "anyone who attacks the state, even verbally, becomes a revolutionary and an enemy by definition. They are the enemy and must be destroyed." On December 30, 1975, after it was signed into law by Gov. Edmund G. (Jerry) Brown, Jr., the California National Guard announced that they were prepared to provide emergency assistance to any local police force in the country. They introduced the 1,200 member Law Enforcement Assistance Force (LEAF), which was a specially trained and equipped military police force to handle mass disturbances and riots, which could be put into place within 12 hours. Although they were phased out in the mid-1980's it appeared that LEAF was the forerunner of a national police force.

This national police force began taking shape through the Multi-Jurisdictional Task Force (MJTF), a creation of the Department of Defense, and is a joint operation of FEMA and the National Guard Bureau. The idea was that, with less military involvement abroad, some of our military personnel could be reassigned to this type of domestic duty. The MJTF was to be the coordinating body of the BATF, FDA, CIA, DEA, IRS, Federal Marshals, National Guard, and local police organizations.

Since 1971, there have been many reports concerning unmarked black helicopters, which, because of their flight paths, are probably equipped for low-flying ground surveillance, and appear to be part of the military's domestic counter-terrorism program. Among the helicopters that have been observed: CH-47 Chinooks (which can carry 64 soldiers), MH-60G Blackhawks, AH-64 Apaches and HH-G0A Night Hawks. It has since been reported by various researchers that they originate from the 160th Special Operations Aviation Regiment, which is based in Ft. Campbell (Hopkinsville), Kentucky, and Hunter Army Airfield in Georgia (although they have helicopters staged at various areas of the country for their use). They carry no markings, and they are the only helicopter unit in the U.S. military allowed to use the color of black (a special paint that is chemically resistant and invisible to radar) because they are a special operations unit that was initially used by the Delta Force, and now are being used by FEMA. They call themselves the 'Night Stalkers,' and their motto is "Death Waits in the Dark."

It has been reported that a growing number of American military aircraft, with the exception of the Coast Guard, have been painted dark gray or dark green, and either have no visible markings identifying them as U.S. aircraft, or have low-visibility markings. It is believed that the purpose for this is so our equipment can be easily transitioned for use as part of any United Nations operations.

Since 1987, the U.S. Army has been training the police, local National Guard units, and the Drug Enforcement Agency (DEA), in how to break in and enter private property, as part of their new urban warfare training. The U.S. Army's Office of Public Affairs announced that the Defense Department Authorization

Act passed by Congress in 1987, initiated this new training, which was being carried out in military bases such as Fort Hood (TX), Fort Benning (GA), and Fort McClellan (AL).

There have been reports of anti-terrorist training missions which have taken place throughout the country. Marines from the 22nd Marine Expeditionary Unit at Camp Lejeune (NC), along with air support from the unmarked black helicopters, carried out a late-night raid in July, 1993, on Tybee Island, near the mouth of the Savannah River. In early 1994, the Army and the Alaska State Police held a joint operation on the Kenai Peninsula, near Anchorage. In July, 1994, Marines from the 13th Marine Expeditionary Unit at Camp Pendleton (CA), held urban warfare training in different locations around Sacramento. In October, 1994, Army Special Forces and the Detroit Police SWAT team, engaged in anti-terrorist training missions at a vacant 6-story apartment house on West Alexandrine Street, and at a group of abandoned houses in Van Buren Township, a suburb of Detroit, near the Willow Run Airport.

A mock city was constructed in the northern area of Fort Polk, in Louisiana, one of the Joint Readiness Training Centers (there are others in Fort Ord, CA and Fort Chaffee, AR), which was labeled a "Military Operations in Urban Terrain Complex" (MOUT). It is also the location of the North American Training Center for the United Nations. Smaller MOUTs are located in Fort Drum (NY) and Fort Indiantown Gap (PA), who have a model town called Johnson City that is used for urban warfare training. The FBI had established an anti-terrorist training compound at the abandoned Brown and Root, Inc. construction yard in Belie Chasse, Louisiana, just south of New Orleans. The purpose of this urban warfare training was nothing more than the perfection of "house-to-house searches and controls on the civilian population," which will be used to disarm the American people through force. It has been suggested that the UN operations in Somalia and Haiti were used as practice runs for disarming the civilian population.

However, before this can happen, a massive gun law will have to be passed, so that all the guns will be confiscated. In 1970, the FBI estimated that the private citizens of the country had a total of 90 million weapons, including 35 million rifles, 31 million shotguns, and 24 million handguns (while the armed forces only had a small arms inventory of 4.8 million guns). Estimates in the early 1990's placed the number of registered handguns in this country at 70 million, and the number of unregistered at 50 million. The Illuminati will not instigate any kind of uprising if Americans will be able to defend themselves. Because of this, there has been a massive attack on our constitutional right "to keep and bear arms."

The extended waiting period mandated by the Brady Bill was only the beginning, there have been other Bills introduced in Congress to ban guns. Sen. Howard Metzenbaum said during a 1993 Senate hearing: "Until we can ban all of them, then we might as well ban none." He also said: "The best way to keep handguns out of the wrong hands is through licensing. Licensing is a barrier to gun crime." At his Senate Confirmation Hearings in 1993, FBI Director Louis Freeh said: "The strongest gun legislation ... I will enforce diligently and exhaustively." U.S. Surgeon General Joycelyn Elders said: "Handguns are a public health issue." Senator Joseph Biden said: "(Banning guns) is an idea whose time has come." Rep. Mel Reynolds said on CNN's *Crossfire:* "If it were up to me we'd ban them all." From the 1970's to 1990's the incidence of violent crimes have more than doubled. They have become more heinous— to the point of being repulsive, and the Government's view is to disarm the criminal, but also at the same time, they want to also disarm law abiding citizens.

Bill Clinton (as quoted in *USA Today*, March 11, 1993, page 2A) said: "We can't be so fixated on our desire to preserve the rights of ordinary Americans..."

The move for gun control is snowballing, and that is part of their plan. In 1994, the National Rifle Association got their hands on a secret document which represented the blueprint for the gun-control lobby in this country. The first step was to use the media to create a clamor for gun control in this country, and this would in turn sway the opinion of a large portion of the population to support such a measure. The second step would be the initiation of gun control legislation that would establish annual licensing fees, and surcharges on ammunition. After two years, the third step would involve a massive increase in the licensing fees. The reason given, would be because of the costs involved to enforce the law, when in fact, it would be to discourage ownership. The failure to get a license would result in a $1,000 fine and/or six months in jail; and if your license lapses, your failure to turn your guns over to the government, would result in a $15,000 fine and/or eighteen months in jail. Both instances also result in the loss of the right to own a firearm.

After two more years, the fourth step would call for further legislation to increase the licensing fees even more. Their ultimate goal "is to reduce the number of licensees to zero." In this way, the Second Amendment to the Constitution of the United States will be circumvented in order to take the guns out of the hands of the American people. After that, the population will be defenseless against government forces. They hoped to accomplish this within 15 years. Noah Webster said in 1787: "Before a standing army or a tyrannical government can rule, the people must be disarmed; as they are in almost every kingdom in Europe."

There was a law passed that tells us what the mentality of the government is concerning this issue. On September 26, 1961, Public Law 87-297 or "The Arms Control and Disarmament Act" was signed. It created the U.S. Arms Control and Disarmament Agency as an "agency of peace to deal with the problem of reduction and control of armaments looking toward ultimate world disarmament." Section 3(a) describes disarmament as the "control, reduction, or elimination, of armed forces and armaments of all kinds." Section 31(a) indicates that the Agency is to engage in study and research to achieve the "limitation, reduction, control, and elimination of armed forces and armaments..." This information can be found in the United States Code, Volume 9, Title 22 (Foreign Relations), Chapter 35 (Arms Control and Disarmament), Sections 2551-2595. Even though the Agency is active in negotiations regarding foreign policy, you can be sure that all such negotiations include the same concessions for America.

In the February 14, 1963 edition of the *Washington Report*, Congressman James B. Utt said that this "Disarmament Act sets up a super-agency with power greater than the power of Congress, which delegated it. The law was almost a duplication, word for word, of a disarmament proposal by the Kremlin in 1959 ... The Disarmament legislation was passed for the purpose of implementing the Department of State Publication 7277, entitled *Freedom from War - The United*

States Program for General and Complete Disarmament in a Peaceful World."

Will the U.S. military go against American citizens if so ordered by the Federal Government? It was reported that a 46-question survey was handed out in May, 1994, to "300 randomly selected" Marines (veterans of the Panama operation and the Persian Gulf War) at the Twentynine Palms Marine Corps Base in the Mohave Desert about 70 miles east of San Bernadino, California. The soldiers were asked for their reaction to various statements, such as U.S. military troops being commanded by UN officers, whether the President "has the authority to pass his responsibilities as Commander-in-Chief to the UN Secretary-General," and if they would serve in a United Nations military force to "maintain world peace." The survey was concluded with this: "The U.S. Government declares a ban on the possession, sale, transportation, and transfer of all non-sporting firearms. A thirty (30) day amnesty period is permitted for these firearms to be turned over to the local authorities. At the end of this period, a number of citizen groups refuse to turn over their firearms. Consider the following statement: I would fire upon U.S. citizens who refuse or resist confiscation of firearms banned by the U.S. Government."

After the news of this survey surfaced (in *The Spotlight*, and the November issue of *American Legion Magazine*), it was later reported that it was part of a soldier's Master Thesis at the Naval Postgraduate School in Monterey, California, and did not "reflect any government program." However, the February, 1994 issue of *Modern Gun* magazine reported that a similar survey had been given to some Navy SEALS.

The Thesis, called *Peacekeeping and UN Operational Control: A Study of Their Effect on Unit Cohesion*, had been classified, until March, 1995, when it was approved for public dissemination. In response to the question about swearing allegiance to the UN, 208 Marines said they could not do so (117 of those strongly disapproved), and 71 said they could (with 19 of those strongly approving). And, in regard to the infamous question 46, of the 264 Marines who responded, 185 said they would be opposed to firing at Americans (with 127 strongly opposing), and 79 said they would be willing to shoot if ordered (with 23 strongly affirming). So, the bottom line is, if ordered, one out of every four Marines would shoot American citizens.

What this survey revealed was that, for the most part, our military probably could not be relied on to act as a cohesive force to fire upon the citizens of this country. However, with increased indoctrination, that could change, but I don't think there is time for that. Therefore, the deck had to be stacked.

On November 11, 1990, President George Bush signed an Executive Order that authorized the presence of UN Battle Groups in the U.S., and there are 15 reported to be here. Before leaving office, in a major speech to the United Nations, Bush said that the United States would permit UN troops to use various military bases for "training purposes," and "multi-national field exercises."

The military staff of the UN Secretary-General had called for a "Rapid Response Peace Force" of 60,000 soldiers, for instant deployment; a "Permanent Peace-Keeping Force" of 275,000 soldiers, for conflict control; and a "Standing Reserve Peace Force" of 500,000 soldiers for UN duty wherever necessary. On March 16, 1993, Senate Joint Resolution No. 65 called for the "establishment of a commission to study the creation of a standing international military force under the United Nations Charter." In 1993, Clinton issued Presidential Review Directive (PRD) #13, supporting Boutros-Ghali's (UN Secretary-General) proposal for a UN military force, substantially made up of Americans. However, Gen. Colin Powell, Commander of the Joint Chiefs of Staff insisted on a codicil that said, if any U.S. commander believed his orders violated the U.S. Constitution, or placed our country or military forces at risk, the orders could be disregarded. On May 3, 1994, Clinton signed the Presidential Review Directive #25, which put U.S. military commanders under the authority of the UN during UN military operations, and instructed the Department of Defense to establish a U.S. military organizational structure which included the United Nations. It was PRD #13 without the Powell codicil.

On June 24, 1994, the National Guard Bureau, an agency of the Department of Defense (which coordinates all the state National Guard units), developed the "National Guard State Partnerships with the Russian Federation" which enabled troops from 14 of the newly formed Russian Federation (as well as other countries in east and central Europe), to train in this country with the National Guard units of some states. According to Clinton's "Bridge to America" proposal, the purpose of these partnerships was to "assist the participating nations' transition to democratic military institutions with peacetime utility in providing military support of civilian authorities..." Troops who were attached to the Russian Interior Ministry were seen training with the U.S. 10th Special Forces Group, who were being reassigned to Fort Carson, Colorado. The Russian soldiers were still wearing the red berets bearing the hammer and sickle, the symbol of Communism. Russians have also been seen training with the SWAT team of Las Vegas, Nevada, and were reportedly involved in joint military training operations in Alaska and Alabama.

Belgian troops were seen in North Dakota and Montana. German soldiers were seen training at Luke Air Force Base near Phoenix, Arizona; as well as Fort Bliss (TX), and Fort McClelland (AL). There have been reports of 19,000 UN troops in Fort Polk (alleged site of a large underground facility), Louisiana, consisting of French, Pakistani, and 2 battalions of Russian soldiers; 600 UN troops near Dulce, New Mexico; 40,000 UN troops staged in Sacramento, California, as well as 40,000 UN troops in San Diego, 22,000 UN troops just south of Los Angeles, 50,000 National Guard and UN troops located near Barstow; 43,000 UN troops in the Texas panhandle; and 14,000 UN troops in Anchorage, Alaska.

The use of Fort Dix in New Jersey (a major east coast base, in an area of 50 square miles, right next to McGuire Air Force Base) was fully committed for UN purposes. Razor wire now surrounds some parts of this base, and there was a sign pointing the way to an Enemy Prisoner of War compound. In addition, in May, 1991, the German government negotiated a deal with our government, which gave them permission to establish a German military facility in our country. There hasn't been a foreign military presence here since Great Britain's occupation during the War of 1812.

Foreign soldiers have been training with American troops in order to function as a cohesive multi-national unit that will operate under the authority of the United Nations. A multi-national UN military force stationed in this country would fire upon American citizens.

Journalist Pam Schuffert, author of *Premonitions of an American Holocaust*, while she was in Germany, asked some soldiers if they knew that German troops were training at Fort Bliss and Holloman, and if they were there "for the hour of martial law, to help arrest Americans and seize their weapons and fire upon them if they resist." One of them replied: "Yes, we have heard all this, and it is true."

Russia-made T-72 main battle tanks have been spotted on our nation's highways, being hauled on flatbed trailers. It is reported that at least 30 may have been brought here. One government response was that they were being used in military war games. Also seen, were Soviet surface-to-air missiles and surface-to-surface missiles. A Soviet Hind-D attack helicopter, and a Soviet Helix anti-submarine naval attack helicopter were seen at the Gulf port National Guard facility in Mississippi. Hundreds of railroad flat cars have been seen with both Russian and UN equipment. Rep. Gene Taylor (D-MS) reported that the aircraft, as well as hundreds of other pieces Russian-built equipment were being purchased and used for training purposes. And he's right, urban warfare training.

Hundreds of Soviet Z1L-131 military trucks were photographed in Saucier, Mississippi, which were imported from East Germany with a UN bill of lading by Airmar Resources Corporation. They were said to be used, and were to be reconditioned and sold. However, many only had a little more than 1,000 miles on them. They were to be painted white, marked for UN use and shipped to Africa, yet many of them have been sent to destinations in this country. There was a report from Montana concerning three train loads of military vehicles, some painted white and marked with the UN designation.

The evidence seems clear, that our government is stockpiling military equipment in preparation for a massive assault against the American people— if necessary. It is believed that there are now over 30 foreign military bases in this country under the United Nations flag, that are manned with a million foreign troops. Because our soldiers could not be counted on to fire upon American citizens, they have been sent overseas as UN peacekeepers, while foreign troops have been brought in that will follow orders to detain, and shoot, anyone who is a threat to the New World Order.

The attack on David Koresh and the Branch Davidians in Waco, Texas may have been just a glimpse of what is going to happen in the future to groups who don't toe the government line. In order to control the population, rather than the wholesale slaughter of people that would further turn public opinion against them, large groups of people will be rounded up to be sent to detention centers for questioning, incarceration, or worse. Michael Maholy, who for 20 years was a CIA-Naval Intelligence agent, said about the detention centers: "Oh, all of us in the intelligence community know about the concentration camps in America. We all know that they are to terminate the resisters of the New World Order under martial law."

Detention Facilities

On August 24, 1939, F.B.I. Director J. Edgar Hoover met with President Roosevelt to talk about a detention plan for the United States, conceivably to deal with a wartime scenario. This was implemented in March, 1942 for Japanese-Americans in the western United States, after the attack on Pearl Harbor, when Roosevelt signed Executive Order #9066, which directed the Army to intern up to 112,000 in concentration camps.

On August 3, 1948, Hoover met with Attorney General J. Howard McGrath to come up with a plan that would enable President Truman to suspend the constitution in the event of a national emergency. The plan was called "Security Portfolio," and if activated, would authorize the FBI to summarily arrest up to 20,000 people and have them placed in national security detention camps without the right of a hearing. It charged the FBI to develop a 'watch list' of the type of people who would be detained, as well as information about their physical appearance, their family, and place of employment.

With the Internal Security Act of 1950, a declaration of war by Congress, an invasion of the U.S. or any its territories, or a domestic insurrection, would enable the President to declare an emergency, and give the Justice Department special powers to "apprehend and by order detain each person as to whom he, the Attorney General or such officer so designated, finds that there is a reasonable ground to believe that such person may engage in, or may conspire with others to engage in acts of espionage or sabotage."

These detention centers were setup at Army facilities in Avon Park (FL), Tulelake (CA), Wickenburg (AZ), and Allenwood (PA).

However, Hoover wasn't happy with the law because it did not suspend the constitution, and it guaranteed the right to a court hearing (habeas corpus), and the FBI continued to secretly establish detention camps, and detailed seizure plans for thousands of people; while Hoover continued to pressure McGrath to officially change his position and allow Hoover to ignore the 1950 law in lieu of the original plan of 1948. On November 25, 1952, the Attorney General gave in to Hoover.

In 1968, during the riots, a Congressional committee stated that acts by 'guerrillas' in the United States was compared to being in a 'state of war,' and detention areas were discussed "for the temporary imprisonment of warring guerrillas." Americans were concerned about this talk, and in 1971 Congress passed legislation that repealed the Emergency Detention Act of 1950. However, there was other legislation that provided for the existence of detention centers.

In December, 1975, the Senate held hearings which revealed the continuing plans for internment. The report "Intelligence Activities, Senate Resolution 21" revealed their secret agenda. The hearings revealed documents, memos, and testimony by government informants which painted the picture of a government that wanted to monitor, infiltrate, arrest and incarcerate a segment of Americans.

The existence of the Master Search Warrant (which authorized the FBI Director to "search certain premises where it is believed that there may be found contraband, prohibited articles, and other materials in violation of the Proclamation of the President of the United States.") and the Master Arrest Warrant (by authorization of the U.S. Attorney General, the head of the FBI is empowered to "arrest persons who I deem dangerous to the public peace and safety. These persons are to be detained and confined until further order.") were revealed.

In 1982, the Reagan Administration initiated the National Security Directive 58 which allowed Robert McFarlane and Oliver North to use the National Security Council to reorganize FEMA (Federal Emergency Management Agency) into an agency that would be equipped to manage the country during a national emergency.

During the Reagan years, a secret program identified as "Operation Rex 84," was initiated by our National Security Council, and authorized the establishment of 23 "emergency detention centers" for the purpose of detaining a large number of "potentially subversive" people. Rex would enable the President to declare a state of emergency, suspend the constitution, and empower the head of FEMA to take control of the internal infrastructure of the country.

The "Rex exercises" simulated an act of civil unrest that culminated in a national crisis that initiated a contingency plan to be able to accommodate the detention of 400,000 people. It was so secretive, that there were reports that special metal security doors were installed on the fifth floor of FEMA's building, and even long-time officials of the Civil Defense Office were denied entry. The cover story for the exercise was to see how our country would handle an influx of refugees resulting from a war in Central America. But in truth— it was about the detainment of American citizens.

Through the Rex 84 program, it had been reported that the following bases were to be used for civilian detention centers: Ft. Huachuca (AZ), Ft. Chaffee (AR), Vandenburg Air Force Base (CA), Eglin Air Force Base (FL), Camp Krome (FL), Ft. Benning (GA), Ft. Indiantown Gap (PA), Camp A.P. Hill (VA) , Ft. Drum (NY), Wickenburg (AZ), Elmendorf Air Force Base (AK), Eilson Air Force Base (AK), Tulelake (CA), El Reno (OK), Tulsa (OK), Florence (AZ), Maxwell Air Force Base (AL), Mill Point (WV), Allenwood (PA), Oakdale (CA), and Ft. McCoy (WI). An additional 20 centers were funded with the 1990-91 defense budget and another 43 were commissioned. An insider has said that there are at least 130 detention facilities in the country.

Even though the directives that brought about Rex 84 have been eliminated, it is believed that the government's plans for these detention centers are now being carried out under the guise of the U.S. Military Base Closure and Realignment Commission (BRAC). Coincidentally, Huachuca, Chaffee, Eglin, and Indiantown Gap were on early BRAC lists. Another 100 bases may be 'closed' or 'realigned' in 2005.

The Federal Bureau of Prisons has priority to use any excess space on U.S. Government property. Army documents have indicated plans for "establishing civilian camps on (Army) installations." One such base that was closed was the Seneca Army Depot, near Seneca Falls, in northern New York. It was discovered that major construction was underway, and it was reported by *The Spotlight*, that it was being prepared for conversion into a massive civilian detention center. The office of Sen. Alfonse D'Amato (R-NY) announced that a large part of the base was going to be turned over to the National Guard, who, it was believed, would oversee the facility. At nearby Fort Drum, the location of the Army's 10th Mountain Division (who have been utilized as UN 'peacekeepers') was also slated to be used as a detention facility.

In 1997, it was revealed, that since 1989, a Civilian Inmate Labor program was in place at Fort Bliss (TX), Fort Dix (NJ), and Camp Atterbury (IN), where the Army was using incarcerated civilians to perform building maintenance and renovation, landscaping and grounds work, and custodial work. Under the facade of

Civilian Labor Camps, it is believed that some detention facilities are being established or renovated.

In the mid-1990's an important discovery was made that really hit home about Government's plans for martial law. At the Amtrak Railcar Repair Facility at Beech Grove, in Indianapolis, Indiana, there were about 10 maintenance barns, covering 129 acres, which is secured by 2 separate fences that lean inward. There are 3 helicopter 25-knot aviation wind socks (as opposed to 10-knot socks which are required for chemical storage), high security turnstiles, and high intensity security lighting. The box car building fence was marked with a "Red/Blue Zone" sign.

One of the barns is large enough to put four box cars in it, and at the top are motorized vents to vent fumes out of the building after the cars have been fumigated. Since the initial observations and photographs were taken in August, 1994, a January 27, 1995 article in the *Indianapolis News* about the lay-offs at the facility said: "Late last year, Congress ordered Amtrak to spend at least $5.9 million patching holes in the roof and fixing masonry on the walls of the giant machine sheds at Beech Grove." Now they are airtight and have been outfitted with newly installed 6 inch pipes, and 2-story hot air furnaces. It was done with the "hopes the yard may be able to solicit work repairing private train cars, and perhaps subway cars from Washington, D.C., or other urban areas." Yet the complex was closed.

The consensus among researchers and patriots is that when martial law is declared, this facility will become a death camp, and be used as a Nazi-style gas chamber, that will be manned by foreign troops.

On 7420 South MacArthur Boulevard in Oklahoma City, OK, (south of the Will Rogers World Airport), built at a cost of $80 million, is the only Federal Transfer Center (FTC) facility in the Federal Bureau of Prisons. It can process up to 100,000 people at a time, and it is believed that this will be the central destination for all detainees. It is likely that it will be coordinating their efforts with Federal Detention Centers (FDC) which are located in: Honolulu (HI), Seattle (WA), Los Angeles (CA), Houston (TX), Miami (FL), Oakdale (LA), and Philadelphia (PA)

Information about the 'Red/Blue' (that appeared on the sign) lists surfaced in June of 1996 when an FBI agent had gotten a copy of the Region 3 Blue list from a CIA agent, and found that his name was on it, as well as other people that he knew in Virginia. It is the same system used by the Nazi's, according to the 1966 book *The Story of the Nazi SS: The Order of the Death's Head* by Heinz Hohne. The sign indicates that this facility will handle Category One (Red) and Category Two (Blue) detainees, and will be used for executions.

A U.S. Air Force Manual (Garden Plot, Plan 55-2) outlined a plan called "Operation Cablesplicer to identify and target resisters, and to detain and incarcerate them.

Martial law is established when the writ of Habeus Corpus, or the right to have a trial by jury, is suspended, and you are taken right to jail. People on the Red list are slated to be picked up immediately upon the initiation of martial law. The scenario is that it will be done late at night, with detainees from that area being taken to a black, unmarked CH-47 Chinook (64 passenger) helicopters where they will flown to one of 38 cities, then put on a jet to a detention facility where they will be executed. People on the Blue List will be picked up within 6 weeks after the declaration of martial law, and they could either be transferred to another detention center for 'reeducation' or be executed. The Green List is for those people who are ignorant of the secret machinations of the New World Order, and do not present a threat to what they are doing.

In the past few years researchers have combed public records, solicited eye witness accounts, and have sought informers in order to piece together the locations of detention centers or 'concentration camps,' which are now reported to be in place all over the country— mostly in sparsely populated areas. There are several lists on the Internet, all variations of the same one. I considered reproducing the list for this book, but I decided against it because I preferred to have a more substantiated and corroborated list. One tell-tale sign of these facilities is that they have fences that point inward (as well as barbed wire), which means they are intended to keep people in, not out. They are usually located near a body of fresh water or freshwater source, a railway system, major highway, or a large airport; have guard towers or buildings; have wind socks, maybe a helicopter landing pad; and contain a large number of buildings which would have the capability of holding a large number of people.

The Government Underground

One of the first publicly revealed underground facilities was the Cheyenne Mountain Operations Center. Construction began in May, 1961, and was completed December, 1965. The main tunnel is a third of a mile long and leads to a pair of 25-ton blast doors which are 50 feet apart. Beyond the second door is an underground complex consisting of a 4-1/2 acre area of chambers and tunnels nearly a mile long. The main chamber consists of three areas 45 feet wide, 60 feet high, and 588 feet long, which are intersected by four chambers 32 feet wide, 56 feet high, and 335 feet long. Within the inner complex, there are fifteen free-standing buildings— a one story, a two story, and 11 three-story buildings.

Although the primary source of electricity is the city of Colorado Springs (a back-up power source comes from six 1,750 kilowatt, 2,800 horse-powered diesel generators), it is essentially a self-contained complex in that all the support services necessary to maintain the operation is contained within, such as a dining facility, medical and dental facility, pharmacy, two physical fitness centers, a base exchange, chapel, and a barbershop. Water is stored in four excavated reservoirs (three are for industrial purposes, and the other is the complex's primary domestic water source) which have the potential to store 1.5 million gallons of water.

This underground complex contains facilities for Air Warning (providing aerospace warning and control for North America), Missile Warning Center (for attacks against the United States or U.S. forces overseas), and Space Control Center (to detect, track, identify and catalog all man-made objects orbiting the earth).

During the Cold War, many Federal Relocation Centers were built for the purpose of the "Continuity of Government," to maintain essential government services and emergency functions during any event which affects national security. It had been reported that there was a system of 96 facilities established around Washington, D.C., in what is called the Federal Arc, which are earmarked for critical governmental personnel from specific agencies, and are located in North Carolina, Virginia, West Virginia, Maryland, and Pennsylvania. After 9-11 it was revealed in an ABC television special with Peter Jennings, that there are 19 emergency operating facilities for sheltering federal government officials within 300 miles of Washington. The administrative nerve center for the whole system is Mount Weather.

Mount Weather

On December 1, 1974, a T.W.A. Boeing 727 jet crashed into a foggy mountain in northern Virginia, killing all 92 people onboard, after that, it was discovered that there was a secret government compound nearby called Mount Weather.

Mount Weather (Western Virginia Office of Controlled Conflict Operations) is an 561 acre installation located about 48 miles (by air, and 54 via the roads) west of Washington, and 1,725 feet above sea level, near the town of Bluemont (5 miles northeast), Virginia. As you drive on route 7, west of Leesburg, you'll turn left on Route 601 just west of Bluemont, and that will lead you right to the gates (actual address is 19844 Blue Ridge Mountain Road). In case of an all-encompassing national emergency, a hand-picked list of civilian and military leaders will be taken to this huge underground shelter in order to form the nucleus of a postwar government. It is run under the auspices of FEMA who refer to it as the "special facility," but it is officially called the "Continuity of Government Program."

Mount Weather has been owned by the federal government since 1902, when the 94 acre site was purchased by the U.S. Department of Agriculture. President Coolidge even talked about building a summer White House there. During World War I it was used as an artillery range, and then during the Depression it was used as a work farm for homeless people. The Bureau of Mines began using the site for experiments in 1936. Initiated by the Federal Civil Defense Administration (later known as the Federal Preparedness Agency), construction began in 1954, and was completed on 1959. Eisenhower told the director of Mt. Weather (code-named "High Point"): "I expect your people to save our government."

It was reported that Millard F. Caldwell, former governor of Florida, suggested that it be used as an alternate capital, because it was believed that the fallout shelter beneath the East Wing of the White House (known as the President's Emergency Operation Center) did not offer sufficient protection from a nuclear attack against Washington.

The plan is for the President, and key administration officials to be flown out of Washington on Air Force One, which, at an altitude of 45,000 feet, is said to be safer that any area on the ground, can be refueled in the air, and stay airborne for up to three days when the engine will fail because of lack of oil. They will be taken to Mount Weather.

It is named for the weather station that was formerly maintained on the mountain by the Department of Agriculture. The facility was constructed inside a mountain made of greenstone and striated granite, the 4th hardest rock known to man; the entrance is sealed with a door, similar to that of a bank vault, only much larger; and it is guarded around the clock. There are also about 65 primary buildings on the surface that is part of this complex. There are 403 people there to take care of the needs of the 1,000 to 2,500 that work there everyday, around the clock.

Richard Pollack, a reporter for Progressive Magazine, in the mid-1970's, interviewed a number of people who had been inside the man-made cavern, and revealed that it is an underground city with roads, sidewalks, office buildings, cafeterias, dormitories, medical facilities, a television station, law enforcement unit, fire department, and a battery-powered subway. It is illuminated with fluorescent lighting. It has a spring-fed artificial lake (large enough for water skiing), its own waterworks, a power plant, and one of the most sophisticated computer systems in the world. It even has a chamber for members of Congress to meet. It can support a population of 200 for up to 30 days, although it can accommodate up to 2,000 people. Only the President, his Cabinet, and the Supreme Court would have private sleeping quarters.

The President or the next in line of succession, would take his place in an area there known as the White House. But until then, a FEMA official is performing the function as Mount Weather is now performing the duties of a back-up United States Government. Pollack wrote: "High-level government sources, speaking under the promise of strict anonymity, told me that each of the federal departments (Agriculture, Commerce, Health and Human Services, Housing and Urban Development, Interior, Labor, State, Transportation, and the Treasury) represented at Mount Weather is headed by a single person on whom is conferred the rank of a Cabinet-level official. Protocol even demands that subordinates address them as 'Mr. Secretary.' Each of the Mount Weather 'Cabinet members' is apparently appointed by the White House and serves an indefinite term. Many of the 'Secretaries' have held their positions through several administrations."

There are also parallel versions of the Selective Service, the Veteran's Administration, the Federal Communications Commission, the Post Office, the Civil Service Commission, the Federal Power Commission, and the Federal Reserve.

In 1975, Senator John Tunney (D-CA) made the accusation that Mount Weather had records on more than 100,000 Americans, and a computer system that gave them access to detailed information on virtually every American. He said they were "out of control."

In 1975, General Leslie Bray, director of the Federal Preparedness Agency (which became FEMA as a result of Executive Order 12148 on July 20, 1979, who also took over the duties and responsibilities of the Defense Civil Preparedness Agency and Federal Disaster Assistance Administration), told the Senate that Mount Weather has extensive files on "military installations, government facilities, communications, transportation, energy and power, agriculture, manufacturing, wholesale and retail services, manpower, financial, medical and educational institutions, sanitary facilities, population, housing shelter, and stockpiles." Bray also told the Senate that the list of those chosen to go there in the event of an emergency had 6,500 names on it. All those on the list have a photo I.D. card with the following inscription: "The person described on this card has essential emergency duties with the Federal Government. Request full assistance and unrestricted movement be afforded the person to whom this card is issued."

In 1961 (Cuban Missile Crisis), 1963 (JFK assassination), and 2001 (September 11th terrorist attacks), the facility was activated to assume governmental responsibilities.

Raven Rock

At Raven Rock Mountain, at the 4,667 acre Raven Rock State Park in Franklin County (near Fountain Dale), on Blue Ridge Summit, is an Alternate Joint Communications Center (AJCC) simply known as 'Site R' (for Raven Rock) or 'The Rock,' which is just over the state line near Waynesboro, PA. It is about 6 miles north of the Presidential retreat of Camp David in Catoctin Mountains near Thurmont (MD), and it is believed by some to be connected with it via a tunnel. In 1950, President Truman approved the 716 acres as part of Camp Albert C. Ritchie in Maryland. Construction began in 1950, and it became operational in 1953. It came under the auspices of Fort Detrick (MD) when Fort Ritchie closed in September, 1998, as part of the 1995 Base Realignment and Closure Act. Because of its 'back-up' status, it is known as the 'underground Pentagon.' It is actually a duplicate of the Pentagon's Command and Control Center, and was used by Deputy Defense Secretary Paul Wolfowitz during the September 11th terrorist attacks. It provides computer services, functions as a disaster recovery site, and oversees over 38 communications systems.

The 260,000 square foot facility lies 650 feet beneath the 1,529 foot summit, and can be accessed by 4 tunnels, which is secured by a chain link fence.

There are five buildings within the complex— with at least three of them being 3-story structures. Inside this massive bunker, which can accommodate 3000 people, there is an underground reservoir containing millions of gallons of water, fluorescent lighting, medical/dental facilities, dining facilities, a fitness center, a convenience store (Post exchange), a barber shop, a chapel, 35 miles of phone lines, and six 1,000-watt generators.

In 2002, in a Department of Defense briefing, in response to a question as to why $74 billion needed to be allocated for upgrades to the facility for power, cooling, and staff accommodation, it was revealed that "…it fits into the overall continuity of government plans."

According to the 1994 U.S. Army Military Police publication *Physical Security of the Alternate Joint Communications Center* they reference a location known as 'Site Creed' which is the "limited area on the west side of the AJCC with an underground building complex." Highly secured, most personnel at 'Site R' did not even know it existed. It is a Presidential Emergency Facility (PEF) that is code-named the "Lucy and Desi Suite."

Greenbrier Facility

Code-named "Project Greek Island," (and sometimes "Casper") only a half-dozen members of Congress, at any one time, knew of its existence. On Sunday, May 31, 1992, an article by Ted Gup, a Washington correspondent for *Time* magazine, appeared in the *Washington Post* (pg. W-11), which revealed that this secret 112,000 square foot facility was located under and beside the Greenbrier Resort Hotel, which is located on 6,500 acres in the Allegheny Mountains in White Sulpher Springs in West Virginia. About 250 miles from Washington D.C., it is an hour away by plane.

The luxury hotel actually looks like the White House. In the winter of 1941-42, it served as an internment area for Japanese, Italian, and German diplomats. In 1949, Secretary of Defense Louis Johnson held a meeting there with the Joint Chiefs of Staff and the Secretaries of the Army, Air Force and Navy for a "top-secret discussion of postwar military strategy." In 1956, Eisenhower had an international meeting there with the leaders of Canada and Mexico.

In 1960, when they began work on their new West Virginia Wing (which contains a complete medical clinic), the Greenbrier website indicates that the "top secret relocation center for the U.S. Congress" was constructed underneath. It was completed 2-1/2 years later. Supposedly deactivated, there are actually public tours of the "former government relocation facility" now.

Its purpose was to house the Congress in the event of a nuclear attack. It has an area for the Senate, House, and a large hall for joint sessions. According to former House Speaker Thomas P. "Tip" O'Neill, who received an annual briefing about the site, spouses would not be allowed in during a nuclear event.

The relocation center's largest room is actually part of the Wing's design. It is 89 by 186 feet, and has a 20 foot high ceiling supported by 18 huge columns. It is now called the Exhibition Hall, and is used for conference events. It has a vehicular, as well as pedestrian entrance, both of which can be sealed off quickly by blast doors hidden behind a false wall. To hotel guests, it appears only to be a very large room. However, its purpose is for joint sessions of Congress.

Behind the hall is a 470-seat auditorium for the House of Representative and a 130-seat auditorium for the Senate. Not too far from these areas is a large white door leading to a corridor about 20 yards long, which culminates with a locked door, and a sign that says: "Danger: High Voltage Keep Out."

Beyond that is an underground installation having 2 foot thick concrete walls reinforced with steel, and a concrete roof under 20 feet of dirt; and contains an infirmary with an operating table, hundreds of metal bunk beds, a shower room, numerous offices, a television studio, radio and communications room, dining room, an internal power plant (with two 2-story high diesel generators); and a "pathological waste incinerator," or cremation oven, which would be used to dispose of bodies, because once the doors are sealed, they can not be opened again until the crisis has passed. A tunnel for vehicles was constructed through the hill to a secret location at the rear of the property which easily accesses Route 60 and a railroad.

The facility was connected, via an underground cable, to a microwave communications outpost at nearby Kates Mountain Road, in the Greenbrier State Forest.

Though this facility is said to be decommissioned, my feeling is that the Government didn't spend millions of dollars on such a facility for it not to be used.

Mount Pony

Mount Pony, east of Culpeper, Virginia, near the intersection of Routes 658 and 3, about 70 miles southwest of Washington, is a 20-1/2 acre site, which contains a 140,000 square foot underground facility with a 400 foot long bunker built of steel reinforced concrete a foot thick and covered with 2 to 4 feet of dirt. It was built in

1969 as a "Continuity of Government" facility and operated by the Federal Reserve Bank of Richmond, where 7 computers became the central point for all American electronic fund transfers. It is self-sustaining, with its own wells, power system, electrical generator, indoor pistol range, incinerator, maintenance shops, cafeteria and storage for water and fuel. It was able to house 540 people for 30 days.

Until 1988, it stored several billion dollars of currency that would be used "to replenish currency supplies east of the Mississippi," and reactivate the economy after a nuclear attack, including a large quantity of $2 bills, in its 23,500 square foot vault with ceilings over 11 feet high, which were shrink-wrapped and stacked on pallets 9 feet high.

It was decommissioned in July, 1992, and in 1997, Congress approved its transfer to the Library of Congress who is using use the installation to protect its collection of 150,000 movies and recordings.

Warrenton Training Center

The Warrenton Training Center (WTC) was initially established in June, 1951, and is believed to contain an underground relocation center for an unknown Federal Agency. According to a report on the Environmental Protection Agency website, the WTC is identified as a "closed and classified communications training and support facility of the National Communications System." The NCS was established in 1963 by President Kennedy to coordinate intra-government communications between 23 Federal Agencies (including U.S. Information Agency and Postal Service), as well as the State Department and CIA.

In June, 1973 it was transferred to the Department of the Army, and redesignated as the U.S. Army Training Group and U.S. Army Security Agency. In September, 1982, it was placed under the auspices of the Defense Department.

The WTC encompasses four sites all secured by a chain link fence. There are 2 underground facilities (Site A and B), on Vinetree Mountain, which some say are connected by a tunnel, because they are only a couple of miles apart.

Site A is at the intersection of Routes 802 and 744, southwest of Warrenton, Virginia. It seems to be the only place where training actually occurs, and contains several small buildings in a heavily wooded area.

Site B is on top of the mountain at Bear Wallow Road on Route 690, and is about 2 miles northwest of Warrenton. Located on 346 acres, this is the official headquarters for the WTC. It has many multi-story buildings, many built in the late 1980's, and is nearly impossible to see from any publicly accessible areas. Its facilities include 2 microwave towers, a large water tank, the Brushwood Conference center, and a pond. There is testimony attesting to the fact that it contains underground facilities. It is part of a fiber optic system that runs from Site C and D, and connects to other intelligence outposts for Washington like Site E, the microwave station in Tysons Corner, Virginia.

These two are code-named "Yogurt" and "Byjams."

Site C, code-named "Brandy," because of the nearby town Brandy Station, is a few miles southeast of Remington on Routes 651 and 654, and has a lot of high frequency antennas, including several directional antennas.

These 3 sites are located in Fauquier County.

Site D is located at Routes 669 and 672, just north of State Route 3, in Culpeper County, 10 miles east of Culpeper, Virginia. It also has a lot of antennas, though fewer of them are high frequency. There is more activity here, and the buildings are larger.

Some Other Underground Facilities in the Federal Arc

The Office of Emergency Preparedness (OEP, now known as FEMA) built a 'hardened' (protected against nuclear attack) underground facility in 1971 at 5231 Riggs Road (Gaithersburg), near junction of Routes 97 and 108, beneath a cow pasture, in Montgomery County, MD, between Olney and Laytonsville. It is entered by a staircase from a small surface building, although there is a horizontal entrance that is used to unload freight. The Federal Regional Center at the Olney Special Facility had served as the Alternate National Warning Center (contained a National Civil Defense Computer system) and was one of two centers (the other being at the North American Aerospace Defense Command or NORAD in Cheyenne Mountain) that would issue a warning in case of a nuclear attack on the United States. It was believed by some to be at least 10 levels deep, however the report of 2 levels seems to be more realistic. It takes up an area of 65,000 square feet. With the Warning Center supposedly transferred to Thomasville, Georgia, it now serves as a Satellite Teleregistration Facility, along with other Regional Centers.

There was a bunker located under the north lawn of the National Park Service's Stephen P. Mather Training Center (formerly Storer College) off Fillmore Street in Harper's Ferry, Virginia. It was to be the emergency relocation center (ERC) for the Department of Interior. Containing only pedestrian access, the door is set into a retaining wall adjacent to the driveway. The facility is now used by the NPS Interpretive Design Center.

There is an abandoned bunker, code-named "Cannonball," on top of Cross Mountain in Franklin County, near the town of Shimpstown, PA (south of Mercersburg), that served as a FEMA V.I.P. Evacuation and Support Center. It is a 103 foot high cylindrical tower, that is 25 foot in diameter, with reinforced concrete walls 15 inches thick. The tower, accessed through a blast door on its side at ground level, contained microwave communications equipment, and served as a microwave relay station. It is believed to have one underground level, which is now flooded. The site also contains an 8,000 gallon fuel tank.

A similar looking facility, part of the same network of facilities, known as a V.I.P. Evacuation and Support facility (code-named "Corkscrew"), is located at Boonesboro, Maryland, between Middletown and Rohersville, on the spine of South Mountain, called Lambs Knoll. On Reno Mountain Road, near the monument of the Civil War officer (Reno), there is an unmarked black-topped service road (marked "Private") that leads to the gate of this installation and around to the back of a silo-like structure, where, a short distance away, is a metal door below ground level. There are no other visible surface structures, which makes it obvious that its facilities are underground. It is fenced in, not marked with any signs, and has an unmanned electric gate. On the grounds there are a couple of collapsible antenna masts and fire tower, and an AT&T relay tower. On the USGS map it is referred to as a fire tower and helipad; while local people refer to it as a missile site, missile silo, weather station, radar site or atmospheric test facility. It is not only a microwave relay station; it is also a complete Presidential Emergency Facility (PEF) which contains a 2-level underground circular bunker (it is divided into wedge-shaped rooms like a pie) about 100 feet in diameter.

Another underground FEMA V.I.P. Evacuation and Support Facility has been identified at Hearthstone Mountain, west of Hagerstown, MD. One of 60 (20 are underground 'hardened' installations) built around the country, it housed an AUTOVON (Automatic Voice Network) center, terrestrial microwave links and troposcatter radio equipment. They were typically large, multi-level installations built to withstand a nuclear attack, with walls 1-1/2 feet thick, and shielded with copper to repel electromagnetic pulse. There is a decontamination chamber and internal filtering system, power generators (with fuel storage), bunks, medical supplies, and enough food to accommodate a staff of 30 for about three weeks. This site is said to be abandoned.

Other Underground FEMA Facilities

During the 1950's, it was reported that there was a large underground facility underneath the AT&T building in downtown Santa Rose, California, which was believed to have tunnels extending a couple miles away to a nearby military base. In 1992, about 15 miles southeast of Santa Rosa, in the mountains near the Napa and Sonoma County line, another underground facility was built. Investigated by the *Napa Sentinel*, they were told by officials at Travis Air Force Base and Hamilton AFB, that it was to be a FEMA base. There is a large microwave transmitter there.

East of Santa Rosa, in a remote area of Napa, in Oakville, near the top of the mountain, is the Oakville Grade Facility, which is another secret underground installation that is part of the Continuity of Government system. Constructed of reinforced steel, it replaced other sites which were located in Benicia, and an old railway tunnel in Ukiah.

The first concrete reinforced underground FEMA Federal Regional Center (FRC) in the country (representing Region VI and states of Arkansas, Louisiana, New Mexico, Oklahoma, Texas) was constructed on a 20 acre parcel of land in Denton, Texas (800 North Loop 288). The FRC for Region X (Alaska, Idaho, Oregon, Washington) is an underground office facility located in a refurbished decommissioned Nike missile site in Bothell, Washington (130 228th Street SW). The FRC complex for Region I (Maine, New Hampshire, Vermont, Rhode Island, Connecticut, Massachusetts) is at 63 (Bldg. A) and 65 (Bldg. B) on Old Marlboro Road, in Maynard, MA (Middlesex County), and has an underground facility containing 2 levels. The FRC for Region IV (Alabama, Florida, Georgia, Kentucky, Missouri, N. Carolina, S. Carolina, Tennesse) in Thomasville, Georgia is located on a 38 acre site, and is a 37,734 square foot underground facility that was built in the early 1970's. It has its own independent water, power and support systems, as well as a telecommunications center.

The FRC for Region VIII (Colorado, Montana, N. Dakota, S. Dakota, Utah, Wyoming) is located at the Denver Federal Center (accessed through Gate 1 at W. 6th Avenue and Kipling Street in Lakewood, CO). During World War II, a 2,080 acre area west of Denver was the site of the Denver Ordnance Plant, which produced ammunition for the war. Afterwards, the Government kept 690 acres, which became the single largest concentration of federal offices outside of Washington, DC. In 1963, the FEMA center was located in building 50, with a 96 foot by 22 foot Quonset-type (corrugated steel structure with arched ribs) bunker submerged in the ground west of it. In 1969 they moved to building 710, a self-contained, two-level underground installation that can provide working and living space for 300 government personnel for up to 30 days. It is accessed through a lobby that protrudes from the earth, and beyond the blast door is a command center, offices, reception area, living area (male and female dormitories with 3-tier bunk beds, pantry, dining facilities, lockers, restrooms, and showers) and communications center (with computers, high frequency radios, ham radio, and a 10,000 watt transmitter which is protected against electromagnetic pulse, lightning and electrical surge). It can operate independently of public utilities, has a main and back-up generators, an 800 foot well, and a 5,000 gallon water tank. A 40 acre antenna field contains 10 above-ground, and 2 buried antenna (which can be raised to the surface in the event the others are damaged).

Because these installations were constructed during the Cold War, when there was a constant threat of nuclear attack, their locations were kept a highly-guarded secret. The information I outlined on the FEMA installations within the Federal Arc is all that is known about the facilities near the seat of power in Washington— which means there are many others. In addition, because officials from Washington could be anywhere in the country on a given day, it is necessary to have underground facilities around the country. For instance, when the terrorist attacks occurred on September 11th President Bush was at an elementary school in Sarasota, Florida. With the skies being a very dangerous place, his plane redirected to Offutt Air Force Base, outside Omaha, Nebraska, where he was taken to a blast-proof bunker beneath a tiny brick building. So, basically there are probably a lot of underground facilities around the country. Besides serving as Emergency Relocation Centers, there are also regional installations for FEMA operations, as well as bunkers that are used for military purposes.

Although it is not known how many are still operational, most likely a lot of them are. Again, just like the detention centers, there is a list available on the internet of underground installations throughout the country. Though I would love to reproduce the list here, I struggled with the fact that, for the most part, these lists are not totally accurate.

It is admitted that most of these underground facilities would not be able withstand the direct hit of a nuclear blast, which is why the secrecy of their locations was so important. However, were their primary purpose to really be functional bomb shelters? It's safe to say that billions of dollars were spent to build these installations within a twenty-year period. It's almost as if government officials were expecting our country to be totally decimated. I believe there was a secondary reason for their construction. In a time of martial law, they will be able to protect Government officials from any sort of paramilitary attack from the citizenry. No matter what is happening on the surface, they will be able to run the country and direct events from below.

CONCLUSION

> *"A patriot must always be ready to defend his country against the government."*
> —Edward Abbey (1927-89, Western novelist and essayist)

Even though the Illuminati ceased to exist as an organization in the 1790's, the organization's leaders kept the conspiracy alive, and continued working towards their goal of a one world socialist government. Since then, as you have read, various organizations have been established to perpetuate these goals, but the term 'Illuminati' continues to be used as the name for the engineers of this Master Conspiracy, since it is more recognizable than the various secret, and little known organizations that are carrying out this Satanic plot. It is believed, that at the pinnacle of the Illuminati, is a group of nine men, who, for the most part are the descendants of the original Illuminati conspirators. It has been reported that they met on June 12, 1952 in France, at the Castle of Arginy (which is where Hugues de Paynes founded the Knights Templar in 1118), under the name "Order of the Temple," to set their final plans in motion for the establishment of a one-world government; also on March 21, 1981, in Switzerland, in a mansion once owned by the Order of the Knights of Malta; then again in France, 1984, as the "International Order of Chivalry, Solar Tradition."

In October, 1977, the John Birch Society printed a secret report retrieved from the office of C. (Clarence) Douglas Dillon (CFR member, head of Dillon, Read and Company, former Chairman of the Rockefeller Foundation, and former Secretary of the Treasury under Kennedy and Johnson) that indicated that the proponents of one-world government had hoped to establish a new World Order by 1976, but by 1970, the date appeared to be impractical, and a new agenda was drawn up, which had required about 15 years for completion. However, 1985 also came without their goals being realized.

The sweeping social reforms of the past, brought us the Social Security and Welfare system, and now the move is on for a National Health Care program. On April 18, 1994, the Associated Press reported that Sen. Jay Rockefeller (D-WV) said: "We're going to push through health care reform regardless of the views of the American people." This is all part of the Master Plan, because it is the ultimate goal of the Illuminati, for the American citizen to eventually be totally dependent upon the government for their security, food, electricity, heat, clothing, and other necessities. Once that potential exists, one-world government is right around the corner.

Slowly our country is being globalized, to fit into the world marketplace. In the Trade Act of 1988, the Commerce Department was charged with the responsibility of instituting the conversion to the metric system, which is now known as the International System. Federal law now mandates that all products must list both metric and non-metric measurements. One world— with one form of measurement.

The economy of the United States, which has been allowed to erode for years, began to experience what may have been the beginning of the final assault, when the North American Free Trade Agreement (NAFTA) was adopted. This two-volume document, nearly 1,100 pages in length, which incorporates most of the provisions of the 1988 Canadian Free Trade Agreement (CFTA), makes the United States, Canada, and Mexico unequal partners in trade. On December 31, 1988, President Ronald Reagan signed Executive Order #12662 which said, that regardless of the constitutionality of decisions made by the bi-national committees of the CFTA, the United States had to accept it.

When NAFTA was approved by Congress, more of our national sovereignty was given up to Mexico. Since Mexican workers do not have minimum wage protection and do not have the right to bargain collectively, the agreement has made Mexico fertile territory for American companies to relocate, thus creating a huge loss of American jobs, and the exploitation of the Mexican workforce. That is only part of the inequities that are contained in this agreement.

Since the inception of NAFTA (January 1, 1994), some of the initial results, were that net exports to Mexico had fallen by nearly $500 million, our trade surplus with Mexico had been cut in half, more than 230 companies had moved to Mexico, and there had been a tremendous increase in America's investment in Mexico. Mattel, the toy manufacturing giant, said that NAFTA would create more American jobs, yet the Public Citizen's Global Trade Watch reported that they laid off 520 workers at their Medina, New York facility. The report further stated that "As of mid-August 1995, the Department of Labor had certified 38,148 workers as having lost their jobs to NAFTA." Months later, the Clinton Administration reported that 127,000 jobs were created by NAFTA (as of 2001, according to Raul Hinojosa-Ojeda, research director of the North American Integration & Development Center at University of California at Los Angeles, only about 100,000 new jobs have been added), but what they didn't reveal, was that a report by the Joint Economic Committee of Congress indicated that the nation had lost 137,000 jobs (this total had risen to 316,000 by 2001).

During the first nine months of 1994, our trade surplus with Mexico shrunk by 27 percent. This report further said that this was "only the tip of the job displacement iceberg." According to Rep. Marcy Kaptur (D-OH), NAFTA promoters said that 60,000 American manufactured cars would be exported to Mexico in 1994, but only 28,000 were. Not only that, we ended up importing 278,000 cars from Mexico.

The highly skilled, well-paying positions have gone to Mexico, while low-paying, low-skilled jobs have been created in the United States. This stems from the fact that the raw materials and parts are exported to Mexico, assembled, then imported back into the country at a far greater value. Rep. Peter DeFazio (D-OR) said: "There's also a conspiracy of silence on the part of the Republican leadership in Congress who provided the votes needed to pass this turkey."

In 1848, Karl Marx said: "Free trade breaks up old nationalities ... in a word, the free trade system hastens social revolution." Henry Kissinger said that NAFTA represented "the most creative step toward a New World Order."

The General Agreement on Tariffs and Trade (GATT) came into existence in 1947 as the overseer of the multilateral trading system. It was an instrument of the United Nations. On January 1, 1995 the World Trade Organization (WTO), the descendant of the proposed International Trade Organization (1948) and Organization for Trade Cooperation (1954), replaced GATT, presenting a new agreement which included "GATT 1994." During the 1940's and 1950's the Congress and the country was not ready to have their economic authority transferred to international control. In 1958, Sen. George Malone of Nevada said: "The global theory of free trade is siphoning off America's wealth and bringing her economy to the level of others. The theory is displacing American workers who otherwise would be employed."

"GATT 1994" was a document consisting of 22,000 pages of information, tariff schedules, rules and regulations; and 650 pages of enabling legislation. Based on its size, how many of our legislators do you think read every word of this trade agreement; and based on its complexity, if it was read— was it understood?

It is the only international agreement which sets the global rules for world trade, and provides for the mediation of disputes, which is argued by many to be the best way to open up foreign markets to U.S. exports, because protectionist countries, as well as the U.S. would have to lower their tariffs (producing a loss in revenue), to create an even playing field. However, critics familiar with its contents say that it will succeed in seriously damaging our national sovereignty and independence. Proponents disagree, saying that any country can withdraw from membership after giving a six month notice. As one of the 146 member nations, the United States would only have one vote, yet it would have to pay nearly 25% of the cost. The GATT agreement would have the power to force Congress to change laws by declaring them to be "protectionist" (WTO Charter, Article 16, Section 4), and if we don't comply, we would be subject to trade sanctions.

Financier, Sir James Goldsmith, a member of the European Parliament, said in his testimony before Congress, that GATT would "cause a global social upheaval the likes of which Karl Marx never envisioned." The October 24, 1994 issue of *Barron's*, indicated that the WTO is a de facto world government. William Holder, deputy general counsel of the UN's International Monetary Fund, said that the WTO is a de jure (by law) world government. In all actuality, this legislation is a Treaty, and as such, should have required approval by two-thirds of the Senate; instead, it was considered a Trade Agreement, which only required a majority vote.

Even though, during the midterm elections of November, 1994, the country overwhelmingly voted to change the course our country has taken, GATT was still brought to a vote during the lame duck session of the 103rd Congress and passed, rather than waiting for the Republican-majority Congress that was elected. Some opponents believe, that if the vote had been postponed, it may never have been ratified, at least, in its present form, But that was unlikely, since its passage was a bipartisan effort spearheaded by a group of key Republicans lead by Majority leader, Sen. Bob Dole of Kansas, and Speaker of the House Rep. Newt Gingrich of Georgia (a member of the CFR); and conservative think-tanks like the Heritage Foundation and the American Enterprise Institute.

The question looms before us as to whether we are actually better off as a country now, compared to the way we were prior to the initiation of everything that has been outlined in this book. I think the answer is a resounding "No!" Right now, the world is a very volatile place— hostilities in foreign countries are threatening, the world economy is teetering, and democracy hangs in the balance, as a handful of men patiently wait for a few more pieces of the puzzle to fall into place, so they can spring their trap.

It would be impossible, within the confines of this format, to fully explore the complex structure of deceit that has been put into place. However, after looking at many pieces of this puzzle, though the picture is incomplete, enough have been put together so that we can now step back and get a panoramic view of how we got to where we are. It's not going to be a pretty picture. Our way of life is going to be drastically changed because of the tyranny of a government out of control. How did this happen— right under our nose?

In 1999, Warner Brothers released a little movie called *The Matrix*. Not considered a major project, it was shot in Australia to save money. Expectations were not high for this edgy sci-fi action film, however, after its opening, it was quite clear that its writers, the Wachowski Brothers had struck gold by tapping into the collective intellectual consciousness of a nation that was preparing to enter a new millennium. Most movies are made to entertain, and are fairly straight forward in their approach, but *The Matrix* challenged its viewers. Incredibly unique was the fact that different people, who saw it, had different interpretations of its meaning.

The plot revolves around Neo, a computer hacker (played by Keanu Reaves) who discovers that the world he lives in is nothing more than a computer simulation that is being fed into his brain as his body rests in a pod, in the real world, along with endless numbers of others, providing the energy that sustains the machines that run the world.

When I read the original script, there were lines in there that did not appear in the movie. For instance, "Anthony" (whose name was changed to Choi in the movie) says to DuJour about Neo: "I told you, honey, he may look like just another geek but this here is all we got left standing between Big Brother (a term from George Orwell's book *1984*) and the New World Order." Also, in a chatroom called "The Matrix," we find the following comments:

Quark: "The Matrix is a euphemism for the government."
Superastic: "No, the Matrix is the system controlling our lives."

It's not hard to see that these lines were removed, so the movie wouldn't come across as being a political commentary that was intended to convey their contention that we are living in the "Matrix," which is being controlled in the real world by the boys in the New World Order.

Especially revealing is the scene in the movie when Neo meets Morpheus (Lawrence Fishburne), the leader of the resistance, at the Lafayette Hotel, and tells him what the Matrix is:

"The Matrix is everywhere. It is all around us. Even now, in this very room. You can see it when you look out your window, or when you turn

FINAL WARNING 343

on your television. You can feel it when you go to work, when you go to church, when you pay your taxes. It is the world that has been pulled over your eyes, to blind you from the truth."

Applying the Wachowski's innuendo to our current situation, we find that they have described a system of 'Command and Control' that has been able to so dominate and overwhelm that we have been completely deceived into believing a lie.

In the movie, Neo is unplugged from the Matrix, enabling him to see the real world. It is my hope, that with the knowledge you gain from reading this book, you will be 'unplugged' from the Matrix, and begin to see for yourself that things aren't what they seem. That the world you thought you were living in— doesn't really exist.

PART TWO

THE SPIRITUAL CONSPIRACY

CHAPTER TEN

SETTING THE STAGE FOR DESTRUCTION

WHEN THE CONSPIRACY ACTUALLY BEGAN

By now, there should be no doubt in your mind that there is an orchestrated effort by a small group of men to establish a one-world government. Even though we have gone back to look at the roots, and evolution of this movement, the actual motive goes back much farther than that. Just think, what motivation could there be to fuel that kind of desire. The answer is that you have to look at things with a spiritual eye, in order to comprehend the complexities that the New World Order actually represents. And when you do that, then you can understand how it has been able to progress through all these years, and why it will continue.

This Part will deal with the application of the First Part to Biblical research and end-time prophecy. Although space constraints will only allow a general treatise of the major elements, I will be dealing with these matters in a much more detailed fashion on my website (www.viewfromthewall.com) in the near future.

When you read Genesis 1:1-2, it says: "In the beginning God created the heaven and the earth. And the earth was without form, and void; and darkness was upon the face of the deep. And the spirit of God moved upon the face of the waters." The Rotherham translation of the Bible, which was taken from the original Hebrew, says: "Now the earth had become waste and empty." You have to understand that there was an undetermined amount of time which passed between these two verses. However, we do have some clues about certain events which occurred before Adam, and the refurbishing of this world for his habitation.

Just as God told Noah and his sons in Genesis 9:1 to "replenish" the earth after the flood, God had told Adam and Eve the same thing in Genesis 1:28. This seems to indicate that there were men on the earth before Adam. Proof of this can be found in Jeremiah 4:23-26. Now you can understand the time frame, and the circumstances regarding Lucifer (the 'lightbringer'). He was a "cherub" (the highest classification of angels), and is described in the Bible as being wise and perfect. It was his job to bring light. Eventually he became proud of himself, and sought to take the place of God (Isaiah 14:12-17, Ezekiel 28:2, I Timothy 3:6). He led a third of the angels (Revelation 12:4) in a revolt against Michael, the archangel, and the remaining angels (Jude 1:6, II Peter 2:4-5) for the control of Heaven. This battle for the control of Heaven nearly destroyed the earth. After his defeat, Lucifer was cast down to earth, where he became known as "Satan" (which means 'adversary'), the leader of the fallen angels (or demons), and the "god of this world." (2 Corinthians 4:4)

When God renewed the earth, and created man in His image, He gave Adam dominion over the earth, which infuriated Satan, who had the impression that he was to rule over the earth. Again, Satan plotted against God, and caused Adam and Eve to sin by eating the fruit of the tree which was forbidden by God. For their sin, they were banished from the Garden of Eden. Ever since then, Satan has been carrying out his plan to corrupt and control the earth. For six thousand years, a small group of satanically empowered men have been feverishly working to eliminate God and to enslave mankind. The New World Order is nothing more than the culmination of these efforts; the final step of a plan that will enable Satan to again challenge God, and the angelic forces of Heaven.

Helping Things Along

In the story about Cain and Abel, when Cain killed his brother, he was cursed by God (Gen. 4:11) and exiled. Genesis 4:12 says: "When thou tillest the ground, it shall not henceforth yield unto thee her strength..." Yet, we find that Cain established the city of Enoch; and his descendants Jubal, was the father of those who became proficient in the harp and organ, and Tubalcain, was a teacher of brass and iron works. We also find, that it wasn't until Enos, the son of Seth, that men began "to call upon the name of the Lord." (Gen. 4:26) Though it doesn't say, the implication is that the line of Cain was ungodly.

The apocryphal Second Book of Adam and Eve, bluntly gives details about this. In chapter 20:2-4, it says: "But as to this Genun (a son of Lamech), Satan came into him in his childhood; and he made sundry trumpets and horns, and string instruments, cymbals and psalteries, and lyres and harps, and flutes; and he played on them at all times and at every hour. And when he played on them, Satan came into them, so that from among them were heard beautiful and sweet sounds, that ravished the heart. Then he gathered companies upon companies to play on them; and when they played, it pleased well the children of Cain, who inflamed themselves with sin among themselves, and burnt as with fire; while Satan inflamed their hearts, one with another, and increased lust among them."

Although the origin and truth of this apocryphal book can never be ascertained, and it never became part of the holy canon, it is believed that the writings were part of an older, more ancient document that accurately reflected upon the events of this historical period. For a family line that has been perceived as being ungodly, they developed musical instruments, and the expertise and ability of producing weapons of war from metal mined out of the earth. Was the knowledge of these things God-given? I have concluded that they were not, and even though the evidence is circumstantial, I believe that Satan, through demons, divulged this information.

FINAL WARNING

Ezekiel 28:13 relates that there were musical instruments created within the body of Lucifer, and it has been said that every time he moved, he played music. He led the angelic praise and worship of God. So when he fell, he knew the importance of music, and how to use it to his advantage. It seems likely that he would have bestowed the knowledge of music. Primitive cultures, American Indian ceremonies, and occult rituals are well known to have used the hypnotic and influential properties of music to enhance their activities.

And through weapons, and the means to wage war, people are controlled.

So, yes, I believe that there was some Satanic influence on the technology of the people at the time, because he was laying the groundwork for his plans to regain control of the world that he once ruled.

According to Tom Van Asperen there is a language of Twice Speak in the Bible, which is a separate code language, much like Equidistant Letter Sequencing, and Mathematical Signature. Basically, it is a revealing of the "secret" talked about in Amos 3:7 that has unlocked the typical and anti-typical method of recording Biblical history, and at the same time, end-time prophetic events. Asperen believes there is so much of this type of prophecy in the Old Testament, that, in a sense, it becomes another New Testament.

I have found some of the Twice Speak revelations to be fascinating in as far as it acts as an underlying witness to the Scriptures. However, when the interpretations provide new information that can not be found in the Biblical text then I have to question it. But, although this concept may be new to you, and may seem kind of off the wall, let's just assume for argument's sake that it is a divine Biblical code that proves the word of God, gives us a better understanding of it, and further reveals end-time prophetic events; and let's assume that the events concerning the line of Cain is also a prophecy concerning the last days.

In 1997, Simon and Schuster published a book called *The Day After Roswell*, by Col. Philip J. Corso (Ret.). The cover proclaimed: "The truth exposed after fifty years- A former Pentagon official reveals the U.S. Government's shocking UFO cover-up." The subject of the book was the alleged crash of a flying saucer in Roswell, New Mexico, where alien bodies and pieces of the aircraft were recovered back in 1947. The government has long denied this happened, and indeed continues to deny the existence of flying saucers and extraterrestrial life. You might not believe in flying saucers. But bear with me, I don't want you to question my credibility now.

Let's look at the time period this occurred. It was 1947, which was around the time that flying saucers were first sighted. Now what else happened about that time? The United Nations was established in 1945, and Israel became an independent nation in 1948. These two events occurring around the same time was not a coincidence, because it set the stage for Armageddon, and the fulfillment of all things. The United Nations, or the foundation for a world government, was the prophetic trigger, and with the time-sensitive prophecies contained in the Bible, Satan knew that he was running out of time.

It was initially reported that a flying saucer crashed at Roswell, and also at that time, there were enough sightings and pictures in other parts of the country to give the report credibility. Since then, there has been so much evidence for the existence of flying saucers and aliens, that it's become pretty much an accepted fact, even though the government continues to deny their existence. In fact, there is so much information and evidence, that now, the Christian church has said that, yes, there is something to it all.. The Christian perspective, and growing consensus, is that aliens are actually demonic manifestations. There have been four or five Christian books on the subject. So, again, let's assume that there was a flying saucer that crashed at Roswell.

Philip Corso, is his book *The Day After Roswell*, relates, that as a member of President Eisenhower's National Security Council, his Research and Development team at the Pentagon analyzed and integrated the alien artifacts found at Roswell into the private business sector. According to him, major companies such as IBM, Hughes Aircraft, Bell Labs, and Dow Corning, were unknowingly given the alien technology, which became the integrated circuit chips, fiber optics, lasers, and the super-tenacity fibers of today.

What I want to hone in on, is the information in Chapter 12, which discusses the "Integrated Circuit Chip: From the Roswell Crash Site to Silicon Valley." Among the wreckage, Corso said that charred quarter-size, cracker-shaped, silicon wafers were found, which had grid lines etched on them, which was actually microscopic circuitry. An analysis of the craft's remains failed to turn up any wiring, so it was determined that these chips actually represented the nerve center of the vehicle, carrying signals through the ship, just like impulses are carried throughout the nervous system of our body. Corso wrote (page 167): "Although IBM and Bell Labs were investing huge sums of development money into designing a computer that had a lower operational and maintenance overhead, it seemed, given the technology of the digital computer circa 1947, that there was no place it could go. It was simply an expensive-to-build, expensive-to-run, lumbering elephant at the end of the line. And then an alien spacecraft fell out of the skies over Roswell, scattered across the desert floor, and in one evening everything changed."

In 1948, it was revealed that the first junction silicon transistor had been developed by Bell Telephone Laboratories, and the technological capabilities of the computer industry took a huge leap in a short period of time. Even Corso wondered about where it would all lead (page 172): "..what if an enemy wanted to implant the perfect spying or sabotage mechanism into a culture? Then the implantation of the microchip-based circuit into our technology by the EBEs (aliens) would be the perfect method. Was it planted as sabotage or as something akin to the gift of fire? Maybe the Roswell crash in 1947 was an event waiting to happen, like poisoned fruit dropping from the tree into a playground."

Now, instead of aliens, think demons, and I believe we have an anti-typical fulfillment of the prophetic event that took place when the line of Cain was given hidden knowledge. I believe that our computer technology, which developed into the Internet, is part of Satan's plan for the last days, and will be used to carry out his devious end-time plot. Only God is omnipotent and omnipresent, however, through a world-wide computer network, Satan will be able to falsely misrepresent his power. For years, it was believed that the huge computer in Brussels, Belgium would be the one that would be used to record the files of everyone on Earth. Now it has come to light that our National Security Agency has a huge classified underground database at Fort Meade, Maryland, that covers an area of ten acres.

THE BEGINNING OF THE END:

The Prophetic Trigger of God's Timeline

For hundreds of years, it has been common knowledge within the Church, that mankind's life span upon this earth would be 6,000 years. This was gleaned from Exodus 20:9-10, which says: "Six days shalt thou labor ... But the seventh day is the Sabbath of the Lord thy God." Like many things in the Scriptures, it had a deeper meaning beyond what was being conveyed about their calendar, which was later revealed in 2 Peter 3:8 — "But, beloved, be not ignorant of this one thing, that one day is with the Lord as a thousand years, and a thousand years as one day."

In 1650, using these Scriptures, Archbishop Jacob Ussher of Armagh in Ireland, attempted to calculate when the Creation took place by using chronological information from the Bible and counting backward from the date of the birth of Christ. At that time, it was believed that Christ was born in 4 BC (some calculations had indicated that it may have been as late as 1 BC or as early as 6 BC; however, recent evidence have determined it to be 3 BC), so Ussher theorized that the Creation took place in 4004 BC, and the passing of four "days" (two thousand years before the law, and two thousand years after the law) took us to Christ's birth in 4 BC, so two more 'days' would end the six 'days' at 1996. The Sabbath, or the seventh 'day,' is the Millennium, or the thousand-year reign of Jesus Christ upon the Earth, which is referred to in the 20th chapter of Revelation.

An apocryphal book known as the Epistle of Barnabas, which early church leaders such as Origen and Jerome believed had been written by the first recruit of the Apostle Paul, Barnabas, said: "And God made in six days the works of His hands; and He finished them on the seventh day, and rested on the seventh day and sanctified it. Consider, my children, what that signifies, He finished them in six days. The meaning of it is this: that in six thousand years the Lord God will bring all things to an end. For with him, one day is a thousand years; as Himself testifieth, saying, behold this day shall be as a thousand years. Therefore children, in six days, that is, in six thousand years, shall all things be accomplished. And what is it that He saith, and He rested the seventh day; He meaneth this; that when his Son shall come, and abolish the season of the wicked one, and judge the ungodly; and shall change the sun and the moon, and the stars, then He shall gloriously rest in that seventh day."

Irenaeus, an early church leader, while writing in 150 AD about the book of Genesis in his book *Against Heresies* said: "This is an account of the things formerly created, as also it is a prophecy of what is to come. For the day of the Lord is as a thousand years; and in six days created things were completed; it is evident, therefore, that they will come to an end at the sixth thousand years." Around 300 AD, in the writings of Christian scholar Lactantius, he said: "Because all the works of God were finished in six days, it is necessary that the world should remain in this state six ages, that is six thousand years. Because having finished the works He rested on the seventh day and blessed it; it is necessary that at the end of the sixth thousandth year all the wickedness should be abolished out of the earth and justice should reign a thousand years." Other writers during the early Christian era also reflected this premise.

Some researchers have sought to adjust the calculations of this theory. The Jewish calendar conformed to the solar year, which contained 360 days, or 12 months of 30 days. In 1583, the Gregorian calendar was adopted, which added an extra 5.25 days to that year. If you add 2,160,000 days (6,000 years X 360 days) to 2,173.50 days (414 years of 5.25 days), you get 2,162,173.50 days, which divided by the Jewish year of 360 days, would make the end of the sixth day, the year 2002. When you deduct from that figure, the seven year period which is commonly referred to as the Tribulation period, that leaves us with the year of 1995 as the culmination of the efforts to establish a New World Order.

There is another theory, which has to do with the amount of time that the Jewish race would be dispersed across the Earth. The Jews were in bondage in Egypt for 430 years and later for 70 years in Babylon. These dates were foretold. The purpose of the prophecy which is given in Ezekiel 4:1-8 was to show how long the Jews would be scattered as a people. Other Scriptures deal with the extent of the dispersal: Deut. 28:25, Deut. 28:64, Jer. 24:9, and Amos 9:9. Adding the 390 and 40 years, gives you 430 years. Leviticus 26:18 says: "And if ye will not yet for all this hearken unto me, then I will punish you seven times more for your sins." From 430, subtract the 70 years they were punished in Babylon, and what God was telling Moses, was that the Jewish people would be dispersed for 2,520 years (360 years X 7).

Now here is where it gets a little tricky. Nebuchadnezaar's first return of his Jewish captives was in 536 BC, and the final return was in 516 BC. Again, using the adjustment for the two calendars, and using the earliest date of 536 BC, we get these calculations: 907,200 days (2520 years X 360 days) plus 2,110.50 days (402 years X 5.25 days) is 909,310.50 days divided by 360 days of the Jewish calendar is 2525.86 years, or the year 1990. But then, the latter date of 516 BC, would give us the year 2010.

The Bible also says that the events of the end times would not take place until all of the Jews returned to their homeland, and this return is referred to in: Isa. 5:26, Isa. 11:11-12, Isa. 43:5-6, Jer. 16:15, Jer. 30:3, Eze. 34:11-13, Eze. 36:24, and Zech. 10:8. This return of God's chosen people, only refers to pure, full-blooded Jews (Gen. 6:1-4, Ezra 10:2-18, Neh. 13:27, Jude 1:7). In 1800, Palestine had a population of 150 Jews; 1827- 1,500 Jews; 1850- 8,000; 1910- 41,000; 1914- 100,000; 1930- 170,000; 1935- 300,000; 1939- 450,000; 1948- 650,000; 1953- 1,300,000; 1962- 2,000,000; and 1970- 2,500,000. Now there are nearly five million Jews in Israel which have been gathered up from over 102 different nations.

A gentleman by the name of Joe Marler had proposed a theory based on Daniel 9:25-26 which says: "Know therefore and understand, that from the going forth of the commandment to restore and build Jerusalem unto the Messiah the Prince shall be seven weeks, and three score and two weeks: the street shall be built again, and the wall, even in troublous times. And after threescore and two weeks shall Messiah be cut off..." The Hebrew word for "week" is 'shabula' which means 'seven,' indicating that a 'week' is actually 7 'weeks' of years, or 49 years, which is known as the Jubilee cycle (Lev. 25:8).

The 62 weeks began when the city of Jerusalem, and its Temple, which was destroyed in 586 BC, was rebuilt. Three such decrees were given. The first came during the first year of the reign of Cyrus (King of Persia, 536-527 BC), who ruled for nine years; after which his son Cambyses (527-520 BC) took over, and all the work on the Temple was stopped for seven years. The second decree was made by Darius I, in the second year of his 35-year reign (520-485 BC). Construction resumed on the Temple in 520 under Zerubbabel, the Persian governor, and was completed between 516-514 BC. Then Xerxes reigned 21 years (485-464 BC). Artaxerxes ruled 40 years (464-424 BC), and during his seventh year, in 457 BC, he decreed that Jerusalem be restored. Nehemiah, the cupbearer to Artaxerxes, was sent to Jerusalem in 444 BC to complete the work on the walls of the city to fortify it. Thus the period of 62 weeks represents 434 years, which added to 444 BC, indicates the date of 10 BC, which is close to the time of the birth of Christ.

Marler's research somehow led him to the period of 440-438 BC, and adding 434 years to 438 BC led to 4 BC, which is closer to the actual date of the birth of Jesus. Marler believes that the other seven 'weeks' or 49 years apply to the second coming of Jesus. Rather than using the date of May 14, 1948, when Israel officially became an independent country, he used the date of November 29, 1947, when the United Nations voted 33-13 to approve a Jewish homeland. Adding 49 years indicated a date of November 29, 1996, as the end of man's rule on this Earth. By counting back 3-1/2 years, he theorized that the period known as the Tribulation would begin May 29, 1993. The irony here is a story that was reported in the news on May 19, 1993. Big Ben, the renowned tower clock famous for its accuracy, which was installed in 1859 at the eastern end of the Houses of Parliament in London, had mysteriously stopped running. Was the most recognized time piece in the world stopped through divine means to signal the beginning of the end? No. And another 'date' had come and gone.

There are also those researchers who have chosen to totally base all of their calculations on the premise of 360 days indicating a Biblical year. For instance, in Hosea 6:1-2 it says: "Come, and let us return unto the Lord: for he hath torn, and he will heal us; he hath smitten, and he will bind us up. After two days will he revive us: in the third day he will raise us up, and we shall live in his sight." From the initiation of Christ's ministry, in the fall of 28 AD, and adding two "days" (2 years X 360 days) would give us 720,000 days, which adjusted to our calendar by dividing into that 365.25 results in 1971.25 years, which added to 28.75, takes us to the year 2000.

Another one has to do with the cleansing of the Temple. In 168 BC, the Syrian King Antiochus IV Epiphanes attacked Israel, and sacrificed a pig to Zeus on the Temple altar, an event that is referred to as the Abomination of Desolation. The period till cleansing, according to Daniel 8:14, was 2,300 days, which some scholars feel refers to 2,300 morning and evening rituals, or 1,150 days (3 years, 2 months and 10 days), which seemingly points to the ritual cleansing performed by Judas Maccabaeus three years later, after the success of the Hasmonean revolt. However, according to the apocryphal book of the Maccabees, the Temple was cleansed in 1,080 days.

To make matters worse, while the King James version states 2,300 days for this period, the Greek Septuagint, which was used during the time of Christ, says 2,400 days. In his 1754 book *Dissertations on the Prophecies*, Bishop Thomas

Newton wrote about the existence of a third manuscript of the book of Daniel, which was mentioned in a Commentary of Jerome, the early church leader. This manuscript gives the figure of 2,200 days. Since this figure can not be applied literally to the events of that time, it is believed that the figure should be considered as years. This assumption is based upon Ezekiel 4:6, which says: "I have appointed thee each day for a year"; and Numbers 14:31, which talks of "each day for a year." If the figure of 2,200 'days' is used, the following calculation is then applied: 2,200 years X 360 days = 792,000 days, which adjusted for our calendar year of 365.25, results in 2,168 years. When this figure is added to 168 BC, it leads us to the year 2000.

Another theory deals with the Times of the Gentiles. This phrase stems from a statement by Jesus in Luke 21:24: "...and Jerusalem shall be trodden down of the Gentiles, until the times of the Gentiles be fulfilled." This refers to a period which began in 606 BC when the Babylonians conquered Jerusalem. In Daniel 4:23, according to Nebuchadnezzar's vision (who is represented by a tree, as men sometimes were: Psalms 1:3, Psalms 37:35, Ez. 31:3), "seven times" were to pass over him. Revelation 11:2-3 ("42 months" X 30= 1,260 days), Rev. 12:6 ("a thousand two hundred and threescore days" or 1,260 days), Rev. 12:14 ("a time, and times, and half a time" or 360 + 720 + 180= 1,260 days) indicates that a "time" is 360 days, which means that seven "times" would be 2,520 'days' or years (on top of referring to the seven years God struck him down with a period of insanity to show his power).

The calculation would go like this: 2,520 years X 360 days = 907,200 days, which adjusted to our calendar year of 365.25 days, results in 2,483.78 years. When this figure is added to 606 BC, it leads us to the year 1878, which is believed to be the end of "the times of the Gentiles." Now comes an interesting proposal. When Jesus spoke of the way things were in the "days of Noah," when God gave mankind an additional 120 years (Gen. 6:3) to repent, before he sent the flood; this period has been added to the year 1878 (of course in the adjusted form of 118.28 of our calendar years), which indicates the year of 1997 as the end of "the times of the Gentiles" and the beginning of the judgment period known as the Tribulation, which when you add this 3-1/2 years, and leads us to the year 2000.

Let me throw one more at you, which came to me from an e-mail, and the website of Torstein Langesaeter from Norway, who made a very detailed mathematical calculation to determine the number of years between Adam, and Jesus; and believes that the period of 6,000 years will conclude in 2028.

All of these calculations can be somewhat correlated to the six 'day' theory, in that it indicates a time frame for events within this 6,000 year period. Jesus was very specific when He spoke about the signs of His return, and He exhorted His disciples to watch, and pray. Because of the symbolism, type and anti-types, and dual prophecies used in the Bible, was there something that would signal the end of time as we got closer to the end of the six 'days' or 6,000 years? In Luke 21:25, Jesus talked about the "signs ... upon the earth distress of nations, with perplexity..."

There was a period in our history when a sequence of events occurred which seemed to set the stage for the fulfillment of Bible prophecy. Let's look at the events which happened during the three year period of 1945 - 1948:

1) On June 26, 1945, at a San Francisco conference, 50 nations met to adopt the United Nations charter. The UN General Assembly held their first meeting in London on January 10, 1946.

2) A UFO was reported to have crashed in Roswell, New Mexico on July 4, 1947.

3) On November 29, 1947, the UN voted to approve a Jewish homeland, and on May 14, 1948, Israel became a nation.

4) It has been long accepted that the Dead Sea Scrolls were discovered in 1947, but according to Randall Price in his book *Secrets of the Dead Sea Scrolls* he found out that they may have actually been discovered as early as 1936. However, 1947 was time when their existence was revealed.

5) The World Council of Churches was established on August 23, 1948.

Just as we are able to interpret prophecy, and determine the signs of the times—so has Satan. He knew the time that Israel would prophetically be resurrected as a nation, and he had to make sure his plans would be in place, so, when the time came, he would be able to deceive the world into accepting the Antichrist as the messiah.

Let's look at the events surrounding Israel becoming a nation. The establishment of the United Nations would herald the move toward one-world government. As discussed earlier, recent exposé has shown that there was a UFO crash at Roswell, and among the technology gleaned from it was integrated circuit chips, fiber optics, and lasers. The treasure of ancient documents found at Qumran has yielded copies of nearly every Old Testament book, however, it has also turned up documents from a Jewish sect known as the Essenes. As these Dead Sea Scrolls were translated in secret, the scholars behind them began to use them to undermine the divinity Jesus, by saying that the Essenes were the true originators of what became known as Christianity. And the World Council of Churches would begin the move toward ecumenicalism that is seeking to bring all the world's religions together into one unified body.

Now let's put these events in perspective with Bible prophecy.

Jesus said in Matthew 24:34 — "Verily I say unto you, This generation shall not pass, till all these things be fulfilled." Jesus was speaking to his disciples concerning the last days, and had just told them about the parable of the fig tree. Some Bible scholars have interpreted Ezekiel 36:8 to mean that the fig tree represented the nation of Israel. So it is believed that Jesus was referring to the generation that would be alive when Israel became a nation on May 14, 1948. Job 42:16 refers to a generation as being 35 years, while Webster's Dictionary indicates that it is forty years. The figure of 40 years is echoed in Hebrews 3:9-10 which says: "When your fathers tempted me, proved me, and saw my works forty years. Wherefore I was grieved with that generation..." Adding 40 years to 1948 would give us the year 1988.

But let me add another wrinkle to this theory. It is no secret that Bible prophecy, and the understanding of it, revolves around Israel. Israel is the only nation that is referred to in the masculine gender. According to Jewish custom, a male is labeled under the following age categories: child (1-12), young man (13-19), warrior (20-29), and mature man (30-50, who is able to officiate in the Temple). The age of 50 is the age of retirement (and Jubilee). So if you interpret this as being symbolic and add 50 years to 1948, you get the year 1998, which is more closely aligned with the other calculations.

I think you'll agree that this sequence of events was unprecedented, and that it was no coincidence that these major events happened in such a short period of time. This is why I believe, that collectively, they represent the prophetic trigger that has set into motion the time which has come to be known as the "last days." These events began the toppling of the prophetic dominoes that will eventually lead to the fulfillment of all things, and the culmination of the events foretold in the books of Daniel, Ezekiel, and Revelation.

Though Jesus said in Matthew 24:36 "... of that day and hour knoweth no man," the prophetic outline He gave indicated the warning signs we are to look for. When it is cloudy, it is a sign that it is going to rain. Much the same, Jesus told his disciples what to look for, and in Matt. 24:33 explained that "when ye shall see all these things, know that it is near..." I for one will not try to calculate a date. I believe that it's okay to come up with a time frame, but in the context that we also consider the signs that Jesus told us to look for. We have been seeing the signs. Without a doubt the end is near. Make sure that your heart is right with God. Watch, and pray.

THE RAPTURE

When this manuscript was initially printed in 1984, I had included a brief section on the Rapture, just to basically cover all the different Rapture theories. Since I grew up being taught in church that there was going to be a Pre-Tribulation Rapture, I sort of leaned that way. But because of all my research, and actually getting into the Scriptures myself, I began to rethink Pre-Trib. When the book was published in 1994, I did not include anything about the Rapture, either way, for fear that it would alienate people and detract from the message I was presenting.

However, things are quite different now. With the juggernaut of the "Left Behind" series consuming this country with best-selling books, audio books, movies, videos and DVD's with their Pre-Tribulation Rapture theory, I felt it was necessary to weigh in with the results of my research. Believe it or not, it's pretty straight forward, and the Scripture doesn't require a theological scholar to interpret its meaning.

The word 'rapture' is not in the Bible. It actually comes from the Latin word 'rapturo,' which means 'to seize or be carried away in one's spirit,' or the transporting from one place to another, and comes from the 1 Thessalonians 4:17 term "caught up." The original Greek word was 'harpazo,' and refers to the same thing. The notion of the Rapture, with its Pre-Tribulation, Mid-Tribulation, Partial Tribu-

FINAL WARNING

lation, and Post-Tribulation theories have been one of the most divisive issues in the Church, with the Pre-Trib view being the prevailing one. If this is your view, please do not be offended that I would kick this sacred cow until you have read the evidence.

The Rapture is a supernatural event that the Church has said will occur in the end-times to remove them from this world when 'trouble' starts.

"But there shall not an hair of your head perish." (Luke 21:28)

"Behold, I shew you a mystery; We shall not all sleep, but we shall all be changed, In a moment, in the twinkling of an eye, at the last trump: for the trumpet shall sound, and the dead shall be raised incorruptible, and we shall be changed." (1 Corinthians 15:51-52)

The following Scriptures are key—

"For the Lord himself shall descend from heaven with a shout, with the voice of the archangel, and with the trump of God: and the dead in Christ shall rise first: Then we which are alive and remain shall be caught up together with them in the clouds, to meet the Lord in the air: and so shall we ever be with the Lord." (1 Thessalonians 4:16-17)

"So man lieth down, and riseth not: till the heavens be no more, they shall not awake, nor be raised out of their sleep." (Job 14:12)

There is no reason that we can't take these verses literally. We can see that when Jesus returns, there will be a resurrection of the dead, and then a 'catching away' of the living. This will occur when the "heavens be no more." In John 6:44, Jesus says: "No man can come to me, except the Father which hath sent me draw him: and I will raise him up at the last day." If He would return before the Tribulation, that wouldn't be the "last day."

So, when is He going to return?

"And the gospel must first be published among all nations." (Mark 13:10)

"But he that shall endure unto the end, the same shall be saved. And this gospel of the kingdom shall be preached in all the world for a witness unto all nations; and then shall the end come. When ye therefore shall see the abomination of desolation, spoken of by Daniel the prophet, stand in the holy place ... For then shall be great tribulation, such as was not since the beginning of the world to this time, no, nor ever shall be ... Then if any man shall say unto you, Lo, here is Christ, or there; believe it not. For there shall arise false Christs, and false prophets, and shall shew great signs and wonders; insomuch that, if it were possible, they shall deceive the very elect ... Wherefore if they shall say unto you, Behold, he is in the desert; go not forth: behold, he is in the secret chambers; believe it not. For as the lightning cometh out of the east, and shineth even unto the west; so shall also the coming of the Son of man be. For as the lightning cometh out of the east, and shineth even unto the west; so shall also the coming of the Son of man be. Immediately after the tribulation of those days shall the sun be darkened, and the moon shall not give her light, and the stars shall fall from heaven, and the powers of the heavens shall be shaken: And then shall appear the sign of the Son of man in heaven: and then shall all the tribes of the earth mourn, and they shall see the Son of man coming in the clouds of heaven with power and great glory." (Matthew 24:13-30)

"And they shall say to you, See here; or, see there: go not after them, nor follow them. For as the lightning, that lighteneth out of the one part under heaven, shineth unto the other part under heaven; so shall also the Son of man be in his day." (Luke 17:23-24)

"Now we beseech you, brethren, by the coming of our Lord Jesus Christ, and by our gathering together unto him ... Let no man deceive you by any means: for that day shall not come, except there come a falling away first, and that man of sin be revealed, the son of perdition; Who opposeth and exalteth himself above all that is called God, or that is worshipped; so that he as God sitteth in the temple of God, shewing himself that he is God ... And now ye know what withholdeth that he might be revealed in his time." (2 Thessalonians 2:1-6)

These four Scriptures give you an absolute time frame for the coming of Jesus. There's only one resurrection— not two; He's only coming one time— not twice. There is nowhere in the Scripture that indicates the He is coming twice. It really irritates me when I hear well-meaning ministers on the radio or television who say that 'Jesus could come back tonight— are you ready?' No, Jesus is not coming back tonight! How do I know that? Because God's Word says so. Christ will not return to this earth until—

The Gospel is preached and distributed to the entire world.

A "falling away" will occur.

The "abomination of desolation" and the revealing of the "man of sin" takes place.

The three things that have to happen before Christ's return is that the Gospel has to be presented to the entire world (which quite possibly has been fulfilled), there must be a "falling away," (which has not occurred yet), and the "abomination of desolation," which is when the Antichrist will reveal himself as the Messiah in the Temple. Then the Tribulation will come.

"Confirming the souls of the disciples, and exhorting them to continue in the faith, and that we must through much tribulation enter into the king-

FINAL WARNING

dom of God." (Acts 14:22)

Jesus tells his disciple that He will return "immediately after the tribulation." Of the period after the Tribulation, Jesus says:

> "Watch ye therefore, and pray always, that ye may be accounted worthy to escape all these things that shall come to pass, and to stand before the Son of man." (Luke 21:36)

Though Christians can't even consider being on the earth during the Tribulation, there are examples, and Scripture to support the case for this. Jesus Himself (Luke 17:26-30, see also Isaiah 43:2) in His discussion about the end-times, used the days of Noah and Lot as examples. Noah, and his family endured the Flood in an ark of protection. Lot and his family escaped the destruction of Sodom only by being obedient and turning their backs on the city. If you remember, Lot's wife didn't listen. Jesus even pointed that out in Luke 17:32 when He said: "Remember Lot's wife." In addition, the Hebrews were protected from the plagues that were brought against Pharaoh and Egypt. We can also take note of Shadrach, Meshach and Abednego surviving the fiery furnace, as well as Daniel going through the ordeal in the Lion's Den. These examples also lead us into another aspect of end-time theology which further explains the flow of events.

It is important to delineate between the Tribulation period, and the time of Armageddon. The Tribulation, or the time when the Antichrist influences the world, is man's wrath on man. The time of the end, when Jesus returns, will be God's wrath on man. The examples of Noah, Lot, and the Hebrews were examples of God's wrath, and a separation from it. The examples of Shadrach and the boys, and Daniel, were examples of going through tribulation, man's wrath, and being protected. And you'll notice that these incidents are in the book of Daniel, the prophetic book that gives information about the time of the Antichrist.

The time when Jesus is to return has been referred to as the 'day of the Lord.' So let's look at what that is.

> "Behold, the day of the LORD cometh, cruel both with wrath and fierce anger, to lay the land desolate: and he shall destroy the sinners thereof out of it." (Isaiah 13:9)

> "For the indignation of the LORD is upon all nations, and his fury upon all their armies: he hath utterly destroyed them, he hath delivered them to the slaughter ... For it is the day of the LORD's vengeance, and the year of recompences for the controversy of Zion." (Isaiah 34:2, :8)

> "Alas for the day! for the day of the LORD is at hand, and as a destruction from the Almighty shall it come." (Joel 1:15)

> "Woe unto you that desire the day of the LORD! to what end is it for you? the day of the LORD is darkness, and not light." (Amos 5:18)

"The sun shall be turned into darkness, and the moon into blood, before the great and notable day of the Lord come:" (Acts 2:20)

"But the day of the Lord will come as a thief in the night; in the which the heavens shall pass away with a great noise, and the elements shall melt with fervent heat, the earth also and the works that are therein shall be burned up." (2 Peter 3:10)

"And the angel thrust in his sickle into the earth, and gathered the vine of the earth, and cast it into the great winepress of the wrath of God." (Revelation 14:9)

The 'day of the Lord' is associated with His vengeance and wrath, and is most detailed in the book of Revelation. This is the "last day" that Jesus talked about. God's wrath is not meant for His people— His Church. You can see this in 1 Thessalonians 5:9: "For God hath not appointed us to wrath, but to obtain salvation by our Lord Jesus Christ." Rev. 3:10 says: "Because thou hast kept the word of my patience, I also will keep thee from the hour of temptation, which shall come upon all the world, to try them that dwell upon the earth." This is the time that Jesus will return, before God's wrath is brought upon the earth.

Even though we are given the seasons in time when the Rapture will occur, Jesus said in Matthew 24:36: "But of that day and hour knoweth no man, no, not the angels of heaven, but my Father only." However, the following portions of Scripture definitively illustrates the time frame that the Rapture will take place, and to me, it can't be any plainer.

"And I saw three unclean spirits like frogs come out of the mouth of the dragon, and out of the mouth of the beast, and out of the mouth of the false prophet. For they are the spirits of devils, working miracles, which go forth unto the kings of the earth and of the whole world, to gather them to the battle of that great day of God Almighty. Behold, I come as a thief. Blessed is he that watcheth, and keepeth his garments, lest he walk naked, and they see his shame. And he gathered them together into a place called in the Hebrew tongue Armageddon." (Revelation 16:13-16)

"For yourselves know perfectly that the day of the Lord so cometh as a thief in the night. For when they shall say, Peace and safety; then sudden But ye, brethren, are not in darkness, that that day should overtake you as a thief. destruction cometh upon them, as travail upon a woman with child; and they shall not escape ... Therefore let us not sleep, as do others; but let us watch and be sober." (1 Thessalonians 5:2-6)

These passages indicate that the Antichrist and False Prophet are preparing for Armageddon, which will be the "great day of God Almighty." Jesus will come as a "thief," a term used to indicate the Rapture, and the admonition of 'watching' and 'keeping your garments,' is a warning to keep your heart right, and not be a part of the "falling away."

There has been some much-criticized research by Dave MacPherson to indicate that the Pre-Tribulation Rapture may be a fairly recent creation. Great men of God like John Wesley, Charles Wesley, Charles Spurgeon, Matthew Henry, John Knox, John Calvin, Isaac Newton, George Whitfield, John Newton, Jonathan Edwards and John Wycliffe never talked about a Pre-Trib Rapture, because the concept literally did not exist. In 1993, after years of investigation, in a well-researched, well-articulated manner, MacPherson was able to put the whole story together about the actual origin of the Pre-Tribulation Rapture teaching.

A gentleman by the name of John Nelson Darby (1800-82), a founding father of the Plymouth Brethren Church in England, is the guy who has received the most attention for teaching the Pre-Trib theory. Some researchers maintain that he was expressing this view as early as 1827, yet it was an article he wrote in 1850 which squarely places him in the Pre-Trib corner:

"It is this passage (2 Thessalonians 2:1-2) which, twenty years ago, made me understand the rapture of the saints before— perhaps a considerable time before— the day of the Lord (that is, before the judgment of the living.)"

By his own admission, he claims 1830 as the year he gained this revelation. It is therefore believed that Darby heard it from Edward Irving (1792-1834), of the Apostolic Catholic Church; and Irving actually found out about it from Margaret Macdonald (c. 1815-40), a 15-year old, chronically sick girl from Port Glasgow, Scotland, a member of his church (along with her sister and brothers) who apparently manifested the charismatic gifts of prophecy, speaking in tongues, and visions. After being sick for a year and a half, and a Christian for only a year, in the spring of 1830 she had a vision, which she gave copies of to various clerical leaders, including Irving.

The most unique part of her long, scripture-laden message, was the earliest known documentation of the Pre-Tribulation theory: "Only those who have the light of God within them will see the sign of his appearance. No need to follow them who say, see here, or see there, for his day shall be as the lightning to those in whom the living Christ is. 'Tis Christ in us that will lift us up— he is the light— 'tis only those that are alive in him that will be caught up to meet him in the air."

Macdonald's vision was first published in 1840 by Dr. Robert Norton (who heard and recorded the words in person), a long-time friend of the family, in the book *Memoirs of James & George Macdonald, of Port-Glasgow*, a biography of her older brothers. Norton quoted a May 18, 1830 letter written by Margaret's older sister Mary that indicated that "the house has been filled with people every day from all parts of England, Scotland, and Ireland," listening to her expound on the Rapture and end-time events. He did not attribute the vision to Margaret until his 1861 book *The Restoration of Apostles and Prophets; In the Catholic Apostolic Church*.

He said that during her long convalescence she had access to her family's "extensive library" which could have included Bibles like the *Self Interpreting Bible* (1778), and the *Columbian Family Bible* (1822) which contained cross references and marginal notes similar to that in study Bibles; as well as a host of other sources which MacPherson believes could have been used as a basis to develop her idea.

In the March, 1830 edition of *The Morning Watch*, a quarterly prophecy magazine that Irving edited, he wrote an article that stated that the "translation of the saints taketh place ... before the judgments which fall upon the earth at the coming of the Son of Man ... just before the great consummation of wrath." However, in a letter dated June 2, 1830, Irving wrote that the "substance of ... Mcdonald's visions ... carry to me a spiritual conviction and a spiritual reproof which I cannot express."

In Part 1 of an article called "Commentary on the Epistles to the Seven Churches in the Apocalypse," in the June issue of *The Morning Watch*, by an author who identified himself only as "Fidus," wrote from a Post-Trib view. Yet, when Part 2 appeared three months later in the September, 1830 edition, he clearly elaborated a Pre-trib view when he wrote that the Philadelphia church "which receives the answer of its faith in being caught up to meet him; which is thus kept from the hour of temptation..." while the Laodicea Church is described as "the last and dying stage of the Gentile church, before the gathering of the Jews..."

Subsequently, Dr. Cyrus I. Scofield discovered the new teaching on a trip to England, and he took it back with him to his church in Dallas, Texas; where it became part of the *Scofield Study Bible* as theological concept, and then became the official position of the Dallas Theological Seminary, as well as the Moody Bible Institute.

I believe that the Word of God clearly bares me out that there will not be a Pre-Tribulation Rapture, and I shudder to think what will happen when those expecting one don't get it. Will this be the source of the "falling away," as those whose faith is not strong enough to endure acquiesce to the strong-arm tactics of a political leadership bent on establishing world government. Without a doubt, this period of time will be a tremendously trying period, and I can only say that God's word is true, and there is a place of protection.

Psalm 91

He that dwelleth in the secret place of the most High shall abide under the shadow of the Almighty. I will say of the LORD, He is my refuge and my fortress: my God; in him will I trust. Surely he shall deliver thee from the snare of the fowler, and from the noisome pestilence. He shall cover thee with his feathers, and under his wings shalt thou trust: his truth shall be thy shield and buckler. Thou shalt not be afraid for the terror by night; nor for the arrow that flieth by day; Nor for the pestilence that walketh in darkness; nor for the destruction that wasteth at noonday. A thousand shall fall at thy side, and ten thousand at thy right hand; but it shall not come nigh thee. Only with thine eyes shalt thou behold and see the reward of the wicked. Because thou hast made the LORD, which is my refuge, even the most High, thy habitation; There shall no evil befall thee, neither shall any plague come nigh thy dwelling. For he shall give his angels charge over thee, to keep thee in all thy ways. They shall bear thee up in their hands, lest thou dash thy foot against a stone. Thou shalt tread upon the lion and adder: the young lion and the dragon shalt thou trample under feet. Because he hath set his love upon me, therefore will I deliver him: I will set him on high, because he hath known my name. He shall call upon me, and I will answer him: I will be with him in trouble; I will deliver him, and honour him. With long life will I satisfy him, and shew him my salvation.

THE DEAD SEA SCROLLS

The ruins of the settlement of Khirbet Qumran stand on a cliff, a mile away from the northwest shore of the Dead Sea, in the Jordan Valley. It is there, just south of Jericho, and twenty miles east of Jerusalem, that one of the most important archaeological discoveries in religious history was made.

Early in 1947, three Bedouin shepherds from the Ta'amireh tribe had their flock in the area, and while Jum'a Muhammad was looking for a stray goat, he discovered a cave in the cliffs. He threw a rock into the hole, and heard the sound of breaking pottery. Two days later, his cousin, Muhammed Ahmed el-Hamed, returned and crawled into the small cave, which measured 6 feet by 20 feet. The cave contained many earthenware jars, about 2 feet high and 10 inches wide. Though many were broken, 9 were believed to be intact. Inside one of the jars, he discovered three leather rolls wrapped in linen. In a subsequent visit, four more leather rolls were discovered. These rolls turned out to be ancient scrolls, which have been referred to as the 'Dead Sea Scrolls.'

A Christian shopkeeper, Khalil Iskander Shahin (known as "Kando"), and George Ishaya (Isaiah) Shamoun, members of the Syrian Jacobite Church in Jerusalem, heard about the discovery and went to Qumran to verify the Bedouin's claims, finding some scroll fragments. They later met with the three shepherds to examine their findings.

One of the Bedouins sold 3 of the scrolls to the Muslim sheik of Bethlehem, and Kando purchased the other 4, which consisted of a 22-foot long scroll containing the entire text of the *Book of Isaiah*, the *Genesis Apocryphon*, the *Habakkuk Commentary*, and the *Manual of Discipline* (also known as the *Community Rule*), which had split into two. These 4 were in turn sold to the Syrian Metropolitan (Archbishop) Athanasius Yeshua Samuel, head of the Syrian Jacobite Church. Samuel later sent George Isaiah back to Qumran to carry out secret extensive excavations. It is believed that other scrolls were discovered, the contents of which have not been revealed.

In September, 1947, Samuel took the four scrolls to Homs (north of Damascus), Syria, where he met with the Patriarch of the Church. During his return trip, he again sent a team to Qumran.

Samuel got in touch with Professor Eleazar Sukenik of the Hebrew University's Department of Archaeology in order to have the age of the scrolls determined. Meanwhile, in November, 1947, Sukenik was contacted by someone identifying himself only as an Armenian antique dealer, and he was able to purchase the other three scrolls, which turned out to be *The War of the Sons of Light With the Sons of Darkness* (also called *The War Scroll*), the *Book of Hymns* (also known as the *Psalm of Thanksgiving Scroll*), and another copy of Isaiah.

In January, 1948, Sukenik received one of Samuel's scrolls, a copy of the *Isaiah* scroll, which he was able to inspect. Although he was interested in purchasing the four scrolls, he couldn't raise the money necessary to make the transaction.

Samuel then contacted the William F. Albright Institute of Archaeological Research in Jerusalem, where the scrolls were inspected by John C. Trever and William H. Brownlee, who felt they were as old, if not older, than the 2nd century Nash Papyrus fragment, which up to then, was the oldest known example of Biblical Hebrew. A set of prints were forwarded to Professor William Foxwell Albright at Johns Hopkins University in Baltimore, Maryland, who was the leading Hebrew epigraphist in the world. He dated the material back to 100 BC. Upon examination of all these Hebrew and Aramaic scrolls and fragments which have been discovered at Qumran, it is generally accepted that they were written between 250 BC and 68 AD, when the Romans destroyed the Qumran settlement.

The scrolls were taken to a bank in Beirut, and then in January, 1949, to a New York City bank vault. Up to 1954, only three of the scrolls had been published. Samuel, labeled a 'smuggler,' was anxious to sell the scrolls, and would not allow the fourth to be published until all of them had been purchased.

In February, 1949, Gerald Lankester Harding, director of the Department of Antiquities for Transjordan and Arab Palestine; and Father Roland de Vaux, director of the Dominican-controlled Ecole Biblique in the Jordanian sector of East Jerusalem, went to the cave at Qumran, where they found the remains of 30 identifiable texts, and a number of unidentifiable fragments. Harding made it known that he was interested in all subsequent finds made by the Ta'amireh tribe. They would sell the results of their excavation to Kando, who would then sell the items to Harding. Meanwhile, de Vaux, Harding, and a group of fifteen workers continued to excavate around Qumran until 1956, where they uncovered the buildings of what they felt were an Essene community.

For nearly two weeks in mid-March, 1952, de Vaux, three members of the Ecole Biblique, William Reed (director of the Albright Institute), and 24 Bedouins under the supervision of three Jordanian and Palestinian archaeologists, embarked on an effort to conduct a survey of all the caves in the area. This survey indicated the existence of 40 caves, and the umbrella term of the Dead Sea Scrolls refers to the scrolls and fragments that were found in eleven of the caves.

In September, 1952, in Cave 4, located about 50 feet away from some of the Qumran ruins, the largest number of scroll fragments were discovered— the remains of over 500 different scrolls.

By 1959, all the scroll fragments were kept in a room known as the 'Scrollery' in the Rockefeller Museum (formerly known as the Palestine Archaeological Museum), which had been built with funds provided by John D. Rockefeller. The Museum was run by an international Board of Trustees, and later fell under the control of the Jordanian government. After the Six Day War in June, 1967, when Israel took over control of the entire city of Jerusalem, the contents of the Museum were considered spoils of war, so the Israeli government became the guardian of the fragments.

The Museum contained laboratories, photographic facilities, and the Department of Antiquities, however, the headquarters of the entire operation was actually located at the Ecole Biblique which contained a research library totally dedicated to Qumran research, which was not open to the public. They also published two journals, the *Revue Biblique*, printed since 1892, and the *Revue de Qumran*, started in 1958 to publish information on the scrolls.

This may be one of the keys to understanding what may be going on here behind the scenes. In 1882, on the site where, according to tradition, St. Stephen, the first Christian martyr was stoned to death, a French Dominican monk established a Dominican church and monastery in Jerusalem. At the urging of Pope Leo XIII, a Biblical school was begun there in 1890 by Father Albert Lagrange to train scholars with the knowledge necessary to protect the Church against the potential of damaging archaeological discoveries. Originally known as the Ecole Practique d'Etudes Bibliques, it was later renamed the Ecole Biblique et Archeologique Francaise de Jerusalem.

Lagrange became a member of the Pontifical Biblical Commission, which had been started by Pope Leo to 'monitor' the work of Catholic scriptural scholarship. In 1956, de Vaux became a consultant to this Commission until his death in 1971, as did his successors Father Pierre Benoit, and Jean-Luc Vesco in 1987. The head of the Pontifical Biblical Commission is Cardinal Joseph Ratzinger who is also the executive head of the Congregation for the Doctrine of the Faith, which prior to 1965 had been known as the Holy Office; and prior to 1542, as the Holy Inquisition. After 1971, with many common members, the two groups were virtually combined, sharing the same offices at the Palace of the Congregation at the Holy Office Square in Rome. Because of this connection, the implication had been made that the Vatican was exerting influence over the Scrolls, in order to control what information is released.

The team that de Vaux chose in 1953, to assemble and translate the Scrolls were primarily Catholic:

1) Frank Cross: Harvard Professor, of the McCormick Theological Seminary in Chicago and the Albright Institute in Jerusalem. The only Protestant on the team.

2) Monsignor Patrick Skehan: From the United States, who was director of the Albright Institute. He was quoted as saying that the Biblical scholar should adhere to Church doctrine and "be subject always to the sovereign right of the Holy Mother Church to witness definitively what is in fact concordant with the teaching she has received from Christ." When he died in 1980, he was replaced by Professor Eugene Ulrich of Notre Dame University.

3) Father Jean Starcky: From France, who, after his death, was replaced by Father Emile Puech of the Ecole Biblique.

4) Dr. Claus-Hunno Hunzinger: From Germany, who was later replaced by a French priest, Father Maurice Baillet.

5) Father Josef Milik: A priest from Poland.

6) John M. Allegro: An ex-Methodist turned agnostic from Oxford, who revealed that certain material was being kept secret because of the con-

troversial nature, and de Vaux did not want the Church to be embarrassed. He was replaced by Oxford Professor John Strugnell, who in 1960 became Assistant Professor of Old Testament Studies at Duke University; and in 1968 became the Professor of Christian Origins at the Harvard Divinity School.

After de Vaux's death in 1971, his handpicked successor was another Dominican, Father Pierre Benoit, who became the head of the Ecole Biblique and the overseer of the international team, until his death in 1987. Strugnell, who converted to Catholicism, then became the leader of the team.

As you can see, this small group of Catholic scholars had complete control of all of the Dead Sea Scroll fragments that were found.

In 1954, Yigael Yadin, the former Chief of Staff for the Israeli Defense Forces, who taught Archaeology at Hebrew University, purchased Samuel's four scrolls for $250,000. Ironically, he was the son of Professor Sukenik. These four scrolls, and the three purchased by his father were then housed in a building known as the Shrine of the Book. While the Israelis worked on these scrolls, across town at the Rockefeller Museum, de Vaux and his group of international scholars were working on the fragments they discovered.

In 1967, Yadin interrogated Kando, who subsequently relinquished possession of a scroll he had for six years, which had been found in Cave 11. Known as the Temple Scroll, at 27 feet, it is the longest scroll, and has been dated between 150-125 BC. It has references to the building of the Temple in Jerusalem, and the rituals to be performed there, however, because of the laws found in it in regard to general matters, and quotes from the Pentateuch (the first 5 books of the Bible, known as the Torah of Moses), it has been referred to as the Sixth Book of the Law, and may contain the information referred to in 1 Chronicles 28:11-19 and 1 Samuel 8:11.

The Pentateuch was compiled by Ezra (Ezra 7:14) about 458 BC, and it is believed that what was edited out, became part of the Temple Scroll. Five separate sources were compiled to form the Temple Scroll, and it is now considered a supplement to the Torah. In addition to the content, another reason that it is considered a Biblical text, is that in all established Biblical books, the name of God, YHWH (Yahweh), is written in the square Aramaic script like the rest of the text; while in non-Biblical writings, the name is written in Paleo-Hebrew, while the rest of the text is in Aramaic.

The goal of de Vaux's international team was for the Oxford University Press to publish all Qumran scrolls by 1962 in a series called the *Discoveries in the Judaean Desert of Jordan*. That didn't happen. The first, in 1955, contained the fragments found in the original cave, known as Cave 1. In 1961, the second volume appeared, however, it contained material discovered in the four caves of Wadi Murabba'at, eleven miles south of Qumran, and was dated from 70-135 AD. This find included the Hebrew versions of all the minor prophets, including Hosea, Joel, Amos, Obadiah, Jonah, Micah, Nahum, Habakkuk, Zephaniah, Haggai, Zechariah, and Malachi. In 1963, the third volume was published, containing fragments from Cave 2, Cave 3, and Caves 5 - 10; including the Copper Scroll found in Cave 3, and fragments from two copies of *The Book of Jubilees*, a copy of which was later found at Masada. Some researchers believe that the Copper scroll should be put in a different category, and separated from the other texts that have been found, because it is the only document that was recorded on metal, it was written in a different variation of Hebrew, and was discovered in an isolated section of the cave; which could indicate a different origin. The fourth volume, in 1965, was a collection of Psalms found in Cave 11. The fifth volume, in 1968, under the direction of Allegro, contained some material from Cave 4, however, most of the scrolls from this cave continued to be withheld from the public, even though Allegro had said in 1964 that the compilation and translation had been nearly completed by 1961. The sixth installment of the series appeared in 1977, the seventh in 1982, and the eighth, which didn't even deal with the texts of Qumran, was released in 1990.

These eight volumes are said to represent only 25% of the information contained in the Scrolls, even though Father Benoit had said in December, 1985, that everything would be published by 1993. Strugnell would later set a deadline of 1996. Then it was announced that it would be done by 2000.

Edmund Wilson, author of *The Scrolls of the Dead Sea*, said in 1955 that de Vaux's team wanted to isolate the sectarian non-Biblical scrolls from being connected with Christianity and Judaism, and concentrated only on the Biblical literature. In 1956, tired of de Vaux's attempts to prevent the Scrolls from being linked to Christianity, John Allegro was a guest on a series of three radio shows in northern England. The third interview resulted in a *New York Times* article which said: "The origins of some Christian ritual and doctrines can be seen in the documents of an extremist Jewish sect that existed for more than 100 years before the birth of Jesus Christ. This is the interpretation placed on the 'fabulous' collection of Dead Sea Scrolls by one of an international team of seven scholars ... John Allegro ... (who) said last night in a broadcast that the historical basis of the Lord's Supper and part at least of the Lord's prayer and the New Testament teaching of Jesus were attributable to the Qumranians."

In 1987, he quit, calling the team's delays "inexcusable," saying that for years they had been "sitting on material which is not only of outstanding importance, but also quite the most religiously sensitive." He died in 1988.

Robert Eisenman, a former Research Fellow at the Albright Institute, who was a Professor of Middle East Religions and Chairman of Religious Studies at California State University at Long Beach, was denied access to photographs of the Scroll fragments by Strugnell. In 1989, he said publicly, that during the last 40 years, all of the research on the Dead Sea Scrolls was controlled by a handful of scholars who had revealed only a small portion. He called for access to the Scrolls by qualified scholars, and for AMS (Accelerator Mass Spectroscopy) Carbon-14 dating to be performed on the documents to verify the dating, which up to that point had been relying on the original, obsolete form of dating, which had been done shortly after their discovery.

In April, 1989, the Israeli Archaeological Council created a Scroll Oversight Committee to oversee the publication of all Qumran texts, and to make sure the international team completed their assignments, and in July, 1989, Amir Drori, Director of the Israeli Department of Antiquities, a member of that Committee, told the *Los Angeles Times*, that "if someone does not complete his work on time we have the right to deliver the scrolls to someone else."

After the Israeli government took full possession of Jerusalem in June of 1967, many were surprised that de Vaux was allowed to continue in his capacity as the leader of the team of scholars, even though it was a known fact that he was anti-Semitic, which was why he would not allow any Jewish scholars into the project. In the mid-1980's, Strugnell brought in Israeli scholar Elisha Qimron; Talmud scholar Jacob Sussman; Devorah Dimant of Haifa University; and Emmanuel Tov, Shemaryahu Talmon, Joseph Baumgarten, and Jonas Greenfield, of Baltimore's Hebrew University, to work on some unpublished text.

In November, 1990, without informing Strugnell, the Israeli government assigned Emmanuel Tov to become the 'joint editor-in-chief' of the project to finish the translation and publication of the Scrolls. Then, in December, 1990, the *New York Times* quoted from an October 28, 1990 interview Strugnell had with the Israeli paper *Ha-Aretz*, where he said that Judaism was a "horrible religion," a "racist" religion, and that Israel was "founded on a lie." Magen Broshi, curator of Jerusalem's Shrine of the Book, said: "We've known for twenty years that he was an anti-Semite." On another occasion, he referred to Strugnell's "rabid anti-Semitism." These anti-Semitic comments resulted in him being dismissed from the project as editor-in-chief, even though he still controlled his portion of the texts. Tov became chief editor, along with Professor Eugene Ulrich and Emile Puech.

In September, 1991, Professor Ben-Zion Wacholder, and one of his doctoral students, Martin G. Abegg, from Hebrew Union College in Cincinnati, Ohio, released their compilation of the Qumran texts, which was published by the Biblical Archaeological Society. In 1988, Strugnell had printed 30 copies of a 52,000 word concordance of words found in the scroll, which had been created by de Vaux's team in the 1950's, so it could be used by the team. Wacholder and Abegg used a computer to reconstruct these words, and it was purported to be 80% accurate. Later that month, the Huntington Library in San Marine, California revealed that it had a complete set of negatives, from photographs, of photographs of the original scrolls, which had been given to them in 1987 by Elizabeth Hay Bechtel of the Bechtel Corporation, who had founded the Ancient Biblical Manuscript Center in Claremont, California (who also had a copy). They made microfilm copies available to any scholar who requested it. The Hebrew Union College also have a partial set; and the Oxford Centre for Postgraduate Hebrew Studies in England has a full set, which had been given to them in May, 1991, by the Israeli Oversight Committee.

The Qumran texts, written in Hebrew and Aramaic, are believed to have been written between 250 BC and 68 AD. They have been divided into two groups — Biblical and non-Biblical. About 20% are Biblical. Copies of every book in the Hebrew Bible have been found, except for Esther (which, coincidentally, was the only book that didn't mention the name of God). In Cave 4, one of the most complete manuscripts which they have been able to reconstruct, is the First Book of Samuel, which was found to contain passages not contained in our Bible, and is being used to fill in some of the narrative gaps. The non-Biblical fragments consist of hymns and psalms, biblical commentaries, legal documents, a letter, apocryphal writings, and an inventory of the Temple treasure. Of the non-Biblical, there are

FINAL WARNING

texts referred to as sectarian writings, which were produced by a unique sect of Jews who have been identified as the Essenes.

The seven intact scrolls that were found in Cave 1, were quickly published by Israeli and American scholars, but the fragments collected by de Vaux were a different story. Just in Cave 4, there was believed to be well over 15,000 fragments (and perhaps as many as 100,000) from 500 different manuscripts. In all, the find was said to represent about 800 manuscripts. Of the Biblical writings, 25 copies of *Deuteronomy* were found, 18 copies of *Isaiah*, and 27 copies of the *Psalter*. Among the non-Biblical, 11 copies of the *Community Rule*, 9 *Songs of the Sabbath Sacrifice*, 8 of the *Thanksgiving Hymn*, and 7 of the *Sons of Light Against the Sons of Darkness*.

Prior to the discovery of the Scrolls, the oldest known Old Testament texts were copies which dated back to 1100 AD, yet they were nearly identical. Originally, only the linen surrounding the scrolls were tested with the Carbon-14 dating process, which indicated a date around the 2nd century BC and the beginning of the 1st century AD. In 1991, new tests by a Swiss laboratory confirmed these results. A palaeographical analysis was done on the script used in writing the texts which revealed a similarity to styles that were used from 250 - 150 BC, 150 - 30 BC, and 30 BC - 70 AD. Archaeological dating was also done with the help of several hundred coins which were found in the Qumran complex. The earliest structures were built between 130 - 110 BC, then rebuilt and enlarged from 110-40 BC. They discovered evidence of an earthquake which had been recorded as occurring in 31 BC, after which they rebuilt the settlement and occupied it until 68 AD when it was destroyed by Vespasian's Roman legions.

During the Maccabean period, in the 2nd century BC, there were three main Jewish groups, the Pharisees, the Sadduccees, and the Essenes. The Essenes were known to be the 'strict' Order. Early historians, such as Pliny the Elder (the 1st century Roman writer), Josephus, and Philo, indicated that the Essenes lived in the area between Jericho and Ein Gedi, on the shores of the Dead Sea, which is where the Qumran ruins are located.

The Sadducees, whose religious principles differed from the Pharisees, separated from them after the Maccabean revolt (168-164 BC). A document identified as *Miqsat Ma'aseh he-Torah*, or *Some Rulings Pertaining to the Torah* (also known as the *Halakhic Letter*), which was found in Cave 4, contains about 22 religious laws, and appears to be the basis of the Qumran philosophy. Discovered in 1952, its contents weren't revealed until 1984, and it has led some researchers to believe that the Qumran group seceded from the established religious center in Jerusalem, and became the group known as the Essenes. Yet the Essene name is never used.

How this break occurred is not really known. According to one theory, when Judea, under Judas Maccabeus, revolted in 165 BC against the Syrian tyrant King Antiochus IV, thus beginning the Hasmonean line of Kings with Judas (165-160 BC), his brother Jonathan (160-143 BC), then his brother Simon (143-134 BC), maintained a friendly relationship with Rome; and in 152 BC when Jonathan made himself the High Priest, this upset the hardline Jews who chose to follow a man they referred to as the "Teacher of Righteousness," who was of the Zadokite (who were descendants of the priestly line of Aaron) line. They went to the desert where they could observe the laws of God.

A document found at Qumran was an earlier version of the *Damascus Document*, which was discovered (2 copies) in a Cairo synagogue in 1896. Dated between 80 - 75 BC, a copy was found in Cave 6, and 7 copies in Cave 4. The fragments recovered at Qumran have proven the Cairo text to be incomplete. The text refers to a contingent of Jews that remained faithful to the Law. A 'Teacher of Righteousness' came to them, and led them into Damascus so they could renew their 'Covenant' with God. This Covenant is referred to in the *Community Rule*. It is believed that there was an Essene community in Damascus. In the book of the Acts of the Apostles, Saul was going to Damascus to persecute these early Christians.

Another theory says that after the destruction of the First Temple in 586 BC, when the Jews were exiled to Babylon, the Essenes were formed as a strict Order because they believed they were being punished by God for their disobedience. When the Jews returned to Jerusalem after the Maccabean victories, they became disenchanted and went to Qumran.

It was believed that the Essenes were a pacifist, monastic Order who wanted to separate themselves from the revolutionary-minded Zealots, yet some of the evidence seems to indicate otherwise. Originally thought to have been celibate, the graves of two women and a child were discovered; plus the *Community Rule* contained marriage laws. The Essenes did not engage in animal sacrifice, yet the Temple Scroll contains instructions for such rituals, and animal bones have been found. Thought to have been peaceful, their scrolls seem to indicate the knowledge of military strategy; and the ruins of a military defense tower and a forge have been excavated. Several manuscripts from Qumran, were also found at the Zealot stronghold on Masada, and there has been some researchers who believe that there was a connection between the two groups.

While de Vaux and his team were trying to distance the Scrolls from Judaism and Christianity, saying there were no connections, the texts which were already published seem to indicate otherwise. Either the early Christians were just living at the Qumran community, or the early Christians and the Qumran community were one and the same. Though Essene in nature, the group in Qumran has been compared to the early Church which was based in Jerusalem. The Habakkuk Commentary said that Qumran's governing body, the Council of the Community, was in Jerusalem. In fact, it is believed that the scrolls were taken to Qumran from Jerusalem for protection. Professor Norman Golb of the University of Chicago has theorized that the Scrolls were from the library of the Jewish Temple, and taken to Qumran, a military installation, during the first Jewish revolt to keep them safe. The vital link for this belief comes from the Copper scroll, which lists 64 locations of hidden Temple treasure. This seems to indicate that perhaps the Qumran settlement was a retreat for the early Christians. But wait, 'Christians' before Christ? This is one of the controversial developments that have emerged from the discovery of the Dead Sea Scrolls.

The New Testament was written in Greek, and Jesus spoke in Aramaic. The Qumran texts are written in Hebrew and sometimes Aramaic, and has been shown to contain information that is echoed in the New Testament. Prior to the discovery of the Scrolls, the teachings of Jesus had been considered as original, though influenced by Old Testament teaching. However, the Qumran documents now indicate the existence of a basis for His message. The *Community Rule*, which was discovered in Cave 1, has proven to be one of the most important discoveries in Qumran. It is a record of the rules and regulations of the Qumran community, where all must make a "Covenant before God to obey all his commandments." One of the basic tenets of Christianity, the baptism of purification, is discussed. It says that the convert "shall be cleansed from all his sins by the spirit of holiness uniting him to its truth ... And when his flesh is sprinkled with purifying water and sanctified by cleansing water, it shall be made clean by the humble submission of his soul to all the precepts of God." This has led to the theory that John the Baptist had lived at Qumran until he was called by God to be the forerunner of Jesus. Author Charles Francis Potter, in his book *The Lost Years of Jesus*, attempted to explain the "eighteen silent years" of Jesus, between the ages of 12 and 30, as being spent at Qumran.

In the Acts of the Apostles (Acts 2:44-46), it says: "And all that believed were together, and had all things in common; And sold their possessions and goods, and parted them to all men, as every man had need. And they, continuing daily with one accord in the temple..." This shows that common ownership was part of the early Christian philosophy. The *Community Rule* stated: "All ... shall bring all their knowledge, powers and possessions into the Community..."; "They shall eat in common and pray in common..." and "...his property shall be merged and he shall offer his counsel and judgment to the Community."

Also in Acts, the Church leadership is shown to be made up of twelve Apostles, which according to Galatians, were led by James (the brother of Jesus), John and Peter. In the *Community Rule*, the Qumran group were governed by a 'Council' of twelve people, with three priests that were in leadership roles, though it is not known if they were part of the twelve.

It also talks about a 'Meal of the Congregation' which is a ritual very much like the 'Last Supper' and the subsequent communion ceremony; while other documents contain parallels with the Sermon on the Mount, and the concept of the battle between the darkness and the light.

The Qumran texts contain references to what's been identified as a messianic figure known as the "Teacher of Righteousness," which some have tried to identify as being Jesus, however, there are no references as to the divinity of this person, so it couldn't be Jesus. In addition, because of the age of the document, this person would have been living well before the time of Christ. However, recently released fragments do allude to Jesus. An unpublished Aramaic scroll fragment out of Cave 4, mention the "Son of God" and the "Son of the Most High," in a similar manner as Luke 1:32, 35. It is the first time these references have appeared in any outside text. Newly released fragments out of Cave 4 even prophecy the coming the coming of Jesus, as the Messiah. Fragment 4Q285 said that a "staff shall rise from the root of Jesse ... the Branch of David ... and they will put to death the Leader of the Community." Fragment 4Q521 said: "The Heavens and the earth will obey his Messiah ... He will not turn aside from the Commandments of the Holy Ones ... For the Lord will visit the Pious Ones and the Righteous will call by name ... He shall release the captives, make the blind to see, raise up the downtrodden ... He will heal the sick, resurrect the dead, and to the Meek announce glad tidings."

Much has been made about this small group of men, who for forty years had been silent about the contents of the Dead Sea Scrolls which were in their possession. With some being considered as emissaries of the Catholic Church, was it because the Scrolls are contrary to the Bible in respect to the origin of Christianity, or was it, as some maintain, because of the power it gave them; or, as Randall Price maintains (in his book *Secrets of the Dead Sea Scrolls*), is all of this talk just an effort to prevent serious consideration of the Scrolls as verification and corroboration of the Bible.

Price quotes Professor Tov who said: "I would completely brush aside any accusations of suppressed material. There is no evidence whatsoever for this having been done by any Catholic source." He also quotes Joseph A. Fitzmyer, a Catholic scholar, and member of the Scroll team who said: "The whole idea of a Vatican conspiracy to suppress the Scrolls that it (the book *The Dead Sea Scrolls Deception* by Baigent and Leigh) portrays is ludicrous nonsense." Randall Price then proceeds to completely unravel the whole conspiratorial argument behind the delays as being because of the "condition of the texts ... accessibility of the materials ... the political situation ... the nature of the text assignments ... scholastic responsibilities ... financial problems ... (and) human problems." His argument is just as convincing.

My concern is that, where there is smoke, there may also be fire. Any kind of association with the Rockefeller name brings with it the influence of the ecumenical movement; and any kind of connection to Catholicism brings with it the baggage of their pagan origins (see my on-line book *Controlled by the Calendar*). Many eminent scholars have tried to make a connection between the Scrolls and the Essenes, even when the evidence for this is circumstantial at best. As I will discuss in the next chapter, those who have tried to prove that Jesus faked his crucifixion have also tried to link him with the Essenes. Even though the Scrolls themselves indicate that the inhabitants of Qumran engaged in the study of astrology and mysticism, this group has been identified as the starting point for the philosophy which became Christianity. So, if we are to believe some of the interpretations of the Scrolls, that the teachings of Jesus were based on the philosophy of the Essenes; this seriously damages His image as being the father of a Religion that bears His name. Not only that, but it further diminishes His divinity, which has increasingly come under attack.

When the last remnants of the Scrolls are published, those discovered so far, and those yet to be discovered, some scholars have expressed a wish for new versions of the Bible to reflect the 'new' information gleaned from the Scrolls. If this happens, will the new material be used to buttress the scriptures as being Holy Spirit inspired- or will they take on the spin of a pre-Christ Christianity, and further contribute to the taking of Christ out of the Christianity of main-line churches, so that the role of Jesus is reduced to that of just a teacher or a political visionary.

Since I believe that Jesus taught only what was given unto Him through the inspiration of the Holy Spirit, what legitimacy should be given to the Dead Sea Scrolls, if any.

Beyond a shadow of a doubt, they are legitimate documents, and not the result of an incredible forgery, as far as being done shortly before their discovery. Therefore, we have to look in another direction. Now that other scholars have access to them, I would think that any incorrect translations would be revised; which brings us to the reconstruction of the actual fragments themselves. We have been forced to rely on the accuracy of de Vaux's team, and their ability to fit the quagmire of pieces together into some sort of coherency. It would seem that gaps in the assembled fragments of text (especially in the case of the Essene documents) would make it difficult to actually grasp its full meaning, especially since missing words may have a bearing on how other words are translated. The complex techniques utilized in this process have brought very little criticism in regard to its accuracy.

Another point of contention is the procedure used to date the Scrolls. Carbon-14 dating has long been criticized as being inaccurate. Originally only the wrapping around them were tested, because they didn't want to destroy any text in order to date them. However, new techniques need less material to achieve the same results. But remember, what is being dated is the material that was written on. If a fragment was dated back to 200 BC, there is no way of knowing whether it was actually written on at that time, or maybe 300 years later. This knowledge makes it difficult to assume the accuracy of any dating.

We must also take into account, whether or not a document is describing actual events, or if it is just plain fiction. For example, it is commonly accepted that some apocryphal books such as *Tobit*, and *Bel and the Dragon* were works of fiction, and for that reason were not included in the Bible. Many apocryphal writings were found at Qumran. When it comes to analyzing the contents of a text, how do you decide that it is a historically accurate document, if you don't know the intention of the writer, or even who the writer was. Just as the writers of the Gospels have been accused of embellishment, do some of the Qumran texts contain embellishments.

Because of the initial secrecy surrounding the Scrolls, how will we really know that all of the fragments found, will be released. It was said that some fragments had been taken to the Ecole Biblique. Were they ever returned to the Rockefeller Museum? I guess, what I am thinking here, is that if they had discovered something that would have shaken the very foundation of the Christian Church, would the Scroll team have allowed it to remain, or would it have found its way into the dark recesses of the Vatican, never again to see the light of day, or perhaps only locked away for a short time, to be released when the time is right.

As Price maintains, there may very well be nothing to the negative slant that has been applied to the Scrolls; and yet, it is very hard not to think conspiratorially because of all the circumstances surrounding them. I believe that the Scrolls are part of the 'last days' trigger, and as such, I believe that they are going to be used in some way to perpetuate an end-time deception.

In addition, how about the existence of other scrolls which haven't made their way into official hands so they can scrutinized by scholars. Strugnell revealed the existence of four other scrolls from Cave 11. Of the two he saw, one was a complete copy of the *Book of Enoch*. On his deathbed, Lankester Harding, the director of Jordan's Department of Antiquities, claimed to have seen two more scrolls that Strugnell had not seen. All four are located in Jordan. Stories have also circulated about Bedouin discoveries which were not given to de Vaux, and have yet to surface. Plus there have been other optimistic forays into the area which could eventually turn up more scrolls or fragments. In one case, archaeologists Dr. Gary Collett and Dr. Aubry L. Richardson, using sophisticated equipment developed by NASA (which can sense non-visible elements of the electromagnetic spectrum and interpret the type of molecules found in its makeup), claimed that there were still unexplored caves, including one which may contain up to 40 intact jars, of the kind used to store manuscripts, and evidence of another copper scroll. A dig was initiated, sanctioned by the Israeli government, to reach this cave, which had not turned up anything.

My feeling is that there hasn't been enough substantiation from the Scrolls to make the kind of claims that have been made. For example, various books in the Bible contain the same information, and are used to cross reference each other; and that wasn't possible with the Scrolls, so, because of that, should their scholarship be accepted, especially when some of the rituals that are similar to the early Christian Church may be nothing more than natural progression— or theological evolution.

Because of further archaeological excavation, we may continue to get a steady flow of information from Qumran for years to come, and how it will affect the perception of Christianity is yet to be seen. All we can do is to evaluate what is available now, and how some of the questionable texts may be use to manipulate religion in this country.

It would be nice to know how much influence the Rockefeller family has on the Rockefeller Museum, where all the fragments were housed. Believe the fact that they have not lent their name, or given money to anything they haven't been able to influence. Their name also figures prominently in the talk concerning the rebuilding of the Jewish Temple. Knowing that they have a huge role in establishing the New World Order, their involvement in the various affairs of Israel has ominous overtones.

SATANISM

The underlying power to all occult practices, is Satanism— the worship of Satan (or Lucifer) in opposition to the worship of God. It is the worship of Satan which has been the driving force behind the handful of men who have perpetuated the Illuminati conspiracy. It has been reported that the spread of the occult has been the job of an inner circle of the Illuminati, which is known as the Council of 13, or the Grand Druid Council.

Through its various incarnations, the spread of the occult has enabled the Illuminati to create a social climate that has welcomed the advent of the New World Order, one-world government, and the one-world church that will accompany it.

The Druids

The occult movement basically began with the Druids, who were found among the ancient Celts (the people of Gaul in France, Switzerland, Belgium, Bohemia, Galicia in Spain, as well as Galatia in what is now known as Turkey), and the forerunners of those living today in the British Isles, Scotland, and Ireland. Their culture flourished for hundreds of years before the Christian era, peaking around 1200 BC, when they became caught up between the encroachment of the Roman Empire and the invasions from barbaric Germanic tribes.

The Druids were members of a priesthood who came from the upper class of Celtic society, and were exempt from taxes and manual labor. Their name comes from the Celtic word 'daur' which means 'oak tree,' which was sacred to them; and in the Gaelic, it means "knowing the oak tree." They performed their rituals and ceremonies in sacred oak groves, as well as river sources and lakes, because they also considered water to be sacred.

Around 98-180 AD, the Druid religion was outlawed, and they were forced to go underground, where it has been secretly active, in various forms, ever since.

The earliest mention of these "men of the oak," was in the 3rd century BC, from Julius Caesar, and what little information that is available, comes from 30 references in Greek and Roman writings from the second century BC to the fourth century AD, and ancient records found in Ireland. For the most part, their legacy has been passed down orally from generation to generation, because they considered it "profane" to write down their teachings.

In the writings of an ancient Greek, he compared the Druids to the Magi of Persia, who were the group from which the Wise Men came. They could also be compared to the Medicine Man of the American Indians. In fact, I kind of thought they might have been a Satanic perversion of the Levite tribe of Israel, from which came the priests.

An aura of mystery surrounded the Druids, and they were considered evil. It was alleged that they possessed strange powers, such as being able to produce mists, storms, floods, and cast spells. As it turned out, there was reason to fear these men, because some of their rituals included both animal and human sacrifice.

The Druids worshipped the Sun God, Hu; the moon, and the stars. Many of their rites centered around such astronomical occurrences as equinoxes and solstices. It is believed that Stonehenge, built in 2750 BC on the Salisbury Plain in southwest England, and transformed into a solar observatory by 1900 BC, was later used by the Druids as a temple for sacrifices. A similar structure in Avebury, 20 miles north, was also used.

Their biggest night of the year, was the ceremony known as the 'Vigil of Samhein,' on October 31st, in honor of Samhein, the Horned Hunter of the Night (Satan, as seen in the Pentagram), the Oak God of the Underworld, and the God of the Dead. It is this ritual that evolved into the annual tradition of Halloween.

Witchcraft

The lineal successor to the religion of the Druids was British witchcraft, which became strong in the 1200's, and considers itself to be the world's oldest religion. The word Witchcraft is derived from the Anglo-Saxon word 'wiccecraeft' ('wiccacraft') or "craft of the wise."

Witches say that their religion is not anti-Christian, because they worship deities that were in existence before the advent of the Christian era. They worship nature and earth, and as polytheists, they believe this power to be manifested in the form of various gods and goddesses. In this pluralistic system, there is a Mother (Moon) goddess, who controls fertility rites, and the process of birth and life; and also a horned god, who represents the masculine side of nature. Known as Cernunnos, the god of hunting, fertility, and wild animals, he is the god of the underworld who controls the gates of life and death.

Even though witches say that they don't believe in Satan, unknown to them, this 'horned hunter of the night' is a descendant of Nimrod, who became the sun god, and was the symbolic representation of Satan. You must remember, that Nimrod, and his wife, Semiramis, were the prototypes for all gods and goddesses that permeated all subsequent cultures and societies.

According to former witches and Satanists, the deities that witches worship are actually demons.

One thing that a lot of people try to do, is to pigeonhole witchcraft into one single category, and you can't do it. Within the realm of Christianity, you have many religions, such as Catholics, Lutherans, Methodists, Baptists, Presbyterians, etc. And within each of these, you have a further breakdown, which divides the various churches according to their own variations in philosophies. Well, since Witchcraft is a religion, the same divisions also exist. There are different denominations, so-to-speak. The terms most used are White and Black Witchcraft, Traditional (who believe power must be inherited through family lineage), Modernist, Gardnerian (revival of the 'old religion' established by anthropologist Gerald Gardner), and Alexandrian (offshoot of the Gardnerian tradition by Alexander Sanders). But there are many others.

White Sorcery is practiced out of the *La Clavicule de Solomon* (*The Key of Solomon*), which was said to be written by King Solomon, but was actually written in the 14th or 15th century. The *Lemegeton* (*Lesser Key*) is known as the *Book of Shadows*. Black Magic comes from the 6th and 7th Book of Moses, mistakenly alleged to have been written by Moses.

There has been a connotation of evil given to witchcraft as a whole, but it can't be as easily defined as that, because there are some gray areas that require an understanding. I am not condoning any aspect of witchcraft, but I do have to be fair.

The most well-known of the witchcraft sects are the Wiccans, who represent what could be considered White Witchcraft. I have talked to some Wiccans, and they do not fit the stereotype that one expects to find when they meet a witch. They do not dress in all black, and in fact, do not dress any differently than anyone else. You have probably talked to a witch, and never even knew it.

As serious as you may be about your religion, and faith; they are just as serious about their religion. Besides their holy days, some covens even have weekly meetings, just like a traditional church.

Wiccans have become more open in their religion in the past few years, as they try to dispel the myth, fear, and discrimination that surround them.

In August, 1995, our local paper had a front page article about a couple local witches, and how their religious activities were just like anyone else's. They have distanced themselves from Satanism, by emphasizing that they don't believe in Satan or demons. They have tried to separate themselves from the dark side of the

FINAL WARNING

occult, by saying that it is against their religion to harm anyone, that they're not out there trying to get people, by putting curses on them. In fact, their primary directive (known as the Witch's Rede) is: "An it harm none— do what thou wilt." This gives them the freedom to do what they want, just as long as it doesn't affect the rights of others, or cause physical harm.

And indeed, Wiccans have gone out of their way to help people. Out of their yearning to help, many enter helping professions, such as social workers, nurses, and counselors. They also do tarot card readings, and are the driving force behind the onslaught of the psychic phone hot lines.

Thousands have been drawn to the spiritualistic aspects of witchcraft, and it is estimated that there could be as many as 800,000 Wiccans in this country, and since 1987, they have "grown tremendously." They are out there spreading their word through books in secular bookstores, occult bookstores, classes, and pagan festivals. They are filling what they see as a void, and are presenting a religion that is more accepting of women in leadership positions, gays, interracial couples and unmarried couples. It is marked by solemn ritualistic ceremonies that makes one feel like they're part of a family; and a religion that offers real power.

We live in a time where the constitutional right of religious freedom has forced us to tolerate and accept any religion, no matter how foreign it is to our belief system, and how contrary it is to the Bible. But on the other hand, in a growing anti-Christian climate in this country, we are also being allowed to exercise our faith because of those same rights. So, we have a responsibility to treat someone else's beliefs with respect, because they have the same rights we do. However, I don't have to agree with them, or like it, and I don't have to allow this false doctrine to permeate our society unanswered.

No matter how honorable Wiccans intentions are, as a Christian, I must abide by the tenets of the Holy Scriptures in my assessment of their religion and practices. Do I hate them. No. In fact, the witches that I talked to were very pleasant, very nice, and very respectful of my religious beliefs. Which is more than I can say about some Jehovah Witnesses and Mormons that have come knocking on my door. It is very easy to forget a very fundamental Biblical teaching, that we must hate the sin, but love the sinner. God loves everyone, even a witch. So as a Christian, we need to let witches know, if ever given the opportunity, that they are living a lie. That the gods and goddesses they are worshipping do not exist, and that they have been deceived by a very real Satan, who is the father of lies.

As I said earlier, witches have a golden rule that prohibits them from hurting anyone. But, not all witches are 'good' witches. And not all witches share that philosophy. Irene Park, a former witch, and author of the book *The Witch Who Switched*, said the worst thing she had ever done to someone was to "demolish them. To see them removed off the face of the earth." She further elaborated: "You can kill them, or else they will commit suicide ... you drive them to do that ... you can do it by thought ... or something like making a potion ... and chanting and doing an incantation, and it works, the spirits work."

Chapter Six of the book *Mastering Witchcraft: A Practical Guide for Witches, Warlocks and Covens* is called "Vengeance and Attack." On page 196 it says: "With all the power of your imagination, and all the faith and intent you can muster, you must actually try to see your spell working its mischief, visualizing your victim suffering all the pangs you wish on him. This type of spell is perhaps best employed for encouraging general misfortune rather than any specific disaster..." It goes on to provide actual instructions and incantations for various curses.

Now, this book was written by a well-known witch named Paul Huson, a Traditionalist from San Francisco, who studied under Dr. Raymond Buckland, who, as I said, is probably the leading Wiccan authority in this country. Compare that with this, from *The Satanic Bible*: "Be certain you do not care if the intended victim lives or dies, before you throw your curse, and having caused their destruction, revel, rather than feel remorse." So you can see, with their own writings, regardless of any moral code they claim to have, the seduction of power and the ability of being able to use it, may be a more overriding determinant in regard to the actions of a witch.

Observing the sacred Celtic calendar of the Druids, witches have eight special holy days through the year, which are known as 'Sabbats.' The April 25, 1989 edition of *USA Today* reported that Patricia Hutchins, a self-proclaimed Wiccan serving in the U.S. Air Force, was granted religious leave by the military to observe the eight Sabbats of her 'religion.'

Some researchers have purported that the Sabbat is the witches sabbath, a corruption of the Jewish day of rest, Others have said that the word 'sabbath' is taken from Shabbathai, or Saturn, the planet which governs the seventh day; while 'sabbat' comes from Sabadius (or Sabazius), which was the title of Dionysus, the god of ecstasy, who was worshipped with partying and orgies. However, just like the Jewish calendar, the Sabbat mirrors the Celtic day, which began at sunset, and ended the next sunset.

There are two great fire festivals, known as Grand Sabbats, which divide the Celtic year in half. October 31st, Halloween (also known as the October Festival), which celebrates the beginning of winter, and is also the beginning of the witches New Year; and April 30th, Beltane (also known as Bealtaine), which celebrates the beginning of summer. Known as the day of Bel's fire because of the bonfires that accompanied their fertility rituals, the Druids held this feast in honor of Bel, a derivative of Baal (mentioned in the Old Testament) and can be associated with Apollo. This day has become connected to Walpurgis Night, a festival to honor Walburga (Walpurga), the daughter of King Richard the Lion-Hearted, a nun who moved to Germany and became abbess of the monastery of Eichstatt. After she died in 779, she was canonized by the Church, and is recognized as the protector against magic. However, witches are actually honoring Waldborg, a fertility goddess. The spirits of the dead are said to be very active on this day.

According to Anton LaVey, the self-proclaimed high priest of the Church of Satan in San Francisco, the two major Satanic observances are also Halloween and Walpurgisnacht.

There are two other minor feasts, which divide the half-year into quarters. February 2nd, Imbolg, the Winter festival (also known as Imbolc or Oimelc), which was a pagan celebration marked with a torchlight procession to honor the various deities associated with agriculture, which was to purify and fertilize the fields prior to the planting season. As the Catholic Church Christianized pagan celebrations, it became known as the Feast of Purification of the Blessed Virgin Mary which is celebrated by the Roman, Creek, and Anglican churches, It is supposedly held to observe the event described in the 2nd chapter of Luke, when Mary went to the Temple for purification, which according to tradition iy happened forty days after the birth of Jesus.

It was originally observed on February 14th, when Jesus was thought to have been born on the day of Epiphany. But when the date of his birth was changed to December 25th, the day was moved. It became known as Candlemas, because church candles are blessed that day, due to Simeon's reference to the "light to lighten the Gentiles." It was believed that these blessed candles, when put in a home, would protect it from evil. Pope Innocent XII (1691-1700) said: "Why do we in this feast carry candles? Because the Gentiles dedicated the month of February to the infernal gods, and at the beginning of it Pluto stole Proserpine, and her mother Ceres sought her in the night with lighted candles, so they, at the beginning of the month, walked about the city with lighted candles. Because the holy fathers could not extirpate the custom, they ordained that Christians should carry about candles in honor of the Blessed Virgin; and thus what was done before in honor of Ceres is now done in honor of the Blessed Virgin."

The other day is August 1st (July 31st according to *A Witches' Bible*) the Summer festival, when the first corn was harvested. This was the Druid festival of Lughnasadh, which was dedicated to Lugh, the Celtic sun god. It has become known as Lammas ('loaf-mass'). Witches celebrate this day to honor the sacred union of the goddess and the horned god.

Also celebrated, to a lesser extent, are the four solar fire festivals: The vernal equinox of March 21st (Alban Eilir, or the spring festival), and the autumnal equinox of September 23rd (September 21st according to *A Witches' Bible*, Alban Elfrad, or the autumn festival); and the two solstices (a Latin word which means "the sun stops").

June 22nd (Alban Hefin, or the mid-summer night festival) has become associated with the eve of St. John's Day (June 24), which is when the Feast of Saint John the Baptist is held. This is the oldest Church observance, and is celebrated on the day of his birth. The exact day is unknown, but the Bible indicates that he was born six months before Jesus. It became part of the mid-summer celebrations because of the summer solstice, which is the beginning of summer (June 20), and the longest day of the year.

December 22nd, known as Yule (Alban Arthan or the mid-winter festival), has become associated with the eve of St. Thomas Day (December 21), which is when the Feast of Saint Thomas is held. The observance was initiated in the 12th century to honor the apostle Jesus appeared to and showed his wounds after the Resurrection, because of his doubts. He is known as the patron saint of masons and architects. It became part of the winter celebrations because of the winter solstice, which is the beginning of winter (December 21), and the longest night of the year.

Whether you know it or not, the Church of Wicca, the largest church in the country devoted to the practice of Witchcraft, is a federally recognized, tax exempt, non-profit, religious organization in the United States. The Church of Satan, which was founded in San Francisco in 1966, is also considered a tax exempt religious organization.

Some other well-known churches are the Wicca Church of America, Church of All Worlds, Universal Church of Wicca, Aquarian Tabernacle Church, The Church of the Iron Oak, and the Church of Universal Brotherhood. Witches are so organized that they hold seminars and conventions that are publicized by the media. In 1970, the New York City Parks Department issued a permit for the Witches International Craft Associates (WICA) to have a "Witch-In" in Sheep Meadow on Halloween. Over 1,000 people attended.

In 1980, Joyce Clemow, a director of the New York Center for the Strange (a non-profit research group that investigates "the myriad aspects of prognostication, prophecy, and divination") said that among America's practicing witches, were three Congressmen, a syndicated financial columnist, the President of one of the nation's banks, a well-known television newscaster, and a man who held a top foreign affairs position in the Nixon Administration. Margot Adler, a reporter for National Public Radio, was a well-known witch, and author of a book on neo-Paganism called *Drawing Down the Moon.*

The Bible is very clear concerning the occult. Exodus 22:18 says: "Thou shalt not suffer a witch to live." Witchcraft practitioners claim that this verse doesn't refer to witchcraft, because the word "witch" is translated from the Hebrew word "chasaph" which actually means "a poisoner."

However, *Strong's Exhaustive Concordance of the Bible* identifies the original word out of the Massoretic text to be "kashaph" (#3784), a root word which means to "whisper a spell, i.e. to inchant (sic) or practise (sic) magic." The word "kesheph" (#3785) is magic or witchcraft, as used in 2 Kings 9:22, Micah 5:12, and Nahum 3:4; and "kashshaph" (#3786) is a magician or sorcerer. The Hebrew word "chemah" (#2534) means "poison." Another verse that corresponds to this sentiment can be found in Leviticus 20:27, which says: "A man also or woman that hath a familiar spirit, or that is a wizard, shall surely be put to death: they shall stone them with stones: their blood shall be upon them."

Jeremiah 10:2 says: "...Learn not the way of the heathen..." Deuteronomy 18:10-12 says: "There shall not be found among you anyone that maketh his son or his daughter to pass through the fire, or that useth divination, or an observer of times, or an enchanter, or a witch, or a charmer, or a consulter with familiar spirits, or a wizard, or a neocromancer. For all that do these things are an abomination unto the Lord..." 1 Peter 5:8 charges us to "be vigilant; because your adversary the devil, as a roaring lion, walketh about, seeking whom he may devour." Ephesians 5:11 says that we are to "have no fellowship with the unfruitful works of darkness, but rather reprove them." And 2 Corinthians 6:11, says: "Be not unequally yoked together with unbelievers: for what fellowship has righteousness with unrighteousness? and what communion has light with darkness?"

In 1980, Skip Tarrant, a head witch in the Church of Wicca, said: "Being a witch makes one feel more alive." According to the testimony of former witches and Satanists, the ancient religion of Witchcraft and its 'white magic' is nothing more than a "little white lie." The deities they worship are actually demons, and the 'horned hunter of the night' is actually Satan. Many witches have come to realize, that in order to get more 'power,' they have to surrender more of themselves, moving into the darker side of Witchcraft, and sometimes into Satanism. Satan does not care what he does, or who he destroys, in order to achieve his goals.

THE NEW AGE MOVEMENT

In 1908, Annie Besant (1847-1933, sister of Sir Walter Besant, a Mason), an outspoken atheist who was converted to Satanism by Pike, a member of the Fabian Society, who became president of the Theosophical Society (whose goal was to "gain access to the universal spiritual reality beyond material existence") after the death of Helena Petrovna Blavatsky (1831-1891, who became a Satanist in 1856 and founded the Society in New York in 1875); and Charles W. Leadbeater, former Anglican priest, a Theosophist, and 33rd degree Mason; discovered Jiddu Krishnamurti, who they believed to be the reincarnation of the being that inhabited Jesus, Krishna and Buddha. They founded the Order of the Star to spread his word. Those who listened to him speak at a Star of the East convocation in 1911 said he "spoke in the first person as a god." Others witnessed "a great coronet of brilliant, shimmering blue" appearing above his head. Many knelt to worship him as the "world teacher" and the "guiding spirit of the universe."

A biographer later wrote: "Although he was only a little boy when she brought him from India to London, and although he hardly moved and did not speak when introduced at a party at Charing Cross, those who were present professed to feel a strange 'vibration' coming from him. Years later this same vibration caused thousands to fall at his feet in homage, accepting him as their Messiah, when he addressed a huge International Conference of Theosophists in Holland. A visitor to the conference afterwards testified, 'When he spoke, it was awe inspiring. I am not easily moved, but there was something there— impalpable, but resistless'."

However, when he came to America in 1926, his occult powers failed him, and his spirit guides left him. The *New York Times* reported him to be "a shy, badly frightened, nice-looking Hindu." His speaking engagements were canceled, and he later denied that he was the 'Christ,' and renounced the Theosophical Society. Because America, at that time, was still, for the most part, a Christian, Bible-believing nation, the spirit that inhabited Jiddu had to leave him.

He retired in 1929, broke all connections with organized philosophy, and became a popular mystic writer and speaker. In 1969, he established the Krishnamurti Foundation of America to publish and distribute his teachings. He said that his only concern was "to set men absolutely, unconditionally free." He died in 1986. However, his library and archives are continuing to feed a new generation his brand of New Age teaching. He was listed as a contributing editor of the *Bruce Lee* magazine, the official publication and voice of the Jun Fan Jeet Kune Do nucleus.

Besant was later replaced with Alice Bailey, a witch, and an occult writer who, back in the 1940's, was the first to use the term 'New Age.' Collaborating with other occultists, she claimed to be working out mankind's spiritual destiny from a remote Himalayan retreat, and that her writings were telepathically sent to her by the Tibetan Djuhal Khul, who said that there was going to be a new world government and a new world religion.

In 1922, Bailey, established the Lucifer Publishing Co. of New York to print and distribute their Satanic doctrine. The name was later changed to the Lucis Publishing Co. Years later, their president, Perry Coles, tried to downplay the sinister overtones, by saying that 'lucis' comes from the Latin word 'lux' which means 'of light,' and the word is used in the context of being "bringers of light," and doesn't have anything to do with Satanism. Yet they are one of the biggest publishers of occult material in the country.

Lucis Publishing, the Arcane School, and World Goodwill (founded in 1933 to promote Luciferian views, is composed of individuals who are referred to as the "New Group of World Servers"), are run under the auspices of the Lucis Trust Co., which had been located at 866 United Nations Plaza in New York City (suite 566 & 567), but later relocated to 120 Wall Street, 24th floor, in New York. They seem to be the coordinating force behind the New Age movement. Some of the people who have served on their Board: Robert McNamara, Donald Regan, Henry Kissinger, David Rockefeller, Paul Volcker, and George Shultz.

Bailey wrote a few books detailing the New Age plan and said that the new world order will be the "reappearance of the Christ." In her *Externalization of the Hierarchy* she said that the New Age will be in full bloom after the global crisis occurs and the world turns to 'Christ' for leadership. She felt that the term 'Christ' could be applied to any person who reached an elevated state of consciousness, thereby achieving a divine status. Only a few souls found enough favor with the spiritual hierarchy of the reincarnated ancient Masters to be chosen to return to earth as an avatar. New Agers claim that Mohammed, Buddha, and Jesus were avatars, and therefore each was a 'Christ.'

Alice Bailey has said:

> "The Christ who will return will not be like the Christ who (apparently) departed. He will not be a 'man of sorrows'; He will not be a silent, pensive figure; He will be the enunciator of spiritual statements which will not necessitate interpretation (and give rise to misinterpretation) because He will be present to indicate the true meaning ... He recognizes and loves those who are not Christian but who retain allegiance to their Founders— the Buddha, Mohammed, and others. He cares not what the faith is, if the objective is love of God and of humanity. If men look for the Christ who left his disciples centuries ago they will fail to recognize the Christ who is in the process of returning."

Bailey said that her "hidden Masters" told her that 1975 was the time to begin open propagation of their plans. Although Maharishi Mahesh Yogi (who brought Transcendental Meditation to America) taught that the New Age began in 1975 when he inaugurated the "Age of Enlightenment," the 1980 book *The Aquarian Conspiracy: Personal and Social Transformation in the 1980's* by Marilyn Ferguson (published by J. P. Tarcher, Inc. in Los Angeles, CA) ignited the New Age movement into one of the fastest growing 'religions' today.

Ferguson said that the New Age movement had "triggered the most rapid cultural realignment in history," and that the movement had grown to such an extent, that thousand of groups were now a part of the network, including: Human Potential Movement, New Thought, Consciousness Movement, Holistic Movement, Whole Earth, and Unity. Some of their front-groups include: Association for Humanistic Psychology, the Holistic Health Organizing Committee, Association for World Organization, Political Science Committee of the Institute for the New Age, Institute for the Study of Conscious Evolution, Naropa Institute, Hunger

Project, Planetary Citizens, Planetary Initiative for the World We Choose, and the Movement for a New Society.

This handbook for action by the New Age movement was introduced at the World Congress on Futurology in Toronto, Canada to be used as a blueprint to begin a new campaign for recruitment into the occult.

The December, 1986 issue of the *Omega-Letter* reported that the New Age movement was the fastest growing religion in America. People are being drawn into the New Age movement because of its propaganda regarding social injustices, environmental concerns, and ending world hunger. Some of the well-known people who were involved: singer John Denver, former astronaut Edgar Mitchell, former University of Notre Dame president Theodore Hesburgh, former German Chancellor Willy Brandt, science fiction writer Isaac Asimov, physicist Fritjof Capra, and *Megatrends* author John Naisbitt.

California New Age minister and writer Terry Cole-Whittaker told *Magical Blend* magazine: "I feel that we are right on the edge and we are going to 'pop' into a new dimension. Everybody senses it."

The central theme of the New Age movement is "the emergence of a new planetary consciousness." They hope to usher in the "Age of Aquarius" and their goal is a one-world religion. It is nothing more than a revival of the ancient Babylonian religion, a dressed-up version of witchcraft, a politically-correct form of witchcraft, which they hope to introduce to every aspect of society.

The spirit guides they refer to are demons. They are working to integrate New Age teaching into religion, and in the process, they are trying to discredit Christianity. For instance, New Agers have latched onto the 'lost years' of Jesus, the period between his boyhood and the beginning of his ministry, which are omitted from the Bible. Kevin Ryerson, the demon channeler for actress Shirley Maclaine, says that his spirit guides told him that "the man Jesus studied for 18 years in India before he returned to Jerusalem. He was studying the teachings of Buddha and became an adept Yogi himself." Elizabeth Clare Prophet in her book *The Lost Years of Jesus*, said that she discovered, through documents she found in the Himalayas, that when Jesus was a youth, he joined a caravan to the East, and studied under "wise men" who taught him mysticism. Edgar Cayce's demon guides also gave him similar revelations. He claimed that Jesus traveled through Egypt, India and Persia; and it was in Persia that he learned from the Mystery Religion teachers. New Age leaders claim this information was censored in the 6th century by the Church. A book called *Jesus Lived in India* by Holger Kerston, has gone as far as to say that after the "resurrection" of Jesus, he returned to India, and that his tomb in Kashmir can still be seen today.

Ruth Montgomery was told by her spirit guides: "...We are as much God as God is part of us ... each of us is God ... together we are God." Corinne and Theodore Heline, authors of many New Age books, including *New Age Bible Interpretation*, said that with the dawning of a New Age, an evil Satan who doesn't exist will vanish from man's memory. Christians unfit for the New Age will also cease to exist, being wiped off the earth by the New Age 'Christ.' New Ager Ken Eyers was quoted in *Parade* magazine (August 9, 1987) as saying: "Those who can not be enlightened will not be permitted to dwell in this world. They will be sent to some equally appropriate place to work their way to understanding."

In the New Age book *Reflections on the Christ* by David Spangler (Director of the UN Planetary Initiative, and a leader in the Planetary Citizens), he wrote that Lucifer is "an agent of God's love." and that "Christ is the same force as Lucifer." He also wrote: "Lucifer prepares man for the experience of Christhood ... (he is) the great Initiator ... Lucifer works within each of us to bring us to wholeness, as we move into a new age ... each of us in some way is brought to that point which I term the Luciferic Initiation, the particular doorway through which the individual must pass if he is to come 'fully' into the presence of his light and his wholeness ... It is one that many people now, and in the days ahead, will be facing, for it is an initiation into the new age." He also made a connection to one world government when he wrote: "No one will enter the New World Order unless he or she will make a pledge to worship Lucifer. No one will enter the New Age unless he will take a Luciferian initiation." New Agers refer to the writings of a 14th century gnostic group, called Luciferians, who worshiped him, believing him to be the brother of God, and taught that he was wrongly cast out of Heaven, and would someday be vindicated. He was praised as the "bright and morning star."

Lola Davis, author of *Toward a World Religion for the New Age*, identified the New Age 'Christ' as Lord Maitreya, who has been labeled as an avatar and a world teacher. She said "he will bring new revelations and further guidance for establishing the World Religion." She also said that the "World Council of Churches ... has the potential to serve as a source of unity among the diversity of religions." On April 25, 1982, the Tara Center (headquartered in London and N. Hollywood, CA), a New Age group led by Benjamin Crème, ran a full page ad in twenty major papers around the world proclaiming that the New Age Messiah, Lord Maitreya, was alive and ready to institute their plan, which included "the installation of a new world government and a new world religion under Maitreya." The ad said: "Since July, 1977, the Christ has been emerging as a spokesman for a group or community in a well-known modern country." It promised that the 'Christ' would appear "within the next two months" and that "his message will be heard inwardly, telepathically, by all people in their own language. From that time, with his help, we will build a new world."

A similar ad ran five years later, on January 12, 1987, in *USA Today*, under the headline "The Christ is in the World," describing Lord Maitreya as "a great world teacher for people of every religion and no religion." He never did appear, and according to Creme, Maitreya, was living in a Hindu-Pakistani community in southeast London, and attending Oxford University, where he is studying the sacred writings of the world's major religions.

When Creme spoke in Detroit on November 4, 1981, he was asked if he had met Maitreya, and he said: "No, I've never met the Christ, but I've met the human body he is inhabiting several times— but never as the Christ." According to the Huntington House book *New Age Messiah Identified* by Troy Lawrence, this man was identified as Rahmat Ahmad, and is the great-great grandson of Mirza Ghulam Ahmad, who was born in the 1800's in India, and claimed that he was the Messiah, sent to unite the entire world in a New World Religion. It was revealed that he was born in February, 1962 in Rabwah, Pakistan, then went to England in July, 1977, in preparation for his role. Lord Maitreya never did appear, and as it turns out, in 1991, Lawrence (real name, Darrick Evenson) was exposed as a fraud, and now his exposé has been pretty much ignored.

Just as the birth of Jesus was prophesied by many Old Testament prophets, New Agers believed that the birth of the new 'Christ,' was prophesied by Jeanne Dixon. Shortly before sunrise on February 5, 1962, Dixon had an unusual experience. For several months, astrologers had predicted that an earth-shaking event on that day, because of a rare conjunction of Jupiter, Saturn and Venus in the constellation of Pisces. A similar conjunction which occurred nearly 2,000 years ago is believed by some to explain the "bright star in the east" at the time of the birth of Jesus.

As she looked outside, she didn't see any trees, or the street, just a blue sky, above a barren desert. In the sky, the sun was shining brighter than she had ever seen. Coming from the sun in every direction were brilliant rays which seemed to be drawing the earth toward it like a magnet. Stepping out of the brightness of the sun's rays, hand-in-hand was a Pharaoh (later identified as Pharaoh Amenhotep) and Queen Nefertiti. In her arms was a baby in ragged soiled clothing. The eyes of the child were "all-knowing" (the all-seeing eye on the Illuminati seal?), full of wisdom and knowledge. To one side of the Queen, Dixon could see a pyramid (the Illuminati?).

The couple came before her, as if to offer the baby to the world. Within the sun, Joseph was guiding the tableau like a puppeteer pulling strings (Bible teacher David Ebaugh has linked Genesis 41:14-36, dealing with Joseph's interpretations of the Pharaoh's dreams, with the Book of Revelation; in addition, Joseph was known as the "dreamer"). Rays of light burst forth from the baby, blending with those of the sun, obliterating the Pharaoh from her sight. Off to the left, Dixon saw Queen Nefertiti walking away, thousands of miles into the past. She paused beside a large brown water jug, and as she stooped to cup her hands and drink, she was stabbed in the back by a dagger. She died and vanished. The baby, meanwhile, had grown to manhood, and a small cross formed above him, expanding until it dripped over the earth in every direction. At the same time, people of every race, religion, and color, all knelt and lifted their arms in worship; and were all as one.

Dixon interpreted this to mean that there was a child born somewhere in the Middle East, shortly after February 5, 1962, of humble peasant origin, possibly a direct descendent of Queen Nefertiti. Her husband, Pharaoh Amenhotep IV (known as the great "Heretic King") had changed his name to Ikhnaton (which means, "He in whom Aton is satisfied"), and built a city, Tell-el-Amarna, protected by impregnable cliffs, to worship the sun god Aton (in 1375 BC). They had seven daughters, but no sons. After his death, the priests of Amon took over. Tutankhaton, who married the third daughter, became Pharaoh at the age of twelve, and changed his name to Tutankhamon (the "image of Amon"), destroying all traces of Atonism, and returning to the worship of earlier gods. If the child isn't a direct descendent, the sun could be a symbol of the one world religion that is to come. When the Illuminati was established, their secret code utilized the planetary symbol for the sun to signify the Order. Dixon said: "There is no doubt in my mind that the 'child' is the actual person of the Antichrist, the one who will deceive the world in Satan's name."

Robert Mueller, a New Ager, is a former Assistant Secretary-General of the UN, and a member of the board of Planetary Citizens. He suggested that religions should "create common world religious institutions," and "display the UN flag in all houses of worship." He has even called for a universal Bible to be written. He said: "We must move as quickly as possible to a one-world government; a one-world religion; under a one-world leader." He also said: "My great personal dream is to get a tremendous alliance between all major religions and the UN." He said in 1982: "The human person and planetary citizenship must be given absolute priority over national citizenship."

Some of Mueller's views were molded by the third UN Secretary-General U Thant, a Buddhist and a one-worlder. In Thant's book *The New Genesis*, he calls for the New Age to be ushered in by the year 2000. Mueller dedicated one of his books to Dag Hammarskjold, the second UN Secretary-General, who he referred to as his "spiritual master."

Dag was behind the renovating of the UN Meditation Room, and even helped raise funds for it. John D. Rockefeller, Jr. gave $5,000 for it. In the book *Spiritual Politics: Changing the World From the Inside*, New Agers Corinne McLaughlin and Gordon Davidson referred to it as a "place of quiet stillness and has been referred to as one of the holiest of holies on the planet ..."

The Meditation Room is shaped like a pyramid without a capstone, sometimes described as a trapezoid, which Satanists believe is the shape that is the most conducive for the manifestation of demonic manifestation. The room is illuminated only from a single beam of light from the ceiling upon a black stone altar. Hammarskjold said that the altar was "dedicated to the God whom man worships under many names and in many forms." On one of the walls is a mural which contains occult symbolism, and at it center is the 'all-seeing eye' of the Illuminati. David Meyer, a former witch, said about the room:

> "I stood in the meditation room, which contains Satan's altar ... The black stone block has a certain kind of magnetism about it, and when I walked into the room with my praying wife, I could sense the intense presence of an evil force beyond description. This is where the world leaders and Illuminati masterminds go to meditate, which is why it is open to the public only in the mornings. Once the sun moves from ante meridian to post meridian only the adept in witchcraft are allowed into that room, for that is witchcraft doctrine regarding meditation. As the sun gives way to waning light and the female power of the moon goddess, the meditation room at the UN becomes off-limits to what they call the 'profane'."

New Ager William Irwin Thompson said in 1991: "We have a new spirituality, what has been called the New Age movement. The planetization of the esoteric has been going on for some time ... The independent sovereign state, with the sovereign individual in his private property are over just as the Christian fundamentalist days are about to be over. We are fast becoming a planetary culture." He also said: "The new spirituality does not reject the earlier patterns of the great universal religions. Priest and church will not disappear; they will not be forced out of existence in the New Age, they will be absorbed into the existence of the New Age."

We can see New Age philosophy being advocated on television, and in the movies. Even though there are New Age bookstores, New Age material has become so popular that it is showing up in regular stores. New Age meditation techniques have been secretly introduced into our public schools as a means of handling problem kid. Subtly the New Age message is entering the mainstream church. The 1970 song by former Beatle member, George Harrison, "My Sweet Lord" (from the album *All Things Must Pass*, which was, in fact, a rip-off of the Chiffon's song "He's So Fine") was accepted by many churches as a Christian song, when in fact it was a song of dedication to Krishna, and contained a chant to summon spirits (demons). He had been involved with the Maharishi Mahesh Yogi, and later converted to Hinduism. I believe that the legal and societal headway gained in recognizing same-sex relationships has to do with the fact that New Age philosophy has weakened, watered-down, and worn-out the message of the Church.

Robert Mueller said, while speaking at the Parliament of World Religions: "Do not worry if not all the religions will join the United Religions organization. Many nations did not join the UN at its beginning, but later regretted it and made every effort to join. It was the same with the European Community and it will be the case with the world's religions because whoever stays out or aloof will sooner or later regret it."

Dick Sutphen, a New Age advocate said that fundamentalism "is extremely dangerous to the future of this planet and potential for a New Age." Barbara Marx Hubbard, Executive Director of the World Future Society, has said in regard to Christians:

> "No worldly peace can prevail until the self-centered members of the planetary body either change or die ... This act is as horrible as killing a cancer cell. It must be done for the sake of the future of the whole ... There have always been defective seeds. In the past they were permitted to die a 'natural death' ... We, the elders have been patiently waiting until the very last moment before the quantum transformation, to take action to cut out this corrupted and corrupting element in the body of humanity. It is like watching a cancer grow; something must be done before the whole body is destroyed..."

The facts speak for themselves here. The New Age movement is a facade whose purpose is to deceive. John Randolph Price, a New Age leader, said that "there are more than half a billion New Age advocates on the planet at this time, working among various religious groups." It is likely that the New Age movement will be the vehicle that will dilute the major religions enough, so that they will be able to find enough common ground to join together in a new World Religion.

THE WORLD CHURCH

Just as there have been signs that the political powers of this world are coming together in a New World Order, so it has been with the Church. The establishment of a World Church would seem to go hand-in-hand with a World Government. We will go back to the early history of man, and follow the history of the church, and what its relationship may be to the World Church.

In the Bible, according to the book of Genesis, Noah had three sons, Ham, Shem, and Japheth. Ham had a son by the name of Cush, and Cush's son was called Nimrod, and was known as the "mighty hunter." It was Nimrod who attempted to build a tower that would reach to Heaven. God confused their language, so they couldn't understand each other, and they were scattered over the face of the Earth. Nimrod (purported to be the founder of Masonry) established a religious system, with the help of his mother and father, to control the people through political methods. This was the beginning of the occult, which became known as Baal (Satan) worship. A common practice was to sacrifice babies.

Nimrod's great-uncle Shem became so enraged over Nimrod's activities, and with the help of a group of Egyptians, killed him, chopped his body up into little pieces, and sent the pieces to different cities as a warning to those who dabbled in the occult.

Nimrod's mother, Semiramis (who had married her son Nimrod), took over the religion, and proclaimed Nimrod a god. She gathered all of Nimrod's pieces, except for his penis, which she couldn't find. She created the symbol of the obelisk and established phallus worship. She claimed that an Evergreen tree sprouted from a tree stump, which she said indicated the entry of new life into the deceased Nimrod. Every year on the anniversary of Nimrod's birth, said to be on December 25th, she would leave gifts at this Evergreen tree, which was the origin of the Christmas tree.

The religion was pushed underground. Those joining had to take oaths of secrecy, and had to tell their priests everything they did wrong. In this way, via the 'confessional,' they could blackmail anyone who didn't yield to their will. Semiramis became known as the 'Queen of Heaven' and was symbolized by the figure of the Moon. Nimrod, her son/husband, was now called Baal, the Sun God, or the 'Divine Son of Heaven.' Statues were produced showing Semiramis holding the baby Nimrod.

When Babylon fell, the religion grew in Egypt and Pergamos (in Asia Minor), where Semiramis became known as Isis, and Nimrod became known as Horus (or Osiris) the Sun God. In Deuteronomy 4:19, Moses warned against Sun worship. In other lands, forms of Baal worship became dominant among various religious practices. In China, Semiramis was called 'Sing Moo' ('Holy Mother'); in ancient Phoenecia, she was called 'Ashtoreth,' and in Asia Minor, 'Diana.'

So, God established a nation of Jews, called Israel, and gave them laws to live by. They were to be the light to a world ravaged with sin, but they too became caught up in idol worship. Even though prophets, anointed by God, warned them, they did not heed the warning. As a punishment, God allowed them to become enslaved by other nations.

When Attalus, King of Pergamos, died in 133 B.C., he bequeathed the Babylonian priesthood to Rome. Thus, Julius Caesar became the Supreme Pontiff of the Babylonian Order. All Roman emperors served in this capacity until 376

FINAL WARNING

A.D., when Emperor Gratian refused it, and Damascus, a Church Bishop, was appointed the Supreme Pontiff.

Jesus Christ, whose birth was prophesied by Isaiah (Isa. 7:14), was sent by God to be the Saviour of the Jews. However, He wasn't recognized as the awaited Messiah, and was despised by religious leaders who plotted against Him. These Jewish leaders became His judges, presenting phony witnesses, and breaking eighteen Jewish laws in order to have Him sentenced to death. Satan, who three years before, had tempted Jesus in the wilderness, believed that through His crucifixion, he had defeated Christ. But, as you know, He rose from the dead three days later; and forty days later was transfigured into heaven. With the Great Commission, Jesus had instructed His disciples to go to all the world to spread the gospel, and Satan tried his best to defeat the Christian movement.

Two years after the establishment of the true Christian Church, Satan raised up a man known as Simon Magus, a Babylonian priest, to do his bidding. According to Acts 8:9-11, Simon "used sorcery, and bewitched the people ... giving out that himself was some great one." Many people, "from the least to the greatest" were impressed with him, thinking him to be "the great power of God." When the apostle Philip began to preach the gospel, and perform miracles in Samaria, Satan saw the potential of being able to use Christianity for his own purpose, and Simon tried to buy his way into an apostleship, without the repenting his sins, in order to gain this mysterious new power. Simon adopted some of the Christian teachings interweaving it with his own pagan religion, and called it Christianity.

The *Dictionary of Christian Biography* (Vol. 4, page 682) says: "...when Justin Martyr wrote his 'Apology' (152 A.D.), the sect of the Simonians appears to have been formidable, for he speaks four times of their founder, Simon ... and tells that he came to Rome in the days of Claudius Caesar (45 A.D.), and made such an impression by his magical powers, that he was honored as a god, a statue being erected to him on the Tiber, between the two bridges, bearing the inscription 'Simoni deo Sancto' ('the holy god Simon')."

Besides his attempt to dilute Christian teaching, Satan zeroed in on its leaders.

Stephen, who was a deacon in the first Christian church in Jerusalem, was stoned to death in 29 A.D.; James, the son of Zebedee, was beheaded in Jerusalem in 45 A.D.; Philip was tied to a pillar at Phrygia in 54 A.D. and stoned; James, the son of Alpheus, was dragged from the Temple, stoned, and beaten to death with a club in 63 A.D.; in 64 A.D., Mark (author of one of the Gospels) was seized by a mob of pagan priests and idol worshipers, who tied a rope around his neck, and dragged him through the streets of Alexandria till he died; Paul (Saul of Tarsus) was persecuted, then beheaded in Rome, in 69 A.D.; Simon Peter was crucified upside-down in Rome in 69 A.D.; Andrew was tied to a cross, and left there three days before he died; Bartholomew was severely beaten in Armenia in 70 A.D., then beheaded; at Calaminia in 70 A.D., Thomas was thrown into a furnace, then speared to death with javelins; at Nad-davar in 70 A.D., Matthew was nailed to the ground, then beheaded; Simon, the Canaanite, was crucified in Syria in 70 A.D.; Judas Thaddeus was beaten to death with sticks in 70 A.D.; Matthias (who replaced Judas Iscariot as a disciple/apostle after Judas committed suicide) was tied to a cross, stoned, and then beheaded in 70 A.D.; Luke (another writer of the Gospels) was hung from an olive tree in Greece in 93 A.D.; and Timothy was stoned to death by idol worshipers in 98 A.D.

Being that Rome, who ruled the known world, was under the influence of a form of Baal worship, Christians who refused to worship the Emperor were persecuted, beginning with Nero, in the middle of the first century. They were arrested and put to death in various ways, such as crucifixion, being tied inside animal skins and attacked by wild dogs, fed to lions, and tied to stakes to be burned as human torches to light Nero's gardens at night. These persecutions, which lasted until early in the fourth century, caused the Christians to literally go underground, to worship secretly. They took refuge in the subterranean catacombs of Rome, which extended for miles underneath the city. There are said to be over two million Christian graves in these caverns. This persecution of the Christians was Satan's attempt to get rid of the Biblical teaching. Various religions, cults, and sects, were established to alter the Holy Scriptures in order to change them, and confuse the world.

Although the Christians were persecuted, their faith in God stood fast. John, the brother of James, the last of the disciples, was exiled to a penal colony on the island of Patmos in 97 A.D. He was instrumental in preserving our Holy Bible, by informing Christians which of the manuscripts were genuine. These manuscripts were then hidden by Christians in the cellars of the great monasteries.

The Roman Catholic Church

In 305, the two Roman emperors, Diocletian and Maximian, stepped down, and were succeeded by their deputies, Galerius and Constantius. Constantius was then replaced by Maximinus Daia in the east, and Severus in the west, and he sent for his son Constantine to help him reclaim the throne. After Constantius died, Constantine was proclaimed emperor by his father's army, and he led them in a march against Rome.

On the evening of October 27, 312, he came face to face with the legions of Maxentius at the Milvian Bridge on the Tiber River. As he prepared to pit his small army against the military might of Rome, so the legend goes, he vowed that if God would help him conquer Rome, he would institute Christian rule. Eusebius wrote in *The Life of Constantine*, that above the setting sun, Constantine and his troops saw a cross in the sky, and above it were the words: "Hoc signo victor eris," which means: "In this sign you shall be victorious." That night, Christ appeared to him with the cross, and told him to use it as a guardian. The next morning, he had this 'sign of God' placed on his helmet, and the shields of his men.

Eusebius was given this account by the emperor himself, years afterward, but he didn't write about it till after Constantine's death. Most historians never acknowledged this glorified account, and not one man in his army of 40,000 ever mentioned it. Lactantius, a Christian, a few years later, wrote that Constantine had a vision of Apollo at the temple in Gaul, who instructed him to place the "celestial sign of God" on their shields prior to going into battle.

Constantine felt that Christ was a manifestation of the Sun God, Sol, or Apollo, even though Christians didn't know it. The emblem he used, was not the cross he allegedly seen, but the symbol, known as the labarum, which was the first two Greek letters of the word 'Christos,' Chi and Rho which had been discovered as part of an inscription found on a Pompeii tomb 250 years earlier.

Regardless of what did happen, he won the battle, and took over the government of Rome. The next year, in 313, he issued the Edict of Milan (also known as the Edict of Toleration), which bestowed religious freedom, in order to show tolerance towards Christianity, and all other forms of monotheism were forbidden. He had his troops sprinkled in baptism, proclaiming them to be Christians, although spiritually they weren't. Constantine made Christianity the official religion of Rome. A document discovered in the eighth century, called the 'Donation of Constantine' was said to have conferred some of his secular power upon the Pope, and it was used by the Church to gain some authority in the government, but it was later proved to be a forgery.

In 325, he set up the Council of Nicaea, and ruled it as the 'Summus Pontifex' (which is the official title of the Pope). He considered himself to be the head of the Church, although the Bishop of Rome was the recognized head, later to be known as the Pope (Italian for 'father'). Constantine ordered all writings that challenged Church teaching to be gathered up and destroyed, and in 331 he commissioned a new Bible. In 303, pagan emperor Diocletian had already destroyed most of the Christian writings around Rome, so of all the manuscripts of the New Testament available, not one had been produced before the fourth century, which made it easy for the Church to alter the Scriptures to fit the point of view they wanted to convey.

Although all Romans were baptized into the Christian faith, there were those who wanted to remain loyal to the Babylonian mysteries, and sought to retain some aspects of their religion in the new Christian religion. Thus, paganism was allowed to infiltrate the Church. Although Constantine claimed to have converted to Christianity, he secretly worshipped the Sun God. He made Sunday a day of rest, not because it was supposed to be the Lord's day, but being that it was the first day of the week, it was to be a tribute to the Sun God.

St. Peter was said to be the first Bishop (or Pope) of the Church, and each Pope is said to be his successor. The rationale being that Jesus said to Peter (originally known as Simeon, or Simon, Jesus called him Cephas, or 'rock,' and the name Peter comes from the Latin 'petrus,' which means 'rock'): "That thou art Peter, and upon this rock I will build my church..." This is a tradition that is historically inaccurate, because Peter never professed that distinction. There is no evidence that the Apostle Peter had ever been in Rome, at any time. In that verse, in the original Greek, 'Peter' is translated from 'petros' (Strong's #4074, a small rock) and 'rock' is translated from 'petra' (Strong's # 4073, a mass of rock). What this means is that Jesus is the rock, the foundation of the Church, while Peter was just going to help build it.

However, secular history explains that there was a "Simon Peter" in Rome during the first century. The pagan gods of the Babylonians and Greeks were identified by the name Peter (or Patres). The Romans referred to Neptune, Saturn, Mars, and Liber, as 'gods' of the Peter-rank. Going back as far as Nimrod, Deuteronomy 23:4 says that Balaam of Pethor was a sacred high place where there was an oracle temple. 'Pethor' meant "place of interpretation," and 'Balaam' was the chief Pantora (Peter) and successor to Nimrod. The Hebrew Lexicon indicates that the consonantal word P-T-R or Peter means "to interpret." Thus, Simon Magus, who had become the interpreter of the Babylonian Mysteries, became known as Simon Peter. The *Vaticano Illustrato II* says that the Babylonian statue of Jupiter was renamed 'Peter.'

Eusebius (264-340), the Bishop of Caesarea, a Church historian (who was imprisoned by the Romans as they searched for Bibles to destroy them), was Constantine's chief religious advisor. He studied at Origen's (184-254) school of Religion and Philosophy in Alexandria, where many gnostic scholars lived and studied. The school became a center for 'Christian' learning and culture. Eusebius and his scribes were instructed by Constantine to prepare fifty Bibles for the churches in Constantinople (Byzantium, or the 'new Rome').

Eusebius wasn't a true Christian, because he believed Jesus to be a lesser god, and was guided by that fact when he produced his version of the Scriptures. For instance, he eliminated the verse in 1 John 5:7, which says: "For there are three that bear record in heaven, the Father, the Word, and the Holy Ghost: and these three are one." These altered manuscripts were prepared into Bibles for the newly formed Roman Catholic Church, and it was out of Eusebius' translation, that the Latin Vulgate Bible emerged (a revision of the old Latin version translated from the Greek Septuagint), written by Jerome (382-404), which became the official Bible for all Roman Catholics. All other versions were banned, discarded, and destroyed.

Emperor Theodosius (378-398) made Christianity the official State religion, and church membership was mandatory. This forced conversion brought many heathens, idol worshipers, and pagans into the Church. Soon these pagans succeeded in getting statues of Semiramis and Nimrod into the Church, as the Babylonian system of 'mother and child' worship eventually evolved into the Madonna and child symbol (prominent at Christmas), and referred to them as the Virgin Mary and the baby Jesus. The halos around their heads were symbolic of the sun. Confessionals were established, just as they were in Babylon, and soon the Church began to grow in power.

Several Christian sects and semi-Christian orders criticized the Catholic Church, and taught from the original manuscripts, which they guarded with their lives, in order to insure the survival of God's word.

The Waldenses were founded in 1170 by a rich merchant from Lyons, in southern France, called Peter Waldo. He separated from the Catholic Church, and sold all of his possessions. He taught from the non-Latin version of the Bible, and said that the Catholic Church wasn't the Church of Christ, and referred to them as the World Church mention in the Book of Revelation. The Christian movement spread to Spain, northern France, Germany, Italy, Poland, Hungary, and Switzerland. The Anabaptists and Lollards were two groups which sprang from the Waldenses.

The Anabaptists was the name for various groups from the radical branch of the Protestant Reformation in the 16th century. They were active in Germany, Holland, and Switzerland, and were nicknamed the 'rebaptizers' because they rejected the idea of infant baptism, which was practiced by the Roman Catholic Church, as a means of saving souls, and demanded rebaptism. Severely persecuted, they eventually rallied behind Menno Simons (1496-1561) who started the group which eventually became known as the Mennonites.

John Wycliffe, a professor of Divinity at Oxford University, linked the Pope with the Antichrist. He translated the Bible from Latin to English, and produced the first English Bible in 1382, paving the way for the Reformation. He organized a group called the Order of Poor Preachers, and began distributing his new Bible. They were called 'Lollards' (or 'idle babblers'). Eventually Wycliffe's writings were banned, and the Pope ordered him to Rome to undergo trial. He died of a stroke in 1384 before he was able to go. By 1425, the Catholic Church was so upset with the increase in the number of Lollards, that they ordered Wycliffe's bones to be exhumed, and they were burned together with the 200 books he had written.

In May, 1163, at a Council in Toulouse, France, which was attended by 17 Cardinals, 124 Bishops, and hundreds of Priests from the Roman Catholic Church, the Inquisition (from the Latin verb 'inquire,' or 'to inquire into') was forged. As one speaker said: "An accursed heresy has recently arisen in the neighborhood of Toulouse, and it is the duty of the bishops to put it down with all the rigor of the ecclesiastical law." Anyone who didn't profess Catholicism was sought out, and again, Satan attempted to destroy Christianity.

In 1198, Pope Innocent III sent two Inquisitors to France with the following order: "The foxes called Waldenses, Cathari, and Patari, who, though they have different faces, yet all hang together by their tails, are sent by Satan to devastate the vineyard of the Lord," and they were "to be judged and killed." In 1200, the Pope instructed a Spanish priest named Dominique de Guzmán (1170-1221) to form an Order to vanquish all opposing religious groups. In 1215, these Dominican monks (Order of the Friar Preachers, or Black Friars), known as the 'Militia of Christ,' were dispatched to speak out against the Albigensians (a semi-Christian group prominent in France, which had Manichaean influence, as did the Cathari), who condemned the Catholic Church for worshipping images. A missionary, Peter of Castelnau, was sent to preach against the Albigensians, who killed him, and in 1208, in response to the murder, the Pope instigated a holy war against the Albigensians, and the Cathari of Toulouse, killing many.

At the Fourth Council of the Lateran in 1227, Pope Honorius III sanctioned the Inquisition, and said that all heretics should be turned over to the government, and their property confiscated. Catholics sympathetic to the views of these groups were excommunicated. The Inquisition sought to eliminate anyone who wasn't Catholic and refused to submit to the Pope. Christians were labeled as enemies of the State. Torture was used to obtain confessions and information, which was authorized by Pope Innocent IV in 1252. Christians were tortured by hoisting them in the air to dislocate their shoulders, tearing their arms out of the sockets. Other methods of torture included lacerating their backs with spikes, suffocation, pouring oil on them and setting them on fire. Female prisoners were often raped and beaten. Most, however, were killed by being burned at the stake.

The Roman Catholic Church had become so powerful, that through their control of the royalty in Europe, the Church and State had combined in an effort to make Catholicism the universal religion.

In Spain, within an eighteen year period, the Chief Inquisitor, Torquemada (1420-1498), imprisoned 97,000, and burned 10,200 to death. From Spain, the

Inquisition spread to northern Italy, southern France, Germany, the Netherlands, Mexico, Latin America, Austria, and Poland. In all, the massive campaign, which ran into the early 1800's, was believed to have claimed about 68 million victims.

In the 1500's, in order to get financing to build St. Peter's Basilica in Rome, 'indulgences' were sold. They were certificates, signed by the Pope, which pardoned sins without confession and repentance.

Martin Luther (1483-1546), who turned away from Catholicism after reading the Syrian text of the Bible from Antioch, witnessed John Tetzel (Archbishop of Mainz and Magdeburg) selling these indulgences, and compiled a list of 95 'points' against indulgences, and nailed them on a church door on October 31, 1517, in Wittenberg, Germany. Those siding with Luther were called 'Protestants' because they protested the power of the Catholic Church. This initiated an era that became known as the Reformation Period. In 1520, a Papal Bull was issued, that officially excommunicated Luther. It called for his death because of his heresy, unless his document was retracted within 60 days. He publicly burned the Order. He went on to translate the New Testament into German, and soon the Lutheran religion (derived from his last name) became the dominant religion in northern Germany.

William Tyndale (1494-1536) translated the Greek version of the New Testament into English, but Church authorities prevented him from publishing it in England, so he published it in Germany in 1525. By 1536 he finished translating the Old Testament, but before it could be printed and distributed, he was burned at the stake in Belgium as a religious heretic, by the order of King Henry VIII of England. A year later, King Henry broke away from the Catholic Church, forming the Church of England, and in 1537, authorized the Tyndale Bible to be distributed as the official Bible of the Church. His translation became the basis of the King James Version.

Soon the Catholic Church was in trouble, and in 1534, Pope Paul III instructed a Spanish priest, Ignatius de Loyola, to organize the 'Order of the Jesuits' (also known as the 'Society of Jesus') in order to oppose the Protestant movement. Loyola, as a soldier, had been maimed in battle, and while recuperating, claimed a conversion to Catholicism. He wrote a guidebook called *Spiritual Exercises* to help people get spiritually closer to Christ. On August 15, 1534, in Paris, Loyola and six other men, joined together in taking vows of poverty and chastity, and to accept any assignment requested by the Pope. The group was officially sanctioned by the Pope in 1540. The head of the Jesuits became known as the 'Black Pope.'

Those taking the Jesuit Oath swore allegiance to "his holiness, the Pope, (who) is Christ's Vice-Regent, and is the true and only head of the Catholic or Universal Church throughout the Earth." The oath contained a pledge to "make and wage relentless war, secretly or openly, against all heretics, Protestants and Liberals, as I am directed to do to extirpate and exterminate them from the face of the whole earth, and that I will spare neither sex, age, nor condition, and that I will hang, waste, boil, flay, strangle, and bury alive these infamous heretics; rip up the stomachs and wombs of their women and crush their infants' heads against the wall, in order to annihilate forever their excrable."

While the Dominicans worked publicly, the Jesuits worked secretly. They had planned the massacre of St. Bartholomew in 1572 that killed 70,000 Huguenots (French Protestants, who later established the Reformed Church of France). Carried out by Dominican monks and Roman Catholic troops, most of the French Christian leaders were killed, which practically stopped the Christian movement in France. To celebrate, the Pope ordered the Rosary said in every church to thank the Virgin Mary for victory, and had a medal struck to commemorate the occasion.

In England, Jesuit priests translated Origen's Alexandrian manuscripts into English in 1582, but the new Bible was rejected. Some researchers feel that this was the real reason behind the attack of the Spanish Armada in 1588. Spain's mighty fleet was defeated. The Jesuit movement grew, and by 1626, there were 15,000 members; and by 1749, over 22,000. It became the largest single Roman Catholic Order.

On June, 1773, Pope Clement XIV (1769-75), pressured by France, Spain, and Portugal, said that the group was "immoral and a menace to the Church and the Faith," and abolished the Order. In Germany, the government established a Commission to liquidate and inventory Jesuit assets. Councilor Zuytgens was appointed to inventory all articles at their college in Ruremonde, and to forward all documents to the government. He discovered the *Secreta Monita*, which was recorded in the "Protocol of the Transactions of the Committee Appointed in Consequence of the Suppression of the Society of Jesus in the Low Countries" which is on file in the archives in Brussels. The book contained secret instructions for the Jesuits, and its leaders, and warned against its discovery, because of people getting the wrong idea about the Order.

The Jesuits continued to operate secretly, establishing their headquarters in Russia. It is believed that they survived by joining Masonic lodges. Napoleon had Pope Plus VII (1800-23) jailed at Avignon until he agreed to reinstate the Jesuits, and at the Congress of Vienna (1814-15) the demand for their services, allegedly to "make America Catholic," led Pope Plus VII to reestablish the Order.

In 1302, Pope Boniface VIII (1294-1303) said: "We declare, affirm, and define as a truth necessary for salvation that every human being is subject to the Roman Pontiff."

Pope Leo X (1513-21) proclaimed that all human beings must be subject to the Roman Pontiff for salvation. He said: "It has served us well, this myth of Christ." He sold indulgences and ordered that heretics be burned.

In 1542, Pope Paul III (1534-50) established the Roman Inquisition to battle Protestantism in Italy. The operation was carried out by a Commission governed by six Cardinals, called the Congregation of the Inquisition. As Catholicism expanded, they concerned themselves only with maintaining religious order, and in 1908, Pope Plus X renamed them the Holy Office, and they were charged with maintaining the purity of the faith. In 1965, Pope Paul VI (1963-78) reorganized the group, and renamed it the Congregation for the Doctrine of the Faith.

Pope Pius (1846-78) said that Protestantism is "no form of Christian religion" and Pope Leo XIII (1878-1903) condemned religious freedom and Bible translations, and said that "everyone separated from the Roman Catholic Church, however unblamable in other respects, has no part in Eternal Life." He also said that he was the head of all rulers, that he was God's earthly ruler, and that the Protestants were the "enemies of the Christian name."

Pope Plus X (1903-14), when he was Archbishop of Venice, said: "The Pope is not only the representative of Jesus Christ, but he is Jesus Christ himself, hidden under the veil of flesh. Does the Pope speak? It is Jesus Christ who speaks (as reported in the *Catholic Nationale*, July 13, 1895)." As Pope, he said that the Reformation leaders were "enemies of the Cross of Christ." Pope Plus XI (1922-39) said in 1928, that the Roman Catholic Church was the only Church of Christ.

In the 1800's, the Vatican wasn't doing very well financially. Their credit was so bad that no Christian banker would help them. In 1835, James Mayer Rothschild (1792-1868) stepped in and lent them $200,000. Pope Gregory XVI (1831-46) was so grateful that he awarded the Rothschild family with a Papal decoration. Ever since then, the Rothschilds have been one of the financial agents of the Vatican. But that still wasn't enough. Properties were sold, relics of the saints were sold, a percentage of the money received at the Shrine of Lourdes was taken, annulments were sold; and they also raised money by selling straw from the Pope's bed, candles, rosaries, and images of the Madonna. They also tried to raise money in 1868 by establishing the Peter's Pence in the United States, a year after the U.S. broke off diplomatic relations with the Vatican (which were later reestablished in 1984).

For years, the Popes ruled a 16,000 square mile area in central Italy, which was referred to as the Papal States. That was reduced to about 4,891 square miles in 1860 when the Kingdom of Italy was formed. In September, 1870, Italian troops marched on Rome and ended the temporal power of the Pope, and limited his sovereignty to the palaces of the Vatican, the Lateran in Rome, and the villa of Castel Gandolfo. On February 11, 1929, Cardinal Gasparri and Italian Premier Benito Mussolini signed the Treaty of Conciliation (known as the Lateran Agreement), which established the independent state of Vatican City, and also made Catholicism the official religion of Italy. The agreement compensated the Vatican for their lost land ($40,000,000), and transferred about 5% of the government's bonds (about $50,000,000) to them. The Lateran Treaty was made part of the Italian Constitution (Article 7) in 1947.

Vatican City in Rome is the world's smallest independent country, taking in an area of nearly 109 acres. It includes St. Peters's Basilica, which covers an area of 163,200 square feet, making it the world's largest church; the Vatican Palace, which has 1,400 rooms, 200 staircases, and is the largest residence in the world; the Vatican Museum, which sits on thirteen acres, and contains the Sistine Chapel, where Michelangelo painted his "Last Judgment" on the ceiling; various buildings between Viale Vaticano and the Church; and the Vatican Gardens. Thirteen buildings outside the boundaries possess extraterritorial rights, and house people necessary for the administration of the Church. The name 'Vatican,' means 'center of divination.'

With a population of 800, about 3,000 employees, and an operating budget of over $100 million annually, the Vatican is the central administrative office of the Roman Catholic Church. Here the Pope wields executive and judicial powers over a religious empire of over 63,000,000 members in thousands of churches. They have extensive real estate holdings (they own one-third of Rome), own major companies and utilities and have controlling interests in others, possess priceless works of art, religious artifacts, and massive deposits in Italian and foreign banks (including America and Switzerland). It is rumored, that the Vatican owns 40-50% of the shares quoted on the Italian Stock Exchanges, which is worth about $5 billion.

Vatican City has their own flag, their own bank, their own license plates (numbered from 1-142), their own radio station (Radio Vatican, which reaches every country on earth with broadcasts in thirty languages), their own newspaper (*l'Osservatore Romano*), their own post office (issuing their own stamps), their own telephone system, the Institute for Religious Works (established in 1942, which provides about $10 million a year towards their budget), a pharmacy, a bar, a gas station, a train depot, and a printing plant. There are no taxes; and they issue their own passports and citizenship papers. The neutral country is protected by 100 Swiss guards, and 150 Italian police.

Despite the efforts of the Catholic Church to destroy the Holy Bible, the Scriptures survived, and in 1603, King James of England gathered 54 English scholars to assemble manuscripts to prepare a Bible. They used the Antioch manuscripts, and the Jewish Massoretic text, completing their work in 1611. The result was the King James Version of the Bible that was used by the Episcopalians in England, and the Scottish Presbyterians. Today, it is the most widely accepted version of the Scriptures in the world.

In England, two groups opposed the Church of England, because of the centralized control of the Anglican Church and their elaborate rituals: the Puritans, who wanted to try and purify it from within; and the Separatists, who felt that the Church was so corrupt, that it was beyond the possibility of reform. To escape the persecution of King James, William Bradford led many to Holland, in 1608; and in 1619, they joined a larger group in England and sailed to America on the Mayflower, where the Separatists became known as Pilgrims. They had intended to land at Virginia, but was blown off course, hundreds of miles north, where the 103 settlers floated into the peninsula of Cape Cod in Massachusetts, in November of 1620.

Some of the Pilgrim leaders became worried about the group who had come from London and Southampton, and to control their actions, 41 of them drew up plans for a civil government, based on Christian principles, which became known as the Mayflower Compact. Bradford was elected as their first Governor, and he established a system that was unlike the Jamestown colony in Virginia (who were Anglicans), which was based on the communal theories of Plato and Francis Bacon. Although half of the settlers died during the harsh winter, the success of the Plymouth colony brought an influx of others seeking religious freedom from the dominance of the Anglican Church of England. To protect their newly found freedom, their government took on the form of a theocracy, which only allowed propertied church members to vote; and there was no tolerance towards other religions.

As the population grew, the Puritans were unable to maintain their strict control, and other colonies in New England were established as a haven from those frustrated with their rigidity. Even though Puritan control was broken in the late 1600's, the New England colonies which welcomed Quakers and Jews, continued to ban Roman Catholic worship until 1783.

In 1624 the Dutch established a colony known as New Netherland, which was seized by the British in 1664, and renamed New York. Various religious groups flourished there, such as the Dutch Reformed, Swedish Lutherans, French Protestant (Huguenots), Quakers, and Jews. In 1682, responding to William Penn's (a Quaker) 'Holy Experiment,' Quakers, Scotch-Irish Presbyterians, Mennonites, and other pietists from Germany settled in Pennsylvania. Although Maryland was founded in 1634 as a Catholic colony, it was soon overwhelmed with Protestants, who dominated religion in America until the Civil War.

The World Council of Churches

In 1910, J. R. Mott, a 45-year old American Methodist minister, chaired the World Congress in Edinburgh to foster inter-church relations and to eliminate overlapping by spreading out their manpower in the missionary field. Out of that, came the Universal Christian Council of Life and Work, at Stockholm, Sweden in 1925; and the World Conference of Faith and Order, at Lausanne in 1927. Eventually, it developed into the World Council of Churches (WCC) at Amsterdam (the Netherlands) on August 23, 1948, when representatives from 147 churches in 44 countries met. The banner over the stage said: "One World-One Church."

Six co-Presidents were appointed to run the organization, including an American, G. Bromley Oxham, who was a 33rd degree Mason, and Vice-President of a communist-front organization known as the Methodist Federation for Social Action. In the 1945 book *Labor and Tomorrow's World*, he wrote: "The workers of Russia speak. They say that the American demand for life, liberty, and the pursuit of happiness can never be realized until it is complemented by the universal obligation to work in a society in which the means of production are owned by the people, and the fruits of the production go to the people..."

Another co-President, T. C. Chao, was the Dean of Yenching University's School of Religion in Peiping (known as the 'Harvard of China,' which was partially funded by the Rockefellers). When the Communists were taking over China, Chao and his students welcomed their actions, and he was later given an official position in the Red Chinese government. Josef L. Hromadka, from Prague (Czechoslovakia), a founding member of the WCC's Central Committee, was a Communist Party member, and said in a January, 1959 speech: "Communism is no embodiment of evil, no 'murder of souls' as some people in the West believe. It is our task to demonstrate that this view is mistaken. Communism has grown out of the humanitarian efforts of many philosophers and poets who desired to create a more just and happy human society."

According to its members, the WCC is a "fellowship of churches which confess the Lord Jesus Christ as God and Savior according to the Scriptures and therefore seek to fulfill together their common calling to the glory of the One God, Father, Son and Holy Spirit." However, the facts seem to point to a much different agenda. The Founding Assembly of the WCC, at their first meeting in 1948, approved and sent to its member churches, a report called, *The Church and the Disorder of Society*, which said:

> "The Christian Church should reject the ideologies of both communism and capitalism ... Communism ideology ... promise that freedom will come automatically after the completion of the revolution. Capitalism puts the emphasis on freedom and promises that justice will follow as a by-product of free enterprise. That, too, is an ideology which has been proven

false ... It is the responsibility of Christians to seek new creative solutions which never allow either justice or freedom to destroy the other."

In 1952, Dr. O. Frederick Nolde, Director of the Commission of the Churches on International Affairs, said: "Our real enemy is not the Soviet Government..." In 1966, the Central Committee of the WCC (their chief policy-making body), said than an "American victory in Vietnam would cause long-range difficulties." They "called upon the United States to halt its bombing of North Vietnam and 'review and modify' its policy of trying to contain communism." They also called for the United Nations to accept Red China as a member. In May, 1967, Dr. Martin Niemoeller, President of the WCC, was awarded the Lenin Peace Prize by Russia.

The Central Committee of the WCC, made up of 120 members, meets annually to carry out policies and decisions. The Executive Committee meets twice a year, in order to keep things going between Central Committee meetings. The entire organization meets in seven year intervals. Their avowed objective is to uphold the ecumenical movement, and to establish an all-inclusive church. The WCC is made up of liberals, evangelicals, neo-Orthodox, Armenians, Calvinists, Protestants, Lutherans, Anglicans, and Russian Orthodox. Most of the non-Roman Catholic Churches belong, and they have been extending invitations to groups such as Hindus, Buddhists, Muslims, and Jews. They have 342 member churches in 120 countries, which represent a membership of nearly 400 million Christians, and most of the world's Orthodox churches.

In October, 1979, Dr. Lukas Vischu, a Swiss Reform Minister, and Eastern Orthodox leader Dimitrios I, urged the Roman Catholic Church to merge with the WCC. An affiliated arm of the WCC, called the American Friends of the World Council of Churches was headquartered at the liberal Riverside Church in New York City, which had been pastored by Skull and Bones member Rev. William Sloane Coffin, a leader in the National Council of Churches.

In May, 1969, the WCC recommended that its churches support violence to overthrow political tyranny and "combat racism." Since then, they have been giving financial aid to nearly 46 revolutionary groups in 17 countries. Some of the groups are communist, while others had been getting arms from Russia. They gave $125,000 to the South West Africa People's Organization in Angola, $65,000 to the African National Congress in Mozambique (whose leader, Joe Slovo, was a member of the Communist Party, and a colonel in the Russian KGB), and $85,000 to Robert Mugabe's Patriotic Front. After the takeover of Zimbabwe (formerly known as Rhodesia, named after Cecil Rhodes, who took over the area in 1897), Mugabe, a well known communist terrorist, told a delegation from the WCC: "This is the moment for the forthright acknowledgment of the support from the World Council of Churches for our struggle." During the Melbourne Conference in May, 1980, three Zimbabwe delegates told the assembly: "Our hard-won victory did not come only through our own determination. We were sustained and reinforced by the support— material, oral, and spiritual— accorded to us by the World Council of Churches, and its member churches."

In 1972, they voted to increase this funding to $1,000,000. Between 1969 and 1979, this Committee, known as the Program to Combat Racism, had provided an average of $2,600,000 a year. Within a ten-year period, ending with the Vietnam

War in 1975, the WCC gave millions of dollars to the Vietcong in North Vietnam. One $500,000 grant went towards their "new economic zones." A $200,000 grant was provided to four anti-government groups in Africa. Between 1980 and 1985 the WCC gave $362,000 to African National Congress, whose leader, Nelson Mandela, who had been called a "cold-blooded communist killer," a "hard-line communist," a "Marxist," and an "unrepentant terrorist." By 1992, they had given them over $1.3 million in grants.

Dr. John C. Bennett, a member of the WCC Executive Committee (as well as a member of the National Council of Churches) said the following: "Communism is to be seen as an instrument of modernization of national unification and increasing social welfare."

The largest U.S. Church donors to the WCC had been the Presbyterian Church (USA), United Methodist, Disciples of Christ, Evangelical Lutheran Church in America, United Church of Christ, Episcopal, and the American Baptist Churches.

Other ecumenical organizations are: National Association of Evangelicals (1950), and its parent organization, the World Evangelical Fellowship (1951); the American Council of Churches (1941), and its parent organization, the International Council of Christian Churches (1948).

The National Council of Churches

The National Council of Churches of Christ in America (NCC), the American subsidiary of the WCC, is an interdenominational group founded on November 29, 1950, after fourteen interdenominational organizations merged. Actually, it was just a reorganization of the pro-communist Federal Council of Churches (FCC), that was founded in 1908 (consisting of 31 major American denominations) by Dr. Walter Rauschenbusch (a Baptist, and the leading spokesman of socialist Christianity, who called for "a new order that would rest on Christian principles of equal rights and democratic distribution of economic power.") and Dr. Harry F. Ward, a top communist. The founding document of the National Council of Churches was adopted from Ward's "The Social Creed of Churches," which said that the Church must stand for "the most equitable division of the product of industry that can ultimately be devised." This was a subtle way of advocating the communistic principle of the confiscation of private property.

In 1927, Rep. Arthur M. Free introduced a resolution in the House that identified the FCC as a "Communist organization aimed at the establishment of a state-church..." In 1936, they were identified by the Office of Naval Intelligence, as being one of the several organizations which "give aid and comfort to the Communist movement and Party," and said they were "one of the most dangerous, subversive organizations in the country." Later that year, Admiral William H. Standley, Chief of Naval Operations, publicly accused the Federal Council of Churches of collaborating with the Communists. The *Congressional Record* (December 9, 1987) quoted from an FBI report on *Soviet Active Measures in the United States*, under the section called "The Soviet Campaign to Influence Religious Organizations," which said: "It is clear ... that the Soviet Union is increasingly interested in influencing and/or manipulating American churches, religious organizations, and their leaders within the United States…" It revealed that "the campaign 'has targeted the members and leaders of a broad range of religious organizations within the United States' and uses several channels for its campaign of disinformation."

In 1933, Rev. Albert W. Beaven, a past president of the FCC (along with 44 others), wrote a letter to President Franklin Roosevelt to try to convince him to socialize America because they believed "there can be no recovery so long as the nation depends on palliative legislation inside the capitalistic system." In 1942, their platform called for "a world government, international control of all armies and navies, a universal system of money, and a democratically-controlled international bank."

Andrew Carnegie gave money to the FCC to promote his goal of "world peace through world government." From 1926 to 1929 John D. Rockefeller donated over $137,000 to the group. In 1948, the FCC received $2,959 from the Russell Sage Foundation (well known supporter of Communist causes, and Planned Parenthood), $1 million from the Henry Luce Foundation (publisher of *Time* and *Life* magazines), and $1 million from the Rockefeller Brothers Fund, as well as others.

When the Rothschilds charged Schiff with the task of undermining religion in America, Schiff delegated certain responsibilities to John D. Rockefeller, Jr. who later recruited Ward, who had taught religion at the Union Theological Seminary (which Rockefeller helped establish) in New York for 25 years. The Seminary was so liberal that it was known as the 'Red Seminary," because of how many students graduates and faculty members had ties to communist groups. Manning Johnson, a Communist Party member, referred to Ward as "the chief architect for Communist infiltration and subversion in the religious field." In 1907, Rockefeller financed Ward's establishment of the Methodist Foundation of Social Service, which was America's first Communist-front organization. This religious institution cast serious doubts as to the virgin birth and divinity of Jesus. In 1953, Ward was identified as a Communist by the House Committee on Un-American Activities. In 1908, they reorganized and changed their name to the Federal Council of Churches.

Raised as a Baptist, Rockefeller began noticing all of the competition between Protestant groups, and after World War II, got involved with the Interchurch World Movement, contributing over $1 million to its initial budget of $40 million, and traveling the country on a national speaking tour. It soon went under. Rockefeller was a well-known supporter of evangelist Billy Sunday, and forty years later, donated $75,000 to Billy Graham's New York crusade. He also donated $26 million to build the Riverside Church, which opened in 1930, which was pastored by Rev. Harry Emerson Fosdick (NCC leader, former President of the Rockefeller Foundation, who didn't believe in the deity of Christ or the virgin birth; and was the brother of Raymond Fosdick, a member of the CFR), who had formerly been the pastor at the old First Presbyterian Church at 11th Street and 5th Avenue in New York. The interdenominational church was located on Riverside Drive in Morningside Heights, a block from Columbia University, and across from the Union Theological Seminary (to whom Rockefeller contributed $1,083,333 in 1922). He was also a large contributor to the World Council of Churches.

Rockefeller provided the land (across the street from the Riverside Church, which it is connected to via an underground tunnel) for the 15-story triangular-shaped Interchurch Center (475 Riverside Drive, suite 880) that serves as the headquarters for the National Council of Churches in New York City.

The membership of the National Council of Churches of Christ in America consists of 36 Protestant, Anglican, and Orthodox denominations. They are the biggest advocate of the ecumenical movement in the country, having well over 140,000 churches, and nearly 50,000,000 members:

African Methodist Episcopal Church (2,500,000 members), 12th largest U.S. Church
African Methodist Episcopal Zion Church (1,296,662), 20th largest U.S. Church
Alliance of Baptists
American Baptist Churches in the USA (1,436,909), 18th largest U.S. Church
Antiochian Orthodox Christian Archdiocese of North America (250,000)
Diocese of the Armenian Church of America (414,000)
Christian Church/Disciples of Christ (1,011,502)
Christian Methodist Episcopal Church (718,922)
Church of the Brethren (13,132)
Coptic Orthodox Church in North America (180,000)
Episcopal Church in the USA (2,311,398), 14th largest U.S. Church
Evangelical Lutheran Church in America (5,125,919), 6th largest U.S. Church
Friends United Meeting (50,803)
Greek Orthodox Archdiocese of America (1,500,000), 15th largest U.S. Church
Hungarian Reformed Church in America (9,780)
International Council of Community Churches (500,000)
Korean Presbyterian Church in America
Malankara Orthodox Syrian Church
Mar Thoma Church
Moravian Church in America-North and South Province (50,982)
National Baptist Convention of America (3,500,000), 7th largest U.S. Church
National Baptist Convention, USA (8,200,000)
National Missionary Baptist Convention of America (2,500,000), 13th largest U.S. Church
Orthodox Church in America (1,000,000), 23rd largest U.S. Church
Patriarchal Parishes of the Russian Orthodox Church in the USA (9,780)
Philadelphia Yearly Meeting of the Religious Society of Friends
Polish National Catholic Church of America (282,411)
Presbyterian Church, USA (3,485,332), 8th largest U.S. Church
Progressive National Baptist Convention (2,500,000), 11th largest U.S. Church
Reformed Church in America (274,521)
Serbian Orthodox Church of USA and Canada (67,000)
Swedenborgian Church (2,475)

Syrian Orthodox Church of Antioch (33,000)
Ukranian Orthodox Church of America (5,000)
United Church of Christ (1,377,320), 19th largest U.S. Church
United Methodist Church (8,340,954), 3rd largest U.S. Church

In the January 1926 issue of the Masonic *New Age* magazine, members were urged to "cast his lot with the Church— to help vitalize it, liberalize it, modernize it, and render it aggressive and efficient— to do less is treason to your country, to your Creator, and to the obligation you have promised to obey." Many NCC pastors are Masons, and in the May 22, 1989 edition of *Time* magazine, Dr. Richard Mouw of the Fuller Theological Seminary in California, said that NCC member churches are teaching "magic and the occult and the New Age."

The National Council of Churches is responsible for the Revised Standard Version of the Bible. They have concerned themselves with civil liberties, social justice, and the theological critique of U.S. foreign policy, particularly in respect to China and Indo-China. The have said that the United States should become a subordinate of the United Nations. They supported the Supreme Court decision that removed prayer and Bible reading from the nation's public school system. In 1960, a Congressional Committee investigation revealed: "Thus far of the leadership of the National Council of Churches of Christ in America, we have found over 100 persons in leadership capacity with either Communist-front records or records of service to communist causes."

The Foundation for Community Organization, which has its offices in the New York headquarters of the National Council of Churches, had made grants to the Mozambique Liberation Front, and the Zimbabwe African National Union. The Church World Service (CWS), a relief and development arm of the NCC, have sent money to "groups supporting the Palestine Liberation Organization, the governments of Cuba and Vietnam, the pro-Soviet movement in Latin America, Asia, Africa, and several political fringe groups in the U.S." The Domestic Hunger Network, which is also coordinated through the NCC, gave a hefty sum to political groups throughout the world.

Hundreds of thousands of NCC dollars have been given to groups who supported the Palestine Liberation Organization; the communist and pro-Soviet governments of Cuba and Vietnam, and countries in Latin America, Asia and Africa. In 1982, $5.5 million in NCC money made its way to Communist guerillas in Zimbabwe, Naminia, Mozambique, and Angola; and in 1983, Communists in El Salvador and Nicaragua were receiving NCC funds.

In 1980, the Methodist Church donated $8 million to the NCC; the United Presbyterian Church (who merged with the Presbyterian Church USA in 1983, after being separated since 1861) gave $3 million; United Churches of Christ, $2 million; the Episcopal Church, $1 million; and the Disciples of Christ, $1 million.

In the July 15, 1968 issue of *Approach*, Gus Hall, the General Secretary of the U.S. Communist Party said that the Communist goals for America were "almost identical to those espoused by the Liberal Church. We can and we should work together for the same things." The socialist message of the NCC was emphasized even more in May, 1972, when a religious ecumenical assembly of 400 Americans met as the "Christians for Socialism." The May 4th edition of the *New York Times*, said that the newly organized group called for the purpose of achieving socialism throughout Latin America (since) socialism appears to be the only acceptable alternative for bringing an end to the exploitation of the class society."

The Support Behind Billy Graham

At a Los Angeles tent meeting in 1949, on a night when Billy Graham was deciding whether to extend or end his revival, the place was suddenly crawling with reporters and photographers. Afterwards, he was told: "You have been kissed by William Randolph Hearst." Hearst was a major newspaper publisher in the country, and also owned many magazines, including *Cosmopolitan*, *Town and Country*, *Harper's Bazaar*, and *Good Housekeeping*. From that day on, the Illuminati-controlled media supported him. Not only did Hearst write favorably about him, but he also helped finance his Crusades for the first three years.

I approached this section of the book with great trepidation, because I know how well respected Rev. Billy Graham is by many people. You may wonder how Graham, one of the country's greatest Christian leaders, could be linked to the Illuminati. Well, by now, you should understand how they work, so what better person to use, then somebody who is admired and respected by millions, even though his impact for their cause is subtle and rather indirect. Throughout his life, Graham has established relationships with people and made alliances with organizations that seem to counteract the message of salvation that he has brought to the world. For instance, he considered his relationship with Henry Luce as an "enduring friendship." Luce, the publisher of magazines like *People*, *Life*, *Time*, *Fortune*, and *Money*, was a Yale graduate, a member of the Skull and Bones and the Council on Foreign Relations.

In 1954, Secretary of State (for Pres. Eisenhower) John Foster Dulles (founding member of the Council on Foreign Relations, Chairman of Rockefeller Foundation, and very active in the Federal Council of Churches) used his influence to help Graham's 1954 Crusade in London, England. Through the Federal Council of Churches, Dulles was chairman for their Commission on a Just and Durable Peace who issued a report calling for a "world government."

In 1957, the Protestant Council of New York, affiliated with the NCC, invited Graham to speak at Madison Square Garden in New York. John D. Rockefeller donated $75,000 to the Crusade, and then afterwards, Graham donated $67,618 to the Protestant Council.

In 1959 at the San Francisco Crusade, and in 1960 at the Detroit Crusade, Graham invited Bishop James A. Pike to the platform to pray. Pike, a member of the Episcopal Church, was very vocal on his denial of the virgin birth, the Trinity, and salvation solely through Christ. In the November, 1960 issue of *Pacific Churchman*, Pike said that anyone who opposed Communism was doing the bidding of hell. After his oldest son committed suicide in 1966, Pike began to consult with various mediums to try to contact him. In 1969 when he died, *Newsweek* even declared that he had "rejected orthodox Christianity."

In 1959, Martin Luther King delivered the opening prayer at one of Graham's

Crusades, and in a 1963 interview with the *New York Times* said that King was his "good personal friend." As discussed in Chapter Four, King was a known communist. In addition to his adulterous behavior, he denied the virgin birth and resurrection of Christ. In a 1961 interview for *Ebony* magazine he said: "I do not believe in hell as a place of a literal burning fire."

In fact, Graham's views in that regard also underwent a metamorphosis. In the July, 1978, issue of *McCall's* magazine he said: "I used to think that pagans in far-off countries were lost— were going to hell— if they did not have the Gospel of Jesus Christ preached to them. I no longer believe that ... I believe there are other ways of recognizing the existence of God— through nature, for instance— and plenty of other opportunities, therefore, of saying yes to God." He elaborated in the book *A Prophet With Honor* by saying that he "did not automatically consign to hell all who never heard the Christian gospel preached."

In an interview in the April 10, 1983 *Orlando Sentinel*, Graham said in response to why many Americans didn't accept the concept of hell: "I think that hell essentially is separation from God forever. And that is the worst hell that I can think of. But I think people have a hard time believing God is going to allow people to burn in a literal fire forever." In a July, 1983 book written by Graham for distribution at his International Conference for Itinerant Evangelists in Amsterdam, he said:

> "Hell is not the most popular of preaching topics. I don't like to preach on it. But I must if I am to proclaim the whole counsel of God. We must not avoid warning of it. The most outspoken messages on hell, and the most graphic references to it, came from Jesus Himself ... Jesus used three words to describe hell ... The third word that He used is 'fire.' Jesus used this symbol over and over. This could be a literal fire, as many believe. Or it could be symbolic ... I've often thought that this could possibly be a burning thirst for God that is never quenched. What a terrible fire that would be— never to find satisfaction, joy or fulfillment."

In the November 15, 1993 edition of *Time* magazine, he is quoted as saying: "When it comes to a literal fire, I don't preach it because I'm not sure about it." And finally, in a television interview in England he said: "I do not believe in a literal hell now."

Tom Allen, a socialist from Scotland, who is a friend of Graham, said that "Billy Graham has one of the most acute and social consciences of any man I ever met."

Billy Graham has been the personal friend and confidant of every President since Eisenhower. Apparently Billy's 'bar' was not raised too high, because he saw our country's leaders (as well as other political leaders) as Christians, yet their fruit did not bear that out. Even though he was a Democrat, in 1960, he wrote an article for *Life* magazine to endorse Richard Nixon's presidential candidacy, who was his "closest friend in the political world." Henry Luce refused to publish it because of pressure from the Kennedy camp.

He described President Johnson as a man whose "spiritual roots are deep in Texas," and "a man reared in deep religious faith that has prevailed in this Southwest country since the beginning."

Graham said that "Nixon held such noble standards of ethics and morality for the nation," and also said that he had "given moral and spiritual leadership to the nation at a time when we desperately need it…" He claimed that Nixon had a "deep personal faith in God … Although he doesn't flaunt his faith publicly, I know him to be a deeply religious man." When Nixon was the recipient of quite a backlash from the American people for planning a trip to Red China, Billy Graham flew to Washington, DC, and called a meeting at the White House of leading ministers from across the country. Both he and Henry Kissinger were able to convince them that the trip to Communist China was necessary. At his May, 1968 Crusade, he said that there was "no American I admire more than Richard Nixon."

He wrote about President Ford (a Mason, and member of the CFR): "I knew him to be a professing Christian, and we had several times of prayer together. He was always warm, friendly, and outgoing to me … A lot of us Christians saw him as a spiritual leader as well as a political one."

In an interview with the *U.S. News and World Report* on May 3, 1993 he said about President Bill Clinton (pro-gay, pro-abortion, and adulterer): "I am quite impressed with his charisma and with some of the things he believes. If he chose to preach the gospel instead of politics, he would make a great evangelist." His autobiography *Just As I Am* talks about being with Clinton on May 1, 1996, and said: "It was a time of warm fellowship with a man who has not always won the approval of his fellow Christians but who has in his heart a desire to serve God and do His will." At a luncheon for 500 newspaper editors during their annual convention in Washington, D.C., Graham said that Clinton's personal life and character were "irrelevant" and referred to him as a "man of God." He said: "I believe Bill has gone to his knees many times and asked God to help him."

There was a time (as reported by *Parade* magazine on February 1, 1981), when Graham said: "Communism is inspired, directed, and motivated by the devil himself. America is at a crossroad. Will we turn to the left-wingers and atheists, or will we turn to the right and embrace the Cross?" There was a time when he called the communists, "satan worshipers," and said in 1954: "Either Communism must die, or Christianity must die, because it is actually a battle between Christ and the Antichrist."

In May 28, 1973, the *Mainichi Daily News*, in Tokyo, Japan, quoted Graham as saying:

> "I think communisms' appeal to youth is its structure and promise of a future utopia. Mao Tse-tung's (China's communist leader) eight precepts are basically the same as the Ten Commandments. In fact, if we can't have the Ten Commandments read in our schools, I'll settle for Mao's precepts."

In 1977, on a trip to Hungary, a Communist country, a deceived Graham talked about the "religious freedom" there. In May, 1982, Graham was invited to speak at the World Conference of Religious Workers for Saving the Sacred Gift of Life from Nuclear Catastrophe (which was attended by 600 clergymen from around the world), which was sponsored by the Russian Orthodox Church. The Reagan Administration tried to convince him not to go fearing that he would become a victim of communist propaganda. While he was there, he said that he didn't see any evidence of religious repression, and said: "There are differences, of course, in religion as it is practiced here and, let's say, in the U.S. But that doesn't mean there is no religious freedom." That was hardly an accurate statement concerning the religious status of the Soviet Union, an atheistic country, who at the time was still dominated by Communism, and persecuted those who worshipped God.

When he returned to America, Graham was asked if his views towards communism had changed, and he said: "I've changed a little at this point, but I am not a pro-Communist." In Franklin Graham's book *Rebel With a Cause*, he said that on one particular trip to Russia, Soviet government officials completely controlled his schedule, "but never hindered his preaching ... (because) Daddy never spoke against Communism in his sermons."

In 1957, Graham was quoted as saying that Catholicism was "a stench in the nostrils of God," yet leaders in his own organization, the Billy Graham Evangelistic Association, have tried to assure supporters that Billy is not catering to the Catholic Church.

In the early 1950's, Cardinal Richard Cushing, the Archbishop of Boston, said that "if he had half a dozen Billy Grahams, he would not worry about the future of his Church." After meeting with him in 1964, Cushing said: "I am 100% for the evangelist. I have never known a religious crusade that was more effective than Dr. Graham's. I have never heard the slightest criticism of anything he has ever said from a Catholic source." In response, Graham said: "I feel much closer to Roman Catholic tradition than to some of the more liberal Protestants…" In 1966, he said: "I find myself closer to Catholics than the radical Protestants." In 1978, Billy said: "I found that my beliefs are essentially the same as those of orthodox Catholics."

When Billy was in Poland in 1978, he praised the "greatness" of Pope Paul VI, even though leaders of his own church criticized him for catering to Communists. Pope Paul was the first Pope to visit the West, and the first place he went was the United Nations, where he gave a speech on October 4, 1965, and then was taken to the Meditation Room.

Graham admitted to being an admirer of Pope John II, and said on the Phil Donahue Show in 1979:

"I think the American people are looking for a leader, a moral spiritual leader that believes something. And he does. He didn't mince words on a single subject. As a matter of fact, his subject in Boston was really an evangelical address in which he asked the people to come to Christ, to give their lives to Christ. I said, 'Thank God I've got somebody to quote now with some real authority'."

Graham has called Pope John a "great evangelist," the "greatest religious leader of the modern world and one of the greatest moral and spiritual leaders of this century." Another time, he said that the Pope was "God's instrument for revival in our generation." In 1994 when *Time* magazine declared Pope John as its "Man of the Year," Graham said: "He'll go down in history as the greatest of our modern popes ... He's been the strong conscience of the whole Christian world." In an interview with Associated Press reporter Richard Ostling, he said he would choose Pope John as the 'Man of the Century,' because he admired "his courage, determination, intellectual abilities and his understanding of Catholic, Protestant and Orthodox differences, and the attempt at some form of reconciliation." He even wrote the Foreword to the book *Pope John Paul II: A Tribute.*

The *Pittsburgh Sun-Telegraph* quoted an insider as saying: "Many of the people who reached a decision for Christ at our meetings (1952 Pittsburgh Crusade) have joined the Catholic Church ... This happened both in Boston and Washington. After all, one of our prime purposes is to help the churches in the community..." As early as 1956, Graham said that he was going to "send them to their own churches— Roman Catholic, Protestant or Jewish ... The rest will be up to God." He has said: "My goal, I always made clear, was not to preach against Catholic beliefs or to proselytize people who were already committed to Christ within the Catholic Church."

When a Crusade is planned, a Committee is brought together, made up of leaders from local churches. Within that group is an Executive Committee. Whenever someone walks down the aisle to receive Salvation, the decision card is given to these leaders, and their respective churches. For instance, the Committee for the 1957 New York Crusade consisted of around 120 modernists (those denying the virgin birth, Christ's resurrection, the divine inspiration of Scripture, and the existence of a literal heaven and hell), and 20 fundamentalists. The June 19, 1969 issue of the *New York Times* outlined his follow-up procedure:

> "After inquirers are dealt with by 'counselors' and cards on each are filled out, a 'Co-Labor Corps' sits at long tables until midnight each night counting and sorting the cards and licking envelopes that will go out in the morning mail to ministers of about 1,000 churches ... The 'Corps' sifts through maps and phone books, finding the church nearest the addresses on the cards, regardless of whether or not they are liberal, conservative, Protestant, Catholic or Jewish..."

When he spoke at Notre Dame University (a Catholic institution) in 1977, and gave the 'invitation,' he said: "Many of you want to come tonight and reconfirm your confirmation. You want to reconfirm the decision that you made when you joined the church." Nothing was ever said about the sacrificial death of Jesus on the Cross, or about the repenting of their sins. He even reassured them that his purpose was not to get them to leave the Church to join another denomination.

In 1979, nearly 3,500 decision cards were given to the Catholic Church. The *Florida Catholic* indicated that in 1983, the decision cards for 600 people from the Orlando crusade were given to the Catholic Church. About 500 names from his 1987 Denver Crusade were given to the St. Thomas Moore Roman Catholic Church. Graeme Keith, who was the chairman of the Charlotte (North Carolina) Billy Graham Crusade Committee, told the *Charlotte Observer* (March 1, 1996): "We have Jewish, Catholic, Protestant and other denominations represented on the committee..." At this Crusade, the decision cards of nearly 1700 people answering the altar call were given to the Catholic Diocese in the area.

In one of his 'My Answer' columns, in response to a Roman Catholic who was writing in regard to some of the changes going on in the Catholic Church, Graham responded by telling him not to "pull out of the church! Stay in it, stay close to the Lord, and use these experiences as an opportunity to help your church be what God intends..." Likewise, the counselors at his Crusades are warned not to criticize the church or religious affiliation of any of the people who come forward for Salvation.

Despite all of the evidence to the contrary, Graham's people have denied any sort of theological wrongdoing. In 1964, an assistant to Graham, George Edstrom, wrote: "Mr. Graham has never preached in a Catholic Church, and he does not agree with them in the joining of one church. If you heard this, it is nothing but false rumors." However, in 1963, he did speak at the Roman Catholic Belmont Abbey in North Carolina. Robert Ferm, a member of his team, on many occasions, has informed the faithful that Graham would "never compromise the gospel by consorting with Catholics," yet Ferm was the one who spoke to the students and faculty before the Crusade at Notre Dame (1977). In the early 1990's, a retired missionary wrote the BGEA to find out why he was sending new converts to the Catholic Church. The response from T.W. Wilson was: "I do not know where you got your information— but I'm sure you have been misinformed." As you have seen, he not only has sent converts to Catholic Churches, but also to other churches who do not believe in a literal interpretation of the Bible.

Billy Graham attended the initial assembly of the World Council of Churches as an observer, as well as later meetings, eventually becoming a speaker. In 1960 he attended the National Council of Churches' 50th anniversary celebration in San Francisco, where he was a guest speaker.

Graham had said that one of his best friends is Jessie Bader, who was the Secretary of Evangelism for the National Council of Churches. In a speech to the NCC he said: "My wife is a Presbyterian. Her denomination is in the National Council so perhaps I am here by marriage." In another speech on August 27, 1991 he said:

> "There's no group of people in the world that I would rather be with right now than you all. Because I think of you, I pray for you, and we follow with great interest the things you do ... I don't speak to too many church assemblies any more because I consider myself as belonging to all the churches. And I love everybody equally and I have no problem in fellowship with anybody who says that Jesus Christ is Lord. This has been a great relief to me to come to that conclusion about 20 some years ago."

On April 21, 1972, Billy Graham was given the International Franciscan Award by the Franciscan friars for his "contribution to true ecumenism," and "his sincere and authentic evangelism..." He told the *U.S. News & World Report*: "World travel and getting to know clergy of all denominations has helped mold me into an ecumenical being. We're separated by theology and, in some instances, culture and race, but all of that means nothing to me any more." Even though he is a Baptist, President Bush invited him to lead various prayers at the 1989 inauguration. Graham wrote: "I protested at first, pointing out that it was customary to have clergy from other traditions participate also (often a Jewish rabbi, a Catholic priest, and perhaps an Orthodox leader). He remained adamant, however, saying he felt more comfortable with me; besides, he added, he didn't want people to think he was just trying to play politics by having representatives of different faiths." In 1992 *The Oregonian* quoted Graham in a Portland, Oregon press conference as calling for "one merged church." As you can see, the Rev. Billy Graham is recognized as an ecumenical leader in the Christian community.

Graham has long been a supporter of the United Nations. In his biography *Just As I Am* he talks about his relationship with Dag Hammarskjold, the second UN Secretary-General:

> "In the 1950's, when I was in New York City, I would occasionally slip by to visit Dag Hammarskjold, secretary-general of the United Nations, and have prayer with him. He was a very thoughtful, if lonely, man who was trying to make a difference for world peace, in large part because of his Christian convictions."

If you remember, it was Dag, the Swedish Socialist (who openly advocated communist policies), who designed the Satanic Meditation Room in the UN building. Dag was also a speaker at the 1954 World Council of Churches meeting.

In 1990, Graham received the World Citizen Award from the World Affairs Council (which is associated with the Council on Foreign Relations) for "promoting and fostering international understanding and world peace." When President George H. W. Bush made the decision to engage our country in the Persian Gulf War, he requested that Graham come to Washington. In the ensuing sermon, he said: "Perhaps, out of this war will come a new peace and— as been stated by the President— a New World Order."

Rev. Graham has allowed his message to be watered-down, and in order to maintain his stature as a national leader, has turned a blind eye to sin. He has shown support for churches that are clearly in conflict with Biblical teaching; and he has ignored Scripture like 2 Corinthians 6:17, which says, "Wherefore come out from among them, and be ye separate," in order to promote a unified Christian Church, and even one-world government. Could the guilt of all of this have contributed to the statement he made on January 2, 2000, in an interview with Fox News' Tony Snow, when he said: "I'm not a righteous man. People put me up on a pedestal that I don't belong in my personal life. And they think that I'm better than I am. I'm not the good man that people think I am. Newspapers and magazines and television have made me out to be a saint, I'm not. I'm not a Mother Teresa. And I feel that very much."

Ecumenical Movement of the Catholic Church

The Pope, leader of the Catholic Church, has been referred to as His Holiness, Holy Father, Vicar of Christ, Head of the Church, Father of Princes and Kings, Father of All Christians, Supreme Teacher of the Universal Church, Supreme Pontiff of the Universal Church, Viceroy of Jesus Christ, Bishop of Rome, and Rector of the World upon Earth. When he is elected, he is crowned with a triple tiara, which, according to the *Catholic Dictionary* signifies the following:

> "...first circlet symbolizes the Pope's universal episcopate, the second his supremacy of jurisdiction, and third his temporal supremacy. It is placed on his head at his coronation by the second cardinal deacon, with the words, 'Receive the tiara adorned with three crowns and know that thou art Father of princes and kings, Ruler of the World, Vicar of our Saviour Jesus Christ' ... The triple crown the Pope wears symbolizes his authority in heaven, on earth, and in the underworld— as king of heaven, king of earth, and king of hell— in that through his absolutions [pardons] souls are admitted to heaven, on the earth he attempts to exercise political as well as spiritual power, and through his special jurisdiction over the soul's in purgatory and his exercise of 'the power of the keys' he can release whatever souls he pleases from further suffering and those whom he refuses to release are continued in their suffering, the decisions he makes on earth being ratified in heaven..."

On the fish-shaped hat worn by the Pope are the words "Vicarirs Feleii Dei" which indicates that he is a "substitute for the Son of God."

In 1864, the position of the Catholic Church in regard to unity with other groups was: "Of course, nothing is more important for a Catholic than that schisms and dissensions among Christians be radically abolished and that all Christians be united ... But under no circumstances can it be tolerated that faithful Christians and ecclesiastics be under the leadership of heretics (non-Catholic)..."

Pope Pius XI (1922-39) said: "The Apostolic See has never allowed Catholics to attend meetings of non-Catholics; the union of Christians can only go forward by encouraging the dissidents to return to the one true church."

Pope John XX III (1958-63) wrote: "When we have realized this enormous task (ecumenism), eliminating what, from a human point of view, would be an obstacle, on a path we seek to make more easy, we shall present the church in all her splendor, without spot or wrinkle, and we shall say to all the others who are separated from us, Orthodox, Protestants, etc.: 'See brothers, here is the Church of Christ! We have done our best to be true to her'."

His Papal Encyclical *Pacem in Terris*, was a bit more radical as it "called for world government, disarmament and socialism," and was compared to the program advocated by Communism.

On October 11, 1962, Pope John held the first Ecumenical Council at St. Peter's Basilica in Rome to modernize the Church. Over 2,700 gathered, including the entire Roman Catholic hierarchy, 28 non-Catholic prelates, representatives from most major Protestant denominations, and dignitaries from Eastern Orthodox Churches in the Middle East. A few months after the initial meeting, the Council reconvened with 2,500 ecclesiastical dignitaries, and 50 observers from non-Catholic denominations. After Pope John died, Billy Graham said at a press conference in Bonn, Germany: "Pope John brought an entirely new era to the world. It would be a great tragedy if the cardinals elect a Pope who would react against the policies of Pope John and bring back the walls between Christian faiths."

A year later, on September 29, 1963, Pope Paul VI (1963-78) made an appeal for Christian unity, and said that the Ecumenical Council's ultimate goal was the universal union of all Christians. He wrote:

> "The restoration of unity among all Christians is one of the principal concerns of the Second Vatican Council. Christ the Lord founded one Church and one Church only ... For it is only through Christ's Catholic Church, which is 'the all-embracing means of salvation,' that they can benefit fully from the means of salvation..."

On March 26, 1967, Pope Paul wrote:

> "Who can fail to see the need and importance of thus gradually coming to the establishment of a world authority capable of taking effective action on the juridical and political planes? ... Delegates to international organizations, public officials, gentlemen of the press, teachers and educators— all of you must realize that you have your part to play in the construction of a new world order."

One observation that was made about him was that he was elected in the 6th year of the previous Pope's reign, in the sixth month (June), he was 66 years old, and he had completed four sets of 66 Popes. There had been talk of a merger with the World Council of Churches, to form the Christian Catholic Church of the United Church of Christ, and Pope Paul even contributed $10,000 to the WCC's Faith and Order Commission. He wrote a Papal Encyclical that "called on the nations to abandon sovereignty to form a world government."

From October 24 to 28, 1999, Pope John Paul II (1978-) held an interfaith meeting at the Vatican that included Jews, Hindus, Muslims, Buddhists, Shintoists, as well as representatives from Orthodox, Anglican, Lutheran, and evangelical churches. The Dalai Lama, a Buddhist, Tibet's exiled spiritual leader, who Pope John called "a great spiritual leader," was invited on stage as the Pope spoke to the gathering.

On September 5, 2000, the Catholic Church issued a document called *Dominus Iesus* which declared "the Roman Catholic Church to be the only 'instrument for the salvation of all humanity'." Pope John Paul II said that "Rome must always be the center of all Christianity and the pope must be the head."

For two years, a group of eight Protestants, led by Charles Colson, the former Nixon aide (echoing sentiments expressed in his book *The Body*), and seven Roman Catholics, led by Father Richard John Neuhaus (former Lutheran, who denies the virgin birth of Christ, his miracles, and his resurrection), worked on an 25-page, 8000-word document known as "Evangelicals and Catholics Together: The Christian Mission in the Third Millennium." (or ECT) It calls for Protestants and Catholics to discontinue their opposition in order to unite against enemies which are common to both of their religious philosophies. In the November, 1994, issue of *Christianity Today* (the magazine started by Billy Graham), an editorial by Colson was titled "Why Catholics Are Our Allies." This seems to be part of a campaign to bring the two religions closer together in ideology. Since accepting the "Prize for Progress in Religion" (which included a $1 million gift), from New Age leader John Templeton, at the 1993 Parliament of World's Religions in Chicago; and revelations of a United Nations connection to his Prison Fellowship ministry, Colson's motivations are highly suspect.

In addition to many Roman Catholic leaders, some major Protestant leaders have signed this agreement, including Pat Robertson (700 Club), Bill Seiple (World Vision), Bill Bright (Campus Crusade for Christ), J. I. Packer (a Senior Editor at *Christianity Today* magazine), Larry Lewis (Home Missions Board of the Southern Baptist Convention), and Richard Land (Christian Life Commission of the Southern Baptist Church).

Needless to say, the agreement came under heavy fire from many Evangelicals, and on January 19, 1995, Colson, Bright, and Packer met with some of the ECT critics at the Coral Ridge Presbyterian Church in Fort Lauderdale, Florida, in a conciliatory meeting which including its pastor D. James Kennedy, John MacArthur (pastor of the Grace Community Church in Sun Valley, CA), R. C. Sproul (Lignonier Ministries), and John Ankerberg (evangelist). Though the two groups were able to hammer out a five-point statement to clarify the support of those Evangelical leaders that signed the agreement, it still retained the aura of religious unity. A Catholic signer, Keith Fournier (author of *Evangelical Catholics* and *A House United: Evangelicals and Catholics Together*), praised the results of the meeting, and said that it represented the "true spirit of ecumenism."

Besides signing the agreement, Pat Robertson had Colson on his show, and brought in Neuhaus to be a keynote speaker at the Christian Coalition's (700 Club's political action group) "1994— Road to Victory Conference" held in Virginia Beach, Virginia. Also in 1994, Pat Robertson presented the Christian Coalition's "Catholic Layman of the Year" Award to Pennsylvania Governor Robert P. Casey, a Democrat who was very vocal in his stand against abortion. Pat Robertson, in the eyes of some Christians, lost credibility, when he entered the 1992 Presidential campaign, saying God told him to run. Though he didn't win, it gave him more political clout and visibility in the Christian community, garnering some of the attention that had previously been bestowed on Billy Graham. Even though he had written a book about the New World Order; as a guest on Larry King's national radio show, he refused to comment on a caller's question about an element of the New World Order. In December, 2003, while I was in the process of reediting this book, on the "Bring It On" segment of his broadcast, he answered a viewers question about the NWO by saying that it wasn't possible for one group to be able to have enough influence to control the affairs of the world. I can't say 'amen' to that, just 'oh my.'

In Pat Robertson's book, *The New Millennium*, published in 1990 by Word Publishing, at the top of every page, to the right of the page number, is the symbol of a circle with a dot in the middle. An unusual symbol, it is used as an astronomical symbol for the sun; and for proofreaders, it is used to indicate a place where a comma should be inserted; and it is sometimes used as a mathematical sign for a circle. However, none of these applications seemed appropriate in this instance. There is one more use for this symbol. According to documents discovered by the German government in 1785, it was the secret symbol which represented the Illuminati's name.

I contacted Word Publishing to ask them about the use of the symbol, since I didn't want to be accused of making an irresponsible accusation. They told me that various symbols, called "dingbats," are sometimes incorporated into the header design of a page. In this case, the symbol was randomly chosen, and nobody at Word was even aware of the symbol's connotations. I had even considered that perhaps the symbol was used to sabotage the book, but Word maintains that everyone there is a committed Christian. If it was randomly chosen, it would really be a coincidence, because there are no other symbols that I know of, that would lend itself to having any connections with the New World Order. Without a doubt, this book is a companion volume to Robertson's *The New World Order* published by Word in 1991.

Because I personally like Pat, and have nothing but respect for him, I guess we have to chalk it up as being an amazing coincidence. However, what I can not ignore is the disturbing trend towards tolerance and coexistence that is succeeding to bring us closer to a united Church, which he, and others, seems to advocate.

One night, I caught Jack van Impe on his show, saying that he agreed with the Pope on almost every issue. Now here is a man who has done a tremendous amount of prophetic research, and yet by condoning the Catholic Church, he is contributing to the ecumenical movement. Paul Crouch of the Trinity Broadcasting Network has said: "I'm eradicating the word Protestant even out of my vocabulary ... I (am) not protesting anything ... (it's) time for Catholics and non-Catholics to come together as one in the Spirit and one in the Lord." Robert Schuller (called the Norman Vincent Peale of the West Coast), who is known to be accepting of Islam, New Age and other cult groups, and has met with the Pope four times, has said: "It's time for Protestants to go to the shepherd (or the Pope) and say, What do we have to do to come home?"

It seems inevitable that sometime in the near future, the last remaining obstacles to a merger between the Roman Catholic Church and the World Council of Churches, into a World Church, will take place, and will contribute to the influence exercised by the New World Order.

The Development of the One-World Church

> *"For false Christs and false prophets shall rise, and shall shew signs and wonders, to seduce, if it were possible, even the elect."*
> (Mark 13:22)

> *"For such are false apostles, deceitful workers, transforming themselves into the apostles of Christ."*
> (2 Corinthians 11:13)

The Bible talks about a religious leader who will come to power, and join forces with the political leader who will rise out of western Europe.

FINAL WARNING

"And I beheld another beast coming up out of the earth; and he had two horns like a lamb, and he spake as a dragon. And he exerciseth all the power of the first beast before him, and causeth the earth and them which dwell therein to worship the first beast, whose deadly wound was healed. And he doeth great wonders, so that he maketh fire come down from heaven on the earth in the sight of men, And deceiveth them that dwell on the earth, by the means of those miracles he had power to do in the sight of the beast; saying to them that dwell on the earth, that they should make an image to the beast, which had the wound by a sword, and did live. And he had power to give life unto the image of the beast, that the image of the beast should both speak, and cause that as many as would not worship the image of the beast should be killed." (Revelation 13:11-15)

The identity of this individual, who has been labeled— the False Prophet, has been the subject of much speculation. However, I think there are some clues as to who this person may be. Matthew 24:26 says: "Wherefore if they shall say unto you, Behold, he is in the desert (Mohammedanism); go not forth: behold, he is in the secret chambers (the Vatican); believe it not." The Catholic Ecclesiastical Dictionary states: "The Pope is not simply a man, but, as it were, God." In light of what has been discussed earlier about the development of a World Church, there seems to be quite a few things which point to the Pope being the leader of this World Church, and perhaps the one who will be known as the False Prophet.

A resolution passed at a Vatican Council, called for the placing of the Pope "on the throne of the world." The Pope is known as the 'Supreme Pontiff of the Universal Church,' as well as a host of other titles mentioned earlier; and in Revelation 17:9, it mentions that the seat of the Antichrist will be in the 'seven mountains'; and Rome, which was built on seven mountains, is known as the 'seven-hilled city.' Rome, the seat of world power in the ancient world, is also the home of the Vatican, which is recognized as an independent government apart from the Italian government. The Pope is literally a god to the Catholic Church, having the authority to forgive sins. Dave Hunt, in his exposé, *A Woman Rides the Beast*, analyzed the title, 'Vicar of Christ,' and he found that the word 'Vicar' comes from the Latin 'vicarius' which means 'anti' (or to be more precise, 'alternate' or 'substitute,' which is in line with what was discussed earlier), which leads to the literal translation of 'Vicar of Christ, as 'Antichrist.'

According to Revelation 17:3-4, the color of the False Prophet will be "scarlet" (red). The primary color of the papacy which is red is said to signify the blood of Jesus. The color has also been associated with Communism and Satanism. It was alleged that Pope Benedict IX (1032-45, 1047-48) practiced sorcery and magic; Pope Boniface VIII (1294-1303) was said to communicate with demons; and it was believed that Pope Sylvester II (999-1003) and Pope Sixtus V (1585-90) were also involved with sorcery. All of these clues could indicate that the False Prophet could be a Pope.

Some researchers indicate that the False Prophet may be Jewish, but that still doesn't rule out the Vatican connection. In 1130, Anacletus II was elected as the

Pope. His great-grandfather was Baruch, a successful Jewish businessman who served as an advisor to Pope Benedict IX. Benedict requested that he convert to Catholicism, which Baruch did, changing his name to that of the Pope. The name 'Benedict' is Latin for 'blessed,' while the name 'Baruch' is Hebrew for the same thing. The conversion was in name only, because Baruch still financed a synagogue in the Jewish quarter of Rome.

Baruch's son, an aide to Pope Leo IX (1049-55), also converted, changing his name to Lee. Lee's son, Petrus Leonis, was the first to use the name Pierleone. His family became an established financial power in the late 11th century, and became active in the affairs of the Catholic Church. His son, Pietro, was sent to a monastery where he worked his way up, attaining the position of cardinal.

When Pope Honorius II (1124-30) was on his deathbed, preparations were made to elect a new Pope. The Pierleone family offered their son, the cardinal; while the Frangipani family, a traditional Catholic family, offered its own candidate. The Frangipani hid the Pope, and after he died in 1130, convened a portion of the cardinals to elect their choice, who adopted the name Innocent II (1130-43). The Pierleone family held an election the same day, with a greater number of cardinals present, and elected Pietro, who took the name Anacletus II (1130-38). Rome sided with Anacletus, and Innocent II fled to France, then later traveled around Europe, accusing Anacletus of being an 'anti-pope.' Despite efforts to remove him, Anacletus remained Pope till he died in 1138. A year later, Innocent II returned, and after Victor IV resigned (also considered to be an anti-pope), was elected, and served till his death in 1143. The Vatican now refers to Anacletus II as an 'anti-pope' ("one who uncanonically claims or exercises the office of the Roman Pontiff"), and has eliminated him from papal history.

Two other Popes were also members of the Jewish Pierleone family: Gregory VI (1045-46) and Gregory VII (1073-86, known as 'Hildebrand,' who was a descendant of a daughter of Lee, and was later made a saint).

On May 13, 1917, Lucia dos Santos and her cousins Jacinta and Francisco Marta, who were tending their sheep near Cova da Iria, saw their first of 6 visions of the Virgin Mary in the hilly terrain of Fatima, Portugal. A series of others followed on the same day every month till October. Mary gave three prophecies concerning the end of World War I, World War II, and Russia. One prophecy said that when an unknown light was seen in the sky, it would be a sign from God that he would punish the world through war, persecution, and famine. On the day of Mary's sixth appearance, October 13, she had promised a miracle. Over 70,000 people showed up in the pouring rain to observe the event. In a ten-minute display, the sun came up, spun in the sky, plunged downward, then rose again. The crowd, as well as the ground, were dried.

Lucia later became a Carmelite nun in Coimbra, Portugal, and in 1927 reported that Jesus had appeared to her and made several prophecies.

This is the text of the first two prophecies in 1917—

> "The first part is the vision of hell. Our Lady showed us a great sea of fire which seemed to be under the earth. Plunged in this fire were demons and

souls in human form, like transparent burning embers, all blackened or burnished bronze, floating about in the conflagration, now raised into the air by the flames that issued from within themselves together with great clouds of smoke, now falling back on every side like sparks in a huge fire, without weight or equilibrium, and amid shrieks and groans of pain and despair, which horrified us and made us tremble with fear. The demons could be distinguished by their terrifying and repulsive likeness to frightful and unknown animals, all black and transparent. This vision lasted but an instant. How can we ever be grateful enough to our kind heavenly Mother, who had already prepared us by promising, in the first Apparition, to take us to heaven. Otherwise, I think we would have died of fear and terror."

"We then looked up at Our Lady, who said to us so kindly and so sadly: 'You have seen hell where the souls of poor sinners go. To save them, God wishes to establish in the world devotion to my Immaculate Heart. If what I say to you is done, many souls will be saved and there will be peace. The war is going to end: but if people do not cease offending God, a worse one will break out during the Pontificate of Pius XI. When you see a night illumined by an unknown light, know that this is the great sign given you by God that he is about to punish the world for its crimes, by means of war, famine, and persecutions of the Church and of the Holy Father. To prevent this, I shall come to ask for the consecration of Russia to my Immaculate Heart, and the Communion of reparation on the First Saturdays. If my requests are heeded, Russia will be converted, and there will be peace; if not, she will spread her errors throughout the world, causing wars and persecutions of the Church. The good will be martyred; the Holy Father will have much to suffer; various nations will be annihilated. In the end, my Immaculate Heart will triumph. The Holy Father will consecrate Russia to me, and she shall be converted, and a period of peace will be granted to the world'."

Mary had asked that her last prophecy be kept secret until 1960 (when, incidentally, John F. Kennedy, the first Roman Catholic President took office). In 1944, after recuperating from a grave illness, she was instructed to write the prophecy down. It was, and it was then sealed and given to the Bishop of Portugal, and it became known as the "Third Secret." It was hand-delivered to the Vatican on April 4, 1957, and kept in the Secret Archive.

When Pope John XXIII read the prophecy, on August 17, 1959, it was said that he was visibly shaken, and he wouldn't reveal its contents, because he said that it didn't "concern our time." Likewise on March 27, 1965, Pope Paul VI read it, and decided not to publish it. Many believed it had to do with Armageddon, and in recent years, various people have become privy to the words written in Lucia's letter, which contained the third prophecy. After the assassination attempt against him, Pope John Paul decided to read it on July 18, 1981. Yet, it still was not released until May 13, 2000.

It was reported that the prophecy indicated that the world was to be punished for disobeying the laws of God and turning away from Him. When the prophecy was unsealed by the Pope in 1960, it was to be published so that the whole world would know about it; and then the country of Russia was to be consecrated to Mary by the Pope and all the bishops. If these two things were done, the wrath of God would not fall upon the Earth. It wasn't done, therefore the country of Russia was to become the instrument of God's punishment upon the nations.

In 1957, Cardinal Ottaviani, in referring to the prophecy, said it had to be buried "in the most hidden, the deepest, the most obscure and inaccessible place on earth." In 1978, John Paul II said that his predecessors "preferred to postpone publication so as not to encourage the world power of Communism to make certain moves." In 1980, while speaking to a group of German Catholics, John Paul II admitted that the "Third Secret" did indeed refer to impending punishment from God and that because Pope John XXIII, for diplomatic reasons, failed to honor the stipulations, the prophecy had been set into motion, and couldn't be stopped.

The "Third Secret" (given July 13, 1917)—

"After the two parts which I have already explained, at the left of Our Lady and a little above, we saw an Angel with a flaming sword in his left hand; flashing, it gave out flames that looked as though they would set the world on fire; but they died out in contact with the splendour that Our Lady radiated towards him from her right hand: pointing to the earth with his right hand, the Angel cried out in a loud voice: 'Penance, Penance, Penance!' And we saw in an immense light that is God: 'something similar to how people appear in a mirror when they pass in front of it' a Bishop dressed in White 'we had the impression that it was the Holy Father.' Other Bishops, Priests, men and women Religious going up a steep mountain, at the top of which there was a big Cross of rough-hewn trunks as of a cork-tree with the bark; before reaching there the Holy Father passed through a big city half in ruins and half trembling with halting step, afflicted with pain and sorrow, he prayed for the souls of the corpses he met on his way; having reached the top of the mountain, on his knees at the foot of the big Cross he was killed by a group of soldiers who fired bullets and arrows at him, and in the same way there died one after another the other Bishops, Priests, men and women Religious, and various lay people of different ranks and positions. Beneath the two arms of the Cross there were two Angels each with a crystal aspersorium in his hand, in which they gathered up the blood of the Martyrs and with it sprinkled the souls that were making their way to God."

It was very interesting that many years ago, Jeane Dixon had a vision with the word "Fatima" in it. She saw the throne of the Pope, but it was empty. Off to one side, she saw a Pope, with blood running down his face, dripping over his left shoulder. She interpreted this vision to mean, that within this century, a Pope will be bodily harmed. She saw hands reaching out for the throne. She said that the new head of the Church would have a different insignia than that of the Pope. Because of the unearthly light, she knew that the power would still be there, but not in the person of the Pope.

St. Malachy, Archbishop of Armagh (an Irish monk who died in 1148), had made prophecies concerning future Popes. His predictions ended with a Pope called "Peter the Roman" who was the seventh Pope after a Pope whose description resembled Pope Plus X. During his reign, "the City of the Seven Hills will be destroyed, and the Awful Judge will judge his people." The seventh Pope is John Paul II (Karol Wojtyla), from Krakow, Poland, who began his reign in 1978.

On April 7, 1970, it was reported that Mary appeared to Veronica Lueken, and had made subsequent appearances to her at the St. Robert Bellarmine Church in Bayside, New York, on the eve of the great feast days of the Church. The messages received during these visitations were recorded on tape, portions of which were revealed in a newsletter known as *Directives*. The message given on October 6, 1976 said: "The plan of ... communism is to overthrow the rule in the Eternal City, gain control in politics in a manner to control the world. They seek to overthrow Rome, these agents of hell and atheism, My child; they seek to overthrow Rome and gain control of the power of the House of My Son throughout the world. They will subvert it from within." On May 13, 1978 came this message: "How I warned and warned that Satan would enter into the highest realm of the hierarchy in Rome. The Third Secret, My child, is that Satan would enter into My Son's Church." Another message given on September 7, 1978 gave more details: "Satan, Lucifer in human form, entered into Rome in the year 1972. He cut off the rule, the role of the Holy Father, Pope Paul VI. Lucifer controlled Rome and continues this control now."

This seemed to echo what Pope Paul VI said on June 29, 1972, on the anniversary of his coronation: "From some fissure the smoke of Satan entered into the Temple of God."

The "Third Secret" has become highly suspect, in that Speckin Forensic Laboratories, a respected international firm, has analyzed the document and compared it with past writings of Lucia, and concluded that, "...based on the documents examined, that the questioned document 'Third Secret' can not be identified with the purported known writings of Sister Lucy." In addition, she claimed to have written it on one sheet of paper, which was confirmed by Cardinal Ottaviani, who read it, and Bishop Venancio who was able to see it through the envelope. Yet, what the Vatican released was four pages. On top of that, while the language in the first two secrets was fairly straight forward; whereas, in the third, Mary does not speak, it is symbolic, and also contains grammatical differences. While the Vatican sought to consider it a fulfillment of the May 13, 1981 assassination attempt on Pope John, the Third Secret actually ends with the death of the Pope. It was also revealed that Sister Lucia wrote to Pope John in May, 1982, to say that the complete fulfillment of the prophecy had not occurred.

What this all seems to add up to is a fraudulently produced 'Secret' intended to divert attention away from what could actually be going on. Though, as a fundamental Christian I have to question 'appearances' of Mary, visions from false prophets, and prophecies from an unreliable source; I do have to consider what Pope Paul VI may be referring to.

In the 1990 book *The Keys of This Blood* by Malachi Martin, a scholar and Vatican insider (as a Jesuit priest, from 1958-64, he served as a close aide to Cardinal Augustin Bea and the Pope), he wrote the following (pg. 632):

"Most frighteningly for [Pope] John Paul [II], he had come up against the irremovable presence of a malign strength in his own Vatican and in certain bishops' chanceries. It was what knowledgeable Churchmen called the 'superforce.' Rumors, always difficult to verify, tied its installation to the beginning of Pope Paul VI's reign in 1963. Indeed Paul had alluded somberly to 'the smoke of Satan which has entered the Sanctuary' ... an oblique reference to an enthronement ceremony by Satanists in the Vatican. Besides, the incidence of Satanic pedophilia— rites and practices— was already documented among certain bishops and priests as widely dispersed as Turin, in Italy, and South Carolina, in the United States. The cultic acts of Satanic pedophilia are considered by professionals to be the culmination of the Fallen Archangel's rites."

In his 1996 book *Windswept House: A Vatican Novel*, which addresses the Vatican's relationship to the New World Order and the next level civilization is to take, Martin begins the story with a description of a ritual known as the "Enthronement of the Fallen Archangel Lucifer" which took place on June 29, 1963, in St. Paul's Chapel at the Vatican, less than a week after Pope Paul's election. It was linked, on the telephone, to a parallel ceremony which took place in South Carolina. The book ends up with the Pope, before dying, leaving a written account about it on his desk for the next Pope (a thinly-veiled description of John Paul II) to find.

According to *The New American*, Martin reiterated that the Satanic rite took place: "Oh yes, it is true; very much so, but the only way I could put that down into print is in novelistic form." He also confirmed it to John Loeffler, host of the *Steel on Steel* radio show, where he was a frequent guest, and said that the Pope did not even know about it.

On January 24, 1979, at the Vatican, the Pope met for two hours with the Soviet foreign minister, Andrei Gromyko. Afterward, Gromyko referred to him as "a man with a worldview." John Paul said that the meeting was to talk about "the prospects for world peace."

On Sunday, April 3, 1994, the *Parade* magazine featured a front page picture of Pope John, with the quote: "We trust that, with the approach of the year 2000, Jerusalem will become the city of peace for the entire world and that all the people will be able to meet there, in particular the believers in the religions that find their birthright in the faith of Abraham." Note the global implication. The interview inside by Tad Szulc focused on the Vatican's establishment of diplomatic relations with Israel on December 30, 1993, which came during a time when Israel was also trying to work out their own peace accord in the Middle East.

This agreement will allow the Vatican to have a seat at the negotiations on the final determination of Jerusalem. The Vatican embassy will be in Tel Aviv, where most other embassies are located, because Jerusalem is not recognized as Israel's capital. In March, 1994, the Vatican also established relations with the Moslem country of Jordan, on Israel's eastern border, and it indicated the beginnings of a move by the Vatican to become more involved in the Middle East situation. Pope John said: "It must be understood that Jews, who for 2000 years were dispersed among the nations of the world, had decided to return to the land of their ancestors. That is their right." Vatican hardliners have criticized the Pope's growing role as the "protector of Jews," but maybe this is just a fulfillment of prophecy.

There does not appear to be any other figure on the world scene that could be considered as a candidate for the False Prophet other than the Pope, with the Roman Catholic Church being the World Church. However, do not misconstrue this as anti-Catholic rhetoric. The real history of the Catholic Church is not known to a large majority of its membership, and therefore, even though they have been deceived, it is wrong to indict those who have sincerely tried to live their lives according to the basic Christian tenets as they know them. It is probable that the Catholic Church, as well as the Protestant churches which make up the World Council of Churches, in the coming years, will be radically different, as liberalism and New Age become more pervasive in Religion— transforming these churches into shadows of their former selves.

CHAPTER ELEVEN

THE SHINING STAR

THE WAR TORN HISTORY OF ISRAEL

In the near future, the country of Israel is going to take a more prominent role in world affairs, so let's take a brief look at their historical development to see why tensions have continued to increase in the Middle East.

The northern kingdom of Israel was conquered by the Assyrians around 722 BC, and the threat of captivity and slaughter forced them to flee. Those people became known as the "ten lost tribes." The other two tribes, Benjamin and Judah (where the word "Jew" came from), remained in the south. Through the years, Jerusalem and Palestine became one of the most overrun areas in the world: Babylonian (587 BC-536 BC), Medo-Persian (536 BC-533 BC), Greek (331 BC-301 BC), Egyptian (301 BC-198 BC), Syrian (198 BC-63 BC), and Roman (63 BC-395 AD). Most of the Jews had fled from the land, and only a small group remained in Jerusalem until 70 AD, when the Romans burned the city. By 135, all of the Jews had been driven out. Still the area continued to be the subject of contention as it was conquered by the Byzantine (396-638), Mohammedan (639-1099), Crusader (1100-1291), Moslem (1292), Egyptian-Mamaluke (1292-1917), and Turks (1917).

In 1895, Theodor Herzl, an Austrian Jew, wrote a book called *The Jewish State* (*Der Judenstadt*) that began the movement towards the establishment of an independent Jewish state. In 1897, he arranged the first World Zionist Congress in Basle, Switzerland. Now known as 'Zionists' (for Mount Zion in Palestine), a fund was started to raise money to buy land, and a blue and white flag was chosen, the colors of the tallith prayer shawl. Herzl traveled around the world, especially in Europe, to lobby for his group. In 1903, a year before he died, England offered the Jews the African country of Uganda, which they rejected, because they knew that Palestine was their country. According to the Bible (Gen. 15:18), Israel's promised land stretches from the Nile River in Egypt to the Euphrates in Syria, and includes the countries of Syria and Lebanon.

In 1904, Dr. Chaim Weizmann (who would become Israel's first President), was made Assistant Professor of Biological Chemistry at the University of Manchester in England. The Polish-born Jew had studied Chemistry in Germany, and taught in Switzerland and England. During World War I, Germany was producing 250,000 shells a day, while England was only producing 2,500, due to a shortage of acetone because of the lack of wood alcohol. Weizmann isolated an organism capable of transforming the starch of cereals, most notably that of maize, and later chestnuts, into acetone butyl alcohol. Because of these advanced experimentations and the contribution of explosives (TNT) to the allied cause, Weizmann was credited with saving the British Army. The only thanks he wanted, was for Palestine to be established as a national homeland for the Jews.

The Sykes-Picat Agreement was a secret wartime agreement between England and France to divide between them the lands of the Ottoman Empire once World War 1 ended. Among the terms was the establishment of an Arab state in 'southern Palestine.' However, the Arabs became upset that Britain decided to instead engineer its own rule over all Palestine through the League of Nations. England essentially ruled Palestine as a colony until 1948.

On November 2, 1917, the British Foreign Secretary Lord Arthur James Balfour sent this declaration to Lord Lionel Walter Rothschild:

"His Majesty's Government views with favor the establishment in Palestine of a national home land for the Jewish people, and will use their best endeavors to facilitate the achievement of this object, it being clearly understood that nothing shall be done which may prejudice the civil and religious rights of existing non-Jewish communities in Palestine or the rights and political status enjoyed by Jews in any other country."

On December 9, 1917, Gen. Edmund Allenby marched into Jerusalem, and when the Turks heard that he was on his way, they interpreted 'Allenby' to mean 'Allah Nebi' ('Prophet of God'), and took it as a sign that God was against them. They were also worried about the accompanying airplanes (from the 14th Bomber Squadron of the Royal Flying Corp), which they had never seen before. They were thinking about the promise in Isaiah 31:5: "As birds flying, so will the Lord of Hosts defend Jerusalem; defending also he will deliver it; and passing over he will preserve it." The Turks left the city.

An interesting fact to add to this narrative can be found in Daniel 12:12. Some believe that the 1335 'days' may refer to the actual date that Palestine was delivered from Moslem rule. Since the land in Daniel's day was under Moslem rule, the date given would most likely be in Moslem terms, not in Jewish or Gregorian. A coin minted in Turkey showed the Gregorian date of 1917 on one side, and the Moslem date of 1335 on the other side. Is this a fulfillment of prophecy?

After the War, the 1919 Paris Peace Conference at Versailles established the League of Nations, who approved the Balfour Declaration and granted a mandate for Great Britain to govern the Palestine area. Within a couple of years, a Select Committee on Estimates, of the British House of Commons, reported that "large numbers of Jews, almost amounting to a second Exodus, have been migrating from Eastern Europe to the American zones of Germany and Austria with the intention in the majority of cases of finally making their way to Palestine. It is clear that it is a highly organized movement, with ample funds and great influence behind it, but the Subcommittee was unable to obtain any real evidence who are the real instigators." A U.S. Senate War Investigating Committee report said that a "heavy migration of Jews from Eastern Europe into the American Zone of Germany is part of a carefully organized plan financed by special groups in the United States." Even though nobody was to leave the Soviet Union without government permission, many Jews were allowed to leave, so they could return to their homeland.

In 1937, a Royal Commission was established by England which divided the country of Palestine into three sections: Jewish, Arab and English. With the increased tension, the UN Security Council later went soft, and the Truman Administration reversed their earlier support, urging that the partition proposal be suspended, in lieu of a 'trusteeship.' Jewish terrorist groups, such as the Stern gang, and the Irgun Zvai Leumi (led by Menachem Begin), worried that a Jewish State would not materialize, began attacking Arabs. *Time* magazine reported that they "stormed the village of Deir Yasin and butchered everyone in sight. The corpses of 250 Arabs, mostly women and small children, were tossed into wells." Rather than risking the possibility of further massacres, the Arab settlers fled the country to live in neighboring countries.

On April 29, 1947, the UN took on the responsibility of settling the Palestinian situation. Facing a Jewish refugee crisis because of mass emigration into Palestine that they could no longer control, England acceded to Resolution 181 of the newly-founded United Nations which called for a partition of the British-ruled area into separate Jewish and Arab states, with Jerusalem as a separate entity administered by the UN. Palestinian Jews approved the plan, but Palestinian Arabs and neighboring Arab countries rejected it.

On May 14, 1948, the British Union Jack in Jerusalem was lowered, and at 4 p.m., David Ben-Gurion (the first Prime Minister) read the Declaration of Independence over the airwaves in a radio broadcast from the Tel Aviv Museum. At 6:10 p.m. President Truman made an official statement of recognition, making the United States one of the first countries to extend diplomatic recognition to the new independent state of Israel.

In a speech to the UN General Assembly, Andrei Gromyko, the Russian Ambassador, announced his support for an independent Jewish State in Palestine, and urged the Arabs to accommodate them. The entire Communist bloc voted to support Israel. They followed their show of support with a strong program which included financial support and military equipment. The Soviet Union was hoping that Israel would become another communist satellite. When it became apparent that Israel would not go communist, Russia discontinued diplomatic relations with them on February 23, 1953, and the Cominform denounced Zionism as an "agency of American imperialism."

Another variation of one of the numerical theories given earlier purports to indicate the foretelling of the establishment of Israel as an independent Jewish State, and the end of the dispersal of the Jewish people throughout the world. The calculation goes like this: 2,520 biblical years X 360 biblical days = 907,200 days, divided by our calendar year of 365.25 days = 2,483.8 calendar years, which added to the end of the Babylonian captivity in 536 BC, leads us to the year of 1948.

When British troops left the area, they said it would be a matter of weeks before the Arabs would take over the new country. On May 15th, the official date of statehood, when Ben-Gurion was broadcasting Israel's appreciation to the U.S. for their recognition, an explosion sounded, after which he said: "A bomb has just fallen on this city from an enemy aircraft flying overhead." An Arab alliance of Egypt, Iraq, Saudi Arabia, Syria, Yemen, Lebanon, and Jordan had attacked Israel.

Even though the newly formed nation was poorly armed, they survived, and actually increased their territory by 600 miles. The 1949 Armistice gave them 21% more land than they had originally been given by the United Nations.

Prior to 1948, the Jewish people were known as 'Palestinians.' There was a *Palestinian Post* newspaper, a Palestinian Brigade of Jewish volunteers in the British Army during World War II, and an all-Jewish Palestinian Symphony Orchestra. Arab inhabitants living in the new country of Israel wanted to differentiate themselves from the Jews, and began called themselves Palestinians. However, the underlying purpose for this was to generate the misconception that it was a distinct nationality, and that 'Palestine' was their ancestral homeland, when in fact, they are actually similar in language and customs to the Arabs of Syria and Jordan, where their ancestors probably came from.

On July 26, 1956, Gamal Abdel Nassar, President of Egypt, seized control of the Suez Canal, and announced that the profits would go towards building the Aswan Dam. Egypt moved into a close alliance with Russia as billions of dollars worth of military equipment, along with Soviet advisors, poured into the country. On October 29th, Israeli forces overran the Gaza Strip, and had it not been for the UN Resolution that ordered a cease fire, Egypt would have fallen to Israel.

Many years ago I came across this unsubstantiated report. On November 7, 1957, the *Jerusalem Post* reported that at 6:03 a.m., Moshe Dayan radioed to twenty of his soldiers stationed in the Sinai Desert, that three Egyptian divisions, 18,000 men, were on their way. They men bowed down, and prayed to the 'God of their Fathers' to have the strength to die, rather than face being captured. When they got up, they saw the Egyptian strike force engaged in retreat. Behind these lines was a car, which the Israelis captured. Inside the car was one of Nassar's commanding generals, who said that they were retreating because they had been surrounded by an army dressed in white. Israel had no such army there. The 18,000 soldiers were never heard from again. A six-week search in Israel, the Sinai Desert, and Egypt failed to turn up any clues. Since it was already established that Israel did not have the resources to capture such a large number of men, what could have happened? *National Geographic* reported that on November 7, 1957, at 6:33 a.m. there was an earthquake of substantial proportions on the Sinai peninsula, which lead to the speculation that the army could have been swallowed up by the earth. If this report was true, it most certainly was a sign that the Jews were indeed God's chosen people.

The Soviet Union began sending equipment to Iraq and Syria, while they continued to interfere in the internal affairs of other Arab nations through military coups and political assassinations. Only U.S. and British intervention prevented Communist takeovers in the Middle East, as in July 1958, when the Marines landed in Lebanon; and British forces, supporting King Hussein, landed in Jordan.

On March 16, 1965, Nassar promised the Arabs an all-out offensive effort against Israel, if they would unite under him, as he hoped to become the President of the United States of Africa. He said: "We must arm 5,000,000 men and overwhelm the Israelis by sheer military might."

In 1967, Russia sent exaggerated reports to Egypt and Syria that Israel was preparing for war against Syria. This was a move by Syria to unify the Arab bloc countries. In a book written by Nassar, he revealed that his chief goal was to eliminate Israel as a nation, and to push them into the sea. On May 26th he said: "The Arab people want to fight. We have been waiting for the right time when we will be completely ready." On May 28th he said: "We will not accept any co-existence with Israel." On June 4th he said, concerning Israel: "We are facing you in battle and are burning with desire for it to start to obtain revenge." The source of Nassar's hatred for Israel can be traced back to a statement he made in December, 1962: "We feel the soil of Palestine is the soil of Egypt, and the whole Arab world. Why do we mobilize? Because we feel that the land of Palestine is part of our land, and we are ready to sacrifice ourselves for it."

Nassar ordered the UN to remove their troops, which they did; and he closed the crucial port of Eliat, on the Gulf of Aquaba, and blockaded the Tiran Straits. He then taunted Israel's Chief of Staff Yitzhak Rabin by saying: "Let him come, I'm waiting." The armies of Egypt, Jordan, Syria, and Lebanon surrounded Israel on all sides. Joining them were Iraq, Algeria, Kuwait, Sudan, and other Arab nations, which represented 25 times more manpower than Israel could field. On the evening of June 4, 1967, Nassar moved his Russian-made tanks and artillery into position. He knew that with America caught up in the Vietnam War, there would be no help for Israel.

As daylight broke on June 5th, Israeli jets flew low from the north and began bombing the Egyptian Air Force. Israeli ships traded fire with Egypt's naval power, and Israeli tanks rolled into the Sinai. As the events unfolded, Russia warned the major countries of the world to back-off, so the world sat back and waited, expecting a swift Arab victory. The victory never came. By the second day, Arab leaders watched their military being ground to bits. After six days, the Arab alliance was in retreat as Israeli soldiers captured the Sinai peninsula up to the Suez Canal, the Golan Heights including Mount Hermon (which would then become the "eyes and ears of Israel," the entire West Bank of the River Jordan, and reclaimed the city of Jerusalem. Schlomo Goren, Ashkenazic (of Eastern European origin) Chief Rabbi of Israel, carried the Scrolls of the Law, and sounded the ram's horn of repentance. In Hebrew, 'shofar' (ram's horn) is the word that 'jubilee' is derived from. In Leviticus 25:8-9, a 'jubilee' is represented as 49 years. There was a 49 year difference between 1917, when Gen. Allenby entered Jerusalem, and 1967, when the Jews took complete control. Gen. Moshe Dayan said: "We have returned to our holiest of holy places, never to be parted from it again ... No power on earth will remove us from this spot again."

Seeing that their plan was failing, Russia called for a ceasefire. In those six short days, the Arabs lost three billion dollars of military equipment, and the Israelis captured $700 million in new Soviet military hardware. Over 15,000 Arab lives were lost, but only 776 Israelis. Israel increased their territory from 8,000 to 34,000 square miles. Moshe Dayan, Israel's Minister of Defense, said afterwards: "Our next war will be with Russia."

After the Israeli victory over the Arabs in 1948, Jordan maintained possession of Judea, Samaria, and the eastern part of Jerusalem, and expelled all the Jews and destroyed their synagogues. They renamed the area the 'West Bank.' Their purpose was to convince the world that these territories were the ancestral lands of the Jordanian Kingdom, when in fact it is well documented that the land belonged to the Jews. Even after the Arabs were driven out of this area during the 1967 war, they still referred to this territory as the West Bank in an effort to continue swaying public opinion.

In the years that followed, Russia continued to arm Egypt, Syria, and other Arab countries. However, by 1972, Enwar Sadat, the President of Egypt, felt that Russia was trying to control the Middle East, and he ended his country's alliance with them. Egypt and Saudi Arabia joined forces so they wouldn't have to rely on Russia. Syria then became the main recipient of Soviet arms.

In 1973, Egypt's War Minister announced that the headquarters for all Arab fronts would be established in Cairo. On October 6, 1973, which was Yom Kippur, the Jewish Day of Atonement, Egypt, Syria, Jordan and eight other Arab nations joined together in a surprise attack against Israel. Much of the Israeli air force was destroyed by Soviet SAM ground-to-air missiles, and only 100 of 265 Israeli tanks survived the first wave, giving the Arabs a 5 to 1 edge in armor superiority. Nixon was very adamant about the U.S. position when he said: "If Russia disturbs the balance of power in the Middle East, the United States will move to assure Israel's security." With reports that the Soviets were airlifting supplies to Egypt, and Iraqi troops were on their way to support Syria, Israeli Prime Minister Golda Meir began considering the nuclear option, and made an urgent plea to the U.S.

Israel no longer had the military hardware to wage an effective war. They needed missiles, ammunition, tanks, and planes. An amazing story that came out of this war had to do with Tzvika Greengold, who was the leader of a group of three Israeli tanks on the Golan Heights, where they were to hold off oncoming Syrian tanks. Somehow he got separated from the other two, so he drove up a hill and destroyed three enemy tanks. He repositioned himself only to see a column of thirty Syrian tanks heading his way. He shot the first, changed positions, and kept shooting. By the time he was done, he had destroyed ten of the tanks, and the Syrians began to retreat because they thought they were being attacked by a larger Israeli force.

Nixon responded to Meir's appeal by saying: "Send everything that can fly." In a commitment to stand by them in their darkest hour, he also sent in two carrier battle groups to the eastern Mediterranean Sea, and when the Soviets threatened to intervene by dropping paratroopers into the Sinai, our military alert level was raised to DEFCON 3. In a 31-day airlift, a $2.2 billion emergency aid shipment codenamed Operation Nickel Grass, the U.S. sent in shipments of ammunition, fighter-bombers, and tanks. Meir would later say: "For generations to come, all will be told of the miracle of the immense planes from the United States bringing in the material that meant life to our people."

In a swift, often reckless counterattack, Israel pushed their way to the west bank of the Suez, and came within 100 miles of Cairo, the Egyptian capital; and witin artillery range of the airfields of Damascus, the Syrian capital. With the tide turned, Israel again prevailed, taking even more territory. Again Russia urged the UN to order a ceasefire. Sadat's terms for a ceasefire was for Israel to withdraw from all territory it took during the 1967 war. American and Soviet pressure turned this Israeli victory into a negotiated compromise. The Arabs punished the world for their support of Israel by initiating an oil embargo against all the nations, such us the United States, who were partial to Israel. This move created worldwide economic chaos.

In 1977, Israeli Chief of Staff Mordechai Gur said publicly that Egypt was again preparing for war, basing his assumption on an unprecedented military buildup that was part of a two-year $6 billion arms modernization plan. Jimmy Carter, said in a 1978 meeting with Israeli Prime Minister Menachem Begin: "I can say, without reservation, as President of the United States of America, that we will continue to do so (remain committed to Israel's security), not just for thirty years, but forever." However, in 1978, President Carter was able to get Prime Minister Menachem Begin (Israel) and Enwar Sadat (Egypt) together to sign the Camp David Peace Accord, which led to the return of the Sinai to Egypt, and full recognition of Israel by Egypt, including the establishment of embassies and trade relations.

On November 5, 1978, the 21-nation Arab League met in Baghdad and established a $3.5 billion war fund "to continue the armed confrontation with the Jewish State"; and in 1980, a 37-nation Islamic Summit called for a 'Holy War' to liberate all Arab land, including Jerusalem, to establish an independent Palestinian state, with an Arab Jerusalem as its capital. The proposal was rejected by Egypt because of their commitment to the Peace Accord.

During 1980-81, Israel passed two key laws that changed the nature of the Middle East conflict: they named Jerusalem, including East Jerusalem and the Old City (captured from Jordan in 1967) as Israel's Eternal Capital (although most of the world still maintains embassies in Tel Aviv); and annexed the Golan Heights (captured from Syria in 1967).

In June, 1982, while responding to a PLO attack from a terrorist base in southern Lebanon, Israeli Intelligence discovered that Russia had enough arms and foodstuffs in huge caves under the town of Sidon to supply a million-man army, including uniforms, assault rifles, ammunition, shells, missiles, and tanks. They found two huge digging machines that were used to dig the underground fortress. The smaller one of the two was able to dig a hole 30 feet wide, 24 feet high, and 60 feet deep, in eight hours. They were part of a six-machine shipment to Austria by a U.S. manufacturer. The whereabouts of the other four were not known. The shocking implication of that discovery, was that the shelf life of the K-rations (meal packets) were only six months, which led many to believe the Israel thwarted a Russian invasion of Israel that was planned for the fall of 1982.

After an eight-year long war with Iran, in 1988, Saddam Hussein, in a bid to become the preeminent leader of the Arab world, offered to put his military at the disposal of the Palestinian effort. Iraq had been a partner in most of Arab attacks on Israel, and during the Persian Gulf War, Hussein threatened to "burn half of Israel." However, in 1989, Yasser Arafat showed his willingness to seek a solution to the Mid-East situation by acknowledging Israel's right to exist, and expressing a desire to begin negotiations to establish a Palestinian political authority that could coexist with Israel.

Salah Khalaf Abu Iyad, Yasir Arafat's chief deputy, said on January 1, 1991: "Now we accept the formation of the Palestinian state in part of Palestine, in the Gaza Strip and West Bank. We will start from that part and we will liberate Palestine, inch by inch."

In August 20, 1993, in the Norwegian capital of Oslo, Yitzhak Rabin (Israel) and Yasser Arafat (head of the Palestinian Liberation Organization) reached an agreement, known as the Declaration of Principles (or Oslo Accords), in an attempt to end its armed struggle in exchange for gradual Palestinian autonomy (through the creation of the Palestinian Authority) over parts of the West Bank and the Gaza Strip, which was later extended to Nablus, Jenin, Bethlehem, Ramallah, Qalqilya, Tulkarm, and Hebron in 1995. The two leaders also signed Letters of Mutual Recognition, in which the Israeli government recognized the PLO as the legitimate representative of the Palestinian people; and the PLO recognized Israel's right to exist, and also renounced terrorism, violence, and their desire for the destruction of the State of Israel.

In a September 9, 1993 letter to Israeli Prime Minister Yitzhak Rabin, Arafat renounced his terrorist activities and said: "The PLO recognizes the right of the state of Israel to exist in peace and security."

The Oslo Accords were signed by both leaders in Washington, D.C. on September 13th, yet, on September 19th, P.L.O. Chairman Arafat said before a group of 19 Arab ministers meeting in Cairo: "Our first goal is the liberation of all occupied territories ... and the establishment of a Palestinian state whose capital is Jerusalem. The agreement we arrived at is not a complete solution ... it is only the basis for an interim solution and the forerunner of a final settlement, which must be based on a complete withdrawal from all occupied Palestinian lands, especially holy Jerusalem."

On September 14, 1993, Jordan signed an agenda for peace with Israel, which culminated with Peace Treaty that was signed in October, 1994. Also in October, 1994, Farouk Kaddoumi, head of the PLO's political department and their foreign minister, said in a speech: "There is a state which was established through historical force and it must be destroyed. This is the Palestinian way." Arafat later told Rabin, the Israeli Prime Minister, that his comment did not reflect the view of the PLO.

On November 4, 1995, Rabin, like Sadat before him, paid for peace with his life.

An October, 1998 summit at Wye Mills, MD, became the first serious peace negotiations in two years, as Israel Prime Minister Benjamin Netanyahu and Arafat met to settle various important issues that had been negotiated during the 1993 Oslo Accords. It ended with Israel surrendering 13% of their land to the Palestinians as part of a land for peace agreement brokered by the U.S.

Pope John Paul II met with Yasser Arafat at the Vatican on February 15, 2000, where they agreed that Jerusalem must be made into an international city. The agreement they signed was in the form of a covenant. The Pope called for an end to the violence and said that the Palestinian State should be created out of the land of Israel. The Vatican said that Israel's annexation of east Jerusalem was illegal, and they didn't recognize Israeli sovereignty there.

In March of the same year, the Pope traveled to the Middle East where he visited Jordan, Israel, and the Palestine territories. *Time* magazine (4/30/00 pg. 36) quoted Yasser Arafat's wife Suha, who had been a devout Catholic before her marriage, as saying that the Holy Father's very presence there was "a clear message for an independent Palestinian state".

Billed as Camp David II, in July, 2000, hoping for a final settlement before he left office, President Bill Clinton hosted a meeting between Israeli Prime Minister Ehud Barak and Arafat. For the first time, Israel offered part of East Jerusalem as the Palestinian capital, and most of the West Bank. The talks failed because of Arafat's demand for the 'right of return' for Palestinian refugees living abroad.

On August 2, 2001, Arafat and Pope John Paul met for a private meeting at the papal summer residence in Castel Gandolfo, where the Pope again called for an end to violence, and said he supported the rights of the Palestinians.

In June, 2003 current Prime Minister Ariel Sharon did a complete about-face (he had promised to use his military experience to end terrorism once and for all) by agreeing with President Bush and Palestinian Prime Minister Abbas that a Palestinian State is the common goal of the U.S., Israel and the Palestinians, and even described Israel's control of their own land as an "occupation."

In July, 2003, Israeli opposition leader, former Prime Minister of Israel, Shimon Peres, publicly proposed that Jerusalem become the 'World Capital' of the world government that is developing. His press release said that the claims on the city being made by Moslems, Christians, and Jews could be placated by the presence of an overriding governing body that had jurisdiction over the city. Peres suggested that the Secretary-General of the UN, Kofi Annan, be the mayor of the city.

In November, 2003, in an attempt to get more support from the U.S. for more Israeli concessions towards the Palestinians, Arafat said in a speech that Israel has a right to live in peace. However groups like Hizballah ('Party of God'), Hamas, Islamic Jihad, and Fatah continued their terrorist attacks, possibly believing that Arafat has become 'soft' in his diplomatic approach to the Middle East situation.

Today, the Israeli military force is probably the most respected in the world, despite its small size. They have a fighting spirit that can not be denied. Their military officers are sworn in with a ceremony at the ancient fortress of Masada, where in 70 AD, unable to hold off the Roman attack any longer, 950 men, women, and children committed suicide, rather than be captured. Part of their oath says: "Masada shall never fall again." This commitment has nurtured that incredible fighting spirit, making them the most elite fighting force in the world— literally unbeatable. They are God's chosen people, and because of that, Israel will never fall, but that won't stop someone from trying. The region will continue to be a powder keg waiting to explode. It seems likely that the Pope (the yet to come False Prophet) will be asked to be the mediator of the Middle East situation, and be the one who facilitates it becoming a Universal City for all religions.

Focusing on Israel

A map drawn by monks during the Crusades, still hangs in the Herford Cathedral, and identifies Jerusalem as the geographic center of the world, which is so marked on the floor of the Holy Sepulcher. The attention of the world will become more focused on this area of the world as this nation continues to prosper. What is it about this country, besides the religious significance, which has made it the most fought over pieces of land in history.

The Dead Sea, located between Israel and Jordan, which is 1,296 feet below sea level, is the lowest spot on the surface of the Earth. It is fifty miles long and eleven miles wide (about 500 square miles), and has a depth of 1,200 feet at its deepest point. Known as the 'Sea of Salt,' because it is ten times saltier than ocean water, it is fed by the Jordan River, and has no outlet. Its waters have evaporated for hundreds of years in the extreme heat, at a rate of 280 million cubic feet per day, leaving behind a variety of minerals. With a concentration of 32% of dissolved ingredients, in a "unique composition" of mostly sodium chloride (salt), while regular ocean water has only 3.5% to 4%; it is the richest mineral source in the world.

The water contains potassium chloride, or potash, which is used as a fertilizer and for making explosives. It is of high quality becomes it doesn't come from rock. It is believed that this ingredient will become a very valuable commodity.

The water also contains magnesium bromide (used to make plastics and rubber), magnesium chloride (used in magnesium metal production and in the manufacturing of a cement used for heavy duty flooring), and hydrogen sulfide (used in chemical laboratories as an analytical re-agent). Because of its sulfuric content, the water is said to have therapeutic properties.

Solar ponds have been built on the Sea. The sun heats the shallow salt water, and the heat is trapped in the dense salt layer on the bottom, and becomes hot enough to turn a turbine, thus producing electricity.

Scientists have also discovered an algae, known as Dunaliella, which can survive in, and has adapted to, the extremely salty conditions. It is being grown in algae farms where they double their numbers every two days. The algae is used to produce a green paste, which, when dried, makes an excellent animal feed because of its high protein content, and it is easy to digest because the algae have no cell walls. It also yields beta carotene (a pigment which gives carrots its color), which is used for food coloring; and also glycerol, which is used for eye shadow and other cosmetics, paints, resins, and toothpaste. When the algae decomposes, it forms the raw material that nature uses to form oil.

The value of the mineral deposits in the Dead Sea has been estimated at over a trillion dollars. However, the Dead Sea has been shrinking in size as the sea level has fallen. The Mediterranean Dead Sea Co. initiated a $1.4 billion project to funnel water to the Dead Sea from the Mediterranean, which is about 70 miles away.

Geological surveys have indicated that there is plenty of steam under Israel to provide power through the harnessing of geo-thermal energy, which is a very economical source of energy. Oil and natural gas deposits have also been discovered. Cutting diamonds is a major industry, as is the exporting citrus fruit to Europe and Japan.

It seems there are plenty of resources in this small country that could be garnished for the benefit of an attacking nation.

THE ARK OF THE COVENANT

The purpose of building the Temple was to house the Ark of the Covenant, so the discovery of the most sacred item in Jewish history may be all that is needed to initiate the rebuilding of the Temple. However, Jeremiah 27:22 seems to indicate a connection between the Temple treasures, and the existence of the Temple. According to Ezra, after the first Temple was destroyed, the Temple vessels had to be returned or refabricated before the Temple could be rebuilt. Thus, only the existence of the Temple vessels may be all that is needed to rebuild the Temple, since it is believed that the Ark was not in the second Temple.

The Ark was a rectangular box four feet long, and two feet high, made of acacia wood (distinguished as a type of wood that does not decay), and covered with gold; with two cherubs (a rank of angels) looking down and facing each other on its lid with outstretched wings, which was known as the mercy seat. It was constructed at Mount Sinai by Bezalel, according to the instructions Moses received from God. Inside was placed the rod of Aaron, a pot of manna (which had been sent by God to feed the Israelites during their time of wandering in the wilderness), and the two tablets of the Law given to Moses (known as the Ten Commandments). Some sources also claim that it contains the original Books of Moses. It represented the divine presence of God, and was the point where the literal manifestation of God on this Earth took place. Just looking at it was known to cause death. The Bible tells us of the power it possessed. It caused the Jordan River to part (Joshua 3:8 - 4:11), aided in the destruction of Jericho (Joshua 6:4-21), and brought about numerous military victories when it was present. Needless to say, it developed quite a mystique.

Inside the Temple, the Ark was placed in a dark, windowless room known as the Holy of Holies. A vale was placed around the Ark, and only once a year, on the Day of Atonement, the high priest was allowed to enter. Even then, he was to carry a container of burning incense, which filled the room with smoke, thus obscuring his view of the Ark. He would sprinkle the blood of a bullock on the ground in front of the Ark, and on the mercy seat, as atonement for the sins of the priests; and then the blood of a goat, as a symbolic atonement for the sins of the people. A rope would be tied around his waist, so if for some reason he accidentally touched the Ark and was killed, he could be pulled out without risk by the other priests.

In the Bible, there are 200 references to the Ark of the Covenant up to the time of Jeremiah, but nothing afterward. It has since disappeared, and nobody is really sure where it's at. The common belief is that the Temple will not be rebuilt unless the Ark is found.

The Ark had not been removed from the Temple during or after the reign of King Josiah, which had begun in 640 BC, and it was in place in the Holy of Holies in 701 BC, which leaves 61 years in which it could have disappeared. It is unlikely that Hezekiah (716-687 BC) would have allowed the Ark to be taken away. Between the time of his death, and Josiah's reign, there were two other rulers, Manasseh (687-642 BC) and Amon (642-640 BC). Amon discovered that Manasseh had been involved in a form of Baal worship, and had erected an image of Astarte (Asherah) in the Temple (2 Kings 21:4-7, 2 Chronicles 33:7), and it is believed that he would have ordered the Levites to remove the Ark. The Ark reappeared in 622 BC (2 Kings 22:1-7, 2 Chronicles 34:8-33, 2 Chronicles 35:3), during the reign of Manasseh's grandson, King Josiah, who vanquished idolatry, repaired and purified the Temple.

However, idolatry took root again, and the actions of Rehoboam, Solomon's son, caused the kingdom to be divided, with Judah (Judea) in the south, and Israel to the north. Judgment came upon the Northern Kingdom in 721 BC when the Assyrians attacked them; and the Southern Kingdom paid the price for they idolatry when the armies of Nebuchadnezzar, the Babylonian king, swept through the land in 606 BC, and then again in 597 BC. During the second invasion, 2 Kings 24:13 says that "all the treasures of the house of the Lord, and the treasure of the king's house" were taken, and "all the vessels of gold which Solomon king of Israel had made in the temple of the Lord" had been cut in pieces. The original Temple was destroyed in 586 BC by the Babylonian commander, Nebuzaradan (2 Kings 25:8-9), and the rest of the treasures were plundered and taken to a Babylonian temple at Shinar (Daniel 1:2), which has led some to theorize that what was taken previously came from the Temple treasury, since Nubuchadnezzar's initial action against Judah was in response to them not paying tribute to him.

Through all of this, the Ark was not mentioned. Lists of Temple items (2 Kings 25:13-17, Jeremiah 52:17-23) do not refer to any Temple treasures from the Holy of Holies, and it is this silence that could indicate that it wasn't captured, since there is a Biblical record of the time when the Philistines captured the Ark. In addition, Ezra 1:7-11 states that all the captured items were later returned by the Persians, but the Ark was not discussed. So, either the Ark was destroyed along with the Temple (possibly indicated by the destruction of the "goodly vessels" in 2 Chronicles 36:19), or the Ark was hidden before it could be found.

When Rome invaded Judea in 63 BC, and the Roman General Pompey swept through Jerusalem, entering the Temple, and the Holy of Holies, it was empty. Jewish history records the high priest making his offering upon the foundation stone of the Holy of Holies, and not the Ark. After Titus returned to Rome with some of the Temple treasure, the Arch of Triumph (or Arch of Titus) was built in 81 AD at the entrance to the Forum, in the Palatine section of Rome, to commemorate his victory. It depicted the seven-branched candelabra known as the menorah (with an octagonal base, rather than a three-legged stand, which it actually has; which could indicate that it was a duplicate kept in the Treasury), the golden table of the showbread, and the seven trumpets of the Jubilee. The Ark is not pictured, thus adding to the evidence that the Ark was not in the second Temple, and has been hidden.

According to the Mishnah (Sotah 9a), after the Temple was built, the Tabernacle was stored under the "crypts of the Temple." It is believed that King Solomon constructed a secret chamber in the recesses of the Temple Mount to hide the Ark, which is where it was placed during the reign of Manasseh. Jewish tradition has held that the Ark and the Altar of Incense were hidden in a secret location under a woodshed on the western side of the Temple, near the Holy of Holies.

This is not such a far-fetched idea when you realize that under the city of Jerusalem there is an underground city consisting of a number of tunnels, chambers, and cisterns; which were created to establish a water storage system, as quarters for guards, chambers to hold sacrificial animals, rooms containing ritual bathing areas, prison cells, and storage areas for Temple treasures. The best known of these subterranean areas is Hezekiah's Tunnel, which was constructed to make sure Jerusalem would have fresh water in case the city was attacked. It started at Gihon Spring, and ran for a third of a mile, through solid rock, spilling into the Pool of Siloam. An escape tunnel used by King Zedekiah which ran from the Tower of Antonia, to a point near the Eastern Gate, emerging outside the walls of the city, covering a distance of over 8,000 feet.

The nine original members of the Knights Templar were received by King Baldwin I (Baudouin) in Jerusalem in 1119, and they established their headquarters in a wing of the al-Aqsa Mosque, which had been converted to a palace. They were given complete access to the palace and various outbuildings which were on the site where Solomon's Temple originally stood, which was adjacent to the Dome of the Rock. Although their goal was "to keep the road from the coast to Jerusalem free from bandits," for nine years they rarely left the palace grounds. It was an unrealistic pledge, because it would have been difficult for the nine to patrol this fifty mile road; besides, a military order known as the Knights of Saint John were already performing that task before the Templars showed up. It is now known that they had some knowledge about the Temple treasures, because there is evidence which indicates that they were engaged in a massive excavation project.

Vast arched subterranean rooms were used by Knights during the Crusades to keep horses, and were known as "Solomon's Stables." The Templars were aware of these hidden areas underneath the Temple grounds, and believed that the Ark would be found there. They mounted an operation to plunder whatever treasurers they could find. Although it is questionable that they found the Ark, it is believed that they discovered treasure, relics and ancient manuscripts dating back to the time of Moses. Israeli archaeologists, engaged in excavations on the southern side of the Mount, found the exit point of a tunnel which had been dug by the Templars. It lead inward about 30 yards, where it was blocked by stone and debris.

There has been many stories concerning the location of the Ark of the Covenant. Some believe it is still buried in a secret chamber on the Temple Mount. Jewish historian Eupolemus wrote that many of the Temple treasures had been plundered by Babylon, "except for the Ark and the tablets in it. This Jeremiah preserved." According to the apocryphal Second Book of Maccabees 2:4-8, which has been dated to 163 BC, the prophet Jeremiah had concealed the Ark (as well as the Tabernacle, and the Altar of Incense) in a cave on "the mountain where Moses went up and beheld the heritage of God." Some researchers believe that this could refer to either Mount Sinai or Mount Nebo, which is located in what is now the country of Jordan, and is the traditional burial place of Moses. The contention was made, that since these articles were made under the leadership of Moses, they may have been deposited at the site of his burial. Various archaeological expeditions had failed to turn up anything there.

During the 1920's, American explorer, Antonio Frederick Futterer, searched various locations in Jordan for the Ark, based on the clues in 2 Maccabees, and believed the location to be on Mount Pisgah, the highest peak on the Mount Nebo range. He claimed to have found an inscription on the sealed entrance of a tunnel which said: "Herein lies the golden Ark of the Covenant." In 1981, while following Futterer's map of Mount Pisgah, a gully was discovered by Tom Crotser, an American explorer, which led to a 4' X 7' tunnel that plunged 600 feet into the ground, ending at a wall, which when broken down, revealed a 10' X 12' crypt which held a rectangular chest 62" long, 37" high and 37" wide, wrapped in a blue cloth, which he believed to be the Ark. Beside it was another bundle, which he thought contained the carrying poles, the cherubim which had been mounted on the top, and the legs. The cave is located near the Church of the Franciscan Fathers of Terra Santa, and is under a building which contains the remains of an old Byzantine church. He didn't disturb the find, thus he doesn't know for sure what he saw. He reported it to the media, and he claimed that God told him to send the photographs he took to London banker David Rothschild, who some people have claimed is a direct descendant of Jesus, and has been chosen to build the third Temple. Rothschild refused to accept the pictures, and they were returned to Crotser. Noted archaeologist Siegfried Horn visited his home in Winfield, Kansas to see the pictures. Only two had any images at all— one is fuzzy, but does show a chamber with a yellow box in the center. His opinion was that it was "not an ancient artifact but of modern fabrication..."

In January, 1979, archaeologist Ronald Wyatt, while sightseeing near the Damascus Gate, felt that the location of Jeremiah's Grotto was near an ancient stone quarry on the northern extension of Mt. Moriah, that is sometimes referred to as the 'Calvary Escarpment' (because it contains the skull face configuration that has been connected to the Golgotha). He believed that during the Babylonian siege of Jerusalem from 587-586 BC, when the city was surrounded, it would have been impossible to remove the Ark, so it had to be there. With the permission of the landowner, and a permit from Israeli officials, he excavated the area. On January 6, 1982, he entered a chamber that contained the Ark, and other artifacts from the first Temple, which had been hidden there by Jeremiah. The 22-foot long cave is actually located directly beneath the area where Christ was crucified. According to Wyatt's research, when Jesus was crucified, his blood flowed down to the ground, through a split in the rock, and onto the Ark.

Most serious researchers doubt his claim, saying that, as far back as the first Temple, the area of Mt. Calvary was used as burial grounds, so it is highly unlikely that the Ark would have been placed on defiled ground. Scholars have questioned his lack of archaeological training, and his techniques; yet Wyatt's work gained more acceptance because of other discoveries, such as the true Mt. Sinai, the location on the Red Sea crossing, Noah's Ark, the 12 altars erected by Moses, Sodom and Gomorrah, and Abraham's family tomb in Hebron. Plus, his work has produced the most information on the Ark, all of which seems to be compatible with Scripture.

Dr. Gary Collett believes that Maccabees actually refers to Qumran, and says that the layout of Cave IV is similar to the Temple, and that its lower level may have been the containment room used by Jeremiah to temporarily protect the Ark. In 1992, two scientists from the Department of Geophysics and Planetary Science at Tel-Aviv University used a ground-breaking radar known as a molecular frequency analyzer and a seismic-reflection device near two caves at the Wadi la-Chippah ('the dome of the bridge') which indicated the presence of a room containing the same sort of pottery known to contain scrolls. Preliminary trenches dug in 1993 failed to turn up anything substantial.

Once Christianity became the official religion of Rome, the treasures plundered by its legions fell into the possession of the Catholic Church. Nelson Canode, of Amarillo, Texas, a former Benedictine monk at a monastery at Subiaco, Italy, about 30 miles from Rome, said that he was taken to a cave, four levels below the monastery, where ancient artifacts were being shuttled from there to the underground vaults of the Vatican, and included the Ark and the disassembled Tabernacle. There are many who believe that once Jerusalem becomes an international city, the Vatican will return any Temple items in their possession.

Because of the research done by Graham Hancock for his book *The Sign and the Seal*, some people think the Ark may be in Ethiopia. Menelik I, the royal son of King Solomon, returned to Ethiopia, after his mother, the Queen of Sheba, died. When he was twenty years old, he returned to Israel, and Solomon treated him with so much favor, that the elders were jealous and wanted him to return home. Solomon agreed to send him home, on the condition that the first born sons of all the elders would go with him. Solomon wanted to give him a replica of the Ark to take with him. However, Azarius, the son of Zadok, the High Priest, worried about the idol worship which was flourishing, switched the Arks, and took the real one.

The Ark was taken to Egypt, on the island of Elephantine in the middle of the Nile, near Aswan, where a temple was built to protect it. It remained there for 200 years, until the temple was destroyed. The Ark was carried along the Nile, and the Takazze tributary into Ethiopia. They arrived at Lake Tana, which was considered a holy place. The Ark stayed on the island of Tana Kirkos for 800 years, where it was taken to the Church of St. Mary of Zion, which had been built in 372 to hold the Ark. During the 1530's, when the Muslims attacked, it was moved to safety, but returned a hundred years later to a rebuilt St. Mary's, which had been constructed on the ruins of the first. It remained there until 1965, when Emperor Haile Selassie (who called himself the "Conquering Lion of Judah" and claimed to be a direct descendent of King Solomon) moved it to the Church of Zion near the center of Aksum (Axum), in northern Ethiopia. Though the communists overthrew the monarchy in 1974, killed Selassie, and imprisoned much of the Royal family, the Ark remained safe because of its reputation for possessing an awesome amount of power, which has generated enough superstition to prevent people from trying to get to it. During all these years, the Ark has been guarded by Menelik's descendents, and the descendents of those who accompanied him, who became known as 'Falasha' (exile) Jews, or the 'Black Jews' This area became part of the independent nation of Eritrea in 1993.

It was alleged, that when Israel became a nation, an appeal was made to Emperor Salassie to return the Ark. He said: "In principle, I agree that the Ark should be returned to the Temple, but the correct time has not yet come." Many researchers believe that the Ark is at the chapel at Aksum, although it has never been seen.

Is Israel waiting for the discovery of the Ark, so they can rebuild the Temple; or are they waiting for the time when they can freely rebuild their Temple, so they can retrieve the Ark and place it in the Holy of Holies? There are some who share the suspicion, that Israel already knows where the Ark is, but also know that the political climate of their homeland is too volatile to take a chance on revealing its location until the right time.

Unlike the Temple, the Ark is not mentioned in Biblical prophecy. As we have discovered, the Ark was not in the second Temple, so the existence of the Ark is not necessary for the Temple to be rebuilt. However, if you turn on the 6 o'clock news, and you see that Israel is announcing the discovery of the Ark of the Covenant, this certainly will have a bearing on the prophetic timetable.

REBUILDING THE JEWISH TEMPLE

There is a school of thought that believes that only the Messiah can rebuild the Temple, because He would be the only one who knows the actual location of its foundation. This sentiment is the official position of the Israeli government. However, there is some evidence that seems to indicate that the Temple will be rebuilt prior to the return of Jesus.

The Antichrist will sign a seven-year protectionary treaty with Israel (and perhaps other nations), but will break it halfway through when he causes the sacrifices to be discontinued (Dan. 9:27, Dan. 12:11), so that he will be able to take "his seat in the Temple of God, displaying himself as being God (2 Thessalonians 2:4, see also Rev. 11:1)." Matthew 24:15 refers to this area as the 'holy place.' This seems to indicate that the Temple will already be in existence by this time.

Moses prophesied that Israel would be punished twice. The first was 430 years of captivity in Egypt, and the second was 70 years of slavery under the Babylonians. After that, three things were foretold: the Jewish nation would be reborn in Palestine, they would repossess old Jerusalem, and they would rebuild their ancient Temple on its original site. In 1948, the nation of Israel was established; in 1967, they took complete control of the city of Jerusalem; which leaves only one prophecy unfulfilled, and that is the rebuilding of the Jewish Temple. Amos 9:11 says: "In that day will I raise up the tabernacle of David that is fallen, and close up the breaches thereof; and I will raise up his ruins, and I will build it as in the days of old..."

Prior to the construction of the Temple, God made His divine presence known in a miqdash ('holy place'), which was a temporary structure known as the Tabernacle, that was erected in various locations around Israel, such as Shiloh, Bethel, Dan, Gilgal, Mizpah, and Hebron. This continued until the Israelites became united, both politically and spiritually, which took place when David conquered Jerusalem, thus creating a central location for their civil government and religious worship. When David realized the big difference between his own house, and the fact that the Ark was protected only by a tent (2 Sam. 7:12), he knew that he had to build a house of God, which according to the Davidic Covenant (2 Sam. 7:4-17), seems to indicate that the site chosen would be a permanent location.

In the 24th chapter of 2 Samuel, it is recorded how David counted his men to see if his army was going to be of sufficient military strength. Because he didn't trust God for his victory, so the Lord sent a destroying angel that brought a plague against the people of Jerusalem. David built an altar and made peace offerings to the Lord. This area on Mount Moriah (Mount Zion), was the site where God tested Abraham's faith by commanding him to sacrifice his son Isaac, and was known as the threshing floor of Araunah the Jebusite. David purchased the land in 990 BC, and in 960 BC, King Solomon began construction of the sacred Temple, which was to provide a shelter for the Ark of the Covenant, the most sacred object in Israel. It took a workforce of 200,000 men seven years to complete this magnificent edifice, with funds gathered by David in a royal treasury. It was destroyed in 586 BC by Babylonian invaders.

The Persians conquered the Babylonians, and Cyrus, the Persian king, allowed 50,000 Jews to return to Jerusalem in 538 BC. In 537 BC, under the direction of King Cyrus, Zerubabbel (a descendant of King David), supervised a contingent of Phoenician workers who laid the foundation stones for the second Temple. All the Temple vessels had been returned, the altar built, and the sacrifices resumed. Opposition by the Samaritans (descendants of Israelite and Assyrian intermarriage) in the north, who had a temple at Mount Gerizim, caused construction to be discontinued until 520 BC, when Darius, the Persian king, instituted taxes to pay for its construction. The Temple was dedicated sometime between 516-514 BC. Another Persian king, Artaxerxes, appointed a Jew named Nehemiah as governor of Jerusalem, and he repaired the walls to protect the Temple, and began rebuilding the city.

Judea soon came under the control of the Greeks (Alexander the Great); and the Egyptian Greeks (or Ptolemies), who allowed governorship by the high priests. A third ruler, a Syrian Greek (Seleucid) known as Antiochus IV (Epiphanes), who sided with the Jewish faction known as the Hellenists, appointed a high priest who initiated pagan worship in opposition to the Orthodox faction. An attack in 170 BC killed many Jews, and again Temple treasures were taken. Antiochus desecrated the Temple by sacrificing a pig on the altar, placing a pagan idol in the Holy of Holies, and burning copies of the Torah. An Orthodox priest named Mattathias Maccabee ("the hammerer") began a revolt, which ended in 164 BC when his third son, Judas took control of Jerusalem, purified the Temple, and resumed the daily offerings. However, their control ended in 63 BC when Rome invaded.

Over the years, the condition of the building declined, and around 20-19 BC, Herod the Great undertook the restoration of the Temple in order to win the favor of the Jews. Most of the construction was completed within ten years, although minor restoration work continued until 64 AD. The rebuilt Temple, known as the Temple of Herod, was twice as high, and much wider. During this period of Roman rule, an imperial sacrifice had to be offered to the emperor, in addition to the traditional Jewish sacrifice. This came to an end in 66 AD, when Eleazar, the son of a captain of the Temple, initiated an uprising of Jewish zealots, which brought the Tenth Legion from Rome. They failed to defeat the Jewish freedom fighters and a massive revolt ensued, which resulted in Judea being returned to the control of the Jews. Emperor Nero then sent Vespasian, Rome's best military leader, and his army, to end the rebellion. By 69 AD, Rome regained control of all Judea, except for Jerusalem. Vespasian, who became the new emperor, gave his son Titus the task of securing Jerusalem. A military operation was launched which ended in 70 AD, when the Temple was set on fire by the Roman Tenth Legion (consisting of 80,000 men) under Titus, who pried the Temple apart stone by stone, and threw them into the valley southeast of Jerusalem. A portion of the Western Wall (Kotel Maarabi), known as the Wailing Wall, was left standing by the Romans as a symbol of how powerful they were. Titus later returned to Rome with some of the Temple treasure.

When Constantine died in 361, his nephew, Flavius Claudius Julianus, the last emperor of Rome (361-363), ruled for 19 months, and attempted to reinstate paganism, and emperor worship. Although he had grown up under the teachings of Eusebius, Bishop of Cesarea, he turned away from those teachings, and pushed for religious tolerance. His hatred of Christianity drove him to return Jerusalem back to the Jews, to restore Jewish law, and to advocate the rebuilding of the Jewish

Temple. He freed them from taxes, and gave his support for the reestablishment of animal sacrifices, but he was told that the Jews no longer practiced the ritual because they had no Temple. Julian appointed Alypius of Antioch to oversee its building, while the governors of Syria and Palestine were instructed to assist. Workmen cleared the debris, and work was begun in 363. When they tried to dig into the foundation, an earthquake occurred, which ignited pockets of natural gas underground, causing fires and explosions, destroying all the stones, wood and metal which were being stored on the site. A number of workers were killed. This was taken as a divine sign that the Temple was not to be rebuilt at that time, and construction was halted after Julian died in the battle against the Persians. After the return to power by the Christian Roman Emperors, the idea was forgotten.

The Church of the Holy Sepulcher was built on higher ground in 326 by Byzantine Christians during Constantine's rule, on the traditional site (according to Catholics) of Jesus' crucifixion, burial and resurrection. Across from the Temple Mount, it was actually intended to symbolically replace the Temple, which is why its layout is reminiscent of the Temple. As a way of offending Jews, the condition of the Temple area was allowed to deteriorate and was even used as a repository for human waste and other refuse.

In 614, the Persians broke through Byzantine defenses, and with the help of the Jews, defeated Heraclius. Chosroes II, the Persian King, placed a Jew named, ironically, Nehemiah, as the governor of the city, and gave them permission to rebuild the Temple. Although it is believed that the sacrifices were resumed, no construction was initiated. About fifteen years later, Heraclius returned to take over the city, building an octagonal church on the site. After the death of Muhammed (570-632), his follower Omar (Umar Abu Ibn el-Khattab, or Umar I) became Caliph, taking over Jerusalem in 638, with the help of his Islamic army. In 643-44 he built a wooden mosque on the Temple site, which stood for 44 years. In 687, Abd al-Malik ibn Marwan, the 10th Caliph, began work on the Qubbat as-Sakhra or the Dome of the Rock (also known as the Mosque of Omar), which was completed in 691.

The Mosque was built to rival the Church of the Holy Sepulcher showing its religious claim on the city by symbolizing the ideology of their new faith, and to be a protection for the rock believed to be the threshing floor purchased by David. No Islamic tradition was connected to the site. Even the Quran (Surah V, v. 21), the Islamic holy scripture, states that the Jews have a historic claim on the land. However, the event known as the 'Night Journey of Muhammad' (or 'hijrah'), when he fled from Mecca to Medina, was connected to Jerusalem, because it mentioned al-Aqsa, which is the name of the Mosque south of the Dome of the Rock. Linguistically, 'al-aqsa,' when it is translated, means 'far corner,' and could very well refer to Mecca. Therefore, the Temple Mount is said to be the rock where Muhammed received his instructions from God, and ascended into Heaven. Some historians believe that the story was concocted during the rule of Umayyad prince, al-Walid I (705-715) to raise the funds necessary to build the al-Aqsa Mosque into an edifice comparable to the Dome of the Rock.

From 1099-1187, the Crusaders occupied Jerusalem, and the Dome of the Rock became a Christian church, while the al-Aqsa Mosque became the headquarters of the Knights Templar. When Jerusalem was overthrown by the Muslim leader

Saladin (Salanad-Din), the Temple Mount complex, containing both the Dome of the Rock and the al-Aqsa Mosque, which is referred to as the Haram ash-Sharif, became the third holiest site in the Islamic faith (after Mecca and Medina), even though all prayers are directed toward Mecca.

Today, the obstacle for rebuilding the Temple, is the Islamic holy site, the Dome of the Rock. It is maintained that the Arabs have had a claim on it for 5,000 years, and that there was never a Jewish temple on that area. The Israeli Antiquities Authority, and most Israeli archaeologists agree that this traditional location was the site of the Temple. In 1967, even though Israel captured East Jerusalem during the Six-Day War, a month later, as a gesture of peace and cooperation, Israeli Defense Minister Moshe Dayan returned control of the Temple Mount back to the Wakf (Islamic authority). It was later reported that he had an underlying fear that the ground would be razed to make way for the rebuilding of the Temple.

Only the tip of the huge rock, on the summit of Mt. Moriah, juts up into the center of the Dome of the Rock. It is unclear whether the rock was the sacrificial altar, or the Holy of Holies where the Ark was placed, but the presence of drain holes bored into the surface, which leads to a cave below the Mosque, may indicate that it was the area of the Temple used for sacrifices. The purpose of the holes was for the blood from animal sacrifices to runoff into a canal which carried the fluids out of the complex. This would place the Holy of Holies in an area which slopes downward, and creates a conflict with archaeological evidence and historical tradition.

There is some support for the idea that the rock was the foundation stone for the Holy of Holies. The argument for this is based on the assumption that one of the Temple gates, known as Warren's Gate (which was beneath the Gate Babel-Mat'hara, and up to 1967 was the location of an Arab latrine), opened directly in front of the Holy of Holies. In 1867, Charles Warren found an ancient gate to the Temple Mount, and since then, the entire Western Wall, and a tunnel running along it, called the Rabbinic Tunnel, was discovered and excavated by 1986; along with four other entrances, by Israel's Ministry of Religious Affairs and the Western Wall Heritage Foundation. The Western Wall of the Temple, left standing by Rome as a symbol of their authority, was part of the retaining wall which was erected to support the immense platform which held the Temple.

In March, 1979, where excavations were being done at the Western Wall, an unsubstantiated report was circulated, that a workman, digging with his fingers, 80 feet below the existing floor, discovered the Arch of King Solomon from the original Temple, which led to the Holy of Holies. The archway of stone was constructed with a special mortar containing broken glass, as per God's instructions. Tests taken of the glistening mortar indicated that it was produced during that period. They would not break through the Wall, because according to the Law, only a Jew from the tribe of Levi, and the family of Aaron, can enter the Holy of Holies.

In July, 1981, Rabbi Meir Yehuda Getz, chief rabbi of the Western Wall, while building a new synagogue behind the Western Wall, investigated water emanating from the Wall, and discovered a great hall (26' wide X 98' high x 82' long) behind a former cistern which contained an arch, believed to be one of the entrances to the Temple. It turned out to be the gate discovered by Warren, which led to the Temple court, and was the closest gate to the Holy of Holies. A group of ten men, some from the Ateret Cohanim Yeshiva, began clearing the hall, working their way toward the Holy of Holies. If the Rock was the foundation stone of the Holy of Holies, then tradition holds that beneath this stone there is a chamber created by Solomon which was later used to hide the Ark. Getz believes that this secret chamber contains the Ark, the table, and the menorah. After breaking down another wall, the Muslim authorities were made aware of what was going on, and the Arabs instigated a riot which led to the excavation site being shut down. A wall was placed over the entrance to the tunnel, and was later reinforced with another wall of steel and plaster, which in 1992 was redone to give it an appearance of natural rock. Rabbi Schlomo Goren believes that they came within 300 feet of this room, and rumors have circulated that Getz saw the Ark, which he denied, saying that the area is under water. Getz said: "The treasures of the First Temple are under the Mount, and we know exactly where they are..."

There was an unsubstantiated report that there is a lower cave, blocked by a slab, which was discovered in 1911. It had been alleged that the Crown of David, the Sword of Solomon, the Ark of the Covenant, the Tables of the Law, and a large amount of gold was discovered there, having been hidden by the priests when the Temple was destroyed. It is believed that these articles were removed, and their whereabouts are unknown.

The Israelis have been kept from rebuilding, or even doing much archaeological excavation because of their strained relationship with the Arabs, and because the Moslems fear that such excavations would weaken the structure of the Mosque. Others would argue that it's because any significant archaeological discoveries on the site would prove Israel's ancient claim to the Mount. Because of the lack of any substantial information, there is even a lot of doubt as to where on the Temple Mount the sanctuary was actually located.

Father Bellarmino Begatti, A Franciscan researcher, published a report in 1979, that, based on measurements and information in ancient documents, the Temple was located on the southern end of the Mount between the Dome of the Rock, and the al-Aqsa Mosque, and seems to be supported by the existence of underground reservoirs and tunnels. The Holy of Holies is believed to be located over the Al Kas Foundation.

Dr. Ze'ev Yeiven, and Dr. Asher Kaufman believe that Arab construction on the northern end exposed an ancient wall near the Dome of the Rock, which is believed to be the eastern wall of the Temple's Court of Women. Of particular interest is an exposed area of rock in an open area of the Mount, about 330 feet north of the Dome of the Rock, which is covered by a small building (cupola), known as the Qubbat el-Arwah (Dome of the Spirits), which is on an east-west alignment with the Eastern Gate and the Mount of Olives. It is also called the Qubbat el-Alouah (Dome of the Tablets), because it is believed that this was the location of the Holy of Holies in the original Temple, where the Ark of the Covenant was placed. If this is true, that means that the Temple can be rebuilt without disturbing the Arab site, because the Mosque, which takes up an area of 34 acres, would actually be separated from most of the Temple foundation by many feet of rubble. Proponents of this theory claim they have identified the area on the Mount of Olives which was used for the sacrifice of the Red Heifer, which further indicates that the Temple was not on the site of the Dome of the Rock.

Ernest Martin, a scholar, and author of many books, said that the Temple was built over the Gihon Spring.

Some Orthodox Jews believe that before the Temple can be rebuilt, both the Dome of the Rock and the al-Aqsa Mosque would have to be removed, because their presence defiles the sacred ground.

Before the Six-Day War, a quarter-page ad appeared in the *Washington Post*, seeking aid for the rebuilding of the Temple. They have been selling bonds to finance its building since 1948. The document known as the 'Temple Scroll,' which was part of the Dead Sea Scrolls found at Qumran, give distinct instructions concerning the construction of the Temple, and a group known as the Ne'emanei Har Habayit (Faithful of the Temple Mount) commissioned a model of the Temple to be built. It has been reported that the cornerstones are already cut and ready. Harvey A. Smith, a Jewish Assemblies of God minister, wrote in his book, that they have the biggest and heaviest stones cut, and secretly placed under the Temple Mount behind Warren Gate. The Temple music has even been deciphered.

After the Six-Day War, Israel Eldad, a noted historian who was interviewed by *Time* magazine, said: "We are at the stage where David was when he liberated Jerusalem. From that time until the construction of the Temple by Solomon, only one generation passed. So it will be with us."

In December, 1970, a special school called "Yeshiva Avodas Hakodesh" founded by Rabbi Hirsh Ha-Cohen (Cohens have been identified as the descendants of the priests in the original Jewish temple), was established to train students from the tribe of Levi in the ancient ritual of animal sacrifice. It was dedicated during the Feast of Dedication (Chanuka). Only students who can trace their lineage back to Aaron can be admitted. Motti Dan (Ha-Cohen), who is said to be a descendent of the priestly line, studied all the rules in regard to the Temple service, and established the "Ateret Cohanim Yeshiva" in the 1970's as a religious school to educate and train others, of similar descent, for the priesthood.

In 1978, Hebrew University began offering a two-year course in the restoration of animal sacrifice, including all methods and Old Testament requirements. The first class graduated on June 1, 1980, and among their graduation exercises, was to perform the ancient rite of animal sacrifice. An episode of "60 Minutes" in March, 1985, in a segment called "One Step in Heaven," indicated that rabbinical students in Jerusalem were studying the Jewish rites of animal sacrifice under Rabbi Shlomo Goren, the former Chief Rabbi of the Israeli Defense Forces, who had said in a November, 1981 *Newsweek* interview that the secret of the location of the Ark would be revealed just prior to the third Temple being built. The animal sacrifices will resume when the Temple is rebuilt.

The Institute for Talmudic Commentaries, run by Rabbi Nahman Kahane (a descendent of the priestly line), which is located in the Young Israel Synagogue, is involved in the study of the Temple rituals and ceremonies, and have been involved in research to catalog all known cohanim (priests) in Israel. The Atara L'yoshna ("restoring the crown to its original form"), a branch of Kahane's group, has established a Study and Tourist Center near the Western Wall, where they have models of the Tabernacle, the two original Temples, the new Temple, the Ark of the Covenant, a menorah, as well as other Temple implements.

A group called the Temple Mount Faithful (or the Temple Mount and Eretz Yisrael Faithful Movement), started by Gershon Salomon, a professor of Oriental Studies at the Hebrew University in Jerusalem, sought to take sole control of the Temple Mount to rebuild the Temple. It was a reactionary movement to protest the move by Moshe Dayan, the Israeli Defense Minister, who allowed the Muslims to maintain control of the Temple Mount area in 1967. He went to court in 1987 with claims by physicist Dr. Asher Kaufman, and archaeologist Dan Bahat, that the Arabs were destroying valuable archaeological evidence from the first and second Temples. The group has also made attempts to lay a special 4-ton cornerstone on the Mount.

The Temple Institute was esablished in Israel, in 1988, by Rabbi Israel Ariel, who in 1967, was the first paratrooper to reach the Western Wall. *Time* magazine printed a two-page article on the group in October, 1989, and ABC-TV's news show "20/20" televised a segment on them. On October 18, 1989, the first bi-annual Conference on Temple Research was held. This joint venture between the Temple Institute and the Ministry of Religious Affairs brought together rabbis, scientists, archaeologists in an attempt to better coordinate their efforts in making the Temple a reality.

Outside the Temple Institute, a sign in Hebrew reads: "Exhibition of Temple Vessels" (while a sign in English says "Treasures of the Temple"). Based on years of research, historical tradition and the Scriptures, the Temple Institute has produced the actual items which will be used in the Temple when it is rebuilt. Many of the 103 items which were used in the original Temple have been produced, or are in various stages of fabrication, including the gold crown of the high priest, the Temple garments, a copper washbasin to be used for purification purposes, incense utensils, and silver trumpets to beckon worshippers to the Temple. In the planning stages was the breastplate of the high priest, which will contain twelve gemstones; and the gold electroplated menorah which will contain 94.6 pounds of gold, giving it an estimated value of $10 million.

In January, 2003, the President of Israel, Moshe Katzav, asked the Prime Minister of the Vatican, Cardinal Angelo Sudano about what Temple treasures were in the possession of the Vatican, and to prepare a list of them.

Before Temple services can be legally reinstated according to Biblical Law, a ritual cleansing must be performed which involves the sacrifice of the Red Heifer (Numbers 19:1-22). The ceremony has only been performed seven times. The priest would sacrifice an unblemished, unbroken Red Heifer, after which the remaining ashes were collected and added to the ashes of the next sacrifice. It took place on the western slope of the Mount of Olives, within sight of the Holy of Holies. The ashes were then sprinkled upon the waters of a large cistern under the Temple to prepare them to be used as the water of purification to cleanse sin and defilement. The last sacrifice occurred in 70 AD, prior to the destruction of the Temple, after which the ashes were secretly buried. This ritual cleansing would have to be performed on the Temple Mount in order to reinstate Temple worship as commanded by the Laws of God.

Originally kept in a containment building near the Eastern Gate, archaeological excavations have been initiated to find the ashes, which according to the 'Copper Scroll' found at Qumran, were buried in a container made of clay, and dung from the Red Heifer. If they can not be located, the Temple Institute, on the belief that the tradition of the "ashes of continuity" is a mistranslation, maintains that the original ashes are not necessary. In October, 1989, the Chief Rabbi of Israel dispatched a team of scientists to Sweden to purchase the frozen embryos of a particular breed of red heifers in order to impregnate a heifer in Israel and breed an animal that would fulfill the scriptural requirements. However, the latest report is that a herd of red Angus cattle have been discovered in Mississippi, and a group of these have been sent to Israel for later use.

Vendyl Jones, a former Baptist minister turned archaeologist in 1977, said to be the inspiration for the creation of the fictional movie character Indiana Jones (though producers Steven Spielberg and George Lucas deny it), while searching in Jericho area caves for the Ark of the Covenant, found a clay jar containing a unique incense oil which dated back to the time of the second Jewish Temple, and contained the five ingredients the Bible identified as being part of the oil used to anoint kings. One of these ingredients was an oil called afars'mon, which was taken from the sap of the rare balsam tree that grew near Jericho at a wadi known as Ein Gedi, near the area of Qumran. The oil was very rare, and when Rome invaded the Qumran community before 70 AD, the Essenes burned the only known grove of these balsam trees, which are now considered extinct.

This special anointing oil is listed in the Copper Scroll, and in 1988, using the clues given there, a worker, Benny Ayers, who was with a group of Christian archaeologists and volunteers (including Dr. Gary Collett and Dr. Nathan Meyers), under the direction of Dr. Joseph Patrich from the Hebrew University's Institute of Archaeology, found an ancient clay container wrapped in palm leaves, in a hole three feet deep, on the floor of a cave adjacent to the one where Vendyl Jones would later discover some incense. Professor Ze'ev Aisenshtat and Dorit Aschengrau at the laboratory of Hebrew Univeristy's Casali Institute of Applied Chemistry, used Carbon-14 dating and said that the oil was put in the container during the first century, and is believed to be the anointing oil that was used in the Temple. The oil's chemical composition was such, that one drop placed in water, turned it a milky white, just as ancient documents indicated. The substance was given to the Chief Rabbi of Israel, and it will be used to anoint the Messiah when he returns.

Chief Rabbi Isaac Herzog believes that the dye used to achieve the blue-colored thread on the Temple garments (Numbers 15:37-40), comes from the Segulit snail, which because of its scarcity, is very expensive. According to the Talmud (Menahot 44a), Israel is inundated every 70 years with these snails. In October, 1990, they were found in large numbers on the Mediterranean beaches of Israel.

In April, 1992, Jones announced that on the floor of a cave, north of Qumran, at the Wadi Jafet Zaben, he discovered about 900 pounds of a reddish-colored material which was tested by the Weizmann Institute of Science, and found to be the remnants of a special mixture of incense believed to be used in the Temple service. Jones felt that this was one of the items listed in the Copper Scroll. However, the Temple Institute believes that since the incense was not found in a container, it had been improperly prepared and disposed of, and thus is not acceptable for use.

Little by little, all the elements seem to be coming together in preparation for the day when the Temple will be rebuilt. The closer we come to that reality, the opposition to it increases within certain religious circles. The destruction of the second Temple in 70 AD, according to some Christian leaders, indicated that the Jews were being punished for rejecting Jesus as the Messiah, and that Judaism was being usurped by Christianity, which had become the new temple of God. They feel that because He spiritually dwells within all who believe and follow His teachings, the rebuilding of the Temple would be a denial of Jesus' atonement for our sins on the cross, which eliminated the necessity of Temple sacrifice. This sort of theological debate is pointless, because the Bible plainly eludes to the existence of the Temple in the last days, regardless of how right or wrong it is.

Now bear in mind, I have been told by Pastor Milt Maiman, (formerly of the Messianic Hebrew Christian Fellowship in Harrisburg, PA) that to fulfill the prophecy, the Temple doesn't have to be rebuilt. Just as the Tent of the Tabernacle was originally used to house the Ark, it could again be erected on the Temple grounds, and used for Temple observances.

So, when you turn on the 6 o'clock news, and you see that Israel has put up the Tent, or that construction on the Temple has begun, know that this is one of the major events in the prophetic timetable, and that the end is near.

CHAPTER TWELVE

THE CURTAIN FALLS

PRIEURÉ DE SION

In the mid-1980's, an incredible revelation was been made in regard to the unity of Europe, the forces behind it, and its relationship to the man who will rise to prominence in Europe's political community. First, let me relate the information as I have gathered it, and then afterward I will comment on how it may fit into the prophetic scheme of things. However, before embarking on this section, I have to warn you that you are going to be reading a mixture of factual history, as well revisionist history that represents a radical departure from the views traditionally held by Christians. I do not share these views, or advocate them in any way, but include them only for you to see how it may possibly have a bearing on end-time prophecy.

In 1891, in Rennes-le-Chateau, a tiny southern French mountaintop village, parish priest Berenger Sauniere, made a discovery while doing renovations to restore a church which had been dedicated to Mary Magdalene in 1059. The altar stone had been removed, which rested on two old Visigoth columns, one of which was found to be hollow. Inside were four parchments sealed in wooden tubes. Two were genealogies, one dated from 1244, which carried the seal of Queen Blanche de Castille, mother of King Louis IX; and the other dated from 1644 by Francois-Pierre d'Hautpoul. Of the other two documents, the Testament of Henri d'Hautpoul, which was dated 1695, was written in French, and is believed to be a complex code detailing a state secret; and the other parchment, written in the 1780's by a priest, Antoine Bigou, was written in Latin, and contained two coded Biblical texts, one on each side of the page, which were excerpts from the New Testament. Sauniere went to Paris to present the parchments to Church authorities.

Also during the restoration, a flagstone dating to the 7th or 8th century was removed, allegedly revealing a burial chamber, which contained skeletons; and because of the amount of money he would soon begin to spend— a treasure of some sort. There has been much speculation about what this treasure could have been.

Some talk had centered around the Holy Grail. The Grail was believed to be a chalice made of gold, which was first used by Melchizedek as he offered bread and wine to Abraham on Mount Moriah. It was guarded in a Phoenician temple in Tyre, the city of Hiram, the king who designed and built Solomon's Temple. It fell into the hands of the Queen of Sheba, who gave it to King Solomon, and it was last used by Jesus and the disciples during the Last Supper. Other traditions have said that it was used by Mary Magdalene or Joseph of Arimathea to catch the blood of Jesus as it dripped off of His body while He hung on the cross. It was believed that Joseph took the cup to Glastonbury in England; while others claim that Mary took it with her to Marseilles in France.

The Cathars, who descended from the Bogomils in Bulgaria, and existed around the 10th and the 11th centuries, were perceived to be a wealthy people, and were said to possess a treasure beyond material wealth. In January, 1244, three months before the fall of their fortress in Montsegur, two men got out with the gold, silver, and money. As their defeat seemed eminent, the northern invaders served them with terms of surrender in March, and gave the Cathars two weeks to make a decision. One of the terms of this 'cease-fire,' was that if anyone tried to escape, they would be killed. A day before the surrender, when they would have been released, four men escaped on a rope, down the sheer western face of the fortress. According to legend, the risk was made to protect their treasure. But if all their gold and silver had been smuggled out three months before, what did they risk their lives to protect. Was it the Holy Grail?

The Knights of King Arthur's Round Table searched for the Grail, and legend has it that three of them seen it— Galahad, Percival, and Bors. Later stories revealed that the Grail was kept at the Church of St. Mary Magdalene in Rennes-le-Chateau, which is where she made her home.

Others believe that the treasure Sauniere found may have been the Temple treasure. In 70 AD when Rome ransacked Jerusalem, carrying its treasure back to Rome, it was believed that they may have gotten all of the Temple wealth, including the Ark of the Covenant. In 410, when the Visigoths invaded Rome, they carried away, "the treasures of Solomon, the King of the Hebrews, a sight most worthy to be seen, for they were adorned in the most part with emerald's and in the olden time they had been taken from Jerusalem by the Romans."

Or, could the treasure discovered by Sauniere been the treasure plundered from the Temple grounds by the Knights Templar.

Many of the Crusaders who went to Palestine to fight against the Moslem invaders were French Catholics, and by 1061, they had conquered Jerusalem, and put Godfroi de Bouillon (1061-1100), Duke of Lower Lorraine, on the throne of Jerusalem. Known as the 'Guardian of the Holy Sepulcher,' he claimed to be of the lineage of David, and between 1090 and 1099, organized a secret society called the Prieuré de Sion (Order of Sion). His aims were to possess the wealth of the world, including the Temple treasure, and to establish world government which would be controlled by a Merovingian king in Jerusalem.

Though deposed in the 8th century, the Merovingian dynasty and bloodline continued, and was perpetuated with Dagobert II, and his son, Sigisbert IV. Through alliances and intermarriages, this line continued through Godfroi. This bloodline was known as a "royal tradition ... founded on the rock of Sion," which was considered to be equal to other European dynasties.

Their headquarters was at the Abbey of Notre Dame du Mont de Sion, in southern Jerusalem on Mount Sion, where the ruins of a Byzantine basilica from the 4th century stood, which was called the Mother of All Churches. It was Godfroi's younger brother, Baudouin I, who became the first king of Jerusalem; it was the Prieuré de Sion that created the Knights Templar as its military arm.

In 1118, Hugues de Payen, a nobleman from Champagne, and Godfroi de St. Omer, a French Knight, along with seven other Knights, founded the Order of the Knights Templar (Order of the Poor Knights of Christ and the Temple of Solomon). They swore to live according to the rules of St. Augustine, and to use their swords, arms, and strength to defend the Christian faith. They also took vows of chastity and poverty, and promised not to join any other organization. They pledged to "keep the roads and highways safe ... for the protection of pilgrims" and not to surrender any wall, or foot of land. They offered their services to Baudouin I, the King of Jerusalem, and an entire wing of the royal palace on the Temple Mount (the site of Solomon's Temple) was given to them to be used as a living quarters. In 1139, Pope Innocent II decreed that these Knights of Christ owed their allegiance to no one but the Pope (thus becoming a military arm of the Catholic Church), and they began to wear white robes with a red cross on the front. They carried a black and white striped banner which displayed the cross, and the words: "Non nobis, Domine, sed nomini tuo da gloriam," which became their battle cry. Their meetings were carried out in secret.

It is known, that for nine years, the Knights were searching for something beneath the Temple grounds, and evidence points to the fact that they might have found something. In March, 1952, a copper scroll found in cave III at Qumran, near the Dead Sea, revealed that more than 138 tons of gold and silver were buried in 64 locations, before the Romans destroyed the Temple. It is believed that 24 of these locations were under the Temple Mount, which was plundered by the Knights Templar and taken to Europe, where it became the basis for the establishment of the international banking system.

In 1153, a nobleman, Bertrand de Blanchefort, who lived only a couple of miles from Rennes-le-Chateau, became the 4th Grand Master of the Knights Templar He escalated their growth into the diplomatic and political circles, and established a Templar presence in the area. Their numbers soon increased to 9,000, and the Order spread to Tripoli, Antioch, Cyprus, Portugal, Castile, Leon, Arragon, France, Flanders, the Netherlands, England, Scotland, Ireland, Germany, Italy and Sicily. They had a presence in most areas adhering to Christianity.

In 1187, after the fall of Jerusalem to Saladin, they were forced to move their headquarters to the island of Cyprus; and in 1188, the Prieuré de Sion withdrew their control from the Knights Templar and separated from them. They moved their headquarters to a Temple in Paris, and through their organization and wealth, the Knights became the bankers of Europe.

By the end of the 12th century, they had 30,000 members (mostly French), and they fought in the wars of their own countries. They soon gained so much power, that their Grand Master Jacques du Molay became a challenge to the authority of King Philip IV ('the Fair'). Between 1303-05, King Philip had Pope Boniface VIII (1294-1303) kidnapped and killed, and had his successor, Pope Benedict XI (1303-05) poisoned; then had his own man, Clement V (1305-16), elected to the vacant papal throne. Pope Clement worked with Philip to begin a campaign to destroy the power and the influence of the Knights, the Merovingian bloodline, and to confiscate their treasures.

In Germany, Spain, and Cyprus, they were acquitted of any charges; but not in England, Italy, and France. On October 13, 1307, all the Templars in France were arrested, amidst charges by a former member (Esquian de Horian), and an investigation by Pope Clement, who said that they appeared to serve Christ, but actually worshipped Lucifer. Accusations included: immorality, heresy, denying Christ and the Virgin Mary; spitting and stepping on the cross; burning the bodies of dead Templars and giving the ashes to initiates to mix in with their food and drink; carrying out rituals with a skull, believed to be that of founder Hugues de Payen; and worshipping a demon who took on the form of a cat. When King Philip's men broke into the Templar castle in Paris, they discovered a silver bust of a woman's head, with a hinged top, which when opened, contained two head bones wrapped in a white cloth, with a red cloth around that. They were believed to be part of the skeletal remains of Mary Magdalene.

It was revealed, that part of the initiation, required the initiate to deny, curse, and spit at the cross, as part of a gesture symbolizing St. Peter's denial of Christ, thus introducing the candidate to the Order as a sinner, so they could teach him the ways of Christianity. In actuality, the Knights had actually become opposed to the Pope, when they realized the Vatican's pagan relationship to sun worship; and since the Catholic Church had become so identified with St. Peter, the Knights had renounced Peter, and became followers of John.

In 1312, Pope Clement ordered that the Knights Templar were to be suppressed. On March 18, 1314, Jacques de Molay, the 22nd Grand Master of the Knights, Geoffrey de Charney (who possessed the Shroud of Turin, which was stolen from Constantinople), and two of their highest officers were burned at the stake for trying to overthrow the government. In England, Edward II joined in the denunciation by arresting and torturing 140 knights, 54 of whom were burned at the stake.

Some of the remaining Templars fled to Portugal, where there were protected by King Dinis II. Most however took refuge in Scotland, where they stayed for 400 years, developing the Scottish Rite branch of Masonry. In England, where the Templars established the first modern Masonic lodge at York, it was identified as the York Rite; while in France, it became known as the Scottish Rite. To signify the accomplishments of the Order, it was made the highest attainable degree in Masonry. It is said that "every true Mason is a Knight Templar..."

Meanwhile, the Prieuré de Sion existed for another 300 years, until 1619, when the historical record dried up.

According to recent information, it is believed that Sauniere's 'treasure' was actually the knowledge gleaned from the parchments, that the crucifixion of Jesus was a set-up, and that He was alive as of 45 AD. Sauniere's niece, Madame James of Montazels, inherited the parchments in 1917, and kept them until 1965 when she sold them to Capt. Roland Stanmore and Sir Thomas Frazier, who keep them in a safe deposit box in Lloyds Bank Europe Limited of London. Only two of the parchments have been released, the contents of the other two have not been revealed.

In the original sources concerning the Holy Grail, references are not to a cup, but to a mystery.

In the 1180's, "Le Roman de Perceval" (or "Le Conte du Graal"), a poem by

Chretien de Troyes, chronicles one, Perceval, who seeks his knighthood. At the castle of the "Fisher King" he sees the Grail, which is golden and is studded with jewels. It is not linked to Jesus. Perceval discovers that he is a member of the "Grail family" because the custodian of the Grail is his uncle. Chretian died before completing his work, and no copies exist. However, the story lived on, becoming closely aligned with King Arthur. "Roman de l'Estoire dou Saint Graal" by Robert de Baron in the 1190's was the version that Christianized the story, claiming that Joseph of Arimathea filled the cup with Christ's blood, and that his family became the keeper of the Grail. Galahad was purported to be Joseph's son, and the Grail was passed onto his brother-in-law, Brons, who took it with him to England, becoming the "Fisher King." In this version, Perceval is the grandson.

The most noted version is "Parzival," which was written between 1195 and 1216 by Wolfram von Eschenbach, a Bavarian Knight who claimed that Chretien's version was inaccurate because Wolfram received his information from a more reliable source. He said that the Grail is some sort of stone. But more important, is his preoccupation with the Grail family, the genealogy, or bloodline.

In early stories, the Grail is called the Sangraal and Sangreal, which was divided to read 'San Graal' or 'San Greal,' when in fact, it should have read 'Sang Raal' or 'Sang Real,' meaning 'Royal Blood.' So therefore, the Grail actually had more to do with blood, and not a cup which held blood.

The "Queste del Saint Graal" written between 1215 and 1230, indicated that the Grail was brought to France by Mary Magdalene, and that the Grail story occurred about 456 years after the resurrection of Jesus, or about 487, which was about the time of the rise in Merovingian power.

In 1964, according to the book *The Jesus Scroll* (1972) by Donovan Joyce, an ancient parchment scroll was excavated on the western shore of the Dead Sea, at the ruins of the fortress of Masada. It was there that 965 Jewish men, women, and children, burned the complex, killed each other, and committed suicide, rather than be captured by the Romans.

The Jewish rebellion against Roman rule and their occupancy force came to a head in 66 AD when several thousand zealots stormed Masada and seized King Herod's fortress. From there, the movement spread, as loyalists hoped to restore the throne of the Maccabean kings, which has been usurped a century earlier. One part of the rebel army stayed at Masada, while the other marched on Jerusalem. The attempt to recapture the city failed, and the survivors retreated back to Masada. Rome struck back, and four years later, with nearly a million dead, and many enslaved, Jerusalem was firmly in their grasp, the Temple was destroyed, and the entire country was overrun. The Roman Tenth Legion, under the command of Flavius Silva, spent three years with a legion of 6,000 men, and 15,000 Jewish slaves, to build an assault tower in order to destroy the last vestiges of Jewish resistance at Masada.

When the Roman soldiers breached the walls of the fortress, they found only corpses, as the occupants preferred death to being captured and enslaved.

In 1963, Masada was excavated by the Israeli Dept. of Antiquities in a massive archaeological operation led by Israeli scholar and soldier, Gen. Yigael Yadin. They discovered coins, tools, weapons, catapult ammunition, wine jars, beads, rings, buckles, jewelry, cosmetics, ovens, pots, pans, lamps, dishes, baskets, and remnants of woven fabric clothing, as well as 14 parchment scrolls containing Biblical text (Leviticus, Deuteronomy, Psalms, Ezekiel), the apocryphal Wisdom of Ben-Sira, and Book of Jubilees, and a sectarian scroll which provided a link between the zealots and the Essenes of Qumran, 30 miles north of Masada.

In a cave on the upper face of the southern-most cliff below the plateau, reached by descending to it with a rope, 25 skeletons were found: 14 males, ages 22-60; a man between 70 and 80; six females between 15-22; four children from 8-12; and a fetus. It had been believed that all of the bodies had been thrown over the side; so either the Roman centurions were unaware of this group which were separated from the main complex, or they were allowed to remain where they had fallen, just as the three skeletons found in Herod's palace at the northern end of the complex, which were believed to be that of Eleazar ben Yáir, the Jewish commander, his wife and child, and left there as a tribute to his valor. The three were formally buried in July, 1969, at the foot of Masada in a common grave, with full military honors.

It seems likely that there was an easier access to the cave, back at that time, which had since eroded away, the face of which was clearly visible from at least two nearby camps, so it had to have been searched. Which means Silva may have known that this was a special group, and also left them untouched.

If the purpose of the rebel's presence at Masada was to restore the Hasmonean throne, then why did the war continue another six years after the death of their leader Mennahem at the battle in Jerusalem. The prevailing evidence suggested that there was someone at Masada more senior than either Eleazar or Mennahem. Because of the discovery of this document, it is now believed that the Zealots on Masada were actually a bodyguard contingent for the Hasmonean Royal Family, headed by Jesus, their king and Messiah, who they swore to defend till the death.

Another document which was discovered, had been written on the evening of April 15, 73 AD, just after the Roman battering ram had compromised the fortress gate, and was pulled back, to await the Roman attack which would come at first light. The document was signed by Yeshua ben Yákob ben Gennesareth, who described himself as a "son of eighty years" (this would have placed his birth at 7 BC) and the last heir of the Hasmonean (Maccabean) King of Israel. Translated, the name was 'Jesus of Gennesareth, son of Jacob.' This document was the 15th parchment to be discovered on Masada, and it is believed that it was smuggled out of Israel by a rogue archaeologist, and taken to Russia. Because it can not be located, the details given about it were only hearsay. The contents were allegedly revealed to the Vatican in February, 1967, because after a meeting between Podgorny of the U.S.R.R. and Pope Paul, the Vatican did an about face, and began supporting the Moslems in their quest for a homeland in Palestine.

Let me interject, that Yadin, in his book *Masada: Herod's Fortress and the Zealots' Last Stand* says of the 25 bodies, that the "only feasible assumption is that they were flung here irreverently by the Roman troops when they cleared the bodies after their victory." Plus, he never mentions the discovery of a 15th scroll.

So, how could the veracity of this story even be considered? There is a developing trend that purports that Jesus was not the product of a virgin birth, that He was a normal man with a messianic complex, who was part of a conspiracy to fake his own death in order to fulfill Old Testament prophecy. It is believed that the Last

Supper was actually a meeting to plan a way for Jesus to cheat death.

Dr. Hugh J. Schonfield, in his book *The Passover Plot* (1965), theorized that the vinegar-soaked sponge given to Jesus during the crucifixion, actually contained a drug that made Jesus appear as though He were dead, when he really wasn't. This insured the prophetic fulfillment that his legs would not be broken (which was done to bring death quicker). Joseph of Arimathea (a member of the Sanhedrin) then went to Pilate to ask for permission to claim the body, so that it could be interred in a tomb owned by Joseph. Pilate sent a centurion to confirm that Jesus was dead. When Joseph asked for the body, he referred to it as 'soma,' (living); while Pilate referred to the body as 'ptoma' (dead).

To substantiate these facts, it is pointed out that the place of the crucifixion had to be near the tomb. While the other gospels state that He was crucified at Golgotha, "the place of the skull," John 19:41 says that he was crucified in a garden, where a new sepulcher had been hewn by Joseph. This garden was actually 'Golgeth,' the 'wheel press,' where olives were pressed into oil, which was the Garden of Gethsemane. Some have even theorized that Joseph was actually the former husband of Mary, who had left Nazareth, and established himself at Jerusalem. After the story about Jesus in the Temple, Joseph is not mentioned again. The 'angels' seen at the tomb were said to be Essene physicians who were sent to revive Jesus, thus creating the illusion of a resurrection.

The apocryphal Gospel of Peter, discovered in an upper Nile valley in 1886, had existed as early as 180 AD, and reveals that Joseph of Arimathea was a friend of Pontius Pilate, and that Jesus was buried in the "garden of Joseph." Basilides, an Alexandrian scholar, who wrote various commentaries on the Gospels between 120 and 130 AD, believed that Jesus did not die on the cross. In December, 1945, an Egyptian peasant discovered a pot near the village of Nag Hammadi in northern Egypt, which contained 13 scrolls, which consisted of copies of Biblical texts, which dated to about 400 AD, and were based on writings that were no older than 150 AD, and provides a good historical reference because they were not altered by the Roman Catholic Church.

In one, the Second Treatise of the Great Seth, it talks about Jesus escaping His death on the cross through substitution, who was identified as Simon of Cyrene. An ancient document, found in the 4th century, in the library of a building used by Greek monks, said that Nicodemus and Joseph conspired to retrieve the body of Jesus so that it could be revived by Essene physicians.

A document found in the 19th century by a member of the Societe Francaise Commerciale in Abyssinia, in the library of an old building formerly occupied by Greek monks, said that Jesus was born in Nazareth, was an Essene, and that after the crucifixion, Nicodemus told Joseph that he was going to resuscitate Jesus, but that John was not to know it. Inside the tomb, using Essene medical knowledge, stimulative substances were burned, and strips of ointment-covered linen were applied to the body. After the treatment, the stone put over the tomb opening held the vapors in. Three days later, an Essene brother, in festive garments, went to the tomb, and the soldiers, thinking him to be an angel, ran away. Then 24 Essenes showed up, and spirited Jesus away to their commune. However, Jesus insisted on leaving and went to his disciples, and they believed him to have risen from the dead.

A document known as *The Crucifixion by an Eye Witness*, was a Latin manuscript in the possession of a Masonic library in Germany, which surfaced near the end of the 1800's, and was said to have been copied from a letter written by a member of the Essene Order, to another in Alexandria, only seven years after the crucifixion. It revealed that Jesus was the son of Mary and an Essene teacher who was not identified. It talked about the crucifixion, Jesus' removal from the cross, and the Essene medical intervention which enabled him to survive the crucifixion; and by appearing to His disciples afterwards, made it seem as though He had risen from the dead. It was first published in 1873, but was withdrawn from circulation, its plates destroyed, as well as most copies. One copy did find its way into the possession of a Mason in Massachusetts, and in 1907, it was republished in Chicago.

The letter says of the birth of Jesus:

"I will tell you of the parentage of this man, who loved all men and for whom we feel the highest esteem. He was from his infancy brought up for our brotherhood. Indeed, he was predicted by an Essene, whom the woman thought to be an angel. This woman was given to many imaginings, delving into the supernatural and into the mysteries of life. Our brother the Essene has acknowledged his part in these things and has persuaded the brotherhood to search for and protect the child secretly."

"Joseph, who was a man of great experience is life and of deep devotion to the immortal truth, was influenced, through a messenger of our Order, not to leave the woman nor disturb her faith in the sacredness of her experience. He was told to be a father to the child until our brotherhood should admit him as a novice. Thus, during their flight to Egypt, Joseph, his wife and the child were secretly protected and guided by our brotherhood."

Apocryphal writings indicate that while in Egypt, Joseph and Mary stayed at the monasteries of Wadi-el-Natrun, Mataria, and al-Moharraq, which were run by the Essenes.

According to Josephus, the Essenes were "the most perfect of all sects in Palestine." He wrote that "they despise riches and worldly gains and live in communes," and "are the most honest people in the world ... exercise justice and equality ... never marry, and they keep no servants. They all live the same simple, industrious and frugal life." He described them as a secret brotherhood that were against the Pharisees and Sadducees, abhorred violence, wore white robes, were vegetarians, did not believe in animal sacrifice, studied the healing properties of herbs, possessed a high moral standard, and observed celibacy.

In 1963, scrolls known as the Talmud of Jmmanuel, were discovered by Greek Catholic priest, Isa Rashid, in a cave he claimed was the burial cave of Jesus. Written in old Aramaic, sealed in protective resin, and buried under a flat rock, it is believed to have been written by Judas Iscariot. Pieces of the scrolls were missing, some unreadable, some deteriorating, yet, what had survived, was completely contrary to the story of Jesus as related in the Bible.

The document claims that Joseph of Arimathea realized that Jesus was still alive, and quickly went to Pilate to request the body, taking it back to his own tomb. There was a secret second entrance, and it was through here that his friends were able to bring the herbs and salves necessary to provide medical treatment. In three days he was strong enough to walk. After a few appearances to his disciples, he went to Syria, then to India, and the area now known as West Pakistan, Afghanistan, and the Himalayas, where he continued to teach. He married and had children, and it was believed that he died at the age of, between 110-115 years old, in Anzimar in Khanyar Srinagar, which is located in Kashmir, India. These scrolls were in the possession of his first born son, who returned to Jerusalem, and hid them in the burial cave of Joseph of Arimathea where Jesus had been taken.

The 'sacred tomb in Kashmir' is the burial site of a man known as Yazu Asaph (also written as Yuz Asaf), who was known as a prophet. He came to this valley about 2000 years ago from Egypt, teaching the same things as Jesus. Located in a small, rectangular brick and wood structure, he is buried in a wooden sepulcher which contains an inner wooden sarcophagus that is covered with a sacred shroud, and a rectangular stone slab.

The structure seems to be built over an ancient stone structure which actually contains the remains of Asaph. A tiny opening allows you to see into the crypt below the floor, and into the burial chamber.

Inside the shrine is a smaller tombstone, which is that of an Islamic saint Syed Nasir-ud Din, who was buried there in the 15th century. Both tombstones are aligned north-to-south, following Islamic custom, but the sarcophagus in the crypt below containing Asaph's remains are aligned east-to-west, which is a Jewish custom.

Chiseled on a stone slab are the impressions of his two feet which bear the traces of crucifixion wounds, conceivably of the man who is buried there. The nature of the wounds indicate that the man was crucified with the left foot over the right, with one nail going through both feet— which matches the pattern of the figure on the Shroud of Turin, which is purported to be the burial cloth of Jesus.

It is also believed that Mary, the mother of Jesus, accompanied Jesus and Mary Magdalene to India. She died when she was 70 years old, trying to escape when the Kushans attacked the region of Taxila. The place she was buried in Pakistan (45 miles east of Taxila) was called 'Mari' until 1875, when the spelling was changed to 'Murree.' The tomb is called 'Mai-Mari-de-Asthan' or 'resting place of mother Mary.' No other tombs in the world are purported to be that of Mary. Mary Magdalene is reported to have died at Kashgar, in central Asia, and it was actually Martha, that took her son, along with some other followers of Jesus, to France, where she lived till her death.

Then came the story of St. Hazrat Issa. Around 1887, Nicolas Notovitch, a Russian journalist, while traveling in Ladakh in Tibet, had fallen from his horse and broke his right leg, below the knee, and was taken to the monastery at Hemis (Himis), 25 miles from Leh, the capital of Ladakh (400 miles north of Delhi), located in a hidden valley of the Himalayas, some 11,000 feet above sea level. There, the chief lama read him the story of Issa, the man he knew as Jesus, which said that during the 17 years in which he is not mentioned in the scriptures, Jesus was in India.

He was told that they had many scrolls describing the "life and acts of the

Buddha Issa, who preached the holy doctrine in India and among the children of Israel." He visited the monastery at Mulbekh, and was told that at the archives at Lhasa, the capital of Tibet, there were several thousand ancient scrolls detailing the life of Issa, and that some of the principal monasteries also had copies.

The documents, which had been brought from India, to Nepal, and then to Tibet, were originally written in Pali, the religious language of the Buddhists, and then translated into Tibetan. Notovitch believed that the verses "may have been actually been spoken by St. Thomas— historical sketches traced by his own hand or under his direction."

There are various references to the apostle Thomas (also known as Didymus, Judas, and "twin brother of Christ, apostle of the Highest who shares in the knowledge of the hidden words of Christ…"), who, according to religious tradition, introduced Christianity to India in 52 AD

The apocryphal *Acta Thomae* (*The Acts of St. Thomas*) written in the early 3rd century, said: "When the Apostles had been for a time in Jerusalem, they divided the countries among them in order that each might preach in the region which fell to him; and India (Parthia, northwest region of India, from the Euphrates to Indus and India proper), fell to the lot of Thomas." He went to India as a carpenter, and preached the gospel to the Parthians, Medes, Persians, Bactrians, Indians, and Hyrecaneans.

One story said that he arrived at the coast of Malabar in 52, and established his first church there. Another story said that after spending some time in the North, he went south, along the coast of the Arabian Sea. And yet another story said he arrived in the state of Kerala in 52, where it is believed that Thomas established seven churches: Cranganore, Palur, Kottakavu, Kokkamangalam, Niram, Chayal, and Quilon. After a couple years he went to South Tamil, and Tamil Najd.

According to a 2nd century Syrian manuscript called *The Doctrine of the Apostles*, it says:

"After the death of the Apostles, there were Guides and Rulers in the Churches; and whatever the Apostles communicated to them, and they had received from them, they taught to the multitudes. They, again, at their deaths also committed and delivered to their disciples after them everything which they had received from the Apostles; also what James had written from Jerusalem and Simon from the City of Rome, and John from Ephesus and Mark from the great Alexandria, and Andrew from Phrygia and Luke from Macedonia and Thomas from India, that the epistles of an Apostle might be received and read in the churches in every place … India and all its own countries and those bordering on it even to the farthest sea, received the Apostles' Hand of Priesthood from Thomas, who was Guide and Ruler in the Church which he built there and ministered there."

His writings speak of the conversion of a king named Gundaphar, and in the 19th century, some coins were discovered in Afghanistan, near the capital city of Kabul, and in the western and southern regions on the Indian Punjab, which bear the name Godophares, and date back to 20 and 40 AD

He went from the west coast to the east, to Mylapore (near Madras in southern India, now called St. Thomas Mount), on the Bay of Bengal, where in 72, he was killed by an assassin sent by the ministers of the king, while he was kneeling in prayer. After being pierced by the spear, he fell on a hand-carved stone cross. This cross was rediscovered by some Portuguese workers on March 22, 1547, as they were digging the foundation for the church that was built on the site. His relics were preserved in a cathedral dedicated to him. The Roman Catholic Church considers the Cathedral of St. Thomas a Basilica, because it was erected over his tomb. However, another source said he was buried six miles away at the church he built, near Fort St. George in Tamil Nadj in India

Notovich published his findings in New York in 1890 as *The Life of Saint Issa*, and in London in 1894, as *The Unknown Life of Christ*. He said that the Roman Catholic Church was aware of the existence of these manuscripts, and in fact have 63 complete, or partial copies of similar manuscripts in various languages.

Notovich was treated by Dr. Karl Marx (not the Russian Revolutionary), who recorded the information in his diary that is in the possession of the Moravian Christian Mission at Leh. However, the *New York Times* published a story about J. Archibald Douglas who visited the same monastery, and they told him they never saw Notovich, and knew nothing of a Saint Issa. They labeled Notovich's book a forgery.

In 1921, a tourist named Henrietta Merrick visited the monastery at Hemis, was told about Issa, and that there were documents that had been in their possession for 1500 years that talked about him.

In 1922, Swami Abhedananda, a scholar, Hindu monk, and a disciple of Ramakrishna, went to India, visited the same monastery at Hemis, and was also told about St. Issa from their copy of the scroll; and he was shown an original copy of the scroll at the monastery in Lhasa, Tibet, which vindicated the incredible claims of Notovitch. He translated it into English, and then in 1929 to Bengali.

In 1928, Professor Nicolai Roerich also traveled to Ladakh and Kashmir, where he visited the Hemis monastery, saw many scrolls, and found out that the writings concerning Issa were kept in the most isolated part of the subterranean storage areas.

Roerich said that the Tibetan scroll he found indicated that Issa was 13 years old when he secretly left his father's house left for India, and Notovich records in his book that he was 14 when he went to India, as does the Natha Namavali (or Sutra). He didn't want to marry, which pushed him into leaving home. He traveled east with a caravan of merchants to Pakistan.

The apocryphal *Gospel of the Hebrews* (also known as the *Gospel According to the Hebrews*) said that Jesus traveled to India by way of Assyria and Chaldea with a group of merchants. His first stop was Sindh, where the Indus River and its tributaries flow into the Arabian Sea. He then went to Punjab and Rajputana, and then to Orissa. The evidence suggested that Issa stayed at the Temple of Jagannath in Puri for 6 years. He also visited Rajagriha, Varanasi (Benares) and other holy cities.

Issa then left the temple so he could visit the birthplace of Buddha, and lived in the Buddhist monastery there, where he was educated in the teachings of Buddha.

Sakyamuni Buddha (563 - 483 BC) was a well-educated prince who renounced his royalty (his father was the Chief of the Shakya Clain in Kapilavastu, in Nepal), because of his disillusionment with the ravages of illness and old age. At Gaya, while meditating under a Bodhi tree, he had a vision, and became 'enlightened.' He taught about "non-violence, peace, and compassion." About 300 years later, Ashoka Maurya (269-232 BC), emperor of northern India, converted to Buddhism, and sent missionaries to many countries. In fact, it has been suggested that the Pythagoreans in Greece, and Essene community in Judea, was the result of missionary work by Buddhists. The man known as Issa was considered to be the incarnate of the spirit of Buddha, and was revered as a great prophet and teacher.

After 6 years in the foothills of the Himalayas in southern Nepal, he was recognized as a Master, and "had become a perfect expositor of the sacred writings." He left, traveling westward. He passed through Punjab, and met up with a caravan of merchants from Kashmir, and he performed miracles among them, including the healing of the sick.

He returned to Egypt where he appeared before the Essene brotherhood, where he passed 7 tests, after which he was proclaimed the Christ. In a meeting before the 7 'Sages' Issa said:

> "The history of life is well condensed in these immortal postulates: 'There are seven hills on which the holy city shall be built; there are seven sure foundation stones on which the universal church shall stand.' The words I speak are not my own; they are the words of him whose will I do."

> "And from men of low estate I will select twelve men, who represent twelve immortal thoughts, and these will be the model of the church. And when a better age shall come, the universal church will stand upon the seven postulates. And in the name of God, our Father God, the kingdom of the soul shall be established on the seven hills. And all the peoples, tribes, and tongues of the earth shall enter in. The prince of peace will take his seat upon the throne of power; the triune God will then be All in All."

He returned to Palestine when he was 29 years old, and the remainder of the narrative pretty much parallels the New Testament, except that the Jewish priests and elders are portrayed as supporting him, and Pilate is the one working behind the scenes to bring about his death. The text then ends with the persecution of his followers, and the disciples being sent forth to preach.

According to tradition, Issa died when he was 125 years old.

In 367, Bishop Athanasius of Alexandria made a list of writings which were to become what we now know as the New Testament. His selections were ratified by the Church Council of Hippo in 393, and again four years later, by the Council of Carthage. Therefore certain 'books' were left out, and were 'lost' even though some may have been historically accurate. One of the primary duties of the Church fathers between the 7th and 12th centuries was to obtain manuscripts from collections in Eastern countries, which contained information that differed from the version accepted and taught by the Church. These original documents may still be in the Vatican archives.

The first mention of the resurrection of Jesus appears in 1 Corinthians 15:3- 8, because it is believed that this was actually written about ten years before Mark was written. Therefore the stories concerning the resurrection of Jesus were unknown to Paul. In 1 Corinthians 9:1, Paul says: "...have I not seen Jesus Christ our Lord?" yet there is no historical reference that he knew Jesus. The word "seen" was translated from the Greek word 'ophthe,' which means to have one's eyes opened to realms beyond this physical world, which refers to visions. It is the same verb which is used by Isaiah (Isa. 6:1) when he said: "I saw the Lord sitting upon a throne..." It was also used in Luke 24:34 to say that Jesus "appeared to Simon" and in the Book of Acts to describe the resurrection. Paul never spoke of a physical resurrection, because in light of the proper translation, it was only in a spiritual resurrection, where Jesus now "sitteth on the right hand of God." (Col. 3:10)

Nearly a hundred "gospels" appeared during the first three centuries, and to preserve continuity and protect the new Christian religion, the four gospels of Matthew, Mark, Luke and John were chosen. Despite some gaps and contradictions, they were very similar. These books were not written during Jesus' lifetime, but date from a time of major revolution in Judea, 66-74 and 132-135, and the earlier writings that they had been based upon have since been lost.

The argument has been made, that though some apocryphal gospels are derived from some sects that are doctrinely different from Christianity, their appearance, some in the early 2nd century, suggest that they were closer to the actual events than the four gospels, and possibly more historically accurate.

What all the writers of the Gospels had, concerning Jesus, was just an outline of the man. There were no eyewitnesses to consult, so where there was a void in detail, they just referred to the Hebrew Scriptures to fill in the blanks. For example, the removal of Jesus to Egypt by His earthly father Joseph, hearkens back to the patriarch Joseph in the Book of Genesis; the story about the young Jesus in the Temple, was modeled after Samuel's Temple experiences; the Sermon on the Mount was an attempt to paint Him as another Moses; the story of Jesus' raising of the widow's son at Nain, was taken from Elijah's raising of the widow's son in 1 Kings 17:17; Jesus' feeding of the 5,000 was just a retelling of God's providing for Moses' people as they wondered in the wilderness; the story of Jesus walking on the water, was a misunderstanding of the Greek preposition which could mean 'on' or 'alongside of'; and the ascension of Jesus was taken from the story of Elijah being taken up into Heaven.

The earliest Gospel was considered to be Mark, which was compiled between 66-74 in Rome, and was believed to address a Greco-Roman readership, and if he wanted it to survive, he could not make it appear as though the Romans were responsible for the death of Jesus. It actually ends without the disciples' assertion that Jesus rose from the dead, and only says that the women were told that He had risen. Mark never mentions whether He was ever seen after the crucifixion.

In 1958, in a monastery near Jerusalem, Professor Morton Smith of Columbia University, discovered a letter that contained a missing fragment of the Gospel of Mark, which through the years had been suppressed by Bishop Clement of Alexandria, who was informed that a gnostic sect known as the Carpocratians were interpreting various passages in the Gospel of Mark for their own purposes, which did not coincide with Church doctrine. The passage was part of the story about Lazarus being raised from the dead, and hinted that he wasn't actually dead. Along with the exclusion, there was also an addition, because the original manuscript ended with the death and burial of Christ, and the discovery of an empty tomb. Yet, the version that exists today, includes the Resurrection, which was added in the 2nd century, making the last twelve verses of Mark fraudulent. However, research by Ivan Panin (outlined in a booklet called *The Last Twelve Verses of Mark*), utilizing analysis of numeric design, has done a lot to reaffirm its authenticity.

The gospels of Luke and Matthew used Mark as a source for their writings. Luke (who also wrote the Book of Acts) dates to about 80, and was composed for a Roman official at Caesarea, and therefore was not anti-Roman. While Matthew's genealogy of Jesus only goes back to Abraham, Luke's goes back to Adam. Where Mark mentions only an empty tomb, in Luke, the women actually go in and see for themselves that it is empty. They encounter not one, but two angelic beings. Luke goes more into depth regarding the subsequent physical appearances of Jesus.

Matthew was put together about 85, and allegedly not by the disciple Matthew. It was intended to be a revision of Mark, in order to put more emphasis on the divine nature of Jesus, and borrowed references from the Book of Joshua who referred to placing guards at a cave in which he had five captured kings imprisoned, and having the cave sealed with a huge stone. It also alluded to Daniel in the lion's den, and how he came out alive, when he applied the story to Jesus in regard to him surviving the tomb. In Mark, Peter is quoted to have said to Jesus, "Thou art the Christ," and in Matthew, he is quoted to have said, "Thou art the Christ, the Son of the living God." The disciples were told to baptize "in the name of the Father, and of the Son, and of the Holy Ghost," which it is alleged that Jesus could not have said, because it actually represented a theological premise that didn't occur till much later.

Barnabas, a follower of Jesus, uncle of Mark, and a companion of Paul, who traveled around Palestine preaching the good news, wrote an apocryphal book, known as the *Gospel of Barnabas*. It was accepted as a canonical gospel in the Alexandrian churches until 325 AD, when the Nicene Council ordered all copies of it to be destroyed, and anyone who had it in there possession was to be put to death.

In the 5th century, a copy, written in his own hand, was found lying on his chest, in his tomb in Cyprus, which made its way into the library of Pope Sixtus V (1585-1590) and was made available by a monk named Frater Marino.

Though there is no major deviation from the authorized gospels, one subtle difference appeared in the Sermon on the Mount, which seems to indicate that the account which in written in Matthew may have been embellished, to make it sound better. Barnabas writes: ""Blessed are they that mourn this earthly life, for they shall be comforted. Blessed are the poor who truly hate the delights of the world, for they shall abound in the delights of the Kingdom of God. Blessed are they that eat at the table of God, for the angels shall minister unto them."

Polycarp, author of a letter to the Philippians, wrote about the first three Gospels, but not the fourth, because it didn't exist, and it wasn't mentioned until 180 by Theophilus of Antioch. John has come to be regarded as the most accurate of the Gospels, even though it is believed to have been written over a period of years by theologians, at the Greek city of Ephesus, who in 100 AD, sought to fill the void in the contents of the other three. John has the risen Jesus being seen by only Mary Magdalene, where in other books, other women accompanied her; and also singles her out as being a primary mourner. This hint at a more intimate relationship has given rise to a theory as to the actual role that Mary had in the life of Jesus. In the other three gospels, the Last Supper is portrayed as a Passover meal, after which Jesus was crucified; however in John, the crucifixion occurred before the Passover, whereby John puts more emphasis on the foot washing that occurred. This discrepancy had been explained by saying that John was using the lunar calendar, while the others were using the solar calendar, however, it is now believed that John's purpose was to present Jesus as the Passover Lamb of the Jews, who is killed as their sacrifice. Where in Luke, only Peter goes to inspect the tomb; in John, it was Peter and John. Critics claim that the story of Doubting Thomas (John 20:19-31) wasn't true, based on the premise that Jesus was tied to the cross, rather than nailed. Some have even claimed that there was "no historical proof that he (John) ever existed."

Simon Peter, the "Rock" upon whom Jesus said He would build His church, was believed to be the first to 'see' Jesus after the resurrection, and it was through his efforts that the philosophy of Christianity was perpetuated. The primary contention is that the New Testament was doctored to present Jesus as being divine. Because Jesus was not of the priestly tribe of the Levites, it was necessary to validate His claims so that He would be accepted by the early Christians. In the Book of Hebrews, completed before the fall of Rome around 68, Jesus was described as being a perfect priest after the order of Melchizedek, who in Genesis was referred to as a priest of the most high God, yet neither was he a Levite. The Book of Hebrews, said to be written by Paul, also refers to the presence of Jesus in Heaven, but never refers to a physical resurrection.

Books such as *Forgotten Worlds* by Robert Charroux (1971), and *Resurrection: Myth or Reality?* by John Shelby Spong (1994), have questioned the authenticity of the Bible. In a 1977 book, called *The Myth of God Incarnate*, 7 scholars and professors from prominent American seminaries seriously questioned whether Jesus was Lord, and said that the Bible should be updated by having all traces of the deity of Jesus removed. They said that Jesus didn't claim to be divine, but was promoted to that status by early Christians who were under pagan influences. Another book, *The Five Gospels: What Did Jesus Really Say?*, a report by 77 Biblical scholars, which were part of the Jesus Seminar, said that Jesus did not say about 80% of the words which are attributed to him in the four gospels. They claim that the words were inserted by Christians after His death. In October, 1994, the Seminar convened and decided that the virgin birth of Jesus was fabricated. One participant called it "theological fiction." This group began working on a new Bible commentary to reflect all of its findings.

The Gospel of John doesn't mention the birth of Jesus, but it covers the conclusion of his ministry. The incident of the wedding at Cana is only mentioned in John, and is unusual in that the bride and groom are not identified, yet Jesus, His disciples, and His mother were there. When they ran out of wine, it was Jesus who performed the miracle of turning water into wine. The question was asked— why

FINAL WARNING

would Jesus use His divine powers for such an insignificant purpose— unless it was His own wedding. Researchers have analyzed John 2:9-10, and feel that where the head of the feast is speaking to the bridegroom, it is actually Jesus that he is addressing. It is argued that this marriage was Jesus being married to Mary Magdalene, who it is believed was the woman whom Jesus cast the demons out of, who washed and anointed the feet of Jesus, and who is identified as Mary of Bethany (sister of Lazarus and Martha). She figures heavily in the gospels, and it was to her that Jesus first revealed Himself after the Resurrection.

Since the Essene law forbade marriage, Jesus may have been forced to withdraw from his relationship with her, because it would interfere with His work.

The *Gospel of the Ebionites* ('ebionim' Hebrew for 'the humble' or 'poor' were purists that believed only the poor could receive Salvation, observed the Law of Moses, and considered Jesus to only be a prophet) or *Gospel of the Hebrews*, supposedly shed so much light on Jesus, that it was suppressed by Church leaders. In fact, all books of the Ebionite sect have mysteriously disappeared. In the *Gospel of Mary*, Peter says: "Sister, we know that the Saviour loved you more than the rest of women. Tell us the words of the Saviour which you remember— which you know but we do not, nor have we heard them." The apocryphal *Gospel of Philip* refers to Mary as his "spouse," and says: "There were three who always walked with the Lord; Mary his mother and her sister (Salome) and Magdalen, the one who is called His companion (partner) ... the spouse (companion) of the Saviour is Mary Magdalen ... (He) loved her more than all the disciples and used to kiss her often on the mouth." Near the end of the book, it says: "There is the Son of Man and there is the son of the Son of Man. The Lord is the Son of Man, and the son of the Son of Man is he who is created through the Son of Man." It was Mary Magdalene, who carried the Grail, Sangraal, or 'Royal Blood' to France.

Around 70 AD, Mary, the wife of Jesus, took his children, and fled the Holy Land to escape the Roman destruction of Jerusalem. They made their way to a Jewish community in Provence, in southern France, where the lineage of Jesus, through marriage, was joined with the royal family of the Franks (during the 5th century, the Sicambrians, a Germanic tribe called the Franks, crossed the Rhine River into Gaul into what is now Belgium and northern France), thus creating the royal Merovingian dynasty. Within the Merovingian royal family, there were many Judaic names. It is believed that she later died at Saint Baume.

It could be that the Holy Grail, 'Sang Raal,' or 'Royal Blood,' could actually represent the womb of Mary Magdalene, which produced the bloodline. It is even conjectured that French cathedrals like Notre Dame, were built in honor of Mary Magdalene, and not the mother of Jesus.

In 2003, according to a novel by Dan Brown called *The Da Vinci Code*, the Prieuré de Sion deliberately manipulated the record of Mary's role in the life of Jesus to spare her family from Roman Catholic leaders who sought to maintain the Biblical depiction. They used a code and symbols to represent and preserve her story, which evolved into the Holy Grail. In a ABC television documentary exploring the possibility of Jesus being married, Brown uses Da Vinci's (a Prieuré de Sion member) painting of *The Last Supper* (c. 1495) as an example. A close examination of the figure on Jesus' right, long believed to be John, actually looks like a woman, and he believes that it is actually a representation of Mary. Art historians, however, only need to refer to his painting 1516 painting of John the Baptist as proof of his penchant for portraying Biblical figures as effeminate men.

Joseph of Arimathea, uncle to Mary, an Essene and well-to-do merchant in the tin market, who was a member of the Sanhedrin, appears to have been a guardian to Jesus. There is a legend that during one of his trips to Britain, Jesus was with him, and they stayed at a small house at Glastonbury. St. Augustine later wrote to Pope Gregory that Jesus had established a church there. Gildas (516-570), an early British historian, said that "Jesus afforded His light to this island during the height of the reign of Tiberius (who ruled 14-37 AD, with the 'height' being around 25-27)."

It is explained that Jesus may have possibly been in the area to learn about the Druids. It is a long-held tradition that after the crucifixion, around 37 AD, Joseph led a group of people who settled in Glastonbury; and a wattle church was built on what became the location of the Abbey, which existed until the 1100's. It is from this group which came the Culdees (quidam advanae) or Christianized Druids, who lived on the islands off the west coast of Britain.

Merovee was the first king of the Merovingian bloodline, and he is surrounded in legend. He was said to have been fathered by two. When his mother was already pregnant by King Clodio, she went swimming in the ocean, where she was raped by a sea creature "similar to a Quinotaur," so that when Merovee was born, the blood that coursed through his veins was a combination of both, which gave him superhuman powers. Merovee claimed he descended from Odin, a Norse God (which is where we get Wednesday, Woden's Day, or Odin's Day), which some researchers believe actually referred to Dan, one of the twelve tribes of Israel, because the Merovingian kings claimed to be the descendants of the Spartans and Trojans.

The tribe of Dan declined to accept their land when Joshua divided it up, and they marched up the Jordan valley to the city of Laish, conquered it, and called it the city of Dan. They immigrated to what is now known as Greece, where they dominated the people who were living there, the Pelasgians. They became known as the Danaoi. They established the settlement of Ionia on the Ionian Isles. A branch migrated to Ireland and were known as the "Tuatha de Danaan," then went to Denmark as the Danes, and another branch eventually made their way to Britain. The Celts claim they came from the tribe of Dan, and that the name Denmark, and the Danube River, give evidence of their migration.

The Spartans lived in the southern Greek peninsula of Arcadia, later migrating across the Aegean Sea to build the city of Troy. According to the Iliad, by the Greek poet Homer, the founder of Troy was Dar-dan-us. Over the centuries the Spartans made their way into southern France, while the Trojans moved north and west into Germany, Belgium and northern France, following the Danube River, eventually settling in the province of Lorraine. In the apocryphal book of 1 Maccabees, it was written that the Spartans were related to the Jews and were of the stock of Abraham, and for various reasons, were believed to have been from the tribe of Dan.

When the tomb of Childeric I, son of Merovee, was opened in 1653, 300 miniature bees of gold were found, which Napoleon had sewn into his coronation robe. In the Bible, the Danites were represented by a serpent, an eagle, a lion, and bees. The eagle's wings on the back of the lion in the 7th chapter of Dan may symbolize Dan breaking away from the tribe of Judah. The tribe of Dan lived in the territory west of Jerusalem, near the coast of the Mediterranean, and after the death of Samson, lost their lands, and went north into the area now known as Lebanon, where they lived for 600 years. In 721 BC, when the Assyrians took ten of the tribes captive, there was no mention of Dan, thus they soon lost their identity.

In Genesis 49:17, Jacob gave a prophetic statement in regard to his sons in that "last days," and said that, "Dan shall be a serpent by the way, an adder in the path, that biteth the horse heels, so that his rider shall fall backward." In the *Testaments of the Twelve Patriarchs*, an apocryphal book written about 150 BC, which is said to represent the final words of Jacob's twelve sons to their families, attributes this statement to Dan, made when he was 125 years old: "I read in the Book of Enoch, the Righteous, that your prince is Satan ... I know that in the last days you will defect from the Lord, you will be offended at Levi, and revolt against Judah (the bloodline of Jesus), but you will not prevail over them."

When Moses built the Tabernacle, he chose two men to head up the project, Bezaleel, of the tribe of Judah, and Aholiab of the tribe of Dan; and after it was completed, the tribes were positioned around it, and instructed to display their standard. Dan was in the north, and given the symbol of Scorpio, which according to the Egyptian Zodiac was a snake; and yet, Ahiezer, captain of the tribe, chose an eagle, considered a hunter of snakes. The symbol of ancient Spartan Greece was an eagle, as was the symbol of ancient Trojan Rome. In recent history, the symbol of the Hapsburg dynasty was an eagle.

The offspring of Merovee were noted for a birthmark, a small red cross, above their heart or between their shoulder blades, which became their symbol. The Merovingians were known as sorcerer-kings, who could heal, had clairvoyant powers, and could telepathically communicate with animals. They wore powerful amulets, and were called the 'long-haired Kings' because they didn't cut their hair. Merovee (447-58) was a practitioner of the religious cult of Diana. His son, Childeric I (458-96) practiced witchcraft. Childeric's son, Clovis I (496-511) adopted Christianity, converting to Catholicism, and in 496, he was given the title "Novus Constantinus" ('New Constantine') by the Bishop of Rome, giving him the authority to preside over the rebirth of a "Christianized" Roman Empire, consolidating the power of the Church, and creating a tie between Church and State. During his rule, the Frank kingdom grew to cover most of France and Germany. It is believed that the Vatican knew the secret of the bloodline.

Merovingian Bloodline
Merovee (447-58)
Childeric I (458-96)
Clovis I (496-511)
Clotaire I (511-58)
Chilperic I (561-84)
Clotaire II (584-628)
Dagobert I (602-38)
Sigisbert III (629-56)

Dagobert II (651-79)
Childeric III (deposed)

The Church had a hand in the assassination of Dagobert II, and Childeric III was deposed by Pepin III, the first of the Carolingian dynasty. The removal of the Merovingians was culminated with the coronation of Charles the Great, Carolus Magnus, or Charlemagne, who in 800 became the Holy Roman Emperor, thus betraying the pact made with the Merovingian bloodline, ending their dynasty. But the bloodline continued in the personage of Sigisbert IV (son of Dagobert II), who fled southward, taking on the surname "Plant-Ard" (eventually "Plantard"), and the title of the Count of Razes.

In 1956, the Prieuré de Sion was registered with the French Government, with the objective of "studies and mutual aid to members." They were headquartered in Sous-Cassan, and within the group they circulated a magazine called *CIRCUIT*, which was an abbreviation for "Chivalry of Catholic Rules and Institutions of the Independent and Traditionalist Union."

In 1976, the excommunication of traditionalist Archbishop Marcel Lefebvre by Pope Paul VI was expected. He represented the conservative branch of the Roman Catholic Church, who fought against the modernization of the Church. In the end, the Pope backed down, and the *Guardian* (8/30/76) revealed their theory why: "The Archbishop's team of priests in England ... believe their leader still has a powerful ecclesiastical weapon to use in his dispute with the Vatican. No one will gave any hint of its nature, but Father Peter Morgan, the group's leader ... describes it as being something 'earth-shaking'."

The Order held a convent at Blois on January 17, 1981, the first since the one in Paris in 1956. The 121 at the meeting were all figures in high finance and international politics. A man named Pierre Plantard de Saint-Clair was elected as their Grand Master. His name figures prominently in many Prieuré documents. He is the lineal descendant of King Dagobert II and the Merovingian dynasty. In 1960, he spoke of an "international secret" hidden at Gisors. His grandfather was a personal friend of Berenger Sauniere, and he owns land in the area of Rennes-le-Chateau. In French records, he was listed as the Secretary-General of the Prieuré de Sion. When asked what their objectives were, he said: "I cannot tell you that. The Society to which I am attached is extremely ancient. I merely succeed others, a point in a sequence. We are the guardians of certain things. And without publicity."

The organization is not limited to just restoring the Merovingian bloodline, and has many Jewish members, though the full extent of the membership is unknown. Documents on file indicate that their organizational hierarchy is similar to the Masons.

In 1979, in Paris, Plantard told reporters of the BBC, when asked if his organization had the treasures of the ancient Jewish Temple, he said: "Yes ... they will be returned to Jerusalem when the time is right." He claimed that the real treasure was "spiritual" and consisted of a "secret" that would create a major social change regarding the restoration of the monarchy. In talking about France, Plantard said that Mitterand was "a necessary stepping-stone." He revealed that their Order is on a timetable, and that their plans were unstoppable.

Plantard talked about unrest within the membership of the Prieuré's Anglo-American contingent. The signatures of Gaylord Freeman, John Drick, and A. Robert Abboud were found on their official correspondence. They were associated with the First National Bank of Chicago. Drick was the President, and on the Board of Directors of other companies, including Stepan Chemical, MCA, Oak Industries, and Central Illinois Public Service. Freeman, an Illinois lawyer, was Chairman of the Board of First National, and on the Boards of other companies, including First Chicago Corporation, Atlantic-Richfield, Bankers Life and Casualty Co., Baxter Travenol Labs, and Northwest Industries. He also chaired a Committee on Inflation for the American Bankers Association. He was a member of the MacArthur Foundation and a trustee of the Aspen Institute of Humanistic Studies. Robert Abboud had also been Chairman of the Board of First National, and later became President of Occidental Petroleum Corp. It was originally believed that the signatures were forged from a 1974 Annual Report, but it was later discovered they were produced with rubber stamps. Though Freeman denied membership in the Prieuré de Sion, or of having any knowledge of their activities, Plantard has corroborated the information and said that their association with Freeman and other financiers had more to do with their goal of European unity, which had become their primary concern.

Plantard resigned as Grand Master, and member of the Order in July, 1984, "for reasons of health," plus other personal reasons, foremost being that he didn't agree with "certain maneuvers" by "our English and American brethren."

During the 19th century, the Prieuré de Sion, working through Freemasonry and the Hiéron du Val d'Or, attempted to establish a revival of the Holy Roman Empire, which was to be a theocratic United States of Europe, ruled simultaneously by the Hapsburgs and by a radically reformed Church. Their goals were thwarted by World War I and the fall of Europe's reigning dynasties. However, they continued to work for a United Europe as a protection against the Soviets, and as a neutral power to serve as a balance between Russia and the United States.

Out of the Merovingian bloodline had come most of the ruling families of Europe, and some Roman Catholic Popes. The genealogy of Dagobert's son, Sigisbert IV, can be traced through a dozen families, including the Houses of Luxembourg, Montpezat, Montesquiou, Sinclair, Stuart, Devonshire, Plantard, and ending with the Hapsburgs. Even though the Hapsburg empire no longer exists, when the first parliament of the European Economic Community met in 1979, one of its primary delegates was Dr. Otto von Hapsburg, the oldest son of Charles I, the last Hapsburg emperor. He and son Karl have been among the leading proponents of a United Europe. Karl von Hapsburg is the heir apparent to the Hapsburg legacy.

In 1909, Hitler found out about the legend behind the Holy Lance of Longinus (the Spear of Destiny, said to be the one used to pierce the side of Jesus during the crucifixion). It was said, that whoever possessed the Spear, would rule the world. It was in the possession of 45 Merovingian rulers from 752-1806, and when Hitler saw it, it was on display at the Hapsburg Treasure House Museum in Vienna. His obsession for the Spear ended, when he began his European military campaign against Austria for the purpose of getting this holy relic, which he did on October 13, 1938. He placed it in the Hall of St. Katherine's Church in Nuremberg. When the War got closer to Germany, the Spear and other treasures were secured in a protective vault. On March 30, 1945, when the American invasion was expected, the treasures were moved again, however, the holy spear was accidentally left behind, where it was found by the Americans. Upon the order of Eisenhower, the Supreme Commander of the Allied forces in Europe, it was returned to the Hapsburgs.

It is believed that the Prieuré de Sion has "incontrovertible proof" concerning Jesus and His continuing bloodline, and has been working to again bring this bloodline to power.

With this type of research, which purports to give you 'evidence' of their claims, it can be rather unsettling. All of these theories and revelations seem so incredible, that they border on the impossible, because they are completely contrary to everything we have been taught to believe. The arguments are so strong and persuasive, but one thing you must always remember about what is going on, is that it is a Satanic conspiracy— planned from the very beginning. With that said, bear in mind what it says in John 8:44— "Ye are of your father the devil, and the lusts of your father ye will do. He was a murderer from the beginning, and abode not in the truth, because there is no truth in him. When he speaketh a lie, he speaketh of his own: for he is a liar, and the father of it." The three main things that Satan does, is that he kills, steals, and destroys; so if any new information seeks to deviate from what is found in the Word of God, then it must be considered highly suspect. You must use spiritual discernment to separate fact from Satanic lies and deceit.

When I found out about the Prieuré de Sion there seemed to be something here, but for the longest time I just couldn't put my finger on it. But soon, the deeper I got, certain things stood out. By approaching these theories as being untruths, which they are; and isolating certain aspects of the premise, I think that the Prieuré de Sion becomes an important piece of the puzzle which I have been trying to assemble.

My theological beliefs are based on the fact that Jesus Christ was, and is the Messiah, the son of God; that He was crucified, and died on the cross for the sins of the world; and that after three days, He rose from the dead, and commissioned His disciples to preach the gospel to all people. I was raised to believe that, and as I have gotten older, it continues to be an undeniable fact. Since I consider this to be the truth, there must be a reason why people would go to such lengths to disprove the resurrection of Jesus, and develop a fraudulent background story.

There seems to be a poison that is slowly spreading in Religion. For years, the story has been building that Jesus planned the crucifixion to fake his death in order to fulfill Old Testament prophecies. This basically says that the concept of Christianity is based on a lie, and that Christ was only a man, who was transformed into the Son of God by early Church leaders. There weren't that many people that held to this belief. However, with knowledge gleaned from archaeological excavations, the discovery and translation of new apocryphal and biblical texts, and new interpretations of Scripture, the liberals have been successful in spreading this propaganda. Even though Jesus has been accepted as a great man, a great teacher, and credited for the establishment of the largest religious group in the world, this movement has sought to strip away his divinity by saying that the Resurrection was concocted to draw people into the Church.

When the revelation of the Prieuré de Sion began to surface amidst talk that not only was the Crucifixion planned, but that Jesus was married to Mary Magdalene, and had children whose descendants became part of the Merovingian Royal Family— there had to be a reason. Although not a lot is known about this group, there seems to be evidence that they may have found much of the Temple treasure, and used this wealth to establish themselves as a financial power in the world. The Merovingians ruled in Europe, and the Prieuré de Sion has been working behind the scenes to unite Europe under a single form of government. With the advent of the European Union, their efforts have been realized. Their goal has been to establish a World Government that would be ruled by the Merovingian bloodline. After all these years, why does this group continue to work towards this goal? The implication has been made that the group represents the Merovingian bloodline, and by extension, are the living descendants of Jesus Christ.

Biblical references in Daniel and Revelation strongly suggest the rise of a future leader out of the reestablished Holy Roman Empire, which is actually Europe. This leader will have to be a man capable of gaining the political support of all the European states. He will be a military genius who will be able to give Europe a sense of security, and a brilliant statesman whose words and deeds will make him a champion of justice. He will understand the problems of Europe, who will be able to bring peace and prosperity to the land.

As time goes on, and more propaganda is spread concerning this bloodline of Jesus, more people will begin to believe it. Remember what Joseph Goebbels (1897-1945, Nazi Minister of Propaganda) said: "The great masses of people will more easily fall victims to a 'big lie' than a small one, if it is repeated often enough." And remember, only two of the four documents discovered by Sauniere have been revealed; plus, it is believed that the Prieuré de Sion is also in possession of documentation that will prove their contention. Something else that has to be considered, because of all the controversy and secrecy surrounding the Dead Sea Scrolls, is there something there that will contribute to this massive deception. When the time is right, this information will be revealed, and it may be the final blow which will allow all of their plans to come together.

Much of the information about Jesus that is cited by the proponents of the various claims that have been made, come from ancient apocryphal documents. Even though some have been proven to be an accurate historical record; others could just be the writings of individuals who refused to accept to truth, and instead came up with their own version of events.

Some of you have probably heard of the British-Israel theory in regard to the migrations of the Jews. Proponents of this theory claim that those populating the country of Israel now are not actually Jews, that the Jewish race actually migrated west to the area of Europe and became the progenitors of the European nations.

The patriarch Jacob produced twelve sons, each of whom became the father of one of the tribes of Israel: Reuben, Simeon, Levi, Judah, Issachar, Zebulun, Joseph, Benjamin, Dan, Naphtali, Gad, and Asher. They each settled in a different part of the land of Canaan on each side of the Jordan River. After the death of King Solomon, Israel was split into two Kingdoms, along territorial and political lines. Judah and Benjamin in the South remained loyal to the House of David; while the rest of the tribes to the North were ruled by a succession of monarchies.

The Assyrian conquest of Israel mentioned earlier was a bit more complex than what is generally known. The downfall of the country began in 734 BC, and ended with the defeat of their capital at Samaria in 722 BC. Plus there was another incursion into Samaria in 720 BC. The actual deportation of Israelites which began with the initial Assyrian attacks from 734-732 BC, actually continued until 715 BC. Three different Assyrian kings were responsible for the forced deportation of Israelites to Assyria: Tiglath-pileser III (745-727 BC), Shalmaneser V (727-722 BC) and Sargon II (722-705 BC). The result was that the Israelite population in northern Israel was virtually wiped out.

In 722-721 BC, Shalmanser V, the King of Assyria conquered the Northern Kingdom of Israel, captured Samaria, and took these ten tribes to Assyria where they were imprisoned in Halah, Habor, Hara, and the river of Gozan. For all intents and purposes, these tribes seemingly disappeared, and they became known as the Ten Lost Tribes of Israel. It is believed, for the most part, that the southern tribes of Judah and Benjamin make up what is known as the Jewish people of today. However, Biblical evidence points to the fact that it was known where these tribes were.

In 2 Chronicles 30:1-10, recorded many years after the exile of the Northern tribes, you'll find this passage:

> "And (King) Hezekiah sent to all Israel and Judah, and wrote letters also to Ephraim and Manasseh, that they should come to the house of the LORD at Jerusalem, to keep the passover unto the LORD God of Israel ... So they established a decree to make proclamation throughout all Israel, from Beersheba even to Dan, that they should come to keep the passover unto the LORD God of Israel at Jerusalem: for they had not done it of a long time in such sort as it was written. So the posts went with the letters from the king and his princes throughout all Israel and Judah, and according to the commandment of the king, saying, Ye children of Israel, turn again unto the LORD God of Abraham, Isaac, and Israel, and he will return to the remnant of you, that are escaped out of the hand of the kings of Assyria ... So the posts passed from city to city through the country of Ephraim and Manasseh even unto Zebulun: but they laughed them to scorn, and mocked them."

This indicates that the King knew where the tribes were and was able to send them correspondence, so they were never really lost at all.

Genesis relates that Cain made his way to a land where he built "a city, and called the name of the city, after the name of his son Enoch." (Genesis 4:17) Although there has been extensive archeological research around the area where Eden was believed to have been located, no remains of such a city has been found. But there is a city that bears the name— Tenochtitlan. However, this was the capital of the Aztec empire, which later became known as Mexico City.

In 1 Chronicles 1:19 it says: "And unto Eber were born two sons: the name of the one was Peleg; because in his days the earth was divided: and his brother's name was Joktan." Peleg was born around 2248 BC and the confounding of speech took place at the Tower of Babel around 2234 BC. The text in Chronicles could be referring to people dividing up into various groups— according to language similarity. However, some researchers believe that this passage reflects the fact that prior to Peleg, all the continents were connected. This confirms the scientific concept known as the Continental Drift Theory (even though it happened much later), and illustrates that the descendants of Noah were able to migrate to lands all around the world on natural land bridges.

In Genesis 35:11, Israel is referred to as a "nation and a company of nations," and is a veiled prophetic reference to what would later occur. Undoubtedly the ten 'lost' tribes were assimilated into local populations, and branches also eventually migrated west.

In 1165, Benjamin of Tudela (son of Jonah), in Spain, set out to explore the world, recording his adventures in his *Book of Travels*. In the mountains of Persia, he ran across Jewish tribesmen who he believed were descendants of the tribes of Dan, Zebulun, Asher, and Naphtali. In Arabia, he discovered the largest Jewish settlement in the region— the Jews of Kheibar, who he identified as being from the tribes of Reuben and Gad.

In the early 16th century, Bartholeme de Las Casas, wrote of the Indians in the West Indies, Peru, and Guatemala: "Indeed, I can bring proofs from the Bible that they are of the Lost Tribes." A report 120 years later by Portuguese traveler Antonio Montezinos indicated that there was an Indian tribe living beyond the mountain passes of the Andes that represented a remnant of a Jewish tribe. He wrote: "I myself heard them recite the Shéma (the expression of Jewish faith) and saw them observe the Jewish rituals."

There is also evidence of Israelites in this country before the Assyrian deportation, such as the unusual custom of the American Indian tribes referring to themselves as nations.

In North Carolina, the Machapunga Indians circumcise their babies and have some traditions that are similar to the Jews, as do the Savanna Indians from the banks of the Mississippi River.

The Yuchi Indians in Oklahoma have a custom which is unique among other American Indian tribes, which proves that they are racially and linguistically different from their neighbors. In *True Discoverers of America,* William Dankenbring wrote: "Every year on the fifteenth day of the sacred month of harvest, in the fall, they make a pilgrimage. For eight days they live in 'booths' with roofs open to the sky, covered with branches and leaves and foliage. During this festival, they dance around the sacred fire, and called upon the name of God." This ritual is similar to the Israelite Feast of Tabernacles (details of which are found in Leviticus 23). Dr. Cyrus B. Gordon (professor of Mediterranean Studies at Brandeis University in Boston Massachusetts), an expert in Hebrew, Minoan, and many other Middle Eastern languages, was allowed to witness one of their fall harvest festivals, and said to his companion, "They are speaking the Hebrew names for God!"

So, what we have is documented proof that the Jews did indeed migrate to other countries. In the course of this migration, they produced many branches which assimilated themselves into the local populations of these various countries. With the establishment of the nation of Israel, and in fulfillment of prophecy, many Jews from many lands have returned to their home. The seventh chapter of Revelation speaks of a 'sealing' of 144,000 Jews from the following tribes: Judah,

Reuben, Gad, Asher, Naphtali, Simeon, Levi, Issachar, Zebulon, Joseph, Benjamin, and Manasses (substituted for Dan). It is assumed that they will be from within the population of the nation of Israel. Is it possible that there is still pure-blood descendents of these tribes? One would assume that if they are not, can they still be considered members of the tribe? If so, and with their Jewish roots lost, are the various branches that migrated to other countries, where they still continue to live, able to consider themselves as representative of their respective tribes?

Following this course of speculative thinking, can we use this as another confirmation to prove that the ten 'lost' tribes, which migrated westward into the area now known as Europe, is actually the "ten horns" or "ten kings," which is believed to be Europe.

I mentioned earlier that Leonardo da Vinci was a member of the Prieuré de Sion. As a matter of fact, from 1510-1519, he was the Nautonnier ('helmsman') or Grand Master of the group. One interesting piece of information I found out was that da Vinci was alleged to have been the one who forged and painted the Shroud of Turin, which is purported to be the burial cloth of Jesus, which is now in possession of the Catholic Church. The authenticity of this cloth has been debated for many years. After it was carbon dated and determined that it is not old enough to have been the burial cloth, then came testing which proved that there was an organic bacterial coating over it which distorts carbon dating results.

It was Dr. Leoncio A. Garza-Valdes, a microbiologist who reached that determination. In a quest to once and for all prove its authenticity, he went a bit farther. There were 'sticky tape' samples taken from areas of the shroud that appeared to be blood. Garza-Valdes had these remnants from the left hand (by the STURP group in 1978), and from the occipital region (by Riggi in 1988). Not only was he able to determine that it was actually blood, but that it was the blood (AB group) of a human male.

Since the secret of the Holy Grail centers on the 'blood' or to be more precise, the 'bloodline,' is the shroud a piece of the puzzle. Dr. Garza-Valdes has allayed any fears of the possibility that someone could try to extract DNA from it in an attempt to clone the man on the shroud, because he said that any blood samples which could be retrieved from it would be so degraded that it would be insufficient to allow the possibility of cloning. However, is the quality of it good enough to prove a bloodline?

The story that has been outlined up to now refers to Jesus and Mary Magdalene being married and having a child. As Christians we know that not to be true. However, it is no secret that Jesus had brothers (James, Joses, Simon, Judas or Juda) and sisters (Mathew 13:55), and their bloodline could have very well survived through their descendents.

Eusebius states that "…there still survived of the Lord's family the grandsons of Jude (James and Jude), who was said to be His brother, humanly speaking. These were informed against as being of David's line and brought … before Domitian Caesar … (who) asked them whether they were descended from David, and they admitted it…" Eusebius said that the descendents of Jesus' family became leaders of various Christian churches, and traced them to the time of the Emperor Trajan (98-117 AD). A Roman Catholic account documents a fourth century incident in 318, when the Bishop of Rome, now referred to as Pope Sylvester

I, met with eight Desposyni (descendents of Jesus' family) leaders. Each of them was a leader of a branch of the Church at the Lateran Palace. They demanded that the confirmation of the bishops of Jerusalem, Antioch, Ephesus and Alexandria be revoked, and that the titles be conferred on members of their family, and that their Church in Jerusalem be considered the Mother Church. Sylvester refused, and there was no subsequent contact reported. The New Testament (Galatians 2:9) bears out the fact that "James, Cephas (Peter), and John" were the leaders of the Church in Jerusalem, and by virtue of the order they were mentioned, and blood-line, James was probably the head of it.

As far as the Shroud of Turin— it could very well be the actual burial cloth of Christ. But if it is a forgery, to believe that Leonardo da Vinci (1452-1519) fabricated it may be a stretch, since the earliest report of its existence was in 1357. Of course, if anybody could have done it, da Vinci is probably the most likely suspect in that he had trained to be an engineer, and was a scientific genius, as well as an artist. So, we must consider the fact, that if the shroud is a fake, either somebody else did it, or da Vinci did it and substituted it for the real one.

Just for kicks and giggles, let's assume that at some point, it will be determined that the Shroud is the authentic burial shroud of Christ (even if it may not be). When some international leader rises to power, and it appears that he embodies every quality that the world is looking for in a leader, and even seems to fulfill the Biblical prophecies of a coming Messiah, what would happen if the DNA of his blood would match the DNA of the blood on the shroud? Who better to lead a united Europe, then a living descendant of Jesus Christ, who could also use New Age philosophy to claim that he is a reincarnation of the Son of God.

In light of this possibility, and the obvious longevity of this group, circumstantial evidence would seem to point to the fact, that the Prieuré de Sion could be the ultimate power behind the Illuminati, using them to bring the world to a point where this man would be accepted with open arms, as the answer to the world's problems. Once this leader takes his place as the head of the revived Holy Roman Empire, it will not be long before he is revealed to be the antagonist referred to in the Bible as the Antichrist.

After wading through all of the information and speculation I have presented to you, finally you have reached the point where you can understand the whole premise upon which this book was based. It is my belief that the purpose of the movement towards a New World Order, is to establish a one-world government, and to set the stage for the rise of the Antichrist.

THE ANTICHRIST

Waiting for a Man

Paul-Henri Spaak (1888-1972), the socialist leader, President of the Consultive Assembly of the Council of Europe from 1949-51, and former Secretary-General of NATO, who was one of the three major proponents of a united Europe said: "We do not want another committee. We have too many already. What we want is a man of sufficient stature to hold the allegiance of all people, and to lift us out of the economic morass into which we are sinking. Send us such a man and, be he God, or the devil, we will receive him."

Such a man will arise, and his ascent to power is discussed in various places in the Bible. This chapter is the culmination of everything you have read up to now. I believe that the Illuminati has been working behind the scenes to create an environment that will enable one man to gain enough power to finally pull the countries of Europe together into one political entity.

> "And four great beasts came up from the sea, diverse one from another. The first was like a lion, and had eaglés wings (Babylon) ... a second, like to a bear (Media and Persia) ... another, like a leopard (Greece) ... and behold a fourth beast, dreadful and terrible, and strong exceedingly; and it had great iron teeth (Rome) ... and it was diverse from all the beasts that were before it; and it had ten horns ... there came up among them another little horn, before whom there were three of the first horns plucked up by the roots: and, behold, in this horn were eyes like the eyes of a man, and a mouth speaking great things." (Daniel 7:3-8)

> "...the fourth beast, which was diverse from all the others, exceeding dreadful, whose teeth were of iron, and his nails of brass; which devoured ... And of the ten horns that were in his head, and of the other which came up, and before whom three fell; even of that horn that had eyes, and a mouth that spake very great things, whose look was more stout than his fellow ... the same horn made war with the saints and prevailed against them ... The fourth beast shall be the fourth kingdom upon the earth ... and shall devour the whole earth, and shall trod it down, and break it in pieces. And the ten horns out of this kingdom are ten kings that shall arise: and another shall rise after them: and he shall be diverse from the first, and he shall subdue three kings. And he shall speak great words against the most High, and think to change times and laws: and they shall be given into his hand until a time and times and the dividing of time (3_ years)." (Daniel 7:19-25)

> "...behold, there stood before the river a ram which had two horns (Media and Persia) ... I saw the ram pushing westward, and northward, and southward ... he did according to his will, and became great ... an he goat (Greece), came from the west ... and touched not the ground: and the goat had a notable horn (Alexander the Great) ... and smote the ram, and brake his two horns ... Therefore the he goat waxed very great: and when he was strong, the great horn was broken, and for it came up four notable ones (Greece, Turkey, Syria, and Egypt) ... And out of one of them came forth a little horn, which waxed exceedingly great, toward the south, and toward the east, and toward the pleasant land (Israel) ... he magnified himself even to the prince of the host, and by him the daily sacrifice was taken away, and the place of his sanctuary was cast down ... How long shall be ... to give both the sanctuary and the host to be trodden under foot

FINAL WARNING

... two thousand and three hundred days." (Daniel 8:3-14)

"And in the latter time of their kingdom, when the transgressors are come to the full, a king of fierce countenance, and understanding dark sentences, shall stand up. And his power shall be mighty, but not by his own power: and he shall destroy wonderfully, and shall prosper, and practice, and shall destroy the mighty and the holy people. And through his policy also he shall cause craft to prosper in his hand; and he shall magnify himself in his heart, and by peace shall destroy many." (Daniel 8:23-25)

"And there appeared another wonder in heaven; and behold a great red dragon (Satan), having seven heads (the five fallen kingdoms of Egypt, Assyria, Babylon, Medo-Persia, and Greece; the current, Rome; and the one yet to come) and ten horns, and seven crowns upon his heads." (Revelation 12:3)

"And I stood upon the sand of the sea (Mediterranean), and saw a beast rise up out of the sea, having seven heads and ten horns, and upon his horns ten crowns ... And the beast which I saw was like unto a leopard, and his feet were as the feet of a bear, and his mouth as the mouth of a lion: and the dragon gave him his power, and his seat, and great authority. And I saw one of his heads as it were wounded to death; and his deadly wound was healed: and all the world wondered after the beast. And they worshipped the dragon which gave power unto the beast: and they worshipped the beast, saying, Who is like unto the beast? who is able to make war with him? And there was given unto him a mouth speaking great things and blasphemies; and power was given unto him to continue forty and two months. And he opened his mouth in blasphemy against God, to blaspheme his name, and his tabernacle ... And it was given unto him to make war with the saints, and to overcome them: and power was given him over all kindreds, and tongues, and nations." (Revelation 13:1-7)

"And there are seven kings: five are fallen, and one is, and the other is not yet come; and when he cometh, he must continue a short space. And the beast that was, and is not, even he is the eighth, and is of the seven, and goeth into perdition. And the ten horns which thou sawest are ten kings, which have received no kingdom yet; but receive power as kings one hour with the beast. These have one mind, and shall give their power and strength unto the beast." (Revelation 17:10-13)

The Scriptures have given us an excellent indication of the origin of the man who will be known as the Antichrist. The term "Antichrist" is first used in 1 John 2:18, and an indirect reference in 2 Thessalonians 2:4, refers to his opposition to God, which has given rise to the prevalent thought that Antichrist meant "against" Christ, when in fact, as Pastor Milt Maiman (formerly of the Messianic Hebrew Christian Fellowship in Harrisburg, PA) pointed out to me, the prefix 'anti' doesn't refer to the Latin which means 'against'; but it is actually derived from the Greek 'ante' which was used to indicate a contrast or substitution, and means 'to take the place of,' or 'in front of,' or 'before or prior to.'

Daniel 8:8 refers to the four powers who are Greece, Turkey, Syria, and Egypt; and Daniel 7:7-8 speaks of the seventh world empire, consisting of ten kingdoms, and the rise of another. The second chapter of Daniel, which refers to the dream of Nebuchadnezzar, clearly points out that the ten toes (kingdoms) are an extension of the previous world empire, or Rome, which would then encompass all of the countries that fell within the boundaries of the Holy Roman Empire: parts of Morocco, Algeria, Tunisia, and Libya; Egypt; part of Saudi Arabia; Jordan, Israel, Syria, and Turkey; Portugal, Spain, France, Belgium, Luxembourg, part of the Netherlands, England, part of Germany, Switzerland, Austria, Italy, Greece, part of Hungary, part of Yugoslavia, part of Romania, Bulgaria, Macedonia, Albania, Slovenia, Croatia, and Bosnia and Herzegovina.

Let's look at the ten horns or kingdoms, which many initially thought was represented by the original Common Market countries of France, West Germany, Italy, Belgium, the Netherlands, Luxembourg, England, Denmark, Ireland, and Greece. The impact of the theory was lessened upon the later addition of Spain, Portugal, and Austria, which made a total of thirteen nations in what is now called the European Union. However, some still tried to make the argument, because Denmark and Ireland were not part of the Roman Empire.

Another fact that supports the theory that the ten kings symbolically represent the area of western Europe is that there are only ten kingdoms, or monarchies now in western Europe: Belgium, Denmark, Liechtenstein, Luxembourg, Monaco, Netherlands, Norway, Spain, Sweden, and the United Kingdom (Northern Ireland; Great Britain— England, Wales, Scotland).

Another confirming theory emanates from Daniel 9:26 which says: "...the people of the prince that shall come shall destroy the city and the sanctuary..." The people that destroyed Jerusalem and the Temple in 70 AD were the Romans. Revelation 14:8 says: "Babylon (sometimes perceived as a symbolic name for Rome) is fallen, that great city, because she made all nations drink of the wine of the wrath of her fornication."

According to Daniel 7:20, this leader of the eleventh country, will go against three of these nations, and defeat them. Yet, Revelation speaks of the ten kings pledging their allegiance to the Antichrist. Do these ten include the eleventh nation of the Antichrist? Will he defeat the three nations, and replace them in the federation with his, and two others? Or will the three defeated nations remain, under the leadership of the eleventh? What is the purpose for the Antichrist to go against these three nations? Is it because they were not originally part of the revived Holy Roman Empire; or if they were, what else could prompt him to attack these countries?

This beckons the theory about the ten tribes that lived in the area of Rome. Three were defeated because they were Aryans who opposed the papacy— Herulians, Vandals, and Ostrogoths; while the other seven became the nations of western Europe— Visigoths, Franks, Anglo-Saxons, Sueves, Burgundians, Alamanni, and Alans. One possible clue is that these nations may be apprehensive about uniting behind the political leadership of the Antichrist. For example, when the European Community met in Maastricht, the Netherlands, in 1991, Great Britain and Denmark voted against the initiation of a common currency. Another theory that somebody e-mailed me, was that the three nations are Afghanistan (Media), Iraq (Babylon), and Iran (Persia), by virtue of the fact that the U.S. has occupied Afghanistan and Iraq.

There are other theories concerning the origin of the Antichrist. Some researchers believe that he has to come from Greece, Turkey, Syria, or Egypt; but not one of the countries which make up the ten nation federation. That would eliminate Greece. Could this country be Syria. In Isaiah 10:5, 10:24, 14:25, 30:31, he is referred to as the "Assyrian." In Micah 5:5 it says: "And this man shall be the peace, when the Assyrian shall come into our land: and when he shall tread in our palaces, then we shall raise against him..." The Aramaeans, a semi-nomadic people who migrated from the Arabian desert around the third century BC, into Syria and Mesopotamia, have also been called Syrians. Let's also look at Habakkuk 1:6— "For, lo, I raise up the Chaldeans, that bitter and hasty nation, which shall march through the breadth of the land, to possess dwelling-places that are not theirs." The land of the Chaldeans was in southern Babylonia, in what is now southern Iraq. These references seem to point to an Arabic background, and are given credence because they consider themselves the enemies of Israel.

A reference in Daniel 11:37 says: "Neither shall he regard the God of his fathers..." This may be an indication of Jewish ancestry, and some researchers believe that the Antichrist will be a Jew from the tribe of Dan. In Genesis 49:17, when the patriarch Jacob is speaking to his sons, he said: "Dan shall be a serpent by the way..." and Jeremiah 8:16 refers to the armies of Dan devouring the land. In the seventh chapter of Revelation, John omitted the name of Dan when he listed the tribes of Israel. Dan and Ephraim were the first to lead Israel into adultery. Dan was replaced by the tribe of Manasseh (Joseph's oldest son).

Though we can't be sure of the area of his origin, in the end, the Antichrist will succeed in doing what no man has been able to do since the fall of the Roman Empire in 476 AD. Charlemagne, Charles V, Louis XIV, Napoleon, Kaiser Wilhelm, Benito Mussolini, and Hitler all tried to take over Europe to unify it, but failed. The Antichrist will be a strong political leader, who will gain strength through statesmanship and promises of peace. On December 6, 1961, McGeorge Bundy (of the CFR), Special Assistant to President Kennedy, told the Economic Club of Europe, that if Western Europe would unite as one power to have economic, military and political unity, they would be a truly great power. *Time* magazine even wrote that the real aim of the Common Market was to become a single country.

The political policies of the Antichrist will bring strength, stability and unity to Europe, while his economic policies will bring prosperity to industry, agriculture, and commerce. His success in doing that will give him international stature.

Candidates for the Antichrist

As the end times quickly engulf us, and prophetic events begin to unfold, many researchers have made suggestions in regard to the identity of the Antichrist.

One of the first was King Don Juan-Carlos I of Spain, born in Rome (January

5, 1938), who is a direct descendant of Queen Victoria of England. In 1948 he was given over to Generalissimo Francisco Franco by his exiled parents, to be educated in Spain. He first attended the Instituto San Isidro, and then was given a private tutor in 1949. In 1955, he graduated from the Navy Orphans College; then attended the Academia General Militar at Zaragoza, where he received a commission in the Spanish Army as a lieutenant (where he graduated 3rd out of a class of 271). Until 1959, he received training from the Naval Academy (attaining the rank of Midshipman in the Spanish Navy) and the Aviation Academy in San Xavier (where he received an officer's commission in the Spanish Air Force). In 1960, he entered the University of Madrid to study law, political science, economics, and philosophy. Carlos became King in 1975, and is recognized as Western Europe's most capable military leader. A new Constitution ratified in 1978, made Carlos the most powerful monarch on the continent.

Prince Charles Philip Arthur George Windsor, who was born November 14, 1948 (a significant year), became the 21st Prince of Wales in 1969. The oldest child of Queen Elizabeth II (and Prince Philip, Duke of Edinburgh) is the heir-apparent to King George VI. His wedding in 1981 captured the attention of the world, and it was rumored that his mother was considering abdicating the throne to him, which would have made him one of the most powerful figures in Europe, by virtue of the fact that England is the most dominant country in Western Europe.

In recent years, especially with books like *The Antichrist and a Cup of Tea*, by Tim Cohen, Prince Charles has become a more serious candidate because of the following facts:

His heraldic coat of arms bears the symbols presented in Revelation 13, and Daniel 7.

His name breaks down into the number 666 in both English and Hebrew using the Biblical system.

He has documentation that proves his bloodline descent from King David, Jesus and Mohammed; but is most likely from the tribe of Dan.

He has requested to be the King of Europe.

It is believed that his power base is behind the New World Order, and he is very involved in the prospect of world government.

He has already taken a traceable bio-chip implant.

Zaki Badawi, principal of the Muslim College, described him as "the most popular world leader in the Muslim community throughout the world ... a man of such stature, and is able to speak for all of us."

In the spring of 2002, came the report that Prince Charles was to have a bronze statue erected in his honor in the square of Palmas, the capital of Tocantins State in central Brazil. Although he will already become the 'Defender of the Faith' should he become King of England, he appears as a muscular, winged god dressed in a loincloth, with an inscription touting him as the "Savior of the World." The statue was commissioned by civic leaders because of Charles' work to publicize the threat to the rainforests from global warming. Jose Wilson Sequeira Campos, the Governor of Tocantins, said: "It is Prince Charles saving the world. We think he is deserving of it." It is already being compared to the statue of Christ overlooking Rio de Janeiro from Corcovado. When the sculptor Mauricio Bentes presented a miniature copy to the Prince during his visit to Brazil, he said: "I am amazed and deeply touched."

One thing you need to realize, is that in the United States, we don't hear about much of the news that occurs overseas, especially with issues that are germane to Europe only, and have no international bearing. Though his international stature seems rather insignificant from our standpoint, it is actually quite prolific in that region of the world. He has been an ardent supporter of a united Europe, and he has used his political weight to help achieve that goal.

James Lloyd, author on the 1992 book *Beyond Babylon*, who has an excellent reputation for his intensive research, believes that Dr. Boutros Boutros-Ghali, the 6th Secretary-General of the UN, will be the Antichrist. In an interview broadcast on Lloyd's shortwave broadcast, Boutros-Ghali maintained that the UN needed a "drastic change" if it was going to be able to take its place as the world government. He said it was important for the UN to get a "consensus of the international community." Asked if the support of organized religion could help convince people to support world government, he said, "Why not?" Citing Revelation 17:11 which says that the Beast has 7 heads (or leaders), and that "even he is the eighth, and is of the seven, and goeth into perdition," Lloyd believes that the 7th head of the UN, Kofi Annan, will not finish his term, and that Boutros-Ghali will be appointed to serve out the remainder of it.

THE MARK OF THE BEAST

The Number of his Name

The Antichrist will use economic terrorism to force the people of the world to follow him.

> "And he (the False Prophet) causeth all, both small and great, rich and poor, free and bond, to receive a mark in their right hand, or in their foreheads: And that no man might buy and sell, save he that had the mark, or the name of the beast, or the number of his name. Here is wisdom. Let him that hath understanding count the number of the beast: for it is the number of a man; and his number is Six hundred threescore and six." (Revelation 13:16-18)

> "...If any man worship the beast and his image, and receive his mark in his forehead, or in his hand, The same shall drink of the wine of the wrath of God ... And the smoke of their torment ascendeth up for ever and ever: and they have no rest day nor night, who worship the beast and his image, and whosoever receiveth the mark of his name." (Revelation 14:9-11)

Many people believe that the number 666 will be his mark, but the Bible doesn't make itself clear on that point. Six is the number of man, because he was created on the sixth day, and given six 'days' to live. The number 666 is the Satanic trinity, and will be the manner in which the Antichrist will be recognized.

Iranaeus (140-202), Bishop of Lyons, a pupil of Polycarp (who was a student of the Apostle John), thought the number 666 was the Greek word "Lateinos": L (30), A (1), T (300), E (5), I (10), N (50), 0 (70), S (200), which adds up to 666. The word means "Latin kingdom," and it was later believed that this referred to the religion of the Vatican, because Latin is their official language, which is used in their canons, missals, prayers, and blessings.

Rev. Jerry R. Church, founder and director of Prophecy in the News ministry in Oklahoma City, Oklahoma, reported that the Sumerians of Noah's time, who lived in what is now southern Iraq, used a sexagesimal system of numerics, which means that their numerical system was based on the number six, instead of ten. He theorized that since all language had a common base, and civilization's first numbering system was based on six, then a code could be devised to "count the number of the beast." The English alphabet is based on the root value of six: 6" X 2= 1 foot, 6" X 6= 1 yard, 6 'forties' = 1 section, 6 sections X 6= 1 township, 1 township = a 6 square mile area, etc. What he came up with was an alphanumeric code: A = 6, B = 12, C = 18, D = 24, E = 30, F = 36, etc. Using this code, he discovered that various words and sequences or words, such as 'Mark of the Beast,' 'Computer,' and 'New York' were equivalent to the numerical value of 666.

The number 666 became quite prominent in order to get people familiar with it, and to eliminate the evil connotations that the number has. Listed below are only some of the areas where the number 666 has been used:

1) Koehring and Clark equipment companies used 666 as part of the product identification number on certain models.
2) Stickers distributed at DuPont Co. plants said: "To be in the know, call 'Mom' (666)."
3) Products of the Bliss-Hastings Co. contained the number 666.
4) The 85th Annual Frontiers Days Festival, held in Cheyenne, Wyoming, promoted July 23, 1981 as "666 Rodeo Day."
5) The logo of Australia's National Bank card contained a configuration of the number 666.
6) In August, 1980, the Chesapeake and Potomac Telephone Co. of Virginia notified their customers that the telephone number of the U.S. Weather Service was being changed from 936-1212, to 666-1212.
7) Men's dress shirts produced in China, and sold in the U.S., had the number 666 on the label, forming the trademark of Kerman Scott Ltd.
8) At the official reopening of the Suez Canal on June 5, 1975, the first Egyptian warship entering it, which was carrying Egyptian President Anwar Sadat, had the number 666 on its bow.
9) The World Bank code number was 666.
10) Some credit cards in the U.S. had the numerical prefix of 666.
11) The Olivetti Computer System P6060, used processing numbers which began with 666.
12) Sears, Belk, J. C. Penney, and Montgomery Ward computers were

prefixing their transactions with the number 666, as mandated by its computer programming.

13) Shoes made in Italy had 666 stamped on the inside label. It consisted of a circle, divided in half; with a horned lamb (see Rev. 13:11) on top, and the number 666 on the bottom. It was later put on all Common Market products.

14) IBM computer equipment in supermarkets had the number 3X666 on them.

15) Visa credit cards represent the number 666: the Roman numeral for 6 is "VI"; the number 6 in ancient Greek was taken from the sixth letter of their alphabet, the letter "stigma," which looks like the English "S"; and in the Babylonian sexagesimal system, and "A" represented 6. Thus the word VISA forms the number 666.

16) Computers manufactured by Lear Siegler, Inc. in the U.S. and shipped to Israel, had a seal on the side stamped with the number 666, which was later discontinued.

17) The Federal Government Medicaid Service Employees Division number was 666.

18) The Internal Revenue Service's ATF (Alcohol, Tobacco and Firearms) Division had the number 666 on their employeés badges.

19) In 1977, the IRS began requiring the number 666 as a prefix on forms for tax payments on Individual Retirement Accounts (form W-2P): Disability is 666.3, death is 666.4, etc. After a lot of protest, it was omitted in 1978-79, but resumed in 1980-81.

20) IRS instructions for the 1979 non-profit Corporation Employee W-2 form, required the prefix 666.

21) Some states had the number 666 on their requisition paperwork.

22) President Carter's secret security force had patches with the number 666 on them.

23) Chrysler Corporation manufactured tanks for President Carter's secret security force that had the number 666 on the side.

24) A contest sponsored by the Israeli Dept. of Education in 1980, featured a tic-tac-toe game, that allowed you to win money if you scratched off the numbers 666.

25) The McGregor Clothing Co. had introduced a "666 Collection" of menswear.

26) A telephone company in the mid-west had its credit cards encoded with the number 666.

27) Identification tags on Japanese-made parts for the Caterpillar Co. in Peoria, Illinois, had the number 666 on them as part of the product code.

28) FLXO Mens Chore Gloves made by the Boss Glove Co., were stamped with the number 666 as a style number,

29) The Crow's Hybrid Corn Co. of Iowa offered a '666' seed as its top yielding hybrid.

30) Scotty had offered a new improved 666 fertilizer.

31) South Central Bell's Telco Credit Union cards had the prefix 666, and then the person's Social Security number.

32) Metric rulers which were distributed in 1979 throughout the country had the number 666 on them.
33) I.D. tags on 1979 General Motor cars manufactured in Flint, Michigan, had the number 666 on them.
34) U.S. Selective Service cards had the number 666 as part of its code.
35) The overseas telephone operator number from Israel was 666.
36) After 1973, Arab-owned vehicles in Jerusalem had the prefix of 666 on their license plates, for the purpose of being able to identify the enemy in case of war.
37) An album by the heavy metal band Black Sabbath was called *666*.
38) There was an elementary grade algebra book published by the Thomas Corwell Co. in New York, titled *666 Jellybeans*.
39) Mastercard had started to use the number '66' on their statements in August, 1980.
40) The formula for the NCR model 304 Supermarket Computer was 6 60 6(which is six, three score, and six).
41) The 'Sundial' style floor tile manufactured by Armstrong, were prefixed with the number 666-13.
42) The cutter boom governing heads on coal mining equipment in Beckley, West Virginia, produced by the Lee Morse Co., were coded with the number 666.
43) Financial institutions in Florida were using the number 666.
44) Parent and Teacher Training books from the Channing L. Bete Co. in Greenfield, Massachusetts, were catalog coded with the number C-666.
45) It has been reported that on one occasion, when Pope John Paul II offered free tickets for papal audiences in Rome, the lower left portion of the ticket displayed a group of numbers followed by the number 666.

The mark may be some sort of identification number, such as your Social Security number, which will serve to identify everyone. In *None Dare Call It Conspiracy*, author Gary Allen wrote (pg. 13): "...his (the individual's) freedom and choice will be controlled within very narrow alternatives by the fact that he will be numbered from birth and followed, as a number ... (until) his final retirement and death benefits." It could be that your Social Security number could be used for such a system, since U.S. law requires every citizen to have such a number by the time they enter the first grade.

The move is on for everyone in the United States to have an identification card. A Special Presidential Commission on Immigration and Refugees had recommended a national identification card in an attempt to keep illegal aliens in check. The *U.S. News and World Report*, in their September 15, 1980 issue, ran an article called "A National Identity Card?" It reported that the Federal Government was planning an identification card that would prevent anyone without one from working or transacting any sort of business. This computerized system would keep track of every citizen, According to a 1994 proposal by the Congressional Commission on Immigration Reform, all American citizens and legal immigrants would be given a national identification card. The project was later shelved, but elsewhere the move is on. In 1995, the European Union was to begin issuing identification cards to all the citizens of western Europe.

In California, driver's licenses were to be issued that would contain a microchip with personal information, motor vehicle records, criminal records, a photograph, and fingerprints. The Department of Defense at the Pentagon issued the MARC (Multi-Technology Automatic Reader) card to their soldiers. It contained a bar code, a magnetic strip, a digitized photograph, and an integrated circuit computer chip. An internal Pentagon memo stated that the card would encode all of a soldier's records. This 6.6 megabyte Laser Card from Drexler Technology Corporation can store nearly 2,000 pages of information, which is more than enough for identification numbers, biographical information, school records, photographs, signature, voice print, fingerprints, medical and health care records, credit and banking information, job information and activities. It is believed that this card will be the prototype for any national identification card that will be issued to U.S. citizens.

With all of this computerization going on, it's obvious that there needs to be a data base to store it all this information so that it can be accessed and used.

Starting back in 1973 it was being reported (most notably in the August, 1976 issue of *Christian Life* magazine) that three floors of the thirteen-floor headquarters of the European Common Market in Brussels, Belgium was occupied by a massive computer. Dr. Hanrick Eldeman, Chief Analyst for the Common Market, said in a 1974 meeting of Common Market leaders during the unveiling of the huge, self-programming computer known as 'The Beast,' that a computerized revitalization project is being prepared to "straighten out world chaos," and that the computer has the potential of "numbering every human on earth." In 1977 (according to a 1990 *Moody* magazine article), this same Dr. Eldeman is reported to have said that he was preparing to assign a number to everyone in the world. By using three entries of six digits each, he said it would be possible for everyone in the world to be given a distinctive number.

As it turns out, the information was actually taken from the novel *Beyond a Pale Horse* by Joe Musser, who later adapted it as a screenplay for a David Wilkerson film called *The Rapture*. It is believed that the confusion between fact and fiction came because there were mock newspapers produced to promote the movie which contained things having to do with the end times, and the 'Beast' computer was part of it.

And then came the report that the 'Beast' computer had taken a backseat to the computer in the Jean Monnet Building (rue Alcide de Gasperi) in Luxembourg, which has been called the largest in the world. Paul Peterson wrote in his book *Sinister World Computerization*: "I saw the center in Luxembourg that can compute facts and figures on everyone in the world."

I suspect that this is also a rumor since I have not been able to find out anything about this book, nor can I connect this author with this type of research. You can see why the association was made when you look at some of the occupants of this building: Commission of European Communities (the European Union's executive arm), European Bank of Investments, European Court of Justice, and the Secretariat of the European Parliament (who also work out of Strasbourg and Luxembourg).

Well, enough with the fiction. The fact is, there is a worldwide communications network already in place. Established in 1973, with only 239 banks from 15 countries, SWIFT (Society for Worldwide Interbank Financial Telecommunication, headquartered at Avenue Adèle 1, La Hulpe, Belgium— a southern suberb of Brussels) now has 7,500 members in 200 countries. This system links member banks across the globe in a manner designed to accommodate any type of computer system. The Burroughs Corporation (who acquired Sperry Corp. in 1986 and is now known as Unisys Corp.) developed the data processing and communications system equipment that is used as a private communications system for the transmission of payment and other international banking transactions. Tata Consultancy Services, Asia's largest global software and services company provided the on-site support. It is made up of switching centers in Brussels (Belgium) and Amsterdam (Netherlands), which have been linked to Burroughs data concentrators in Amsterdam, Brussels, Copenhagen, Frankfurt, Helsinki, London, Milan, Lux, Montreal, New York, Oslo, Paris, Stockholm, Vienna, and Zurich. These data concentrators are linked to terminals in all the member banks of those countries.

According to the book *SWIFT: Banking and Business*, Dr. T. Hugh Moreton said: "In early 1982 we are ready to believe every country in the world will be connected in one way or another to SWIFT." The United States SWIFT Bank, built at a cost of $15 million, is located near the Federal Reserve Office in Culpepper, Virginia.

The biggest concentration of super computers in the world can be found at Fort Meade, Maryland, between Washington and Baltimore, at the headquarters of the National Security Agency, which is the most secret intelligence agency in our government. Occupying an area of a thousand acres, the NSA contains a $47,000,000 subterranean computer facility that stretches for blocks and has ten acres of Cray supercomputers. The supercomputers are tied into each other with 52 separate computer systems from around the world.

It's just a matter of time before everyone living in the major industrial nations are tied into an international computer system through Social Security numbers, Driver's License numbers, Credit Card numbers, Checking and Savings Account numbers, Birth Certificates, and Passports. All of your personal and financial information will be on record, including your employment and medical record, taxes paid, banking transactions, and property acquisitions. Basically, any type of information on you that has to be entered into a computer, will ultimately find its way into a database that can be accessed by the government.

In 1798, Adam Clarke, a Methodist minister, said: "The Mark of the Beast will be an 18 digit number, 6 + 6 + 6." In this digital age, it seems possible that a universal number could be used to identify people, rather than all different kinds of numbers. All other numbers, such as driver's license numbers, banking account numbers, and credit card numbers would be phased out in lieu of your Social Security number, since it is already tied into your banking transactions, tax returns, and medical history. If any type of personal identification is every issued for the citizens of the United States, it will most likely adapt your Social Security number so that it can be used to accomplish personal and financial transactions electronically.

In the course of research for her books *When Your Money Fails ... The "666 System" Is Here*, and *The New Money System*, Mary Stewart Relfe, Ph.D., found out that Christians who sent back credit cards with a '666' prefix were told that by 1982, the number would be on all cards. If that is the case, it must be encoded into the magnetic strip, which can only be read with a scanner. Relfe came to believe that if a Personal Identification Card (PIT) was issued, it would contain a magnetic strip, bar code, photograph, signature, and an 18-digit identification number that would look something like this:

666-110-202-123-45-6789
666- (International Code to Activate the World Computer)
110- (National Code to Activate Central U.S. Computer)
202- (Telephone Area Code)
123-45-6789 (Social Security Number)

The Cashless Society

In 1974, Gary Allen wrote in *A Decade Left- Has Orwell's 1984 Come Early?*: "Federal planners forsee the day when every citizen will have a money card instead of money to spend. The cards will be placed in a machine at each point of purchase, and the charge would be electronically subtracted from the customer's Federal Reserve Account." The November, 1975 issue of *Progressive Grocer* reported: "The day will come when one card will be good at any terminal, in any state..." In the September 21, 1976 issue of the *Daily Oklahoman*, was an article titled, "The Cashless Society Expected to Become Reality Soon," which said: "The long-talked about cashless society is almost here. Bank debit cards are expected to go into nationwide use soon." In the December 27, 1979 issue of *Electronic Fund Transfer Report*, there was an article titled "Electronic Money" which revealed: "A sophisticated point of sale system is quietly operated by the Chase Manhattan Bank in one of the banking industry's best kept secrets. Chase is now directly linked to hundreds of electronic cash registers or P.O.S. terminals in department and specialty stores ... by offering this service to merchants on a nationwide basis, a network will be created that will allow the Chase Manhattan Bank to have a national E.F.T. present."

On May 29, 1980, during ABC-TV's Good Morning America show, a Federal Reserve official talked about the existence of a new Federal debit card: "A thin piece of plastic which is to be inserted in automatic machines. One must then punch in his own secret code number ... You are not to write your number down, tell it to anyone, or record it anywhere. It must be memorized." Giant Food, Inc. and the Safeway Stores were the first to install the Point-of-Sale computerized Electronic Fund Transfer checkout machines in their supermarkets to take bank debit cards. They were later joined by Mobil Oil who installed the system in all of its gas stations throughout the country. Since then, debit cards have quickly assimilated themselves into all aspects of the retail industry.

The plan was to combine the credit card and the debit card into a single multi-use card which could be used to make deposits, pay bills, transfer money, make withdrawals, make purchases, and borrow money. On March 3, 1979, the Knight

News Service in Miami, Florida reported: "By 1980, many bankers predict, most shoppers will exchange the wallet full of credit cards they now carry for a single, all-purpose card and number." In the September 17, 1979 issue of the *Electronic Fund Transfer Report*, in an article called "MasterCard," it said:

> "In a speech, John J. Reynolds, President of Interbank Card Association, said that 'the newly named MasterCard (formerly known as Master Charge) will be a full transaction card, rather than just a credit card ... In significant ways, Interbank now had brought its EFT strategy in line with Visa's. The debit card will bear the familiar red and ochre logo, in the same way that all Visa cards are blue, white and gold. Even the magnetic stripe specification adopted for the new MasterCard now embraces an element introduced by Visa's three digit service code in the discretionary datafield of track two. With this code, it will be possible to determine if a card from one country many be used ... in another country. D. Sean Miller, Interbank Senior Vice-President, told *EFT Report*: 'the real reason it's there is that it would be very difficult to put it in later'."

According to the October 26, 1981 issue of *Business Week*, Russell E. Hogg, President of MasterCard International, Inc. predicted: "Within five to seven years, there will be more debit cards in America than credit cards." An article in *Time* magazine, September 29, 1980 reported: "It looks and feels like a credit card, payment takes place instantly. A computer deducts funds from the shopper's bank account and transfers them into that of the store or restaurant where purchases have been made..." The cover of the January 18, 1982 issue of *Business Week*, depicted a single debit card for nationwide electronic banking. The accompanying article said: "One month ago key executives from a dozen of the largest U.S. and Canadian banks flew to a secret meeting at Chicago's O'Hare Hilton Hotel to form a joint venture that would create the first National Retail-Banking Network ... the new networks should be far more powerful than Visa and MasterCard because they will operate with the debit card."

One of the reasons being given to move towards the cashless society, is the effect it would have on crime. An attorney wrote in the *American Bar* magazine: "Crime would be virtually eliminated if cash became obsolete. Cash is the only real motive for 90% of the robberies. Hence its liquidation would create miracles in ridding earth's citizens of muggings and holdups." A cashless society would also eliminate extortion and blackmail for money; and the purchase of illegal contraband, such as drugs and untaxed alcohol. However, it's obvious that the real reason for going cashless is that the population can be monitored, controlled and manipulated.

On the reverse side of all credit and debit cards is a $1/2$" X 3" magnetic stripe, which is called a 'magstripe' and contains three tracks (each about one-tenth of an inch long):

> Track 1 is 210 bits per inch (bpi), and holds 79 6-bit plus parity bit read-only characters. The information is contained in two formats— (A) Reserved for propriety use of the card issuer; (B) Start Sentinel (1 charac-

ter), Format Code="B" (1 alpha character), Primary Account Number (up to 19), Separator (1), Country Code (3), Name (2-26), Separator (1), Expiration Date or Separator (4 or 1), Discretionary Data (enough characters to fill out remaining maximum capacity of 79 character), End Sentinel (1), Longitudinal Redundancy Check Character (1)

Track 2 is 75 bpi, and holds 40 4-bit plus parity bit characters. The format was developed by the banking industry— Start Sentinel (1 character), Primary Account Number (up to 19), Separator (1), Country Code (3), Expiration Date or Separator (4 or 1), Discretionary Data (enough characters to fill out remaining maximum capacity of 40 character), End Sentinel (1), Longitudinal Redundancy Check Character (1)

Track 3 is 210 bpi, and holds 107 4-bit plus parity bit characters. It is a read/write track which includes an encrypted PIN, country code, currency units, and amount authorized, but its use is not universal among banks.

However, technology is changing so rapidly, that the magnetic strip has been rendered obsolete by the 'Smart Card,' which has a 2 line display screen, yet is only slightly larger than a credit card. Instead of a magnetic strip, it is imbedded with an integrated circuit chip for the storage of information, and it can be updated each time the card is used. With this card, a person could shop, bank, and receive social services; and it could be used to store their medical history, Social Security records and other personal information. It eliminates credit card fraud because there is no number on it. However, since the chip card costs between $20-$50 to produce, and the magnetic strip only costs 60¢ to produce; and most electronic systems have already been set up for the magnetic strip, it is unlikely that the industry will convert.

In the April, 1980 edition of *Business Week*, there was an advertisement for National Cash Register, for the financial (cashless) terminals, which featured a card called the "Worldwide Money Card" which they said will replace all the world's currencies. Another advertisement in the November 5, 1981 edition of the *Wall Street Journal* read: "A new banking era has begun and Citibank invites you to be in the forefront ... A global system linking every major city in America to a bank with a financial service network that circles the entire world." Dr. Emil Gaverluk (who has a doctorate in Educational Technology and is an expert in Communications Science), of the Southwest Radio Church, said: "The next card beyond Visa's stage will be a universal card, and will probably be issued out of Europe. It will be issued to all industrialized nations and they'll tell you this is the best card you've ever had in your life ... the next stage after that is the number on the forehead or hand."

Paper currency and checks will be phased out in lieu of debit cards, and the plan seems to be for debit cards to be converted to the International Card, as all the nations do away with their monetary systems to do business through computers. But people will lose their card, or have it stolen, or accidentally mutilate it. You have probably noticed that the magnetic strip on your credit cards does not hold up well. The constant rubbing against each other, and against your wallet, causes scratches and drop outs on the strips which can not be read by scanners. These arguments will result in numbers being lasered directly on the body.

Professor B. A. Hodson, director of the Computer Center at the University of Manitoba, had recommended an identifying mark to be put on the forehead of every person. The cover of the September 20, 1973 issue of *Senior Scholastics*, a high school publication, showed a group of kids with numbers tattooed on their foreheads, and the feature article was titled, "Public Needs and Private Rights - Who Is Watching You?" An advertisement by the First Tennessee Bank, showed a man with his bank number tattooed on his arm, implying that this was the only way to remember your number.

Initially, a process had been developed to create a permanent non-toxic fluid that could be invisibly tattooed on human flesh, until a particular light, such as infrared or ultraviolet, shown on it. The process was tested by tattooing Social Security numbers on babies. In 1974, a Washington State University professor, Dr. R. Keith Farrell, invented a laser gun, which he used to number fish, which accomplished the task in less than a second. When asked if the gun could be used to put numbers on people, he said: "It could indeed be used for such a purpose." The laser beam can not be felt, the number can not be seen with the naked eye, and it is as permanent as your fingerprints. In the October, 1980 edition of *Advertising Age* magazine, TeleResearch Item Movement, Inc. (TRIM) had a full page advertisement for their supermarket computer scanner, which featured the picture of a man with a UPC symbol printed on his forehead. Dr. Ray Brubaker wrote in his book, *Is the Antichrist Now Here?*: "In Cincinnati, Ohio, an experiment was conducted in which there was affixed on the back of each hand a number that was read by a scanner in the supermarket where these people did their shopping. As each item was checked out, the cash register simultaneously flashed it to the proper bank, where it was automatically deducted from that person's account." A full-page illustration which appeared in a 1993 issue of the *London Daily Mail*, showed housewives in Europe making purchases by putting their hands on a computer screen at the cash register.

Another alternative has to be considered here also. Note that in Revelation 13:16, it says that the "mark" will be placed "in" the right hand or forehead, not "on" it. An article in the October 2, 1980 edition of the *Seattle Post-Intelligencer* reported: "Race horses and house cats or other domestic animals may be injected with minute electronic wafers that will help owners trace their animals. Vern Taylor, President of Identification Devices, Inc., said that the wafer is printed with a serial number and injected into the animal, When an electronic wand is passed over the area, the serial number is displayed on a digital readout. He said that the microchip will be sold to vetinarians. A computer data bank, known as the Animal Bureau of Identification, will also help law enforcement officials as well as animal control officers identify animals."

An article in the June 21, 1981 edition of the *Denver Post* reported that "a chip ... about the diameter of the lead in an automatic pencil ... can be injected with a simple insulin-type syringe into a human (or animal) ... one wafer is encoded with a 12-digit unique number." It can also be placed on inanimate objects to electronically monitor the whereabouts of store merchandise and leased equipment. A *Washington Times* article (October 11, 1993) contained a report by Martin Anderson, Senior Fellow at the Hoover Institute, concerning a solution for the problem of people losing their identification cards. He said: "You see, there is an identification system you can't lose. It's the Syringe Implantable Transponder, a permanent method of identification using radio waves. A tiny microchip, the size of a grain of rice, is simply injected under the skin." With this microchip, satellites can identify your location within 15 feet.

I've read reports that suggested that the government was using the mandatory infant immunization program to secretly implant these chips. That was never proven. Besides, I believe that part of the end-time plan is for you to make a choice as to who you are going to serve.

Now, ten years later, the system has been refined and perfected. The Palm Beach, Florida-based company, Applied Digital Solutions has made its VeriChip available for insertion into humans. The microchip, about the size of a tip of a ball point pen (12 mm X 2.1 mm), which contains a unique verification number, is implanted in the (right) arm or the hip, using a syringe-like device and a local anesthetic for the pain. The advantages being touted is that hospital officials and security personnel can access a person's medical history and confirm identity. The company has said that they are also developing technology that will enable satellites to track people who have been kidnapped. Details about their product is sketchy. The company has said that the chip does not contain any information, it is not known what the information storage capacity is. It appears that this may be just a prototype system, in that a chip costs $150, there is a $50 annual maintenance fee, and the scanning equipment and software cost $1,200.

The Universal Product Code System

I am sure you have seen the horizontal scanners at the grocery stores which are used to read the UPC symbols off of the items you are buying, so that the computer will automatically print the price of that item. They obviously have the capability of scanning your hand. For a time, a few years ago, I began to see upright scanners. With a flat scanner, the cashier only had to slide the item across the scanning plate; but with the upright scanner, the cashier has to lift the item up in front of the scanner. I was amazed the first time I seen one, because right away I knew that its purpose wasn't to make things easier for the cashier, it was to make it easier to scan your forehead and hand. Recent versions have placed them lower on the checkout station. I haven't seen a lot of them, so I don't know if the retail industry as a whole is going to upgrade to this version of the scanner.

We have been talking about future developments, so let's talk about the present. Do you realize that with the Universal Product Code (UPC), we are already buying and selling under the number 666.

In 1970, the National Association of Food Chains, and five other major trade associations representing manufacturers, wholesalers, and retailers, met, and formed an ad hoc committee to set up guidelines for an encoding system that could be accepted by the entire industry. In 1971, a code management committee came up with the concept of a ten-digit numerical code: the first five to identify the manufacturer, and the last five to identify the specific item. In 1972, the Uniform Grocery Product Code Council, Inc. and Distribution Codes, Inc. (in charge of assigning numbers) was established, with thousands of companies invited to become members. On April 3, 1973, the ad hoc committee announced that they had selected a twelve-digit bar code that could be printed by conventional methods, and be scanned omni-directionally by an automated system. By the end of 1974, the Uniform Grocery Product Code Council had changed their name to the Uniform Product Code Council, Inc., and had 21 representatives from manufacturers, distributors, and trade associations on their Board. Around 2,600 companies, representing a total of $70.7 billion in annual sales, had become members of the Code Council, and were utilizing the bar coding on their products.

The UPC system functions like this. The prices are marked on the shelf and not the item (although some chains continue to put prices on the items). As the items are carried down the conveyer belt, the cashier pulls the item, symbol downward, across the scanner, and bags the item. The scanner contains a laser beam which emits a beam of light. The white bars or spaces will reflect more light than the black bars, which is measured by a light detector. A time measurement of how long the beam takes to move across the bar and space, is also used for decoding. The scanner reads the symbol, no matter what direction it is passed over the scanner, from several inches, to a foot away, decoding the number and sending the number to a computer. The computer transmits to the electronic cash register, the price of the product, which is indicated on a display, and printed on the receipt tape.

Checkout time is speeded up by 60-70% over the conventional method, eliminating the need for as many employees. When the register totals the purchase, the printed receipt tape usually indicates the store name, number, and location, item name, item price, whether it is taxable, and the total. It allows for payment in cash, food stamps, check, debit card, or credit card; and deducts the coupons which are presented. It tells how much change is received, the date, time, and lane number. Besides the quickness and efficiency, another feature of the system is the ability to automatically keep track of inventory.

> Left Hand Guide Bar (101— 2 black bars and 1 white bar) represents the number 6, and tells the computer that information is coming.
>
> Center Bar (01010— 3 white bars and 2 black bars) which represents the number 6, and separates the design.
>
> Right Hand Guide Bar (101— 2 black bars and 1 white bar) represents the number 6, and tells the computer that the information is complete.

> The regular size of the bar code is 1.469" X 1.020," but it can be printed from 80% of that size, to twice that size. It must appear in a rectangular block on the bottom, side or back panel of a product, or anywhere it can be scanned. The bar code is a series of black and white parallel bars, 30 black and 31 white (for 10 digits), with white margins on each side. Each digit of the code is represented by two black bars, and two white bars, which is composed of seven data elements or 'modules.' A module may

be white or black. A white or black bar can be made up of 1, 2, 3, or 4 modules. Modules are all the same width, being that they are the foundation of the system, and create the bars which are visible to the naked eye.

If you look at the diagram of the UPC symbol, you will notice that the symbol is split into two sides, a left-hand side, using an odd number of modules; and a right-hand side, using an even number of modules, making them opposite of each other. Thus, it doesn't matter if the symbol is entered upside-down. For each set of 7 modules is a number, and each number is represented by a field whose optical bars are broken down into the following binary codes, where 0 = a blank space, and 1 = a black bar:

Set 1 (left side)
0 - 0001101
1 - 0011001
2 - 0010011
3 - 0111101
4 - 0100011
5 - 0110001
6 - 0101111
7 - 0111011
8 - 0110111
9 - 0001011

Set 2 (right side)
0 - 1110010
1 - 1100110
2 - 1101100
3 - 1000010
4 - 1011100
5 - 1001110
6 - 1010000
7 - 1000100
8 - 1001000
9 - 1110100

The UPS Code begins with a Number System Character (on the left of the symbol):

0 = Grocery
1 = Unknown
2 = Variable weight items such as fruit, meat and produce
3 = National Drug Code and Health Related Items
4 = Reserved for NDC and HRIC, if manufacturer identification code on left has to be expanded to 11 digits (1st five on the left side, 6th will be placed at the right of the symbol)
5 = Reserved for use on coupons

6 = Encodes a 12-digit code when the code must be expanded
7 = Unknown
8 = Unknown
9 = Encodes a 12-digit code in stores where more information is needed on symbol

The first group of numbers (generally 5) is the Manufacturer's Code, and the second group of numbers (generally 5) is the Manufacturer Product Code (such as an item number). The Code ends with a Check Character (to the right of the symbol) whose purpose is to check for errors, such as an unauthorized addition of lines that could result in the computer reading the wrong number.

There are various other UPC Code designs that have been utilized such as the Zero Suppression Method (Design #2, 2nd most commonly used design) which permits zeros to be eliminated from the ten digit code number, thereby narrowing it to six numbers, which reduces the width of the symbol so it can fit on a product with a smaller package. Known as truncation, this method also reduces the height by shortening the length of the vertical lines; but it also reduces the computer's effectiveness in reading the symbol omni-directionally. It is the second most commonly used UPC design. Mary Stewart Relfe believed that the intention of this alternate design was to insure that the general public would not crack the UPC code. It actually represents half of the regular symbol. The design incorporates bar codes from the first and second sets, and from a third set created from the second set.

There is an extended version of the main design (Design #3) for use on magazines and books. While the main portion of the design will only use bar codes from the first and second sets; the extended area on the right side of the symbol will use bar codes from all three sets.

Going back to Revelation 13:17, it says: "And that no man might buy or sell, save he that had the mark, or the name of the beast, or the number of his name." Incredibly, as you have seen, through the use of the UPC system of encoding products, we are actually buying and selling with the number 666. The left and right-hand guides, and center bar patterns in Design #1, is designated by the following binary codes:

left-hand guide: 101
center bar pattern: 01010
right-hand guide: 101

Just to verify, when you consider the number 6 when used as a Data Character, as in the second set, the number 6 is encoded as 1010000. In other words, the only visible modules of the number 6, is the designation of 101, which is used in the left and right-hand guides, and the center bar pattern. Since the Data Characters use a seven module encodation, and the two guides and center pattern consist of three and five modules, it is obvious that the two numerical encodations are different. While the numbers at the middle of the UPC symbol represent the Manufacturer Code, and the Manufacturer Product Code; the numbers encoded in the two guide bars and center bar pattern, represent the number "666." This "666" code can be found in every UPC symbol. In Design #2, which is half of Design #1, it incorporates a third bar code for the number six, which is represented by half of the center bar pattern, or a module pattern of 010.

The number 6 is a prominent part of the UPC, symbol. In Design #1, there are six numbers on the left side, and six numbers on the right side. There are six numbers in Design #2. There are six different variations of the UPC symbol. Six is the perfect computer number, a fact, which, according to the *Wall Street Journal* (November 11, 1981), led Apple Computer, Inc. to introduce their Apple I units at a price of $666.66.

Richard J. Mindlin, Executive Vice-President of the Uniform Product Code Council had said: "There are no unidentified characters in the symbol, as each encodation serves either as data characters or for information to indicate to the scanner to start or stop reading. These start and stop characters are not the same as the encodation for the digit '6'."

George J. Laurer, who invented the UPC in 1973 has said: "There is nothing sinister about this nor does it have anything to do with the Bible's 'mark of the beast.' It is simply a coincidence like the fact that my first, middle, and last name all have six letters. There is no connection with an international money code either." As of November 2000, Mr. Laurer has stopped responding to questions about this.

I can understand his contention that he is being accused of creating something that is inherently evil. We have been quick to attach a negative connotation to it, but the fact of the matter is, Bible prophecy has been fulfilled, we are buying and selling with the number 666. That is undeniable. The Apostle John made a prophetic observation— he gave us a sign to look for. So, regardless of all the mechanics of how we got there, we are there.

Those stores who already have electronic fund transfer (EFT) capabilities, and are accepting debit cards, are pulling funds directly from a customer's checking account, and transferring it to the store's account at the bank. At this point, it is not known if the system can accept an international debit card, however it is reasonably safe to assume that the system was created to accommodate the final step, or the 'mark of the beast.' Besides the warning in Revelation 14:10 not to take this Mark; the Law of Moses in Leviticus 19:28 said: "Ye shall not ... print any marks upon you..." Revelation 16:2 indicates that those who take the Mark will be stricken with a "grievous sore."

Sen. Frank Church said in August, 1975, that "the government has the technological capacity to impose 'total tyranny' if ever a dictator came to power. There would be no place to hide." The Antichrist will be that dictator. With the potential of money and debit cards being lost or stolen, the idea of a number being applied with a laser to your skin may also be going by the wayside because of it being exposed to external conditions. It seems as though VeriChip technology being tested now will be the means through which people will be made part of the 'beast system.' The purpose of the Mark is to make a person totally dependent upon the government, and to serve as a surveillance tool. When Revelation 14:17 says that you won't be able to "buy or sell" without the "mark," this is an obvious financial connection. When the economic infrastructure of this country is totally converted to a system that is completely cashless, everything will then be in place for the implantable identification technology. Your pay will be direct deposited, your bills will be automatically withdrawn from your checking account; and when you go to the grocery store, to the doctor, or to get gas, if you don't have a chip, you will not be able to "buy or sell," because you will not have a means to access your account. Those who do not take the Mark will be harassed by the government, and eventually be targeted for arrest and detention. True Christians, who refuse to take the Mark, will become fugitives when their rights are taken away.

THE INVASION OF ISRAEL

Bible prophecy and Biblical interpretation have come a long way in the past 40 years. I grew up reading the works and research of many great men of God, which certainly had an influence on how I viewed end-time events. At times, I would just take things for granted, or just assume that someone was right on how they saw things. But as I got older, and started my own research, and I began to put everything together, somehow things just were not meshing. If you are a student of Bible prophecy, like I am, you have probably heard a number of end-time theories and scenarios. Many seem plausible. But again, they don't always seem to totally fit into the scheme of things.

As I said earlier, space just did not permit a detailed examination, so I have been relegated to just providing an overview of things. Throughout this book, I have tried to give various alternatives for different aspects of prophetic events, rather than concretely saying that, 'This is the way it is.' The writings of Ezekiel, Daniel, and Revelation are a collection of very mysterious writings; and Daniel is specifically, because of its concept of using dual prophecy.

In pooling the resources together that I have, I have been slowly developing a picture to provide a sort of chronology of end-time events. As a child, when I would be in church listening to ministers talking about the Antichrist and the last days, I always wondered how all that could be possible— how the world could ever be brought to the place where one man could exercise so much authority over it. When I found out about the Illuminati that seemed to answer all my questions. However, the ensuing research actually created more questions, because the direction it seemed to take veered away from the traditionally held views of Bible prophecy. I actually considered stopping here, rather then taking the chance of compromising this entire body of research, but, being a writer, I have to bring everything to its logical conclusion. So, here we go ...

The Antichrist is Revealed

"I am Antichrist, I am Antichrist, I know what I want, I know how to get it; I want to destroy."
—(from a song by the Sex Pistols, a punk-rock band)

Daniel 9:27 says that the Antichrist will "confirm the covenant with many for one week." Obviously to do this, he would have to be in a position of authority to do it.

As of this writing, although Europe is as united as it has ever been, talks aimed at drafting a Constitution have broken down. Therefore, Europe as a truly unified political entity does not yet exist. It is believed that the Antichrist's rise to power will be through that government. Will he be the one that will actually make it happen? Revelation 17:12 says: "And the ten horns which thou sawest are ten kings, which have received no kingdom as yet; but receive power as kings one hour with the beast." So, with the resources of a united Europe behind him, he would definitely have a political base from which to operate from diplomatically.

According to Daniel, "his power shall be mighty," (8:24) and "he shall cause craft to prosper in his hand," (8:25). The success he will achieve in Europe will no doubt give him international recognition. In Daniel 11:7, it says: "...and power was given him over all kindreds, and tongues, and nations." This seems to imply a larger scope of authority. Is it possible that he will become the Secretary-General of a UN that has been transformed into a world government (due to the efforts of the New World Order)? How else would he be in a position to exercise authority over such a large group of people?

The Middle East has been a powder keg for many years because the Arab nations (Esau's descendants) feel they had their birthright taken away by Israel (Jacob's descendants). A covenant is made with "many for a week," or seven years. Because the second part of that verse talks about causing the sacrifices to stop, which is an obvious reference to the reinstitution of Temple sacrifice is Jerusalem, it has been assumed that the covenant was just made with Israel. How can just Israel be referred to as "many?" The terminology dictates that the covenant would have to be made with "many" nations, and it would have to be nations somewhat associated with Israel. This would seem to be a covenant between the Antichrist (leader of the world government), Israel and the Arab nations, in order to seek a peaceful solution to the Middle East crisis. Somehow he will achieve a diplomatic solution that will give the Arabs what they want, and give the Jews the security they want, which will enable them to build or erect a Temple, on its original foundation, so that Temple sacrifice can be resumed. Even though there were 300 specific predictions concerning Jesus, the Jewish people didn't accept Him because they were expecting a great conqueror to deliver them from the Romans. However, it won't take long for this western European leader to be heralded as the Messiah they have been waiting for.

The aim of a world government will be to seek complete disarmament in order to maintain peace. Any country that does not willingly join in will be forced to comply, as it says that "he shall destroy wonderfully..."

Meanwhile, the individual who has emerged as the preeminent religious leader in the world will succeed in bringing together the major religions to form a new coalition of Christianity that will be bound together with New Age philosophy. To legitimize his claim of being called by God to lead the Church, he will use his mastery of the occult to give the illusion of being able to perform "miracles." (Revelation 13:13-14)

In the "midst" (or $3^1/_2$ years) of the covenant, it seems that diplomacy was not enough to bring lasting peace to this region. In Daniel 11:40, we find a conflict between the "king of the north" and the "king of the south." Chapter 11:42-43 and historical prospective (dual prophecy) leads us to believe that the "king of the south" will be Egypt. The "king of the north" has been identified as Syria, and it is believed that this is the country that the Antichrist will come out of. This conflict is identified as the vehicle through which the Antichrist gains control of the nations (10 horns) of the old Holy Roman Empire. Well, that's one scenario.

You have to ask yourself, why would Egypt attack Syria? Since signing a peace treaty with Israel, Egypt has been involved in any armed conflicts. If anything, I could see Syria (who has been very militant) attacking Egypt because of their treaty with Israel. More important, Syria is a small country, and does not have the military capability to do all that is being attributed to it. Anyway, I think that the "king of the north" is referencing western Europe. After the "ten kings" received their power, they were as "one mind." (Rev. 17:13) Therefore, as one unified nation, they could be referred to as a "king." And the nations of the Roman Empire are north.

Who is the "king of the south" actually attacking? Daniel 11:40 doesn't really say that the "king of the south" is attacking Israel. As I said earlier, Egypt does have a treaty with them. Of course, that could be broken. However, the passage seems to indicate that the "king of the south" is attacking the "king of the north." Apparently the European Federation will have a protectionary force (peace keepers) in place in the Middle East, and this is who the attack will be directed at. The "king of the north" will then respond with a major ground and naval offensive. However, in the process of putting down this rebellion, "many countries shall be overthrown." (Dan. 11:41). It is stated that Edom, Moab, and Ammon will not be affected. Ironically, they, along with the Israelites, Arabians, Ishmaelites, and Midianites were the descendants of Arphaxad, the son of Shem, the middle son of Noah. Their land was on the eastern shore of the Dead Sea, in an area now occupied by the country of Jordan. It is logical to assume that the countries involved will be Arab countries, especially in light of the fact that he moves on the country of Egypt and takes spoils. (Dan. 11:42) At this point, Libya and Ethiopia come to the aid of Egypt.

It is apparent by this time that since Egypt had broken the covenant, all bets are off, as the European military force has responded with extreme prejudice. This upheaval in diplomacy now creates an unstable condition world-wide as an aura of war is manifested. Daniel 11:44-45 says: "But tidings out of the east and out of the north shall trouble him: therefore he shall go forth with great fury to destroy, and utterly to make away many. And he shall plant the tabernacles of his palace between the seas in the glorious holy mountain..." He will withdraw from Egypt, killing as many people as he can, before doubling back to Jerusalem. This is the beginning of the end.

Abomination of Desolation

"When ye therefore shall see the abomination of desolation, spoken of by Daniel the prophet, stand in the holy place..." (Matthew 24:15)

"Let no man deceive you by any means: for that day shall not come, except there come a falling away first, and that man of sin be revealed, the son of perdition; Who opposeth and exalteth himself above all that is called God, or that is worshipped; so that he as God sitteth in the temple of God, shewing himself that he is God," (2 Thessalonians 2:3-4)

"And from the time that the daily sacrifice shall be taken away, and the abomination that maketh desolate set up, there shall be a thousand two hundred and ninety days. Blessed is he that waiteth and cometh to the thousand three hundred and five and thirty days." (Daniel 12:11-12)

"And there was given unto him a mouth speaking great things and blasphemies; and power was given unto him to continue forty and two months. And he opened his mouth in blasphemy against God, to blaspheme his name, and his tabernacle, and them that dwell in heaven. And it was given unto him to make war with the saints and to overcome them..." (Revelation 13:5-7)

"I beheld, and the same horn made war with the saints, and prevailed against them..." (Daniel 7:21)

"Then let them which be in Judea flee into the mountains." (Matthew 24:16)

"But when ye shall see the abomination of desolation, spoken of by Daniel the prophet, standing where it ought not, (let him that readeth understand,) then let them that be in Judea flee to the mountains." (Mark 13:14)

"And the woman fled into the wilderness, where she hath a place prepared of God, that they should feed her there a thousand two hundred and threescore days ... And when the dragon saw that he was cast unto the earth, he persecuteth the woman which brought forth the man child. And to the woman were given two wings of a great eagle, that she might fly into the wilderness, into her place, where she is nourished for a time, and times, and half a time, from the face of the serpent ... And the dragon was wroth with the woman, and went to make war with the remnant of her seed, which keep the commandments of God, and have the testimony of Jesus Christ." (Revelation 12:6, 13-17)

When the Antichrist reveals himself by defiling the Jewish Temple with a statue of his image, and his demand that he be worshipped as the Messiah; the eyes of the Jewish people will be opened. He will become the most dreaded being that ever walked the earth. Revelation 13:2 indicates that "the dragon (Satan) gave him his power, and his seat, and great authority," and once his Satanic agenda is realized, the Jews will flee Israel to escape his wrath. With the phrase "two wings of a great eagle" it's possible that an airlift will be mounted to aid the Jews in their escape into the "wilderness."

This area is believed to be the land of Edom, Moab, and Ammon, which will not be overrun by European forces. There in the southern Jordanian wilderness, 180 miles south of the Ammon, and 75 miles north of Aqaba (which is on the Gulf of Aqaba), is a 20-square mile complex known as the ancient city of Petra (a Greek word meaning 'Rock'). Located in a valley, and surrounded by impassable sandstone cliffs, the only entrance is a narrow path known as El Ciq, which is about 6,000 feet long, and varies in width from 12 to 30 feet. The sides are part of nearly perpendicular cliffs which range in heights from 300 to 500 feet.

Known as Mount Seir in the Bible, this was the home of Esau, the father of the Edomites (ancestors of the Palestinian Arabs). During the Babylonian captivity of the Jews, the Edomites moved into Israel, and Petra was inhabited by an Arabic tribe known as the Nabataeans (said to be the descendants of Nebajoth, the oldest son of Ishmael) during the 6th century BC, and became an important trade center. They were defeated by the Romans around 55 BC, and in 32 BC, Marc Antony gave Petra to Cleopatra of Egypt as a gift. Because he was married to Octavia, the sister of Roman Emperor, the Senate stripped him of his rank and ordered him back to Rome. Antony committed suicide in 30 BC, as did Cleopatra later. With the decrease of Roman influence in the 5th century, and after the Islamic invasion during the 7th century, the area became part of the province of Arabia, and remained a ghost town until it was rediscovered in 1812 by Swiss explorer John L. Burckhardt. The last segment of the 1989 Paramount movie *Indiana Jones and the Last Crusade* was filmed at Petra.

Believed to have originally been built inside an extinct volcano, this rock city contains many elaborate facades among its many structures, which include various tombs, monuments, and dwellings, which were carved into the rock of the mountainside. Some date back to the Edomite era, most are Nabataean, and some are Roman and early Christian. There are thousands of natural and man-made caves. Even though it is located in a desert area, there are water cisterns there, and dozens of springs and wells, including the Ain Musa ('Spring of Moses'), two miles from the entrance, which is traditionally identified as one of the two sites where Moses produced water by striking a rock. At one time this spring had been channeled into the city. It has been reported that Petra could hold up to a million people.

In 1935, out of a $5 million trust fund, Dr. William E. Blackstone sent a group of Christians there with Bibles, printed in Hebrew, which were sealed in copper boxes and buried in hewn-out vaults in the mountain. The Bibles are marked at the passages which deal with the Antichrist. In recent years, a construction firm out of Minneapolis, Minnesota, had been hired to restore the water system; and other international teams were schedules to carry out other restoration work.

From this point on is the time referred to as the 'Great Tribulation." Revelation 11:2 says: "...for it is given unto the Gentiles: and the holy city shall they tread under foot forty and two months (or $3^1/_2$ years or 1,260 days)." Although his influence will be worldwide, the Antichrist will have absolute power over 25% of the world (Rev. 6:8), with the main concentration being in the nations of the world controlled by the world government. He will seek out and destroy true Christians and all others who will not worship him or take his Mark. In Matthew 24:9, Jesus said: "Then shall they deliver you up to be afflicted, and shall kill you: and ye shall be hated of all nations for my name's sake." Revelation 20:4 talks about those who were "beheaded for the witness of Jesus, and for the word of God, and which had not worshipped the beast, neither his image, neither had received his mark upon their foreheads, or in their hands..."

It is at this time when "two witnesses" will emerge to "prophesy," according to Revelation 11:3. It says, "I will give power unto my two witnesses," which could indicate that God intends to anoint a couple of ordinary men, who will become 'super evangelists,' possessing extraordinary powers like the prophets of old. However, just as angels have been sent to Earth in various capacities, the consensus seems to be that these two will be prophets sent by God.

There have been two possibilities mentioned as to the identities of the two. Matthew 17:3 and Mark 9:4, refer to Jesus being transfigured with Elijah and Moses. In 2 Kings 2:11, the prophet Elijah was taken to heaven in a fiery chariot; and in Malachi 4:5, this prophecy is given: "Behold, I will send you Elijah the prophet before the coming of the great and dreadful day of the Lord." Moses, unlike Elijah, had died, so it was his spiritual body which had appeared. So the identity of the second witness perhaps points to Enoch, because he was the only other person in the Bible who never died. According to Genesis 5:24, he was taken by God.

These two witnesses, who will preach for 1,260 days, will most likely have a ministry similar to John the Baptist. They will be latter-day prophets, opposing the dictatorship and government of the Antichrist, and spreading the word that the Son of Man, Jesus, the true Messiah, is returning the reclaim the Earth. After their ministry is complete, the Antichrist will succeed in having them killed, and as a warning to others, the Antichrist will demand that their bodies remain unburied, so the world can see the extent of his power. However, God will show his power, and bring them back to life ($3^1/_2$ days later), and they will be taken back to Heaven.

Armageddon—the Main Event

In the 38th and 39th chapters of Ezekiel, the preliminary information is given on the final battle. The Antichrist and the full might of his military forces are now entrenched in Israel. It's a Battle Royale, with the nations of the world converging upon the tiny nation of Israel in a bid for world domination.

The line-up of combatants that appears in chapter 38 includes the descendents of Japheth (3rd chapter of Genesis), a son of Noah: Gomer, Magog, Madai, Javan, Tubal, Meshech, and Tiras, who repopulated the Earth after the Flood.

Magog's descendants settled in the area of Armenia, which is in southern Russia, after being driven north through the Caucasus mountains by the Medes. This race came to be known as the Scythians, and were called 'Magogites' by the Greeks. The Chinese name for the Caucasus mountains running through Russia mean 'Fort of Gog,' while the Russians call their peaks, the 'Gogh.' The Arabic term for the Great Wall of China is 'the wall of Al Magog,' because it was erected with the intention of keeping out the armies of Magog. Their descendants include the Tarters, Cossacks, Kalmuks, and the Mongols. The *Kesses HaSofer*, a Jewish Commentary, indicates that the word 'Mongol,' which identifies the Siberian-Russian people, comes from the word 'Magog.'

In the Septuagint (Greek) translation of the Bible, it describes 'Gog' as the 'prince of Rosh.' Rosh was the name of a tribe living in the area of the Volga. In some languages, Rosh is the word for the country of Russia. The ancient form of the name Russia, is 'Ros.' The Chinese had called the Scythians 'Rosh.' The King James Version translated 'Rosh' to mean 'chief prince,' because in Hebrew it means 'head'; but in the Septuagint version, 'Rosh' is used as the proper name it is believed to be.

An interesting fact from the Oxford Paperback Encyclopedia (from Oxford University Press) is that there is a British legend that identifies Gog and Magog as the survivors of a race of giants destroyed by Brutus the Trojan, the legendary founder of London. They were depicted in statues erected at London's Guildhall during the reign of Henry V, but were destroyed by the Fire of London in 1666. Reconstructed, they were again destroyed during the air raids of the Blitz in 1940. The current statues were created in 1953. Models of these "gods" are carried through the streets during the Lord Mayor's annual procession. No doubt an offshoot of that is the fact that there are two hills called Gog and Magog near Cambridge, in England, where there are huge drawings in the ground that can only see seen from the air.

The descendants of Meshech (known to the Assyrians as 'Mushku'), settled in western Russia, where they established a city called Meshech, later known as Mosach, then Moscovi (Muscovy or Moscow), which is the capital of Russia.

Tubal's descendants lived in the area of the Black Sea, then moved north, settling in the eastern part of Russia, establishing the city of Tobolsk. Their descendants include the Iberians, Georgians, Cappadocians, as well as other Asiatic and European peoples.

This attack will also include Persia (the descendants of Madai, which includes Iran and Iraq), Ethiopia (the descendants of Cush, the son of Ham, another son of Noah), and Libya (the descendants of Phut, the son of Ham). Ethiopia and Libya were the nations that came to Egypt's aid. Since Egypt is not mentioned, we have to assume that they suffered great destruction.

In 1847, Sir Henry Layard discovered the Assyrian capital city of Nineveh, and the Royal Palace, which contained over 23,000 clay tablets describing all kinds of things. After defeating the Israelites, and taking them captive, they were exiled to an area below the Black and Caspian Seas. These reports gave the names used by the Assyrians for the different groups of Israelites that were planted as a buffer between them and their enemies (Medes). The "Royal Letters" date back to 707 BC, which is about 14 years after the defeat of Samaria. Letters #1079 (describes the defeat of the Urartians), and its follow-up #197 (which says it occurred in the land of Gamir) were written by Sennacherib to his father, King Sargon. Letter #112 talks about a people (Iskuza or Isaac) that "went forth" from the midst of the Mannai, into the "land of Urartu," while another letter distinctly separates the Urartians, the Mannai, and the Gamera (or Gimira), which means the people in Letter #112 are Gamerraan, or in English, the 'Cimmerians.'

The Behistun Rock was found in the 1700-foot high Zargos mountains in northwestern Iran, 300 foot above the ground on a sheer face, The relief had been commissioned by Darius the Great in 515 BC, and lists the peoples and nations he defeated and ruled over as part of the Medo-Persian Empire. It is interesting to point out, that while he was putting down the Israelite insurrection, he was helping the Jews to rebuild the Temple.

The Rock (confirmed by Darius' tomb, as well as a golden tablet that talks about the 'Sakka') is inscribed in three languages, is 100 feet high, and 150 feet wide. By 1840, it had been deciphered by Sir Henry C. Rawlinson. The name 'Kana' (Canaan) appears 28 times. 'Saka' or 'Sakka' in Mede, Persian, Elamite, and 'Sacae' in Greek, is 'Gimri' in Babylonian. The Assyrian and Babylonian renditions are nearly the same. 'Sakka' refers to a nomad or one who lives in a tent or 'booth.' The word 'booth' in Hebrew is 'succoth.' 'Sakka' comes from 'Isaac,' (pronounced 'e-sahk' with emphasis on the last syllable) and became 'Saxon.' 'Gimri' comes from the Assyrian 'Khumri' (after Biblical House of 'Omri,' 6th King of Israel) and became Ghumri, Gimira, Gimmira, the Greek 'Kimmeroii,' or English 'Cimmerian.'

According to the apocryphal book of 2 Esdras 13:40-44, they migrated to Europe. While the main body of prisoners remained in the area about a hundred years, the Israelites slowly began moving to the east and the north. When the power of the Assyrians was broken, there were several migrations, with the two main groups moving west under the Black Sea, north through the Dariel Pass of the Caucasas Mountains into the steppes of southern Russia. A large group also migrated east.

Between 650-500 BC, the Cimmerians in Europe moved up the Danube and became known as Celts, eventually migrating to France than England. Between 250-100 BC, when southern Russia was invaded by the Sarmatians from the east, the Scythians (Isaac is believed to be the foundation for this name) were driven northwest through Poland into Germany. After 450 AD, the Romans called the Scythians 'Germans,' meaning 'genuine,' to distinguish them from the Sarmatians in Scythia.

So, Gomer's desecendants (known to the Assyrians as 'Gimirrai' or 'Cimmerians') settled in central Asia Minor, north of the Black Sea, in southern Russia, then moved west along the Danube River, to the area now known as Germany. He was the father of Eastern Europe. Old world maps identify this area as Gomer, Gomerlunt, Gomeria. Their descendants include the Galatians, Phrygians, Gauls, Celts (Greek "Keltoi"), Germans, French, Welsh, Irish, Britons, and other Anglo-Saxon (means 'Isaac's son') peoples. In addition, Togarmah (known to the Assyrians as 'Tilgarimmu'), a son of Gomer, is singled out. His descendants occupied Turkey and Asia Minor, and another branch settled in Estonia, Latvia, and Lithuania, which were later taken over by the Soviet Union. They were granted independence in September, 1991.

Togarmah's 'bands' could also refer to Armenia and Syia, whose ancestors claimed that Haik, the father of their race, was the son of Togarmah. The descendants of another son of Gomer, Ashkenaz, settled in Germany and Austria.

In Ezekiel 38:13, "Sheba, Dedan, and the merchants of Tarshish, with all the young lions thereof," seem to be questioning the motives of the Soviet Union, perhaps because they seem far removed from what appears to be a regional conflict. It is not clear whether they involve themselves in the military action.

Sheba (also Saba), was an ancient kingdom in the area of the southwestern edge of Saudi Arabia which became known as the British colony of Aden, until achieving independence as South Yemen (who united with North Yemen in 1990). This was the traditional kingdom of the Queen of Sheba who ruled over the Sabaeans (who dominated all of southern Arabia), and was labeled in Matthew 12:42 as the 'Queen of the South.' The historian Josephus referred to her as the "Queen of Egypt and Ethiopia." Dedan was the name of a Sabaean oasis in the northern part of Saudi Arabia, which was one of their many colonies in northern Arabia.

Another identifying indication again comes from Biblical genealogy. Cush, the son of Ham, was the father of Ethiopia, and other tribes who settled south of Egypt, in Arabia, Babylonia and India. Cush's sons are identified as Seba (who in Psalms 72:10 is associated with the kings of Sheba, and in Isaiah 43:3 are mentioned with Ethiopia, which indicates that he is the father of the Sabaeans); Havilah (a name associated with the area of the Sinai and northwestern Arabia); Sabtah, Raamah, and Sabtechah (all three of which were associated with tribes in southern Arabia). Sheba and Dedan are listed as sons of Raamah. Thus, the reference to Sheba and Dedan actually identifies the country of Saudi Arabia (as well as the countries of Oman, Yemen, the United Arab Emirates, Qatar, and Bahrain). They were an ally of the Coalition against Iraq during the Gulf War.

The "merchants of Tarshish, with all the young lions thereof" are also named with them. According to Jeremiah 10:9, Tarshish is identified as a land rich with precious metals; and in other passages, such as Isaiah 2:16, are associated with possessing a prominent shipping empire which was used to export goods to places all over the Mediterranean. Some researchers have tried to connect Tarshish with Tartessus (located in the Guadalquivir Valley) in southwestern Spain, where the Phoenicians founded colonies to capitalize on the wealth of minerals found there.

The Phoenicians established the city of Carthage on Africa's northern coast (in what is now Tunisia), and it was these Carthaginians who began colonizing Spain in 654 BC (until they were driven out by the Romans in 206 BC), and exploring the Atlantic coastline from western Africa to Britain. Recent archaeological evidence has shown that they possessed sailing capabilities far beyond what was originally known. An inscription discovered in 1780 on a cliff above Mount Hope Bay in Bristol, Rhode Island, which was written in Tartessian Punic, reads: "Voyagers from Tarshish this stone proclaims." It is believed that this inscription was made about 533 BC. Howard University's Dept. of Archaeology has found five other areas in the United States where Tarshish had colonies 2500 years ago.

Tarshish was a great-grandson of Noah, whose descendants migrated to the areas which later became Spain and Great Britain. Ezekiel 27:12 indicates that Tarshish was a source of tin, and the word 'Britain' means "land of tin." Both Spain, with their Armada, and England, became major naval powers. An analysis of these facts may indicate that Tarshish is referring to one (England) or two countries of the western European alliance. The "young lions" (the lion is a symbol of England) could refer to the United States (who came out of England), Canada, Australia, New Zealand (all part of the English Empire), their possessions and allies. Again, we can't be sure if these countries that are mentioned are participants in this massive assault.

In Revelation 16:12, the 6th angel pours out his vial, which causes the Euphrates River to dry up, so "that the way of the kings of the east might be prepared," and then in Rev. 9:16 we find that "the number of the army of the horsemen were two hundred thousand thousand..." We can connect these two verses together by virtue of numbers and geography.

An estimate made in April, 1961, said that there "were 200 million armed and organized militiamen" in China. The Associated Press reported that one out of every five in China have had military training. Premier Mao Tse-tung publicly boasted the fact that China could field an army of 200 million. A Chinese documentary called *Voice of the Dragon* revealed that China could produce a military force of 200 million. In an Associated Press article by John A. Hightower, on April 28, 1964, he said: "The documents (secret Chinese military plans) make clear that the Red Chinese leaders believe that they cannot be defeated by long range nuclear missiles, such as U.S. missiles, and if they invaded, they could rely on their vast military manpower." To comprehend a number this large, bear in mind that the population of the United States is about to 295,000,000.

Napoleon said: "Let China sleep, for when China awakes, let the nations tremble." In 1953, Premier Mao Tse-tung (who in 1921 founded China's Communist Party) said: "Members of the Chinese Communist Party do not take second place to the members of any Communist Party in the world." China is the last bastion of Communist domination, and they likewise will join the fray in a quest for world domination.

The government of Pakistan, with the help of 12,000 Chinese soldiers, constructed the 549 mile Korakoram superhighway, which had been nicknamed the "roof on top of the world." Starting in Tibet, it weaves its way through the province of Singkiang; the mountains peaks of Manchuria, Mongolia, Nepal, the Himalayas, West Pakistan; and into Afghanistan, to where the Euphrates River rises in Turkey, and runs across Syria. It follows the ancient trans-Asian invasion route used by Alexander the Great, Genghis Khan, and the Mogul invaders. Will China use this highway as a route to Israel?

It is written that the Euphrates River will be dried up at the time of this troop movement. It could be done through supernatural means, as has happened with the Red Sea and the Jordan River (Exodus 14:13-22, Joshua 3:4, 2 Kings 2:8, 14); or it could be the result of manipulation. There are two dams in the Turkish section of the Euphrates, Ataturk and Karakaya. In 1974, Soviet engineers built the Keban dam, and in 1975, built another at Tabka, in Syria. In January, 1990, Turkey began the operation of a dam that caused the river to fall 75% in one day. So, it is quite possible that the river could be made to dry up at just the right time.

Okay, take a deep breath. We have the armies of the Antichrist hunkering down in Israel, we have the Soviet Union and countries of Eastern Europe (perhaps Albania, Bulgaria, Romania, Ukraine, and Yugoslavia) coming down from the north, we have Iraq and Iran coming from the East, we have China coming from the Far East, and we have Ethiopia and Libya coming from the South. What this amounts to is millions upon millions of men bearing down on Israel from three directions. It does not look good.

And Then Shall the End Come

Revelation 16:13-16 identifies the unholy trinity of Satan, the Antichrist, and the False Prophet working to bring together the armies of the world in preparation for the coming battle. There is a hint here that Satanic inspiration will be used to marshal the coming military forces into a cohesive unit that will be arrayed against Christ himself. The place this will happen at is identified: "And he gathered them together into a place called in the Hebrew tongue Armageddon." Armageddon is a combination of the two Hebrew words 'har' and 'magedon,' which roughly translated, means the 'mount of Megiddo.' It is located on a 300 square mile area on the south side of the valley of Megiddo, or the Plain of Esdraelon (Jezreel), southeast of Mt. Carmel, which extends to the Jordan Valley. Megiddo, which stood at the entrance of a pass across the Carmel mountain range, was the capital of the area of Canaan when it was attacked by Joshua. The port city of Haifa is located at the Valley's western entrance, and no doubt will be utilized as the drop-off point for troops who are transported by naval vessels. While this area is identified as the area where the armies of the world gather, Joel 3:2, 12, 14, pinpoints the battle area as the valley of Jehoshaphat, which was known as the "valley of decision" and according to tradition is believed to be located near Jerusalem, in the Kidron valley.

It seems obvious that the military might of the Antichrist will use any means at their disposal to do battle against an invincible adversary, and the extent of our present weapons technology is our nuclear capability.

On August 6, 1945, the first atomic bomb was dropped on Hiroshima, Japan. The heat from this blast was 127,200,000 degrees Fahrenheit, or three times hotter than the center of the sun. Although the 20 kiloton explosion affected only a four square mile area, its intensity killed 50,000 people, and wounded another 55,000, On August 9, 1945, the second bomb, was dropped on Nagasaki, and people ten miles away were paralyzed, and even those with only slight wounds, eventually died. President Harry Truman said: "The force from which the sun draws its power has been loosed against those who brought war to the Far East." In 1953, a movie was produced which recorded the results of "Operation Ivy," a military test of a hydrogen bomb detonation in the Pacific which took place in November, 1952. The blast caused an entire island to disappear, turning it into deadly vapor and radioactive ash.

The concentration of the use of nuclear weapons in such a small area could possibly throw the Earth off of its axis— producing disastrous results. An article in the September, 1975 edition of *Smithsonian* magazine said: "Astronomical theories that attribute climate changes to shifts in the Earth's orbit or rotation on its axis; solar theories that propose that the Earth's climate varies in response to changed in the activity of the sun; and geophysical theories that link climatic changes to events and interactions within the land-ocean-atmosphere..." These theories seem to be corroborated by events described in the book of Genesis.

When the Earth was created, the weather was always clear and sunny. There was never any rain. The vegetation was watered by the morning dew, which was why the people scoffed when Noah warned of an impending flood— because they didn't know what rain was. The pre-Flood calendar was a perfect year of 12 months, lieved to be the five cities of the plain. Excavations made since 1974 at the Tell Mardikh, site of the ancient Ebla, in northern Syria, have turned up tablets from their archives which refer to all five cities of the plain, and on one, even names them in the same sequence as in Genesis 14:2.

Nelson Glueck, while Director of the American School of Oriental Research in Jerusalem (1932-39), made a survey of the southern Transjordan area, east and south of the Dead Sea, and discovered that the area had been settled before 2000 BC, but suddenly had been abandoned. These cities were located at the Vale of Siddim, at the southern end of the Dead Sea in the Great Rift Valley, which extends from Mount Hermon and the Sea of Galilee in the north, as far south as the Gulf of Aquaba, and includes the Jordan Valley and the Dead Sea region. It is part of a huge fracture in the Earth's crust that begins several hundred miles north at the foot of the Taurus Mountains in Asia Minor, and ends beyond the Red Sea in Africa. It is 1,320 feet below the level of the Mediterranean Sea.

The Dead Sea, between Israel and Jordan, is the lowest spot on the Earth's surface, and is fed by the Jordan River. Without an outlet, the water has evaporated for hundreds of years, leaving behind a variety of minerals, including sodium chloride, potassium chloride, magnesium bromine, magnesium chloride and hydrogen sulfide. As the name suggests, fish cannot live in its waters. Along the southern end of the Dead Sea is a ten mile mass of salt called Jebel Usdim (Arabic for 'mountains of Sodom'). The salt at its base is 150 feet deep in places, and geologists have also indicated the presence of sulphur, natural gas, oil, and bitumen. The "slimepits" mentioned in Genesis 14:10, refer to the bitumen, asphalt or pitch, a lustrous black petroleum product which melts and burns. There are vast beds of it on both sides of the Sea, with heavier concentrations at the southern end. The Nabataeans collected the bitumen which floated to the surface for trade.

The southern half of the Dead Sea seems relatively new, and is much shallower than the northern half, which is 1,296 feet deep. It had been written that the ruins were still visible until the first century; and there were even later reports that when the sun was shining in the right direction, the outline of trees were visible under the surface of the water, preserved by the high salt content of the water. These stories were not confirmed by divers, who found no sign of human settlements. However, regardless of any hard evidence, enough circumstantial evidence exists which indicated that the southern end of the Dead Sea was the location of the destruction.

It has been theorized that an earthquake ignited the natural gas deposits, which created a violent explosion, and propelled a mixture of salt, sulphur and bitumen into the air, literally raining fire and brimstone, as the oil basin beneath the cities burned. Some have even gone as far as saying that God leveled the area with an atomic blast.

It appears, that from all descriptions, hell will be unleashed. The very power of the elements themselves will be turned upon the encroaching army.

During the U.S. hydrogen bomb tests on the Marshall Islands, an analysis of the results indicated, that there were also hailstones. The blast caused a tremendous air turbulence to develop, which in turn caused the formation of hailstones large enough to dent the armor plating on surface ships. Similar hailstones are described in Revelation 8:7, and 16:21.

Revelation 8:8 talks about a "great mountain burning with fire" which falls into the sea; and in 8:10, "a great star from heaven, burning as it were a lamp" falls into the rivers. A meteor that fell in Winslow, Arizona, left a crater a mile in diameter. Indentations on the ocean floor off the coats of South Carolina and Georgia indicate a meteor shower which accompanied an asteroid that hit the western area of the Atlantic Ocean. In 1908, in Siberia, what is believed to have been a meteor, fell with such an impact, that trees for 25 miles around were knocked over, and the resulting smoke was visible for hundreds of miles.

In 1937, an asteroid, called Hermes, which was over a mile in diameter, approached the Earth. Scientists plotting its course thought it might hit the planet, but it only came within a million miles, then veered away. They estimated that if it would have hit an ocean, at its speed of 1,800 mph, it would have generated a tidal wave big enough to destroy all nearby coastal cities. Icarus (discovered in 1949), the closest asteroid to the sun, comes dangerously close to the Earth during its orbit around the sun. American geologist Dr. Robert Dietz said that if the asteroid, which is a 1/2 mile in diameter, would ever hit the Earth, its impact would be equivalent to that of a 200-million megaton atomic blast, which would sink islands, initiate earthquakes, disrupt the earth's magnetic field, and maybe knock it off its axis. Another asteroid, Toro (discovered in 1964), over three miles in diameter, also comes close to this planet during its orbit between Venus and the Earth.

In the end, the futile attempt at Armageddon will be in vain, and the combatants will be destroyed within a day (Rev. 18:8). Ezekiel 39:8 says: "Behold, it is come, and it is done, saith the Lord God; this is the day whereof I have spoken." Ezekiel specifically points out that 5/6's of the Soviet Army is destroyed (39:2). For some reason God's wrath is aimed more at them, as far as invading forces, possibly because of what they have done in their past. Or maybe it's because they got there first, since no one else is mentioned. At any rate, the carnage will be so great, that God will command the birds to the area to feast on the flesh of the fallen (Ezekiel 39:4). It will take seven months to bury the dead (39:12). It will take seven years to burn the weapons (39:9).

It was reported a few years ago that Russia was producing war equipment out of a substance invented in the Netherlands, known as 'Lignostone,' which is a compressed laminated wood that is actually five-times harder than solid wood, yet has twice the elasticity. Since it is wood, and not metal, it doesn't show up on radar. The British are said to be using a similar substance for the gears in their large vehicles. The synthetic resin used to bond the layers of wood together under high pressure burns brightly with intense heat, thus making it easier for the weapons to be burned.

This is another one of those pesky little end-time rumors that seem to be so pervasive. A little research bears out the fact that there is no military equipment produced with this material, only electrotechnical materials, sportsgear, industrial supplies, wooden mallets, furniture, and a few other things. Besides, if the stuff burns so easily, who would want to be on a battlefield in a vehicle which can be ignited so easily.

The Millenial Kingdom

Jesus will then establish his kingdom on this Earth (Joel 3:17), and restoration of this area will begin. The earthquake which caused the Mount of Olives to split (Zech. 14:4), will produce a waterway to issue forth from under the Temple, which will split into two separate rivers south of Jerusalem (Ez. 47:1-12, Joel 3:18, Zech. 14:8); one going to the Mediterranean, and the other to the Dead Sea. This will cleanse the waters of the Dead Sea, and enable it to support life; and will change the desert on the eastern slope of Israel's mountains into fertile land (Deut. 30:9).

On July 11, 1927, there was an earthquake that shook Palestine from the Sea of Galilee to the border of Egypt. Afterward, geologists discovered a fault line at the Mount of Olives running east to west. Professor Bailey Willis, of Stanford University, said that because of the fault, the area around Jerusalem could expect to experience seismic disturbances because of the slippage that would occur on the fault the runs under the Mount.

Israel will take possession of the land promised to them in Genesis 15:18. The country of Israel will extend from the Nile to the Euphrates River, and include parts of Lebanon, Syria, Iraq, and Jordan; and from the Red Sea, to almost the Black Sea.

"And I saw thrones, and they sat upon them, and judgment was given unto them: and I saw the souls of them that were beheaded for the witness of Jesus, and for the word of God, and which had not worshipped the beast, neither his image, neither had received his mark upon their foreheads, or in their hands; and they lived and reigned with Christ a thousand years." (Revelation 20:4)

AFTERWORD

When I began this odyssey in 1978, I never really understood the fervency that was put within me. To be quite frank, although I had been taken to church from a young age, at that time I was not even living for the Lord. Yet, I found myself totally consumed and driven in my search for knowledge about an organization through which Bible prophecy was being fulfilled. Most people who don't consider themselves a Christian, generally don't spend all of their free time working on a manuscript about a group whose is paving the way for the coming of the Antichrist. But I guess because of the years that I did spend in Church, God had instilled something in me, which I didn't know was there.

When I was $2^1/_2$ years old, I was hit by a car, and suffered a fractured skull. When I was 29 years old, my appendix ruptured, but because of a misdiagnosis, I was not operated on till the next day. Afterward, someone said to me that people have sometimes died within the hour of an appendix bursting. Without a doubt, God had His hand on me. He had spared me for some reason— for some purpose. I began to realize that I had a destiny to fulfill.

After *Final Warning* was initially published in 1994, God really began working on me. With all the doors that opened, it wasn't hard to see His hand at work. On April 14, 1996, I got down on my knees and gave my heart to the Lord.

My wife was always trying to get me to go to Church, but I was always too busy doing things. One day she said that the Church was having a special service that Saturday, that there was going to be a prophetess there. Whoa, Nelly! A prophetess? Listen, I grew up in a spirit-filled church, and I was accustomed to God speaking to the Church through the gift of tongues. But a prophetess— c'mon. That's Old Testament stuff. God doesn't speak through people anymore. Well, I agreed to go anyway. But I was going as a skeptic.

After the prophetess was finished ministering to the church, she began to have people stand up, and she was saying things to them. To be quite honest, being that I was skeptical; I wasn't even paying attention to what was going on. But then all of a sudden, she asked my wife and I to stand up. Uh oh.

In part, this is what she said to me:

> "There's a day of rebuilding the wall that has been broken down ... We're rebuilding the wall like Nehemiah rebuilt the wall ... the rebuilding of some things that were torn down, that you might know that my plan still lives and that my vision still remains ... There's a rebuilding of the wall, for once it's built, I'm going to show you how to be a watchman upon that wall ... Son, that you might stand tall, knowing that I have appointed you, and I have called you; let me recommission you..."

Now, you have to realize that this lady did not know me, neither did the pastors. When I you a young boy, I was told on two occasions (that I can remember), that I was going to grow up to be a preacher. The only one who knew that was my mother. As I stood there weeping, I knew that I had truly received a Word from the Lord. To say that this moment was a turning point in my life, is an understatement. My destiny had been revealed to me in a very powerful way.

I started to become very frustrated in my efforts to get *Final Warning* printed by a larger publisher who would have the distribution capabilities to market it to a much wider audience. One Sunday morning (March 1, 1998) I got up early to pray, and I said to the Lord that if there was a work He wanted me to do, He would have to give me the tools to do it. Two days later, a brother walked up to me after the Church service and said: "God told me to give you my computer." Earlier, that same night, the guest minister gave me this Word from the Lord:

> "You accurately discerned that the call of God is upon your life. You accurately discerned that there was a future with me. You accurately discerned that the time would come that you would have to serve me, and that you would have to step out…"

My friend from church brought the computer to my house that Saturday and set it up. The night before, our guest minister gave me the following Word from the Lord:

> "There's going to be a day, a time, an hour, that you will have to walk out of where you now stand. You will have to take a step of faith and you will enter into the land. For I will touch your tongue with heaven's fire, and you will preach with a holy desire … Is this not what you've asked of me to do for you this day … Now therefore, hear the word of the Lord, I am going to grant to you the sword. For you have had it in your sheath too long…"

The Lord equipped me, anointed me, and gave me marching orders. Oh yes, and He gave me a lot of grace too, because now I had a computer, and I didn't even know how to use a mouse. For the next eight months I read books, studied manuals, and made many mistakes; but on November 24, 1998, my website went online for the first time, featuring the online version of my book *Final Warning*— for the entire world to read.

I am honored and I am humbled to be able to use my talents, skills and abilities to serve my God, and I have taken my role as a 'watchman of the wall' very seriously. Ezekiel 33:2-9 tells us what our responsibility is as a watchman:

> "Son of man, speak to the children of thy people, and say unto them, When I bring the sword upon a land, if the people of the land take a man of their coasts, and set him for their watchman: If when he seeth the sword come upon the land, he blow the trumpet, and warn the people; Then whosoever heareth the sound of the trumpet, and taketh not warning; if the sword come, and take him away, his blood shall be upon his own

head. He heard the sound of the trumpet, and took not warning; his blood shall be upon him. But he that taketh warning shall deliver his soul. But if the watchman see the sword come, and blow not the trumpet, and the people be not warned; if the sword come, and take any person from among them, he is taken away in his iniquity; but his blood will I require at the watchman's hand. So thou, O son of man, I have set thee a watchman unto the house of Israel; therefore thou shalt hear the word at my mouth, and warn them from me. When I say unto the wicked, O wicked man, thou shalt surely die; if thou dost not speak to warn the wicked from his way, that wicked man shall die in his iniquity; but his blood will I require at thine hand. Nevertheless, if thou warn the wicked of his way to turn from it; if he do not turn from his way, he shall die in his iniquity; but thou hast delivered thy soul."

This has been such an incredible year of getting work done on my house, getting rid of stuff, and reorganizing things. Through it all, the word "positioning" continued to come to me. This year, I began to have more people visiting my website, and all of a sudden, in June, many people wanted copies of *Final Warning*. Four months later, God opened up a door for it to get published. Our God is an awesome God!

I am determined to walk in the destiny that God has planned and purposed for my life. Right now, I don't know where that destiny may lead, but I have committed to go where He leads. Because I have gotten my book published, some people where I work have joked about me becoming famous. Well, I don't know if God has destined me for greatness, but I do know that He has destined to use me greatly.

APPENDIX A

THE SECRET COVENANT

(This document was e-mailed to me— written by an unknown author.)

An illusion it will be, so large, so vast it will escape their perception.
Those who will see it will be thought of as insane.
We will create separate fronts to prevent them from seeing the connection between us.
We will behave as if we are not connected to keep the illusion alive. Our goal will be accomplished one drop at a time so as to never bring suspicion upon ourselves. This will also prevent them from seeing the changes as they occur.
We will always stand above the relative field of their experience for we know the secrets of the absolute.
We will work together always and will remain bound by blood and secrecy. Death will come to he who speaks.
We will keep their lifespan short and their minds weak while pretending to do the opposite.
We will use our knowledge of science and technology in subtle ways so they will never see what is happening.
We will use soft metals, aging accelerators and sedatives in food and water, and also in the air.
They will be blanketed by poisons everywhere they turn.
The soft metals will cause them to lose their minds. We will promise to find a cure from our many fronts, yet we will feed them more poison.
The poisons will be absorbed through their skin and mouths, and they will destroy their minds and reproductive systems.
From all this, their children will be born dead, and we will conceal this information.
The poisons will be hidden in everything that surrounds them, in what they drink, eat, breathe and wear.
We must be ingenious in dispensing the poisons for they can see far.
We will teach them that the poisons are good, with fun images and musical tones.
Those they look up to will help. We will enlist them to push our poisons.
They will see our products being used in film and will grow accustomed to them and will never know their true effect.
When they give birth we will inject poisons into the blood of their children

and convince them it's for their help.

We will start early on, when their minds are young, we will target their children with what children love most, sweet things.

When their teeth decay we will fill them with metals that will kill their mind and steal their future.

When their ability to learn has been affected, we will create medicine that will make them sicker and cause other diseases for which we will create yet more medicine.

We will render them docile and weak before us by our power.
They will grow depressed, slow and obese; and when they come to us for help, we will give them more poison.

We will focus their attention toward money and material goods so they may never connect with their inner self. We will distract them with fornication, external pleasures and games so they may never be one with the oneness of it all.

Their minds will belong to us and they will do as we say. If they refuse we shall find ways to implement mind-altering technology into their lives. We will use fear as our weapon.

We will establish their governments and establish opposites within. We will own both sides.

We will always hide our objective but carry out our plan.

They will perform the labor for us and we shall prosper from their toil.

Our families will never mix with theirs. Our blood must be pure always, for it is the way.

We will make them kill each other when it suits us.

We will keep them separated from the oneness by dogma and religion.

We will control all aspects of their lives and tell them what to think and how.

We will guide them kindly and gently letting them think they are guiding themselves.

We will foment animosity between them through our factions.

When a light shall shine among them, we shall extinguish it by ridicule, or death, whichever suits us best.

We will make them rip each other's hearts apart and kill their own children.

We will accomplish this by using hate as our ally, and anger as our friend.

The hate will blind them totally, and never shall they see that from their conflicts we emerge as their rulers. They will be busy killing each other.

They will bathe in their own blood and kill their neighbors for as long as we see fit.

We will benefit greatly from this, for they will not see us, for they cannot see us.

We will continue to prosper from their wars and their deaths.

We shall repeat this over and over until our ultimate goal is accomplished.

We will continue to make them live in fear and anger though images and sounds.

We will use all the tools we have to accomplish this.

The tools will be provided by their labor.

We will make them hate themselves and their neighbors.

FINAL WARNING

We will always hide the divine truth from them, that we are all one. This they must never know!

They must never know that color is an illusion; they must always think they are not equal.

Drop by drop, drop by drop we will advance our goal.

We will take over their land, resources and wealth to exercise total control over them.

We will deceive them into accepting laws that will steal the little freedom they will have.

We will establish a money system that will imprison them forever, keeping them and their children in debt.

When they shall band together, we shall accuse them of crimes and present a different story to the world for we shall own all the media.

We will use our media to control the flow of information and their sentiment in our favor.

When they shall rise up against us we will crush them like insects, for they are less than that.

They will be helpless to do anything for they will have no weapons.

We will recruit some of their own to carry out our plans, we will promise them eternal life, but eternal life they will never have for they are not of us.

The recruits will be called "initiates" and will be indoctrinated to believe false rites of passage to higher realms. Members of these groups will think they are one with us never knowing the truth. They must never learn this truth for they will turn against us.

For their work they will be rewarded with earthly things and great titles, but never will they become immortal and join us, never will they receive the light and travel the stars.

They will never reach the higher realms, for the killing of their own kind will prevent passage to the realm of enlightenment. This they will never know.

The truth will be hidden in their face, so close they will not be able to focus on it until it's too late.

Oh yes, so grand the illusion of freedom will be, that they will never know they are our slaves.

When all is in place, the reality we will have created for them will own them. This reality will be their prison. They will live in self-delusion.

When our goal is accomplished a new era of domination will begin.

Their minds will be bound by their beliefs, the beliefs we have established from time immemorial.

But if they ever find out they are our equal, we shall perish then. This they must never know.

If they ever find out that together they can vanquish us, they will take action.

They must never, ever find out what we have done, for if they do, we shall have no place to run, for it will be easy to see who we are once the veil has fallen. Our actions will have revealed who we are and they will hunt us down and no person shall give us shelter.

This is the secret covenant by which we shall live the rest of our present and future lives, for this reality will transcend many generations and life spans.

This covenant must never, ever be known to exist. It must never, ever be written or spoken of, for if it is, the consciousness it will spawn will release the fury of the prime creator upon us, and we shall be cast to the depths from whence we came and remain there until the end time of infinity itself.

This covenant is sealed by blood, our blood— We, the ones who from heaven to earth came.

APPENDIX B

DECLARATION

There is nothing that can happen to me today that my God can not handle. When I go to my knees, God will help me stand up to anything. And because I walk by faith, and not by sight, I know that with God, all things are possible. I go where others fear, fight where others fall, and triumph where others fail. No weapon that is formed against me shall prosper, and when the enemy comes in like a flood, the Spirit of the Lord will lift up a standard against him.

I bend, but I will not break. I will go on to the end. I will never give up, and I will never surrender. What doesn't kill me will only make me stronger. I have no fear in what man can do to me, because through Christ, I am more than a conqueror. I am an overcomer and I can do all things through Christ who strengthens me.

It is not important that I be the best, only that I do my best. Without Him I am nothing, with Him I am everything. Champions are not men who never fail, they are men who never quit. Remember, it's hard to beat a person who never gives up. Expect to win. I am a winner and I will walk in victory, because I have put my trust in God. He is my Deliverance and my Salvation. He is my Fortress and my Defense. He is my Shield and my Buckler. He is my Rock and my Strength. It is He, who fights for me, and I shall not be moved.

(Compiled by David Allen Rivera, 2000)

SOURCES CONSULTED

"A Trilateral World Approach," *Current*, April, 1977, vol. 192, pg. 54-61.
"Aides Play, Taxpayers Pay," *Harrisburg Patriot News*, July 21, 1983, pg. A-9.
"AIDS Alert," *The Overcomer*, November, 1994, pg. 6-7.
Gary Allen. "The CFR- Conspiracy To Rule The World," *American Opinion*, April, 1969 (reprint).
___. "Foundations," *American Opinion*, November, 1969 (reprint).
___. *None Dare Call It Conspiracy* (Concord Press: Seal Beach, CA, 1971).
___. "The Looters," *American Opinion*, May, 1974 (reprint).
___. "Federal Reserve: The Trillion Dollar Conspiracy," *American Opinion*, February, 1976 (reprint).
___. *Jimmy Carter, Jimmy Carter* ('76 Press: Seal Beach, CA, 1976), pg. 43, 47, 52-55, 66, 69-80.
___. *Kissinger: The Secret Side of the Secretary of State* ('76 Press: Seal Beach, CA, 1976), pg. 27-35, 40-43, 51, 94-97, 121-126.
___. *The Rockefeller File* ('76 Press: Seal Beach, CA, 1976).
American Opinion Preview Series. *Seventy-Eighty Nine* (American Opinion: Belmont, MA, 1968), pg. 63, 71-130.
American Security Council. *The Salt Syndrome*, 1980 (30 min. TV show).
"The Anatomy of a Revolution," *Bulletin*, Committee to Restore the Constitution, July, 1986, pg. 5-6.
Gene Antonio. *The AIDS Cover-Up?* (Ignatius Press: San Francisco, CA, 1987).
George Armstrong. *The Rothschild Money Trust*, 1940.
"As Kremlin Flexes Muscles Around the World," *U.S. News & World Report*, November 2, 1981, vol. XCI, no. 18, pg. 44-45.
Michael Baigent and Richard Leigh. *The Dead Sea Scrolls Deception* (Touchstone Books/Simon & Schuster: New York, NY, 1991).
Michael Baigent, Richard Leigh, and Henry Lincoln. *Holy Blood, Holy Grail* (Dell: New York, NY, 1983).
___. *The Messianic Legacy* (Dell: New York, NY, 1986).
Jeffrey A. Baker. *Cheque-Mate: The Game of Princes* (The Baker Group, Inc.: St. Petersburg, FL, 1993).
David Balsiger and Charles E. Sellier. *The Lincoln Conspiracy* (Schick-Sunn Classic Books: Los Angeles, CA, 1977).
A. J. Baker. *Pearl Harbor* (Ballantine Books: New York, NY, 1969), pg. 1.
Wade Baskin. *The Sorcerer's Handbook* (Citadel Press: Secaucus, NJ, 1974), pg. 100, 232, 343, 465.
Terry Diane Beck and Alexis Teitz Gersumky (editors). *The Foundation Center Source Book 1975/76 Vol. 1* (Columbia University Press: New York, NY,

1975), pg. 836-875.
Benjamin Haggott Beckhart. *Federal Reserve System* (Columbia University Press: American Institute of Banking, 1972), pg. 1-25.
Nine Lo Bello. *The Vatican Empire* (Trident Press: New York, NY, 1968).
Reed Benson and Robert Lee. "What's Wrong With the United States," *The Review of the News*, September 9, 1970 (reprint).
Charles Berlitz. *Doomsday: 1999 A.D.* (Pocket Books: New York, NY, 1981).
C. J. Bernardo and Eugene H. Bacon. *American Military Policy* (Telegraph Press: Harrisburg, PA, 1957), pg. 480-484.
Dr. Tom Berry. *The Christian During Riot and Revolution* (Bible Baptist Church: Elkton, MD, 1978), pg. 1-13.
Stephen Birmingham. *"Our Crowd": The Great Jewish Families of New York* (Harper & Row: New York, NY, 1967), pg. 155-187.
James Bjornstad. *Twentieth Century Prophecy* (Dimension Books: Minneapolis, MN, 1975).
Fred Blahut. "COS Suffers Two Setbacks," *The Spotlight*, April 24, 1995, pg. 6.
Mike Blair. "Foreign Tanks, Missiles," *The Spotlight*, August 15, 1994, pg. 1, 14.
___. "Hidden Aircraft I.D.'s Seen as Bow to the UN," *The Spotlight*, August 15, 1994, pg. 1, 6.
___. "Marines Quizzed On Loyalty," *The Spotlight,* August 22, 1994, pg. 1, 3.
___. "Citizens Terrorized by Troops," *The Spotlight*, August 29, 1994, pg. 1, 3.
___. "Urban Warfare Training Center Now Taking Shape in Louisiana," *The Spotlight,* August 29, 1994, pg. 4, 5.
___. "Russian Choppers Confirmed," *The Spotlight,* September 5, 1994, pg. 1, 3.
___. "Armed Patriots Confront UN Unit," *The Spotlight*, September 12, 1994, pg. 1, 3.
___. "FEMA Connection Exposed," *The Spotlight*, September 26, 1994, pg. 1, 12, 13.
___. "Military Base to House U.S. Dissidents?" *The Spotlight,* October 10, 1994, pg. 14, 15.
___. "Russian Special Forces Unit Coming," *The Spotlight,* October 10, 1994, pg. 12, 13, 15.
___. "Feds Training to SWAT Enemies Secret Federal Training Facility," *The Spotlight*, November 21, 1994, pg. 1, 5, 6.
___. "Multi-Jurisdictional Task Force Shoot Outs Have Urban Dwellers Fearful They Could Become Targets," *The Spotlight,* December 5, 1994, pg. 11.
___. "Soviet Trucks in South Said to Be for UN Use," *The Spotlight,* August 22, 1994, pg. 15.
___. " 'Shoot Americans' Survey Results," *The Spotlight,* April 24, 1995, pg. 1, 3.
Arthur E. Bloomfield. *The End of the Days* (Bethany Fellowship, Minneapolis, MN, 1961).
___. *Signs of His Coming* (Bethany Fellowship: Minneapolis, MN, 1962).
___. *How To Recognize the Antichrist* (Bethany Fellowship: Minneapolis, MN, 1975).

with 30 days in each month. Now we have 365 a days in a year. According to scientists, the reason for this is that the Earth has been moved away from the sun by a million miles, resulting in 2% less heat; and the tilt of the axis is now $23^1/_2$ degrees, which accounts for the harshness of the seasons. The magnetic field was also changed. This upsetting of the delicate balances of nature has been blamed for the reduction of the human life span. Methuselah lived to be 969 years old, while Moses lived only to be 120.

The movement of the Earth off of its axis would initiate earthquakes, and volcanic activity; affecting the topography of the Earth, and the poisoning of the waters. In addition, the volcanic activity, because its ash, smoke and dust tend to stay in the air for long periods of time, will screen out the light of the sun, as well as the moon and stars. Radioactive particles and the igniting of sulfur deposits (brimstone) will poison the air. Will God allow the possibility of such a devastation to take place— apparently not. It appears that there will be a preemptive first strike.

"The noise of a multitude in the mountains, like as of a great people; a tumultuous noise of the kingdoms of nations gathered together ... for the day of the Lord is at hand; it shall come as a destruction from the Almighty ... Behold the day of the Lord cometh, cruel both with wrath and fierce anger, to lay the land desolate: and he shall destroy the sinners thereof out of it. For the stars of heaven and the constellations thereof shall not give their light: the sun shall be darkened in his going forth, and the moon shall not cause her light to shine ... Therefore I will shake the heavens, and the earth shall remove out of her place, in the wrath of the Lord of hosts, and in the day of his fierce anger ... (it) shall be as when God overthrew Sodom and Gomorrah." (Isaiah 13:4-19)

"...let all the inhabitants of the land tremble: for the day of the Lord cometh, for it is nigh at hand; A day of darkness and of gloominess, a day of clouds and of thick darkness ... A fire devoureth before them; and behind them a flame burneth ... The earth shall quake before them; the heavens shall tremble: the sun and the moon shall be dark, and the stars shall withdraw their shining." (Joel 2:1-10)

"Behold, the day of the Lord cometh ... For I will gather all nations against Jerusalem to battle ... Their flesh shall consume away while they stand on their feet, and their eyes shall consume away in their holes, and their tongue shall consume away in their mouth." (Zechariah 14:1-12)

"But in those days, after that tribulation, the sun shall be darkened, and the moon shall not give her light, And the stars of heaven shall fall, and the powers that are in heaven shall be shaken. And then shall they see the Son of man coming in the clouds with great power and glory." (Mark 13:24-26)

"And I beheld when he had opened the sixth seal, and lo, there was a great earthquake; and the sun became black as sackcloth hair, and the moon became as blood; And the stars of heaven fell unto the earth ... and every mountain and island were moved out of their places ... For the great day of his wrath is come: and who shall be able to stand?" (Revelation 6:12-17)

According to Revelation 11:13, within the hour after the two witnesses leave the earth, a massive earthquake will occur. This same earthquake is referred to in Zechariah 14:4, as Jesus returns to this world at the same point he left it, on the Mount of Olives, a small range of four summits which overlook Jerusalem from the east. The earthquake is again mentioned in Revelation 16:18-21: "And there were voices, and thunders, and lightnings; and there was a great earthquake ... And every island fled away, and the mountains were not found. And there fell upon men a great hail out of heaven, every stone about the weight of a talent (114 pounds)..."

It is interesting to note, that when Jesus died on the cross, there was "darkness over all the land" and "the earth did quake, and the rocks rent (Matthew 27:45, 51)." The 18th century scientist von Hoff wrote: "There have been strange colorings of the heavens and unusual fogs noticed as occurring at the same time of earthquakes; such as the unusual color of the sky at Lisbon on the first of November, 1755, and the dry fog (Nebel), which was so thick as to produce total darkness during the earthquake in Calabria in 1783."

In Revelation 19:11, John writes about this moment: "And I saw heaven open and behold a white horse; and he that sat upon him was called Faithful and True, and in righteousness he doth judge and make war." The rider is none other than Jesus, the King of Kings, and Lord of Lords. He is followed by an army of angels. Verse 19 describes the reception waiting below: "And I saw the beast, and the kings of the earth, and their armies, gathered together to make war against him that sat on the horse, and against his army."

Ezekiel's description of "the fire of my wrath," (38:19) "a great shaking," (38:19) "an overflowing rain, and great hailstones, fire, and brimstone," (38:22) "I will send a fire," (39:6) certainly paints a picture that will be very similar to the destruction meted out by God at Sodom and Gomorrah.

This event, which occurred about 1897 BC, and is discussed in Genesis 19:24-29: "Then the Lord rained upon Sodom and Gomorrah brimstone and fire from the Lord out of heaven; And he overthrew those cities, and all the plain, and all the inhabitants of the cities, and that which grew upon the ground ... and, lo, the smoke of the country went up as the smoke of a furnace."

In 1924, a joint expedition of archaeologists W. F. Albright and Mervyn G. Kyle, from the American School and Xenia Seminary, discovered five oases, on a plain, 500 feet above the level of the southeast corner of the Dead Sea in the Moabite foothills. Evidence of a walled area was discovered at Bab-Edh Dra'a (Bab edh-Dhra) in 1965, part of a fortification built by the Canaanites during the time of Abraham; and from 1975-79, excavations of pots and other items were unearthed, which dated back to 2500 to 2000 BC. Four other sites have been identified on the east side of the Dead Sea as part of the ruins of the five plain cities involved in the turn of events, including Numeira (discovered in 1973), Safi (identified as Zoar), Feifa, and Hanazir. Because of evidence which proves that the area was fertile and densely populated, all of these sites, along with Sodom and Gomorrah, are be-

Janet Bock. *The Jesus Mystery: Of Lost Years and Unknown Travels* (Aura Books: Los Angeles, CA, 1980).
J. Krim Bohren. "The Gold Fringed Flag: Two Flags for US," *Truth Seeker*, 1994, vol. 121, no. 5, pg. 5.
Diana Bowder. *The Age of Constantine and Julian* (Barnes & Noble: New York, NY, 1978), pg. 22-27.
Robert O. Bowen. *The Truth About Communism* (Colonial Press: Northport, AL, 1962), pg. 2-28, 50, 65-66, 86-87, 92, 94, 99, 102, 123.
Samuel Bowles. "The Trilateral Commission: Have Capitalism and Democracy Come To A Parting of the Ways?" *The Progressive*, June, 1977, vol. 41, pg. 20-23.
Thieleman J. van Braght. *The Bloody Theater (or Martyrs Mirror of the Defenseless Christians)* (Herald Press: Scottdale, PA, 1950), pg. 70-98, 270-352.
Charles D. Brennan. "Martin Luther King, Jr.— A Summary View," *Conservative Digest*, September, 1983, vol. 9, no. 9, pg. 29-31.
Ronald Brownstein. "Will It Slow Your Mail," *Parade*, July 19, 1981, pg. 16-18.
Bulletin, Committee to Restore the Constitution, December, 1982, pg. 2.
Dr. Cathy Burns. *Billy Graham and His Friends: A Hidden Agenda?* (Sharing: Mt. Carmel, PA, 2001).
James P. Cannon. *America's Road to Socialism* (Pathfinder Press: New York, NY, 1975), pg. 71-124.
Frank A. Capell. "An Intelligence Report," *The Review of the News*, February 12, 1975, vol. 11, no. 7, pg. 53.
"Carter Assures Trilateral Commission Control of America's Synfuel Program," *The Spotlight*, October 27, 1980, vol. 43, pg. 8.
"Carter's Brain Trusts," *Time*, December 20, 1976, vol. 108, pg. 19.
Marshall Cavendish Corp. *Man, Myth and Magic* (Marshall Cavendish Corp.: New York, NY, 1970), pg. 1402-1404 (Vol. 10).
Richard Cavendish. *The Black Arts* (G. P. Putnam's Sons: New York, NY, 1967), pg. 306.
Robert Charroux. *Forgotten Worlds* (Popular Library: New York, NY, 1973), pg. 5, 77-82, 229-237, 241, 251-284.
Maj.-Gen. Count Cherep-Spiridovich. *The Secret World Government* (Christian Book Club of America: Hawthorne, CA, 1976, originally published in 1926 by the Anti-Bolshevist Publishing Association in New York).
Jack T. Chick. *Angel of Light* (Chick Publications: Chino, CA, 1978).
___. *Spellbound* (Chick Publications: Chino, CA, 1978).
___. *Sabotage* (Chick Publications: Chino, CA, 1979).
J. R. Church. *Guardians of the Grail* (Prophecy Publications: Oklahoma City, OK, 1989).
Doug Clark. *The Coming Oil War* (Harvest House Publishers: California, 1980), pg. 51-103.
___. *The Greatest Banking Scandal in History* (Harvest House Publishers: Eugene, OR, 1981).
"Clean Up the 'Economic Mess'— Repeal Federal Reserve Act," *Bulletin*, Committee to Restore the Constitution, December, 1981.

Norman Cohn. *Warrant for Genocide* (Harper & Row, Publishers: New York, NY, 1966).

Margaret Cole. *The Story of Fabian Socialism* (Stanford University Press: Stanford, CA, 1961), pg. 3-8, 18, 347.

Robert Glenn Cole. *Masonic Gleanings* (Kable Printing Co.: Chicago, IL, 1954), pg. 105, 141-150.

Dr. John Coleman. *Conspirators' Hierarchy: The Story of the Committee of 300* (American West Publishers: Carson City, NV, 1992).

Peter Collier and David Horowitz. *The Rockefellers: An American Dynasty* (Holt, Rinehart and Winston: New York, NY, 1976), pg. 134, 142, 150-55, 485, 497- 498.

Len Colodny and Robert Gettlin. *Silent Coup: The Removal of a President* (St. Martin's Press: New York, NY, 1992).

"Confab of States Exposed as Plan to Change Constitution," *The Spotlight*, March 27, 1995, pg. 12, 13.

Terry Cook. "The Mark of the New World Order," *Today's Front Page*, October, 1994, pg. 1, 2.

Milton William Cooper. *Behold A Pale Horse* (Light Technology Publishing: Flagstaff, AZ, 1991).

Count Egon Caesar Corti. *The Rise of the House of Rothschild (1770-1830)* (Grosset & Dunlap, Publishers: New York, NY, 1928), pg. 151-159.

___. *The Reign of the House of Rothschild (1830-1871)* (Cosmopolitan Book Corp.: New York, NY, 1928), pg. 434.

Phoebe Courtney. *The CFR Is Still In Control* (The Independent American: Littleton, CO, 1981).

Virginia Cowles. *The Rothschilds: A Family of Fortune* (Alfred A. Knopf, Inc.: New York, NY, 1973), pg. 1- 54.

John Daniel. *Scarlet and the Beast: Vol. 1, A History of the War Between English and French Freemasonry* (Jon Kregal, Inc.: Tyler, TX, 1994).

___. *Scarlet and the Beast: Vol. 2, English Freemasonry, Mother of Modern Cults, Vis-A-Vis Mystery Babylon, Mother of Harlots* (JKI Publishing: Tyler, TX, 1994).

Arkan Daraul. *A History of Secret Societies* (Citadel Press: New York, NY, 1961), pg. 220-232.

Nord Davis Jr. "Dallas Conspiracy," *PARDON ME, but... #2*, Northpoint Teams (Topton, NC), April, 1992, pg. 30, 32.

___. "Sui Juris," *PARDON ME, but... #5*, Northpoint Teams (Topton, NC), August, 1994.

Delma Dennis. *The Will and Way to Win* (John Birch Society: Belmont, MA, 1973), pg. 20-23.

Jeane Dixon. *My Life and Prophecies* (William Morrow and Co., Inc.: New York, NY, 1969), pg. 160-192.

William Joseph Doran. *Trinity of Terror* (Maverick Publications: Bend, OR, 1980), pg. 19, 25, 36-39.

William Campbell Douglass MD. "WHO Murdered Africa," *The Patriot Review*, November, 1987, Vol. 11, no. 9.

Nevill Drury and Gregory Tillett. *The Occult Source Book* (Routledge and

Kegan Paul: London, 1978), pg. 144-147, 155, 188, 200-219, 226, 373-375.
Charles Duncombe. "The World Today in Prophecy: The Chip Is Down," *Christ for the Nations*, May, 1981, vol. 34, no. 2, pg. 14.
___. "The World Today in Prophecy: Euphrates River," *Christ for the Nations*, October, 1983, vol. 36, no. 7, pg. 15.
David P. Ebaugh. *The Key to the Book of Revelation* (self-published, Harrisburg, PA, 1971).
David Eells. *The Church in Tribulation* (The Prophecy Club: Topeka, KS, 2003), 2-tape cassette presentation.
Robert Eisenman and Michael Wise. *The Dead Sea Scrolls Uncovered* (Penguin Books: New York, NY, 1992).
Encyclopedia Britannica, 1977 edition (many entries were consulted here).
Ralph A. Epperson. *The Unseen Hand* (Publius Press: Tucson, AZ, 1985).
___. *The New World Order* (Publius Press: Tucson, AZ, 1990).
Europa Yearbook. *1976: A World Study*, Vols. 1 & 2 (Europa Publications Ltd.: London, 1977).
Mike Evans. "Countdown to Armageddon," *Christ for the Nations*, August, 1982, pg. 4-5, 13.
___. "Israel: America's Key to Survival," *The Evangelist*, January, 1983, pg. 33-35.
Myron Fagan. *The Illuminati-CFR* (Emissary Publications: South Pasadena, CA, 2-cassette set).
David Farrer. *The Warburgs: The Story of a Family* (Stein and Day, Publishers: New York, NY, 1974), pg. 36-41, 58-62, 83, 117-118, 179, 196, 247.
"Federal Call for Con-Con," *The Spotlight*, April 10, 1995, pg. 8.
Federal Register, Presidential Executive Orders, National Archives, Washington, DC:
#10312 12-12-51, vol. 16, no. 16, pg. 12452
#10346 04-19-52, vol. 17, no. 78, pg. 3477
#10995-#11005 02-20-62, vol. 27, no. 35, pg. 1519-1547
#11051 10-02-62, vol. 27, no. 191, pg. 9683
#11087-#11095 02-28-63, vol. 28, no. 41, pg. 1835-1862
#11310 10-13-66, vol. 31, no. 199, pg. 13199
#11490 10-30-69, vol. 34, no. 209, pg. 17567
#11647 02-12-72, vol. 37, no. 30, pg. 3167
#11921 06-15-76, vol. 41, no. 116, pg. 24293
#12148 07-24-79, vol. 44, no. 143, pg. 43239
#12149 07-24-79, vol. 44, no. 143, pg. 43247
Rev. Francis E. Fenton. *The Treason of the Churches* (American Opinion: Belmont, MA, 1972).
Thomas Ferguson and Joel Rogers. "Another Trilateral Election," *The Nation*, June 28, 1980, pg. 769, 783-787.
Annie Fremantle. *This Little Band of Prophets: The Story of the Gentle Fabians* (MacMillan Co.: New York, NY, 1960), pg. 17, 33, 69-70, 81, 94.
Rupert Furneaux. *Ancient Mysteries* (Ballantine Books: New York, NY, 1977), pg. 209-212.
Dr. Leoncio A. Garza-Valdes. *The DNA of God?* (Berkley Books: New York,

NY, 1999).

"Gen. Marshall Asked Dewey Silence on Japanese Codes," *The Patriot*, Harrisburg, PA, August 18, 1981, pg. 3.

Jerome M. Gilison. *The Soviet Image of Utopia* (Johns Hopkins University Press: Baltimore, MD, 1975), pg. 1, 101-164.

Stephen Gill. *American Hegemony and the Trilateral Commission* (Cambridge University Press: Cambridge, Great Britain, 1990), pg. 131-132, 137-141, 150 165, 243.

William R. Goetz. *Apocalypse Next* (Horizon House Publishers: Beaverlodge, Alberta, Canada, 1980), pg. 136-137, 167, 175, 195, 216-217.

M. Hirsh Goldberg. *The Jewish Connection* (Bantam Books: New York, NY, 1977), pg. 17, 27-29, 51-52, 72-73, 114-119, 145, 163-164, 224, 239.

Sen. Barry M. Goldwater. *The Conscience of a Conservative* (Victor Publishing Co.: New York, NY, 1960), pg. 107-108.

___. *With No Apologies* (William Morrow & Co., Inc.: New York, NY, 1979), pg. 85, 128, 130, 132, 152, 231, 277-300.

Robert Goldwin (editor). *Readings in World Politics* (Oxford University Press: New York, NY, 1959), pg. 383-393, 411-424.

Joseph F. Goodavage. *Our Threatened Planet* (Pocket Books: New York, NY, 1978), pg. 40, 89-93, 129-133, 149, 251.

"GOP Report Attacks Global Trade Treaty," *The Spotlight*, November 7, 1994, pg. 8.

W. V. Grant. *After the Rapture— Then What?* (Dallas, TX).

___. *I Saw the Antichrist in America* (Dallas, TX).

___. *The Great Dictator* (Dallas, TX).

___. *The Man Child* (Dallas, TX).

William Greider. *Secrets of the Temple* (Touchstone/Simon & Schuster: New York, NY, 1987).

"Greatest Men's Party Shakes Up Feminists, Activists," *The Patriot*, Harrisburg, PA, July 9, 1981, pg. 6.

Des Griffin. *Descent Into Slavery* (Emissary Publications: South Pasadena, CA, 1980).

___. *Fourth Reich of the Rich* (Emissary Publications: South Pasadena, CA, 1983).

G. Edward Griffin. *The Fearful Master: A Second Look at the United Nations* (Western Islands: Belmont, MA, 1964), pg. 68, 70, 73, 87, 110, 113, 176-177.

___. *The Grand Design* (Thousand Oaks American Media: California, 1968), pg. 15.

Dr. Elgin Groseclose. *Fifty Years of Managed Money: The Story of the Federal Reserve* (Spartan Books: New York, NY, 1966).

"Guilt By Association," *Macleans*, March 10, 1980, vol. 93, pg. 33.

Edward Vose Gulick. *Europe's Classical Balance of Power* (Cornell University Press: Ithica, NY, 1955), pg. 186-187, 286-287.

Ted Gup. "The Doomsday Blueprints," *Time*, August 10, 1992, pg. 32-39.

Murat Halstead. *The Life and Distinguished Services of William McKinley, Our Martyr President* (Memorial Association Publishers: New York, NY, 1901), pg. 504 - 508.

Graham Hancock. *The Sign and the Seal* (Crown Publishers, Inc.: New York, NY, 1992).

Billy James Hargis. "Billy Graham Duped and Deceived," *Christian Crusade*, July, 1982, vol. 29, no. 5, pg. 1-2, 4.

___. "Billy In Moscow," *Christian Crusade*, July, 1982, vol. 29, no. 5, pg. 3- 4.

___. "The Russian Pipeline: Update," *Christian Crusade*, December, 1982, vol. 29, no. 8, pg. 3.

Dr. Billy James Hargis and Dr. Jose Hernandez, *Disaster File* (Crusader Books: Tulsa, OK, 1978).

Fida M. Hassnain. *A Search For Historical Jesus* (Gateway Books: Great Britain, 1994).

Gal Hawthorne. "Fairy Tales: Proof of Life After Death," *Examiner*, September 20, 1983, pg. 22.

George R. Hawtin. "Portrait of Things to Come," *The Page*, pg. 8-11.

___. "Six Days Shalt Thou Labour," *The Page*, Nov. 1968, pg. 3-4.

___. "Iron Mixed With Clay," *The Page*, June/July, 1972, vol. 12, no. 6, pg. 6-14.

___. "As We See the Day Approaching," *The Page*, December, 1972, vol. 12, no. 11.

___. "The End of the Days," *The Page*, Sept. 1977, vol. 16, no. 9.

Charles William Heckethorn. *The Secret Societies of All Ages and Countries* (University Books: New York, NY, 1965), Vols. 1 & 2.

Lawrence E. Hicks. *Universal Product Code* (American Management Association: New York, NY, 1975).

Douglas Hill and Pat Williams. *The Supernatural* (Signet Books: New York, NY, 1965),

"Historian Says FDR Destroyed Constitution with 1933 Action," *The Spotlight*, October 9, 1995, pg. 10-11.

"Hitler Took 75 Drugs, Used Leeches During War," *The Harrisburg Patriot News*, April 22, 1983, D-16.

H. V. Hodson (editor). *The International Foundation Dictionary* (Europa Publications: London, 1974), pg. 292-343.

Stanley Hoffman (editor). *Conditions of World Order* (Houghton Mifflin Co.: Boston, MA, 1968), pg. viii, ix, 224-226.

William Hoffman. *David: Report on a Rockefeller* (Lyle Stewart, Inc.: New York, NY, 1971), pg. 14-17, 25-36, 41-53, 187.

Richard Hofstadter. *The American Political Tradition* (Vintage Books: New York, NY, 1967), pg. 33-34.

Robert B. Holtman. *The Napoleonic Revolution* (J. B. Lippincott Co.: New York, NY, 1979).

Hans Holzer. *The Directory of the Occult* (Henry Regnery Co.: Chicago, IL, 1974), pg. 91-92, 153-188.

"Homosexual Mob Attacks San Francisco Churchgoers," *The Overcomer*, July, 1994.

J. Edgar Hoover. *Master of Deceit* (Henry Holt and Co.: New York, NY, 1958), pg. 3-78.

Warren Hough. "UN Gets U.S. Troops; Moves Into 'Phase 2'," *The Spotlight*, August 22, 1994, pg. 1, 6.

___. "Key U.S. Units Internationalized," *The Spotlight*, December 5, 1994, pg. 3.

Edwin P. Hoyt, Jr. *The House of Morgan* (Dodd, Mead & Co.: New York, NY, 1958), pg. 4, 44, 48, 65, 97, 105, 109-110, 134-135, 163, 196, 202, 214.

David Hudson. "U.S. Currency Change Aimed at 'Cash Only' Group," *The Spotlight*, May 21, 1984, pg. 20-21.

N. W. Hutchings. "New Money," *The Gospel Truth*, Southwest Radio Church, February, 1984, vol. 25, no. 3.

___. *Petra: In History and Prophecy* (Hearthstone Publishing: Oklahoma City, OK, 1991).

___. "Getting Ready for the Cashless Society," *Prophetic Observer*, October, 1994, pg. 1-4.

J. Bernard Hutton. *The Subverters* (Arlington House: New York, NY, 1972).

Dr. Jack Van Impe. *The Coming War With Russia* (LP Recording, 1979).

___. *The 80's, the Antichrist and Your Startling Future!* (Jack Van Impe Ministries: Royal Oak, MI, 1982).

___. "Was World War III Averted in Lebanon?" *Perhaps Today*, July / August, 1983, vol. 4, no. 2, pg. 1-2.

___. *Revelation Revealed Verse by Verse* (Enterprise Printers, Inc.: Mt. Pleasant, MI, 1982), pg. 150-156, 194-196.

___. *11:59 ... and Counting* (JVI Books, 1983).

Dr. Jack Van Impe and Roger F. Campbell. *Israel's Final Holocaust* (Thomas Nelson Publishers: Nashville, TN, 1979).

Rael Jean Isaac. "Do You Know Where Your Church Offerings Go?" *Readers Digest*, January, 1983 (reprint).

Grant R. Jeffrey. *Armageddon: Appointment With Destiny* (Bantam Books: New York, NY, 1988).

___. *Messiah: War in the Middle East & the Road to Armageddon* (Bantam Books: New York, NY, 1992).

A. H. M. Jones. *Constantine and the Conversion of Europe* (English Universities Press, Ltd.: London, 1949), pg. 94-97, 100.

Emanuel M. Josephson. *The Federal Reserve Conspiracy and the Rockefellers* (Chedney Press: New York, NY, 1968).

Donovan Joyce. *The Jesus Scroll* (Signet: New York, NY, 1972), pg. 7-13, 17-18, 25, 35-36, 81-85, 127-128, 145-149, 151, 154, 156-159, 166.

"Just What Is the Trilateral Commission," *U.S. News and World Report*, April 7, 1980, vol. 88, pg. 37.

Gary H. Kah. *En Route to Global Occupation* (Huntington House Publishers: Lafayette, LA, 1992).

Trisha Katson. "Sovereignty-Robbing Treaty Still Alive on Capitol Hill," *The Spotlight*, September 26, 1994, pg. 4.

___. "Last Minute Hold On GATT Vote," *The Spotlight*, October 17, 1994, pg. 1, 3.

___. "Defeat of Balanced Budget Amendment Hikes COS Threat," *The Spotlight*, March 27, 1995, pg. 12-13.

___. "Global Connection Exposed," *The Spotlight*, April 3, 1995. pg. B3.
___. "Opposition in Grassroots to Constitution Changes Grow," *The Spotlight*, April 3, 1995, pg. B2-B3.
___. "Powers of COS in the Process," *The Spotlight*, April 3, 1995, pg. B3.
___. "Supreme Court Would Ignore Con-Con Political Questions," *The Spotlight*, April 3, 1995, pg. B2-B3.
___. "COS Hits Populist Roadblock," *The Spotlight*, April 10, 1995, pg. 3.
Walter Kaufmann. *Nietzsche* (Vintage Books: New York, NY, 1950), pg. 284.
Jim Keith. *Black Helicopters Over America: Strikeforce for the New World Order* (Illuminet Press: Lilburn, GA, 1994).
Werner Keller. *The Bible As History* (Bantam Books: New York, NY, 1956), pg. 81, 385-395.
Rev. Clarence Kelly. *Conspiracy Against God and Man* (Western Islands: Boston, MA, 1974).
Holger Kersten. *Jesus Living In India* (Element Books: Rockport, MA, 1986, 1994).
Devvy Kidd. *Why A Bankrupt America?* (POWER: Redding, CA, 1993).
Dwight Kinman. *The New World Order* (Mary E. Royer: Elizabethtown, PA, 1992).
Salem Kirban. *The Day Israel Dies* (Salem Kirban, Inc.: Huntingdon Valley, PA, 1975).
___. *Satan's Angels Exposed* (Salem Kirban, Inc.: Huntingdon Valley, PA, 1980).
___. *The New Age Secret Plan for World Conquest* (AMG Publishers: Chattanooga, TN, 1992).
Mina C. Klein and H. Arthur Klein. *Temple Beyond Time: The Story of the Site of Solomon's Temple* (Van Nostrand Reinhold Co.: New York, NY), pg. 81-86, 129-130, 151-152.
E. C. Knuth. *Empire of the City* (The Noontide Press, 1944).
Roger P. Labrie (editor). *SALT Handbook* (American Enterprise Institute: Washington, DC, 1979).
Tim LaHaye. *Rapture Under Attack* (Multnomah Publishers: Sisters, OR, 1998).
Martin A. Larson. *The Federal Reserve and Our Manipulated Dollar* (Devon-Adair Co.: Connecticut, 1975).
Victor Lasky. *Jimmy Carter: The Man and the Myth* (Richard Marek Publishers: New York, NY, 1979), pg. 159-161, 326-327, 333-334, 387.
Troy Lawrence. *The Antichrist Is Now Here!: The New Age "Messiah" Identified* (People United for Christ: Upland, CA, 1988).
"Lenin Offered 4 / 5's of Land, Wilson Passed Say Scholar," *The Harrisburg Patriot News*, Harrisburg, PA, April, 19, 1981, pg. 19.
John Heron Lepper. *Famous Secret Societies* (Gryphon Books: Michigan, 1971), pg. 106-122.
J. C. Lewis. *The Trilateral Commission*, cassette tape.
Liberty Lobby. "Spotlight on the Bilderbergers," published by *The Spotlight*.
Gordon Lindsay. *The Antichrists Have Come* (Voice of Healing Publishing Co.: Dallas, TX).
___. *The Book of Revelation Made Easy* (Voice of Healing Publishing Co.:

Dallas, TX), vols. 1-16.

___. *The End of the Age* (Voice of Healing Publishing Co.: Dallas, TX), vols. 1-9.

___. *The Second Coming of Christ* (Voice of Healing Publishing Co.: Dallas, TX).

___. *Will the Antichrist Come Out of Russia* (Voice of Healing Publishing Co.: Dallas, TX, 1966).

___. *America, Russia and Antichrist* (Voice of Healing Publishing Co.: Dallas, TX, 1969).

___. *Will Christians Go Through the Great Tribulation* (Christ for the Nations Publishing Co.: Dallas, TX, 1970).

Mrs. Gordon (Freda) Lindsay. *World Prayer and Share Letter*, Christ for the Nations, Dallas, TX, July, 1983, pg. 2.

Hal Lindsey. *There's A New World Coming* (Bantam Books: New York, NY, 1975).

___. *The 1980's: Countdown to Armageddon* (Bantam Books: New York, NY, 1980), pg. 29-30, 74, 76, 81, 105, 122-128, 136-137, 150-152.

Hal Lindsey and C.C. Carlson. *The Late Great Planet Earth* (Zondervan Publishing House: Grand Rapids, MI, 1977).

Daniel Logan. *The Reluctant Prophet* (Avon Books: New York, NY, 1969), pg. 148-149.

J. Anthony Lukas. "The CFR— Is It A Club? Seminar? Presidium? 'Invisible Government?'" *New York Times Magazine*, Sunday, November 21, 1977, pg. 34, 123-126, 128-131, 138, 142.

Ferdinand Lundberg. *The Rich and the Super Rich* (Lyle Stuart, Inc.: New York, NY, 1968), pg. 154-169, 386, 601-602.

___. *The Rockefeller Syndrome* (Lyle Stuart, Inc.: New York, NY, 1975).

Norman MacKenzie (editor). *Secret Societies* (Holt, Rinehart and Winston: New York, NY, 1976), pg. 169-170, 300, 303.

Norman MacKenzie and Jeanne MacKenzie. *H. G. Wells: A Biography* (Simon and Schuster: New York, NY, 1973), pg. 62, 168-170, 184-190, 196-235, 355.

Dave MacPherson. *The Rapture Plot* (Millennium III Publishers: Simpsonville, SC, 1994).

Ian MacPherson. *News of the World to Come* (Christian Communications, Ltd.: Hong Kong, 1975).

Joe Marler. *Tribulation*, The Overcomer Ministry, Walterboro, SC, 1992, 2 cassette set.

Texe Marrs. *Dark Secrets of the New Age* (Crossway Books: Wheaton, IL, 1987).

___. *Dark Majesty* (Living Truth Publishers: Austin, TX, 1992).

___. "The New MARC Card— Don't Leave Home Without It!" *Flashpoint*, October, 1994, pg. 1, 2.

___. "Beware the Dead Sea Scroll: Is There An Illuminati Plot to Pollute the Word of God?" *Intelligence Examiner Special Edition*, 1994, 60 min. cassette tape.

___. "Chuck Colson's Historic Secret Mission: Undo the Protestant Reforma-

tion," *Flashpoint*, November, 1994, pg. 1.
___. "Priest Richard Neuhaus Exposed— He's a Marxist Heretic!" *Flashpoint*, November, 1994, pg. 2, 3.
___. "Foreign Occupation Troops in America?" *Flashpoint*, December, 1994, pg. 3.
Joe Maxwell. "Evangelicals Clarify Accord with Catholics," *Christianity Today*, March 6, 1995, pg. 52-53.
Allen Mayer, Merwin Sigale, Deborah Witherspoon, and Phyllis Malamud. "The Trilateral Elite," *Newsweek*, March 24, 1980, vol. 95, pg. 38.
William S. McBirnie. *Anti-Christ* (Acclaimed Books: Dallas, TX, 1978).
Burke McCarty. *The Suppressed Truth About the Assassination of Abraham Lincoln* (Taiwan), pg. 6-16.
U.S. Rep. Larry McDonald. "No Holidays Until King Files Public," *Conservative Digest*, September, 1983, vol. 9, no. 9, pg. 27.
James McKinley. "Playboy's History of Assassination in America, Part 1: Death to Tyrants!" *Playboy*, January, 1976, pg. 96-102, 170, 222, 224-226, 228, 232-237.
C. F. McQuaig. *The Masonic Report*, pg. 3, 5.
D. A. Miller. *Forbidden Knowledge Or Is It...* (Joy Publishing: San Juan Capistrano, CA, 1991).
Ed Mitchell, Jody Scharf Mitchell, and Dori Webster. *The 1981-1985 Tribulation Report: Part I* (Victory Press: Tucson, AZ, 1981), pg. 52-75.
Robert H. Montgomery. "Dictatorship and the Growing Presidential Power," *American Opinion*, January, 1967(reprint).
Ruth Montgomery. *A Gift of Prophecy* (Bantam Books: New York, NY, 1965), pg. 173-183.
Frederic Morton. *The Rothschilds: A Family Portrait* (Atheneum: New York, NY, 1961), pg. 1-55.
Alvin Moscow. *The Rockefeller Inheritance* (Doubleday & Co., Inc.: New York, NY, 1977), pg. 4, 15, 19, 62-108, 225-226, 265, 407-437.
Robert Moss. "Reaching for Oil: The Soviets Bold Mideast Strategy," *Saturday Review*, April 12, 1980, pg. 14-22.
Zygmunt Nagorski. "A Member of the CFR Talks Back," *National Review*, December 9, 1977, vol. 29, pg. 1416-1419.
Gary Null. "AIDS: A Man-Made Plague?" *Penthouse*.
Carl Oglesby. *The Yankee and Cowboy War* (Berkley Publishing Corp.: 1977), pg. 23-27, 268-311.
"Old Congress Preps for GATT Vote," *The Spotlight*, December 5, 1994, pg. 8.
"PR Man for Army Says 'No', But the Facts Say 'Yes'," *The Spotlight*, November 7, 1994, pg· 14, 15.
James Peltz. " 'Smart Card' Has Its Own Information Storehouse," *Sunday Patriot News*, Harrisburg, PA, October 9, 1983, pg. B-10.
Ross Perot and Pat Choate. *Save Your Job, Save Our Country: Why NAFTA Must Be Stopped— Now!* (Hyperion: New York, NY), 1993.
lain Phelps-Fetherston. *Soviet International Front Organizations* (Frederick A. Praeger, Publishers: New York, NY, 1965), pg. 1-8.
Nicholas Piediscalzi and Robert G. Thobaben (editors). *From Hope to Libera-*

tion: Towards A New Marxist-Christian Dialogue (Fortress Press: Philadelphia, PA, 1974), pg. 33.

Daniel J. Pilla. "Pilla Predicts 'The Demise of Cash,' Says Government Is Lying," *The Spotlight*, September 16, 1994, pg. 16-17.

Alain Pilote. "Country With Honest Money Would Defeat Bankers," *Spotlight*, December 12, 1994, pg. 16-18.

John Pollock. *Billy Graham* (McGraw-Hill Book Co.: New York, NY, 1966), pg. 59.

Randall Price. *Secrets of the Dead Sea Scrolls* (Harvest House Publishers: Eugene, OR. 1996)

___. *In Search of Temple Treasures* (Harvest House Publishers: Eugene, OR, 1994).

Randall Price and Thomas Ice. *Ready to Rebuild* (Harvest House Publishers: Eugene, OR, 1992).

Elizabeth Clare Prophet. *The Lost Years of Jesus* (Summit University Press: Livingston, MT, 1984, 1987).

George J. Prpic. *A Century of World Communism* (Barron's Educational Series, Inc.: New York, NY, 1970).

Carroll Quigley. *Tragedy and Hope: A History of the World In Our Time* (Macmillan: New York, NY, 1966).

Ayn Rand. *Atlas Shrugged* (Random House: New York, NY, 1957).

___. *Capitalism: The Unknown Ideal* (Signet: New York, NY, 1966), pg. 150-166.

Rep. John R. Rarick. "The Anatomy of a Revolution" (Extensions of Remarks), *Congressional Record*, October 19, 1968, pg. 30311-30315.

Lorman Ratner. *Antimasonry: The Crusade and the Party* (Prentice-Hall, Inc.: Englewood Cliffs, NJ, 1969), pg. 21-23.

Readers Digest. *Family Encyclopedia of American History* (The Readers Digest Association, Inc.: Pleasantville, NY, 1975).

___. *The Story of America* (Readers Digest Association, Inc.: Pleasantville, NY, 1975).

___. *The World's Last Mysteries* (Readers Digest Association, Inc.: Pleasantville, NY, 1978), pg. 83-91.

John Rees. "Communists Back August 27 'March on Washington'," *Conservative Digest*, September, 1983, vol. 9, no. 9, pg. 32.

Dr. Mary Stewart Relfe. *Introducing the 666 Age* (Ministries, Inc.: Montgomery, AL, 1980, 6 tape set).

___. *Let No Man Deceive You* (Ministries, Inc.: Montgomery, AL, 1980, cassette tape).

___. *The Imminence of Christ's Return* (Ministries, Inc.: Montgomery, AL, 1980, cassette tape).

___. *The One World Government* (Ministries, Inc.: Montgomery, AL, 1980, cassette tape).

___. *When Your Money Fails ... The "666 System" Is Here* (Ministries, Inc.: Montgomery, AL, 1981).

___. "Replacement Currency," *Current Events and Bible Prophecy Newsletter*, Ministries, Inc.: Montgomery, AL, January/February, 1982, pg. 1-2.

___. *The New Money System* (Ministries, Inc.: Montgomery, AL, 1982).
Robert V. Remini. *Andrew Jackson and the Banks War* (W. W. Norton & Co., Inc.: 1967).
"Rhodes Reunion," *People*, July 11, 1983, vol. 20, no. 2, pg. 61-68.
Jasper Ridley. *Garibaldi* (Viking Press: New York, NY, 1974), pg. 584.
John Robison. *Proofs of a Conspiracy Against All the Religions and Governments of Europe, Carried On In the Secret Meetings of the Free Masons, Illuminati, and Reading Societies* (Dobson & Cobbet: Philadelphia, PA, 1798).
Lt. Col. AUS Ret. Archibald E. Roberts. *The Crisis of Federal Regionalism: A Solution* (Betsy Ross Press: Ft. Collins, CO, 1976).
___. *Emerging Struggle for State Sovereignty* (Betsy Ross Press: Fort Collins, CO, 1979).
J. M. Roberts. *The Mythology of the Secret Societies* (Charles Scribner's Sons: New York, NY, 1972), pg. 118-145.
Pat Robertson. *The New Millenium* (Word Publishing: Dallas, TX, 1990).
___. *The New World Order* (Word Publishing: Dallas, TX, 1991).
David Rockefeller. "In Pursuit of a Consistent Foreign Policy," *Vital Speeches of the Day*, June 15, 1980, pg. 517-520.
___. "The Trilateral Commission," *Saturday Evening Post*, October, 1980, pg. 36-38, 84.
Marvin Rosenthal. *The Pre-Wrath Rapture of the Church* (Thomas Nelson Publishers: Nashville, TN, 1990).
Charles C. Ryrie. *Come Quickly, Lord Jesus* (Harvest House Publishers: Eugene, Oregon, 1996).
Anthony Sampson. *The Seven Sisters* (Bantam Books: New York, NY, 1991).
Bill Sampson. "Peace Movement Helps Red Weaken U.S.— Know Your Enemy," *Christian Crusade*, December, 1982, vol. 29, no. 8, pg. 1, 4-6.
Phyllis Schlafly and Chester Ward. *Kissinger on the Couch* (Arlington House Publishers: New Rochelle, NY, 1975), pg. 129, 134-152, 211, 245, 260.
Arthur M. Schlesinger. *The Age of Jackson* (New American Library: New York, NY, 1945), pg. 88-89, 93-94.
Dr. Hugh J. Schonfield. *The Passover Plot* (Bantam Books: New York, NY, 1965).
Albert Shadowitz and Peter Walsh. *The Dark Side of Knowledge* (Addison-Wesley Publishing Co., Inc.: Reading, MA, 1976), pg. 43-44.
Hershel Shanks. *Understanding the Dead Sea Scrolls* (Vintage Books/Random House: New York, NY, 1992).
Lawrence H. Shoup and William Minter. *Imperial Brain Trust: The Council on Foreign Relations and United States Foreign Policy* (Monthly Review Press: New York, NY, 1977).
W. Cleon Skousen. *The Naked Capitalist* (Salt Lake City, UT, 1970).
Jim Shaw and Tom McKenny. *The Deadly Deception* (Huntington House: Lafayette, LA, 1988).
Leslie Sheppard. *Encyclopedia of Occult and Parapsychology* (Gale Research Co.: Detroit, MI, 1978), vol. 1, pg. 460.
Leonard Silk and Mark Silk. *The American Establishment* (Basic Books, Inc.:

New York, NY, 1980).
Philip W. Smith. "Nuclear Alert," *Sunday Patriot News*, July 26, 1981, pg. A-5.
Dan Smoot. *The Invisible Government* (Western Islands: Boston, MA, 1962).
Anthony Solomon. "Trilateralists At the Top— New Foreign Policy Elite," *U. S. News and World Report*, February 21, 1977, vol. 82, pg. 31.
"Soviet Threat: The Shadow Lengthens," *Army Reserve Magazine*, Spring, 1980, pg. 22-25.
Horace Smythe. "New Money Plans Remain Unclear," *The Spotlight*, August 6, 1984, pg. 19, 29.
Lewis Spence. *An Encyclopedia of Occultism* (University Books: New Hyde Park, NY, 1960), pg. 38-41, 68-70, 85-92, 96-97, 123-124, 173-175, 213, 223, 314, 372-373, 405-408, 425, 431-436.
Robert Keith Spenser. *The Cult of the All-Seeing Eye* (Monte Carlo Press: 1964).
John Shelby Spong. *Resurrection: Myth or Reality?* (Harper Collins Publishers: New York, NY, 1994).
Alan Stang. "Policrats: Plans for a National Police Force," *American Opinion*, February, 1974 (reprint).
___. "Crimes of the World Council of Churches," *American Opinion*, January, 1982 (reprint).
Vernon Stauffer. "The New England and the Bavarian Illuminati," *Columbia University Studies in Political Science* (Columbia University Press: New York, NY, 1919), vol. 82, no. 1, pg. 9-374.
Louis Stewart. *Life Forces* (Andrews and McMeel, Inc.: New York, NY, 1980), pg. 373-375.
William T. Still. *New World Order: The Ancient Plan of Secret Societies* (Huntington House Publishers: Lafayette, LA, 1990).
John A. Stormer. *None Dare Call It Treason* (Liberty Bell Press: Florissant, MO, 1964).
___. *The Death of A Nation* (Liberty Bell Press: Florissant, MO, 1968).
"Supreme Law of the Land," *Bulletin*, Committee to Restore the Constitution, January, 1982.
Antony C. Sutton. *Energy: The Created Crisis* (Books In Focus, Inc.: New York, NY, 1979), pg. 3-4, 9, 12-15, 25-30, 36, 40-43, 69-71, 117, 153.
Antony C. Sutton and Patrick M. Wood. *Trilaterals Over Washington* (The August Corp.: Scottsdale, AZ, 1978).
___. *Trilaterals Over Washington II* (The August Corp.: Scottsdale, AZ, 1981).
Jimmy Swaggart and Dr. Marvin Solum. *The Book of Daniel* (Jimmy Swaggart Ministries: Baton Rouge, LA, 1981).
Charles R. Taylor. *World War III and the Destiny of America* (Sceptre Books: Nashville, TN, 1979).
Merrill C. Tenney (editor). *Pictorial Bible Dictionary* (Zondervan Publishing House: Grand Rapids, MI, 1963).
"These Are American Leaders?" *Conservative Digest*, September, 1983, vol. 9, no. 9, pg. 23.
Dana L. Thomas. *The Money Crowd* (G. P. Putnam's Sons: New York, NY, 1972), pg. 38-50.
Richard H. Timberlake, Jr. *The Origins of Central Banking in the United States*

(Harvard University Press: MA, 1978).
John Todd. *Witchcraft* (60 min. cassette tape recorded in February, 1978, at the Open Door Church in Chambersburg, PA, pastored by Dino Pedrone).
Max Toth and Greg Nielsen. *Pyramid Power* (Freeway Press: New York, NY, 1974), pg. 114-115.
"The Trilateral Commission," *Congressional Record* (Senate), June 3, 1980, pg. 6200-6208.
"The Trilateral Commission: How Influential?" *U. S. News and World Report*, May 22, 1978, vol. 84, pg. 74-77.
TRIM (Tax Reform IMmediately). *Bulletin*, Summer, 1980, pg. 2-3 (a non-profit, non- partisan, nationwide network of educational committees founded by the John Birch Society).
James P. Tucker Jr. "It's Time To Call Washington," *The Spotlight*, August 15, 1994, pg. 13.
___. "NAFTA Exposed as Destroyer of U.S. Jobs," *The Spotlight*, December 26, 1994, pg. 1.
___. "One Worlders Take A Giant Step," *The Spotlight*, December 26, 1994, pg. 9.
___. "Students to Be 'World Citizens'," *The Spotlight*, December 26, 1994, pg. 5.
"UNESCO Withdrawal," *Christian Inquirer*, April, 1984, pg. 20.
Merrill F. Unger. *Unger's Bible Handbook* (Moody Press: Chicago, IL, 1966).
Tom Valentine. *The Great Pyramid* (Pinnacle Books, Inc.: New York, NY, 1975), pg. 55.
Antonia Vallentin. *H. G. Wells: Prophet of Our Day* (The John Day Co.: New York, NY, 1950), pg. 48, 141, 249, 256-259, 315.
Robert Van Kampen. *The Rapture Question Answered: Plain & Simple* (Fleming H. Revell: Grand Rapids, MI, 1997).
Harold Lord Varney. "Tax-Free Cash," *American Opinion*, November, 1968 (reprint).
Immanuel Velikovsky. *Earth in Upheaval* (Dell Publishing Co.: New York, NY, 1955), pg. 120.
"WCC, NCC, Continue to Fund Revolution," *Christian Inquirer*, April, 1984, pg. 23.
W. Warren Wagar. *H. G. Wells and the World State* (Books for Libraries Press: New York, NY, 1961), pg. 165, 174, 182-205.
Arthur Edward Waite. *A New Encyclopedia of Free Masonry* (Weathervane Books: New York, NY, 1970), vol. 1, pg. 21, 46-53, 64, 386-388, 484; vol. 2, pg. 105-106, 191, 251-263, 413.
Amy Wallace, David Wallechinsky, and Irving Wallace. *The Book of Lists #3* (Bantam Books: New York, NY, 1983), pg. 40, 151-152.
John F. Walvoord. *The Rapture Question* (Zondervan Publishing House: Grand Rapids, Michigan, 1979).
Wes Ward. "Jekyll Island," *Saturday Evening Post*, January/February, 1981, pg. 108-111, 128.
James W. Wardner. *The Planned Destruction of America* (Longwood Communications: Longwood, FL, 1993).

Watch Tower Bible and Tract Society of New York. *Our Incoming World Government- God's Kingdom* (1977).
Roy Wayne. "UN Troops Deployed in US?" *The National Educator*, August, 1994, pg. 1, 10.
Sir Charles Webster. *The Congress of Vienna 1814-1815* (Barnes and Noble, Inc.: New York, NY, 1963), pg. 75-79, 161-164.
Nesta H. Webster. *World Revolution: The Plot Against Civilization* (Small, Maynard and Co.: Boston, MA, 1921).
Robert Welch. *The John Birch Society Bulletin*, Belmont, MA, February, 1975, pg. 1-15.
___. *The John Birch Society Bulletin*, Belmont, MA, July, 1976, pg. 1- 65.
H. G. Wells. *The Open Conspiracy: Blue Prints For A World Revolution* (Doubleday, Doran & Co., Inc.: New York, NY, 1928), pg. 126-163.
Robert Craig West. *Banking Reform and the Federal Reserve 1863-1923* (Cornell University Press: New York, NY, 1977).
William J. Whalen. *The Handbook of Secret Organizations* (Bruce Publishing Co.: Milwaukee, WI, 1966), pg. 46-65.
John Wesley White. *Re-entry* (World Wide Publications: Minneapolis, MN, 1971).
___. *WW III* (Zondervan Publishing House: Grand Rapids, MI, 1977).
"Who are the UN Peacekeepers?" *Parade*, January 8, 1995, pg. 18.
Lindsey Williams. *There Is No True Energy Crisis*, Life Messengers: Seattle, WA, 1980.
Derek Wilson. *Rothschild: The Wealth and Power of a Dynasty* (Charles Scribner's Sons/Macmillan Publishing Co.: New York, NY, 1988), pg. 42, 57-58, 81, 101, 157, 177-78, 185, 188, 303-5.
Alan Wolfe. "Carter's Russia Watchers— The Trilateral Straddle," *Nation*, December 31, 1977, vol. 84, pg. 712-715.
World Almanac. *Book of the Strange* (Signet: New York, NY, 1977), pg. 162-169, 180-183, 189-191, 246-248, 468-471.
Ronald E. Wyatt. *Discovered: Noah's Ark!* (World Bible Society: 1989), pg. 34-36.
Yigael Yadin. *Masada: Herod's Fortress and the Zealots' Last Stand* (Steimatzky Ltd: Jerusalem, 1966), pg. 168-199.
Franklin V. York. "The ACLU Con Game," *The Review of the News*, August 13, 1975 (reprint).
J. H. Zeigler and B. L. Green. *The Talmud of Jmmanuel* (Wildflower Press: Tigard, OR, 1992).

ABOUT THE AUTHOR

David Rivera has been studying and researching the New World Order and its relationship to Bible prophecy for 25 years. He has an Associate in Arts (Paralegal) Degree from the Harrisburg Area Community College, and majored in Psychology and Public Policy at the Pennsylvania State University. As a young man he was very active in grassroots politics and held various positions in the local Democratic Party. He was the recipient of the 1979 and 1981 'Outstanding Young Man of America' Award from the U.S. Jaycees. He completed a 2–year Bible School program through Bill Anderson Ministries International and has undergone ministry training in his Church.

David is the author of *Final Warning: A History of the New World Order* (1994), *Controlled by the Calendar: The Pagan Origins of Our Major Holidays* (1997), and *Being More Than You Can Be: Breaking the Power of the Past, To Be Released Into the Destiny of the Future* (2000). He was the Proofreader and Editor of the book *Double Honor: Uprooting Shame In Your Life* (1999) by Pastor Melodye Hilton. He disseminates his writing and research through his website. He lives in central Pennsylvania with his wife and three children.